T0140114

Lecture Notes in Artificial Intelligence 11508

Subseries of Lecture Notes in Computer Science

More information about this series at http://www.springer.com/series/1244

Leszek Rutkowski · Rafał Scherer ·
Marcin Korytkowski · Witold Pedrycz ·
Ryszard Tadeusiewicz · Jacek M. Zurada (Eds.)

Artificial Intelligence and Soft Computing

18th International Conference, ICAISC 2019
Zakopane, Poland, June 16–20, 2019
Proceedings, Part I

 Springer

Editors
Leszek Rutkowski
Częstochowa University of Technology
Częstochowa, Poland

Marcin Korytkowski
Częstochowa University of Technology
Częstochowa, Poland

Ryszard Tadeusiewicz
AGH University of Science and Technology
Kraków, Poland

Rafał Scherer
Częstochowa University of Technology
Częstochowa, Poland

Witold Pedrycz
University of Alberta
Edmonton, AB, Canada

Jacek M. Zurada
University of Louisville
Louisville, KY, USA

ISSN 0302-9743 ISSN 1611-3349 (electronic)
Lecture Notes in Artificial Intelligence
ISBN 978-3-030-20911-7 ISBN 978-3-030-20912-4 (eBook)
https://doi.org/10.1007/978-3-030-20912-4

LNCS Sublibrary: SL7 – Artificial Intelligence

This Springer imprint is published by the registered company Springer Nature Switzerland AG
The registered company address is: Gewerbestrasse 11, 6330 Cham, Switzerland

Preface

This volume constitutes the proceedings of the 18th International Conference on Artificial Intelligence and Soft Computing ICAISC 2019, held in Zakopane, Poland, during June 16–20, 2019. The conference was organized by the Polish Neural Network Society in cooperation with the University of Social Sciences in Łódź, the Institute of Computational Intelligence at the Częstochowa University of Technology, and the IEEE Computational Intelligence Society, Poland Chapter. Previous conferences took place in Kule (1994), Szczyrk (1996), Kule (1997), and Zakopane (1999, 2000, 2002, 2004, 2006, 2008, 2010, 2012, 2013, 2014, 2015, 2016, 2017 and 2018) and attracted a large number of papers and internationally recognized speakers: Lotfi A. Zadeh, Hojjat Adeli, Rafal Angryk, Igor Aizenberg, Cesare Alippi, Shun-ichi Amari, Daniel Amit, Plamen Angelov, Albert Bifet, Piero P. Bonissone, Jim Bezdek, Zdzisław Bubnicki, Andrzej Cichocki, Swagatam Das, Ewa Dudek-Dyduch, Włodzisław Duch, Pablo A. Estévez, João Gama, Erol Gelenbe, Jerzy Grzymala-Busse, Martin Hagan, Yoichi Hayashi, Akira Hirose, Kaoru Hirota, Adrian Horzyk, Eyke Hüllermeier, Hisao Ishibuchi, Er Meng Joo, Janusz Kacprzyk, Jim Keller, Laszlo T. Koczy, Tomasz Kopacz, Zdzislaw Kowalczuk, Adam Krzyzak, Rudolf Kruse, James Tin-Yau Kwok, Soo-Young Lee, Derong Liu, Robert Marks, Evangelia Micheli-Tzanakou, Kaisa Miettinen, Krystian Mikołajczyk, Henning Müller, Ngoc Thanh Nguyen, Andrzej Obuchowicz, Erkki Oja, Witold Pedrycz, Marios M. Polycarpou, José C. Príncipe, Jagath C. Rajapakse, Šarunas Raudys, Enrique Ruspini, Jörg Siekmann, Andrzej Skowron, Roman Słowiński, Igor Spiridonov, Boris Stilman, Ponnuthurai Nagaratnam Suganthan, Ryszard Tadeusiewicz, Ah-Hwee Tan, Shiro Usui, Thomas Villmann, Fei-Yue Wang, Jun Wang, Bogdan M. Wilamowski, Ronald Y. Yager, Xin Yao, Syozo Yasui, Gary Yen, Ivan Zelinka, and Jacek Zurada. The aim of this conference is to build a bridge between traditional artificial intelligence techniques and so-called soft computing techniques. It was pointed out by Lotfi A. Zadeh that "soft computing (SC) is a coalition of methodologies which are oriented toward the conception and design of information/intelligent systems. The principal members of the coalition are: fuzzy logic (FL), neurocomputing (NC), evolutionary computing (EC), probabilistic computing (PC), chaotic computing (CC), and machine learning (ML). The constituent methodologies of SC are, for the most part, complementary and synergistic rather than competitive." These proceedings present both traditional artificial intelligence methods and soft computing techniques. Our goal is to bring together scientists representing both areas of research. This volume is divided into five parts:

- Neural Networks and Their Applications
- Fuzzy Systems and Their Applications
- Evolutionary Algorithms and Their Applications
- Pattern Classification
- Artificial Intelligence in Modeling and Simulation

The conference attracted a total of 333 submissions from 43 countries and after the review process, 122 papers were accepted for publication.

I would like to thank our participants, invited speakers, and reviewers of the papers for their scientific and personal contribution to the conference.

Finally, I thank my co-workers Łukasz Bartczuk, Piotr Dziwiński, Marcin Gabryel, Marcin Korytkowski as well as the conference secretary, Rafał Scherer, for their enormous efforts to make the conference a very successful event. Moreover, I appreciate the work of Marcin Korytkowski, who was responsible for the Internet submission system.

June 2019   Leszek Rutkowski

Organization

ICAISC 2019 was organized by the Polish Neural Network Society in cooperation with the University of Social Sciences in Łódź and the Institute of Computational Intelligence at Częstochowa University of Technology.

ICAISC Chairs

Honorary Chairs

Hojjat Adeli, USA
Witold Pedrycz, Canada
Jacek Żurada, USA

General Chair

Leszek Rutkowski, Poland

Co-chairs

Włodzisław Duch, Poland
Janusz Kacprzyk, Poland
Józef Korbicz, Poland
Ryszard Tadeusiewicz, Poland

ICAISC Program Committee

Rafał Adamczak, Poland
Cesare Alippi, Italy
Shun-ichi Amari, Japan
Rafal A. Angryk, USA
Jarosław Arabas, Poland
Robert Babuska, The Netherlands
Ildar Z. Batyrshin, Russia
James C. Bezdek, Australia
Marco Block-Berlitz, Germany
Leon Bobrowski, Poland
Piero P. Bonissone, USA
Bernadette Bouchon-Meunier, France
Tadeusz Burczynski, Poland
Andrzej Cader, Poland
Juan Luis Castro, Spain
Yen-Wei Chen, Japan

Wojciech Cholewa, Poland
Kazimierz Choroś, Poland
Fahmida N. Chowdhury, USA
Andrzej Cichocki, Japan
Paweł Cichosz, Poland
Krzysztof Cios, USA
Ian Cloete, Germany
Oscar Cordón, Spain
Bernard De Baets, Belgium
Nabil Derbel, Tunisia
Ewa Dudek-Dyduch, Poland
Ludmiła Dymowa, Poland
Andrzej Dzieliński, Poland
David Elizondo, UK
Meng Joo Er, Singapore
Pablo Estevez, Chile

Raúl Rojas, Germany
Imre J. Rudas, Hungary
Enrique H. Ruspini, USA
Khalid Saeed, Poland
Dominik Sankowski, Poland
Norihide Sano, Japan
Robert Schaefer, Poland
Rudy Setiono, Singapore
Paweł Sewastianow, Poland
Jennie Si, USA
Peter Sincak, Slovakia
Andrzej Skowron, Poland
Ewa Skubalska-Rafajłowicz, Poland
Roman Słowiński, Poland
Tomasz G. Smolinski, USA
Czesław Smutnicki, Poland
Pilar Sobrevilla, Spain
Janusz Starzyk, USA
Jerzy Stefanowski, Poland
Vitomir Štruc, Slovenia
Pawel Strumillo, Poland
Ron Sun, USA
Johan Suykens, Belgium
Piotr Szczepaniak, Poland
Eulalia J. Szmidt, Poland
Przemysław Śliwiński, Poland

Adam Słowik, Poland
Jerzy Świątek, Poland
Hideyuki Takagi, Japan
Yury Tiumentsev, Russia
Vicenç Torra, Spain
Burhan Turksen, Canada
Shiro Usui, Japan
Michael Wagenknecht, Germany
Tomasz Walkowiak, Poland
Deliang Wang, USA
Jun Wang, Hong Kong, SAR China
Lipo Wang, Singapore
Paul Werbos, USA
Slawo Wesolkowski, Canada
Sławomir Wiak, Poland
Bernard Widrow, USA
Kay C. Wiese, Canada
Bogdan M. Wilamowski, USA
Donald C. Wunsch, USA
Maciej Wygralak, Poland
Roman Wyrzykowski, Poland
Ronald R. Yager, USA
Xin-She Yang, UK
Gary Yen, USA
Sławomir Zadrożny, Poland
Ali M. S. Zalzala, United Arab Emirates

Additional Reviewers

M. Baczyński
M. Blachnik
L. Bobrowski
P. Boguś
W. Bozejko
R. Burduk
J. ChandBansal
W. Cholewa
P. Ciskowski
M. Clerc
C. CoelloCoello
B. Cyganek
J. Cytowski
R. Czabański
I. Czarnowski

N. Derbel
L. Diosan
A. Dockhorn
W. Duch
S. Ehteram
B. Filipic
I. Fister
M. Fraś
M. Gavrilova
E. Gelenbe
M. Gorzałczany
G. Gosztolya
D. Grabowski
M. Grzenda
J. Grzymala-Busse

L. Guo
Y. Hayashi
F. Hermann
K. Hirota
A. Horzyk
J. Ishikawa
D. Jakóbczak
E. Jamro
A. Janczak
M. Jirina
W. Kamiński
E. Kerre
F. Klawonn
P. Klęsk
J. Kluska

A. Kołakowska
J. Konopacki
J. Korbicz
P. Korohoda
M. Korytkowski
M. Korzeń
J. Kościelny
L. Kotulski
Z. Kowalczuk
M. Kraft
M. Kretowska
D. Krol
B. Kryzhanovsky
A. Krzyzak
E. Kucharska
P. Kudová
J. Kulikowski
O. Kurasova
V. Kurkova
M. Kurzyński
J. Kwiecień
A. Ligęza
M. Ławryńczuk
J. Łęski
K. Madani
W. Malina
K. Malinowski
A. Materka
R. Matuk Herrera
J. Mazurkiewicz
V. Medvedev
M. Mernik
J. Michalkiewicz
S. Misina
W. Mitkowski

M. Morzy
P. Musilek
H. Nakamoto
G. Nalepa
M. Nashed
S. Nasuto
S. Osowski
A. Owczarek
E. Ozcan
M. Pacholczyk
W. Palacz
G. Papa
A. Parkes
A. Paszyńska
A. Piegat
V. Piuri
P. Prokopowicz
A. Przybył
A. Radzikowska
E. Rafajłowicz
E. Rakus-Andersson
Ł. Rauch
L. Rolka
A. Rusiecki
J. Sas
A. Sashima
R. Sassi
E. Sato-Shimokawara
R. Scherer
F. Scotti
C. Siemers
K. Skrzypczyk
E. Skubalska-Rafajłowicz
D. Słota
C. Smutnicki

A. Sokołowski
B. Strug
P. Strumiłło
P. Suganthan
J. Swacha
P. Szczepaniak
E. Szmidt
G. Ślusarczyk
J. Świątek
R. Tadeusiewicz
Y. Tanigaki
Y. Tiumentsev
K. Tokarz
S. Tomforde
H. Tsang
M. Vajgl
E. Volna
R. Vorobel
T. Walkowiak
L. Wang
T. Wang
Y. Wang
J. Wąs
M. Wojciechowski
M. Wozniak
M. Wygralak
R. Wyrzykowski
Q. Xiao
T. Yamaguchi
X. Yang
J. Yeomans
D. Zaharie
D. Zakrzewska
A. Zamuda

ICAISC Organizing Committee

Rafał Scherer (Secretary)
Łukasz Bartczuk
Piotr Dziwiński
Marcin Gabryel (Finance Chair)
Rafał Grycuk
Marcin Korytkowski (Databases and Internet Submissions)

Contents – Part I

Fuzzy Systems and Their Applications

Evolutionary Algorithms and Their Applications

Pattern Classification

Artificial Intelligence in Modeling and Simulation

Contents – Part II

Computer Vision, Image and Speech Analysis

Bioinformatics, Biometrics and Medical Applications

Various Problems of Artificial Intelligence

Neural Networks and Their Applications

SpikeletFCN: Counting Spikelets from Infield Wheat Crop Images Using Fully Convolutional Networks

Tahani Alkhudaydi[1,2]([✉])[iD], Ji Zhou[1,3,4][iD], and Beatriz De La Iglesia[1][iD]

[1] University of East Anglia, Norwich Research Park, Norwich NR4 7TJ, UK
{t.alkhudaydi,b.iglesia}@uea.ac.uk
[2] Faculty of Computers and IT, University of Tabuk, Tabuk 71491, Saudi Arabia
talkhudaydi@ut.edu.sa
[3] Earlham Institute, Norwich Research Park, Norwich NR4 7UZ, UK
Ji.Zhou@earlham.ac.uk
[4] Plant Phenomics Research Center, China-UK Plant Phenomics Research Centre,
Nanjing Agricultural University, Nanjing 210095, China
Ji.Zhou@njau.edu.cn

Abstract. Currently, crop management through automatic monitoring is growing momentum, but presents various challenges. One key challenge is to quantify yield traits from images captured automatically. Wheat is one of the three major crops in the world with a total demand expected to exceed 850 million tons by 2050. In this paper we attempt estimation of wheat spikelets from high-definition RGB infield images using a fully convolutional model. We propose also the use of transfer learning and segmentation to improve the model. We report cross validated Mean Absolute Error (MAE) and Mean Square Error (MSE) of 53.0, 71.2 respectively on 15 real field images. We produce visualisations which show the good fit of our model to the task. We also concluded that both transfer learning and segmentation lead to a very positive impact for CNN-based models, reducing error by up to 89%, when extracting key traits such as wheat spikelet counts.

Keywords: Wheat · Spikelet counting · Plant phenotyping ·
Image analysis · CNN · Density estimation

1 Introduction

The application of the internet of things (IoT) in agriculture has enabled the monitoring of crop growth through networked remote sensors and non-invasive imaging devices [7,27]. Analysis of the output of such systems with machine learning and image processing techniques can help to extract meaningful information to assist crop management. For example, yield quantification can be tied to other features measured (e.g. temperature, humidity, variety of seed, etc.) to ultimately develop fully automated monitoring systems capable of delivering real-time information to farmers.

© Springer Nature Switzerland AG 2019
L. Rutkowski et al. (Eds.): ICAISC 2019, LNAI 11508, pp. 3–13, 2019.
https://doi.org/10.1007/978-3-030-20912-4_1

Wheat is one of the three major crops in the world with a total demand expected to exceed 850 million tons by 2050 [1]. One of the key challenges for wheat is to stabilise the yield and quality in wheat production [22]. However, climate change and related environmental issues have affected yield production [11].

In this paper, we focus on the task of counting spikelets in wheat images as a form of yield quantification for wheat crops. In particular, we use a density estimation method which has been applied in the context of crowd counting [14], to count spikelets.

The tasks of counting wheat spikelets from infield images (Fig. 1) (as opposed to images obtained in some constrained lab environment) presents some real challenges because of their self-similarity, high volume per image, and severe occlusion as well as the challenges posed by lighting and other variations in the images captured. Image processing or machine-learning approaches for object counting require manual identification of features. Deep learning can automatically extract useful features, and can also lead to high accuracy in image classification tasks [13]. Convolutional Neural Networks (CNNs), a particular type of deep learning model, learn their own features representations and have shown real promise in many areas in computer vision and plant phenotyping [24]. For that reason and because density estimation is considered as structural problem (requiring a prediction for each pixel in the image), we employ a Fully Convolutional Network (FCN) [15] to solve the task.

Fig. 1. Example of images from (a) ACID dataset and (b) CropQuant dataset which shows spikes, and spikelets.

Furthermore, because the data annotation required to extract 'ground truth' from images is expensive in term of time and resources, we utilised transfer learning in the task of density estimation [18,25]. Transfer learning enhances the image training set with further labelled images from other context and those can be used to pre-train some of the parameters improving the model fit.

Our overall approach is as follows. We employ a fully convolutional model (SpikeletFCN) to perform density estimation from dot annotated images. We utilise additional labelled data for the density estimation by means of transfer learning. In addition, we investigate training SpikeletFCN with and without prior segmentation and compare the performance of each. Section 2 presents research that is relevant to our method. Section 3 discusses the datasets we used, the architecture of SpikeletFCN, model optimisation and training procedure details. Section 4 describes the performance results of testing SpikeletFCN and the their interpretation. Finally, Sect. 5 presents our conclusions.

2   Related Work

Object counting from images is a difficult problem that emerges in many different scenarios, for example, monitoring crowds [26], performing wildlife census [2], counting blood cells in images [8] and others. Supervised counting methods required labelled images with ground truth. Methods for supervised counting include counting by detection or by segmentation, regression based methods such as global regression [3,6,12], local regression [4] and density estimation [14].

Many works [2,19,21] have used detection or segmentation in various ways, but they may require intensive labelling. However, when the only task required is to determine the total number of a certain object in an image rather than detecting them or their position, then counting by regression can be more natural and suitable, specially when the number of objects per image is high. It can be divided into three sub-methods: global regression, density estimation and local regression.

Global Regression often maps global image features to a real number [3,6,12]. However, as stated by Lempitsky and Zisserman [14] extracting these features globally discards information about the location of the objects which may be important in some contexts. Also, sufficient labelled images would be required to represent different counts for training purposes.

Learning to count objects through density estimation regression [14] takes into account the spatial information of objects. Density estimation regression learns mapping from local features into pixel level densities. This gives the advantage of integral density estimation over any image regions. Lempitsky and Zisserman [14] used dot annotations to infer density maps and utilised them as training ground truths by applying a normalised 2D Gaussian kernel. Then, they designed a counting cost function that minimises the distance between the target density map and the inferred ground truth one. Subsequently, Fiaschi et al. [5] used random forest regression, which optimised the training process to predict the density map.

On the other hand, Local Regression [4] predicts the local count of a small region in the image directly without the need to predict a density map. However, it uses the density map in the training stage to infer object counts. Also, it employs the concept of redundant counting to ensure maximum counting precision.

Although it captures the local features of objects, it can be expensive and inefficient in term of time and computational resources.

2.1 Counting in Plant Phenotyping

Counting organs or constituent parts of plants is an essential and important task to be tackled in plant phenotyping. For example, TasselNet [16] was developed to count maize tassels from infield maize crop. TasselNet performs counting by local regression using a deep convolutional neural network-based approach. Pound et al. [18] developed a multi-task deep learning model to count and localise wheat spikes and spikelets, achieving good accuracy. They tested the model on wheat crop images captured in a controlled environment inside a glasshouse. Their problem is therefore similar to ours but simpler given the reduced variation in the controlled laboratory environment as opposed to a real field image. Figure 1 shows both type of images.

Also, Madec et al. [17] investigated counting spikes from infield wheat crop images captured by UAV platform using two CNN-based models. The first was Faster-RCNN [20], a CNN based object detection model. The second was an adaptation of TasselNet [16] for this task. They concluded that both models achieved similar results when tested on images containing crops that have a similar distribution of spikes as the images both models trained on. However, they found that Faster-RCNN outperformed other models when tested on images containing more mature crops.

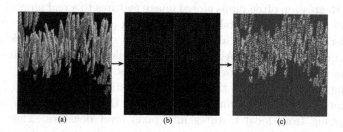

Fig. 2. An example of spikelets density generation where: (a) represents sub-image of a wheat crop, (b) represents corresponding dot annotation and (c) the generated density map from the dot annotation.

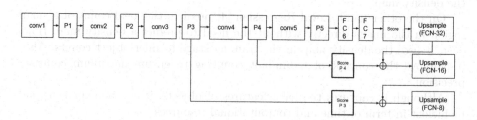

Fig. 3. SpikeletFCN architecture

Also, Hasan et al. [9] tackled the problem of counting spikes by using an R-CNN object detector. They trained four versions of R-CNN on four different growth stages of infield wheat images that vary in growth stage and variety and reported good results.

3 Spikelets Counting Using SpikeletFCN

3.1 Problem Statement

We propose to model the problem of counting spikelets as a density estimation problem. Given N input images $I_1, I_2, \ldots, I_N$ with a size of $H \times W \times D$ that represent infield wheat crop plots, for each image, I_i, there is a corresponding dot map P_i that can be represented as a set of 2D points $P_i = \{P_1, \ldots, P_{SPC_i}\}$, where $|P_i|$ is the number of spikelets in image I_i. Each point is placed at the centre of each spikelet as shown in Fig. 2(b). To generate the ground truth map GT_i (shown in Fig. 2(c)), a 2D Gaussian kernel $\mathcal{N}(p; P, \sigma^2 1_{2 \times 2})$ is applied to the dot map P_i which generates a density for each pixel p of image I_i. Therefore, the size of GT_i is the same as the input image: $GT_i = \{D^{P_1}, \ldots, D^{P_{H \times W}}\}$ where D^{P_j} is the generated density for the jth pixel in image I_i.

The effect of applying the Gaussian kernel is that it can reflect the crowding around a spikelet by taking into account the information of the pixel's neighbourhood when updating its density value. In other words, the more spikelet occlusion in a certain region, the high density values will be assigned to pixels in the region.

The total number of spikelets in a certain image I_i is the sum of all pixels densities in GT_i:

$$|P_i| = SPC_i = \sum_{p \in I_i} D^p \tag{1}$$

3.2 Datasets

CropQuant Dataset [27]. We used 15 high-dimensional RGB image series of 6×1.5 m wheat plots collected at Norwich Research Park (NRP) between May and July 2016. The image series covers one growing stage: flowering. The resolution of images is 2592 by 1944 pixels, which were captured hourly by R-pi camera modules integrated in the CropQuant workstation. Image data were synchronised with HPC data storage infrastructure at NRP. We have dot annotated each image by placing a dot in the centre of each spikelet. The total number of spikelets in all images is 63,006 and the average spikelet number per scene is 4200.4 with a standard deviation of 197.

ACID Dataset. The Annotated Crop Image Dataset (ACID) has 520 images of wheat plants captured from 21 pots in a glasshouse with a resolution of 1956×1530. The imaging is done by 12 MP cameras and all images have a black background. The images show different spike arrangements and leaves and were obtained in consistent lighting. Also, the images were dot annotated by placing a dot in the centre of each spikelet. The total number of spikelets in all images is 48,000 and the average spikelet number per scene is 92.3 with a standard deviation of 28.52.

Figure 1 shows examples of both CropQuant and ACID images which exemplify their similarities and differences.

3.3   SpikeletFCN Architecture

In our approach, we apply a fully convolutional network to tackle the problem of spikelet counting. Figure 3 represents our architecture. The last fully connected layers attached in any CNN-based classifiers are converted to convolutions. This ensures that the semantics of target objects are preserved which are essential for tasks that require structural predictions (predictions for each pixel) because converting those layers to convolutions provide localisation and shape information about target objects. Our model, SpikeletFCN, is composed of a Very Deep Convolutional Network (VGG16) [23] (Fig. 3: conv1-P5), formed by two fully convolutional (Fig. 3: FC6 and FC7) layers and three upsampling layers. The filter size selected for all convolutional layers is 3 × 3 with a stride of 1 and the max-pool layers have a pooling size of 2 × 2 with a stride of 2. We employ the concept of feature fusion by adding two skip connections (Fig. 3: after P3 and P4) to fuse the local features related to spikelets from lower layers to other shape and semantic features related to the wheat crops from higher layers. We added upsampling layers to ensure we recover the original image size affected by the application of repetitive convolutions and subsampling which reduces the input size.

We found that using a pixel-wise $L2$ loss function (Eq. 2) as the cost function for model optimisation gave the best results to regress the per pixel density:

$$\mathcal{L} = \sum_{p \in I_i} (D^p_{GT_i} - D^p_{predicted})^2 \qquad (2)$$

where $D^p_{GT_i}$ is the density ground truth and $D^p_{predicted}$ is the predicted density for a certain pixel p in image I_i.

The weights were updated for every learning iteration using a mini-batch RMSprop optimising algorithm [10] with a learning rate of 0.001 and mini-batch of 20.

3.4   Experimental Set Up

We first formed the training and validation set from the ACID dataset according to the 80:20 split rule. Then, we randomly sampled sub-images with a size of 512 × 512 for each set. After that, we manually selected 1241 sub-images from the training set and 303 sub-images from the validation set that contain spike regions. With those images we trained the model for 100 epochs for the transfer learning experiments described below.

On the other hand, for the CQ_2016 dataset, the limitations imposed by the task of dot annotating, which is time consuming and could therefore only be accomplish for a very reduced number of images, meant we only had 15 images dot annotated for our experiments. We therefore decided to divide them into 3-folds for cross validation, with 5 images per fold. Then, we randomly subsampled 512×512 sub-images from each fold individually.

To investigate whether segmenting spike regions could enhance the spikelets counting task, we manually remove the background using ground truth masks. In future research, we intend to also use a CNN to tackle the segmentation, instead of a manual approach.

We trained the model on each fold of the CQ_2016 dataset, validated and tested on the other two folds in four steps:

1. We first trained the model from scratch on the original images (no segmentation) and the model converged after an average of 155 epochs.
2. We then trained the model from scratch on the images with the spike regions isolated so after this manual segmentation the model converged after an average of 75 epochs.
3. We then loaded parameters learned from training the model on the ACID dataset, as described earlier, and continued fine tuning the model using the original images. The model converged after an average of 36 epochs. This represents transfer learning, using the ACID dataset in the initial stage of parameter initialisation and the CQ_2016 dataset to train the final model.
4. We repeated the previous transfer learning model building step, but then combined it with continued fine tuning on the CQ_2016 dataset images with the spike regions isolated and the model converged after an average of 30 epochs.

For the testing phase, SpikeletFCN predicts the density of each pixel in a certain image. Then, the number of spikelets in the image is calculated by summing all the predicted densities over the whole image according to Eq. 1 in Sect. 3.1.

4 Results

Object counting methods use two evaluation metrics to measure the model performance when applied on testing images: mean absolute error (MAE) and means square error (MSE).

We have calculated the cross-validated performance of the SpikeletFCN model for the different experimental steps described in Sect. 3.4 using the MAE and MSE measures. Table 1 shows our results. Table 1 shows that applying segmentation before counting has decreased the spikelet counting error to 82.2 and 102.0 for MAE and MSE respectively when training SpikeletFCN from scratch. This represents a reduction of 83.5% and 81.2% respectively for MAE and MSE with respect to error measures without segmentation.

In terms of transfer learning, loading ACID pre-trained parameters has a positive impact on the model performance by decreasing MAE and MSE to 53.0 and

Table 1. The MAE and MSE of estimating the number of spikelets for two experimental setups (as columns): training SpikeletFCN from scratch and by loading ACID dataset learned parameters and for pre-segmenting images (in rows) on CQ_2016 images.

	Scratch		ACID [18]	
	MAE	MSE	MAE	MSE
With segmentation	82.2	102.0	53.0	71.2
Without segmentation	498.0	543.5	77.12	107.1

71.2 respectively when segmentation is also applied. This represents a decrease of 35.5% and 30.2% respectively when segmentation is applied with respect to the error from the scratch model. When no segmentation is applied, the transfer learning reduces error by 84.5% and 80.3% respectively for MAE and MSE. Hence both segmentation and transfer learning have a very significant effect on error rates. It is worth noting that the pre-trained ACID model has minimised the gap between the SpikeletFCN performance with and without segmentation. The difference in missed spikelets when training from scratch is 415.8 for MAE and 441.5 for MSE. On the other hand, the comparative difference when loading pre-trained ACID parameters is 24.12 for MAE and 35.9 for MSE. Overall, the difference between the best model (with segmentation and transfer learning) and the worse (the scratch model without segmentation) is over 89% for MAE and over 86% for MSE.

In term of model training time, we can infer from Sect. 3 that loading ACID pre-trained parameters and training the model in images with segmentation have resulted on faster training of the model.

Also, we analysed the results in more detail through visualisation. Figure 4 shows some images with their density maps and respective spikelet counts. They show that visually the density maps obtained appear to be reasonably accurate with respect to the original images and seem to improve with the segmentation, though in some cases the prediction represents under or over-counting.

More detailed visual analysis, in this case for the ACID images, is shown in Fig. 5. By comparing the density maps generated from our models (column (b) of Fig. 5 with the 'ground truth' density maps derived from the dot annotation (column (c)) we can note that in some images, SpikeletFCN may be considered as over-counting because it is able to detect spikelets that were miss-annotated (missed) by accident in the dot annotation. For example, in Fig. 5, SpikeletFCN predicted spikelet number for the second and third images as 53.47 and 49.93 while the ground truth for both images was 46.0 and 46.61. However, in these images, spikes that appear to contain a single row of spikelets in the dot annotation are recognised as having more spikelets by the SpikeletFCN model and this seems to correlate to the images in column (a). We can assume that as the dot annotation gets much more complex in the very crowded infield images, dot annotation may also be more inaccurate, so some of our errors may reflect the inaccuracies of our ground truth.

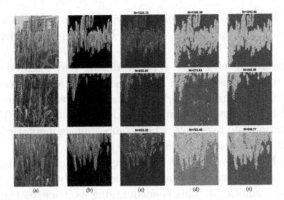

Fig. 4. Visualisation of density map results of testing SpikeletFCN on some CQ_2016 sub-images where (a) represents image patch, (b) image patch without background (c) ground truth for spikelet density map and counts, and (d) and (e) are predicted spikelet density map and count for the original image patch and image patch without background respectively.

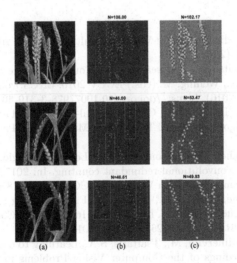

Fig. 5. Visualisation of density maps resulting from testing for the Adapted Spikelet-FCN on ACID dataset. (a) is image patch, (b) is 'ground truth' spikelet density map and count obtained after dot annotation, and (c) is the predicted spikelet density map and count.

5   Conclusion

Counting spikelets from infield wheat crop images is a vital step in quantifying yield traits but is very challenging given the variability, density and occlusion associated with spikelets in real wheat images. In this paper, we trained and tested SpikeletFCN to count spikelets using a density estimation approach. We also attempted to improve our learning by applying transfer learning and segmentation.

Our experimental results were very promising and resulted in good error rates, much improved by using both manual segmentation and transfer learning. In particular transfer learning did help to improve the performance of the models trained on infield crops images. Error rates decreased by over 81% when using manual segmentation and over 86% when combining segmentation with transfer learning. Also, it led to faster training of the model.

Visualisation helped us to discover that the process of obtaining ground truth by dot annotation is imperfect and models may actually uncover spikelets which have not been dot annotated. This is encouraging as it means the model is able to learn features of the spikelets, even in the context of imperfect training data.

In the future, we plan to test our model on more infield wheat crops that vary in year growth, growth stages and other factors. We will also develop CNN-based models to tackle the task of spike segmentation as we have shown that it can play an important role in improving the task of spikelets counting.

References

1. Alexandratos, N., Bruinsma, J.: World agriculture towards 2030/2050. Land Use Policy **20**(4), 275 (2012)
2. Arteta, C., Lempitsky, V., Zisserman, A.: Counting in the wild. In: Leibe, B., Matas, J., Sebe, N., Welling, M. (eds.) ECCV 2016. LNCS, vol. 9911, pp. 483–498. Springer, Cham (2016). https://doi.org/10.1007/978-3-319-46478-7_30
3. Cho, S.Y., Chow, T.W., Leung, C.T.: A neural-based crowd estimation by hybrid global learning algorithm. IEEE Trans. Syst. Man Cybern. Part B Cybern. **29**(4), 535–541 (1999)
4. Cohen, J.P., Boucher, G., Glastonbury, C.A., Lo, H.Z., Bengio, Y.: Count-ception: counting by fully convolutional redundant counting. In: 2017 IEEE International Conference on Computer Vision Workshop (ICCVW), pp. 18–26. IEEE (2017)
5. Fiaschi, L., Koethe, U., Nair, R., Hamprecht, F.A.: Learning to count with regression forest and structured labels. In: 2012 21st International Conference on Pattern Recognition (ICPR), pp. 2685–2688. IEEE (2012)
6. Giuffrida, M.V., Minervini, M., Tsaftaris, S.A.: Learning to count leaves in rosette plants. In: Proceedings of the Computer Vision Problems in Plant Phenotyping (CVPPP), pp. 7–10 (2016)
7. Gubbi, J., Buyya, R., Marusic, S., Palaniswami, M.: Internet of Things (IoT): a vision, architectural elements, and future directions. Future Gener. Comput. Syst. **29**(7), 1645–1660 (2013). https://doi.org/10.1016/j.future.2013.01.010
8. Habibzadeh, M., Krzyżak, A., Fevens, T.: White blood cell differential counts using convolutional neural networks for low resolution images. In: Rutkowski, L., Korytkowski, M., Scherer, R., Tadeusiewicz, R., Zadeh, L.A., Zurada, J.M. (eds.) ICAISC 2013. LNCS (LNAI), vol. 7895, pp. 263–274. Springer, Heidelberg (2013). https://doi.org/10.1007/978-3-642-38610-7_25
9. Hasan, M.M., Chopin, J.P., Laga, H., Miklavcic, S.J.: Detection and analysis of wheat spikes using convolutional neural networks. Plant Methods **14**(1), 100 (2018). https://doi.org/10.1186/s13007-018-0366-8

10. Hinton, G., Srivastava, N., Swersky, K.: Neural networks for machine learning. In: Lecture 6a: Overview of Mini-batch Gradient Descent, p. 14 (2012)

11. Howden, S.M., Soussana, J., Tubiello, F.N., Chhetri, N., Dunlop, M., Meinke, H.: Adapting agriculture to climate change. Proc. Nat. Acad. Sci. U.S.A. **104**(50), 19691–19696 (2007). https://doi.org/10.1073/pnas.0701890104

12. Kong, D., Gray, D., Tao, H.: A viewpoint invariant approach for crowd counting. In: 18th International Conference on Pattern Recognition, ICPR 2006, vol. 3, pp. 1187–1190. IEEE (2006)

13. LeCun, Y., Bengio, Y., Hinton, G.: Deep learning. Nature **521**(7553), 436 (2015)

14. Lempitsky, V., Zisserman, A.: Learning to count objects in images. In: Advances in Neural Information Processing Systems, pp. 1324–1332 (2010)

15. Long, J., Shelhamer, E., Darrell, T.: Fully convolutional networks for semantic segmentation (2015)

16. Lu, H., Cao, Z., Xiao, Y., Zhuang, B., Shen, C.: TasselNet: counting maize tassels in the wild via local counts regression network. Plant Methods **13**(1), 79 (2017)

17. Madec, S., Jin, X., Lu, H., De Solan, B., Liu, S., Duyme, F., Heritier, E., Baret, F.: Ear density estimation from high resolution RGB imagery using deep learning technique. Agric. For. Meteorol. **264**, 225–234 (2019)

18. Pound, M.P., Atkinson, J.A., Wells, D.M., Pridmore, T.P., French, A.P.: Deep learning for multi-task plant phenotyping. In: 2017 IEEE International Conference on Computer Vision Workshop (ICCVW), pp. 2055–2063. IEEE (2017)

19. Ren, M., Zemel, R.S.: End-to-end instance segmentation with recurrent attention. In: CVPR (2017)

20. Ren, S., He, K., Girshick, R., Sun, J.: Faster R-CNN: towards real-time object detection with region proposal networks. In: Advances in Neural Information Processing Systems, pp. 91–99 (2015)

21. Ryan, D., Denman, S., Fookes, C., Sridharan, S.: Crowd counting using multiple local features. In: Digital Image Computing: Techniques and Applications, 2009, DICTA 2009, pp. 81–88. IEEE (2009)

22. Shewry, P.R.: Wheat. J. Exp. Bot. **60**(6), 1537–1553 (2009)

23. Simonyan, K., Zisserman, A.: Very deep convolutional networks for large-scale image recognition. CoRR

24. Tardieu, F., Cabrera-Bosquet, L., Pridmore, T., Bennett, M.: Plant phenomics, from sensors to knowledge. Curr. Biol. **27**(15), R770–R783 (2017)

25. Yosinski, J., Clune, J., Bengio, Y., Lipson, H.: How transferable are features in deep neural networks? In: Advances in Neural Information Processing Systems, pp. 3320–3328 (2014)

26. Zhang, C., Li, H., Wang, X., Yang, X.: Cross-scene crowd counting via deep convolutional neural networks. In: Proceedings of the IEEE Conference on Computer Vision and Pattern Recognition, pp. 833–841 (2015)

27. Zhou, J., et al.: CropQuant: an automated and scalable field phenotyping platform for crop monitoring and trait measurements to facilitate breeding and digital agriculture. bioRxiv. https://doi.org/10.1101/161547

Modifications of the Givens Training Algorithm for Artificial Neural Networks

Jarosław Bilski[1]([⊠]) [iD], Bartosz Kowalczyk[1] [iD], and Andrzej Cader[2,3]

[1] Institute of Computational Intelligence, Częstochowa University of Technology,
Częstochowa, Poland
{Jaroslaw.Bilski,Bartosz.Kowalczyk}@iisi.pcz.pl
[2] Information Technology Institute, University of Social Sciences, Łódź, Poland
acader@san.edu.pl
[3] Clark University, Worcester, MA 01610, USA

Abstract. The Givens algorithm is a supervised training method for neural networks. This paper presents several optimization techniques that could be applied on the top of the Givens algorithm. First, the classic variant of the Givens method is briefly described. The main section of the article contains a detailed description of the proposed retry worst samples, skip best samples, and the Givens epoch update optimization techniques. The paper concludes with the simulation results and an overall summary.

Keywords: Feed-forward neural network · Training algorithm ·
Optimization · QR decomposition · Givens rotation ·
Training acceleration

1 Introduction

The direction of the modern artificial intelligence development is driven by neural networks. Many researchers across the globe focus their attention on developing algorithms and training sets to solve various problems, e.g. human handwriting, image or sound recognition [9,10,15–23]. Neural networks also find numerous uses in the areas of economics, medicine or industry [1,2,8,24–26]. This wide usage of artificial intelligence implies a great need of improving training algorithms for neural networks.

Some learning methods, such as Back Propagation, are well known and easy to implement but they require a huge effort to train advanced models [14]. Many researches have been conducted to improve performance of the classic BP algorithm [13]. There are also more complex algorithms such as Levenberg-Marquardt that is able to speed up a training process to just a few epochs [12]. Many researches have also been carried out in the areas of improving the LM algorithm [3,4,7]. This paper presents a few approaches to the optimization techniques that could be applied for the Givens algorithm [5]. The described methods have been tested on several mathematical problems such as a single

© Springer Nature Switzerland AG 2019
L. Rutkowski et al. (Eds.): ICAISC 2019, LNAI 11508, pp. 14–28, 2019.
https://doi.org/10.1007/978-3-030-20912-4_2

and two real variables functions approximations (logistic curve, hang and sinc) and a two-spirals classification problem.

2   The Classic Givens Algorithm

The Givens rotation is a well known orthogonal transformation method derived from the n-dimensional linear algebra [11]. In neural networks it can be used in a minimization method for the error criterion. The following sections cover the basics of the Givens rotations along with the QR decomposition method in order to compute the weights update for a neural network.

2.1   Rotation Basics

Let $\mathbf{a} \in \mathbb{R}^n$ and $\mathbf{G} \in \mathbb{R}^{n,n}$. The elementary step of the Givens algorithm is to compute a rotation matrix with the following structure

$$
\mathbf{G}_{pq} =
\begin{bmatrix}
1 & & & \cdots & & 0 \\
& \ddots & & & & \\
& & c & \cdots & s & \\
& \vdots & \vdots & \ddots & \vdots & \vdots \\
& & -s & \cdots & c & \\
& & & & & \ddots \\
0 & & & \cdots & & 1
\end{bmatrix}
\begin{matrix} \\ \\ p \\ \\ q \\ \\ \\ \end{matrix}
\tag{1}
$$
$$ p q$$

The given rotation matrix is applied to the transformed vector by the left-sided multiplication

$$
\mathbf{a} \to \bar{\mathbf{a}} = \mathbf{G}_{pq}\mathbf{a}. \tag{2}
$$

Parameters c and s are responsible for the angle of the rotation which is applied to vector $\mathbf{a}$. Due to the structure of matrix $\mathbf{G}_{pq}$, only elements a_p and a_q of vector $\mathbf{a}$ are affected by a single rotation as follows

$$
\begin{aligned}
\bar{a}_p &= ca_p + sa_q \\
\bar{a}_q &= -sa_p + ca_q \\
\bar{a}_i &= a_i \quad (i \neq p, q; i = 1, \ldots, n).
\end{aligned}
\tag{3}
$$

The goal of the Givens elimination step is to manipulate parameters c and s in order to substitute element a_q by 0. To achieve that, the parameters of matrix $\mathbf{G}_{pq}$ are computed as follows

$$
c = \frac{a_p}{\rho} \quad s = \frac{a_q}{\rho}, \tag{4}
$$

where ρ is obtained from equation

$$
\rho =
\begin{cases}
a_p\sqrt{1 + (a_q/a_p)^2} & \text{for } |a_p| \geq |a_q| \\
a_q\sqrt{1 + (a_p/a_q)^2} & \text{for } |a_p| < |a_q|.
\end{cases}
\tag{5}
$$

The application of Eqs. (4) and (5) to Eq. (3) results in

$$\begin{aligned}\bar{a}_p = ca_p + sa_q = \rho \\ \bar{a}_q = -sa_p + ca_q = 0.\end{aligned} \tag{6}$$

2.2 QR Decomposition Based on Rotations

The previous section focuses on a single rotation which leads to elimination of a single element of a vector. The QR decomposition is an iterative method of transforming any non-singular matrix $\mathbf{A} \in \mathbb{R}^{m,n}$ into the product of the orthogonal $\mathbf{Q}$ and the upper-triangle $\mathbf{R}$ matrices as shown in the following equation

$$\mathbf{A} = \mathbf{QR}, \tag{7}$$

where

$$\mathbf{Q}^T\mathbf{Q} = \mathbf{I}, \tag{8}$$

$$\mathbf{Q}^T = \mathbf{Q}^{-1}, \tag{9}$$

$$r_{ij} = 0 \quad \text{for } i > j. \tag{10}$$

Note that the computation of orthogonal matrix $\mathbf{Q}$ is not explicitly needed. In each iteration of the algorithm only parameters c and s of the rotations are calculated. At the final stage the decomposition is accomplished as shown below

$$\mathbf{R} = \mathbf{G}_{m-1}\ldots\mathbf{G}_1\mathbf{A}_1 = \mathbf{G}_{m-1,m}\ldots\mathbf{G}_{23}\ldots\mathbf{G}_{2m}\mathbf{G}_{12}\ldots\mathbf{G}_{1m}\mathbf{A}_1 = \mathbf{Q}^T\mathbf{A}. \tag{11}$$

Nevertheless, matrix $\mathbf{Q}$ can be calculated back by inversion of the respective rotations as shown in the following equation

$$\mathbf{Q} = \mathbf{G}_1^T\ldots\mathbf{G}_{m-1}^T = \mathbf{G}_{1m}^T\ldots\mathbf{G}_{12}^T\mathbf{G}_{2m}^T\ldots\mathbf{G}_{23}^T\ldots\mathbf{G}_{m-1,m}^T. \tag{12}$$

2.3 Weights Update

The Givens training algorithm is assumed to be effective for any multi-layered neural network which uses any differentiable activation function. In order to compute the weights update, the error measure given by Eq. (13) needs to be minimized.

$$J(n) = \sum_{t=1}^{n}\lambda^{n-t}\sum_{j=1}^{N_L}\varepsilon_j^{(L)2}(t) = \sum_{t=1}^{n}\lambda^{n-t}\sum_{j=1}^{N_L}\left[d_j^{(L)}(t) - f\left(\mathbf{x}^{(L)T}(t)\,\mathbf{w}_j^{(L)}(n)\right)\right]^2. \tag{13}$$

At this stage Eq. (13) needs to be derived and linearized to its normal form given by

$$\sum_{t=1}^{n}\lambda^{n-t}f'^2\left(s_i^{(l)}(t)\right)\left[b_i^{(l)}(t) - \mathbf{x}^{(l)T}(t)\,\mathbf{w}_i^{(l)}(n)\right]\mathbf{x}^{(l)T}(t) = \mathbf{0}. \tag{14}$$

To obtain the entry point to the Givens training algorithm, Eq. (14) needs to be transformed into its vector form as follows

$$\mathbf{A}_i^{(l)}(n)\,\mathbf{w}_i^{(l)}(n) = \mathbf{h}_i^{(l)}(n)\,, \tag{15}$$

where

$$\mathbf{A}_i^{(l)}(n) = \sum_{t=1}^{n} \lambda^{n-t} \mathbf{z}_i^{(l)}(t)\, \mathbf{z}_i^{(l)T}(t), \tag{16}$$

$$\mathbf{h}_i^{(l)}(n) = \sum_{t=1}^{n} \lambda^{n-t} f'\left(s_i^{(l)}(t)\right) b_i^{(l)}(t)\, \mathbf{z}_i^{(l)}(t), \tag{17}$$

where

$$\mathbf{z}_i^{(l)}(t) = f'\left(s_i^{(l)}(t)\right) \mathbf{x}^{(l)}(t)\,. \tag{18}$$

$$b_i^{(l)}(n) = \begin{cases} f^{-1}\left(d_i^{(l)}(n)\right) & \text{for } l = L \\ s_i^{(l)}(n) + e_i^{(l)}(n) & \text{for } l = 1 \ldots L - 1, \end{cases} \tag{19}$$

$$e_i^{(k)}(n) = \sum_{j=1}^{N_{k+1}} f'\left(s_i^{(k)}(n)\right) w_{ji}^{(k+1)}(n)\, e_j^{(k+1)}(n) \quad \text{for } k = 1 \ldots L - 1. \tag{20}$$

Since each neuron computes its own linear response ($s_i^{(l)}$) Eq. (15) needs to be applied for all the neurons of a network. In order to solve Eq. (15) the Givens QR decomposition is used as described in the previous section. Orthogonal matrix $\mathbf{Q}^T$ is implicitly acquired during the decomposition process as shown in the following equations

$$\mathbf{Q}_i^{(l)T}(n)\,\mathbf{A}_i^{(l)}(n)\,\mathbf{w}_i^{(l)}(n) = \mathbf{Q}_i^{(l)T}(n)\,\mathbf{h}_i^{(l)}(n)\,, \tag{21}$$

$$\mathbf{R}_i^{(l)}(n)\,\mathbf{w}_i^{(l)}(n) = \mathbf{Q}_i^{(l)T}(n)\,\mathbf{h}_i^{(l)}(n)\,. \tag{22}$$

At this stage matrix $\mathbf{A}$ is fully transformed into upper-triangle matrix $\mathbf{R}$, so its inversion is not that complex anymore. The weights update for i-th neuron is calculated due to the equations

$$\hat{\mathbf{w}}_i^{(l)}(n) = \mathbf{R}_i^{(l)-1}(n)\,\mathbf{Q}_i^{(l)T}(n)\,\mathbf{h}_i^{(l)}(n)\,, \tag{23}$$

$$\mathbf{w}_i^{(l)}(n) = (1 - \eta)\,\mathbf{w}_i^{(l)}(n-1) + \eta\,\hat{\mathbf{w}}_i^{(l)}(n)\,. \tag{24}$$

3   Modifications of the Givens Algorithm

The neural network training process of the Givens method is based on the presentation of consecutive epochs. A single epoch includes all samples of a teaching sequence. Each sample contains input and expected data. The teaching process is assumed to be completed once the overall network's error ε is below a predefined threshold ($\varepsilon < \Theta$)—success or if the epoch limit is exceeded—failure.

The first proposed optimization is to retry the samples whose error was higher than the given multiplication of a target error. The second idea is to skip the samples whose error already fell below a given percent of a target error. In the classic Givens algorithm the weights update occurs after the presentation of each sample. In the last approach weight update is performed only once per epoch, after all the samples have been presented. The convergence criteria for all the modifications are the same as for the classic Givens (CG).

3.1   Retry Worst Samples

The retry worst samples modification (RWS) is based on the idea to run the whole training process again using only a subset of a teaching sequence. The samples that need to be trained again are selected based on the network's error for the given sample

$$e_s = \frac{1}{2} \sum_{i=1}^{N_L} \varepsilon_i^2, \tag{25}$$

where s is a sample index, $i = 1 \ldots N_L$ is an output neuron index, ε is a nonlinear output neuron's error. At the early stage of a network's training the randomly selected weights are barely starting to shape. At this stage it is too early to apply the RWS modification, because all samples from the epoch are most likely to be presented again. To stop this from happening, the RWS modification's activation threshold t is introduced and calculated as shown

$$t = \Theta p, \tag{26}$$

where Θ is an accepted network error threshold and $p \geq 1$ is a RWS modification's parameter. The epoch error is based on the selected error criterion. For the average epoch error criterion it is calculated as follows

$$\bar{\varepsilon} = \frac{\sum_{s=1}^{S} e_s}{S}. \tag{27}$$

For the maximum epoch error criterion it is calculated due to

$$\bar{\varepsilon} = \max(e_s). \tag{28}$$

Once the network error satisfies the RWS modification's prerequisite given by Eq. (29), the individual errors of all samples are being verified by Eq. (30) if they need to be trained again.

$$\bar{\varepsilon} < t \tag{29}$$

$$e_s > t \tag{30}$$

The RWS modification can be summarized by the following steps:

1. Present all samples from the teaching sequence to the network.
2. Verify if the overall network error $\bar{\varepsilon}$ is less than the predefined modification's activation threshold t. If Eq. (29) is satisfied, then continue to step 3. Otherwise, skip the RWS modification, proceed to the next epoch and go back to step 1.
3. For each sample verify if its error e_s is above the modification's activation threshold t. If Eq. (30) is satisfied, then run the teaching process for this sample again. Otherwise continue.

3.2 Skip Best Samples

The skip best samples modification (SBS) is based on the idea to suppress the training process for a subset of a teaching sequence. The samples that can be skipped must satisfy the following equation

$$e_s < \Theta p, \tag{31}$$

where e_s is a network's error for the given sample calculated due to (25), Θ is an accepted network error threshold and $p \in (0 \ldots 1)$ is an SBS modification's parameter. Parameter p in the SBS modification denotes a percentage of the target network's error. The samples with an error below this threshold are treated as well trained, hence the weight update is skipped. The SBS modification can be summarized by the following steps:

1. Present the next sample to the network and calculate its error e_s.
2. If error e_s of the current sample satisfies Eq. (31), then suppress the weight update and go to the next sample. Otherwise, proceed with the training.

3.3 Epoch Weight Update

In the classic Givens algorithm the weight update vector is applied to the neuron in every iteration (23, 24). In the epoch weight update modification (EG - Epoch Givens), the update vector of each iteration $\hat{\mathbf{w}}$ is accumulated in resultant vector $\hat{\mathbf{v}}$. Based on that, in the EG modification Eq. (24) from the CG is substituted by the following

$$\hat{\mathbf{v}}_i^{(l)} = \sum_{n=1}^{N} \hat{\mathbf{w}}_i^{(l)}(n) - \mathbf{w}_i^{(l)}(0). \tag{32}$$

Once the epoch is completed, the resultant vector of consecutive corrections $\hat{\mathbf{v}}$ is created. Then vector $\hat{\mathbf{v}}$ is scaled by teaching step η and applied to the neuron's weights as follows

$$\mathbf{w}_i^{(l)} = \mathbf{w}_i^{(l)}(0) + \eta \hat{\mathbf{v}}_i^{(l)}. \tag{33}$$

The epoch weight update modification can be summarized by the following steps:

1. Perform calculations as for the classic Givens algorithm with respect to Eqs. (13–23).
2. For each sample accumulate the difference between the current update vector and the initial weight vector for the current epoch as shown in Eq. (32).
3. Once all samples have been presented to the network, scale the vector of updates $\hat{\mathbf{v}}$ by η and apply it to the weight's vector as shown in Eq. (33).

4   Simulation Results

The discussed modifications have been tested on an authorial implementation of the neural network. This section is divided into several subsections. Each section is fully devoted to a respective teaching problem. Each section also contains a setup description for the given experiment. The performance factor ξ defined by Eq. (34) has been used to reveal the best combination of parameters across all tested algorithms. The following sections contain the best results in terms of the lowest epoch count and the biggest success ratio selected from all experimental results.

$$\xi_{\text{algorithm}} = \frac{\text{SuccessRatio}}{\text{EpochAverage}} \tag{34}$$

4.1   Single Variable Function Approximation - Logistic Curve

The first approach to the Givens modifications performance tests is approximating the function of a single real variable. The function represents a logistic curve given by

$$f(x) = 4x(1 - x) \quad x \in [0, 1]. \tag{35}$$

During the experiment a fully connected MLP network with the total of 6 neurons (1-5-1) has been used. The teaching sequence consists of 11 samples presented in a random order in each epoch. Target error Θ has been set to 0.001 as a maximum epoch error. A detailed setup description is presented in Table 1. The experiment presents the best results which are given in Table 2.

Table 1. Setup for the logistic function approximation

Target error Θ	0.001
Criterion	Epoch max
Limit	1000
Network topology	1-5-1 full connected
Activation in hidden layers	Hyperbolic tangent
Teaching sequence size	11
Sequence type	Random order
Weights starting range	Random in $[-0.5, 0.5]$
Experiment retry count	100

The classic Givens algorithm (CG) has achieved the best performance with $\eta = 0.006$ and $\lambda = 0.911$. 98 out of 100 teaching trials ended up with a success giving a value of 38.34 as an average of the required epochs for reaching the predefined training goal. A single teaching process took 11.74 ms on average.

Table 2. Results of the logistic function approximation

	CG	RWS	SBS	EG
p	-	1.5	0.9	-
η	0.006	0.006	0.006	0.1
λ	0.911	0.911	0.911	0.962
Success ratio	98%	100%	100%	84%
Epoch avg	38.34	42.18	37.72	86.71
Duration avg [ms]	11.48	12.67	9.11	29.64

The RWS modification achieved the best performance once the repetition threshold was set to $p = 1.5$. The RWS modification proves to be more successful than CG but on average at the cost of a few additional epochs.

The SBS modification has achieved the best performance once the skip sample threshold was set to $p = 0.9$. The SBS modification turns out to be more successful and slightly more epoch efficient on average than CG.

The EG modification has achieved the best performance for $\eta = 0.1$ and $\lambda = 0.962$. Unfortunately, in the case of the logistic curve approximation, the epoch Givens modification does not give any better results in terms of the success ratio nor epoch average.

4.2 Two Variables Function Approximation - Hang

The next approach to the Givens modifications performance tests is approximating the non-linear function of two real variables. The trained Hang function is given by

$$f(x_1, x_2) = \left(1 + x_1^{-2} + \sqrt{x_2^{-3}}\right)^2 \quad x_1, x_2 \in [1, 5]. \tag{36}$$

During the experiment a fully connected MLP network with a total of 16 neurons (2-15-1) has been used. The teaching sequence consists of 50 samples presented in a random order in each epoch. Target error Θ has been set to 0.001 as an average epoch error. A detailed setup description is presented in Table 3. The best results obtained in the experiment are presented in Table 4.

The classic Givens algorithm (CG) has achieved the best performance with $\eta = 0.02$ and $\lambda = 0.966$. 99 out of 100 teaching trials were successful giving a value of 26.04 as an average of the epochs required for reaching a predefined training goal. A single teaching process took 156.16 ms on average.

The RWS modification has achieved the best performance once the repetition threshold was set to $p = 4$. That means a lot of samples can be retried during each epoch. The RWS modification turns out to be more successful than CG with a better average epoch count.

The SBS modification has achieved the best performance once the skip sample threshold was set to $p = 0.6$. The results show that many samples were able to achieve error smaller than 60% of the target error Θ. This is reflected by a short average duration time of a single training. 75.36 ms for SBS comparing to 156.16 ms for CG. The SBS modification turns out to be more successful and slightly more epoch efficient in epoch average than CG, but with twice as big improvement in an average training duration time.

Table 3. Setup for the Hang function approximation

Target error Θ	0.001
Criterion	Epoch average
Limit	1000
Network topology	2-15-1 full connected
Activation in hidden layers	Hyperbolic tangent
Teaching sequence size	50
Sequence type	Random order
Weights starting range	Random in $[-0.5, 0.5]$
Experiment retry count	100

Table 4. The results of the Hang function approximation

	CG	RWS	SBS	EG
p	-	4	0.6	-
η	0.02	0.02	0.02	0.01
λ	0.966	0.966	0.966	0.994
Success ratio	99%	100%	100%	100%
Epoch avg	26.04	24.3	25.38	71.64
Duration avg [ms]	156.16	105.99	75.36	295.4

The EG modification has achieved the best performance for $\eta = 0.01$ and $\lambda = 0.994$. The epoch modification brings the only improvement in terms of success ratio. The epoch average and the average duration time are not improved for the Hang approximation comparing to the classic variant of the Givens algorithm.

4.3   Two Variables Function Approximation - Sinc

The next approach to the Givens modifications performance tests is approximating the non-linear function of two real variables. The Sinc function is given by

$$f(x_1, x_2) = \begin{cases} 1 & x_1 = x_2 = 0 \\ \frac{\sin x_2}{x_2} & x_1 = 0 \wedge x_2 \neq 0 \\ \frac{\sin x_1}{x_1} & x_2 = 0 \wedge x_1 \neq 0 \\ \frac{\sin x_1}{x_1} \frac{\sin x_2}{x_2} \end{cases} \tag{37}$$

During the experiment a fully connected MLP network with a total of 16 neurons (2-15-1) has been used. The teaching sequence consists of 121 samples presented in a random order in each epoch. Target error Θ has been set to 0.005 as an average epoch error. A detailed setup description is presented in Table 5. The experiment reveals the best results presented in Table 6.

Table 5. Setup for the Sinc function approximation

Target error Θ	0.005
Criterion	Epoch average
Limit	1000
Network topology	2-15-1 full connected
Activation in hidden layers	Hyperbolic tangent
Teaching sequence size	121
Sequence type	Random order
Weights starting range	Random in $[-0.5, 0.5]$
Experiment retry count	100

Table 6. The results of the Sinc function approximation

	CG	RWS	SBS	EG
p	-	2	0.2	-
η	0.02	0.02	0.02	0.006
λ	0.984	0.984	0.984	0.972
Success ratio	100%	100%	100%	100%
Epoch avg	92.29	60.09	83.09	86.06
Duration avg [ms]	1197.89	728.75	494.28	1136.44

The classic Givens algorithm (CG) has achieved the best performance with $\eta = 0.02$ and $\lambda = 0.984$. 100% of the teaching trials were successful giving a value of 92.29 as an average of required epochs for reaching a predefined training goal. A single teaching process took 1197.89 ms on average.

The RWS modification has achieved the best performance once the repetition threshold was set to $p = 2$. The RWS modification turns out to be as successful as CG with a much better average epoch count and duration time.

The SBS modification has achieved the best performance once the skip sample threshold was set to $p = 0.2$. The results show that many samples were able to achieve the error smaller than 20% of target error Θ. This is reflected by a short average duration of a single training. 494.28 ms for SBS comparing to 1197.89 ms for CG. The SBS modification turns out to be as successful as CG with a slightly better epoch average and a huge improvement in an average training duration time.

The EG modification has achieved the best performance for $\eta = 0.006$ and $\lambda = 0.972$. The epoch modification is as good as CG in terms of success ratio. The EG modification also shows noticeable improvements in the area of average epoch count and training duration time comparing to the CG method.

4.4   Classification Problem - Two Spirals

The final approach to the Givens modifications performance tests is a two variables classification problem known as the two spirals. During the experiment a fully connected MLP network with a total of 16 neurons (2-5-5-5-1) has been used. The teaching sequence consists of 96 samples presented in a random order in each epoch. Target error Θ has been set to 0.1 as the maximum epoch error. A detailed setup description is presented in Table 7. The experiment presents the best results which are given in Table 8.

Table 7. Setup for the two spirals classification

Target error Θ	0.1
Criterion	Epoch max
Limit	5000
Network topology	2-5-5-5-1 full connected
Activation in hidden layers	Hyperbolic tangent
Teaching sequence size	96
Sequence type	Random order
Weights starting range	Random in $[-0.5, 0.5]$
Experiment retry count	100

The classic Givens algorithm (CG) has achieved the best performance with $\eta = 0.02$ and $\lambda = 0.991$. 90 out of 100 teaching trials ended up with a success giving a value of 51.59 as an average of the epochs required for reaching a predefined training goal. A single teaching process took 1195.99 ms on average.

The RWS modification has achieved the best performance once the repetition threshold was set to $p = 3.5$. Unfortunately, the RWS modification turns out to

Table 8. The results of the two spirals classification

	CG	RWS	SBS	EG
p	-	3.5	0.8	-
η	0.02	0.02	0.02	0.0003
λ	0.991	0.991	0.991	0.996
Success ratio	90%	34%	74%	79%
Epoch avg	51.59	47.74	58.28	306.42
Duration avg [ms]	1195.99	843.53	380.45	6212.55

be rather unstable for a two-spirals problem as the success ratio drops to 34% bringing only a small improvement in the case of epoch average.

The SBS modification has achieved the best performance once the skip sample threshold was set to $p = 0.8$. The SBS modification reduced the success ratio to 74% but the average duration time is also reduced to 380.45 milliseconds per training on average.

The EG modification has achieved the best performance for $\eta = 0.0003$ and $\lambda = 0.996$. The epoch modification does not bring any improvements comparing to the classic Givens algorithm.

5   Conclusions

The paper discusses a rather complex experiment with a great number of statistics data embedded in it. To make the summary section clearer, the usability of each modification is investigated in the areas of success ratio, average epoch count and average duration time of the training process across all tested scenarios. In the following tables number 1 denotes the best performance in a given category and number 4 stands for the worst statistics.

Table 9. The summary in scope of success ratio

	Log	Hang	Sinc	Spirals
CG	2	2	1	1
RWS	1	1	1	4
SBS	1	1	1	3
EG	3	1	1	2

In the area of the success ratio (Table 9), the RWS and SBS modifications manifest the best - 100% - efficiency for the tested approximation problems while performing worst in the two-spirals problem. The EG modification proves to be slightly more efficient than CG only in the Hang simulation.

Table 10. The summary in terms of average epoch count

	Log	Hang	Sinc	Spirals
CG	2	3	4	2
RWS	3	1	1	1
SBS	1	2	2	3
EG	4	4	3	4

In the area of the average epoch count (Table 10), the best performing modification is RWS followed by SBS. The EG modification comes last in the table with the worst overall performance in the area of the average epoch count.

Table 11. The summary in terms of average time duration

	Log	Hang	Sinc	Spirals
CG	2	3	4	3
RWS	3	2	2	2
SBS	1	1	1	1
EG	4	4	3	4

The ability of skipping a training process for given samples turns out to be the key to time optimization even if some additional epochs are required. In the area of the average teaching duration time (Table 11), the SBS modification is the best performing optimization for the Givens algorithm. Again, the EG modification turns out to be less effective and shows its potential only during the sinc experiment.

From the perspective of the selected training problems, the sinc function approximation seems to be the most flexible problem to have teaching modifications applied in it. The classic Givens manifests the worst performance during the Sinc function approximation training.

In the nearest future further research is likely to be attempted. The first idea is to apply more than a single modification to the training process at the same time. Additionally, the proposed modifications could be tested with different training sets. The presented modifications could also be applied to different training algorithms, especially to the parallel Givens implementation as proposed in [6].

This work was supported by the Polish National Science Center under Grant 2017/27/B/ST6/02852.

References

1. Starczewski, A.: A new validity index for crisp clusters. Pattern Anal. Appl. **20**, 687–700 (2017)
2. Alkhazaleh, S., Hazaymeh, A.A.: N-valued refined neutrosophic soft sets and their applications in decision making problems and medical diagnosis. J. Artif. Intell. Soft Comput. Res. **8**(1), 79–86 (2018)
3. Bilski, J., Wilamowski, B.M.: Parallel levenberg-marquardt algorithm without error backpropagation. In: Rutkowski, L., Korytkowski, M., Scherer, R., Tadeusiewicz, R., Zadeh, L.A., Zurada, J.M. (eds.) ICAISC 2017. LNCS (LNAI), vol. 10245, pp. 25–39. Springer, Cham (2017). https://doi.org/10.1007/978-3-319-59063-9_3
4. Bilski, J., Kowalczyk, B., Grzanek, K.: The parallel modification to the levenberg-marquardt algorithm. In: Rutkowski, L., Scherer, R., Korytkowski, M., Pedrycz, W., Tadeusiewicz, R., Zurada, J.M. (eds.) ICAISC 2018. LNCS (LNAI), vol. 10841, pp. 15–24. Springer, Cham (2018). https://doi.org/10.1007/978-3-319-91253-0_2
5. Bilski, J., Kowalczyk, B., Żurada, J.M.: Application of the givens rotations in the neural network learning algorithm. In: Rutkowski, L., Korytkowski, M., Scherer, R., Tadeusiewicz, R., Zadeh, L.A., Zurada, J.M. (eds.) ICAISC 2016. LNCS (LNAI), vol. 9692, pp. 46–56. Springer, Cham (2016). https://doi.org/10.1007/978-3-319-39378-0_5
6. Bilski, J., Kowalczyk, B., Żurada, J.M.: Parallel Implementation of the givens rotations in the neural network learning algorithm. In: Rutkowski, L., Korytkowski, M., Scherer, R., Tadeusiewicz, R., Zadeh, L.A., Zurada, J.M. (eds.) ICAISC 2017. LNCS (LNAI), vol. 10245, pp. 14–24. Springer, Cham (2017). https://doi.org/10.1007/978-3-319-59063-9_2
7. Bilski, J., Smoląg, J., Żurada, J.M.: Parallel approach to the levenberg-marquardt learning algorithm for feedforward neural networks. In: Rutkowski, L., Korytkowski, M., Scherer, R., Tadeusiewicz, R., Zadeh, L.A., Zurada, J.M. (eds.) ICAISC 2015. LNCS (LNAI), vol. 9119, pp. 3–14. Springer, Cham (2015). https://doi.org/10.1007/978-3-319-19324-3_1
8. Bustamam, A., Sarwinda, D., Ardenaswari, G.: Texture and gene expression analysis of the mri brain in detection of alzheimer's disease. J. Artif. Intell. Soft Comput. Res. **8**(2), 111–120 (2018)
9. Chang, O., Constante, P., Gordon, A., Singana, M.: A novel deep neural network that uses space-time features for tracking and recognizing a moving object. J. Artif. Intell. Soft Comput. Res. **7**(2), 125–136 (2017)
10. Pires, R.G., Marananil, A.N., de Souza, G.B., da Silva Santos, D.F., Papa, J.P.: Deep features extraction for robust fingerprint spoofing attack detection. J. Artif. Intell. Soft Comput. Res. **9**(1), 41–49 (2019)
11. Kiełbasiński, A., Schwetlick, H.: Numeryczna Algebra Liniowa. Wydawnictwa Naukowo-Techniczne (1992)
12. Hagan, M.T., Menhaj, M.B.: Training feedforward networks with the marquardt algorithm. IEEE Trans. Neural Netw. **5**, 989–993 (1994)
13. Bilski, J., Smoląg, J., Galushkin, A.I.: The parallel approach to the conjugate gradient learning algorithm for the feedforward neural networks. In: Rutkowski, L., Korytkowski, M., Scherer, R., Tadeusiewicz, R., Zadeh, L.A., Zurada, J.M. (eds.) ICAISC 2014. LNCS (LNAI), vol. 8467, pp. 12–21. Springer, Cham (2014). https://doi.org/10.1007/978-3-319-07173-2_2

14. Werbos, J.: Beyond Regression: New Tools for Prediction and Analysis in the Behavioral Sciences. Harvard University (1974)
15. Jordanov, I., Petrov, N., Petrozziello, A.: Classifiers accuracy improvement based on missing data imputation. J. Artif. Intell. Soft Comput. Res. **8**(1), 31–48 (2018)
16. Kamimura, R., Kitago, T.: Self-assimilation for solving excessive information acquisition in potential learning. J. Artif. Intell. Soft Comput. Res. **8**(1), 5–29 (2018)
17. Ke, Y., Hagiwara, M.: An English neural network that learns texts, finds hidden knowledge, and answers questions. J. Artif. Intell. Soft Comput. Res. **7**(4), 229–242 (2017)
18. Liu, H., Gegov, A., Cocea, M.: Rule based networks: an efficient and interpretable representation of computational models. J. Artif. Intell. Soft Comput. Res. **7**(2), 111–123 (2017)
19. Gabryel, M.: The bag-of-words method with different types of image features and dictionary analysis. J. Univ. Comput. Sci. **24**(4), 357–371 (2018)
20. Wróbel, M., Nieszporek, K., Starczewski, J.T., Cader, A.: A fuzzy measure for recognition of handwritten letter strokes. In: Rutkowski, L., Scherer, R., Korytkowski, M., Pedrycz, W., Tadeusiewicz, R., Zurada, J.M. (eds.) ICAISC 2018. LNCS (LNAI), vol. 10841, pp. 761–770. Springer, Cham (2018). https://doi.org/10.1007/978-3-319-91253-0_70
21. Nowicki, R.K., Starczewski, J.T.: A new method for classification of imprecise data using fuzzy rough fuzzification. Inf. Sci. **414**, 33–52 (2017)
22. Starczewski, J.T., Nieszporek, K., Wróbel, M., Grzanek, K.: A fuzzy SOM for understanding incomplete 3d faces. In: Rutkowski, L., Scherer, R., Korytkowski, M., Pedrycz, W., Tadeusiewicz, R., Zurada, J.M. (eds.) ICAISC 2018. LNCS (LNAI), vol. 10842, pp. 73–80. Springer, Cham (2018). https://doi.org/10.1007/978-3-319-91262-2_7
23. Tambouratzis, G.: Using particle swarm optimization to accurately identify syntactic phrases in free text. J. Artif. Intell. Soft Comput. Res. **8**(1), 63–67 (2018)
24. Yan, P.: Mapreduce and semantics enabled event detection using social media. J. Artif. Intell. Soft Comput. Res. **7**(3), 201–213 (2017)
25. Zalasiński, M., Cpałka, K., Er, M.J.: A new method for the dynamic signature verification based on the stable partitions of the signature. In: Rutkowski, L., Korytkowski, M., Scherer, R., Tadeusiewicz, R., Zadeh, L.A., Zurada, J.M. (eds.) ICAISC 2015. LNCS (LNAI), vol. 9120, pp. 161–174. Springer, Cham (2015). https://doi.org/10.1007/978-3-319-19369-4_16
26. Zalasiński, M., Cpałka, K., Rakus-Andersson, E.: An idea of the dynamic signature verification based on a hybrid approach. In: Rutkowski, L., Korytkowski, M., Scherer, R., Tadeusiewicz, R., Zadeh, L.A., Zurada, J.M. (eds.) ICAISC 2016. LNCS (LNAI), vol. 9693, pp. 232–246. Springer, Cham (2016). https://doi.org/10.1007/978-3-319-39384-1_21

Deep Neural Networks Applied to the Dynamic Helper System in a GPGPU

João Pedro Augusto Costa[1,3], Omar Andres Carmona Cortes[2(✉)],
Valério Breno Santos Nunes de Oliveira[2,3], and Ada Cristina França da Silva[3]

[1] Master Program in Computer Engineering and Systems (PECS),
Stadual University of Maranhão (UEMA), São Luis, MA, Brazil
jpac1207@gmail.com
[2] Computer Department (DComp), Federal Institute of Maranhão (IFMA),
São Luis, MA, Brazil
omar@ifma.edu.br, valerio.nunes@acad.ifma.edu.br
[3] VALE.SA, São Luis, MA, Brazil
ada.silva@vale.com

Abstract. This paper presents a study about the use of two deep neural networks (MLP and LSTM) in the Dynamic Helper System (DHS), which is a system that only exists in the EFC railway. The DHS assists a fully loaded train in sections with slopes and climbs. Therefore, this work shows that it is possible to predict the next action of the DHS using a classification algorithm, specifically, deep neural networks. The training and testing dataset is a real one, and the training task was performed using PyCUDA, Keras, and TensorFlow in a General Purpose GPU. Results using a real-world dataset indicate that deep neural networks can reach an accuracy above 99% and precision about 81% on predicting the next action of the DHS.

Keywords: Deep neural networks · Helper System · GPU

1 Introduction

A railway is an excellent alternative to transport large volumes of materials, like fuel, seeds, and minerals. Particularly in this work, a freight train usually transports ferrous metal from a *mine* to a *port* [16], using an infrastructure that consists of the train by itself, communication networks, and radio equipment. Between these two extreme points, the railway has to deal with many problems, such as vandalism, equipment failures, weather, and geographic conditions.

The tracks generally contain simple segments, known as **CDV** and segments that allow line changing, known as **WT**. This is a simplification of a duplicate railroad, that ignores telecommunication, automation and signaling equipment (Fig. 1).

© Springer Nature Switzerland AG 2019
L. Rutkowski et al. (Eds.): ICAISC 2019, LNAI 11508, pp. 29–38, 2019.
https://doi.org/10.1007/978-3-030-20912-4_3

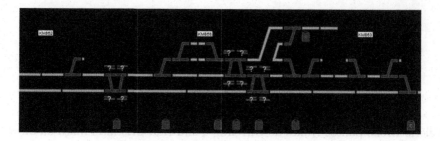

Fig. 1. Railway representation

As previously mentioned, railways are also subjected to many geographic conditions, such as erosions, landslides, and long hills. In this paper, a geographic condition called slope is essential to understand the importance of the DHS. The slope refers to the tangent of the angle from a surface to the horizontal and can be defined by $\{d, \delta h, I, \alpha\}$, where d is the horizontal distance, δh is the high, I is the slope length, and α is the angle of inclination. A slope with $\alpha \neq 0$ is presented as a climb when the train goes from the lowest point to the highest point, as presented in Fig. 2. In this situation, the train needs extra power to continue its journey because the train is usually fully loaded. The DHS gives the required extra power.

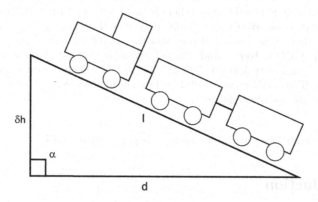

Fig. 2. Railway climb representation

In this context, the main idea of this paper is to identify the next step of the DHS to help the train to overcome the slope using deep neural networks particularly when it is fully loaded. At the best of our knowledge, there are no other works that explore any classification algorithm in the DHS. Moreover, the training task has been conducted in a General Purpose Graphical Unit Processing (GPGPU). The main reason for using GPGPUs is their parallel and high precision computing [14]. In fact, Artificial Neural Networks have been accelerated using GPUs in many types of research as presented in [11,15,23]. Further, using GPUs in Deep Learning is the cutting edge in Deep Neural Networks as shown in [9,10,21,22].

Thus, this paper is divided as follows: Sect. 2 describes how DHS works; Sect. 3 gives a brief introduction to deep neural networks and how the GPGPU was used in this work; Sect. 4 shows the results of the experiment using two different deep neural networks; finally, Sect. 5 presents the conclusions and future directions of this work.

2   The Dynamic Helper System

As previously mentioned, the DHS helps trains to climb slope sections of the railway. In this context, we need two definitions as follows:

Definition 1: A *train* is a set of loaded wagons.

Definition 2: *Helping* is the action of coupling at the end of a fully loaded train to give it the extra power required to overcome a climb [8].

Hence, there are two ways of using the DHS. The first one is called **Conventional Helper**, in which it is necessary to stop the train to start the procedure. In this particular case, the helping locomotive will leave the parallel line and pass to the traffic line. Afterward, the helper locomotive driver is responsible for the manual coupling of the air ducts that will synchronize the two trains brakes. This kind of helping is harmful for two reasons: it increases the required fuel in significant levels because it is necessary a new acceleration of the freight train, and decreases the availability of the line, *i.e.* if there is a train in the line it has to stop as well.

The second way is named **Dynamic Helper** and aims to avoid the problems caused by Conventional Helper. The word dynamic refers to the fact that the coupling between the helper wagon and the freight train occurs in movement. In this context, many electronics and pneumatic types of equipment compose the Dynamic Helper. One of them is called **End Of Train** (EOT), which is electro-pneumatic equipment that couples in the freight train tail and allows the train driver to perform the Helper procedure in a supervised way. Either, there exists a set of equipment that monitors the entire process, ensuring that the DH procedure is agile and secure.

The coupling process happens as follows: once the two locomotives are in the same line, a laser range-finder installed in the front of helper locomotive constantly measures the relative distance between the two trains, from about 100 m. The EOT contains a transducer that monitors the air ducts pressure and a GPS which informs the geographic position and the freight train speed (see simplified diagram in Fig. 3). All these information are given to the train driver by a friendly interface inside the locomotive, which presents alerts If any of the equipment variables are out of their respective limits; thus emergency actions can be taken, for example, the traction cut. Given that the speed and distance are monitored in meters by:

$$\begin{cases} \text{Laser Range-finder} \rightarrow \text{if } x \geq 0 \text{ and } x \leq 100 \\ \quad\text{EOT GPS} \rightarrow \text{if } x \geq 101 \text{ and } x \leq 1000 \end{cases} \tag{1}$$

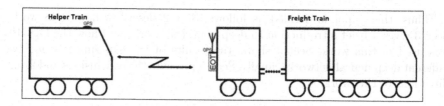

Fig. 3. Dynamic helper representation

with x being the current distance, the train driver is responsible for accelerating and break the Helper Locomotive using all this information. The locomotive interface presents in all routes the next action to be applied.

The entire process, from coupling to decoupling, involves the generation of time series at the end of the process—these series concern to distance and speed as presented in Fig. 4. These data are stored in text logs that are treated and used in this work to training the deep neural networks. Table 1 presents the main attributes we can find in the log file. These features help the driver to achieve a successful helping procedure. In this context, the possible actions are **{ACEL, MANT, FREIE, CTR, EMER, ACOP}**, which mean **accelerate, maintain, brake, traction cut, emergency** and **couple**, respectively.

Table 1. Attributes of Dynamic Helper log

Name	Description
GPS_POS	DH locomotive position from GPS
GPS_SP	DH locomotive speed from GPS
L_DIST	Relative distance from Rangefinder
L_SPEED	Relative speed from Rangefinder
B_PRESS	Brake pressure in moment
EOT_BAT	EOT battery level in moment
EOT_PRESS	Air ducts pressure in moment
EOT_GPS	Freight train position from EOT
EOT_SP	Freight train speed from EOT
AP	Acceleration point applied
REL_SP	Relative speed of persecution
REL_DIS	Relative distance of persecution
TRAC_CUT	Cut-off
ADV_VAL	Advance valve
CONT_GPS	Communication count

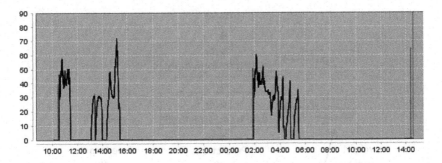

Fig. 4. Speed temporal series

3 Deep Neural Networks

Neural networks stayed out of favor as a general area of research until the eighties [2]. Since then, a significant breakthrough has been made in the field. Especially, after powerful computer architectures have popularized and big data becoming accessible to the general public. This scenario brought up all the condition to evolve a new area called deep learning, which is a field of machine learning consisting of learning successive layers to get increasingly meaningful representations [4]. Modern models of deep learning consist of tens or hundreds of successive layers that apply transformations learned from data to minimize a loss function using an optimizer as presented in Fig. 5. Concerning implementation, these transformations are often matrix and vector operations, which are more costly as the size of the data increases, *i.e.*, the bigger the data size, the higher the cost of training.

Hence, as we can see, Deep-learning networks are distinguished from the more conventional single-hidden-layer neural networks by their depth, *i.e.*, the number of node layers through which data passes in the process of pattern recognition. In deep-learning networks, each layer of nodes can train on a distinct set of features based on the previous layer's output. The further we advance into the neural net, the more complex the features nodes can recognize since they aggregate and recombine features from the previous layer.

In this work, we use two types of deep neural networks, a regular densely neural network, similar to **MLP** and the **LSTM** recurrent neural network [20]. The two chosen models have already been applied in a series of problems [17,18, 24] and are widely known in the literature.

In this work, we use two types of deep neural networks, a regular densely neural network, similar to **MLP** and a **LSTM** recurrent neural network [20]. These models have already been applied in a series of problems [17,18,24] and are widely known in the literature. All in all, the differences between those models are two. Each unit uses information of the current instance to apply weighted-sum operations passing the results to the forward layer in MLP, and each unit has multiple activation functions allowing past data to be used along with current instances, which is an exceptional characteristic given that data is sequential in LSTM.

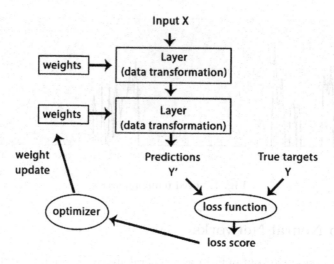

Fig. 5. Deep Default model

3.1   DNN in a GPU

With GPU's prices decreasing along the time, the development of deep neural networks became more forthcoming, allowing the fast development of many types of deep models, using frameworks like TensorFlow [1] and Caffe [12].

Deep neural networks have already been used in GPU in many previous works, generally to make the training process faster. Like in [13], that uses GPU to train of 1.2 million images in a large deep network; [6], that applies a Multi-column DNN in a set of image recognition problems, like the MNIST dataset.

Besides common image processing, GPUs are used to run problems with ample space of states, like in the multi DNN that mastering the famous game GO [18] and for large-vocabulary speech recognition [7]. In the context of this work, the GPUs are used to accelerate the training step, considering a large number of instances in helper procedures. Besides the training stage, we also get predictions faster, that is essential to open the possibility of automatic control. The agility provided by the GPU operations in comparison with CPU's allows faster retraining of the model as the procedure log provides new information.

4   Computational Experiments

In this section, we present the results of the deep neural networks by using a dataset generated by the attributes presented in Table 1. The dataset is devised by 65064 instances and 54 attributes. Table 2 presents the configurations that have been used in the training stage and tests. An expert in the area provided the information on what attributes are more important to the operation. Thus, booth algorithms receive the same 14 attributes as the input. The attributes are scaled and the prediction set **{ACEL, MANT, FREIE, CTR, EMER, ACOP}** are mapped into **{1, 2, 3, 4, 5, 6}** in order to use both of neural networks.

Table 2. Networks configuration

	MLP	LSTM
Architecture	{14,15,6}	{64,6}
Activations	{relu, relu, softmax}	{softmax}
Loss	cat. crossentropy	cat. crossentropy
Optimizer	rmsprop	rmsprop

All the tests were executed using the Keras API [3] over TensorFlow [1]. The algorithms are executed in a **GPU NVIDIA GEFORCE 840M** with 2 GB of video memory and 384 cores. To evaluate the networks we used the k-fold cross-validation method [5], with $k = 10$ and 1000 epochs. Doing so, each folder is tested with 6506 instances, which means about 10% of the dataset.

Tables 3 and 4 shows the accuracy and loss metrics for each fold in training process. Figures 6 and 7 shows the medium values over the epochs from each model. The results of both algorithms show high accuracy, with **MLP** performing better than LSTM for most folds, whereas **LSTM** shows a lower mean loss.

Table 3. Folds accuracy

Fold	MLP	LSTM
1	0.99538	0.99215
2	0.99492	0.99369
3	0.99307	0.99384
4	0.99569	0.99461
5	0.99538	0.99261
6	0.99446	0.99369
7	0.99353	0.99400
8	0.99507	0.99461
9	0.99292	0.99369
10	0.99523	0.99338
Mean	0.99457	0.99363
Std. Dev	0.00010	0.00077

Table 4. Folds loss

Fold	MLP	LSTM
1	0.01834	0.02047
2	0.01418	0.01453
3	0.01539	0.01314
4	0.01915	0.01425
5	0.02697	0.01846
6	0.01312	0.02057
7	0.02418	0.01828
8	0.02587	0.02189
9	0.03827	0.02154
10	0.02922	0.02103
Mean	0.02247	0.01842
Std. Dev	0.00791	0.00329

Precision, recall, and accuracy, defined by Eqs. 2, 3 and 4 respectively, assess the quality of the test phase, in which n is the number of classes, TP_i represents

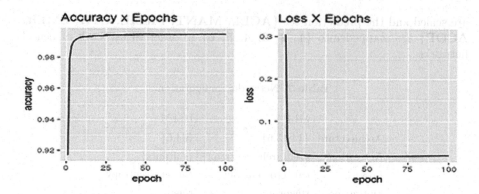

Fig. 6. Accuracy and loss MLP

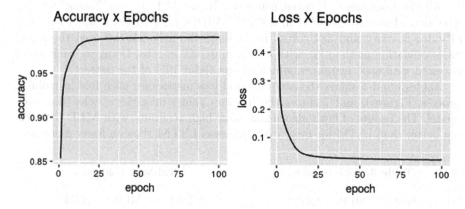

Fig. 7. Accuracy and loss LSTM

the number of observations ranked correctly as class i, TN_i is the number of observations labeled correctly as not belonging to the i class, FP_i represents the observations assigned incorrectly to the class i, and FN_i is the amount of observations wrongly labeled as class i [19].

$$\frac{\sum_{i=1}^{i=n} \frac{TP_i}{TP_i+FP_i}}{n} \tag{2}$$

$$\frac{\sum_{i=1}^{i=n} \frac{TP_i}{TP_i+FN_i}}{n} \tag{3}$$

$$\frac{\sum_{i=1}^{i=n} \frac{TP_i+TN_i}{TP_i+FN_i+FP_i+TN_i}}{n} \tag{4}$$

The Table 5 shows the results for both deep networks.

Table 5. Algorithms configuration

Name	Precision	Recall	Accuracy
MLP	81.79365%	82.03600%	99.81900%
LSTM	81.82288%	81.05381%	99.78772%

According to the tests, the **MLP** architecture achieves the bests results showing a very high accuracy. On the other hand, it is important to note that the **LSTM** also produces very high accuracy, better than in the training step, showing that the model reaches a good generalization from new data.

5   Conclusion and Future Work

This work shows that it is possible to predict the next action in the Dynamic Helper System using deep neural networks with high accuracy. The **MLP** achieved better results than **LSTM** on Recall and Accuracy metrics, whereas the recurrent network achieved a better Precision. Anyway, the differences between these two neural networks might be minimum when enough data is available, which is the case in this work. The results can be improved by using more data, that is available at the cost of more time for re-training.

Future work includes predicting the specific acceleration and breakpoint for the helper locomotive and developing an automatic control for the system by implementing a deep neural network in the locomotive directly.

References

1. Abadi, M., et al.: TensorFlow: a system for large-scale machine learning. OSDI. **16**, 265–283 (2016)
2. Aggarwal, C.C.: Neural Networks and Deep Learning. Springer, Cham (2018). https://doi.org/10.1007/978-3-319-94463-0
3. Arnold, T.B.: kerasR: R interface to the keras deep learning library. J. Open Source Softw. **2** (2017)
4. Chollet, F., Allaire, J.J.: Deep Learning with R. Manning Publications Company, Greenwich (2018)
5. Cigizoglu, H.K., Kişi, Ö.: Flow prediction by three back propagation techniques using k-fold partitioning of neural network training data. Hydrol. Res. **36**(1), 49–64 (2005)
6. Ciresan, D.C., Meier, U., Schmidhuber, J.: Multi-column deep neural networks for image classification. CoRR abs/1202.2745 (2012). http://arxiv.org/abs/1202.2745
7. Dahl, G.E., Yu, D., Deng, L., Acero, A.: Context-dependent pre-trained deep neural networks for large-vocabulary speech recognition. IEEE Trans. Audio Speech Lang. Process **20**(1), 30–42 (2012)
8. Di-eletrons, Marcílio Dias Street, 201, Belo Horizonte, MG - Brasil: Dynamic Helper Manual, e edn. (2010)

9. Dong, S., Gong, X., Sun, Y., Baruah, T., Kaeli, D.: Characterizing the microarchitectural implications of a convolutional neural network (CNN) execution on GPUs. In: Proceedings of the 2018 ACM/SPEC International Conference on Performance Engineering, ICPE 2018, pp. 96–106. ACM, New York (2018)

10. Dong, S., Kaeli, D.: DNNMark: a deep neural network benchmark suite for GPUs. In: Proceedings of the General Purpose GPUs, GPGPU-2010, New York, pp. 63–72 (2017)

11. Ho, T.Y., Lam, P.M., Leung, C.S.: Parallelization of cellular neural networks on GPU. Pattern Recogn. **41**(8), 2684–2692 (2008)

12. Jia, Y., et al.: Caffe: convolutional architecture for fast feature embedding. In: Proceedings of the 22nd ACM International Conference on Multimedia, pp. 675–678. ACM (2014)

13. Krizhevsky, A., Sutskever, I., Hinton, G.E.: ImageNet classification with deep convolutional neural networks. In: Pereira, F., Burges, C.J.C., Bottou, L., Weinberger, K.Q. (eds.) Advances in Neural Information Processing Systems, vol. 25, pp. 1097–1105. Curran Associates, Inc. (2012). http://papers.nips.cc/paper/4824-imagenet-classification-with-deep-convolutional-neural-networks.pdf

14. Mark, W.R., Glanville, R.S., Akeley, K., Kilgard, M.J.: Cg: a system for programming graphics hardware in a c-like language. ACM Trans. Graph. **22**(3), 896–907 (2003)

15. Pendlebury, J., Xiong, H., Walshe, R.: Artificial neural network simulation on cuda. In: Proceedings of the 2012 IEEE/ACM 16th International Symposium on Distributed Simulation and Real Time Applications, DS-RT 2012, pp. 228–233. IEEE Computer Society, Washington, DC (2012)

16. Pinheiro, E., Miranda, E., Oliveira, A.: On the train timetabling problem and heuristics, Brazilian Symposium of Operation Research (2016)

17. Rowley, H.A., Baluja, S., Kanade, T.: Neural network-based face detection. IEEE Trans. Pattern Anal. Mach. Intell. **20**(1), 23–38 (1998)

18. Silver, D., et al.: Mastering the game of go with deep neural networks and tree search. Nature **529**(7587), 484 (2016)

19. Sokolova, M., Lapalme, G.: A systematic analysis of performance measures for classification tasks. Inf. Process. Manage. **45**(4), 427–437 (2009)

20. Sundermeyer, M., Schlüter, R., Ney, H.: LSTM neural networks for language modeling. In: Thirteenth Annual Conference of the International Speech Communication Association (2012)

21. Wang, L., et al.: SuperNeurons: dynamic GPU memory management for training deep neural networks. SIGPLAN Not. **53**(1), 41–53 (2018)

22. Wu, S., Zhang, M., Chen, G., Chen, K.: A new approach to compute CNNs for extremely large images. In: Proceedings of the 2017 ACM on Conference on Information and Knowledge Management, CIKM 2017, pp. 39–48. ACM, New York (2017)

23. Yazdanbakhsh, A., Park, J., Sharma, H., Lotfi-Kamran, P., Esmaeilzadeh, H.: Neural acceleration for GPU throughput processors. In: Proceedings of the 48th International Symposium on Microarchitecture, MICRO-48, pp. 482–493. ACM, New York (2015)

24. Zhou, C., Sun, C., Liu, Z., Lau, F.: A C-LSTM neural network for text classification. arXiv preprint arXiv:1511.08630 (2015)

Combining Neural and Knowledge-Based Approaches to Named Entity Recognition in Polish

Sławomir Dadas[(✉)]

National Information Processing Institute, Warsaw, Poland
`slawomir.dadas@opi.org.pl`

Abstract. Named entity recognition (NER) is one of the tasks in natural language processing that can greatly benefit from the use of external knowledge sources. We propose a named entity recognition framework composed of knowledge-based feature extractors and a deep learning model including contextual word embeddings, long short-term memory (LSTM) layers and conditional random fields (CRF) inference layer. We use an entity linking module to integrate our system with Wikipedia. The combination of effective neural architecture and external resources allows us to obtain state-of-the-art results on recognition of Polish proper names. We evaluate our model on the data from PolEval 2018 (http://2018.poleval.pl/) NER challenge on which it outperforms other methods, reducing the error rate by 22.4% compared to the winning solution.

Keywords: Named entity recognition · Wikipedia · Entity linking

1 Introduction

Named entity recognition (NER) is a problem of finding and classifying instances of named entities in text. NER systems are usually designed to detect entities from a pre-defined set of classes such as person names, temporal expressions, organizations, addresses. Such methods can be used independently but they are often one of the first steps in a complex natural language understanding (NLU) workflows involving multiple models. Therefore the performance of NER systems can affect the performance of NLU downstream tasks. The problem of named entity recognition is challenging because often both contextual information and domain knowledge are required to accurately recognize and categorize named entities.

1.1 Prior Work

Popular approach to named entity recognition is to train a sequence labeling model, i.e. a machine learning model that assigns a label to each word in a sentence indicating whether that word is a part of named entity or not. In

L. Rutkowski et al. (Eds.): ICAISC 2019, LNAI 11508, pp. 39–50, 2019.
https://doi.org/10.1007/978-3-030-20912-4_4

the past few years, methods based on neural networks were the dominant solutions to this problem. Collobert and Weston [6] showed that it is possible to train effective sequence labelling models with neural architecture involving word embeddings. Later, other word embedding approaches became popular, notably Word2Vec [16], GloVe [19] and FastText [2]. Deep learning NER systems utilised those models as well as LSTM layers (long short-term memory) for encoding the sentence level information and CRF (conditional random fields) inference layer [10,11,13,29]. Some studies highlighted the importance of character level features by integrating additional character based representations. To this end, CNNs (convolutional neural networks) [4,13,29] or bidirectional LSTMs [11,12,20,27] were used. Most recently, state-of-the-art NER systems employed word representations based on pre-trained language models, either replacing classic word embedding approaches [20,21] or using both representations jointly [1]. In Polish, early tools for named entity recognition were based on heuristic rules and predefined grammars [9,22] or CRF models with hand-crafted features [15,26,30]. Pohl [24] used OpenCyc and Wikipedia to build purely knowledge-based NER system. Only recently methods involving deep learning were introduced [3,14].

While modern named entity recognition methods have made considerable progress in exploiting contextual information and long term dependencies in text, in some cases it is not sufficient to accurately recognize a named entity. When the context does not provide enough information, model should be able to use external knowledge to help with the detection and classification. Such a need exists, for example, in the case of abbreviations or highly ambiguous phrases that can refer to several different entities. Therefore, we believe that the problem of integrating knowledge sources with NER models should be explored. In this work, we focus on named entity recognition for Polish language. We show how such model can be integrated with Wikipedia and how can we improve its performance by using an external knowledge base.

1.2   Contributions

Our contributions are the following: (1) We propose a named entity recognition system for Polish that combines deep learning architecture with knowledge-based feature extractors, achieving state-of-the art results for this task. (2) We propose a method utilizing an entity linking model based on Wikipedia to improve the accuracy of named entity recognition. Additionally, we release a tool for efficient labeling of Wikipedia's articles. (3) We make the source code of our method available, along with pre-trained models for NER, pre-trained Polish Word2Vec [16] embeddings and ELMo [21] embeddings, labeled data set of articles from Polish Wikipedia and two lexicons.

2   Problem Description and System Architecture

In this section, we describe the problem of Named Entity Recognition for the Polish language, following the guidelines of the National Corpus of Polish (NKJP) [25].

We introduce the challenges that arise from this task. Then, we present the general architecture of our system and show how it addresses those challenges. Finally, we describe language resources and external modules used by the system.

2.1   Problem Description

The National Corpus of Polish (NKJP) is one of the largest text corpora of Polish language. A part of the corpus, so called *"one million subcorpus"*, has been manually annotated which allows to use it as a training set for many natural language processing tasks. Among others, the subcorpus contains annotations of named entities from several entity categories, which in turn may be further divided into subcategories. Therefore, our task is to detect and classify any mention of a named entity in text, assigning the correct category and subcategory if applicable. NKJP identifies the following set of categories: *persName* (names of real and fictional people), *orgName* (organization names), *geogName* (names of geographical and man made structures), *placeName* (geopolitical names), *date*, *time*.

Although the structure of the National Corpus of Polish in the context of named entity recognition requires a few task specific tweaks, our model can still be easily adapted to other sequence labeling tasks, in particular to named entity recognition in other languages. We decided to resolve task specific issues with simple solutions that would not require to change the core model architecture. Here, we provide a brief explanations of those problems and our solutions:

Nested labels - NKJP defines main categories and subcategories for named entities. Out of six main categories, two contain subcategories. For *placeName*, every instance of a named entity can be assigned exactly one of its subcategories. For *persName*, each word in a named entity can possibly have different subcategory, or no subcategory at all. Our solution to this problem was to train two models: one for predicting main categories and another for predicting subcategories. The architecture of both models is identical, except the model for subcategories takes another one-hot feature vector as an input which is the output label of its parent model (the main category label). In this work, we describe the main model only since we use exactly the same training procedure and the same hyperparameters for the subcategory model.

Overlapping entities - Given an example named entity of *"Johns Hopkins Hospital in Baltimore"*, it may be labeled as *geogName* or *orgName* depending on the sentence context. However, fragments of this entity can also be labeled as *persName* (*"Johns Hopkins"*) and *placeName-settlement* (*"Baltimore"*). There is a number of similar cases in the NKJP data set, where fragments of named entity are named entities themselves. That makes this task a multi-label classification problem where most samples are assigned a single label and small number of edge cases have two labels. To avoid transforming our model to multi-label classifier, we decided to move smaller overlapping entities to subcategory model i.e. we train the subcategory model as they were subcategories of the longer entity. It doesn't solve all cases - some cannot be properly labeled with this approach - but the model is able to learn most of them.

2.2   System Architecture

Figure 1 shows a general architecture of our system. The system consists of four modules: an entity linking model based on Wikipedia (described in Sect. 3), a feature extractors module (which integrates the aforementioned entity linker and a number of lexicons) and two deep learning models. Each word or word n-gram in an input sentence is first preprocessed by feature extractors that assign additional labels to it. The extractors used by our system are described in the next subsection. The enriched sequence of words is then used as an input to the neural models. An architecture of such model is shown in Fig. 2. Our model is similar to other recent deep learning NER architectures [10,11,13,29]. First, a vectorized representation of word is constructed by concatenating an output of pre-trained word embedding, a trainable character level encoder and a set of one-hot vectors from feature extraction module. Next, a hidden word representation is computed by a number of bidirectional LSTM layers. Finally, this representation is sent to a CRF output layer, which is responsible for predicting a sequence of labels Y that maximizes the probability $P(Y|X)$, where X is the sequence of word vectors. Two such models are utilised by our system, resulting in two output sequences: Y_{main} for main categories and Y_{sub} for subcategories of named entities. In order to correctly resolve multi word entities, we use BIO (beginning-inside-outside) tagging scheme as the output format of Y_{main} and Y_{sub} sequences.

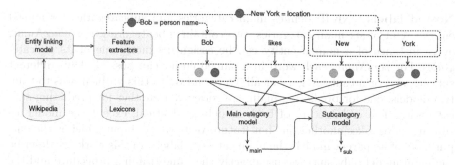

Fig. 1. High level architecture of our named entity recognition system. Entity linking and feature extractor modules are responsible for enriching input with information from lexicons and Wikipedia. Input sequences are then sent to two neural models, predicting main categories and subcategories of named entities. A sequence of predicted main entity classes Y_{main} is used as an input to subcategory model which outputs a sequence of entity subclasses Y_{sub}.

2.3   Feature Extractors

To support the detection of named entities, our system uses a number of additional feature extractors. Some of the features described below use static language resources, other are based on heuristic rules. The Wikipedia module deserves additional attention since it employs an external standalone service based on the Wikipedia-Miner project [18], using the Polish Wikipedia dump as a data source. Here, we present a short descriptions of all extractors, more information on the process of integrating our system with Wikipedia can be found in the Sect. 3. Although the implementation of those feature extractors can vary in complexity, the purpose of each module is to assign a label to a word in the input sequence. Such label is then encoded as a one-hot vector and the vector is concatenated to produce the final word representation, consisting of the word embedding, character-based word representation and all the one-hot vectors provided by the feature modules. The full list of one-hot features used by our system includes:

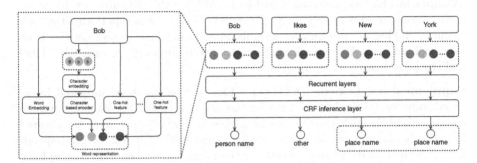

Fig. 2. An architecture of our neural named entity recognition model. The model takes word sequence as an input, in this example *"Bob likes New York"*. For each word in the sequence, a vectorized word representation is built. Figure on the left shows the structure of the module responsible for building word representations. Different components of the resulting vector are represented with different colors - red for word embedding, yellow for character encoder, blue for one-hot feature modules. On the right, complete architecture is shown, featuring recurrent layers and CRF inference layer. (Color figure online)

Capitalization Feature - Following other works on Named Entity Recognition [10,28], we add a capitalization feature providing information about the casing of the input.

PoliMorf - PoliMorf [31] is an open-source Polish morphological dictionary containing over 7 million word forms assigned to over 200 word categories. In addition to the word categories, each entry in the dictionary contains a word lemma, part-of-speech tag and optional supplementary tags describing the word.

PersonNames (lexicon of Polish, English and foreign names) - The lexicon contains about 346 thousand first and last names crawled from various Internet sources. Each name in the dictionary is labeled either as a Polish, English or foreign (other). Additional label indicates if a name is also a common word in Polish or English.

GPNE (Gazetteer for Polish Named Entities) - The gazetteer has been created for the task of Named Entity Recognition in Polish and over the years it has been used by several NER systems i.e. the SProUT platform [22,23] or NERF [30]. It includes forenames and surnames, geographical names, institution names, country names and their derivatives and parts of temporal expressions among others.

NELexicon2 - This resource is a lexicon of named entities, created and maintained in Wroclaw University of Technology [15]. Most of the entries have been extracted automatically from several sources such as Wikipedia infoboxes or Wiktionary. It contains more than 2.3 million names.

Wikipedia (Entity Linking Module) - While other features are based on static resources, this module is a contextual classifier which performs the task of entity linking i.e. recognizing and disambiguating mentions of entities from Wikipedia in text. After the linking phase, each found entity is assigned a label and the label is used as an input to the system.

Supplementary Lexicon (Extras) - This lexicon has been prepared by us specifically for PolEval Named Entity Recognition task. Our intention was to create an additional resource containing classes of words that were not covered by other dictionaries but were essential for a successful NER system. More specifically, the dictionary consists mostly of the names of settlements, geographical regions, countries and continents. Besides that, it also contains common abbreviations of institutions' names. This resource was created in a semi-automatic way, by first extracting the words and their forms from SJP.PL[1] - a free, community driven dictionary of Polish - and then manually filtering out mismatched words.

3   Wikipedia Integration

One of the distinctive features of our system is the use the Wikipedia as a supplementary resource that helps to detect named entities, improving the accuracy of the model. Unlike lexicons and other static resources, modules based on evolving knowledge-bases such as Wikipedia can be automatically updated which is particularly important for named entity recognition systems that need to stay up to date in order to prevent the degradation of their performance over time. Our approach to utilizing Wikipedia involved labeling the articles with tags corresponding to named entity categories. We then used an entity linking method from the Wikipedia Miner [18] toolkit, which we modified slightly to make it suitable for named entity recognition. The linked entities were assigned labels from our data set and the labels were used as an input to the deep learning model. In order to prepare the labeled set, we developed WikiMapper - an open source GUI application for tagging Wikipedia's pages[2]. In this section, we describe the principles of operation of the aforementioned tool, the process of creating the

---

[1] https://sjp.pl.

[2] https://github.com/sdadas/wiki-mapper.

data set and our method of improving named entity recognition by the use of an additional entity linking model.

3.1 Data Set Preparation

The process of manually labeling data sets with millions of samples is usually costly and time-consuming. In some cases, however, it is possible to exploit the structure of data in order to make it more efficient. With regards to Wikipedia, we can take advantage of the fact that the structure is hierarchical i.e. each article is assigned at least one category and each category except the main categories has at least one parent category. When labeling the data, we rarely can benefit from moving down to the level of individual articles, we typically want to assign a label to all articles in a category. Depending on the task, this category can be more specific or general. On the basis of these assumptions, we have developed WikiMapper tool, with the objective of accelerating the workflow of manually tagging Wikipedia. It allows to quickly search articles and categories by title and efficiently traverse the category tree. We can use it to tag an individual article, a category or a set of pages matching specific search criteria. When a label is assigned to a category, it is automatically propagated to its child categories and articles. Since it's legal for an article or category to have multiple parents, every node in a graph can possibly have many inherited labels. In such cases, label conflicts are resolved in the following way: (1) For every path leading from unlabelled node to all of its labelled parent nodes, select the label connected with the shortest path. (2) When there are multiple paths of the same shortest length, select the most frequently occurring label among those paths. In the case of a tie, select the label arbitrarily. Using the WikiMapper tool, we managed to label over 90% of 1.1 million articles in Polish Wikipedia in 5 h.

3.2 Entity Linking Feature Module

Entity linking is the task of detecting and disambiguating named entities defined in a knowledge base (e.g. Wikipedia, BabelNet, DBPedia[3]). Its objective is to create a mapping between mentions of named entities in text and their references in the knowledge base. This is closely related to the task of named entity recognition that can be seen as creating a mapping between instances of named entities and a set of pre-defined labels. Therefore it is possible to utilize entity linking model as a NER model by assigning a set of named entity labels to objects in the knowledge base. Such standalone methods have been proposed before [24], our approach employs the knowledge-based model as a part of a deep learning named entity recognition system. The process works as follows. First, the entity linking model finds references to entities in text. Next, a label assigned to such reference - coming from a data set described earlier - is used to tag this instance of named entity. Labels are then transformed to a one-hot vectors and passed as an input to the neural model.

---

[3] https://www.wikipedia.org, https://babelnet.org, https://wiki.dbpedia.org.

To explain the entity linking method itself, we need to summarize the methodology of the Wikipedia Miner [18] framework. Two important definitions that we will use in this section is the *concept* and the *label*. The concept is an entity existing in the knowledge-base i.e. an article in Wikipedia. The label is a fragment of text that might be referring to a concept. Not all labels are unambiguous, some are used to describe different concepts depending on the context in which they appear. Wikipedia Miner collects several statistics from the dump of Wikipedia, one of them is a set of labels linking to each of the concepts with their frequencies. Additionally, the framework computes prior link probability $p(l)$ for every label l which is the ratio of the number of times the label is used as a link between concepts to a total number of occurrences of this label in text corpus.

The fundamental measure on which the entity linking method is based is the *relatedness*. It reflects how closely two concepts are related and is based on Normalized Google Distance [5]:

$$rel(a,b) = 1 - \frac{log(max(|A|,|B|)) - log(|A \cap B|)}{log(|W|) - log(min(|A|,|B|))} \tag{1}$$

Where $rel(a,b)$ it the relatedness between concepts a and b, $|A|$ is the number of articles linking to a, $|B|$ is the number of articles linking to b, $|A \cap B|$ is the number of articles linking to both a and b, $|W|$ is the number of all articles.

Entity linking in Wikipedia Miner [18] works in the context of a single text document. First, all candidate labels are found in the text. Labels with prior probability $p(l)$ lower than a specified threshold are discarded. From the remaining labels a set of possible concepts is determined. Next, a decision tree classifier called *disambiguator* is used to score every label-concept pair (l, c) found in the text. The model takes as an input three statistics related to the (l, c) pair and outputs a single value from 0 to 1 representing the disambiguation probability i.e. the probability that the label l is referring to the concept c. Originally, the method filtered concepts based on disambiguator outputs, preserving only the highest scoring concepts. In order to make the process more suited for named entity recognition, we modified the concept selection method. First, we apply heuristic rules that discard most likely irrelevant concepts and labels (single character labels, numeric labels, labels consisting of lowercase common words only, labels with person names but not referring to a concept tagged as *persName*). Then, for each ambiguous label, we score its concepts based on the average of disambiguator output and relatedness of the concept to all unambiguous concepts in the document. Finally, the highest scoring concept for the label is selected.

4   System Evaluation

In this section, we evaluate our named entity recognition system on the data from Poleval 2018 competition. PolEval is an evaluation series for natural language processing in Polish inspired by SemEval[4]. PolEval 2018, which was held from

---

[4] https://en.wikipedia.org/wiki/SemEval.

June to August, included an evaluation of named entity recognition tools. A new annotated data set has been prepared specifically for this task in accordance to the guidelines of NKJP. In this competition, the original NKJP set has been used for training while the new data set for evaluation of the models.

Table 1. Evaluation of our model on the data from PolEval 2018 NER task. We compare for variations of our model with three best models from this competition. The final score for this task is based on the combination of *exact match* and *overlap* F1 scores (*Final score = 0.8 * Overlap score + 0.2 * Exact match score*). For computing our scores, we used the official evaluation script provided by the organizers.

Model	Final score	Improvement	Exact score	Overlap score
Liner2 [15]	81.0		77.8	81.8
PolDeepNer [14]	85.1		82.2	85.9
Per group LSTM-CRF with Contextual String Embeddings [3]	86.6		82.6	87.7
Without external resources				
Our model (Word2Vec)	84.6	−2.0/−12.9%	80.2	85.7
Our model (ELMo)	87.9	1.3/9.7%	84.5	88.8
With Wikipedia and lexicons				
Our model (Word2Vec)	87.3	0.7/5.2%	82.9	88.4
Our model (ELMo)	**89.6**	3.0/22.4%	**86.2**	**90.5**

Training and Evaluation Procedure. Our model was trained on the annotated *one million subcorpus* of NKJP. The publicly available version of the subcorpus is already tokenized and includes additional metadata such as lemmas or part-of-speech tags. On the other hand, the PolEval data set has been published in a raw text form. For this reason, it was required to tokenize and lemmatize the data before it could be used for model evaluation. For sentence splitting and tokenization, we used the tokenizer from LanguageTool [17]. For lemmatization, a simple frequency-based lemmatizer was used, selecting the most frequently occurring form in the corpus from the list of word forms suggested by Morfologik[5]. Each of our models was trained for 10 epochs using NADAM optimization algorithm [7] with the learning rate of 0.002, β_1 of 0.9, β_2 of 0.999 and batch size of 32. We used 10-fold cross-validation procedure on the NKJP data set in order to select optimal hyperparameters for our model. Our final architecture used in the evaluation stage included three LSTM layers with 100 hidden units and a CRF inference layer. Variational dropout [8] with the probability of 0.25 has been applied before each recurrent layer. A character level representation based on CharCNN was selected for the final model.

---

[5] https://github.com/morfologik/morfologik-stemming.

In order to highlight the elements of our model that had the greatest impact on the performance in named entity recognition, we present four variations of the model. The best performing model utilizes contextualized ELMo embeddings by Peters et al. [21] trained on a large corpus of Polish and includes external features from Wikipedia and lexicons. As a baseline, we decided to evaluate the same architecture trained with static Word2Vec embeddings. Additionally, those two approaches were trained as standalone neural models, without using any external resources.

Discussion. We compare the performance of our system with three best submissions from PolEval 2018 in Table 1, reporting an absolute and relative improvement over the winning solution. The competing approaches are the following:

– **Per group LSTM-CRF with Contextual String Embeddings** [3] - The winning solution proposed an approach similar to Akbik et al. [1], utilizing contextual embeddings based on shallow pre-trained language model in combination with GloVe word embeddings. To address the problem of overlapping named entities, they trained a few separate NER models, each dedicated for detecting only a subset of NKJP labels.
– **PolDeepNer** [14] - An ensemble of three different deep learning models.
– **Liner2** [15] - A CRF based NER system actively developed since 2013.

The evaluation results show that the contextual word embeddings and knowledge-based features both significantly increase the performance of the model. Of our four models, only the basic version with Word2Vec and no external resources does not improve the score over the winning approach from PolEval. It's interesting to compare our standalone ELMo model with Borchmann et al. [3] since both utilize recently introduced contextual embeddings. Named entity recognition models with Flair [1] and ELMo [21] have already been compared for English. Contrary to English results, ELMo seems to perform better than Flair for Polish. This can be due to the fact that ELMo, with more layers and more parameters, is better suited for complex and challenging languages such as Polish. We can also observe that knowledge-based features have a bigger impact on the model with static embeddings. For Word2Vec, there is a 2.7% absolute improvement in the score, while the improvement for ELMo is 1.7%. However, this is understandable, since the benefits of contextual information and external knowledge are overlapping. Compared with our baseline model, ELMo and language resources combined increase the score of our model by as much as 5%, from 84.6 to 89.6. Compared with the best solution from PolEval, our model improves the score by 3%, reducing the error rate by 22.4%.

5   Conclusions

In this paper, we presented a neural architecture for named entity recognition and demonstrated how to improve its performance by using an entity linking model with a knowledge base such as Wikipedia. We have shown how to exploit the structure of Wikipedia to efficiently create labeled data sets for supervised natural language tasks. The evaluation of our system on data from PolEval 2018 shows that it can produce state-of-the-art performance for named entity recognition tasks in Polish. An improvement over previous approaches is the effect of combining knowledge-based features, contextual word embeddings and optimal hyperparameter selection. Integrating entity linking methods into NER systems is a promising direction that can be pursued to further improve the accuracy of such systems, especially using modern entity linking approaches involving deep learning methods such as graph embeddings that can be easily incorporated into other neural architectures.

References

1. Akbik, A., Blythe, D., Vollgraf, R.: Contextual string embeddings for sequence labeling. In: 27th International Conference on Computational Linguistics, COLING 2018, pp. 1638–1649 (2018)
2. Bojanowski, P., Grave, E., Joulin, A., Mikolov, T.: Enriching word vectors with subword information. Trans. Assoc. Comput. Linguist. **5**, 135–146 (2017)
3. Borchmann, L., Gretkowski, A., Graliński, F.: Approaching nested named entity recognition with parallel LSTM-CRFs. In: Proceedings of AI and NLP Workshop Day 2018 (2018)
4. Chiu, J.P., Nichols, E.: Named entity recognition with bidirectional LSTM-CNNs. Trans. Assoc. Comput. Linguist. **4**, 357–370 (2016)
5. Cilibrasi, R.L., Vitanyi, P.M.: The Google similarity distance. IEEE Trans. Knowl. Data Eng. **19**(3), 370–383 (2007)
6. Collobert, R., Weston, J.: A unified architecture for natural language processing: deep neural networks with multitask learning. In: Proceedings of the 25th International Conference on Machine Learning, pp. 160–167. ACM (2008)
7. Dozat, T.: Incorporating Nesterov momentum into ADAM. In: ICLR (2016)
8. Gal, Y., Ghahramani, Z.: A theoretically grounded application of dropout in recurrent neural networks. In: Advances in Neural Information Processing Systems, pp. 1019–1027 (2016)
9. Graliński, F., Jassem, K., Marcińczuk, M., Wawrzyniak, P.: Named entity recognition in machine anonymization. In: Recent Advances in Intelligent Information Systems (2009)
10. Huang, Z., Xu, W., Yu, K.: Bidirectional LSTM-CRF models for sequence tagging. CoRR abs/1508.01991 (2015)
11. Lample, G., Ballesteros, M., Subramanian, S., Kawakami, K., Dyer, C.: Neural architectures for named entity recognition. In: Proceedings of NAACL-HLT, pp. 260–270 (2016)
12. Liu, L., et al.: Empower sequence labeling with task-aware neural language model. arXiv preprint arXiv:1709.04109 (2017)
13. Ma, X., Hovy, E.: End-to-end sequence labeling via bi-directional LSTM-CNNs-CRF. In: Proceedings of the 54th Annual Meeting of the Association for Computational Linguistics (Volume 1: Long Papers), pp. 1064–1074 (2016)
14. Marcińczuk, M., Kocoń, J., Gawor, M.: Recognition of named entities for Polish-comparison of deep learning and conditional random fields approaches. In: Ogrodniczuk, M., Kobyliński, Ł. (eds.) Proceedings of the PolEval 2018 Workshop, pp. 77–92. Institute of Computer Science, Polish Academy of Science (2018)

15. Marcińczuk, M., Kocoń, J., Janicki, M.: Liner2-a customizable framework for proper names recognition for Polish. In: Bembenik, R., Skonieczny, L., Rybinski, H., Kryszkiewicz, M., Niezgodka, M. (eds.) Intelligent Tools for Building a Scientific Information Platform. SCI, vol. 467, pp. 231–253. Springer, Heidelberg (2013). https://doi.org/10.1007/978-3-642-35647-6_17
16. Mikolov, T., Sutskever, I., Chen, K., Corrado, G.S., Dean, J.: Distributed representations of words and phrases and their compositionality. In: Advances in Neural Information Processing Systems, pp. 3111–3119 (2013)
17. Miłkowski, M.: Developing an open-source, rule-based proofreading tool. Softw. Pract. Exp. **40**(7), 543–566 (2010)
18. Milne, D., Witten, I.H.: An open-source toolkit for mining Wikipedia. Artif. Intell. **194**, 222–239 (2013)
19. Pennington, J., Socher, R., Manning, C.: Glove: global vectors for word representation. In: Proceedings of the 2014 Conference on Empirical Methods in Natural Language Processing (EMNLP), pp. 1532–1543 (2014)
20. Peters, M., Ammar, W., Bhagavatula, C., Power, R.: Semi-supervised sequence tagging with bidirectional language models. In: Proceedings of the 55th Annual Meeting of the Association for Computational Linguistics (Volume 1: Long Papers), pp. 1756–1765 (2017)
21. Peters, M., et al.: Deep contextualized word representations. In: Proceedings of the 2018 Conference of the North American Chapter of the Association for Computational Linguistics: Human Language Technologies (Volume 1: Long Papers), pp. 2227–2237 (2018)
22. Piskorski, J.: Named-entity recognition for Polish with SProUT. In: Bolc, L., Michalewicz, Z., Nishida, T. (eds.) IMTCI 2004. LNCS (LNAI), vol. 3490, pp. 122–133. Springer, Heidelberg (2005). https://doi.org/10.1007/11558637_13
23. Piskorski, J., Schäfer, U., Xu, F.: Shallow processing with unification and typed feature structures-foundations and applications. Knstliche Intelligenz **1**(1), 17–23 (2004)
24. Pohl, A.: Knowledge-based named entity recognition in Polish. In: Federated Conference on Computer Science and Information Systems (FedCSIS), pp. 145–151. IEEE (2013)
25. Przepiórkowski, A., Banko, M., Górski, R.L., Lewandowska-Tomaszczyk, B.: National Corpus of Polish. Polish Scientific Publishers PWN, Warsaw (2012)
26. Radziszewski, A.: A tiered CRF tagger for Polish. Intelligent Tools for Building a Scientific Information Platform, vol. 467, pp. 215–230. Springer, Heidelberg (2013). https://doi.org/10.1007/978-3-642-35647-6_16
27. Rei, M.: Semi-supervised multitask learning for sequence labeling. arXiv preprint arXiv:1704.07156 (2017)
28. Reimers, N., Gurevych, I.: Optimal hyperparameters for deep LSTM-networks for sequence labeling tasks. arXiv preprint arXiv:1707.06799 (2017)
29. dos Santos, C., Guimaraes, V., Niterói, R., de Janeiro, R.: Boosting named entity recognition with neural character embeddings. In: Proceedings of NEWS 2015 the Fifth Named Entities Workshop, p. 25 (2015)
30. Waszczuk, J.: NERF - named entity recognition tool based on linear-chain CRFs (2012). http://zil.ipipan.waw.pl/Nerf
31. Wolinski, M., Milkowski, M., Ogrodniczuk, M., Przepiórkowski, A.: PoliMorf: a (not so) new open morphological dictionary for Polish. In: LREC, pp. 860–864 (2012)

Sensitivity Analysis of the Neural Networks Randomized Learning

Grzegorz Dudek[✉][iD]

Electrical Engineering Faculty, Częstochowa University of Technology,
Częstochowa, Poland
dudek@el.pcz.czest.pl

Abstract. Randomized algorithms for learning feedforward neural networks are increasingly used in practice. They offer very speed training because the only parameters that are learned are the output weights. Parameters of hidden neurons are generated randomly once and need not to be adjusted. The key issue in randomized learning algorithms is to generate parameters in a right way to ensure good approximation and generalization properties of the network. Recently the method of generating hidden nodes parameters was proposed [1], which ensures better adjustment of the random parameters to the target function and better distribution of neurons in the input space, when comparing to the previous approaches. In this work the new method is tested in terms of sensitivity to the number of neurons, noise in data and data deficit. Experiments shows better results for the new method in comparison to the existing approach of generating random parameters of the network.

Keywords: Randomized learning algorithms ·
Neural networks with random hidden nodes ·
Feedforward neural networks

1 Introduction

In conventional learning of neural networks (NNs) all parameters, weights and biases, are required freely adjustable. They are tuned properly during a learning process which usually employs some form of gradient descent method which is known to be time consuming, sensitive to initial values of parameters and converging to local minima. For complex classification or regression problems the training is complicated and inefficient. In recent years randomized learning algorithms for NNs are developed by many researchers. The original idea of building NNs with random weights can be found in [2] and [3]. In these approaches the weights and biases of hidden nodes are assigned with random values and need not to be adjusted during the learning process. Thus, the resulting optimization task solved by NN becomes convex and can be formulated as a linear least-squares

Supported by Grant 2017/27/B/ST6/01804 from the National Science Centre, Poland.

L. Rutkowski et al. (Eds.): ICAISC 2019, LNAI 11508, pp. 51–61, 2019.
https://doi.org/10.1007/978-3-030-20912-4_5

problem [4]. This results in a thousandfold increase in the learning speed over the classical gradient descent-based learning. Many simulation studies reported in the literature show high performance of the randomized neural networks (RNNs) which is compared to fully adaptable ones.

Parameters of the RNN hidden neurons are randomly selected from some intervals according to any continuous sampling distribution and do not change. However, how to select these intervals remains an open question. This issue is considered to be one of the most important research gaps in the field of randomized NN learning [5]. In applications of RNNs reported in literature the ranges for random parameters are selected without scientific justification and could not ensure the universal approximation property. Usually these intervals are assigned as $[-1, 1]$, regardless of the data distribution, complexity of the target function and type of an activation function. Some authors note the influence of these intervals on the model performance and suggest to optimize them in a more appropriate range for a specified application [6,7]. For example in [8] the weights are chosen from a normal distribution with zero mean and some specified variance that can be adjusted to obtain input-to-node values that do not saturate the sigmoids. Then, the biases are computed to center each sigmoid at one of the training points. In [9] authors combine unsupervised placement of network nodes according to the input data density with subsequent supervised or reinforcement learning values of the linear parameters of the network. In [10] a supervisory mechanism of assigning random weights and biases is proposed for the model generated incrementally by stochastic configuration algorithms. The random parameters are generated adaptively selecting the scope for them, ensuring the universal approximation property of the network.

In this work a new method of generating random NN parameters proposed recently in [1] is investigated. The method generates weights and biases separately depending on the data scope and complexity, and activation function type. It ensures an adjustment of the random parameters to the target function and better distribution of neurons in the input space when comparing to the previous approaches with fixed intervals for random parameters. We test the new method in terms of sensitivity to the number of neurons, noise in data and training data deficit.

The rest of this paper is structured as follows. Section 2 introduces randomized learning algorithms in two versions: a classical one with fixed intervals for random parameters and in the new one proposed in [1]. Section 3 reports experimental results concerning sensitivity analysis for both versions of the randomized learning. Conclusions are given in Sect. 4.

2   Randomized Learning Algorithms

In this work feedforward neural networks (FNNs) with a single hidden layer are considered. The network has n inputs, one output and m hidden nodes with activation functions $h(x)$. The training set is $\Phi = \{(\mathbf{x}_l, y_l) | \mathbf{x}_l \in \mathbb{R}^n, y_l \in \mathbb{R}, l = 1, 2, ..., N\}$.

In the first step of learning the parameters of each hidden node are generated by random: weights $\mathbf{a}_i = [a_{i,1}, a_{i,2}, \ldots, a_{i,n}]^T$ and biases $b_i, i = 1, 2, \ldots, m$, according to any continuous sampling distribution. Usually $a_{i,j} \sim U(a_{min}, a_{max})$ and $b_i \sim U(b_{min}, b_{max})$.

In the second step the output matrix for the hidden layer is calculated:

$$\mathbf{H} = \begin{bmatrix} \mathbf{h}(\mathbf{x}_1) \\ \vdots \\ \mathbf{h}(\mathbf{x}_N) \end{bmatrix} = \begin{bmatrix} h_1(\mathbf{x}_1) & \ldots & h_m(\mathbf{x}_1) \\ \vdots & \vdots & \vdots \\ h_1(\mathbf{x}_N) & \ldots & h_m(\mathbf{x}_N) \end{bmatrix} \tag{1}$$

where $h_i(x)$ is an activation function of the i-th node, which is nonlinear piecewise continuous function. In this work a sigmoid activation function is used:

$$h_i(\mathbf{x}) = \frac{1}{1 + \exp\left(-\left(\mathbf{a}_i^T \mathbf{x} + b_i\right)\right)} \tag{2}$$

The i-th column of $\mathbf{H}$ is the i-th hidden node output vector with respect to inputs $\mathbf{x}_1, \mathbf{x}_2, \ldots, \mathbf{x}_N$. Note that hidden nodes map the data from n-dimensional input space to m-dimensional feature space, and $\mathbf{h}(\mathbf{x}) = [h_1(\mathbf{x}), h_2(\mathbf{x}), \ldots, h_m(\mathbf{x})]$ is a nonlinear feature mapping. Because the parameters $\mathbf{a}_i$ and b_i are fixed, the output matrix $\mathbf{H}$ is calculated only once and remains unchanged.

The output weights connecting hidden nodes with output node can be obtained by solving the following linear equation system:

$$\mathbf{H}\boldsymbol{\beta} = \mathbf{Y} \tag{3}$$

where $\boldsymbol{\beta} = [\beta_1, \beta_2, \ldots, \beta_m]^T$ is a vector of output weights and $\mathbf{Y} = [y_1, y_2, \ldots, y_N]^T$ is a vector of target outputs.

A least mean squares solution of (3) can be expressed by $\boldsymbol{\beta} = \mathbf{H}^+\mathbf{Y}$, where $\mathbf{H}^+$ is the Moore-Penrose generalized inverse of matrix $\mathbf{H}$.

The network expresses a linear combination of the activation functions $h_i(\mathbf{x})$ of the form:

$$\varphi(\mathbf{x}) = \sum_{i=1}^{m} \beta_i h_i(\mathbf{x}) = \mathbf{h}(\mathbf{x})\boldsymbol{\beta} \tag{4}$$

It is worth mentioning that the prototype of NN with randomization was Random Vector Functional Link (RVFL) network proposed by Pao and Takefji [3]. This solution has also direct links from the input layer to the output one. In experimental part of this work we use RVFL as a comparative model.

In most of the works on randomized learning algorithms the intervals for random parameters of hidden nodes are assigned as fixed regardless of the data distribution and activation function type. Typically $a_{min} = b_{min} = -1$ and $a_{max} = b_{max} = 1$. In [1] it was demonstrated that the intervals of the random weights and biases are extremely important due to approximation properties of the network. When they are set as $[-1, 1]$ the neurons operate on the saturation fragments of activation functions and accurate fitting to the strongly nonlinear function can be impossible. The method proposed in [1] distributes neurons across the input space and adjusts the activation function slopes to the target function steepness. According to this approach the weights of the i-th hidden node are calculated as follows:

$$a_{i,k} = \zeta_k \frac{\Sigma_i}{\sum_{j=1}^{n} \zeta_j} \tag{5}$$

where $\zeta_1, \zeta_2, \ldots, \zeta_n \sim U(-1,1)$ are i.i.d. numbers and Σ_i is the sum of weights: $\Sigma_i = a_{i,1} + a_{i,2} + \ldots + a_{i,n}$, which is randomly selected from the interval:

$$|\Sigma_i| \in \left[\ln \left(\frac{1-r}{r} \right), s \cdot \ln \left(\frac{1-r}{r} \right) \right] \tag{6}$$

Two parameters in (6), $r \in (0, 0.5)$ and $s > 1$, control the steepness of activation functions. Specifically, they determine two boundary sigmoids between which the activation functions are randomly generated.

Having weights $a_{i,k}$, the bias for the i-th activation function is determined in such a way that the inflection point of the sigmoid is set at some point $\mathbf{x}_*$ randomly generated inside the input space. When the input vectors $\mathbf{x}$ are normalized so that they belong to the n-dimensional unit hypercube $H = [0, 1]^n \subset \mathbb{R}^n$, the point $\mathbf{x}_*$ is selected from H, thus $x_{*,1}, x_{*,2}, \ldots, x_{*,n} \sim U(0, 1)$. The bias for the i-th activation function is calculated from:

$$b_i = -\mathbf{a}_i^T \mathbf{x}_* \tag{7}$$

From (7) we can see that the bias of the i-th hidden node is strictly dependent on the weights of this node. When generating random parameters of the hidden nodes, the weights and biases should be considered separately, because these parameters have different meaning. Thus generating them both from the same interval, usually $[-1, 1]$, is incorrect. More detailed discussion on this topic and derivations of the above equations can be found in [1].

In the next section we compare the new method of generating random parameters with the method based on the fixed intervals of $[-1, 1]$ including RVFL where additional direct connections between input and output layers are introduced.

3   Simulation Study

This section reports some simulation results over the regression problem including a two-variable function approximation task. A target function is defined as follows:

$$g(\mathbf{x}) = \sin \left(20 \cdot \exp \left(x_1 \right) \right) \cdot x_1^2 + \sin \left(20 \cdot \exp \left(x_2 \right) \right) \cdot x_2^2 \tag{8}$$

where $x_1, x_2 \in [0, 1]$.

This function is shown in Fig. 1. Note that a variation of function (8) is the lowest around the corner $[0, 0]$ and gradually increases towards the corner $[1, 1]$.

The training set Φ contains 5000 points $(\mathbf{x}_l, y_l)$. The components of $\mathbf{x}_l, x_{l,1}$ and $x_{l,2}$, are independently uniformly randomly distributed on $[0, 1]$ and y_l are distorted by adding the uniform noise distributed in $[-0.2, 0.2]$. The testing set of the size 100000 points is distributed uniformly in the input space and is not disturbed by noise. It expresses the true target function, which is spanned between -1.64 and 1.78.

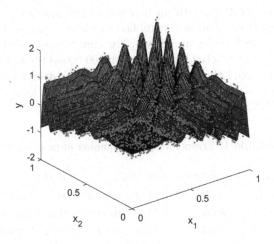

Fig. 1. The target function and training points.

We test three randomized approaches for FNN learning described in the previous section:

- RNN1: FNN with random parameters generated according to (5) and (7),
- RNN2: FNN with random parameters generated from the uniform distribution over $[-1, 1]$,
- RNN3: RVFL network with random parameters generated as in RNN2 from $[-1, 1]$.

In all cases the sigmoidal activation function is used in the hidden nodes. As a measure of accuracy in the comparative studies we use root mean squares error (RMSE). For each experiment 100 independent trials are performed. The r and s parameters for RNN1 were adopted from [1] as 0.1 and 5, respectively. With such values good results were obtained for function (8) approximation.

In the first experiment the impact of the number of hidden nodes on the approximation accuracy of the NNs is investigated. The number of hidden nodes is changed from 100 to 2000 with step of 100. Figure 2 shows the RMSE distributions using box-and-whisker plots for the investigated randomized learning methods. As we can see from this figure, the training error for RNN1 converges to the value of around 0.10. The test error for RNN1 has a minimum $(RMSE = 0.0645)$ for 600 nodes. Adding hidden nodes over 600 increases both

RMSE and its variance. This exhibits an overtraining: too many steep nodes fit into noisy data points. RMSE for RNN2 and RNN3, where random parameters are chosen from $[-1, 1]$, is incomparably greater than for RNN1. It is due to using saturated parts of activation functions to compose strongly nonlinear target function. Adding new neurons does not improve the results. The pattern of the training error distribution for different numbers of nodes is very similar to the pattern of the test error distribution. In RNN2 and RNN3 cases, networks are not prone to overfitting with an increase in the number of neurons. They are strongly underfitted. This is exemplified in Fig. 3 (upper charts), where the fitted surfaces for 2000 nodes are shown. For comparison, bottom charts show the fitting surfaces constructed by RNN1 with 500 (good fitting) and 2000 (overfitting) nodes. In Table 1 the errors are shown for the optimal number of hidden nodes. Note that RMSE for test data are above six times lower for RNN1 than for RNN2 and RNN3.

Table 1. Errors for optimal number of neurons.

Approach	#neurons	$RMSE_{trn}$	$RMSE_{tst}$
RNN1	600	0.1119 ± 0.0012	0.0645 ± 0.0393
RNN2	2000	0.4307 ± 0.0001	0.4196 ± 0.0001
RNN3	2000	0.4304 ± 0.0001	0.4193 ± 0.0001

In the second experiment we test how the results are sensitive to the noise disturbing data. The training data are generated from (8) and are distorted by adding the uniform noise distributed in $[-c, c]$. The noise boundary c changes from 0 to 1 with step of 0.1. It means that the noise level defined as the ratio of the noise range to the target function range (which is 3.42) is from 0 to about 58%. For each noise level 100 independent trials are performed for each randomized NN. The number of hidden nodes was set to 500. Results in Fig. 4 are shown. The training and test errors for RNN1 gradually increase with the noise level. The increase is faster for the training error. This is because the test points expressing the true target function are not disturbed by noise, i.e. they are the same for each noise level in training points. The relationship between the percentage increase in the training error and the percentage noise level can be estimated by the linear regression: $\Delta RMSE_\% = 32.38c_\% - 35.70$. For test data this equation is of the form: $\Delta RMSE_\% = 5.43c_\% - 81.77$. In the case of RNN2 and RNN3, where the flat parts of the activation functions are mostly used by neurons, the fitted surfaces are similar to each other for different noise level in the training data. The training error increases with the noise level because the training points move away from the fitted surface. In the same time, the test error stays at the same level because neither test points nor fitted surfaces change with the noise. But due to modeling using saturated parts of neurons the test error in RNN2 and RNN3 is much bigger than in the case of RNN1.

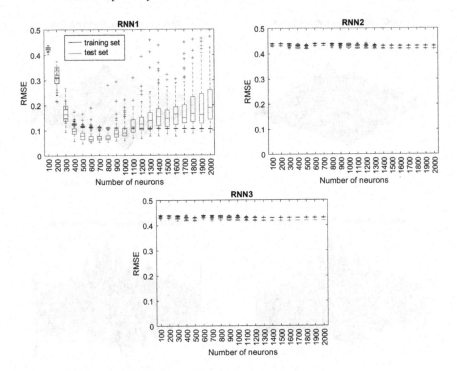

Fig. 2. Impact of the hidden neurons number on the error.

Table 2. Errors for the noise level $c = 1$

Approach	$RMSE_{trn}$	$RMSE_{tst}$
RNN1	0.5570 ± 0.0011	0.2222 ± 0.0747
RNN2	0.6985 ± 0.0011	0.4290 ± 0.0021
RNN3	0.6983 ± 0.0003	0.4282 ± 0.0003

In Table 2 the errors are shown for the noise level $c = 1$ corresponding to the maximum considered disruption of data at level of 58%. In this case the test RMSE for RNN1 increased to 0.2222 from 0.0572 for data without noise. For RNN2 and RNN3 the test RMSE at the maximum noise level was about twice higher than for RNN1.

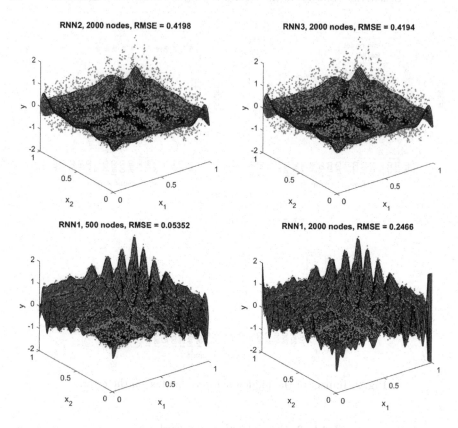

Fig. 3. The surfaces fitted to the training points.

In the third experiment we investigate the influence of the number of training points on accuracy of the randomized NNs. Setting the number of hidden nodes as 500 we change the number of training points from 500 to 5000 with the step of 500. Figure 5 shows the results. For a smaller number of training points the lower training errors are observed. Our 500 steep neurons in RNN1 are able to fit better into a small number of points. But this small set of training points does not reflect sufficiently the target function complexity. Deficit in training points and flexible learning model lead to overfitting (see Fig. 6). This is a cause of bigger test errors for smaller number of training points. Bigger training sets lead to improvement in accuracy on the test set. For RNN2 and RNN3 the fitted surface is not able to fit accurately to the training points (see Fig. 6), and the training error only slightly improves with the number of training points. Due to a poor fitting of the model to the training points, the test error is less sensitive to the training points number when compared to RNN1 case. But in the RNN2 and RNN3 cases the error level is unacceptable high.

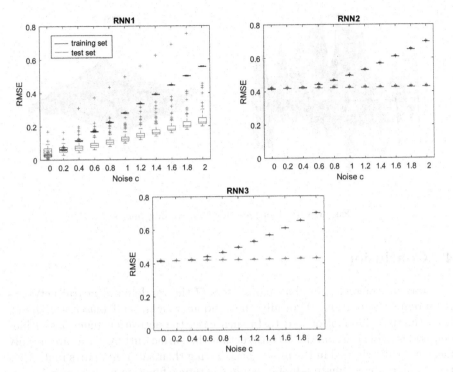

Fig. 4. Impact of the noise level on the error.

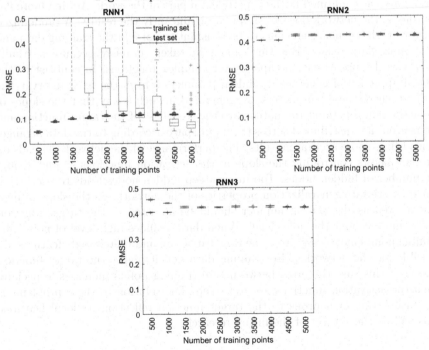

Fig. 5. Impact of the training points number on the error.

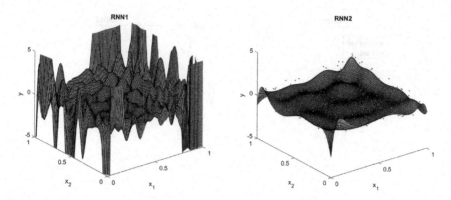

Fig. 6. Fitted surfaces for 500 training points.

4   Conclusion

The way of generating random parameters of the randomized neural networks is extremely important. Typically the random weights and biases are chosen from the fixed interval of $[-1, 1]$. In such case, the activation functions of hidden nodes, which are used for construction the surface fitting data, are usually incorrectly distributed in the input space having their saturated parts in it. Thus they cannot approximate a highly nonlinear target function with required accuracy. This was confirmed in the experimental part of the work. Adding more flat neurons to the network does not improve significantly the results. A randomized network with flat neurons seems to be resistant to noise in the training data and to training data deficit. But this cannot be taken seriously because it results from a weak approximation capacity for complex functions. In contrast to the typical approach of generating random parameters from the fixed interval, the method where these parameters are generated in such a way that the slopes of the activation functions are matched to the steepness of the target function and the neurons are distributed across the input space according to the data arrangement, brings more accurate results. The performance of the network depends on the parameters controlling the slope of the activation functions (r and s) and the number of hidden nodes. Too many steep hidden nodes leads to overfitting which deteriorate generalization properties of the network. So the slope of neurons as well as the neuron number should be adjusted to the target function taking into account the noise level. When data includes high level of noise, the training points move away from the target function and therefore its features are invisible for the network. Also training data deficit makes the target function blurry. In this case the error between rare training points increases, especially when the activation functions are too steep. The solution to these problems is the local fitting of neurons to the target function reflecting its local features. This will be the subject of the future research.

References

1. Dudek, G.: Generating random weights and biases in feedforward neural networks with random hidden nodes. Inf. Sci. **481**, 33–56 (2019)
2. Schmidt, W.F., Kraaijveld, M.A., Duin, R.P.W.: Feedforward neural networks with random weights. In: Proceedings of the 11th IAPR International Conference Pattern Recognition Methodology and Systems, vol. II, pp. 1–4 (1992)
3. Pao, Y.H., Takefji, Y.: Functional-link net computing: theory, system architecture, and functionalities. IEEE Comput. **25**(5), 76–79 (1992)
4. Principe, J., Chen, B.: Universal approximation with convex optimization: gimmick or reality? IEEE Comput. Intell. Mag. **10**, 68–77 (2015)
5. Zhang, L., Suganthan, P.N.: A survey of randomized algorithms for training neural networks. Inf. Sci. **364–365**, 146–155 (2016)
6. Husmeier, D.: Random Vector Functional Link (RVFL) networks. In: Neural Networks for Conditional Probability Estimation: Forecasting Beyond Point Predictions. Perspectives in Neural Computing, Chap. 6, pp. 87–97. Springer, London (1999). https://doi.org/10.1007/978-1-4471-0847-4_6
7. Li, M., Wang, D.: Insights into randomized algorithms for neural networks: practical issues and common pitfalls. Inf. Sci. **382–383**, 170–178 (2017)
8. Ferrari, S., Stengel, R.F.: Smooth function approximation using neural networks. IEEE Trans. Neural Networks **16**(1), 24–38 (2005)
9. Gorban, A.N., Tyukin, I.Y., Prokhorov, D.V., Sofeikov, K.I.: Approximation with random bases: Pro- et Contra. Inf. Sci. **364**, 129–145 (2016)
10. Wang, D., Li, M.: Stochastic configuration networks: fundamentals and algorithms. IEEE Trans. Cybern. **47**(10), 3466–3479 (2017)

On Approximating Metric Nearness
Through Deep Learning

Magzhan Gabidolla[✉], Alisher Iskakov, M. Fatih Demirci, and Adnan Yazici

Department of Computer Science, School of Science and Technology,
Nazarbayev University, Astana, Kazakhstan
{magzhan.gabidolla,alisher.iskakov,muhammed.demirci,adnan.yazici}@nu.edu.kz

Abstract. Many problems require a notion of distance between a set of points in a metric space, e.g., clustering data points in an N-dimensional space, object retrieval in pattern recognition, and image segmentation. However, these applications often require that the distances must be a metric, meaning that they must satisfy a set of conditions, with triangle inequality being the focus of this paper. Given an $N \times N$ dissimilarity matrix with triangle inequality violations, the metric nearness problem requires to find a closest distance matrix, which satisfies the triangle inequality condition. This paper introduces a new deep learning approach for approximating a nearest matrix with more efficient runtime complexity than existing algorithms. We have experimented with several deep learning architectures, and our experimental results demonstrate that deep neural networks can learn to construct a close-distance matrix efficiently by removing most of the triangular inequality violations.

Keywords: Deep learning · Convolutional neural networks ·
Metric nearness problem · Matrix analysis

1 Introduction

Many applications in computer vision, image processing and machine learning are based on computing the distance between a pair of data points in a high dimensional space using a distance function. However, due to measurement errors and noise in the data, the triangle inequality property of the distance function is usually violated. Formally, in a distance function or metric d on a set X, the following conditions are satisfied for all $x, y, z \in X$:

1. $d(x, y) \geq 0$
2. $d(x, y) = 0 \Leftrightarrow x = y$
3. $d(x, y) = d(y, x)$
4. $d(x, z) \leq d(x, y) + d(y, z)$

The fourth condition is the aforementioned triangle inequality, which states that the distance between any two elements in a set must always be less than or equal to the distance reached through another intermediary element in the set.

© Springer Nature Switzerland AG 2019
L. Rutkowski et al. (Eds.): ICAISC 2019, LNAI 11508, pp. 62–72, 2019.
https://doi.org/10.1007/978-3-030-20912-4_6

Fig. 1. Human similarity judgment do not obey triangle inequality.

Since many applications and algorithms only work with metric data, it is important to eliminate triangular inequality violations by changing the distances between data points as small as possible. In [3] the author used a triangle-fixing algorithm from [10] to remove the triangular inequality violations and obtained a significant improvement in computation time. However, the triangle-fixing algorithm takes $O(n^3)$ with n as a size of matrix, therefore finding a faster solution for removing violations will benefit certain applications.

Apart from the noise and measurement errors in real data, the very nature of a problem itself can result in distances disobeying triangle inequality. As an example for this, human judgment of similarity between shapes can be considered [2]. As shown in Fig. 1, while the distance in terms of similarity between the centaur to the person and the horse is small, the distance is large between the person and the horse. By representing the data points and a distance function in this way, it can be seen that these functions are not metric. To describe the problem more formally, we adopt the formulation from [10], where the authors define the metric nearness problem and present its deterministic solution. Firstly, a dissimilarity matrix is defined to be a symmetric, non-negative matrix with zero diagonal, whereas a distance matrix is a dissimilarity matrix whose entries satisfy the triangle inequalities. Given a dissimilarity matrix D as input, the problem is to find a distance matrix M such that:

$$M \in \arg\min_{X} \|X - D\| \tag{1}$$

Although there exist algorithms which accomplish this task, such as the one proposed in [10], in this paper we examine how deep learning can be used to remove triangle inequality violations by minimally modifying the input distance matrix.

It is therefore of theoretical and practical importance to determine whether deep neural networks can learn to eliminate violations of triangle inequalities, while maintaining a minimum distance between input and output matrices. Our main goal in this paper is summarized in Fig. 2, where an input matrix with triangle inequality violations shown in red is provided to the proposed model, producing an output matrix with little or no triangle inequality violations. With the proposed approach, our main contributions are:

- presenting the first work that utilizes deep learning for the metric nearness problem,
- approximating the solution to the metric nearness problem with deep neural networks and comparing it to the deterministic solution described in [10],
- presenting a more efficient solution in terms of runtime complexity to the metric nearness problem than the existing algorithms.

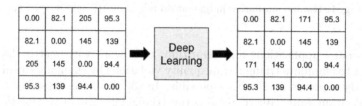

Fig. 2. Proposed deep learning approach

We have experimented our approach extensively with several deep learning architectures and different parameters. Overall, our results show that with adequate training, deep neural networks can learn to remove most of the triangle inequality violations while by maintaining a close distance to the input matrix. Our proposed approach runs in $O(n^2)$ as opposed to $O(n^3)$ of the triangle fixing algorithm in [10], where n is the number of data points in the distance matrix.

After a brief introduction of related work in Sect. 2, we describe our methodology including the dataset, technology, and models used in the proposed framework in Sect. 3. We present our results in Sect. 4 and discussion in Sect. 5. Finally, we conclude the paper in Sect. 6.

2   Related Work

A pioneering work in this area is done by Sra, Dhillon, and Tropp [10]. Their paper introduces a deterministic triangle-fixing algorithm for the metric nearness problem. The authors propose algorithms for l_2, l_1, l_∞, and l_p norms, which show much faster performance over the standard solution using CPLEX - proprietary optimization software. The triangle-fixing algorithm achieves performance that is up to 30 times faster than CPLEX. The authors of [10] also show that by only allowing decreasing changes to an input dissimilarity matrix, we obtain an instance of an all-pairs shortest path (APSP) problem.

Solomonik et al. [9] provide a distributed memory algorithm for the APSP problem. Their aim is to utilize the performance of parallel processing by a careful focus on the efficiency of inter-process communication. The algorithm is based on the divide-and-conquer approach, which according to the authors, provide a high level of temporal locality, thus allowing for a more efficient cache use. The focus on parallel computing might be viewed similar to the way deep learning networks work on GPUs. While the precise formulation of the metric nearness problem requires the minimization of the distance between input and output matrices (according to some norm), Gilbert and Jain [5] propose a slightly different formulation of the problem, whose objective is to modify as few as possible distances so that most of the entries in the original metric would remain unchanged. According to the authors, the main motivation for this reformulation is that in many of the practical applications most of the distances satisfy triangle inequalities, with only few of the entries disobeying it. Thus, metric nearness solutions could unnecessarily perturb many of the distances. The authors refer to this as a sparse metric repair problem, and with some modifications to existing algorithms, they propose different methods to solve different cases of this problem. Although there are many other different variations of the problem, in this paper we focus on the original formulation given in [10].

As far as the applications of the metric nearness problem are concerned, Demirci [3] applies it to a problem in computer vision area, namely shape matching. Shape matching calculates a similarity of a pair of shapes based on some closeness definition. The author argues that while existing algorithms match shapes using a metric distance, according to psychological studies, human judgment is not metric. To find a shape similarity between different shapes, the author proposes to first apply a triangle-fixing algorithm described in [10], and then use an existing algorithm for shape matching. The approach shows lower accuracy, but it has much faster computation time.

One particular study that shows the importance of fixing triangular inequalities is done by Baraty et al. [1], where they consider the impact of these inequality violations on Partition Around Medoids clustering algorithms. The authors perform experiments to test the accuracy of the medoid based clustering algorithm on the randomly generated dissimilarity matrices with triangular inequality violations. The results of the experiment illustrate that the incoherence degree of the algorithm increases as the number and extent of triangular inequality violations grows. Also, by removing these violations using a rectification process, they show that the performance of the algorithm improves.

Another example of adverse effect of triangle inequality violations is shown in [4], where the authors show how this affects the solution to the Vehicle Routing Problem (VRP). VRP is a classic problem of allocating a set of vehicles to a set of customers, with constraints on vehicles and some map topology. The authors consider both frequency and severity of triangle inequality violations, violating a distance matrix by a factor of 2, 3, 4, 5 and with 10%, 20%, 30%, 40%, 50% of violations. Particular algorithms for solving VRPs tested in that study are Simulated Annealing and Ant Colony Optimization. As the authors present, the solution quality is substantially degraded with an increased number of violations, though computation time is not affected.

3   Methodology

Our main approach to the Metric Nearness Problem is to train various neural network architectures end-to-end with input distance matrices containing triangle inequality violations and target distance matrices without violations produced by the triangle fixing algorithm from [10].

3.1 Dataset and Technology

Training deep neural networks requires large amounts of data, so the first task is to generate enough input-output matrices. For this purpose, we created large amounts of distance matrices of sizes 8×8 and 32×32. In general, to produce a dissimilarity matrix of size $N \times N$, we randomly scatter N points in a $2D$ coordinate plane with coordinates ranging from -100 to 100 (random uniformly distributed). Then, the distances between each pair of points are calculated, which results in a distance matrix. By randomly perturbing the values in the matrix, we artificially produce triangular inequality violations. Finally, using the software from [10], the closest matrix in ℓ_2 norm without violations is generated. The summary of the dataset is presented in Table 1. By following normalization practices used in computer vision tasks, a zero-mean and variance-one normalization technique is used.

Table 1. Dataset summary

Matrix size	Dataset size	Mean	Standard deviation	Average violations
8×8	80000	98.83	59.59	4.4
32×32	81213	101.24	52.06	11.9

All the code in this study is written using the PyTorch framework, which handles the backpropagation automatically with an autograd feature. The hardware used for network training and testing is a Tesla K20c GPU with 5 GB of memory and 3.5 TFLOPS performance for single-precision.

3.2 Evaluation

There are two main evaluation criteria for the performance of deep learning on this task. The first is the number of triangle inequality violations in the output matrix, which is expected to be zero, or at least, less than those in the input matrix. The second evaluation criteria is the distance in l_2 norm between output matrices and target matrices generated by the triangle fixing algorithm. This criteria is used to keep the output distance matrix as close as possible to the input. By using mean-squared error loss during training phase of neural networks, the second criteria can be explicitly incorporated into the network. In this case, however, the first criteria is only implicitly considered, as the triangle inequality violations are not taken into account in the calculation of mean-squared error. For this reason, in addition to the standard mean-squared error loss, we define our own loss function, which attempts to capture triangular inequality violations. To calculate this loss, we first find triplets of entries violating the triangle inequality. Then, the same procedure for calculating mean squared error is done, but with violating entries error being multiplied by some factor α greater than 1. For α, we experimented with 1.5 and 2.0 values. By doing this, violating entries contribute more to the loss, thereby encouraging the network to learn fixing the triangle inequality violations. However, searching for violations takes $O(n^3)$ time, which makes the training much slower. For this reason, a limited number of experiments are performed with our own defined loss.

3.3   Models

For almost all of the models, 60000 matrices were used for training, while validation set consisted of 10000 matrices, and the remaining 10000 matrices used for testing. During each training phase, several measurements are collected. First, we keep track of the training loss, which shows how the loss function changes during training. Second, we record how the number of violations of the triangle inequality property changes from random batches in each training epoch. At the end of each epoch, the models are tested against validation data and the losses and changes in triangular inequality violations are recorded.

In general, all the models used can be divided into three broad categories: the models used for image classification tasks, convolutional autoencoders and a stack of convolutional layers.

Image Classification Models: AlexNet's architecture [7] is chosen as a first attempt to be trained and tested for 32×32 matrices. Slight modifications are made for filter sizes and max pooling layers to fit the data properly. The output size of the AlexNet is changed from 1000 to 1024, so that it will match the size of the flattened matrix. Mean squared error (MSE) is chosen as a loss function.

Following AlexNet, deeper models are also experimented. One of these is a class of VGG models [8]. In particular, we trained VGG-16 and VGG-19 variations. Similar type of modifications done in AlexNet are performed for VGG models. The next model is one of the best performing models in image classification tasks, namely ResNet architectures [6]. We used ResNet-50 implementation in our experiments.

Autoencoders: The second group of models that we experimented is the convolutional autoencoders. In particular, we chose an architecture used for image denoising as a basis for our autoencoder models. The structure of the model is relatively straightforward. Firstly, several convolutional layers are stacked together to encode the input. Then, corresponding convolutional layers are used to decode and produce the output of the same size as input (Fig. 3). By varying the depth and filter sizes of this basic model, we trained and tested several architectures.

Stack of Convolutional Layers: Apart from existing popular architectures, we also constructed our own model as a stack of convolutional layers with increasing filter size followed by the corresponding convolutional layers with decreasing

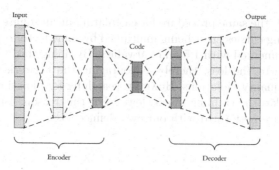

Fig. 3. Autoencoder architecture

filter size, similar to the encoder-decoder architecture (Fig. 4). Starting from a filter size of 32, the number of feature maps grows until 512, by doubling every layer. From then, it decreases to the input layer size of 1, by halving at each consecutive layer.

4   Results

Learning rate plays an important role for the performance of the models. In our experiments, we observe that setting it to a high value yields very erratic behaviour, whereas lower values does not produce adequate learning. We, thus, use an adaptive learning rate by fine-tuning it to lower values during training.

4.1   Image Classification Models

According to our experiments with 32×32 matrices, the learning loss in AlexNet decreases to a certain extent, but the loss is still significant. On the other hand, it produces output matrices with zero triangle inequality violations. After inspecting the individual entries in the output matrix, we observe that zero-triangle inequality violations occur because of a low learning rate, i.e., the model does not learn to construct a significant output because the loss is very high. When you set a higher learning rate and decrease it adaptively, the results of the validation data indicate that the AlexNet architecture does not eliminate triangle inequalities.

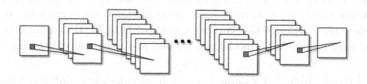

Fig. 4. Stack of convolutional layers

Similar situation also occurs with 8 × 8 matrices with mean-squared error and custom loss. As can be seen from Fig. 5, we can observe that regardless of the number of epochs, the number of violations of the inequality of the triangles remains almost constant, although the violations fall below three on average.

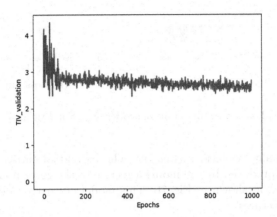

Fig. 5. Triangle inequality violations of AlexNet during validation with 8 × 8 matrices and MSE loss. The vertical axis label (TIV) indicates the number of triangle inequality violations.

ResNet and VGG both display quite similar performances to AlexNet, with a number of triangle inequality violations not decreasing but lower than the average of violations in the original matrices.

4.2 Autoencoders

The learning process is very slow for 32 × 32 matrices in autoencoders, although the loss of validation is slowly decreasing. For this reason, we mainly focus on 8 × 8 matrices.

For the 8 × 8 matrices used in autoencoders, we use our custom loss in experiments. Figure 6a illustrates the loss of validation for this encoder-decoder architecture and Fig. 6b shows how the number of violations of the triangle inequality changes. Both figures show a positive trend for the 1000 epochs and, leaving the model train even further, we could achieve even better results. At the last epoch, on average, the number of triangle inequality violations decreased from 4 to 2 and the loss between the corresponding entries reached 4%.

4.3 Stack of Convolutions

Our custom model with convolution stacks has almost the same performance as the autoencoder, but the validation loss has been reduced to a lower value. With more than 1000 epochs, the model has learned to eliminate about 50%

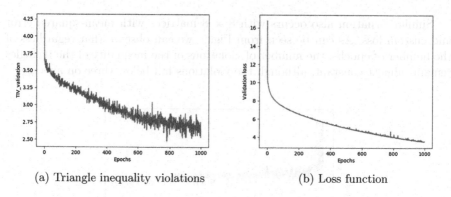

(a) Triangle inequality violations   (b) Loss function

Fig. 6. Validation results of autoencoder, 8×8 matrices, MSE loss

of triangle inequality violations (Fig. 7a). The individual entries in the output distance matrix produced by the model are close to the corresponding entries of the input matrix, as shown in Fig. 7b. This model currently works better than the other architectures.

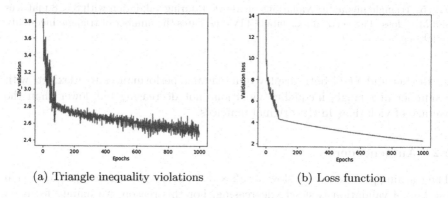

(a) Triangle inequality violations   (b) Loss function

Fig. 7. Validation results of stack of convolutions, 8×8 matrices, MSE loss.

5 Discussion

Since in the image classification models, convolutional layers are used for feature extraction and fully connected layers are utilized for classification, these layers are not suitable for the metric nearness problem. On the other hand, the idea behind autoencoder architectures fits the metric nearness problem much better, due to the fact that their inputs are mapped to the same sized outputs with some modifications. For example, autoencoders are used effectively to remove Gaussian noise in images. Thus, by treating triangular inequality violations as noise, autoencoder architectures can be extended to reduce the number of such violations. In the stack of convolutional layers, by transforming inputs into some high dimensional space, the model learns to eliminate violations of triangle inequalities better than image classification models and autoencoders. Overall, our models have performed well over more than 1000 epochs, suggesting that an increase in the number of epochs and the size of the data set could further improve the results.

One of the advantages of the proposed model over existing deterministic algorithms is its better computational complexity of running time. For all the architectures tested, and in particular for the convolution stack, the runtime complexity is $O(n^2)$, with a constant factor. Whereas, the runtime complexity of all known deterministic algorithms are $O(n^3)$. In particular, the pseudocode of the triangle correction algorithm proposed in [10] checks the existence of triangle inequality violations at each iteration, which requires $O(n^3)$. The parallel nature of the current implementation of deep neural networks adds another advantage to the proposed models, while the derivation and implementation of parallel algorithms to the metric nearness problem is not an easy task.

6   Conclusion

In this paper, we presented a novel deep learning approach to the metric nearness problem. We have experimented with several deep learning architectures and obtained promising results. The autoencoder architecture and the stack of convolutional layers can approximate the solution to the metric nearness problem and produce close output matrices with most of the triangle inequality violations removed. Moreover, the proposed deep learning models has a lower runtime complexity when compared to the triangle-fixing algorithm in [10].

For future work, we plan to use our approach in some of the applications that require metric distance matrices, such as efficient partial image retrieval using vantage objects. Although our current results do not produce outputs with zero-triangle inequality violations, some applications tolerate a small number of such violations. The use of our framework in these applications is also part of our future research plan. At the same time, we aim to improve our models so that they can learn to eliminate all violations of triangle inequality. Our current results show that it is possible to further refine our networks for this purpose.

References

1. Baraty, S., Simovici, D.A., Zara, C.: The impact of triangular inequality violations on medoid-based clustering. In: Kryszkiewicz, M., Rybinski, H., Skowron, A., Raś, Z.W. (eds.) ISMIS 2011. LNCS (LNAI), vol. 6804, pp. 280–289. Springer, Heidelberg (2011). https://doi.org/10.1007/978-3-642-21916-0_31
2. Bronstein, A.M., Bronstein, M.M., Bruckstein, A.M., Kimmel, R.: Partial similarity of objects, or how to compare a centaur to a horse. Int. J. Comput. Vision 84(2), 163 (2008)
3. Demirci, M.F.: Efficient shape retrieval under partial matching. In: 20th International Conference on Pattern Recognition, pp. 3057–3060, August 2010

4. Fleming, C.L., Griffis, S.E., Bell, J.E.: The effects of triangle inequality on the vehicle routing problem. Eur. J. Oper. Res. **224**(1), 1–7 (2013)
5. Gilbert, A.C., Jain, L.: If it ain't broke, don't fix it: sparse metric repair. In: 55th Annual Allerton Conference on Communication, Control, and Computing (Allerton), pp. 612–619, October 2017
6. He, K., Zhang, X., Ren, S., Sun, J.: Deep residual learning for image recognition. CoRR abs/1512.03385 (2015)
7. Krizhevsky, A., Sutskever, I., Hinton, G.E.: Imagenet classification with deep convolutional neural networks. Commun. ACM **60**(6), 84–90 (2017)
8. Simonyan, K., Zisserman, A.: Very deep convolutional networks for large-scale image recognition. CoRR abs/1409.1556 (2014)
9. Solomonik, E., Bulu, A., Demmel, J.: Minimizing communication in all-pairs shortest paths. In: IEEE 27th International Symposium on Parallel and Distributed Processing, pp. 548–559, May 2013
10. Sra, S., Tropp, J., Dhillon, I.S.: Triangle fixing algorithms for the metric nearness problem. In: Saul, L.K., Weiss, Y., Bottou, L. (eds.) Advances in Neural Information Processing Systems, vol. 17, pp. 361–368. MIT Press, Cambridge (2005)

Smart Well Data Generation via Boundary-Seeking Deep Convolutional Generative Adversarial Networks

Allan Gurwicz[✉], Smith Arauco Canchumuni,
and Marco Aurélio Cavalcanti Pacheco

Department of Electrical Engineering,
Pontifical Catholic University of Rio de Janeiro, Rio de Janeiro, Brazil
{agurwicz,marco}@ele.puc-rio.br, saraucoc@uni.pe

Abstract. The current trend in the Oil & Gas industry is the use of more complex and detailed reservoir models, seeking better refinement and uncertainty reduction. Alas, this comes with a great increase in computational time, encumbering the optimization process. With the growing adoption rate for smart wells in oil field development projects, these optimizations are indispensable as to justify the investment on the technology and maximize financial return, by finding the optimal valve control schedule. The present paper seeks to establish a new methodology for creation of smart well data by means of a deep generative model, capable of modeling complex data structures. This generation of data is advantageous to the industry as it can then be used for various other applications. Other benefits besides the reduction of optimization time include the use in data augmentation, where the network is used to diversify existing data as to improve lacking datasets, and data privacy, as the generated data, while next to real, can be shared without the original, protected model. A case study was done in an industry-recognized benchmark model, and the results completely support the use of the proposed methodology, as it was able to achieve all expected objectives.

Keywords: Convolutional neural networks ·
Generative Adversarial Networks · Smart wells

1 Introduction

The use of smart completions steadily grows with each passing year. Since its inception, in the 1990's, operators progressively realize its advantages and adopt it as part of their projects.

This technology allows for the control of individual zones for each well in a reservoir, and can be optimized for increasing the net present value of the project. Alas, these optimizations require a painstakingly great number of simulations, which each one being computationally intensive. This is a challenge for

© Springer Nature Switzerland AG 2019
L. Rutkowski et al. (Eds.): ICAISC 2019, LNAI 11508, pp. 73–84, 2019.
https://doi.org/10.1007/978-3-030-20912-4_7

all optimization algorithms, and has the effect of difficult optimizations in state of the art and complex models, which are, nowadays, common.

This paper proposes the use of deep generative models for the generation of production curves and valve control alternatives, in order to reduce simulation time. These are systems capable of extracting high level representations to generate new samples which follow the same probabilistic distribution function of a given training dataset [10]. Within all the deep generative models, this work focuses on Generative Adversarial Networks (GANs) [11] and implements a modified version of the Boundary-Seeking [13] and Deep Convolutional [18] Generative Adversarial Networks.

This methodology allows for data augmentation, where the generator aims to be accurate enough to improve datasets for other applications and routines, without the need for excessive simulation.

A big concern in the Oil & Gas industry is data confidentiality, mainly in relation to reservoir models. The present application also aims to open barriers in relation to the sharing of data, as the results generated by the model, while not real and subject to secrecy protocols, represent a realistic enough model for other methodologies.

A section aims to describe the smart well technology and benefits, with the next one for a literature review in similar applications. The methodology developed in the paper is then described, followed by a case study, with the objective of applying the methodology in a real world problem. A final section draws conclusions from the obtained results and suggests future work.

2   Smart Wells

Well drilling is one of the crucial areas in the world of petroleum engineering, as efficient and safe wells are paramount to the development of any field. The process can be roughly broken down to two steps, drilling and completion.

While the first one is the act of drilling the formation and connecting the reservoir to the surface, the second is responsible for preparing the well, in a safe manner, for its use along the field production span [19].

The technology of smart completions has been developed as a means to increase profitability, being one of the most significant recent breakthroughs in the field [9]. Not only can it improve existing viable projects, it is able to induce viability in currently non-economic projects.

The smart well usually consists of the following elements [14]:

- Flow control devices, able to restrict or shut production;
- Feedthrough isolation packers, to isolate individual zones while allowing control, communication and power cables;
- Control, communication and power cables, as to transmit power and data through the well;
- Downhole sensors, for the real-time monitoring of multiple parameters, such as flow, temperature and pressure, among others.

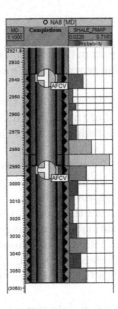

Fig. 1. Example of smart completion, with two flow control valves. Reproduced from Abreu et al. [2]

An example of smart well can be seen in Fig. 1.

Various work exists in the optimization of smart well control, such as a methodology for the evaluation of flexibility under uncertainty and the optimization of flow control strategies [2], the optimization of production using direct search methods [6] and a paper which aims to determine the optimal performance of smart wells via gradient-based optimization techniques [22], among several others. The common denominator among all these is the paramount use of the simulator for all objective function calculations, being the biggest bottleneck for further applications and refinements.

3 Reservoir Simulation

With the objective of optimizing reservoir development projects prior to execution, simulation software allows the user to input model characteristics and project parameters, outputting production curves and various other results.

The present work focuses on changing only the input of valve controls, which means restricting or allowing production for each controlled zone. This translates to setting the parameter in the $[0, 1]$ interval, where 1 means the zone is completely open for production, and 0, that it is shut.

This is usually regulated by specialists, who control the wells aiming for the maximization of oil and gas productions, and the minimization of water production, or the maximization of project net present value.

4   Literature Review

The present application diverges from the common use of Generative Adversarial Networks (GANs) [11] in that the generated and evaluated media are not images, but numerical data.

Boundary-Seeking GANs [13], from which the present model inherits the loss function, aim for the ability of training on discrete data. The paper has an application in continuous data, for which it states that the modification improves stability.

Deep Convolutional GANs [18] aim to improve the application of convolutional neural networks (CNNs) in the GAN context. The paper proposes constraints to the architecture, to improve training and unsupervised learning. The present work takes inspiration from this novel layer configuration.

There are applications in continuous non-image data, such as the use of the network for generation of music [15]. The paper uses recurrent networks as layers in the discriminator, and finds acceptable results. Another paper also generates musical data via GANs, but with CNNs making up the layers of the generator and discriminator [21].

For time-series examples, medical data was generated with the use of recurrent and recurrent conditional GANs [7], electroencephalographic brain signals were generated via the use of CNNs as layers in the GANs [12] and there is work in time-series laboratory data [20]. All of the papers found good results.

As applications in the Oil & Gas industry, there is the generation of pore and reservoir-scale models [16], and work focusing on geophysics [17] and geology [5]. While all applications found acceptable results in their respective fields, no applications could be found on smart wells, which makes the present proposal a novel one.

5   Generative Adversarial Networks

Generative Adversarial Networks are stochastic deep generative networks built by a combination of two networks. A generator network is trained to build new samples, which come from the same distribution function of the training dataset. The discriminator network is the model responsible for evaluating the samples generated by the other network, based on the training dataset. This general structure is shown in Fig. 2. Both the generator and discriminator networks can be constructed from different layer configurations, such as fully connected, convolutional, recurrent and others. The training process is a competition between these two networks, where the generator tries to create new "fake" data to be recognized as "real". Meanwhile, the discriminator is trained to distinguish between "real" and "fake" data.

6   Methodology

The present methodology consists in a routine that harnesses the power of GANs to generate realistic production strategies and curves.

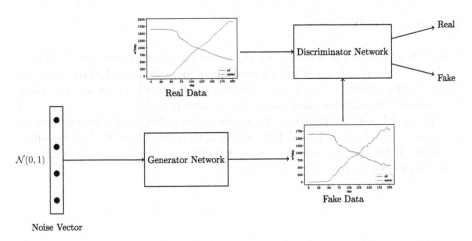

Fig. 2. Structure of the Generative Adversarial Network.

The first step is the definition of a reservoir model, followed by the specification of its smart completions. The model then needs to be simulated, through reservoir simulation software, with diverse enough scenarios, as to build an initial dataset.

The GAN is then constructed, trained and the generator is used for creating a new dataset. This data is then evaluated, and the previous step is repeated several times in order to optimize the parameters and architecture of the networks.

A routine was developed as a means to evaluate the results after training, besides visual inspection. It consists in generating a number of scenarios and simulating the reservoir model with the generated valve controls. The oil and water production results given as outputs of the simulator are then compared to the ones given by the generator, via the Root Mean Square Error, as seen in (1), and the Normalized Root Mean Square Error, as seen in (2), metrics. While the former gives an idea on the magnitude of the error, in terms of the units in question, the latter is non-dimensional, useful for comparing different datasets.

$$RMSE = \sqrt{\frac{1}{n}\sum_{j=1}^{n}(y_j - \hat{y}_j)^2} \tag{1}$$

$$NRMSE = \frac{RMSE}{y_{max} - y_{min}} \tag{2}$$

Where y are the values given by the simulator, $\hat{y}$ are the values given by the generator of the GAN and n is the amount of data in question.

This results in a generator model capable of replicating the behavior of the reservoir, in a fraction of the time spent by the simulator.

7   Case Study

The PUNQ-S3 model [8] was used for the present application, with some adaptations, such as removal of well testing and shut-in periods, as well as the inclusion of smart completions on two wells, allowing for the control of a total of six zones. The porosity map for the final model can be seen in Fig. 3.

The model is a benchmark in the industry, based on a reservoir engineering study on a real field and used for various optimization and history matching problems. It has 11 production wells and no injection ones, on a 19 × 28 × 5 grid. Its production period is of 17 years.

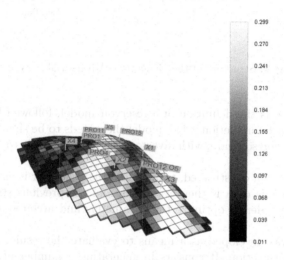

Fig. 3. Porosity map of the adapted PUNQ-S3 model.

7.1   Dataset

The first step before focusing on the GAN was the construction of a robust enough dataset. The IMEX simulator [4] was used for the simulation of 1000 scenarios, dictated by random valve controls, applied in random time steps. This led to a total of 203000 rows of data, with 203 time steps per scenario. Table 1 shows the structure of the dataset, where the first six variable names correspond to the name of the wells, as seen in Fig. 3.

The data was normalized to the [0, 1] interval before being fed to the network.

7.2   Model Construction

The GAN model was built with the Keras framework [3], with a TensorFlow [1] backend. The generator and discriminator configurations were adapted from the

Table 1. Structure of the dataset.

Variable	Possible variable interval	Minimum value	Maximum value
PRO1, layer 3	$[0, 1]$	0	1
PRO1, layer 4	$[0, 1]$	0	1
PRO1, layer 5	$[0, 1]$	0	1
PRO12, layer 3	$[0, 1]$	0	1
PRO12, layer 4	$[0, 1]$	0	1
PRO12, layer 5	$[0, 1]$	0	1
Oil production (m^3/day)	$\mathbb{R}_{\geq 0}$	$4.57 \cdot 10^2$	$2.00 \cdot 10^3$
Water production (m^3/day)	$\mathbb{R}_{\geq 0}$	$2.50 \cdot 10^{-5}$	$2.03 \cdot 10^3$

ones proposed in [18], in order to work with time-series data in lieu of images. These can be seen in Figs. 4 and 5.

Two models were built and tested: a deep convolutional generative adversarial network (DCGAN) and a boundary-seeking deep convolutional generative adversarial network (B-DCGAN).

The convolutional layers were chosen based on experiments that indicated it added a smoothness to the generated data, which made it more similar to the real curves. The loss function was inherited from the proposed in [13], for continuous data[1].

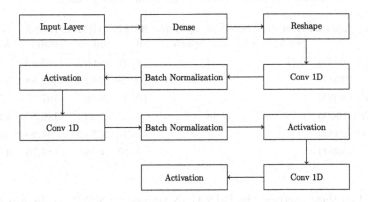

Fig. 4. Generator model architecture.

---

[1] Implementation based on https://wiseodd.github.io/techblog/2017/03/07/boundary-seeking-gan/.

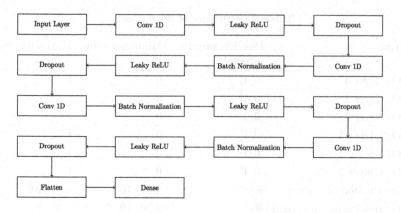

Fig. 5. Discriminator model architecture.

8   Training and Results

Table 2 contains the results obtained after training via the previously described routine, for different configurations and 128 generated scenarios. The column "Average Time per Epoch I" was measured when training in an Intel® Core™ i5 750 CPU, while the column "Average Time per Epoch II" was measured when training in the Intel® AI DevCloud platform, with an Intel® Xeon® Gold 6128 CPU, containing the Intel® optimization for TensorFlow.

Table 2. Results obtained via the developed routine.

Network	Epochs	Average Time per Epoch I	Average Time per Epoch II	RMSE oil	NRMSE oil	RMSE water	NRMSE water
DCGAN	10000	6.71	2.44	83.26	6.66%	96.40	4.78%
DCGAN	20000			100.29	8.02%	109.88	5.45%
DCGAN	30000			106.11	8.49%	107.95	5.35%
B-DCGAN	10000	6.75	2.48	93.20	7.45%	140.37	6.96%
B-DCGAN	20000			59.15	4.73%	91.90	4.56%
B-DCGAN	30000			55.97	4.48%	84.76	4.20%

Based on these metrics, the B-DCGAN trained on 30000 epochs was chosen as the final model.

Figure 6 contains a boxplot of the NRMSE of each scenario, for both oil and water productions. The box extends from the lower to the upper quartile values of the data, and the whiskers extend to the 2nd and 98th percentiles. The circles represent outliers, and the middle line, the median.

As this plot illustrates, not only is the total NRMSE low, the distribution of the NRMSEs has predominantly low values, with a few high outliers that are still acceptable values.

Figure 7 contains boxplots comparing the distribution between the simulated and generated data. It was built in a similar fashion to the previous one, with the difference that the whiskers extend to the maximum and minimum values of the data. It shows that the GAN was able to correctly learn the distribution of the original data, maintaining approximate maximum and minimum values, as well as medians and quartiles.

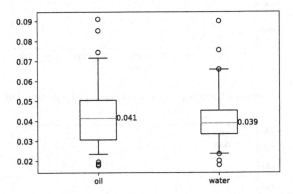

Fig. 6. Boxplot of the NRMSE.

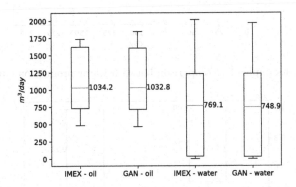

Fig. 7. Boxplots of the simulated and generated oil and water production data.

Figures 8 and 9 show examples of curves generated by the final model, compared to the ones simulated with the same valve controls.

Figure 10 shows a comparison between the valve control data of the original dataset, and the one given by the generator model of the B-DCGAN. The whiskers extend to the maximum and minimum of the data, and the dotted line represents the mean. These results show that the model was able to replicate the distribution of original valve control data, while increasing diversity, as seen by

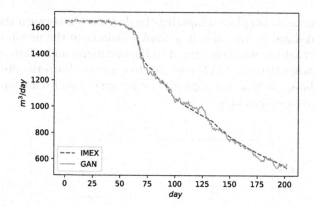

Fig. 8. Example of a comparison between oil production curves.

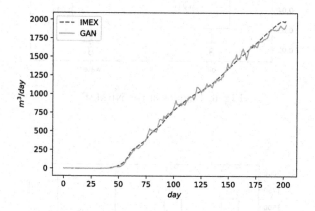

Fig. 9. Example of a comparison between water production curves.

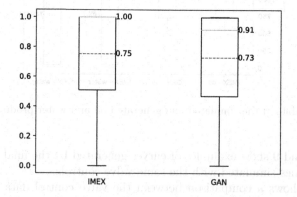

Fig. 10. Boxplots of the original and generated valve data.

the shift in the median. This means that the generated strategies have applied control earlier than the original dataset, and is useful as it increases data variety, for future dataset building.

While the simulation of a scenario takes 5.261 s, the generation of one takes 0.008. These results mean that, after initial training, the model is able to build a whole dataset in a negligible amount of time.

9 Conclusions

The present application of GANs was not only successful, but novel, paving the way for future intersections between the methodology and smart well technology, benefiting the industry.

The network was able to generate realistic-looking production curves, with good evaluation metrics. Therefore, the methodology can now be coupled to other applications, such as reservoir simulator substitution, where another specialized network can be trained on a dataset augmented by the GAN, reducing dataset-building time and enabling various simulation-intensive optimizations.

Acknowledgment. The authors would like to thank Petrobras, Intel, CNPq and CAPES for the resources made available for the development of this work.

References

1. Abadi, M., Agarwal, A., Barham, P., et al.: TensorFlow: large-scale machine learning on heterogeneous systems (2015). https://www.tensorflow.org
2. Abreu, A.C.A.: An approach to value flexibility considering uncertainty and future information: an application to smart wells. Ph.D. thesis, Department of Electrical Engineering, Pontifical Catholic University of Rio de Janeiro, Rio de Janeiro, Brazil (2016)
3. Chollet, F., et al.: Keras (2015). https://keras.io
4. Computer Modelling Group Ltd., CMG: IMEX: three-phase, black-oil reservoir simulator, user's guide (2017)
5. Dupont, E., Zhang, T., Tilke, P., Liang, L., Bailey, W.: Generating realistic geology conditioned on physical measurements with generative adversarial networks. arXiv e-prints (2018). arXiv:1802.03065
6. Emerick, A.A., Portella, R.C.M.: Production optimization with intelligent wells. In: SPE Latin America and Caribbean Petroleum Engineering Conference. Society of Petroleum Engineers, Buenos Aires, Argentina (2007). https://doi.org/10.2118/107261-MS
7. Esteban, C., Hyland, S.L., Rätsch, G.: Real-valued (medical) time series generation with recurrent conditional GANs. arXiv e-prints (2017). arXiv:1706.02633
8. Floris, F.J.T., Bush, M.D., Cuypers, M., Roggero, F., Syversveen, A.R.: Methods for quantifying the uncertainty of production forecasts: a comparative study. Petrol. Geosci. **7**, S87–S96 (2001). https://doi.org/10.1144/petgeo.7.S.S87
9. Gao, C.H., Rajeswaran, R.T., Nakagawa, E.Y.: A literature review on smart well technology. In: SPE Production and Operations Symposium. Society of Petroleum Engineers, Oklahoma City, Oklahoma, USA (2007). https://doi.org/10.2118/106011-MS

10. Goodfellow, I.J., Bengio, Y., Courville, A.: Deep Learning. MIT Press (2016). http://www.deeplearningbook.org
11. Goodfellow, I.J., Pouget-Abadie, J., Mirza, M., et al.: Generative adversarial networks. arXiv e-prints (2014). arXiv:1406.2661
12. Hartmann, K.G., Schirrmeister, R.T., Ball, T.: EEG-GAN: generative adversarial networks for electroencephalographic (EEG) brain signals. arXiv e-prints (2018). arXiv:1806.01875
13. Hjelm, R.D., Jacob, A.P., Che, T., et al.: Boundary-seeking generative adversarial networks. arXiv e-prints (2017). arXiv:1702.08431
14. Konopczynski, M., Ajayi, A., Russel, L.A.: Intelligent well completion: Status and opportunities for developing marginal reserves. In: 27th Annual SPE International Technical Conference and Exhibition. Society of Petroleum Engineers, Abuja, Nigeria (2003). https://doi.org/10.2118/85676-MS
15. Mogren, O.: C-RNN-GAN: continuous recurrent neural networks with adversarial training. In: Constructive Machine Learning Workshop (CML) at NIPS (Conference on Neural Information Processing Systems), Barcelona, Spain (2016)
16. Mosser, L.J., Dubrule, O., Blunt, M.J.: Conditioning of three-dimensional generative adversarial networks for pore and reservoir-scale models. arXiv e-prints (2018). arXiv:1802.05622
17. Mosser, L.J., Dubrule, O., Blunt, M.J.: Stochastic seismic waveform inversion using generative adversarial networks as a geological prior. arXiv e-prints (2018). arXiv:1806.03720
18. Radford, A., Metz, L., Chintala, S.: Unsupervised representation learning with deep convolutional generative adversarial networks. arXiv e-prints (2015). arXiv:1511.06434
19. Thomas, J.E., et al.: Fundamentals of Petroleum Engineering. Petrobras and Interciência (2001). (in Portuguese). ISBN 8571930996
20. Yahi, A., Vanguri, R., Elhadad, N., Tatonetti, N.P.: Generative adversarial networks for electronic health records: a framework for exploring and evaluating methods for predicting drug-induced laboratory test trajectories. In: Machine Learning for Health Workshop (ML4H) at NIPS (Conference on Neural Information Processing Systems), Long Beach, California, USA (2017)
21. Yang, L.C., Chou, S.Y., Yang, Y.H.: MidiNet: a convolutional generative adversarial network for symbolic-domain music generation. arXiv e-prints (2017). arXiv:1703.10847
22. Yeten, B., Brouwer, D.R., Durlofsky, L.J., Aziz, K.: Decision analysis under uncertainty for smart well deployment. J. Petrol. Sci. Eng. 43(3–4), 183–199 (2004). https://doi.org/10.1016/j.petrol.2004.02.013

Resilient Environmental Monitoring Utilizing a Machine Learning Approach

Dan Häberlein[1(✉)], Lars Kafurke[1], Sebastian Höfer[1], Bogdan Franczyk[1], Bernhard Jung[2], and Erik Berger[2]

[1] Institute of Business Information Systems, University of Leipzig, Grimmaische-Str. 12, 04109 Leipzig, Germany
haeberlein@wifa.uni-leipzig.de
[2] Institute of Computer Science, Technical University Bergakademie Freiberg, Bernhard-von-Cotta-Str. 2, 09599 Freiberg, Germany

Abstract. A wide range of regulations is established to protect citizens health from the noxious consequences of aerosols, e.g. particulate matter (PM10). To ensure a public information and the compliance to given regulations, a resilient environmental sensor network is necessary. This paper presents a machine learning approach which utilizes low-cost platforms to build a resilient sensor network. In particular, malfunctions are compensated by learning virtual models of various particulate matter sensors. Such virtualized sensors are already utilized in the field of proprioceptive robotics [1] and are comparable to a digital twins definition. Several experiments show the proposed method yields PM10 estimates and forecasts similar to high-performance sensors.

Keywords: Environmental monitoring · Virtual sensor · Machine learning · Volunteered geographic information

1 Introduction

Environmental monitoring takes an essential role for many stakeholders like scientists, policy makers as well as the public. Although many data sets are expensive to gather and hard to analyze, the advantages outweigh the possible success in question. Longterm measurements help to reveal changes in slowly shifting ecosystems [2]. A development as slow as mentioned has been recorded by German governmental authorities regarding air quality. The *collected data*[1] implies that the particulate matter (PM10) concentration in overall Germany has been reduced by about 38% over the course of twenty years between 1995 and 2015. The availability of this data is based on regulations of the European Union (2008/50/EG). The aim of those regulations is to protect citizens health threatened by consequences when being exposed to noxious high PM10 concentrations [3]. However, many cities still face the violation of PM10 and nitric oxide limits.

---

[1] www.umweltbundesamt.de/daten/luft/luftschadstoff-emissionen-in-deutschland.

© Springer Nature Switzerland AG 2019
L. Rutkowski et al. (Eds.): ICAISC 2019, LNAI 11508, pp. 85–93, 2019.
https://doi.org/10.1007/978-3-030-20912-4_8

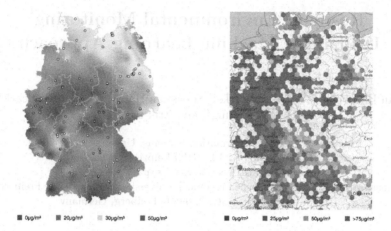

Fig. 1. Different PM10 concentrations measured on the 19/12/2018. Left: An average day measurement acquired from the federal environment agency. Right: A snapshot of the *Luftdaten Info* citizen science project acquired at 2:00 PM.

In those cases, authorities have a limited action scope and must even consider the introduction of driving bans in heavily frequented areas. Additionally, measurement stations are placed at potential high risk areas like cities and inhabited traffic hubs, leaving citizens of certain areas in the dark about their individual PM10 exposure. This circumstance is visualized in the left part of Fig. 1 as it shows fragmentary nature of the *German PM10 monitoring network*[2]. On the other hand, a more finely grained measurement network is not an option either. Accurate PM10 sensors using the gravimetric measurement method are usually expensive, maintenance heavy and consequently not appropriate for rural areas.

To counter this development, scientists have been proposing the term citizen science [4]. They claim that the involvement of non-expert people using broadly available commodity sensors can help to complete monitoring networks. Technologically, this development has been supported by the rise of the internet of things (IoT). The IoT has been the foundation of reflecting physical things into the digital world [7]. Using IoT technology, there are already established projects for citizen science driven aerosol measurements [5,8]. The right part of Fig. 1 shows a similar map of Germany, displaying the *current PM10 exposure*[3] measured using citizen science data [6]. Comparing both figures gives rise to the assumption that the citizen science driven solutions are more fine grained and broader applicable. However, citizen science data sources like [6] are still discarded entirely by authorities, many scientists and regulators. Due to their low-cost nature, many IoT sensors are prone to the production of non-consistent data as well as full data loss [9,10]. To tackle those shortcomings, the here

---

[2] www.umweltbundesamt.de/daten/luftbelastung/aktuelle-luftdaten.
[3] www.maps.luftdaten.info.

presented approach tries to increase the robustness against data loss and erroneous measurements by using machine learning techniques [11].

This paper describes a supervised machine learning approach inspired by similar use in robotics. Robotics are a domain were a multitude of data is produced and evaluated in real time. Moreover, robustness is an inevitable feature of systems and algorithms used. We aim to transfer our gained knowledge in the field of robotics to increase robustness and compensation capabilities also for the PM10 monitoring domain.

2   Approach

The goal of the presented approach is to build a robust low-cost sensor network for the accurate environmental monitoring and forecasting of PM10 concentrations. For this, the proposed approach makes use of supervised machine learning techniques where training data is acquired from multiple low-cost sensor platforms. In more detail, each platform consists of a Raspberry Pi which is equipped with several low-cost **Nova SDS011**[4] PM10 sensors. To the best of the authors knowledge this is the cheapest available sensor platform for measuring PM10 concentrations. These sensors are less accurate and more prone to error than actual high-performance devices. In particular, the high-performance **Dr. Födisch FDS15**[5], of which one device is already a hundred times more expensive than the low-cost platform, is utilized for evaluation purposes. In the following, each step of the presented machine learning approach is explained in more detail.

2.1   Data Acquisition

In this paper, low-cost sensor networks are used for monitoring and forecasting of PM10 measurements. These networks consist of n platforms where each one is equipped with m sensor devices. Here, the usage of multiple sensors $(m >= 2)$ increases the network's robustness against environmental influences and device specific malfunctions. The corresponding low-cost sensor readings $\mathbf{s}^l = (s_1^l, \ldots, s_{n \cdot m}^l)$ are recorded and used as training data

$$\mathbf{D}_{low} = \begin{bmatrix} \mathbf{s}_1^l \\ \vdots \\ \mathbf{s}_t^l \end{bmatrix}, \tag{1}$$

where t describes the number of equidistant samples in time. The recording rate and number of samples depend on the particular application and the required accuracy.

---

[4] www.watterott.com/de/Nova-SDS011-Feinstaub-Sensor.
[5] www.foedisch.de/staubmesstechnik/feinstaub.

In addition to the low-cost sensor data $\mathbf{D}_{low}$, k additional high-performance sensors can be recorded simultaneously

$$\mathbf{D}_{high} = \begin{bmatrix} s_1^h \cdots s_{1,k}^h \\ \vdots \ddots \vdots \\ s_t^h \cdots s_{t,k}^h \end{bmatrix}. \tag{2}$$

This allows comparing the quality of the utilized supervised machine learning approach with an expensive but more accurate state of the art device. Following this basic idea, an experimental data set is introduced and evaluated in Sect. 3.

2.2 Model Learning

The presented approach is inspired by behavior-specific proprioception models (BSPMs) [1], a machine learning approach from the field of robotics. One BSPM mode is the so called *virtual sensor* [12] which replaces a sensor device by employing artificial neural networks. The basic idea is to find a mapping between the robot's available sensors and the expensive sensor devices by applying a machine learning algorithm.

However, in the context of this paper virtual sensors are utilized to compensate malfunctions therefore increasing robustness and forecasting capabilities of the overall network (see Sect. 3.2). Additionally, the usage of $\mathbf{D}_{low}$ for the prediction of $\mathbf{D}_{high}$ is evaluated in Sect. 3.3 and further discussed in Sect. 4. Various artificial neural network architectures are feasible for this. Due to long-term correlations within the data, this paper focuses on recurrent network architectures called *nonlinear autoregressive network with exogenous inputs* (NARX) [13] which was empirically proven to perform better than feed-forward networks and other recurrent architectures. In particular, NARX use actual and previous samples as input neurons to predict the particular output. Furthermore, current predictions are used to increase the quality of future predictions. This is achieved by implementing a loop closure where the actual prediction is directly fed back into the input (autoregressive). Hence, the network is trained by the deviation in the temporal evolution of its predictions. This allows to protect predictions from sudden changes. Broadly speaking, a NARX network smoothly compensates anomaly data points which makes it more robust against noise.

The NARX architecture is configured with two hidden-layers each containing five sigmoidal neurons. The input applies a time window of five measurements observing a four dimensional input while predicting a one dimensional output. An additional forecasting of outputs is then achieved by shifting the particular output data to the actual input data. For example, currently measured inputs are used to predict an output which lies in the future of the recorded time series.

3   Experiments

Different experiments have been conducted to validate the robustness and forecasting capabilities of the proposed virtual sensor method. For this, a data set

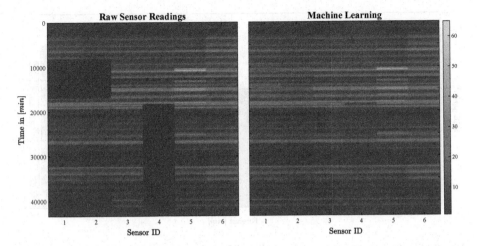

Fig. 2. The PM10 concentration measured by the low-cost sensor network. Left: The raw sensor measurements suffer from temporal and permanent malfunctions which can affect a particular sensor and even a complete sensor platform. Right: Partial malfunctions are compensated by learning a particular virtual sensor from the still functioning sensor devices. As a result, the environmental sensor networks keeps functional.

was acquired from the environmental sensor network mentioned in Sect. 2. In particular, the network consists of three low-cost platforms each equipped with two PM10 sensors (SDS011). These platforms are located in Leipzig (Germany) and cover an area of about $10000 \, m^2$. Figure 2 left shows the error-prone raw measurements of the PM10 sensors which was stored once per minute for a period of about 30 days. In consequence, the overall data $\mathbf{D}_{low}$ contains 43200 six dimensional samples of the three differently located low-cost platforms. This recording is used for training, testing and validation purposes in the following experiments.

In more detail, the compensation capabilities of the low-cost sensor network are evaluated first. Next, the robustness of the forecasting approach is shown for various temporal delays. Finally, the high-performance sensor (FDS15) is virtualized by learning a model from the acquired data.

3.1 Compensation Capabilities

The error susceptibility of such low-cost sensor networks is a common problem (see Sect. 1). In this paper, a machine learning approach is applied to solve this drawback. The recurrent neural network architecture (NARX, see Sect. 2.2) is used to compensate various malfunctions.

For training purposes, only data which contains a fully functional sensor network is applicable. Hence, a subset of data within between minute 3000 and 8000 is selected from the overall data. This subset $\hat{\mathbf{D}}_{low}$ is further split into 50% training, 25% testing and 25% validation data. This is a common trade-off which

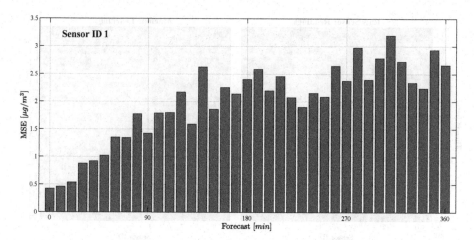

Fig. 3. The first low-cost sensor is predicted from inputs of sensors three to six within between forecast delays of 0 to 360 min. Here, a NARX network is trained 50 times for each delay where only the best result is visualized. The accuracy decreases for increasing delays but remains sufficient to implement an adequate early warning system.

usually decreases the probability of overfitting and increases the reliability of the results. The remaining training data is then used to learn six different NARX networks where learning is stopped when overfitting is detected or after reaching a maximum of 100 epochs. For example, the sensor denoted by ID one is used as output while ID three to six are used as input. The sensor denoted by ID two is explicitly excluded since both sensors are equipped to the same platform and therefore are probably affected by the same source of noise. The resulting approximations achieve a *mean square error* (MSE) of less than $0.5 \, \mu g/m^3$ for each sensor. This accuracy is sufficient for the proposed application but can be enhanced by increasing the network's complexity and the corresponding computational effort spend for learning.

However, each sensor is approximated by sensor readings located at other platforms. During malfunctions, the learned virtual counterparts are used to compensate erroneous and even completely missing sensor readings. Figure 2 right shows the results of the corresponding neural networks. The malfunctioning hardware is replaced by the corresponding virtual sensor so the environmental sensor network keeps functioning. In the following, the forecasting capabilities of the utilized NARX architecture are evaluated.

3.2   Forecasting Robustness

Another goal is to predict a critical increase of PM10 concentrations. For this, the mentioned subset $\hat{D}_{low}$ is used to forecast sensor one's measurements within 0 to 360 min. To achieve comparable results, this learning procedure is repeated 50 times with only the network the lowest MSE being stored. This is necessary since

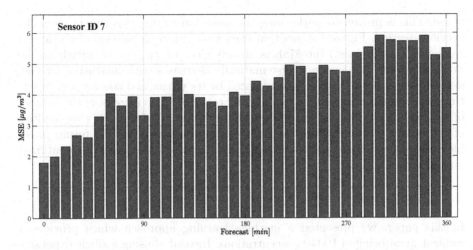

Fig. 4. The high-performance sensor output is predicted from inputs of six low-cost sensors where the forecast delay is between 0 to 360 min. In this experiment, a NARX network has been trained 50 times for each delay with only the best result visualized. The MSE is substantially higher as for forecasting a low-cost sensor. This is due to the different hardware and measurement range of both sensor devices. However, the quality of the virtualized FDS15 is adequate to replace the expensive sensor in settings where forecasting is not required.

each learning procedure begins at a random start initialization and therefore always achieves slightly different results.

Figure 3 presents the corresponding decrease of accuracy when increasing the temporal forecast. As is observable, even a six hour forecast results in a MSE of about $3\,\mu g/m^3$. One possible explanation for the forecasting procedure's robustness is that the NARX network uses temporal patterns which occur due to recurring traffic volume. However, in the context of PM10 limits, which usually lie between $20\,\mu g/m^3$ to $50\,\mu g/m^3$, this is sufficient to detect tendencies and implement an adequate early warning system. In the following, this forecasting procedure is applied to learn a high-performance sensor from the low-cost sensors.

3.3 Learning a Virtual Sensor

In contrast to the previous experiments, this section focuses on learning a virtual high-performance sensor from low-cost sensor inputs. The acquired data set $\mathbf{D}_{low}$ is extended by sensor readings of a seventh sensor $\mathbf{D}_{high}$ which contains the measurements of a simultaneously recorded FDS15. The idea is to learn the NARX network with inputs from the six dimensional low-cost measurements $\hat{\mathbf{D}}_{low}$ to the output of this high-performance sensor $\hat{\mathbf{D}}_{high}$. This allows replacing the expensive hardware with a network of low-cost platforms during runtime. The sensors hardware and consequently its measurements are completely different from the low-cost devices. Hence, the prediction accuracy is also substantially worse. This is proven by performing the same forecasting experiment as in the previous section. Figure 4 shows that even for a direct estimation of the actual value (without forecast) the MSE is already close to $2\,\mu g/m^3$. Similarly to the previous results the accuracy systematically decreases with increasing forecast delays. Hence, the FDS15 can be replaced by its virtualized counterpart in settings where forecasting is not compulsorily required. Also increasing the number of neurons or layers does not particularly enhance the forecasting capabilities of the NARX network. Still, the following conclusions highlight future possible direction which are promising to further increase the quality of the utilized virtual sensor approach.

4   Conclusion

In this paper, we presented a machine learning approach which provides a resilient monitoring of PM10 concentrations. Instead of using a single expensive device, data from multiple low-cost PM10 sensors is gathered to learn a NARX network. The corresponding virtual sensor generates PM10 approximation and consequently can be used to replace measurements of the physical device during malfunctions. In addition, the low-cost characteristic of the sensor platforms allows the usage of this approach in citizen science applications.

The conducted experiments further highlighted that the forecasting accuracy subsequently decreases with increasing temporal delays. For the proposed applications, for example tendency detection, the achieved results are sufficient but can not compete with the quality of a high-performance device. There are several possibilities to further increase estimation and forecasting capabilities of the presented approach. For instance, more data can be acquired using even more platforms as well as the application of further heterogeneous environmental measurements, e.g. temperature, wind and humidity. Regarding machine learning, state-of-the-art deep learning techniques can be applied. For instance, long-term correlations can be detected more accurately by utilizing a *long short-term memory* (LSTM) [14]. Such LSTMs are proven to compete better in various applications than classical neural network architectures [15] but are computational much more expensive.

Regarding the data acquisition process, future work must advance the measuring process as well as the corresponding infrastructure. An appliance of citizen science will ensure better data availability due to the usage of a mobile, more user friendly version. More precisely, we plan to attach sensors to consistently used physical mobile objects (like rear lights in bicycles or tram coaches). Such a more complex system with many non-experts would be concerned with more requirements regarding resilience, robustness and usability. At the moment, the sensor systems are only stationary expert systems. On the other hand, such a system would not only need to include sensor measurements but the monitoring of the sensor's context. Therefore, we would expand our data ingestion infrastructure as well as alter our analysis tool chain to be more flexible and scaleable.

Finally, given our promising results and the success of other citizen science projects as outlined in Fig. 1, one near future step could be the appliance of our work to other data sets, e.g. Luftdaten.info [6]. Utilizing our approach could improve the resilience of more established sensor networks.

References

1. Berger, E.: Behavior-specific proprioception models for robotic force estimation: a machine learning approach, Ph.D. thesis (2018)
2. Lovett, G.M., et al.: Who needs environmental monitoring? Front. Ecol. Environ. **5**(5), 253–260 (2007)
3. Rohr, A., Wyzga, R.: Attributing health effects to individual particulate matter constituents. Atmos. Environ. **62**, 130–152 (2012)
4. Irwin, A.: Citizen Science: A Study of People, Expertise and Sustainable Development. Routledge, London (2002)
5. McCrory, G., Veeckman, C., Claeys, L.: Citizen science is in the air – engagement mechanisms from technology-mediated citizen science projects addressing air pollution. In: Kompatsiaris, I., et al. (eds.) INSCI 2017. LNCS, vol. 10673, pp. 28–38. Springer, Cham (2017). https://doi.org/10.1007/978-3-319-70284-1_3
6. Blon, M.: Research regarding PM measurements. The citizen science project luftdaten.info, M.Sc. thesis, University of Esslingen (2018). (In German)
7. Razzaque, M.A., et al.: Middleware for Internet of Things: a survey. IEEE Internet Things J. **3**(1), 70–95 (2016)
8. Kosmidis, E., Syropoulou, P., Tekes, S., et al.: hackAIR: towards raising awareness about air quality in Europe by developing a collective online platform. ISPRS Int. J. Geo-Inf. **7**, 187 (2018)
9. Schneider, P., Castell, N., Vogt, M., Dauge, F., Lahoz, W., Bartonova, A.: Mapping urban air quality in near real-time using observations from low-cost sensors and model information. Environ. Int. **106**, 234–247 (2017)
10. Castell, N., et al.: Can commercial low-cost sensor platforms contribute to air quality monitoring and exposure estimates? Environ. Int. **99**, 293–302 (2017)
11. Lary, D., Alavi, A., Omi, A., Walker, A.: Machine learning in geosciences and remote sensing. Geosci. Front. **7**, 3–10 (2016)
12. Berger, E., Vogt, D., Grehl, S., Jung, B., Amor, H.B.: Estimating perturbations from experience using neural networks and information transfer. In: IEEE/RSJ International Conference on Intelligent Robots and Systems (IROS), Daejeon, pp. 176–181 (2016)
13. Lin, T., Horne, B.G., Tino, P., Giles, C.L.: Learning long-term dependencies in NARX recurrent neural networks. Trans. Neural Network **7**, 1329–1338 (1996)
14. Gers, F.A., Schmidhuber, J., Cummins, F.: Learning to forget: continual prediction with LSTM. In: Neural Computation, pp. 2451–2471 (2000)
15. Srivastava, R.K., Greff, K., Schmidhuber, J.: Training very deep networks. In: Advances in Neural Information Processing Systems, pp. 2377–2385 (2015)

Study of Learning Ability in Profit Sharing Using Convolutional Neural Network

Kazuki Hashiba and Yuko Osana[✉]

Tokyo University of Technology, 1404-1, Katakura, Hachioji, Tokyo 192-0982, Japan
osana@stf.teu.ac.jp

Abstract. Profit Sharing using Convolutional Neural Network (PS-CNN) has been proposed as a method of deep reinforcement learning. In the previous work, experiments have been conducted using Atari 2600's Asterix in the Profit Sharing using Convolutional Neural Networks, and it is known that a better score can be obtained than Deep Q-Network. However, experiments have not been conducted on games other than Asterix, and sufficient consideration has not been made. In this paper, we report on the results of studying learning ability for some Atari 2600' games in Profit Sharing using Convolution Neural Network. By comparing the results with the results in Deep Q-Network, we confirmed that this method can acquire higher score than the Deep Q-Network in some games. The common feature of these games is that the number of actions and the number of states are relatively large.

Keywords: Convolutional Neural Network · Profit Sharing

1 Introduction

In recent years, as a method which shows better performance than the conventional methods in the field of image/speech recognition, the deep learning has been drawing attention. Deep learning is learning in hierarchical neural networks which have many layers, and the Convolutional Neural Network (CNN) [1] is one of the typical models.

On the other hand, various studies on reinforcement learning are being conducted as learning methods to acquire appropriate policies through interaction with the environment [2]. In reinforcement learning, learning can proceed by repeating trial and error even in an unknown environment by appropriately setting rewards.

The combination of deep learning and reinforcement learning is called Deep Reinforcement Learning. Most of these methods are based on the Q Learning [4], and as one of these methods, the Deep Q-Network [5] which is based on the convolutional neural network and the Q Learning is proposed. In the Deep Q-Network, the game screen is used as observation, and when observation is given as an input to the

© Springer Nature Switzerland AG 2019
L. Rutkowski et al. (Eds.): ICAISC 2019, LNAI 11508, pp. 94–101, 2019.
https://doi.org/10.1007/978-3-030-20912-4_9

convolutional neural network, the action value in Q Learning for each action is output. This method can realize learning that acquires a score equal to or higher than that of a human in plural games. As a deep reinforcement learning using a method other than Q Learning, we have proposed a Deep Q-Network using reward distribution [6] and a Profit Sharing using Convolutional Neural Network(PS-CNN) [7]. The Deep Q-Network using reward distribution learns to not take wrong actions, by distributing negative rewards in the same way as Profit Sharing [3]. Although this method can perform learning with the same degree of precision and speed as Deep Q-Network, it shows that the score that can be finally obtained is same level as Deep Q-Network. In the Profit Sharing using Convolutional Neural Network, the error function based on the update equation for the value function in the Profit Sharing is used instead of the error function based on the updating equation for the value function in the Q Learning in the Deep Q-Network. In the previous work [7], experiments have been conducted using Atari 2600's Asterix in the Profit Sharing using Convolutional Neural Networks, and it is known that a better score can be obtained than Deep Q-Network. However, experiments have not been conducted on games other than Asterix, and sufficient consideration has not been made.

In this paper, we report on the results of studying learning ability for some Atari 2600' games in Profit Sharing using Convolution Neural Network.

2 Profit Sharing Using Convolutional Neural Network

Here, the Profit Sharing using Convolutional Neural Network (PS-CNN) [7] which is examined in this paper is explained.

2.1 Outline

In the PS-CNN, action value in Profit Sharing is learned by convolutional neural network. This is a method that learns the value function of Profit Sharing instead of the value function of Q Learning used in the Deep Q-Network [5]. By changing to an error function based on the value function of Profit Sharing which can acquire probabilistic policy in a shorter time, the proposed method is able to learn in a shorter time than the conventional Deep Q-Network. However, in the Profit Sharing, since temporally continuous data is meaningful in episodes, experience replay used in the Deep Q-Network is not used in the proposed method. The Q Learning uses fixed target Q-Network because the value of other rules is also used when updating the value of the rule. In contrast, the Profit Sharing uses the value of the rule included in the episode in updating the connection weights. Therefore, the proposed method does not use fixed target Q-Network.

2.2 Structure

The structure of the convolutional neural network used in the PS-CNN is shown in Fig. 1. As seen in Fig. 1, the PS-CNN is a model based on the convolutional

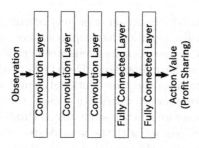

Fig. 1. Structure of PS-CNN.

neural network, consisting of three convolution layers and two fully connected layers as similar as the conventional Deep Q-Network. The play screen of the game (observation) is input to the convolutional neural network, and the action value for each action corresponding to the observation is outputted. For the first to fourth layers, rectified linear function is used as an output function. The number of neurons in the last finally connected layer which is the output layer is the same as the number of actions that can be taken in the problem to be handled. Since the problem learned by the PS-CNN can be regarded as a regression problem to learn the relationship between each observation and the action value of each action in the observation, the output function of the output layer is an identity mapping function.

2.3 Learning

In the PS-CNN, the convolutional neural network learns to output the value of each action corresponding to the play screen of the game (observation) which is given as input. Here, the action value is updated based on the Profit Sharing. So, the error function E is given by

$$E = \frac{1}{2} \left(r_\tau F(\tau) - q(o_\tau, a_\tau) \right)^2 \tag{1}$$

where r is reward, $q(o_\tau, a_\tau)$ is the value of taking action a_τ at observation o_τ. $F(\tau)$ is the reinforcement function at the time τ and is given by

$$F(\tau) = \frac{1}{(|C^A| + 1)^{W - \tau}} \tag{2}$$

where C^A is the set of actions that an agent can take at the observation, $|C^A|$ is the number of actions that an agent can take, W is the length of an episode.

The action is selected based using the ε-greedy as similar as the conventional Deep Q-Network. When the game screen o_τ is given to the PS-CNN, the value of all actions in observation o_τ is output in the output layer. Based on the output action value, action is determined by the ε-greedy method. In the ε-greedy method, one action is selected randomly with the probability ε ($0 \leq \varepsilon \leq 1$), the action whose value is highest with the probability of $1 - \varepsilon$.

The probability to select the action a in observation o_τ, $P(o_\tau, a)$ is given by

$$P(o_\tau, a) = \begin{cases} (1 - \varepsilon) + \dfrac{\varepsilon}{|C^A|} & \left(\text{if } a = \underset{a' \in C^A}{\operatorname{argmax}} \ q(o_\tau, a')\right) \\ \dfrac{\varepsilon}{|C^A|} & (\text{otherwise}) \end{cases} \tag{3}$$

where, $|C^A|$ is the number of action types that the agent can take, which is the same as the number of neurons in the output layer of the PS-CNN.

The selected action a_τ is executed, and the state transits to the next state o_{tau+1}. Also, by taking the action a_τ, the reward r_τ is given based on the score, game state and so on.

3 Computer Experiment Results

To demonstrate the effectiveness of the PS-CNN, computer experiments were conducted on some games of Atari 2600. The results are shown below.

3.1 Task

Beam Rider (Fig. 2(a)), Centipede (Fig. 2(b)) and Chopper Command (Fig. 2(c)) are shooting games. In Beam Rider and Centipede, the actions of the agent are four kinds of movement; moving to left and right, not moving and shooting. In Chopper Command, the actions of the agent are six kinds of movement; moving to up, down, left and right, not moving and shooting.

Fishinf Derby (Fig. 2(d)) is a fishing game. In this game, the actions of the agent are five kinds of movement; moving to up, down, left and right, and not moving.

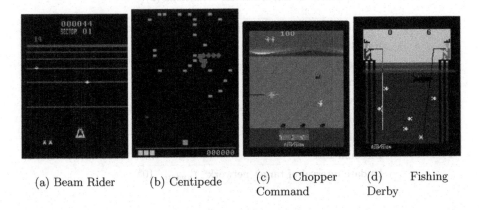

(a) Beam Rider   (b) Centipede   (c)   Chopper   (d)   Fishing
                                           Command   Derby

Fig. 2. Trained games.

3.2 Experimental Conditions

Table 1 shows the conditions for the convolutional neural network used in the PS-CNN and the conventional Deep Q-Network. The game screen used in this research is an RGB image of 400×500. In the experiment, the RGB image is grayscaled, reduced to 84×84 pixels, and an image grouped for 4 frames is used as input.

Table 2 shows other conditions related to learning. An action is selected by ε-greedy. At the start of learning, ε is set to 1 so that actions are randomly selected. After that, ε is decreased until it becomes $1/10^6$ every action (one step). The agent gradually emphasizes the action value and selects an action.

In the PS-CNN, since Profit Sharing is used, as the length of the episode becomes longer, the value of the denominator on the right side of Eq. (2) becomes too large and the reward can not be distributed sufficiently. Therefore, only five steps before acquisition of the score are regarded as episodes.

Table 1. Experimental conditions (1).

	Filter size	Stride	Output size	Output function
Input	–	–	$84 \times 84 \times 4$	–
Convolution Layer 1	8×8	4	$20 \times 20 \times 32$	ReLU
Convolution Layer 2	4×4	2	$9 \times 9 \times 64$	ReLU
Convolution Layer 3	3×3	1	$7 \times 7 \times 64$	ReLU
Full-Connected Layer 1	–	–	512	ReLU
Full-Connected Layer 2	–	–	5 (The number of actions)	Identity function

Table 2. Experimental conditions (2)

The number of learning steps		1.0×10^7
Initial value of ε	ε_{ini}	1
Decrease amount of ε	ε_r	$1/10^6$
Minimum of ε	ε_{min}	0.1
ε in evaluation episodes	ε'	0.05
Size of replay memory	D_{max}	10^6
Size of mini batch	M	32
Discount rate	γ	0.99
Update interval of target network	T_{update}	10^4

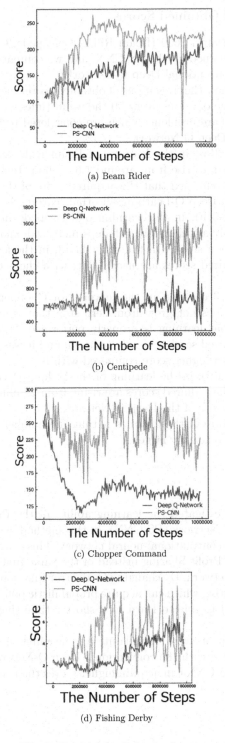

(a) Beam Rider

(b) Centipede

(c) Chopper Command

(d) Fishing Derby

Fig. 3. Transition of obtained scores.

3.3 Transition of Obtained Scores

Here, some games of atari 2600 (Beam Rider, Centipede, Chopper Command, Fishing Derby) are learned by the PS-CNN, and we compared the transition of the score with the conventional Deep Q-Network.

Figure 3(a)–(d) show the transitions of obtained scores in each method. These figures are the average of scores every 50 thousand times.

These four games are problems which are considered to be difficult to learn on the conventional Deep Q-Network.

As shown in Fig. 3(a), in the learning of Beam Rider in the PS-CNN, the acquisition score starts to rise from around 1.6 million steps. Then, for around 3 million steps, it is confirmed that the acquired score of the PS-CNN is 100 or more higher than the Deep Q-Learning and that learning is done properly.

As shown in Fig. 3(b), in the learning of Centipede in the PS-CNN, the score increased sharply as the number of steps increased, and scored about 1800 points around 7 million steps. On the other hand, in the learning of the Deep Q-Network, the acquired scores are nearly flat, with the acquired score scored roughly 100 points.

As shown in Fig. 3(c), even in the learning of Chopper Command in the PS-CNN, the score does not grow from zero step that started randomly, and it can not be said that learning is properly performed. However, in the Deep Q-Learning, the acquired score is clearly reduced, and it was confirmed that the PS-CNN can acquire a higher score compared with it.

As shown in Fig. 3(d), in the learning of the Fishing Derby in the PS-CNN, it is confirmed that the acquired scores are rising from 2 million steps and finally exceed the acquired score of the Deep Q-Network.

The common feature of these games is that the number of actions and the number of states are relatively large.

4   Conclusions

In this paper, we investigated the learning ability of the Profit Sharing using Convolutional Neural Network (PS-CNN). In this method, action value in Profit Sharing is learned by convolutional neural network. This is a method that learns the value function of Profit Sharing instead of the value function of Q Learning used in the Deep Q-Network. By changing to an error function based on the value function of Profit Sharing which can acquire probabilistic policy in a shorter time, the proposed method is able to learn in a shorter time than the conventional Deep Q-Network.

Computer experiments were carried out on some games of Atari 2600, and the PS-CNN was compared with the conventional Deep Q-Network. As a result, we confirmed that the PS-CNN can acquire higher scores than the Deep Q-Network in some games.

References

1. LeCun, Y., Bottou, L., Bengio, Y., Haffner, P.: Gradient-based learning applied to document recognition. Proc. IEEE **86**(11), 2278–2324 (1998)
2. Sutton, R.S., Barto, A.G.: Reinforcement Learning: An Introduction. The MIT Press, Cambridge (1998)
3. Grefenstette, J.J.: Credit assignment in rule discovery systems based on genetic algorithms. Mach. Learn. **3**, 225–245 (1988)
4. Watkins, C.J.C.H., Dayan, P.: Technical note: Q-learning. Mach. Learn. **8**, 55–68 (1992)
5. Mnih, V., et al.: Human-level control through deep reinforcement learning. Nature **518**, 529–533 (2015)
6. Nakaya, Y., Osana, Y.: Deep Q-network using reward distribution. In: Rutkowski, L., Scherer, R., Korytkowski, M., Pedrycz, W., Tadeusiewicz, R., Zurada, J.M. (eds.) ICAISC 2018. LNCS (LNAI), vol. 10841, pp. 160–169. Springer, Cham (2018). https://doi.org/10.1007/978-3-319-91253-0_16
7. Hasuike, N., Osana, Y.: Learning game by profit sharing using convolutional neural network. In: Kůrková, V., Manolopoulos, Y., Hammer, B., Iliadis, L., Maglogiannis, I. (eds.) ICANN 2018. LNCS, vol. 11139, pp. 43–50. Springer, Cham (2018). https://doi.org/10.1007/978-3-030-01418-6_5

Neural Net Model Predictive Controller for Adaptive Active Vibration Suppression of an Unknown System

Mateusz Heesch and Ziemowit Dworakowski[✉] [iD]

AGH University of Science and Technology, Kraków, Poland
zdw@agh.edu.pl.com

Abstract. Active vibration suppression is a well explored area when it comes to simple problems, however as the problem complexity grows to a time variant system, the amount of researched solutions drops by a large margin, which is further increased with the added requirement of very limited knowledge about the controlled system. These conditions make the problem significantly more complicated, often rendering classic approaches suboptimal or unusable, requiring a more intelligent approach - such as utilizing soft computing. This work proposes a Artificial Neural Network (ANN) Model Predictive Control (MPC) scheme, inspired by horizon techniques which are used for MPC. The proposed approach aims to solve the problem of active vibration control of an unknown and largely unobservable time variant system, while attempting to keep the controller fast by introducing several methods of reducing the amount of calculations inside the control loop - which with proper tuning have no negative impact on the controller's performance. The proposed approach outperforms the multi-input Proportional-Derivative (PD) controller preoptimized using a genetic algorithm.

Keywords: Neural network · Adaptive control · Unknown system · System identification · Vibration suppression

1 Introduction

1.1 Vibration Suppression

Vibrations have always been a problem for both structures and machines. They hamper the usability of the object by reducing user comfort, negatively impacting precision of machines, causing quicker wear or even putting people in direct danger. While taking them into account during design phase of the object is often enough, in some cases they need to be further reduced or eliminated altogether. In consequence, the necessity of reducing or eliminating vibrations [12] inevitably led to the development of vibration suppression technologies [9].

The work presented in this paper was supported by the National Science Centre in Poland under the research project no. 2016/21/D/ST8/01678.

L. Rutkowski et al. (Eds.): ICAISC 2019, LNAI 11508, pp. 102–112, 2019.
https://doi.org/10.1007/978-3-030-20912-4_10

There is a multitude of ways to address vibration suppression, the most common ones being stiffening, isolation and damping. In addition, some semi-active (or semi-passive) methods have also been developed - e.g. magnetorheological (MR) fluid damper, with adjustable viscosity of oil [14]. However, this type of a solution is still inherently passive, in opposition to active vibration cancelling, in which an actuator is effectively adding energy into the system to counteract the vibrations, due to which an inadequately controlled active suppression may destabilize the system - but a well controlled one offers higher performance than passive suppression [11].

It is hardly a new approach [4,7], but it is heavily limited in its applications due to several factors, amongst them unknown and changing system dynamics, which in many cases are also complex - e.g. a bridge with constantly shifting mass distribution and multiple excitation points as cars drive through it. Naturally, controlling a system with close to no knowledge of it is a non-trivial task.

1.2   Soft-Computing-Based Adaptive Control Systems

There are two major approaches to design of control algorithms for time-varying systems: robust approach in which the algorithm should work reasonably well under all circumstances possible and adaptive approach in which the control algorithm is able to adjust itself to the changing behavior of the object. In general a robust approach provides lower efficiency and is possible to use when changes in the system are relatively small [16]. For that reason, when either the system changes significantly or the precise control is required, adaptive algorithms are preferred. A schematic view of the adaptive control can be seen in Fig. 1: a regular control system with the addition of adaptation loop that gauges the system performance and adjusts it if necessary [5]. In cases when there is little to no knowledge regarding the system dynamics, a soft-computing approaches can be used to adapt to system changes on-the-fly. While there are numerous advances in utilizing soft computing in many engineering branches for control - including model identification [3] and vibration suppression [9] - the field is far from saturated as these solutions often concern a very limited area of applications, leaving many topics unexplored, or even untouched. Few examples of Artificial-neural-network-based applications of vibration reduction include manipulators [17], buildings [13], beams [15] or spacecrafts [6] but in most of these examples the system is either partially known, assumed to be stationary or is subjected to other artificial constraints that limit the possibility of applying particular control scheme to other cases. In particular, lack of classic solutions to adaptive vibration control did not trigger development of efficient soft-computing ones, even though these methods are naturally suited for such problems.

1.3   Contribution and Organization of the Article

The article introduces a novel adaptive control algorithm based on the Artificial Neural Network. The work uses an approach known as a Neural Net Model Predictive Control (MPC) scheme, inspired by horizon techniques which are used for MPC. The method is designed to work for systems with unknown dynamics with large variability of system parameters. Several ways of computational time reduction were proposed as well.

The article is organized as follows: Sect. 1 provides a brief introduction to the subject; Sect. 2 introduces the adaptive control algorithm, Sect. 3 describes the problem in which the algorithm is to be applied, Sect. 4 provides the results of the numerical experiment, finally, Sect. 5 summarizes and concludes the article.

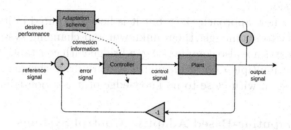

Fig. 1. Basic schematic of an adaptive controller consisting of distinct control and adaptation loops

2   The Method

2.1   Problem Assumptions

While the algorithm wasn't designed for one specific problem, some assumptions regarding the system and available knowledge about it had to be made - as these factors can severely limit viable approaches, and in consequence render some types of algorithm unfeasible. The assumptions for the controlled system are as follows:

- the system is a Multi-Degree-of-Freedom (MDOF) system with at least 3 degrees of freedom
- no knowledge of the system parameters or degrees of freedom is available
- only two points are observable - the object of suppression, and the point of application of the actuator
- these two points are separate, no information about their relation is available
- the system is subject to an unknown external excitation that causes vibrations, applied at a third point
- the system may change over time

2.2   Algorithm Design

The control problem at hand is a complex one, owing it's difficulty to three major factors:

1. The system is completely unknown
2. The system is changing over time
3. The actuator force is not applied directly on the suppression target

In consequence the algorithm design process was centered around addressing each of these issues.

The resulting control algorithm is a variation of neural net based model predictive control - a control approach that makes use of the model of the system to simulate the system response over a set time horizon, and then provide a control signal which best realizes the control goal over this horizon. In other words: the algorithm predicts damped system response for variety of possible inputs and then selects the input which minimizes the response over selected time period. In order to do that the algorithm needs to learn the system so the prediction of responses to particular inputs would be possible.

The usage of such a controller is normally split into 2 phases - model identification, where the neural net is trained using data from the system to reflect its behaviour, and then predictive control, where at each timestep the optimizer - neural net loop - simulates the possible future outcomes and returns optimal control signal.

This type of controller solves issues 1 and 3, as identifying the system via neural network requires no prior knowledge of the system, and giving the net proper information on outputs (such as state of both suppressed and actuated objects) should lead to accurate modelling of the transmission path between these 2 points. Issue no. 2 is then solved by the addition of adaptation loop within which the neural net is periodically retrained.

2.3 Algorithm Schematic

The proposed algorithm is composed of 2 major elements - controller and adaptation control - as seen in Fig. 2 - the former of which provides the input values for the controlled system, while the latter handles the controller's adaptation as well as online-learning capabilities. The schematic does not include reference signal since for vibration control it is simply a static 0 - however if this algorithm was to be applied to a problem where supplying reference signal is necessary, it would be passed into the selection algorithm block inside the controller.

2.4 Controller

The controller itself is built around a neural net, which aims to be a representation of the controlled system. The control algorithm is based on a streamlined predictive control, bearing similarities to fixed and receding horizon optimizations [1]. In both of these, several time steps for the systems output are estimated sequentially, and a control strategy is picked to best realize control goal over this horizon - the difference between these two is in applying this strategy. For fixed horizon, the strategy is realized for however many time-steps the horizon was set for, while in receding horizon only the first time step input is used. If the

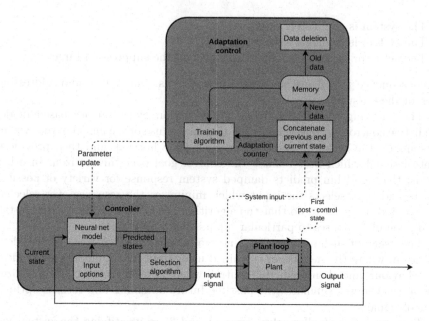

Fig. 2. Schematic of the proposed predictive control algorithm depicting the Controller, responsible for supplying Plant loop with proper control inputs, as well as Adaptation Control which harvests data from Plant loop in order to perform parameter updates on Controller's neural network core. For suppression task the reference signal is static 0

model used for predicting future states was a perfect reflection of the physical model, both of these methods would result in the same control signal, with receding horizon controller requiring more calculations (as they are necessary in each step). However since the identified models are generally not perfect, the extra calculations pay off in higher confidence of the predictions, minimizing the effect of error stacking in recurrent predictions.

The proposed algorithm goes in a different direction to avoid error stacking, as well as reduce the necessary calculations. Instead of performing series of recurrent predictions, the neural net predicts the outcomes for a single timestep, and the optimal input for this timestep is then used as control signal, as seen in Fig. 3.

To further improve performance, a naive approach of control signal persistence (CSP) is proposed - the control signal value which was deemed optimal for the single timestep persists for multiple ones, eliminating the need to recalculate it at every step. The rationale behind this approach is that for a sufficiently small persistence window the state of the controlled system does not undergo a significant change. Logically, if the system state does not change in a big way, neither does the optimal control signal. The calculation amount reduction is given by Eq. 1.

$$1 - \frac{1}{window\_size} \tag{1}$$

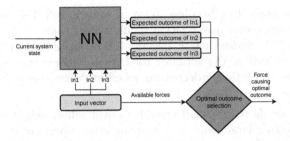

Fig. 3. Schematic of the inner workings of the neural Controller, which predicts outcomes of pre-defined available input forces, and proceeds to select the optimal outcome.

An alternative to CSP was also explored, where instead of predicting 1 step ahead, and setting the control signal for x steps, a single (non-iterative) prediction would be made for x steps ahead, to answer the question of finding the optimal static control signal for these x steps. However this approach was discarded since the controllers simply failed to reach satisfying level of suppression. The assumed reason behind this is that predicting x steps ahead is a considerably more difficult problem to model and - if possible at all - would require much larger neural nets, and in consequence much more training time and slower operation. This stands in opposition to the reason behind implementing such method in the first place - which is to speed the controller up.

In addition to that, the controller is also constrained in what control signals it can use - a quantized vector of possible inputs is specified to avoid free (and time consuming) iterative exploration of options.

A single cycle for the controller is as follows:

1. The controller receives current state of the system.
2. Current state + quantized input vector is fed into the neural net.
3. The net returns predicted system states for each of the proposed inputs, at the end of control time window.
4. The selection algorithm picks the control signal for the time window based on the estimated states.
5. The static (over the duration of the control time window) control signal is passed to the model.

While the computational weight of the control algorithm is lower than horizon-based model predictive control methods, it does require selection of CSP window length, as well as the quantized input vector. Selection of the latter is straightforward, as the actuator output range is generally limited, picking several values from this range is a simple precision vs speed tradeoff. While reducing the continuous range of inputs to a discrete list may seem like a bad idea at first glance, the importance of having a continuous range needs to be reconsidered - e.g. in many cases the difference between applying the force of 0.6N, and 0.603N is very likely to be negligible. Needless to say, if the controlled system is a highly sensitive, the input vector quantization should reflect that.

As for the CSP window length selection, it is dependent on both the controlled system as well as the actuator used, with window size increasing controller speed and theoretically decreasing its effectiveness due to its approximation implications:

1. the window needs to be small enough to still reflect relatively small time steps, not making large leaps and omitting crucial parts of the signal - e.g., if the oscillation frequency is 50 Hz, then picking a window of size 0.05 s will render the controller useless.
2. the window needs to be small enough to fit controller speed requirements.
3. lastly, the window needs to be long enough to allow for actuator reaction.

2.5   Adaptation Control

To deploy the controller, firstly the net is trained on some measured data, preferably one previously controlled with a different method, so that some effects of the input to the system are known. The controller is then operational - however depending on the quality of data provided for initial training, as well as changes that happen within the model - the control may very well be suboptimal, which is why another module is necessary. The adaptation control module of the proposed algorithm is not only devoted to the adaptation of the controller in case of change in the model, but is also responsible for its online learning capabilities.

After each control step it receives the data about it - what inputs were used, and what effects they had. These are then retained in the system's simple "memory" model with a set fixed size, where old entries are replaced with new ones. Periodically, the neural net will undergo a brief re-training process, fitting the neural net to the data stored in its memory, essentially "forgetting" how the model acted in past, and reinforcing knowledge on how it is behaving currently. This process leads to general self-improvement of the model during its operation, including adaptation.

2.6   PD Controller

PD-based controllers are often used in vibration suppression tasks [8,10]. Here, a simple multi-input PD control scheme was included [2] as a reference point for an ANN-based algorithm. The PD method operates based on a following equation:

$$F(t) = \sum P_1, i * y_i(t) + P_2 i * (y_i(t-1) - y_i(t)) \tag{2}$$

where P_i and $P_{2,i}$ refer to adjustable parameters, i refer to the observable mass under investigation, $y_i(t)$ is a displacement of i-th mass at time t while $y_i(t-1)$ is a displacement of i-th mass in time $t-1$. $P_{1,i}$ thus refer to adjustable proportional parameters of a controller while $P_{2,i}$ refer to adjustable derivative parameters of a controller. Depending on the parameters' values, the controller can either be treated as a robust or adaptive one. In this scenario it is pre-trained for a particular system state and then compared with adaptive ANN solution.

3   Problem Definition and Simulation Setup

While the system's parameter change over time is not of concern, the system on which the tests are to be carried out should comply with the other 2 main issues of the control problem that the controller was designed for - the knowledge of the system should be severely limited, and the system itself ought to be a complex MDOF one, with separate points for external disturbance, active component actuation and suppression target. The problem is an extension of the 3-degree-of-freedom unknown system for which the evolutionary-optimized PD controller was proposed before [2]. The resulting system can be seen in Fig. 4.

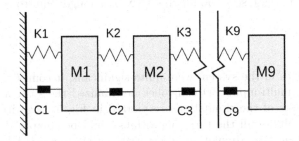

Fig. 4. Schematic of the 9-DOF mechanical system used for suppression simulations

The simulations themselves had following parameters:

- Total time - 15 s
- Simulation timestep - 0.001 s
- External disturbance of a 0.005 s long impulse starting at 0.1 s with the magnitude of 100N applied to m_1
- Suppression target set - m_3
- Actively actuated mass - m_5

The controller was tested in a volatile environment, with random changes to each parameter at every simulation cycle, leaving no time to properly adapt. The system's parameters were selected in following way:

- All masses were initialized at 5 kg, changed by a random number (uniform distribution) between −1 and 1 at every simulation cycle. Masses were kept within 0.1–10 boundaries).
- All damping ratios were initialized at 2.5, changed by a random number (uniform distribution) between −0.2 and 0.2 at every simulation cycle. Damping ratios were kept within 0.01–5 boundaries).
- Spring constants linearily decayed by 20% over the simulation length.

The NN predictive control was initialized with pre-trained net based on PD control of a time-invariant version of this system, reducing the magnitude of weight changes necessary properly fit the constantly changing system during the first few simulation cycles as the net starts at a point where it is familiar with the dynamics of the system in broad sense. The predictive control performance is compared to static multi-input PD control tuned with the use of a simple genetic algorithm: the system state at the beginning of simulation was copied for the genetic algorithm so the adjustable parameters of the PD algorithm were set to optimum for particular state of the system. Although this step would not be possible in practical scenario (usually there is no possibility to freeze the system so the PD controller would be able to learn it properly), this step was performed to provide a worst-case-scenario for the ANN-based algorithm to compete with.

4   Results

Since the changes in the system were quite significant, it comes as no surprise that the static multi-input PD controller destabilized the system on multiple occasions. Results of the simulation are plotted in Fig. 5. Logarithmic scale is used so the results of all the three algorithms could be compared in one plot. It is worth noting that simulation starts with a PD approach being comparable with the NN-based one. That is because of the pre-optimization performed before the experiment. As the experiment progressed, the PD control started to obtain significantly worse results - often destabilizing the system. The fact that all the three solutions seem to be correlated is due to the fact, that the parameters of the system contribute significantly to the vibration suppression. In some configurations (e.g. - higher damping ratios) the algorithms have "less work to do" - therefore they are compared against each other and against the uncontrolled system behavior instead of absolute RMS values.

Various metrics allowing for comparison of all the three solutions are given in Table 1. The superiority of the proposed approach over the pre-optimized multi-input PD one is well pronounced in all the metrics used.

Table 1. Results of the experiment averaged for the whole simulation.

Metric	No control	Multi-input PD	Predictive NN
Total RMS worse than uncontrolled [%]	n/a	36.25	0.65
RMS relative to the uncontrolled [Fraction]	n/a	5.58	0.81
Destabilized system [%]	0	31.90	0.05
Average RMS [m]	0.0286	0.2366	0.0227

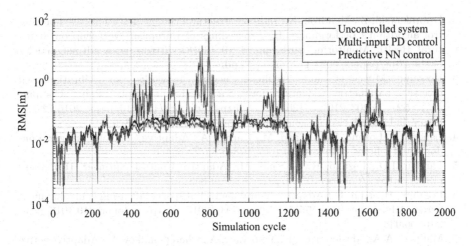

Fig. 5. Total RMS results of the adaptability test. Logarithmic scale was used for y axis for the purpose of better readability.

5   Conclusions

The results of the test bring several important takeaways:

- The proposed algorithm can very quickly fit to an unknown model which is constantly changing.
- The proposed algorithm struggles to achieve a very good performance - at multiple points its control results were worse than those of the multiple-input PD controller.
- While generally not providing optimal control per se, the algorithm was very capable at making adaptations that didn't result in the controller amplifying the systems vibrations, with only 0.65% of the cycles ending up in that state, as opposed to the fixed controller, for which this happened in 36.25% of the cases.
- Even though the stability analysis was not performed in this case, obtained results clearly show the proposed approach is generally stable, and safe enough for practical applications.

Acknowledgement. The work presented in this paper was supported by the National Science Centre in Poland under the research project no. 2016/21/D/ST8/01678.

References

1. Camacho, E., Bordons, C., Alba, C.: Model Predictive Control. Advanced Textbooks in Control and Signal Processing. Springer, London (2004). https://books.google.pl/books?id=Sc1H3f3E8CQC

2. Dworakowski, Z., Mendrok, K.: Indirect structural change detection based on control algorithm's performance. In: Proceedings of European Workshop on Structural Health Monitoring 2018, pp. 1–10 (2018). https://www.ndt.net/article/ewshm2018/papers/0024-Dworakowski.pdf

3. Hossain, M.S., et al.: Artificial neural networks for vibrationbased inverse parametric identifications: a review. Appl. Soft Comput. J. **52**, 203–219 (2016). https://doi.org/10.1016/j.asoc.2016.12.014. http://linkinghub.elsevier.com/retrieve/pii/S1568494616306329

4. Landau, I., Lozano, R., M'Saad, M., Karimi, A.: Adaptive Control. Springer, London (2011). https://doi.org/10.1007/978-0-85729-664-1

5. Landau, I.D., Lozano, R., M'Saad, M.: Adaptive Control. Springer, Heidelberg (1998). https://doi.org/10.1007/978-0-85729-343-5

6. Leeghim, H., Kim, D.: Adaptive neural control of spacecraft using controlmoment gyros. Adv. Space Res. **55**(5), 1382–1393 (2015). https://doi.org/10.1016/j.asr.2014.06.038

7. Mal'tsev, A.A., Maslennikov, R., Khoryaev, A., Cherepennikov, V.: Adaptive active noise and vibration control. Acoust. Phys. **51**(2), 195–208 (2005)

8. Milovanović, M.B., Antić, D.S., Milojković, M.T., Nikolić, S.S., Perić, S.L., Spasić, M.D.: Adaptive PID control based on orthogonal endocrine neural networks. Neural Netw. **84**, 80–90 (2016). https://doi.org/10.1016/j.neunet.2016.08.012

9. Muhammad, B.B., Wan, M., Feng, J., Zhang, W.H.: Dynamic damping of machiningvibration: a review. Int. J. Adv. ManufacturingTechnology (2016). https://doi.org/10.1007/s00170-016-9862-z

10. Pan, Y., Er, M.J., Sun, T., Xu, B., Yu, H.: Adaptive fuzzy PD control with stable H tracking guarantee. Neurocomputing (2016). https://doi.org/10.1016/j.neucom.2016.08.091

11. Preumont, A.: Vibration Control of Active Structures: An Introduction. Solid Mechanics and Its Applications. Springer, Netherlands (2011). https://doi.org/10.1007/978-94-007-2033-6. https://books.google.pl/books?id=MUQUQyB4bEUC

12. Rao, S.S., Fah, Y.F.: Mechanical Vibrations; 5th edn. in SI units. Prentice Hall, Singapore (2011). https://cds.cern.ch/record/1398617

13. Subasri, R., Suresh, S., Natarajan, A.M.: Discrete direct adaptive ELM controller for active vibration control of nonlinear base isolation buildings. Neurocomputing **129**, 246–256 (2014). https://doi.org/10.1016/j.neucom.2013.09.035

14. Terasawa, T., Sano, A.: Fully adaptive semi-active control of vibration isolation by Mr Damper. IFAC **38** (2002). https://doi.org/10.3182/20050703-6-CZ-1902.00254

15. Valoor, M., Chandrashekhara, K., Agarwal, S.: Self-adaptive vibration controlof smart composite beams using recurrent neural architecture. Int. J. Solids Struct. **38**(44–45), 7857–7874 (2001). https://doi.org/10.1016/S0020-7683(01)00125-1. http://linkinghub.elsevier.com/retrieve/pii/S0020768301001251

16. Zak, S.H.: Systems and Control. Oxford University Press, Oxford (2002)

17. Zhao, Z.l., Qiu, Z.c., Zhang, X.m., Han, J.d.: Vibration control of a pneumatic driven piezoelectric flexible manipulator using self-organizing map based multiple models. Mech. Syst. Signal Process. **70–71**, 345–372 (2016). https://doi.org/10.1016/j.ymssp.2015.09.041, http://linkinghub.elsevier.com/retrieve/pii/S0888327015004537, www.sciencedirect.com/science/article/pii/S0888327015004537

Robust Training of Radial Basis Function Neural Networks

Jan Kalina and Petra Vidnerová[✉]

Institute of Computer Science, The Czech Academy of Sciences,
Pod Vodárenskou věží 2, 182 07 Prague 8, Czech Republic
{kalina,petra}@cs.cas.cz

Abstract. Radial basis function (RBF) neural networks represent established machine learning tool with various interesting applications to nonlinear regression modeling. However, their performance may be substantially influenced by outlying measurements (outliers). Promising modifications of RBF network training have been available for the classification of data contaminated by outliers, but there remains a gap of robust training of RBF networks in the regression context. A novel robust approach based on backward subsample selection (i.e. instance selection) is proposed and presented in this paper, which searches sequentially for the most reliable subset of observations and finally performs outlier deletion. The novel approach is investigated in numerical experiments and is also applied to robustify a multilayer perceptron. The results on data containing outliers reveal the improved performance compared to conventional approaches.

Keywords: Machine learning · Outliers · Robustness ·
Subset selection · Anomaly detection

1 Introduction

Regression modeling, i.e. estimating (smoothing, fitting) and predicting a continuous response variable based on a set of features plays a crucial role in the analysis of real data in a tremendous variety of applications. Recently, there is an increasing trend in applying nonlinear estimation tools without assuming a specific shape of the regression function [6]. This is true also for numerous machine learning methods allowing to predict a future development of the response [2]. In this paper, radial basis function (RBF) neural networks are considered, which represent an important class of feedforward artificial neural networks. These have been successfully used in an enormous number of applications [11].

Each analysis of a real dataset requires a careful detection of outlying measurements (outliers, anomalies) [12]. This is true also for RBF networks, which implicitly assume the observed data not to be contaminated by outliers [3,23]. So far, most available applications of RBF networks to real data have not paid sufficient attention to the presence and influence of outliers. Therefore, it is highly

© Springer Nature Switzerland AG 2019
L. Rutkowski et al. (Eds.): ICAISC 2019, LNAI 11508, pp. 113–124, 2019.
https://doi.org/10.1007/978-3-030-20912-4_11

desirable to consider alternative robust approaches to RBF networks training, which represents the interest of the current paper. Here, the most common form of RBF networks is recalled in Sect. 2, together with a review of some available robust approaches to their training. A novel idea for their robust training is described in Sect. 3. The performance of the classical and novel approaches to training RBF networks as well as to multilayer perceptrons is presented on artificial and real datasets in Sect. 4, revealing the strengths of the novel robust approach. Finally, Sect. 5 concludes the paper.

2   Radial Basis Function Neural Networks

This section recalls RBF networks, discusses their non-robustness under the presence of outliers in the data, and proceeds to an overview of available robust methods for their training. We consider the regression task to model a continuous response $Y_1, \ldots, Y_n$ by means of p features (independent variables, regressors, inputs) with $p \geq 1$ available for n observations (measurements, instances), where the values for the i-th observation ($i = 1, \ldots, n$) are denoted as $X_{i1}, \ldots, X_{ip}$. The architecture of the most common RBF network may be described as a hierarchical structure with an input layer containing p inputs, a single hidden layer with N RBF units (neurons), and a linear output layer. The user chooses N together with a radially symmetric function ρ. The selection of these hyperparameters must reflect specific properties of the particular data.

The model for the RBF network (see e.g. [11]) has the form

$$f(x) = \sum_{j=1}^{N} a_j \rho(||x - c_j||) \tag{1}$$

for a given value of the features $x \in \mathbb{R}^p$, where $||.||$ denotes the Euclidean norm, $c_1, \ldots, c_N \in \mathbb{R}^p$ are center vectors and $a_1, \ldots, a_N \in \mathbb{R}$ parameters denoted as weights. It is necessary to estimate these parameters in a learning procedure, which is a nonlinear optimization task to minimize a certain criterion over these parameters and over other possible parameters corresponding to ρ.

Most commonly (although not always), the quadratic loss

$$\min \sum_{i=1}^{n} (Y_i - f(X_i))^2 = \min \sum_{i=1}^{n} \left(Y_i - \sum_{j=1}^{N} a_j \rho(||X_i - c_j||) \right)^2, \tag{2}$$

is minimized over $c_1, \ldots, c_N \in \mathbb{R}^p$, $a_1, \ldots, a_N \in \mathbb{R}$ and over other possible parameters corresponding to ρ. If estimated values of parameters $a_1, \ldots, a_N$ and $c_1, \ldots, c_N$ are denoted as $\hat{a}_1, \ldots, \hat{a}_N$ and $\hat{c}_1, \ldots, \hat{c}_N$, respectively, the RBF network as a function of a variable x can be expressed as

$$f(x) = \sum_{j=1}^{N} \hat{a}_j \rho(||x - \hat{c}_j||) = \sum_{j=1}^{N} \hat{a}_j K(x, c_j), \quad x \in \mathbb{R}^p. \tag{3}$$

The notation using a suitably chosen kernel K reveals the relationship to other kernel-based machine learning tools. It is most common to choose ρ as the Gaussian kernel (Gaussian density), replacing (3) by

$$f(x) = \sum_{j=1}^{N} \hat{a}_j \exp\left\{ -\frac{||x - \hat{c}_j||^2}{2\hat{\sigma}_j^2} \right\}, \quad x \in \mathbb{R}^p, \tag{4}$$

where not only $\hat{a}_1, \ldots, \hat{a}_N$ and $\hat{c}_1, \ldots, \hat{c}_N$ but also $\hat{\sigma}_1^2, \ldots, \hat{\sigma}_N^2$ (i.e. variability parameters or bandwidth of individual Gaussian kernels) must be estimated from the given data; these are obtained by an optimization procedure, which requires to provide an initial solution, i.e. starting point for the parameters. Known theoretical properties of RBF networks include their ability to approximate smooth functions, particularly the universal approximation property [16].

There are numerous available computational tools for training of RBF networks [19], while the backpropagation algorithm is the most common choice. It is however vulnerable to outliers, as it is known from the context of multilayer perceptrons [22]. Other algorithms for RBF networks are influenced by outliers as well and the vulnerability remains also for larger values of N. The reasons for incorrect interpolation of conventional RBF networks under the presence of outliers include minimizing the sum of squares residuals and choosing the Gaussian kernel (4).

2.1   Available Robust Approaches to Training of RBF Networks

Because there seem to be much less robust tools available for RBF networks compared to multilayer perceptrons, this paper is primarily focused on robust training for RBF networks. So far, a few robust alternatives to RBF networks training have been already presented. These are however mostly devoted to the classification task; see ([15], pp. 54) for discussion. Robust approaches to RBF networks for classification are based on two main distinct ideas, namely replacing the sum of squared residuals by a more robust loss function, and detecting outliers (atypical/anomalous instances) by exploiting tools of robust and nonparametric statistics [4,12]; the latter approach allows training of the RBF network only over the non-outlying data points, or to assign small weights to outliers (in an implicit way).

In the classification task, the robust activation function may consider various robust versions of the Mahalanobis distance as used in [3]. Robust training based on outlier detection exploiting the local outlier factor of multivariate data was proposed by [18]. Another outlier detection was proposed by [7], who evaluated a simple outlyingness measure based on the cumulative distribution function; there, anomalous measurements are found in an iterative procedure evaluating confidence coefficients (i.e. percentages for each class in the classification task).

In the regression task, there have been only a few approaches robustifying the activation function. Compositions of sigmoidal activation functions were considered in [17] to robustify the performance for a rather specific task to estimate a response which is almost constant over relatively large intervals. A highly robust regression estimator, namely the least trimmed absolute value estimator, was recommended as the optimization criterion for RBF networks in [21]. If subtractive clustering (SC) is used for an automatic recommendation of the center vectors, a robustified loss function may be subsequently used [23]; still, the popular SC approach remains vulnerable to outliers and consecutive steps of the training cannot improve this. A recent approach to outlier detection for regression RBF networks was developed in [15], which is denoted as generalized edited nearest neighbor (ENN) algorithm, and was also combined with robust versions of the activation function.

3   A Robust Training of RBF Networks Based on Backward Instance Selection

Our novel approach to robust training of RBF networks can be described as a backward subsample selection process, i.e. outlier detection together with their deletion, while the final estimate considers only the selected subset of observations. This is inspired by the forward search (cf. [10]), which can be described as a promising (but not sufficiently appreciated) alternative approach to statistical data analysis. It sequentially adds the most reliable (i.e. least outlying) observations to a subset, while the outlier detection is performed afterwards based on the whole sequence of variance estimates across such subsets [1]. The forward search is comprehensible and powerful and its theoretical properties have been recently derived [5]. However, the forward selection is not suitable for RBF networks because of the nonlinearity of the task.

We propose a backward procedure for selecting individual observations, formally described in Algorithm 1. The approach is based on a gradual (sequential) adding observations to a selected subset. It divides the data points to

(i) a smaller set of outliers,
(ii) a larger set of all the remaining instances,

where the latter are interpreted as the good (consistent) data points.

While Algorithm 1 is self-explaining, we will now interpret its key steps and also its notation. Let $\lfloor x \rfloor$ denote the integer part of $x \in \mathbb{R}$. In the course of the algorithm, sets $S^{n-1}, \ldots, S^{\lfloor n/2 \rfloor}$ of indicators are sequentially constructed, which contain zeros or ones only. Zeros correspond to observations of type (i), which are subsequently ignored, and the RBF network is repeatedly computed only for observations of type (ii). A corresponding sequence $r_{n-1}, \ldots, r_{\lfloor n/2 \rfloor}$ is constructed, which contains the absolute residuals of the most outlying observations. In addition, we always return a single least outlying outlier back to the set of reliable data (i.e. for $k < n - 2$); this allows to improve the optimization procedure and is suitable because of potential masking of outliers (cf. the description of possible complications with outlier detection in multivariate data in [2]). The final outlier detection within Algorithm 1 can be performed either (a) automatically, or (b) subjectively by a visual inspection of figures for various subsets. These two approaches will be now explicated.

Algorithm 1. RRBF: robust training of RBF networks based on backward instance selection

---

Input: Response $Y_1, \ldots, Y_n$, features $X_{i1}, \ldots, X_{ip}$ for $i = 1, \ldots, n$
Input: Hyperparameters selected by the user: number of units N, radially symmetric function ρ
Input: Series of quantiles $c(\lfloor n/2 \rfloor), \ldots, c(n)$
Output: Fitted RRBF network
  $S^n := (1, 1, \ldots, 1)^T \in \mathbb{R}^n$
  for $k = n - 1$ downto $\lfloor n/2 \rfloor$ **do**
    $S^k = (S_1^k, \ldots, S_n^k)^T := S^{k+1}$
    for $t = 1$ to n **do**
      if $S_t^k = 1$ **then**
        $S^* = (S_1^*, \ldots, S_n^*)^T := S^k$
        $S_t^* := 0$
        Fit the RBF network for such $X_1, \ldots, X_n$, which have the indicator in S^* equal to 1
        $\hat{Y}_t :=$ fitted value of the t-th observation
      end if
    end for
    $u := \arg\max |Y_t - \hat{Y}_t|$ over those indexes $t = 1, \ldots, n$, for which $S_t^k = 1$
    $S_u^k := 0$
    $r_k := |Y_u - \hat{Y}_u|$
    if $k < (n - 1)$ **then**
      for $m = 1$ to n **do**
        if $S_m^k = 0$ **then**
          $S^* = (S_1^*, \ldots, S_n^*)^T := S^k$
          $S_m^* := 1$
          Fit the RBF network for such $X_1, \ldots, X_n$, which have the indicator in S^* equal to 1
          $\hat{Y}_m :=$ fitted value of the m-th observation
        end if
      end for
      $v := \arg\min |Y_m - \hat{Y}_m|$ over those indexes $m = 1, \ldots, n$, for which $S_m^k = 0$
      if $u \neq v$ **then**
        $S_v^k := 1$
      end if
    end if
  end for
  $z := \lfloor n/2 \rfloor$
  while $r_z < c(z)$ **do**
    $z := z + 1$
  end while
  Fit the RBF network for such $X_1, \ldots, X_n$, which have the indicator in S^z equal to 1

(a) If the automatic approach is used, which is described in the final part of Algorithm 1, the resulting method is denoted as a robust RBF (RRBF) network. For a particular t in Algorithm 1, i.e. if considering the step from S^t towards S^{t-1}, we use a threshold derived under the assumption of normally distributed errors for the already selected $t - 1$ observations. While the assumption of normality of errors may be limiting, it has been described as a successful strategy also in data-driven nonparametric regression approaches of [6].

The threshold denoted as $c(t)$ for each t is defined as the 99th percentile of the distribution of the random variable $\max\{Z_1, \ldots, Z_{t-1}\}$, where $Z_1, \ldots, Z_{t-1}$ are independent random variables following normal distribution $\mathsf{N}(0, \sigma^2)$. We must approximate $c(t)$ by simulations, while estimating the nuisance parameter σ^2 by means of the median absolute deviation (MAD) [12] computed from residuals of the RBF network across all observations.

(b) A subjective approach may replace the final outlier detection of Algorithm 1 by a visual inspection of the non-decreasing sequence $r_{\lfloor n/2 \rfloor}, \ldots, r_n$. The plot of this sequence reveals a dramatic change of trend as soon as outliers come into play. When the set of selected data points starts to include outliers (for a sufficiently large t), then values of r_t start to rise up enormously. The first such change point in the sequence corresponds to the true contamination level. This approach is inspired by the subjective search for the trimming constant for robust regression of [13].

The computational complexity of the proposed approach is rather high due to the repeated evaluation of the RBF network over subsets of data. Denoting the complexity of the RBF network by $\mathcal{O}(\mathrm{RBF})$, the proposed approach has the order of complexity equal to $n^2 \mathcal{O}(\mathrm{RBF})$, which prohibits its use for large datasets.

4   Numerical Applications

In order to illustrate the vulnerability of a traditional RBF network to outliers and the performance of the novel approach RRBF, we present numerical experiments both on simulated and real data sets. Because Algorithm 1 can be used also for robust fitting of multilayer perceptrons (MLP), we use such an approach (denoted as RMLP) as well. The computations were performed using R software package [20] together with packages RSNNS and neuralnet. Particularly, RBF networks are trained by a backpropagation algorithm, namely a gradient descent method for optimization of all parameters (including variances $\sigma_1^2, \ldots, \sigma_N^2$).

4.1   A Simulated Dataset

We use an artificial dataset with $n = 100$ measurements visualized in Fig. 1, obtained as a sine function contaminated by noise. The horizontal axis is the only feature. We choose the Gaussian kernel for the model and $N = 10$ RBF units for the hidden layer. Such an RBF network seems to be very suitable for fitting the nonlinear trend in the particular dataset. The RSNNS package allows a nice graphical presentation of the RBF network model and yields directly the estimates of all parameters together with fitted values of the response.

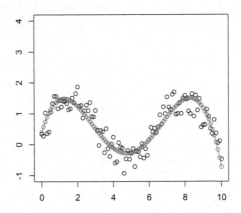

Fig. 1. Raw data of Sect. 4.1 together with trend estimated by a (standard) RBF network with 10 RBF units and Gaussian function ρ.

Figure 1 shows the raw data as well as the trend estimated by the RBF network specified above. Figures 2 and 3 show the RBF and RRBF networks for two different (rather simple) contaminations of the data, respectively.

- Contamination A: A set of 5 observations was replaced by independent random values generated from a normal distribution $N(0, 1/3)$.
- Contamination B: Each fifth observation was replaced by the exact value 3.5.

Figure 2 reveals the effect of outliers on the conventional RBF network. The estimation by the RBF network is clearly deteriorated by outliers in both images of Fig. 2.

Values of prediction error evaluated in a leave-one-out cross-validation are presented in Table 1 for two nonlinear regression methods. The error is evaluated as either the standard mean squared error (MSE), i.e. over all observations, or its robust counterpart denoted as the trimmed mean squares error (TMSE). Using $\alpha = 3/4$ and $h = \lfloor (1 - \alpha)n \rfloor$, these are defined as

$$\text{MSE} = \frac{1}{n} \sum_{i=1}^{n} r_i^2 \quad \text{and} \quad \text{TMSE}(\alpha) = \frac{1}{h} \sum_{i=1}^{h} r_{(i)}^2, \tag{5}$$

where $r_i = Y_i - \hat{Y}_i$ are prediction errors, $\hat{Y}_i$ denotes the fitted value of the i-th observation for $i = 1, \ldots, n$, and squared prediction errors are arranged as $r_{(1)}^2 \leq \cdots \leq r_{(n)}^2$.

Table 1. Results for the simulated data of Sect. 4.1. Error measures (MSE and TMSE(3/4)) evaluated for the RBF and RRBF networks.

Neural network	Raw data		Contam. A		Contam. B	
	MSE	TMSE	MSE	TMSE	MSE	TMSE
RBF	0.111	0.042	0.541	0.057	1.422	0.351
RRBF	0.111	0.042	0.634	0.045	1.769	0.082

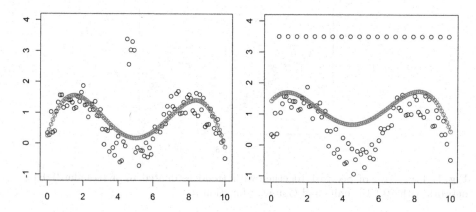

Fig. 2. Two contaminated versions of the dataset of Sect. 4.1 with trend estimated by a (standard) RBF network with 10 RBF units and Gaussian function ρ.

For raw data, the RBF and RRBF networks yield the same results. For contaminated data, MSE is smaller for RBF compared to RRBF networks, as the RBF network minimizes exactly the value of MSE. TMSE is for contaminated data smaller for RRBF networks than for RBF, and at the same time remains only slightly changed compared to TMSE for raw data. On the other hand, MSE for contaminated data is much increased compared to MSE for raw data. On the whole, MSE turns out not to be a suitable error measure, as it is heavily influenced by outliers, while TMSE is able to express that the RRBF networks perform a good fit over the good (non-contaminated) data. In addition, the results of the rigorously derived approach (a) correspond to the intuitive approach (b).

4.2 Real Datasets

We also use two real datasets, which are both larger compared to the simple setup of Sect. 4.1. Both are publicly available datasets coming from the repository [8], where they are recommended for regression modeling.

(I) The Auto MPG dataset. The response, i.e. consumption of each car in miles per gallon (MPG), explained by four continuous features, namely displacement, horsepower, weight, and acceleration. As we omitted missing values (i.e. observations with index 33, 127, 331, 337, 355, and 375), we work with $n = 392$ and $p = 4$.

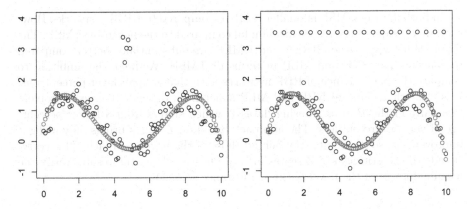

Fig. 3. Two contaminated versions of the dataset of Sect. 4.1 with trend estimated by the RRBF network with 10 RBF units and Gaussian function ρ.

(II) The Boston Housing dataset. As we consider only continuous features (omitting features 4, 7, and 9 from the original dataset) and there are no missing values, we work with $n = 506$ and $p = 11$, while the response represents the per capita crime rate by town.

Because the robust approach of Sect. 3 is directly applicable also to multilayer perceptrons, we illustrate its performance also on them. We also use a simple outlier detection approach by means of Z-scores; we may refer to e.g. [9], where a Z-score algorithm was used to determine anomalies. The method further denoted as RBF-Z will be used in the following way. Let us say that the RBF network has been trained over all available observations. We will consider the observation X_i (for $i = 1, \ldots, n$) to be outlying if and only if

$$0.6745 \cdot \frac{|u_i - \tilde{u}|}{\mathsf{MAD}(u_1, \ldots, u_n)} \geq 2.5, \tag{6}$$

where $u_1, \ldots, u_n$ are residuals corresponding to the RBF network, $\tilde{u}$ is the median over $u_1, \ldots, u_n$, and $\mathsf{MAD}(u_1, \ldots, u_n)$ denotes the median absolute deviation of the residuals. Then, the method RBF-Z fits an RBF network to all the non-outlying measurements. Here, 0.6745 is a consistency factor ensuring consistency of MAD under normally distributed errors [12] and the threshold 2.5 is a standard choice in analogous rules of outlier detection (see e.g. [14]). In the same spirit, MLP-Z denotes outlier detection by Z-scores if the multilayer perceptron is used for the regression task.

For the Auto MPG dataset, we use an RBF network with $N = 40$. A multilayer perceptron with 2 hidden layers is used, which contain 16 and 8 neurons, respectively. A sigmoid activation function is considered in every hidden layer and a linear output layer is used. For the Boston Housing dataset, we use an RBF network with $N = 50$. An analogous multilayer perceptron as for the Auto MPG dataset is used. The results for the networks with such selected architectures are presented in Table 2.

In both datasets, MSE is smaller for RBF compared to RRBF networks. However, we consider TMSE more meaningful compared to the non-robust MSE. The novel robust approaches RRBF and RMLP are substantially better compared to conventional RBF and MLP in terms of TMSE. Without the ambition to compare the performance of RBF networks with that of multilayer perceptrons, it is clear that classical RBF and MLP suffer from outliers. This is a problem especially in the Boston Housing dataset, which suffers from a larger percentage of very severe outliers. The approach based on Z-scores brings only a slight improvement, so its results stay behind those of the novel approach. This corresponds to the criticism of Z-scores in [18]. On the whole, the results verify the meaningfulness of the novel backward instance selection.

Table 2. Results for real datasets of Sect. 4.2. Error measures (MSE and TMSE(3/4)) evaluated for the RBF and RRBF networks.

Neural network	Dataset			
	Auto MPG		Boston housing	
	MSE	TMSE	MSE	TMSE
RBF	46.9	17.2	52.7	4.4
RRBF	51.0	13.3	59.7	3.9
RBF-Z	49.1	16.6	56.5	4.3
MLP	60.8	28.9	57.9	5.3
RMLP	72.8	15.0	65.1	4.3
MLP-Z	68.2	23.6	63.4	5.0

5   Conclusions

RBF networks represent an established tool for nonlinear regression tasks, i.e. for fitting a continuous response in dependence on a set of features, with various real applications. However, their interpolation may be influenced by outliers. Therefore, we propose an alternative training procedure, which can be described as a backward subsample selection inspired by [1,5]. To the best of our knowledge, this procedure is original in the context of machine learning and represents thus one of the few approaches for robust training of RBF networks for regression. The new learning method sequentially orders the observations according to their outlyingness and then performs outlier detection. Contrary to our sequential process, we perceive standard training of neural networks as a mere "snapshot" analyzing (only) all observations at once. The presented forward search philosophy is conceptually simple and comprehensible.

The new approach may be recommended for additive outliers, including severe individual as well as clustered ones, and also for smoothing peaks and/or outlier detection in (possibly high-frequency) data. It is also suitable for time series of positive values, where the outliers are asymmetrically distributed and typically above the trend rather than being symmetrically distributed above and below the majority of the data; such data are common in financial econometrics. If the data are non-contaminated, the approach has the tendency not to detect any outliers (small false positive rate). The approach is flexible and can be used also for other machine learning methods.

Numerical examples of Sect. 4 reveal the efficiency for a non-contaminated illustrative dataset. At the same time, the robustness of the novel approach is documented in contaminated datasets.

Disadvantages and limitations of the novel approach include its computational complexity (while other available robust approaches for RBF networks are computationally tedious as well). General limitation of RBF networks (including numerical instability or unsuitability for data with a constant trend in a certain interval [17]), nonlinear regression (boundary problems if a change of trend appears near the endpoints of the compact support), or backward search, particularly due to the automated process of subset selection, are valid for the novel approach as well. The novel approach is not suitable if the data locally contain more than 50% of outliers, which is, however, true for any available non-linear regression approach. It is also clear that removing outlying values (e.g. in case of relevant peaks) is meaningful only in some (but not all) applications.

As future research, we intend to compare various criteria for outlier detection, to exploit other computational tools than the gradient descent optimization algorithm, to reduce the computational complexity, or to perform more intensive numerical experiments with the robust approach to RBF networks.

Acknowledgements. We thank Barbora Peštová for technical assistance and six anonymous referees for valuable suggestions leading to improvements of the paper. The work is supported by the projects 19-05704S (J. Kalina) and 18-23827S (P. Vidnerová) of the Czech Science Foundation.

References

1. Atkinson, A.C., Riani, M., Cerioli, A.: The forward search: theory and data analysis. J. Korean Stat. Soc. **39**, 117–134 (2010)
2. Ben-Gal, I.: Outlier detection. In: Maimon, O., Rockach, L. (eds.) Data Mining and Knowledge Discovery Handbook: A Complete Guide for Practitioners and Researchers, 2nd edn, pp. 117–130. Springer, New York (2010). https://doi.org/10.1007/978-1-4939-7131-2
3. Borş, A.G., Pitas, I.: Robust RBF networks. In: Howlett, R.J., Jain, L.C., Kacprzyk, J. (eds.) Radial Basis Function Networks 1. Recent Developments in Theory and Applications, pp. 123–133. Physica Verlag Rudolf Liebing KG, Vienna (2001)
4. Broniatowski, M., Jurečková, J., Kalina, J.: Likelihood ratio under measurement errors. Entropy **20**, 966 (2018)
5. Cerioli, A., Riani, M., Atkinson, A.C., Corbellini, A.: The power of monitoring: how to make the most of a contaminated multivariate sample. Stat. Methods Appl. **27**, 559–587 (2018)

6. Davies, L.: Data Analysis and Approximate Models. Model Choice, Location-Scale, Analysis of Variance, Nonparametric Regression and Image Analysis. CRC Press, Boca Raton (2014)
7. Dendek, C., Mańdziuk, J.: Improving performance of a binary classifier by training set selection. In: Kůrková, V., Neruda, R., Koutník, J. (eds.) ICANN 2008. LNCS, vol. 5163, pp. 128–135. Springer, Heidelberg (2008). https://doi.org/10.1007/978-3-540-87536-9_14
8. Frank, A., Asuncion, A.: UCI Machine Learning Repository. University of California, Irvine (2010). http://archive.ics.uci.edu/ml/
9. Grabaskas, N., Si, D.: Anomaly detection from kepler satellite time-series data. In: Perner, P. (ed.) MLDM 2017. LNCS (LNAI), vol. 10358, pp. 220–232. Springer, Cham (2017). https://doi.org/10.1007/978-3-319-62416-7_16
10. Harrell, F.: Regression Modeling Strategies, With Applications to Linear Models, Logistic and Ordinal Regression, and Survival Analysis, 2nd edn. Springer, New York (2015). https://doi.org/10.1007/978-1-4757-3462-1
11. Haykin, S.O.: Neural Networks and Learning Machines: A Comprehensive Foundation, 2nd edn. Prentice Hall, Upper Saddle River (2009)
12. Jurečková, J., Picek, J., Schindler, M.: Robust Statistical Methods with R, 2nd edn. Chapman & Hall/CRC, Boca Raton (2019)
13. Kalina, J.: Three contributions to robust regression diagnostics. J. Appl. Math. Statist. Inf. **11**, 69–78 (2015)
14. Kalina, J.: A robust pre-processing of BeadChip microarray images. Biocybern. Biomed. Eng. **38**, 556–563 (2018)
15. Kordos, M., Rusiecki, A.: Reducing noise impact on MLP training–techniques and algorithms to provide noise-robustness in MLP network training. Soft. Comput. **20**, 46–65 (2016)
16. Kůrková, V., Kainen, P.C.: Comparing fixed and variable-width gaussian networks. Neural Netw. **57**, 23–28 (2014)
17. Lee, C.C., Chung, P.C., Tsai, J.R., Chang, C.I.: Robust radial basis function neural networks. IEEE Trans. Syst. Man Cybern. B **29**, 674–685 (1999)
18. Liu, F.T., Ting, K.M., Zhou, Z.H.: Isolation forest. In: Eighth IEEE International Conference on Data Mining, pp. 413–422. IEEE (2008)
19. Neruda, R., Vidnerová, P.: Learning errors by radial basis function neural networks and regularization networks. Int. J. Grid Distrib. Comput. **1**, 49–57 (2009)
20. R Core Team: R: A language and environment for statistical computing. R Foundation for Statistical Computing, Vienna (2019). https://www.R-project.org/
21. Rusiecki, A.: Robust learning algorithm based on LTA estimator. Neurocomputing **120**, 624–632 (2013)
22. Rusiecki, A., Kordos, M., Kamiński, T., Greń, K.: Training neural networks on noisy data. In: Rutkowski, L., Korytkowski, M., Scherer, R., Tadeusiewicz, R., Zadeh, L.A., Zurada, J.M. (eds.) ICAISC 2014. LNCS (LNAI), vol. 8467, pp. 131–142. Springer, Cham (2014). https://doi.org/10.1007/978-3-319-07173-2_13
23. Su, M., Deng, W.: A fast robust learning algorithm for RBF network against outliers. In: Huang, D.-S., Li, K., Irwin, G.W. (eds.) ICIC 2006. LNCS, vol. 4113, pp. 280–285. Springer, Heidelberg (2006). https://doi.org/10.1007/11816157_28

Sequential Data Mining of Network Traffic in URL Logs

Marcin Korytkowski[1,2], Jakub Nowak[2], Robert Nowicki[2],
Kamila Milkowska[2], Magdalena Scherer[3(✉)], and Piotr Goetzen[4,5]

[1] Intigo Sp. z o.o., Piotrkowska 262/264, 90-361 Lodz, Poland
[2] Computer Vision and Data Mining Lab, Institute of Computational Intelligence,
Częstochowa University of Technology, Al. Armii Krajowej 36,
42-200 Częstochowa, Poland
{marcin.korytkowski,jakub.nowak,robert.nowicki}@iisi.pcz.pl
[3] Faculty of Management, Częstochowa University of Technology,
al. Armii Krajowej 19, 42-200 Częstochowa, Poland
magdalena.scherer@wz.pcz.pl
[4] Information Technology Institute, University of Social Sciences,
90-113 Lodz, Poland
pgoetzen@san.edu.pl
[5] Clark University Worcester, Worcester, MA 01610, USA
http://intigo.ai, http://iisi.pcz.pl

Abstract. One of the roles of website administrators is the activity
registration of WWW sites and users using the services. Along with the
development of data analysis algorithms, there are new possibilities of
using registered actions of many users in logs. In this paper, we present
a way to detect anomalies in URL logs using sequential pattern mining
algorithms. We analyse the registered URL request sequences of the public institution website in order to identify unwanted bots. By detecting
and comparing sequences, we can classify the activity into a normal and
malicious one.

Keywords: URL logs · Sequential data mining · Computer networks

1 Introduction

Efficient computer network intrusion detection and user profiling are substantial for providing computer system security. Recently, the development of deep
learning allowed to efficiently analyse big computer network data [2,8]. It is also
possible to use tree-based classifiers [4,5] to classify network users [9]. There are
also works on using fuzzy logic [13,15] to cybersecurity [7,12]. Many researchers
dealt with the analysis of data contained in logs. One of the known methods is
the use of sequential pattern mining to analyse user trends in order to select an
appropriate commercial offer. Through this procedure, we can influence users'
decisions in order to sell their own products. In the case of large websites,

© Springer Nature Switzerland AG 2019
L. Rutkowski et al. (Eds.): ICAISC 2019, LNAI 11508, pp. 125–130, 2019.
https://doi.org/10.1007/978-3-030-20912-4_12

data analysis is a very difficult and time-consuming task for the administrator. Therefore, in most cases, the analysis of data in logs only occurs when there are clear signs of anomalies on the site. In our research, we analyse data from HTTP request logs (URLs). Initially, we assume that users navigate websites in a predictable way. We base this assumption on how persons use websites when searching for information. The interests of a given user are usually strictly defined, so the transitions between websites is done according to their interests. We compare found sequences by plain vector comparison. It is possible to use various algorithms for fast vector comparison used often in computer vision [14].

This article is based on data collected from a WAN network infrastructure, which is used by residents of four districts in Poland, as well as network users who are employees of the local government offices and their organizational units, e.g. schools, hospitals, etc. Internet access to the analysed network is done with the help of two CISCO ASR edge routers that route packets using RIP version 2. A cluster of PaloAlto devices working in an active-active mode takes care of the network security. The network is routed by the Open Shortest Path First (OSPF) algorithm with virtual routing and forwarding (VRF). In each of the four districts, there is one CISCO core switch.

The remainder of the paper is as follows. Section 1 introduces the subject of this paper. Section 2 describes network data preparation for sequential pattern mining. Section 3 presents the experiments with finding sequences by three sequential pattern mining algorithms.

2   Data Preprocessing

Data from the computer network logs had to be prepared to the machine learning needs. The first step was to detect what addresses the user requested. While preparing the webpage to display, the client's web browser sends many requests to the server, which are registered in the logs. Example requests are presented in Listing 1.1

Listing 1.1. Example HTTP requests.

```
2018−07−16  07:06:09  10.210.50.107  GET
/bundles/modernizr  v=wBEWDufH_8Md−Pbioxomt90vm6tJN2
Pyy9u9zHtWsPo1  80  −  10.10.24.124  Mozilla/
5.0+(Windows+NT+6.3;+Win64;+x64)+AppleWebKit/537.36+
(KHTML,+like+Gecko)+Chrome/67.0.3396.99+Safari/537.36
http://www.xxxxxxxxx.eu/  200  0  0  0
2018−07−16  07:06:09  10.210.50.107  GET
/Content/bootstrap.min.css  −  80  −  10.10.24.124  Mozilla/
5.0+(Windows+NT+6.3;+Win64;+x64)+AppleWebKit/537.36+
(KHTML,+like+Gecko)+Chrome/67.0.3396.99+Safari/537.36
http://www.xxxxxxxxx.eu/  200  0  0  33
2018−07−16  07:06:09  10.210.50.107  GET
/Content/VariantRed.css  −  80  −  10.10.24.124  Mozilla/
```

```
5.0+(Windows+NT+6.3;+Win64;+x64)+AppleWebKit/537.36+
(KHTML,+like+Gecko)+Chrome/67.0.3396.99+Safari/537.36
http://www.xxxxxxxxx.eu/ 200 0 0 0
2018-07-16 07:06:09 10.210.50.107 GET
/Scripts/respond.min.js - 80 - 10.10.24.124 Mozilla/
5.0+(Windows+NT+6.3;+Win64;+x64)+AppleWebKit/537.36+
(KHTML,+like+Gecko)+Chrome/67.0.3396.99+Safari/537.36
http://www.xxxxxxxxx.eu/ 200 0 0 15
2018-07-16 07:06:09 10.210.50.107 GET
/Content/Images/IconContrast.png - 80 - 10.10.24.124
Mozilla/
5.0+(Windows+NT+6.3;+Win64;+x64)+AppleWebKit/537.36+
(KHTML,+like+Gecko)+Chrome/67.0.3396.99+Safari/537.36
http://www.xxxxxxxxx.eu/ 200 0 0 31
2018-07-16 07:06:09 10.210.50.107 GET
/Content/FR.png - 80 - 10.10.24.124 Mozilla/
5.0+(Windows+NT
+6.3;+Win64;+x64)+AppleWebKit/537.36+(KHTML,+like+Gecko)
+Chrome/67.0.3396.99+Safari/537.36
http://www.xxxxxxxxx.eu/ 200 0 0 31
```

We are interested only in entries regarding specific websites. Therefore, we reject all entries concerning scripts, images, CSS styles etc. We have prepared the data similarly to the case of [16]. Then, we group the addresses into a sequence. By this term, we mean the sequence of URLs, i.e. the set of addresses that have been registered for one user of the site at a given time. In our case, we identify users using only IP addresses. During the preliminary analysis of the data, we concluded that the session for one user ends if we have not registered any activity in more than 1 h [18]. In the case of the dataset on which we worked, it did not happen that any of the users visited the site exactly every hour. Therefore, this division should not be a key value during the tests and during the change of this value to 2, 3 and 4 h we obtained identical results. Next, we need to create a dictionary with URLs. We counted that the users in the network requested 681 unique addresses in the considered period. Each address was assigned a unique number. In the presented solution, we examined only sessions consisting of at least 6 addresses. All sessions recorded with fewer addresses have been omitted. We assumed to investigate only the behaviour of users or robots who spend more time on a website. Then, we separated all the sessions that we considered to be unwanted in our website, the ones we want to eliminate in the future. We obtained from the Internet the most popular IP addresses of bots, and then we checked which addresses refer to logs in the file "robot.txt". If an address wanted to download data excluded in "robot.txt", we considered it an intruder. These sequences accounted for approximately 15% of the total traffic recorded.

The final step was to separate test and training data. The test data contained 20% of all sessions recorded at the latest. As a result, we obtained three files:

- training data containing desired user behaviour,
- data with unwanted sequences,
- test data.

Below we present an example of a file with saved sequences:

```
0 1 3 4 5 6 7 8 9 10 -2
18 19 20 0 3 21 22 23 24 -2
0 3 41 9 31 36 66 12 11 67 -2
0 3 38 95 35 66 96 36 41 -2
0 119 140 141 142 143 144 145 146 -2
```

In this case, -2 is the sequence separator.

3   Experiments

The experiment consisted in finding characteristic sequences for users. Sequence detection in URLs is a very difficult task, there are many methods to identify the sequence of addresses [11]. Repetition of exactly the same sequence in visited websites by users is a very rare phenomenon [6]. Our experiment was not intended to prove that the existing sequential pattern mining algorithms can be used for our task. We used Sequential Pattern Mining algorithms implemented in SPMF [3] to detect sequences, BIDE+ [17], PrefixSpan [10] and SPADE [19]. The above algorithms are designed to search only the exact schemes that the users navigated web pages. On their basis, we know that if a user visited pages A, B then he will probably visit page C. The algorithms implemented in SPMF return elements consisting of at least one character. For our applications, it would not be easy to use a sequence consisting of too few characters. If we consider that only one url creates a sequence, then the bot only uses the address immediately will be misidentified. In our experiment, we assumed that the sequence should consist of at least three URL addresses. The sequences obtained were from three addresses up to 5 addresses long. The created sequences form the knowledge base of user behaviour. On its basis, we will assess whether the registered logs belong to the user or the bot. In our case, we do not consider the order of the elements in the sequence, because we assume that the user who is guided by a particular subject does not have to navigate the pages in the same order. The problem is the appropriate programming of the sequence comparison mechanism. The BIDE+, SPADE, PrefixSpan algorithms do not check the order of the elements, nor do they consider whether other elements are woven into the sequence. In other words, if we have two sequences ABCD and ADC, then the common sequence for them is ACD. We must also take this dependence into account when comparing a sequence to a sequence. In the case of our data set, the sessions did not contain a large number of addresses; therefore we did not consider splitting the session into smaller windows, as in the case of DNA analysis [1]. We divided the results

Table 1. Percentage of correctly recognized users and bots with time of each SPM algorithm

SPM Algorithm	Correctly recognized users	Correctly recognized bots	Time [ms]
BIDE+	86.6%	86%	61
PrefixSpan	82.3%	86%	14
SPADE	87.1%	82%	40

into two groups with the recognition of intruders and identification of whether the traffic is appropriate (Table 1).

For each algorithm, we assigned the same minimum support 4% of all sequences in the training sequence. The critical element is the working time of algorithms. In our case, the PrefixSpan algorithm worked best, for which the time was 14 ms. However, it did not find certain sequences specific to users.

4   Conclusion

The presented approach is a novel approach to computer security. We detected sequences of requested web pages by sequential pattern mining algorithms. We used three SPM algorithms, namely BIDE+, Prefixspan and SPADE. We compared the algorithms in terms of accuracy and speed. After finding sequences, we compared sequences by vector similarity. The presented method can detect in nearly real-time security breaches in HTTP traffic.

References

1. Benson, G.: Tandem repeats finder: a program to analyze DNA sequences. Nucleic Acids Res. **27**(2), 573–580 (1999)
2. de Souza, G.B., da Silva Santos, D.F., Pires, R.G., Marananil, A.N., Papa, J.P.: Deep features extraction for robust fingerprint spoofing attack detection. J. Artif. Intell. Soft Comput. Res. **9**(1), 41–49 (2019)
3. Fournier-Viger, P., et al.: The SPMF open-source data mining library version 2. In: Berendt, B., Bringmann, B., Fromont, É., Garriga, G., Miettinen, P., Tatti, N., Tresp, V. (eds.) ECML PKDD 2016. LNCS (LNAI), vol. 9853, pp. 36–40. Springer, Cham (2016). https://doi.org/10.1007/978-3-319-46131-1_8
4. Jordanov, I., Petrov, N., Petrozziello, A.: Classifiers accuracy improvement based on missing data imputation. J. Artif. Intell. Soft Comput. Res. **8**(1), 31–48 (2018)
5. Ono, K., Hanada, Y., Kumano, M., Kimura, M.: Enhancing island model genetic programming by controlling frequent trees. J. Artif. Intell. Soft Comput. Res. **9**(1), 51–65 (2019)
6. Masseglia, F., Poncelet, P., Teisseire, M., Marascu, A.: Web usage mining: extracting unexpected periods from web logs. Data Min. Knowl. Disc. **16**(1), 39–65 (2008)
7. Meng, S., Wang, P.F., Wang, J.C.: Application of fuzzy logic in the network security risk evaluation. In: Advanced Materials Research, vol. 282, pp. 359–362. Trans Tech Publ (2011)

8. Nowak, J., Korytkowski, M., Scherer, R.: Classification of computer network users with convolutional neural networks. In: 2018 Federated Conference on Computer Science and Information Systems (FedCSIS), pp. 501–504, September (2018)

9. Nowak, J., Korytkowski, M., Nowicki, R., Scherer, R., Siwocha, A.: Random forests for profiling computer network users. In: Rutkowski, L., Scherer, R., Korytkowski, M., Pedrycz, W., Tadeusiewicz, R., Zurada, J.M. (eds.) ICAISC 2018. LNCS (LNAI), vol. 10842, pp. 734–739. Springer, Cham (2018). https://doi.org/10.1007/978-3-319-91262-2_64

10. Pei, J., et al.: Mining sequential patterns by pattern-growth: the prefixspan approach. IEEE Trans. Knowl. Data Eng. **16**(11), 1424–1440 (2004)

11. Pei, J., Han, J., Mortazavi-asl, B., Zhu, H.: Mining access patterns efficiently from web logs. In: Terano, T., Liu, H., Chen, A.L.P. (eds.) PAKDD 2000. LNCS (LNAI), vol. 1805, pp. 396–407. Springer, Heidelberg (2000). https://doi.org/10.1007/3-540-45571-X_47

12. Sallam, H.: Cyber security risk assessment using multi fuzzy inference system. IJEIT **4**(8), 13–19 (2015)

13. Scherer, R.: Multiple Fuzzy Classification Systems. Springer, Heidelberg (2012). https://doi.org/10.1007/978-3-642-30604-4_4

14. Scherer, R.: Computer Vision Methods for Fast Image Classification and Retrieval. SCI, vol. 821. Springer, Cham (2020). https://doi.org/10.1007/978-3-030-12195-2

15. Scherer, R., Rutkowski, L.: Neuro-fuzzy relational systems. In: Fuzzy Systems and Knowledge Discovery, pp. 44–48 (2002)

16. Sun, H., Sun, J., Chen, H.: Mining frequent attack sequence in web logs. In: Huang, X., Xiang, Y., Li, K.-C. (eds.) GPC 2016. LNCS, vol. 9663, pp. 243–260. Springer, Cham (2016). https://doi.org/10.1007/978-3-319-39077-2_16

17. Wang, J., Han, J.: BIDE: efficient mining of frequent closed sequences. In: Proceedings 20th International Conference on Data Engineering, pp. 79–90. IEEE (2004)

18. Zaiane, O., Luo, J.: Web usage mining for a better web-based learning environment. In: Proceedings of Conference on Advanced Technology for Education, pp. 60–64. Banff, Alberta (2001)

19. Zaki, M.J.: SPADE: an efficient algorithm for mining frequent sequences. Mac. Learn. **42**(1), 31–60 (2001)

On Learning and Convergence of RBF Networks in Regression Estimation and Classification

Adam Krzyżak[1](✉) and Marian Partyka[2,3]

[1] Department of Computer Science and Software Engineering, Concordia University, 1455 de Maisonneuve Blvd. West, Montreal H3G 1M8, Canada
krzyzak@cs.concordia.ca
[2] Department of Electrical Engineering, Westpomeranian University of Technology, 70-313 Szczecin, Poland
[3] Department of Knowledge Engineering, Faculty of Production Engineering and Logistics, Opole University of Technology, ul. Ozimska 75, 45-370 Opole, Poland
m.partyka@po.opole.pl

Abstract. In the paper we study convergence of the RBF networks with so-called regular radial kernels. The parameters of the network are learned by the empirical risk minimization. Mean square convergence of L_2 error is investigated using the machine learning tools such as VC dimension and covering numbers. RBF network estimates are applied in nonlinear function learning and classification.

Keywords: Nonlinear regression · Classification · RBF networks · Convergence · VC dimension · Covering numbers

1 Introduction

In artificial neural network literature several types of feed-forward neural networks are commonly considered. They include: multilayer perceptrons (MLP), radial basis function (RBF) networks, normalized radial basis function (NRBF) networks and deep networks. These neural network models have been applied in different problems including interpolation, classification, data smoothing and regression. Convergence analysis of MLP can be found among others in, Cybenko [9], White [50], Hornik et al. [24], Barron [2], Anthony and Bartlett [1], Devroye et al. [11], Györfi et al. [21], Ripley [42], Haykin [23], Hastie et al. [22]. Deep networks have been discussed in Bengio et al. [17] and their convergence was recently investigated in Kohler and Krzyżak [26] and Bauer and Kohler [3] (the latter two are one of the first papers to analyze convergence of deep multilayer networks).

Research of the first author was supported by the Alexander von Humboldt Foundation and the Natural Sciences and Engineering Research Council of Canada under Grant RGPIN-2015-06412. He carried out this research at the Westpomeranian University of Technology during his sabbatical leave from Concordia University.

L. Rutkowski et al. (Eds.): ICAISC 2019, LNAI 11508, pp. 131–142, 2019.
https://doi.org/10.1007/978-3-030-20912-4_13

They have been applied in numerous papers, e.g., in [5]. RBF networks have been considered in, e.g., Moody and Darken [37], Park and Sandberg [39, 40], Girosi and Anzellotti [15], Girosi et al. [16], Xu et al. [52], Krzyżak et al. [29], Krzyżak and Linder [30], Krzyżak and Niemann [31], Győrfi et al. [21], Krzyżak and Schäfer [35] and Krzyżak and Partyka [32].

In this paper we consider the radial basis function (RBF) networks with one hidden layer of at most k nodes with a fixed kernel $\phi : \mathcal{R}_+ \to \mathcal{R}$:

$$f_k(x) = \sum_{i=1}^{k} w_i \phi \left(\|x - c_i\|_{A_i} \right) \tag{1}$$

where

$$\|x - c_i\|_{A_i}^2 = [x - c_i]^T A_i [x - c_i]$$

which are class of functions satisfying the following conditions:

(i) radial basis function condition: $\phi : \mathcal{R}_0^+ \to \mathcal{R}^+$ is a left-continuous, monotone decreasing function, the so-called *kernel*.

(ii) centre condition: $c_1, ..., c_k \in \mathcal{R}^d$ are the so-called *centre vectors* with $\|c_i\| \leq R$ for all $i = 1, ..., k$.

(iii) receptive field condition: $A_1, ..., A_k$ are symmetric, positive definite, real $d \times d$-matrices each of which satisfies the eigenvalue inequalities $\ell \leq \lambda_{min}(A_i) \leq \lambda_{max}(A_i) \leq L$. Here, $\lambda_{min}(A_i)$ and $\lambda_{max}(A_i)$ are the minimal and the maximal eigenvalue of A_i, respectively. A_i specifies the *receptive field* about the centre c_i.

(iv) weight condition: $w_1, ..., w_k \in \mathcal{R}$ are the *weights* satisfying $\sum_{i=1}^{k} |w_i| \leq b$ for all $i = 1, ..., k$.

Throughout the paper we use the convention $0/0 = 0$. Common choices for the kernel satisfying (i) are:

- **Window type kernels.** These are kernels for which some $\delta > 0$ exists such that $\phi(t) \notin (0, \delta)$ for all $t \in \mathcal{R}_0^+$. The classical naive kernel $\phi(t) = \mathbf{1}_{[0,1]}(t)$ is a member of this class.
- **Non-window type kernels with bounded support.** These comprise all kernels with support of the form $[0, s]$ which are right-continuous in s. For example, for $\phi(t) = \max\{1 - t, 0\}$, $\phi(x^T x)$ is the Epanechnikov kernel.
- **Regular radial kernels.** These kernels are nonnegative, monotonically decreasing, left continuous, $\int_{\mathcal{R}^d} \phi(\|x\|) dx \neq 0$, and $\int_{\mathcal{R}^d} \phi(\|x\|) dx < \infty$, where $\| \cdot \|$ is the Euclidean norm on $\mathcal{R}^d$. Regular kernels include naive kernels, Epanechnikov kernels, exponential kernels and the Gaussian kernels. Note that the regular kernels are bounded.

Let us denote the parameter vector $(w_0, \ldots, w_k, c_1, \ldots, c_k, A_1, \ldots, A_k)$ by θ. It is assumed that the kernel is fixed, while network parameters $w_i, c_i, A_i, i = 1, \ldots, k$ are learned from the data. The most popular choices of radial function ϕ are:

- $\phi(x) = e^{-x^2}$ (Gaussian kernel)
- $\phi(x) = e^{-x}$ (exponential kernel)
- $\phi(x) = (1 - x^2)_+$ (truncated parabolic or Epanechnikov kernel)
- $\phi(x) = \frac{1}{\sqrt{x^2+c^2}}$ (inverse multiquadratic)

All these kernels are nonincreasing. In the literature on approximation by means of radial basis functions the following monotonically increasing kernels were considered

- $\phi(x) = \sqrt{x^2 + c^2}$ (multiquadratic)
- $\phi(x) = x^{2n} \log x$ (thin plate spline)

They play important role in interpolation and approximation with radial functions [16], but are not considered in the present paper.

Standard RBF networks have been introduced by Broomhead and Lowe [8] and Moody and Darken [37]. Their approximation error was studied by Park and Sandberg [39,40]. These result have been generalized by Krzyżak, Linder and Lugosi [29], who also showed weak and strong universal consistency of RBF networks for a large class of radial kernels in the least squares estimation problem and classification. The rate of approximation of RBF networks was investigated by Girosi and Anzellotti [15]. The rates of convergence of RBF networks trained by complexity regularization have been investigated in regression estimation problem by Krzyżak and Linder [30].

Normalized RBF networks are generalizations of standard RBF networks and are defined by

$$f_k(x) = \frac{\sum_{i=1}^{k} w_i \phi\left(\|x - c_i\|_{A_i}\right)}{\sum_{i=1}^{k} \phi\left(\|x - c_i\|_{A_i}\right)}. \tag{2}$$

Normalized RBF networks (2) have been originally investigated by Moody and Darken [37] and Specht [45]. Further results were obtained by Shorten and Murray-Smith [44]. Normalized RBF networks (NRBF) are related to the classical nonparametric kernel regression estimate also called the Nadaraya-Watson estimate (3):

$$r_n(x) = \frac{\sum_{i=1}^{n} Y_i K\left(\frac{x - X_i}{h_n}\right)}{\sum_{i=1}^{n} K\left(\frac{x - X_i}{h_n}\right)} \tag{3}$$

where $K : \mathcal{R}^d \to \mathcal{R}$ is a kernel and h_n is a smoothing sequence (bandwidth) of positive real numbers. The estimate has been introduced by Nadaraya [38] and Watson [49] and studied by Devroye and Wagner [14], Krzyżak [27], Krzyżak and Pawlak [34] and Györfi et al. [21]. Its recursive versions were investigated in [20,21]. Other nonparametric regression estimation techniques include nearest-neighbor estimate [10,12,21], partitioning estimate [4,21], orthogonal series estimate [19,21], tree estimate [7,22] and Breiman random forest [6,25,43].

In the analysis of the NRBF nets (2) presented in [52] and in [32,33] the authors analyzed convergence of the normalized RBF by exploiting the relationship between their mean integrated square error (MISE) and MISE of the kernel regression estimate, however these results were valid only on the training data, i.e., no generalization was shown. Generalization ability of NRBF networks and their convergence was investigated in [35].

This paper investigates generalization ability and weak convergence of the RBF network (1) with parameters trained by the empirical risk minimization with applications in nonlinear function learning and classification. In this paper we will use specialized tools from computational learning theory such as VC dimension and covering numbers to analyze generalization ability of RBF networks with so-called regular kernels. The paper is organized as follows. In Sect. 2 the algorithm for nonlinear function learning is presented. In Sect. 3 the RBF network classifier is discussed. In Sect. 4 convergence properties of the learning algorithms are investigated and conclusions are provided in Sect. 5.

2   Nonlinear Function Learning

Let (X, Y), (X_1, Y_1), (X_2, Y_2), ..., (X_n, Y_n) be independent, identically distributed, $\mathcal{R}^d \times \mathcal{R}$–valued random variables with $\mathbf{E}Y^2 < \infty$, and let $m(x) = \mathbf{E}(Y|X = x)$ be the corresponding nonlinear regression function. Let μ be the distribution of X. It is well-known that regression function R minimizes L_2 error:

$$\mathbf{E}|m(X) - Y|^2 = \min_{f:\mathcal{R}^d \to \mathcal{R}} \mathbf{E}|f(X) - Y|^2.$$

Our aim is to estimate m from the i.i.d. observations of random vector (X, Y)

$$D_n = \{(X_1, Y_1), \ldots, (X_n, Y_n)\}$$

using RBF network (1). We train the network using so-called empirical risk minimization by choosing its parameters that minimize the empirical L_2 risk

$$\frac{1}{n} \sum_{j=1}^{n} |f(X_j) - Y_j|^2 \tag{4}$$

on the training data D_n, that is we choose RBF network m_n in the class

$$\mathcal{F}_n = \{f_k = f_\theta : \theta \in \Theta_n\} = \left\{ \sum_{i=1}^{k} w_i \phi \left(\|x - c_i\|_{A_i} \right) : \sum_{i=0}^{k_n} |w_i| \leq b_n \right\} \tag{5}$$

where

$$\Theta_n = \{\theta = (w_1, \ldots, w_{k_n}, c_1, \ldots, c_{k_n}, A_1, \ldots, A_{k_n})\}.$$

so that

$$\frac{1}{n} \sum_{j=1}^{n} |m_n(X_j) - Y_j|^2 = \min_{f \in \mathcal{F}_n} \frac{1}{n} \sum_{j=1}^{n} |f_\theta(X_j) - Y_j|^2. \tag{6}$$

We measure the performance of the RBF network estimates by the squared error

$$\mathbf{E}\left[|m_n(X) - m(X)|^2\right] = \mathbf{E}\left[\int |m_n(x) - m(x)|^2 \mu(dx)\right].$$

This approach has been investigated among others by Zeger and Lugosi [36] and by Györfi et al. [21].

Initial analysis of convergence of m_n was carried out in [29] using Vapnik-Chervonenkis dimension concept introduced by Vapnik and Chervonenkis [46, 47] and covering numbers which are basic tools of computational learning theory (CLT) and of machine learning. They were applied in nonparametric regression learning by many researchers (for in-depth survey of the main results in CLT and their applications in nonparametric regression refer to [21]). In this paper we use machine learning tools of CLT to analyze generalization ability and convergence of the RBF networks with regular kernels. In our analysis we are motivated by the results of presented in [21, 29].

3   RBF Classification Rules

Let (Y, X) be a pair of random variables taking values in the set $\{1, ..., M\}$, whose elements are called classes, and in R^d, respectively. The problem is to classify X, i.e. to decide on Y. Let us define *a posteriori* class probabilities

$$p_i(x) = P\{Y = i | X = x\}, i = 1, \cdots, M, x \in R^d.$$

The Bayes classification rule

$$\Psi^*(X) = i \ \text{if} \ p_i(X) > p_j(X), j < i, \ \text{and} \ p_i(X) > p_j(X), j > i$$

minimizes the probability of error. The Bayes risk L^* is defined by

$$P\{\Psi^*(X) \neq Y\} = \inf_{\Psi : R^d \rightarrow \{1, ..., M\}} P\{\Psi(X) \neq Y\}.$$

The local Bayes risk is equal to $P\{\Psi^*(X) \neq Y \mid X = x\}$. Observe that $p_i(x) = E\{I_{\{Y=i\}} \mid X = x\}$ may be viewed as a regression function of the indicator of the event $\{Y = i\}$. Given the learning sequence $V_n = \{(Y_1, X_1), ..., (Y_n, X_n)\}$ of independent observations of the pair (Y, X), we may learn $p_i(x)$ using RBF nets mimicking (6), i.e.,

$$\frac{1}{n} \sum_{j=1}^{n} |\hat{p}_{in}(X_j) - I_{\{Y_j=i\}}|^2 = \min_{f \in \mathcal{F}_n} \frac{1}{n} \sum_{j=1}^{n} |f_Y(X_j) - I_{\{Y_j=i\}}|^2. \quad (7)$$

We propose plug-in RBF classifier with parameters learned by (7) resulting in the classification rule Ψ_n which classifies every $x \in R^d$ to any class maximizing $\hat{p}_{in}(x)$. The global performance of Ψ_n is measured by $L_n = P\{\Psi_n(X) \neq \theta \mid V_n\}$ and the local performance by $L_n(x) = P\{\Psi_n(x) \neq \theta \mid V_n\}$. A rule is said to be weakly, strongly, or completely Bayes risk consistent (BRC) if $L_n \rightarrow L^*$, in probability, almost surely, or completely, respectively, as $n \rightarrow \infty$, see, e.g., Wolverton and Wagner [51] and Greblicki [18].

In the next section we discuss convergence of the RBF regression estimate m_n as well as plug-in classification rule induced by it.

4   Convergence

In this section we present convergence results for the RBF learning function learning and classification algorithms.

4.1   Convergence Results

We have the following convergence results for the RBF network m_n and classification rule Ψ_n with regular radial kernels.

Theorem 1.   *Let $|Y| \leq L < \infty$ a.s.. Consider a family $\mathcal{F}_n$ of RBF networks defined by (5), with $k_n \geq 1$, and let K be a regular radial kernel. If*

$$k_n, b_n \to \infty$$

and

$$k_n b_n^4 \log(k_n b_n^2)/n \to 0$$

as $n \to \infty$, then the RBF network m_n minimizing the empirical L_2 risk over $\mathcal{F}_n = \{f_\theta : \theta \in \Theta_n\}$ is consistent, i.e.,

$$\mathbf{E}\left[|m_n(X) - m(X)|^2\right] \to 0 \ \ as \ n \to \infty \qquad (8)$$

and consequently

$$\mathbf{E}\left[|L_n(X) - L^*(X)|^2\right] \to 0 \ \ as \ n \to \infty \qquad (9)$$

for all distributions of (X, Y) with $|Y| \leq L < \infty$.

Theorem 1 provides conditions for mean square convergence of the RBF regression estimates m_n and classifiers Ψ_n for all distributions of the data with bounded Y. The latter condition is naturally satisfied in classification.

4.2   Outlines of Proofs

We will first introduce basic tools from CLT required in the analysis of convergence of algorithms m_n and Ψ_n discussed in this paper, see [21].

We will start with the definition of the $\epsilon - cover$ and the covering numbers.

Definition 1. *Let $\epsilon > 0$ and let $\mathcal{G}$ be a set of functions $\mathcal{R}^d \to \mathcal{R}$. Every finite collection of functions $g_1, \ldots, g_N : \mathcal{R}^d \to \mathcal{R}$ with the property that for every $g \in \mathcal{G}$ there is a $j = j(g) \in \{1, \ldots, N\}$ such that*

$$\|g - g_j\|_\infty := \sup_z |g(z) - g_j(z)| < \epsilon$$

is called an ϵ-cover of $\mathcal{G}$ with respect to $\|\cdot\|_\infty$.

Definition 2. *Let $\epsilon > 0$ and let $\mathcal{G}$ be a set of functions $\mathcal{R}^d \to \mathcal{R}$. Let $\mathcal{N}(\epsilon, \mathcal{G}, \|\cdot\|_\infty)$ be the size of the smallest ϵ-cover of $\mathcal{G}$ w.r.t. $\|\cdot\|_\infty$. Take $\mathcal{N}(\epsilon, \mathcal{G}, \|\cdot\|_\infty) = \infty$ if no finite ϵ-cover exists. Then $\mathcal{N}(\epsilon, \mathcal{G}, \|\cdot\|_\infty)$ is called an ϵ-covering number of $\mathcal{G}$ w.r.t. $\|\cdot\|_\infty$ and will be abbreviated to $\mathcal{N}_\infty(\epsilon, \mathcal{G})$.*

Next we define the VC dimension. We begin with the shatter coefficient.

Definition 3. *Let $\mathcal{A}$ be a class of subsets of $\mathcal{R}^d$ and let $n \in \mathcal{N}$.*
(a) *For $z_1, \ldots, z_n \in \mathcal{R}^d$ define*

$$s(\mathcal{A}, \{z_1, \ldots, z_n\}) = |\{A \cap \{z_1, \ldots, z_n\} \; : \; A \in \mathcal{A}\}|,$$

that is, $s(\mathcal{A}, \{z_1, \ldots, z_n\})$ is the number of different subsets of $\{z_1, \ldots, z_n\}$ of the form $A \cap \{z_1, \ldots, z_n\}$, $A \in \mathcal{A}$.
(b) *Let G be a subset of $\mathcal{R}^d$ of size n. One says that $\mathcal{A}$ **shatters** G if $s(\mathcal{A}, G) = 2^n$, i.e., if each subset of G can be represented in the form $A \cap G$ for some $A \in \mathcal{A}$.*
(c) *The nth **shatter coefficient** of $\mathcal{A}$ is*

$$S(\mathcal{A}, n) = \max_{\{z_1, \ldots, z_n\} \subseteq \mathcal{R}^d} s(\mathcal{A}, \{z_1, \ldots, z_n\}).$$

That is, the shatter coefficient is the maximal number of different subsets of n points that can be picked out by sets from $\mathcal{A}$.

We can now define the VC dimension.

Definition 4. *Let $\mathcal{A}$ be a class of subsets of $\mathcal{R}^d$ with $\mathcal{A} \neq \emptyset$. The **VC dimension** (or Vapnik–Chervonenkis dimension) $V_{\mathcal{A}}$ of $\mathcal{A}$ is defined by*

$$V_{\mathcal{A}} = \sup \{n \in \mathcal{N} \; : \; S(\mathcal{A}, n) = 2^n\},$$

i.e., the VC dimension $V_{\mathcal{A}}$ is the largest integer n such that there exists a set of n points in $\mathcal{R}^d$ which can be shattered by $\mathcal{A}$.

Convergence of m_n also implies convergence of Ψ_n thanks to plug-in scheme and therefore we will only discuss convergence of m_n. To show convergence of (8) it is sufficient to show for bounded Y that

$$\inf_{f \in \mathcal{F}_n} \int |f(x) - m(x)|^2 \mu(dx) \to 0 \quad (n \to \infty) \tag{10}$$

and

$$\mathbf{E}\left\{ \sup_{f \in \mathcal{F}_n} \left| \frac{1}{n} \sum_{i=1}^{n} |f(X_i) - Y_i|^2 - \mathbf{E}\{|f(X) - Y|^2\} \right| \right\} \to 0 \quad (n \to \infty). \tag{11}$$

Approximation error consistency (10) follows from the Lemma 1 below (stated without proof), which implies that $\bigcup_{k=1}^{\infty} \mathcal{F}_k$ is dense in $L_2(\mu)$ for any probability measure μ on $\mathcal{R}^d$ and for RBF networks with regular radial kernels [29]. It is sufficient to restrict the class RBF nets to a subset of the family $\mathcal{F}_n$ of RBF networks by constraining the receptive field matrices A_i to be diagonal with the equal elements, i.e., $A_i = h_i^{-2} I$. Consequently $\mathcal{F}_n$ becomes

$$f_\theta(x) = \sum_{i=1}^{k} w_i K\left(\left\| \frac{x - c_i}{h_i} \right\|^2 \right) + w_0, \tag{12}$$

where $\theta = (w_0, \ldots, w_k, c_1, \ldots, c_k, h_1, \ldots, h_k)$ is the vector of parameters, $w_0, \ldots, w_k \in \mathcal{R}$, $h_1, \ldots, h_k \in \mathcal{R}$, and $c_1, \ldots, c_k \in \mathcal{R}^d$.

Lemma 1. *Assume that K is a regular radial kernel. Let μ be an arbitrary probability measure on $\mathcal{R}^d$. Then the RBF networks given by (12) are dense in $L_2(\mu)$. In particular, if $m \in L_2(\mu)$, then, for any $\epsilon > 0$, there exist parameters $\theta = (w_0, \ldots, w_k, c_1, \ldots, c_k, h_1, \ldots, h_k)$ such that*

$$\int_{\mathcal{R}^d} |f_\theta(x) - m(x)|^2 \mu(dx) < \epsilon. \tag{13}$$

In the next lemma we consider convergence of estimation error (11).

Lemma 2. *Assume $|Y| \leq L < \infty$ a.s. Consider a family of RBF networks defined by (5), with $k = k_n \geq 1$. Assume that K is a regular radial kernel. If*

$$k_n, b_n \to \infty$$

and

$$k_n b_n^4 \log(k_n b_n^2)/n \to 0$$

as $n \to \infty$, then

$$\mathbf{E} \left\{ \sup_{f \in \mathcal{F}_n} \left| \frac{1}{n} \sum_{i=1}^n |f(X_i) - Y_i|^2 - \mathbf{E}\{|f(X) - Y|^2\} \right| \right\} \to 0 \quad (n \to \infty)$$

for all distributions of (X, Y) with Y bounded.

Outline of Proof. Let K be bounded by k^*. Define the family of functions

$$\mathcal{H}_n = \{h : \mathcal{R}^{d+1} \to \mathcal{R} \ : h(x, y) = (f(x) - T_L y)^2$$
$$((x, y) \in \mathcal{R}^{d+1}) \text{ for some } f \in \mathcal{F}_n\}, \tag{14}$$

where T_L is the usual truncation operator. Thus each member of $\mathcal{H}_n$ maps $\mathcal{R}^{d+1}$ into $\mathcal{R}$. Hence

$$\sup_{f \in \mathcal{F}_n} \left| \frac{1}{n} \sum_{j=1}^n |f(X_j) - Y_j|^2 - \mathbf{E}|f(X) - Y|^2 \right|$$

$$= \sup_{h \in \mathcal{H}_n} \left| \frac{1}{n} \sum_{i=1}^n h(X_i, Y_i) - \mathbf{E}h(X, Y) \right|,$$

and for all $h \in \mathcal{H}_n$ we have $|h(x, y)| \leq 4b_n^2 k^{*2}$ for all $(x, y) \in \mathcal{R}^d \times \mathcal{R}$. Using Pollard's inequality [41] we obtain

$$\mathbf{P} \left\{ \sup_{f \in \mathcal{F}_n} \left| \frac{1}{n} \sum_{j=1}^n |f(X_j) - Y_j|^2 - \mathbf{E}|f(X) - Y|^2 \right| > \epsilon \right\}$$

$$= \mathbf{P} \left\{ \sup_{h \in \mathcal{H}_n} \left| \frac{1}{n} \sum_{i=1}^n h(X_i, Y_i) - \mathbf{E}h(X, Y) \right| > \epsilon \right\}$$

$$\leq 8\mathbf{E} \left\{ \mathcal{N}_1(\epsilon/8, \mathcal{H}_n, Z_1^n) \right\} e^{-n\epsilon^2/128(4k^{*2}b_n^2)^2}. \tag{15}$$

In the remainder of the proof we obtain an upper bound on the L_1 covering number $\mathcal{N}_1(\epsilon/8, \mathcal{H}_n, z_1^n)$, which will be independent of z_1^n. First we relate covering numbers of class $\mathcal{H}$ to the covering numbers of class $\mathcal{F}$. One can show, for n large enough,

$$\mathcal{N}_1\left(\frac{\epsilon}{8}, \mathcal{H}_n, z_1^n\right) \leq \mathcal{N}_1\left(\frac{\epsilon}{32k^*b_n}, \mathcal{F}_n, x_1^n\right).$$

Next we relate the covering numbers of the class of functions in $\mathcal{F}_n$ to covering numbers of the class

$$\mathcal{G} = \{K(\|x - c\|_A) : c \in \mathcal{R}^d\}.$$

One can show

$$\mathcal{N}_1\left(\frac{\epsilon}{32k^*b_n}, \mathcal{F}_n, x_1^n\right)$$
$$\leq \left(\frac{128k^{*2}b_n^2(k_n + 1)}{\epsilon}\right)^{k+1}\left(\mathcal{N}_1\left(\frac{\epsilon}{64k^*b_n^2(k_n + 1)}, \mathcal{G}, x_1^n\right)\right)^k. \quad (16)$$

We can bound $\mathcal{N}_1(\epsilon/(64k^*b_n^2(k_n+1)), \mathcal{G}, x_1^n)$ by relating covering numbers of $\mathcal{G}$ to the VC dimension of graph sets of functions in $\mathcal{G}$.

Since K is left continuous and monotone decreasing we have

$$K\left(\sqrt{[x - c]^T A[x - c]}\right) \geq t \quad \text{if and only if} \quad [x - c]^T A[x - c] \leq \varphi^2(t),$$

where $\varphi(t) = \max\{y : K(y) \geq t\}$. Equivalently, (x, t) must satisfy

$$x^T Ax - x^T(Ac + A^T c) + c^T Ac - \varphi^2(t) \leq 0.$$

Consider now the set of real functions on $\mathcal{R}^{d+1}$ defined for any $(x, s) \in \mathcal{R}^d \times \mathcal{R}$ by

$$g_{A,\alpha,\beta,\gamma}(x, s) = x^T Ax + x^T\alpha + \gamma + \beta s,$$

where A ranges over all $(d \times d)$-matrices, and $\alpha \in \mathcal{R}^d$, $\beta, \gamma \in \mathcal{R}$ are arbitrary. The collection $\{g_{A,\alpha,\beta,\gamma}\}$ is a $(d^2 + d + 2)$-dimensional vector space of functions. Thus the class of sets of the form $\{(x, s) : g_{A,\alpha,\beta,\gamma}(x, s) \leq 0\}$ has VC dimension at most $d^2 + d + 2$ or $V_{\mathcal{G}^+} \leq d^2 + d + 2$, where $\mathcal{G}^+$ is the class of all subgraphs of functions in $\mathcal{G}$. Using the results of van de Geer [48] we obtain for n large enough

$$\mathcal{N}_1\left(\frac{\epsilon}{32k^*b_n}, \mathcal{F}_n, x_1^n\right) \leq \left(\frac{C_1 b_n^2 k_n}{\epsilon}\right)^{C_2 k_n}.$$

Putting all the results together we finally obtain for some constants C_1, C_2 the following bound:

$$\mathbf{P}\left\{\sup_{f \in \mathcal{F}_n}\left|\frac{1}{n}\sum_{j=1}^n |f(X_j) - Y_j|^2 - \mathbf{E}|f(X) - Y|^2\right| > \epsilon\right\}$$
$$\leq 8\exp\left(-\frac{n}{(b_n)^4}[\epsilon^2/C_3 - \frac{C_2 k_n b_n^4}{n}\log\frac{C_1 b_n^2 k_n}{\epsilon}]\right),$$

where C_1, C_2, and C_3 are appropriate constants depending on k^* and d. The proof is complete.

References

1. Anthony, M., Bartlett, P.L.: Neural Network Learning: Theoretical Foundations. Cambridge University Press, Cambridge (1999)
2. Barron, A.R.: Universal approximation bounds for superpositions of a sigmoidal function. IEEE Trans. Inf. Theory **39**, 930–945 (1993)
3. Bauer, B., Kohler, M.: On deep learning as a remedy for the curse of dimensionality in nonparametric regression. Ann. Stat. (2019, to appear)
4. Beirlant, J., Györfi, L.: On the asymptotic L_2-error in partitioning regression estimation. J. Stat. Plann. Infer. **71**, 93–107 (1998)
5. Bologna, G., Hayashi, Y.: Characterization of symbolic rules embedded in deep DIMLP networks: a challenge to transparency of deep learning. J. Artif. Intell. Soft Comput. **7**(4), 265–286 (2017)
6. Breiman, L.: Random forests. Mach. Learn. **45**, 5–32 (2001)
7. Breiman, L., Friedman, J.H., Olshen, R.A., Stone, C.J.: Classification and Regression Trees. Wadsworth Advanced Books and Software, Belmont (1984)
8. Broomhead, D.S., Lowe, D.: Multivariable functional interpolation and adaptive networks. Complex Syst. **2**, 321–323 (1988)
9. Cybenko, G.: Approximations by superpositions of sigmoidal functions. Math. Control Signals Syst. **2**, 303–314 (1989)
10. Biau, G., Devroye, L.: Lectures on the Nearest Neighbor Method. SSDS. Springer, Cham (2015). https://doi.org/10.1007/978-3-319-25388-6
11. Devroye, L., Györfi, L., Lugosi, G.: Probabilistic Theory of Pattern Recognition. Springer, New York (1996). https://doi.org/10.1007/978-1-4612-0711-5
12. Devroye, L., Györfi, L., Krzyżak, A., Lugosi, G.: On the strong universal consistency of nearest neighbor regression function estimates. Ann. Stat. **22**, 1371–1385 (1994)
13. Devroye, L., Krzyżak, A.: An equivalence theorem for L_1 convergence of the kernel regression estimate. J. Stat. Plann. Infer. **23**, 71–82 (1989)
14. Devroye, L.P., Wagner, T.J.: Distribution-free consistency results in nonparametric discrimination and regression function estimation. Ann. Stat. **8**, 231–239 (1980)
15. Girosi, F., Anzellotti, G.: Rates of convergence for radial basis functions and neural networks. In: Mammone, R.J. (ed.) Artificial Neural Networks for Speech and Vision, pp. 97–113. Chapman and Hall, London (1993)
16. Girosi, F., Jones, M., Poggio, T.: Regularization theory and neural network architectures. Neural Comput. **7**, 219–267 (1995)
17. Goodfellow, I., Bengio, Y., Courville, A.: Deep Learning. The MIT Press, Cambridge (2016)
18. Greblicki, W.: Asymptotically Optimal Probabilistic Algorithms for Pattern Recognition and Identification. Monografie No. 3. Prace Naukowe Instytutu Cybernetyki Technicznej Politechniki Wroclawskiej, Nr. 18. Wroclaw, Poland (1974)
19. Greblicki, W., Pawlak, M.: Fourier and Hermite series estimates of regression functions. Ann. Inst. Stat. Math. **37**, 443–454 (1985)
20. Greblicki, W., Pawlak, M.: Necessary and sufficient conditions for Bayes risk consistency of a recursive kernel classification rule. IEEE Trans. Inf. Theory **IT–33**, 408–412 (1987)
21. Györfi, L., Kohler, M., Krzyżak, A., Walk, H.: A Distribution-Free Theory of Nonparametric Regression. Springer, New York (2002). https://doi.org/10.1007/b97848

22. Hastie, T., Tibshirani, R., Friedman, J.: The Elements of Statistical Learning. SSS. Springer, New York (2009). https://doi.org/10.1007/978-0-387-84858-7
23. Haykin, S.O.: Neural Networks and Learning Machines, 3rd edn. Prentice-Hall, New York (2008)
24. Hornik, K., Stinchocombe, S., White, H.: Multilayer feed-forward networks are universal approximators. Neural Netw. **2**, 359–366 (1989)
25. Jordanov, I., Petrov, N., Petrozziello, A.: Classifiers accuracy improvement based on missing data imputation. J. Artif. Intell. Soft Comput. **8**(8), 31–48 (2018)
26. Kohler, M., Krzyżak, A.: Nonparametric regression based on hierarchical interaction models. IEEE Trans. Inf. Theory **63**, 1620–1630 (2017)
27. Krzyżak, A.: The rates of convergence of kernel regression estimates and classification rules. IEEE Trans. Inf. Theory **IT–32**, 668–679 (1986)
28. Krzyżak, A.: Global convergence of recursive kernel regression estimates with applications in classification and nonlinear system estimation. IEEE Trans. Inf. Theory **IT–38**, 1323–1338 (1992)
29. Krzyżak, A., Linder, T., Lugosi, G.: Nonparametric estimation and classification using radial basis function nets and empirical risk minimization. IEEE Trans. Neural Networks **7**(2), 475–487 (1996)
30. Krzyżak, A., Linder, T.: Radial basis function networks and complexity regularization in function learning. IEEE Trans. Neural Networks **9**(2), 247–256 (1998)
31. Krzyżak, A., Niemann, H.: Convergence and rates of convergence of radial basis functions networks in function learning. Nonlinear Anal. **47**, 281–292 (2001)
32. Krzyżak, A., Partyka, M.: Convergence and rates of convergence of recursive radial basis functions networks in function learning and classification. In: Rutkowski, L., Korytkowski, M., Scherer, R., Tadeusiewicz, R., Zadeh, L.A., Zurada, J.M. (eds.) ICAISC 2017. LNCS (LNAI), vol. 10245, pp. 107–117. Springer, Cham (2017). https://doi.org/10.1007/978-3-319-59063-9_10
33. Krzyżak, A., Partyka, M.: Learning and convergence of the normalized radial basis functions networks. In: Rutkowski, L., Scherer, R., Korytkowski, M., Pedrycz, W., Tadeusiewicz, R., Zurada, J.M. (eds.) ICAISC 2018. LNCS (LNAI), vol. 10841, pp. 118–129. Springer, Cham (2018). https://doi.org/10.1007/978-3-319-91253-0_12
34. Krzyżak, A., Pawlak, M.: Distribution-free consistency of a nonparametric kernel regression estimate and classification. IEEE Trans. Inf. Theory **IT–30**, 78–81 (1984)
35. Krzyżak, A., Schäfer, D.: Nonparametric regression estimation by normalized radial basis function networks. IEEE Trans. Inf. Theory **51**, 1003–1010 (2005)
36. Lugosi, G., Zeger, K.: Nonparametric estimation via empirical risk minimization. IEEE Trans. Inf. Theory **41**, 677–687 (1995)
37. Moody, J., Darken, J.: Fast learning in networks of locally-tuned processing units. Neural Comput. **1**, 281–294 (1989)
38. Nadaraya, E.A.: On estimating regression. Theory Probab. Appl. **9**, 141–142 (1964)
39. Park, J., Sandberg, I.W.: Universal approximation using Radial-Basis-Function networks. Neural Comput. **3**, 246–257 (1991)
40. Park, J., Sandberg, I.W.: Approximation and Radial-Basis-Function networks. Neural Comput. **5**, 305–316 (1993)
41. Pollard, D.: Convergence of Stochastic Processes. Springer, New York (1984). https://doi.org/10.1007/978-1-4612-5254-2
42. Ripley, B.D.: Pattern Recognition and Neural Networks. Cambridge University Press, Cambridge (2008)
43. Scornet, E., Biau, G., Vert, J.-P.: Consistency of random forest. Ann. Stat. **43**(4), 1716–1741 (2015)

44. Shorten, R., Murray-Smith, R.: Side effects of normalising radial basis function networks. Int. J. Neural Syst. **7**, 167–179 (1996)
45. Specht, D.F.: Probabilistic neural networks. Neural Netw. **3**, 109–118 (1990)
46. Vapnik, V.N., Chervonenkis, A.Y.: On the uniform convergence of relative frequencies of events to their probabilities. Theory Probab. Appl. **16**, 264–280 (1971)
47. Vapnik, V.N.: Estimation of Dependences Based on Empirical Data, 2nd edn. Springer, New York (1999). https://doi.org/10.1007/0-387-34239-7
48. van de Geer, S.: Empirical Processes in M-Estimation. Cambridge University Press, New York (2000)
49. Watson, G.S.: Smooth regression analysis. Sankhya Ser. A **26**, 359–372 (1964)
50. White, H.: Connectionist nonparametric regression: multilayer feedforward networks that can learn arbitrary mappings. Neural Netw. **3**, 535–549 (1990)
51. Wolverton, C.T., Wagner, T.J.: Asymptotically optimal discriminant functions for pattern classification. IEEE Trans. Inf. Theory **IT–15**, 258–265 (1969)
52. Xu, L., Krzyżak, A., Yuille, A.L.: On radial basis function nets and kernel regression: approximation ability, convergence rate and receptive field size. Neural Netw. **7**, 609–628 (1994)

Application of Deep Neural Networks to Music Composition Based on MIDI Datasets and Graphical Representation

Mateusz Modrzejewski[(✉)], Mateusz Dorobek, and Przemysław Rokita

Division of Computer Graphics, Institute of Computer Science, The Faculty
of Electronics and Information Technology, Warsaw University of Technology,
Nowowiejska 15/19, 00-665 Warsaw, Poland
{M.Modrzejewski,P.Rokita}@ii.pw.edu.pl,
mdorobek@mion.elka.pw.edu.pl

Abstract. In this paper we have presented a method for composing and generating short musical phrases using a deep convolutional generative adversarial network (DCGAN). We have used a dataset of classical and jazz music MIDI recordings in order to train the network. Our approach introduces translating the MIDI data into graphical images in a piano roll format suitable for the DCGAN, using the RGB channels as additional information carriers for improved performance. We show that the network has learned to generate images that are indistinguishable from the input data and, when translated back to MIDI and played back, include several musically interesting rhythmic and harmonic structures. The results of the conducted experiments are described and discussed, with conclusions for further work and a short comparison with selected existing solutions.

Keywords: AI · Artificial intelligence · Neural networks · GAN ·
Music · MIDI

1 Introduction

Music is a vital part of our lives - it's a deeply human phenomenon that has emerged in some form in every civilization throughout history. Music as we know and perceive it today has started developing in the late XVIII century, but its beginnings reach out as far as to 3000 BC [6]. Music is constantly evolving and one hand, we may consider its evolution only in terms of the skills and science behind the brilliance of master instrumentalists, composers, singers, producers and songwriters. However, the second obvious factor of the evolution of music is deeply rooted in technological progress - from instruments such as synthesizers, through digital audio workstations (DAW) up to CPU-consuming algorithms that emulate vintage devices or help us build microtuning systems. The evolution of music is also closely related to achievements such as the magnetic tape, the

© Springer Nature Switzerland AG 2019
L. Rutkowski et al. (Eds.): ICAISC 2019, LNAI 11508, pp. 143–152, 2019.
https://doi.org/10.1007/978-3-030-20912-4_14

compact disc and improvements in amplification systems, just to name a few examples.

Using artificial intelligence for generating music is interesting both in scientific and artistic terms: due to the abstract character and overall complexity of music, it is a very challenging information type for AI solutions. It also expands our overall knowledge of how we perceive music and allows us to investigate the details of our creative process. As an undiscovered and highly experimental form of composition, it may be used to greatly stimulate the artist's creativity and offer new, unconventional forms of expression.

Besides of purely artistic applications, the need of such solutions is clearly visible with the development of such environments like Google Magenta [9] and attempts on music classification [1] and generation [3,7], as well as with the expansion of the content creation market in modern media.

We propose to generate music using a graphic representation. We have created a dataset of images by transforming a quantized MIDI recordings dataset consisting of a classical music part and a jazz music part. The images were used for training the neural network to generate similar ones, which after decoding back to MIDI could be listened back to. Our expectation was therefore to train a network to generate samples capturing the overall character, as well as a certain level of harmonic and rhythmic content that could be found in the training data.

2 Datasets

2.1 Our Approach to Data Representation

MIDI files follow a protocol in which subsequent lines represent key and control actions. It is stored in a binary form and can be converted into a text format [11]. Although MIDI data can be used in the text format, we propose to use a latent graphical representation for the data. Our approach is to use an enhanced piano roll graphic format [12]. Piano roll represents both the time structure of music (rhythm), as well as the harmonic and melodic structure (pitches) in a comprehensible format. Our data processsing consists of:

– redundant information (comments etc.) is removed from the MIDI text,
– the dynamics of the samples are all set to maximum,
– all the samples are quantized to 30 ms (16th note in 120BPM tempo),
– redundant long pauses are removed.

The MIDI data is then compressed to 64 × 64 images as shown on Fig. 1.

The scale of the piano has been reduced to 64 keys from the actual 88 by scaling the far notes by an octave, as the loss of information from these notes does not introduce particular modifications in the overall character of the samples.

The rhythm structure is also compressed by using the RGB channels as additional information carriers: each of the notes is coded using all of the subpixels of the bitmap, therefore stretching the timeline three times. Rhythm values are represented by lighting up the subpixels: this allows to represent 20 s of music

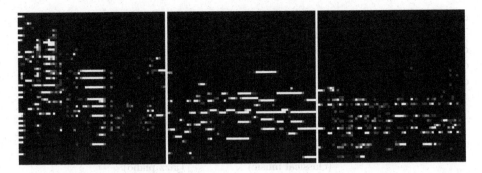

Fig. 1. Example MIDI files coded as R, G, B images, used for training the network.

with each of the R, G, B, C, M, Y, K and W colored images, which is a sample length better than in most available solutions.

In some of the used training files, we have encountered an error as a result of incorrectly closed sustain pedal[1] events. The images containing this error had long white lines followed by an abrupt stop, as shown in Fig. 2. We have decided not to remove these images, but rather to automatically shut the sustain pedal after 3 s (a time long enough for most of the actual situations where a piano player would use the pedal in the considered music examples). This additional processing stage also improved the rhythmic clarity of some of the data, while not introducing significant changes to the overall musical character of the data.

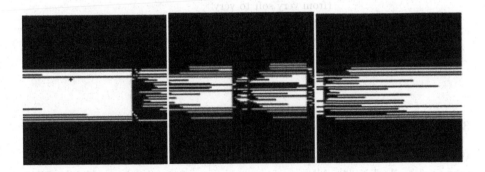

Fig. 2. Example of the error found in some data.

2.2 Qualities of Selected Datasets

Due to a general lack of usable data in the piano roll format, we have decided to transform the MAESTRO MIDI dataset [5] into piano roll images. MAESTRO

---

[1] While the sustain pedal is pressed, the notes of the piano sustain after keys are released by the pianist.

consists of 172 h of virtuoso solo piano classical music in MIDI and WAV format. The files were collected from recordings of different piano players from a piano competition in Minneapolis, USA. We have also used an over 20 h MIDI dataset of jazz pianist Doug McKenzie's recordings [2]. Table 1 shows a brief comparison of the qualities and quantities of the datasets.

Table 1. Features of the samples in the used data sets.

Feature	MAESTRO MIDI (classical music)	Doug McKenzie dataset (jazz piano)
Number of samples	25k images (ca. 172 h)	2,9k images (ca. 20 h)
Overall level of musical technical difficulty	High	High
Overall rhythmic structure	Presence of many non-repetive phrases with fluent tempo changes typical for classical music	Varying, improvised rhythmic structures, presence of triplet phrasing in a swing context
Harmonic structure	Ordered, often very typical for the rules of classical music	Rich, includes more complex harmonies typical for jazz music (some of which are improvised and some are well-known, typical jazz chord progressions)
Dynamic structure	Full range of dynamic (from very soft to very loud)	Full range of dynamic
Instruments	Solo piano	Mostly solo piano, some files with double bass and drums

3 Method and Summary of Our Approach

We have used a DCGAN implementation using PyTorch with the model structure as described in [4]. All experiments were performed using a Nvidia GPU with CUDA architecture. DCGAN contains two concurring convolutional networks: the *generator*, which is trying to create fake images similar to real ones, to fool the *discriminator*, which has to distinguish the training images from the generated images, as shown on Fig. 3. Both of them have a CNN [13] structure to analyze and extract features from 2D matrices - the generator and discriminator may be seen as where deep learning occurs.

All experiments were conducted used the training images that we have created from our MIDI datasets (as described in Table 1).

Upon performing qualitative experiments with the environment proposed above, we have also decided to perform additional experiments with an expanded

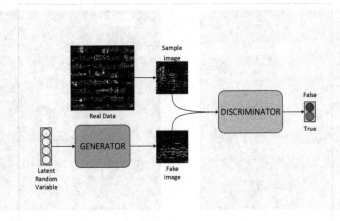

Fig. 3. Structure of the DCGAN.

dynamic range. In our main experiment, we have used flat dynamics set at the maximum value - the full dynamic range experiment was conducted in order to investigate how the dynamic spectrum affects the training process.

4   Results

4.1   MAESTRO Dataset

In first experiment we have used generated images with binary dynamic range (on or off) generated from MAESTRO database. We have trained the network for 50 000 iterations, also trying whether an additional 20 000 iterations would improve the results.

Figure 4 shows the flat dynamic results. At first glance we can't distinguish real images from the fake ones, as the included structures are very similar. Figure 5 shows single sample result images both without and with full dynamics. Figure 6 shows the loss functions for the two experiments.

Upon translation back to MIDI and listening through the generated material, we have found the presence of the following musical composition elements:

- major and minor chords;
- typical voicings and classical music cadenza resolutions;
- 4th chords;
- pronounced bass lines and arpeggios;
- V-I chord progressions (dominant to tonic chord - one of the most important chord progressions in music theory) or a tonic chord at the end of a phrase;

The generated music had mostly a quite chaotic rhythmic structure, but that is due to the dynamic quantization and training using virtuoso performances,

 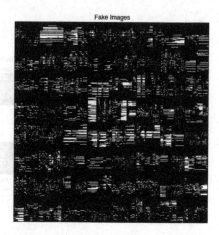

Fig. 4. Real images (left) and fake images (right) generated upon learning with the MAESTRO dataset.

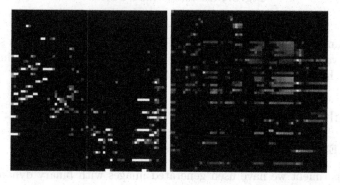

Fig. 5. Example result images with flat (left) and full (right) dynamic with the MAE-STRO set.

often including very fast and difficult pieces. Some of the samples have a much more pronounced and deliberate rhythmic structure, with clear phrases built out of eight and sixteenth notes.

Unfortunately, no significant improvement was introduced in the results after running 20 000 additional iterations, as much of the chaotic character remained unchanged. The harmonic elements were also similar to the previous experiment. The generator's cost is oscillating around a certain value, while the discriminator almost perfectly recognizes false images from real ones, as its loss function is close to 0.

As we can see in Fig. 7, in the full dynamic experiment the discriminator cost went up and generator cost fell down to zero ofter 25 000 iterations, which means that the discriminator couldn't tell any difference between fake and real images. As suspected, the results were more chaotic both rhythmically and harmonically.

a)

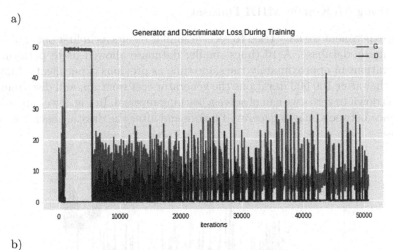

b)

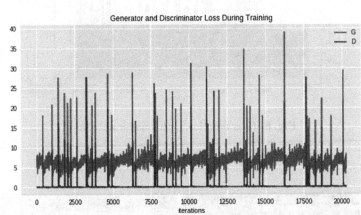

Fig. 6. Loss function for (a) MAESTRO dataset (b) MAESTRO dataset with additional iterations.

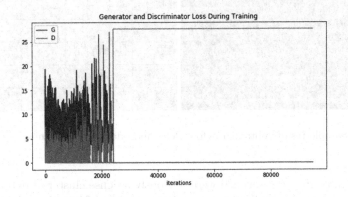

Fig. 7. Cost function in the full dynamic experiment.

4.2   Doug McKenzie MIDI Dataset

In this experiment we have tried to receive similar results as in first one, but using a jazz music database. A 10 times smaller database allowed us to perform 120 000 iterations in approximately the same time as previous experiments. Figure 8 shows that after 100 000 iterations the generator cost went up, and discriminator cost fell down to zero - we can observe a learning reversal. In Fig. 9 we can observe difference between images generated before and after the drastic generator const increase.

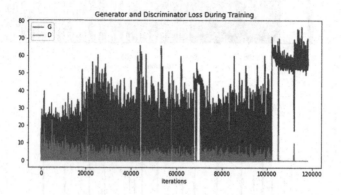

Fig. 8. Loss function with smaller database.

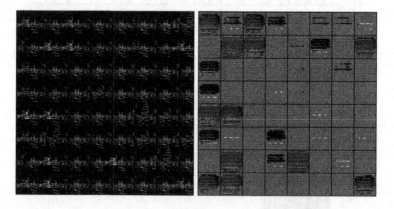

Fig. 9. Sample results obtained before (left) and after (right) learning reversal.

The results after the reversal were obviously a dense cluster of notes lacking major musical sense, but listening back to the results of iterations directly preceding the learning reversal we have observed satisfying results, including the presence of complex altered chords typical for jazz and blues music and phrases finished by these chords **in addition** to the classical music elements mentioned above that can also be found in jazz music.

4.3 Result Summary

Generated images in most cases were indistinguishable at first glance for a human (and in the experiment with full dynamic range even to discriminator). We are able to generate 20 s phrases with 64×64 images and 40 s phrases if dropping the piano keyboard reduction (but also largely increasing the training time). Training with virtuoso piano music resulted in syncopated and chaotic rhythm on many samples, but also long harmonic phrases and chord progressions including major, minor and 4th chords. Melodic and bass lines showed up several times and so did arpeggios and even cadenzas with typical resolutions (like V-I and II-V-I). Advanced jazz chords were also observed. The generated music does not generally contain repeating phrases and loops (structural staples in many genres like pop), but the phrases that we have generated are long and contain many concentrated, cohesive, usable musical ideas. The ideas often span an even number of bars, thus providing a great source of short loops for the composer to choose from.

Existing solutions for a similar problem of generating music (such as Magenta, DeepJazz [8] or Amper Music [10]) create music phrases that are much simpler and shorter, with just basic harmony and certain pre-defined or overfitted solutions. Most of them have a regular rhythm that is less chaotic than in our approach, but music generated by our DCGAN contains advanced progression with resolutions which is our main advantage over other similar projects. Other approaches (based on genetic algorithms, Markov models etc.) often have a much narrower scope of operation and focus closely on certain aspects of the generated music (creating short melodies, operating within certain scales or keys, matching a melody to given harmony etc.), while the harmonic richness of phrases generated in our approach serves as a mean of enhancing and inspiring the composer's creativity.

5   Conclusions and Further Work

In this paper we have proposed a method for composing short musical phrases using a deep convolutional generative-adversarial network and a graphic representation of MIDI input data. The samples generated by our solution are longer and have a richer harmonic structure when compared to results generated by many of the existing solutions. We have selected a set of musical qualitative features (harmony, rhythmic structure etc.) that our network has learned to reproduce. We have also performed additional experiments in order to determine parameters allowing for overall improvement of the quality of the generated samples.

The obtained results allow us to conclude that a GAN and a graphical piano roll data representation for, however unorthodox, is a good choice for further experiments with generating music. In our nearest work we would like to focus on generating long, cohesive musical ideas and genre-specific harmonic and rhythmic content.

References

1. Choi, K., Fazekas, G., Sandler, M., Cho, K.: Convolutional recurrent neural networks for music classification. In: 2017 IEEE International Conference on Acoustics, Speech and Signal Processing (ICASSP), pp. 2392–2396. IEEE (2017)
2. McKenzie, D.: MIDI Collection. https://bushgrafts.com/midi/. Accessed 16 Jan 2019
3. Engel, J., et al.: Neural audio synthesis of musical notes with wavenet autoencoders. In: ICML (2017)
4. Goodfellow, I., et al.: Generative adversarial nets. In: Ghahramani, Z., Welling, M., Cortes, C., Lawrence, N.D., Weinberger, K.Q. (eds.) Advances in Neural Information Processing Systems, vol. 27, pp. 2672–2680. Curran Associates Inc (2014)
5. Hawthorne, C., et al.: Enabling Factorized Piano Music Modeling and Generation with the MAESTRO Dataset (2018)
6. Wilkowska-Chołmińska, K., Chołmiński, J.: Historia Muzyki cz.I. PWM (1989)
7. Johnson, D.D., Keller, R.M., Weintraut, N.: Learning to create jazz melodies using a product of experts. In: ICCC (2017)
8. DeepJazz. https://github.com/jisungk/deepjazz. Accessed 16 Jan 2019
9. Google Magenta - research tool for artistic applications of machine learning. https://magenta.tensorflow.org. Accessed 16 Jan 2019
10. Amper Music. https://www.ampermusic.com/. Accessed 16 Jan 2019
11. The MIDI File Format. https://www.csie.ntu.edu.tw/~r92092/ref/midi/. Accessed 16 Jan 2019
12. What is a Player Piano (Pianola)? http://www.pianola.co.nz/public/index.php/web/about_piano_rolls. Accessed 16 Jan 2019
13. van den Oord, A., Kalchbrenner, N., Espeholt, L., Kavukcuoglu, K., Vinyals, O., Graves, A.: Conditional image generation with PixelCNN decoders. In: Lee, D.D., Sugiyama, M., Luxburg, U.V., Guyon, I., Garnett, R., (eds.) Advances in Neural Information Processing Systems, vol. 29, pp. 4790–4798. Curran Associates Inc (2016)

Dense Multi-focus Fusion Net: A Deep Unsupervised Convolutional Network for Multi-focus Image Fusion

Hafiz Tayyab Mustafa[1(✉)], Fanghui Liu[1], Jie Yang[1(✉)], Zubair Khan[1], and Qiao Huang[2]

[1] Institute of Image Processing and pattern Recognition,
Shanghai Jiao Tong University, Shanghai 200240, China
{analyst21,lfhsgre,jieyang,zubairkhan}@sjtu.edu.cn
[2] Department of Radiology and Medical Imaging, University of Virginia,
Charlottesville, VA, USA
qh2162@gmail.com

Abstract. In this paper, we introduce a novel unsupervised deep learning (DL) method for multi-focus image fusion. Existing multi-focus image fusion (MFIF) methods based on DL treat MFIF as a classification problem with a massive amount of reference images to train networks. Instead, we proposed an end-to-end unsupervised DL model to fuse multi-focus color images without reference ground truth images. As compared to conventional CNN our proposed model only consists of convolutional layers to achieve a promising performance. In our proposed network, all layers in the feature extraction networks are connected to each other in a feed-forward way and aim to extract more useful common low-level features from multi-focus image pair. Instead of using conventional loss functions our model utilizes image structure similarity (SSIM) to calculate loss in the reconstruction process. Our proposed model can process variable size images during testing and validation. Experimental results on various test images validate that our proposed method achieves state-of-the-art performance in both subjective and objective evaluation metrics.

Keywords: Multi-focus image fusion · Convolutional neural network · Unsupervised learning · Structure similarity

1 Introduction

Image fusion integrates information of two or more images into a single one with more information and better visual perception. In static image fusion, we assume source images to be aligned and have no difference of depth or viewpoint of the scenes. It is very challenging for photographers to capture an image with all objects clearly focused. Because of the limited depth of focus in the optical lenses of cameras, it becomes difficult to capture an appropriate image which contains all portion of the site with various depth-of-field (DOF). Hence, some

© Springer Nature Switzerland AG 2019
L. Rutkowski et al. (Eds.): ICAISC 2019, LNAI 11508, pp. 153–163, 2019.
https://doi.org/10.1007/978-3-030-20912-4_15

areas of the image become blurred. Fusion of different DOF images with different focus levels of the same scene into one all-in-focus image is called Multi-Focus Image Fusion (MFIF) [18]. The fused image contains more information for visual perception and highly desirable in various image processing and computer vision tasks such as edge detection and segmentation.

In recent years Deep Learning (DL) has got much attention and gained many advancements in computer vision tasks, for instance classification [10], object recognition [7], segmentation [16], image super-resolution [4] and so on. Recently, in image fusion field some DL-based image fusion approaches have been introduced for digital photography [5,14,20], multi-modality imaging [13,15,27] and remote sensing imaging applications [2,17,26]. Among most of them, for Multi-focus Fusion Convolutional Neural Network (CNN) is used to fuse images. CNN-based methods divide input images into small patches and focus measure is learned for each small patch and fed them to the network. Mostly CNN-based models for MFIF are considered as a classification task. Recently Liu et al. [14] presented a CNN-based method to fuse multi-focus image pairs. Their method learns a classifier to classify between focused and defocused images to get focus maps, binary segmented map, and final decision map. Then in the last step, the image is fused by the pixel-wise weighted-average approach. Following Liu et al. [14], Tang et al. [20] introduced an improved method called pixel CNN for classification of focused and the defocused pixel in images. Du et al. [5] presented DL-based method for MFIF which uses multi-scale input and their network architecture follows the same model as used in [14]. DL-based models which make use of supervised learning require a massive amount of training data with labels. Authors [5,14,20] simulate blur on image patches by using popular image classification datasets to create training samples. However, a common limitation of supervised learning methods is the unavailability of labelled images for image fusion. Furthermore, these methods only utilize the result calculated by the last layers which tend to lose useful information obtained by the middle layers. Recently Prabhakar et al. [19] proposed a DL-based unsupervised architecture for multi-exposure fusion. Although their method achieves better performance for exposure fusion but their architecture is very simple and only performs better for multi-exposure images.

To address these issues, we proposed an unsupervised deep learning architecture for fusing multi-focus images. Our network consists of three subnetworks; Feature extraction, fusion and reconstruction networks. Feature extraction network is designed to extract features of each input image. All these features obtained by feature extraction networks are fused in the fusion process. Finally, fused image is reconstructed by the reconstruction network. The whole network is trained end-to-end by utilizing structural similarity as no-reference image quality loss function. To the best of our knowledge, this is the first end-to-end unsupervised method for fusing color multi-focus image pairs.

The remainder of this paper is organized in three sections. In Sect. 2, we present the proposed network in detail. In Sect. 3, we discuss details of experiments. Section 4 concludes the paper.

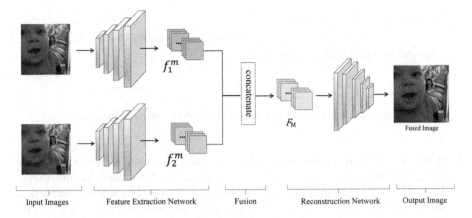

Fig. 1. Schematic diagram of the proposed unsupervised CNN model.

2 Proposed Method

In this section proposed dense multi-focus fusion network is explained in detail. Detailed schematic diagram of the proposed method is illustrated in Fig. 1. From the figure it can be seen that our proposed convolutional network consists of three sub-networks: the feature extraction network, fusion layer and reconstruction network. First, a pair of RGB input images of any size to be fused are fed to feature extraction network separately to output feature maps, then in the second component, the feature maps of input images will merge together to form fused feature maps. Finally, in the last step fused feature maps will go through reconstruction subnetwork to output the final fused image.

2.1 Network Design

We proposed an unsupervised deep learning model to fuse multi-focus images. The network architecture is illustrated in Fig. 2.

Feature Extraction Network. The network is designed for color images with three channels. Pair of source images from the multi-focus pair, I_1 and I_2 of size $h \times w \times 3$ are the inputs to feature extraction networks. Each network consists of a stack of four convolutional layers followed by a bias and rectification layers without any pooling. Images are convolved with 3×3 filters and ReLU activation before passing through the network. We did not use pooling in our network because pooling eliminates some essential image details which are useful later for image reconstruction. All convolutional layers are connected to each other with direct connections among two layers [9]. Both feature extraction networks have tied weights, advantages of tied weights is to reduces the chances of overfitting of the model and preserve as much features as possible. The network is trained in such a way that both feature extraction networks will learn the same features for source images.

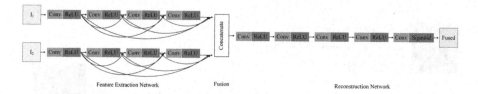

Fig. 2. The detailed network architecture of the proposed method.

Fusion. The feature maps obtained by feature extraction networks are combined in the fusion layer and fused by concatenation into fused feature maps. Suppose f_1^m and f_2^m represents the feature maps obtained by feature extraction network from input images I_1 and I_2 respectively, where $m = \{1, 2, \ldots n\}, n = 64$ represents number of feature maps. F_m denotes the fused feature maps. Concatenation can be formulated by Eq. (1).

$$F_m = concat(f_1^m(x, y), \ f_2^m(x, y)) \tag{1}$$

Reconstruction Network. The aim of this network is to reconstruct desire fused image precisely without losing any details. As illustrated in Fig. 1 it takes concatenated feature maps as input and consists of five convolutional layers out of which first four includes ReLU activation functions. The final output of the RGB fused all-in-focus image is produced by the last convolutional layer with sigmoid activation function.

2.2   Implementation Details

In our proposed method all convolutional layers have 3×3 filters with ReLU activations except for the last layer of reconstruction network where sigmoid is applied. Before applying convolution operation, the parameters of convolutional layers are initialized randomly. We pad zeros around boundaries which helps to preserves the size of feature maps identical to the source images. The final convolutional layer of reconstruction network has 3 output channels because of RGB fused output image. For network training, we use open source image dataset MS COCO [12] as a training dataset, which contains more than 80,000 RGB images. All images are resized to 200×200 for training, the learning rate is set to 10^{-3}.

2.3   Loss Function

For multi-focus image fusion all-in-focus reference images are not available therefore, it is essential to choose proper loss function for the network. Two straightforward and common image quality metrics used widely in many applications are the mean square error and the peak signal-to-noise ratio. These metrics are generally used to compute loss between input and reference images. However, they do not match with the human visual perception because the signal error is not same to the degradation of visual quality in the human visual system (HVS). So instead, we use structure similarity [21], a popular image quality measure to compute the difference between images. The image structure similarity (SSIM) aims to extract structural information of different sliding windows to the corresponding position of the image being compared. The window moves across the image pixel by pixel and SSIM is calculated within the local window. SSIM separates highly structured independent parameters such as luminance, contrast, and structure. We aim to generate a fused image which is same as desired all-in-focus image. Let $r = \{r_i | i = 1, 2, 3, \ldots, n\}$ be the reference image and $t = \{t_i | i = 1, 2, 3, \ldots, n\}$ be the test image and SSIM [21] can be defined as

$$SSIM(r, t|a) = \frac{(2\bar{a}_r \bar{a}_t + C_1)(2\sigma_{a_r a_t} + C_2)}{(\bar{a}_r^2 + \bar{a}_t^2 + C_1)(\sigma^2_{a_r} + \sigma^2_{a_t} C_2)}, \tag{2}$$

where C_1 and C_2 are small constants, a_r is a sliding window in reference image r, $\bar{a}_r$ is the mean of a_r, $\sigma^2_{a_r}$ and $\sigma_{a_r a_t}$ are the variance and covariance of a_r and a_t respectively. Value of $SSIM(r, t|a) \in [-1, 1]$ will be between -1 and 1 and represents the similarity between a_r and a_t. As this value approach towards 1 the more similarity exists between images and 1 state that a_r and a_t are same in structure. To compute SSIM in local window of the image, from Eq. (3) we calculate first $SSIM(r_1, \hat{t}|a)$ and $SSIM(r_2, \hat{t}|a)$. In our method the constants C_1 and C_2 are set to 0.0001 and 0.0009 respectively. Sliding window size is set as 11×11, it moves pixel by pixel in an image from top-left to bottom-right. SSIM loss function [25] on an image patch p can be defined as

$$\mathcal{L}_{SSIM}(p) = \frac{1}{n} \sum_{\hat{p} \in p} 1 - SSIM(\hat{p}), \tag{3}$$

where n represents the total number of sliding windows, due to convolutional nature of network the above equation can be written as

$$\mathcal{L}_{SSIM}(p) = 1 - SSIM(\bar{p}), \tag{4}$$

where $\bar{p}$ is the center pixel of patch p and the loss is back propagated to train the network. Pixel loss is calculated by

$$\mathcal{L}_{\bar{p}} = ||G - I||_2, \tag{5}$$

where G is desired generated all-in-focus image and I is input image. The final Loss is calculated by the combination of structural similarity loss Eq. (5) and pixel loss Eq. (6) given by

$$\mathcal{L} = \mathcal{L}_{SSIM}(p) + \mathcal{L}_{\bar{p}} \tag{6}$$

3   Experimental Results

To validate the efficiency of the proposed model, in this section we demonstrate the comparison on the visual results of our proposed method with some state-of-art multi-focus image fusion (MFIF) methods on benchmark datasets. We select five state-of-the-art MFIF methods to compare with our proposed method. These methods include guided filtering (GF) [11], dense SIFT (DSIFT) [23], boundary finding (BF) [24], convolutional neural network (CNN) [14] and pixel convolutional neural network (p-CNN) [20]. We perform experiments on 20 pair of multi-focus images from an open source available dataset "Lytro" [1]. Objective evaluation in image fusion plays a significant part and it is a difficult task since the ideal fused image is not available. Several quantitative evaluation metrics have been proposed for evaluating MFIF performance. However, there is no ideal standard which can fully summarize the best one. We evaluate our results using four metrics which includes normalized mutual information Q_{MI} [8], image structural similarity Q_{IS} [22], human perception Q_{HP} [3] and visual information fidelity Q_{VIF} [6]. Q_{MI} measures about the amount of mutual information between source and fused images, Q_{IS} is structural similarity-based metric which measure the structural information of source images preservation level. Q_{HP} is image quality metric based on human perception that make use of major features in HVS model and Q_{VIF} measures about visual information fidelity. For all metrics the higher the values the better fusion result.

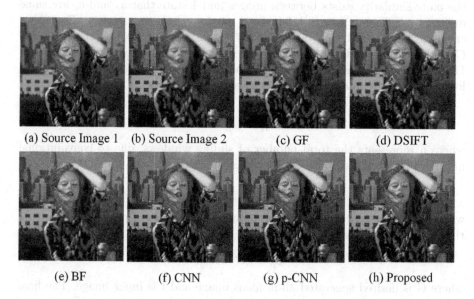

(a) Source Image 1   (b) Source Image 2   (c) GF   (d) DSIFT

(e) BF   (f) CNN   (g) p-CNN   (h) Proposed

Fig. 3. The "Model Girl" source image pairs and its fused output images obtained from various state-of-the-art fusion methods and our proposed method.

3.1   Comparison with Other Methods

For better analysis and effectiveness, we compare the performances of various MFIF methods to validate our proposed method. For this, mainly we provide

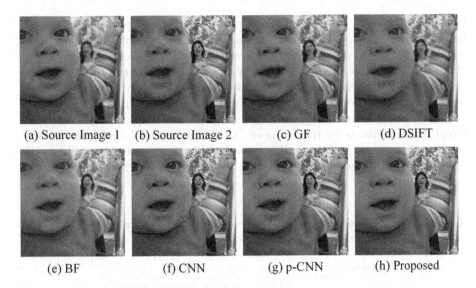

(a) Source Image 1   (b) Source Image 2   (c) GF   (d) DSIFT

(e) BF   (f) CNN   (g) p-CNN   (h) Proposed

Fig. 4. "Baby" source image pairs with their fused results obtained from various fusion methods.

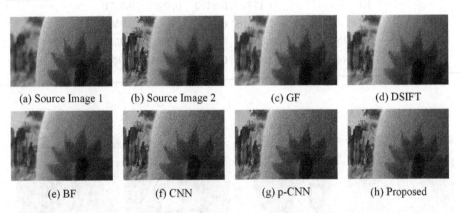

(a) Source Image 1   (b) Source Image 2   (c) GF   (d) DSIFT

(e) BF   (f) CNN   (g) p-CNN   (h) Proposed

Fig. 5. "Painted Egg" source image pairs with their fused results obtained from various fusion methods.

three examples here to exhibit the difference among selected MFIF methods. Figure 3 illustrates the fusion results of the "Model girl" images by other methods and proposed method as well. Figure 3(a) and (b) are the source images, whereas, subfigures (c)–(g) are the output fused images from methods GF, DSIFT, BF, CNN, p-CNN and our proposed method respectively. It is clear that our proposed method has no obvious artifacts in the final results, whereas, fused images from other methods contain some sort of artifacts around edges. Figure 4 compares the result of our proposed method on "Baby" image set. Figure 4(a) and (b) are the source images and the rest of subfigures are the fused results from the other methods mentioned above. From the figure it can be noticed that fused result by our proposed model is the best among others. In the last example, detailed results of "Painted Egg" fused images are shown in Fig. 5. Results clearly shows that other models contain blur artifacts around edges and the result obtained by our proposed method is free from such artifacts. To verify more effectiveness our proposed methods some more fused results are displayed in Fig. 6.

The average scores obtained by our method and compared with other different fusion methods for the fusion of "Model girl", "child" and "painted egg" image sets are listed in Table 1. Highest values are shown in bold to validate the efficiency of our proposed model. Results shows that our method achieves better performance in most cases by using four evaluation metrics.

Table 1. The objective assessment of various fusion methods for the fusion of three pairs of validation mutli-focus source images.

Methods	Q_{MI}	Q_{IS}	Q_{HP}	Q_{VIF}
GF	1.1474	0.9143	0.7613	0.9467
DSIFT	1.1687	0.9291	0.7637	0.9513
BF	1.1715	0.9472	0.7685	0.9576
CNN	**1.1748**	0.9653	0.7829	0.9598
p-CNN	1.1739	0.9661	0.7857	0.9587
Proposed	1.1724	**0.9694**	**0.7869**	**0.9598**

Fig. 6. Some more fused images results obtained by our proposed method.

3.2 Application to Multi-exposure Fusion

Here we will examine the possibility of using our proposed method to other applications of image fusion such as multi-exposure fusion (MEF). When a photograph is captured by a camera which contains shades or tinted regions, it becomes challenging to fix the suitable exposure. In different lighting conditions

(a) Underexposed Image   (b) Overexposed Image   (c) Fused Image

Fig. 7. Fusion result of images with different exposure using proposed method

sometimes, the image becomes too bright or too dark. Fusion of different exposure images into a single one with suitable exposure is known as multi-exposure fusion. To exploit the generalizability of CNN, without fine tuning the network we use it to fuse multi-exposure images. Figure 7 shows that our proposed model successfully fuse images with variable exposure. This indicates that our proposed CNN model is generic and could be applied in MEF.

4   Conclusion

In this paper, we introduced an end-to-end unsupervised model for fusing multi-focus images. The network learns to predict the fused image from an input pair of different focus images. Model directly predicts the fused image using an unsupervised deep learning model which uses the structural similarity (SSIM), no reference image quality metric to compute network training loss. The proposed model first extracts common low-level features from a pair of source images. Then extracted features from both images are fused together to generate a representation or feature map. Finally, this fused representation is passed through reconstruction network to obtain an all-in-focus fused image. We train our model on an open source dataset image and perform extensive experiments as well as quantitative and qualitative evaluations to validate the efficiency of our proposed method. Our proposed CNN model could be used in other digital photography applications of image fusion such as multi-exposure fusion. In the future, we aim to make our model more robust and generic which can fuse over two images.

Acknowledgment. This research is partly supported by NSFC, China (No: 61876107, 61572315, U1803261); and 973 Plan, China (2015CB856004).

References

1. Lytro dataset. http://mansournejati.ece.iut.ac.ir/content/lytro-multi-focus-dataset
2. Azarang, A., Ghassemian, H.: A new pansharpening method using multi resolution analysis framework and deep neural networks. In: 2017 3rd International Conference on Pattern Recognition and Image Analysis (IPRIA), pp. 1–6. IEEE (2017)

3. Chen, H., Varshney, P.K.: A human perception inspired quality metric for image fusion based on regional information. Inf. Fusion **8**(2), 193–207 (2007)
4. Dong, C., Loy, C.C., He, K., Tang, X.: Image super-resolution using deep convolutional networks. IEEE Trans. Pattern Anal. Mach. Intell. **38**(2), 295–307 (2016)
5. Du, C., Gao, S.: Image segmentation-based multi-focus image fusion through multiscale convolutional neural network. IEEE Access **5**(99), 15750–15761 (2017)
6. Han, Y., Cai, Y., Cao, Y., Xu, X.: A new image fusion performance metric based on visual information fidelity. Inf. Fusion **14**(2), 127–135 (2013)
7. He, K., Zhang, X., Ren, S., Sun, J.: Deep residual learning for image recognition. In: Proceedings of the IEEE Conference on Computer Vision and Pattern Recognition, pp. 770–778 (2016)
8. Hossny, M., Nahavandi, S., Creighton, D.: Comments on information measure for performance of image fusion. Electron. Lett. **44**(18), 1066–1067 (2008)
9. Huang, G., Liu, Z., Van Der Maaten, L., Weinberger, K.Q.: Densely connected convolutional networks. In: 2017 IEEE Conference on Computer Vision and Pattern Recognition (CVPR), pp. 2261–2269. IEEE (2017)
10. Krizhevsky, A., Sutskever, I., Hinton, G.E.: Imagenet classification with deep convolutional neural networks. In: Advances in Neural Information Processing Systems, pp. 1097–1105 (2012)
11. Li, S., Kang, X., Hu, J.: Image fusion with guided filtering. IEEE Trans. Image Process. **22**(7), 2864–2875 (2013)
12. Lin, T.-Y., et al.: Microsoft COCO: common objects in context. In: Fleet, D., Pajdla, T., Schiele, B., Tuytelaars, T. (eds.) ECCV 2014. LNCS, vol. 8693, pp. 740–755. Springer, Cham (2014). https://doi.org/10.1007/978-3-319-10602-1_48
13. Liu, Y., Chen, X., Cheng, J., Peng, H.: A medical image fusion method based on convolutional neural networks. In: 2017 20th International Conference on Information Fusion (Fusion), pp. 1–7. IEEE (2017)
14. Liu, Y., Chen, X., Peng, H., Wang, Z.: Multi-focus image fusion with a deep convolutional neural network. Inf. Fusion **36**, 191–207 (2017)
15. Liu, Y., Chen, X., Ward, R.K., Wang, Z.J.: Image fusion with convolutional sparse representation. IEEE Signal Process. Lett. **23**(12), 1882–1886 (2016)
16. Long, J., Shelhamer, E., Darrell, T.: Fully convolutional networks for semantic segmentation. In: Proceedings of the IEEE Conference on Computer Vision and Pattern Recognition, pp. 3431–3440 (2015)
17. Masi, G., Cozzolino, D., Verdoliva, L., Scarpa, G.: Pansharpening by convolutional neural networks. Remote Sens. **8**(7), 594 (2016)
18. Nejati, M., Samavi, S., Shirani, S.: Multi-focus image fusion using dictionary-based sparse representation. Inf. Fusion **25**, 72–84 (2015)
19. Prabhakar, K.R., Srikar, V.S., Babu, R.V.: Deepfuse: a deep unsupervised approach for exposure fusion with extreme exposure image pairs. In: Proceedings of the IEEE International Conference on Computer Vision, pp. 4714–4722 (2017)
20. Tang, H., Xiao, B., Li, W., Wang, G.: Pixel convolutional neural network for multifocus image fusion. Inf. Sci. **433**, 125–141 (2018)
21. Wang, Z., Bovik, A.C., Sheikh, H.R., Simoncelli, E.P.: Image quality assessment: from error visibility to structural similarity. IEEE Trans. Image Process. **13**(4), 600–612 (2004)
22. Yang, C., Zhang, J.Q., Wang, X.R., Liu, X.: A novel similarity based quality metric for image fusion. Inf. Fusion **9**(2), 156–160 (2008)
23. Liu, Y., Liu, S., Wang, Z.: Multi-focus image fusion with dense SIFT. Inf. Fusion **23**, 139–155 (2015). Elsevier

24. Zhang, Y., Bai, X., Wang, T.: Boundary finding based multi-focus image fusion through multi-scale morphological focus-measure. Inf. Fusion **35**, 81–101 (2017)
25. Zhao, H., Gallo, O., Frosio, I., Kautz, J.: Loss functions for image restoration with neural networks. IEEE Trans. Comput. Imaging **3**(1), 47–57 (2017)
26. Zhong, J., Yang, B., Huang, G., Zhong, F., Chen, Z.: Remote sensing image fusion with convolutional neural network. Sens. Imaging **17**(1), 10 (2016)
27. Zhong, J., Yang, B., Li, Y., Zhong, F., Chen, Z.: Image fusion and super-resolution with convolutional neural network. In: Tan, T., Li, X., Chen, X., Zhou, J., Yang, J., Cheng, H. (eds.) CCPR 2016. CCIS, vol. 663, pp. 78–88. Springer, Singapore (2016). https://doi.org/10.1007/978-981-10-3005-5_7

Microscopic Sample Segmentation by Fully Convolutional Network for Parasite Detection

Patryk Najgebauer[1]🆔, Rafał Grycuk[1]🆔, Leszek Rutkowski[1]🆔,
Rafał Scherer[1(✉)]🆔, and Agnieszka Siwocha[2,3]

[1] Institute of Computational Intelligence, Częstochowa University of Technology,
al. Armii Krajowej 36, 42-200 Częstochowa, Poland
{patryk.najgebauer,rafal.grycuk,leszek.rutkowski,
rafal.scherer}@iisi.pcz.pl
http://iisi.pcz.pl
[2] Information Technology Institute, University of Social Sciences,
90-113 Lodz, Poland
asiwocha@san.edu.pl
[3] Clark University, Worcester, MA 01610, USA

Abstract. This paper describes a method of pixel-level segmentation applied to parasite detection. Parasite diseases in most cases are detected by microscopic samples examination or by ELISA blood tests. The microscopic methods are less invasive and often used in veterinary, but they need more time to prepare and visually evaluate samples. Diagnosticians search the entire sample to find parasite eggs and to classify their species. Depending on the species of the diagnosed animal, the samples can contain various types of pollution, e.g. fragments of plants. Most of the objects in the sample by their transparency look similar, and some of parasites eggs might be unintentionally omitted. The presented method based on fully convolutional network allows processing the entire space of the sample and assigning a class to each pixel of the image. Our model was trained to classify parasite eggs and distinguish them from adjacent or overlapped pollution.

Keywords: CNN · FCN · Spatial segmentation · Microscopic sample segmentation

1 Introduction

Methods based on machine learning become quite common in image processing applications. They can more and more accurately interpret images. Initially, the methods were focused on the classification of entire images [7]. The next stage were methods that were able to recognise, localise and mark by bounding box objects in the image content [3,15]. Along with object detection some methods were proposed for image segmentation (class semantic segmentation) [9,12]

© Springer Nature Switzerland AG 2019
L. Rutkowski et al. (Eds.): ICAISC 2019, LNAI 11508, pp. 164–171, 2019.
https://doi.org/10.1007/978-3-030-20912-4_16

that later evolved into object segmentation (class instance segmentation) [4,14]. Now, these methods evolved to panoptic segmentation [6] that is a combination of semantic segmentation and an additional object segmentation to assign the appropriate class to each pixel of the image.

Most of these general purpose models are trained on large data sets such as COCO [8] or ImageNet [16] and can become a framework to build another model to resolve a specific problem [1,2,5,13]. This approach reduces the time needed to train the entire new model from scratch. In microscopic image analysis, the most popular application of segmentation methods in medicine is biopsy analysis in cancer diagnosis.

The rest of this paper is organized as follows. Section 2 describes some problems arising during parasite microscopic samples analysis. Section 3 presents the way of creating dataset, convolutional neural network used in the paper and data augmentation. The results of experiments are shown in Sect. 4.

2   Problem Description

Many existing datasets for microscopy parasite diagnosis are made of ideal samples of egg objects, centred, not covered and not adjoined to other objects. These samples are easily searchable by the image content, and it is easy to train a classifier on them. In a real sample, objects can be covered by any kind of pollution that are remains of undigested food. This objects had a variety of shapes and internal pattern structures. In most cases, more polluted samples are taken from herbivorous species. The internal pattern of most of this additional content is similar to parasite eggs, and we only distinguish it by looking from a further perspective, searching for characteristic shapes. The internal pattern of parasite eggs can also be different depending on an embryo development (Fig. 1) that is influenced by the state of a parasitological disease, and it changes with the time between a sample taken from a patient to the preparation before microscopic analysis. A most stable unchanging feature of eggs is their shell and shape that is characteristic for many parasites and allows to classify them properly.

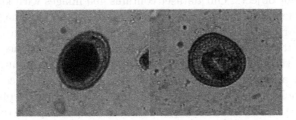

Fig. 1. Examples of eggs of the same species in a different state of embryo development.

The samples can also contain eggs of different than internal parasite species such as insects what may be confusing. They usually have a larger dimension, so the precise information of the magnification rate is also important.

Another but the less significant problem is sample backlight and white balance. High transparency of samples makes them highly influenced by a backlight of the microscope. Acquisition of the same sample on different microscopes provides images in a different colour, contrast and brightness that may affect the classifier and in our solution we take this into consideration during classifier training. The examined samples in microscopic magnification are a considerable space to search. Diagnosticians improve the analysis by dynamic changing the magnification to localise objects faster, but increasing the contamination in the sample makes this process harder. Some parasite eggs may be unrecognised; especially in the case when a disease is still undeveloped, and the presence of eggs is rare. Earlier we tackled the problem of detecting parasite eggs by hand-made descriptors [10,11].

3   Method Description

Our goal in the presented solution is to train a neural network to efficiently detect and classify parasite egg species especially when they are overlapped or appear together with other objects. To solve the problem, we consider using Fully Convolutional Network (FCN) [9] to pixel-level image classification. The most attention is given to the preparation of the appropriate dataset and to developing a method of the model training.

3.1   Parasite Dataset

To create a robust classifier, at first we create data sets that include many aspects of real microscopic samples. Our training set has seven classes with four classes (Fig. 2) of parasite species: whipworms, visceral worm, pinworm, hookworm and three classes of other content: background, air bubble and pollution. We add additional classes for better isolation between parasites and content. In our assumption, the estimator will learn to recognise the differences between patterns more accurately, and we reduce the problem of segmentation expanded on different adjacent objects. Our dataset contains 465 images with labelled masks describing segmentation. Segmentation masks cover the entire image and assign a single class for each pixel of the image. Classes are encoded in the masks by colour starting from the default black class segment that is assigned to the background and fill the entire free space of the image. Class segmentation masks are handcrafted by a human that colourised objects by appropriate colour assigned to the class. Each of the parasite eggs was marked with some surplus (Fig. 3) to better preserve the information of egg shells and to speed up the dataset preparation. Additional minor objects such as bubbles and pollution were selectively marked only for contrast learning.

3.2   Fully Convolutional Network Model

Our FCN model uses four blocks of pooling and convolution layers imported from the VGG16 model that transform the input to a multidimensional feature map

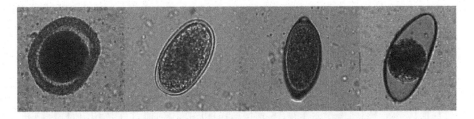

Fig. 2. Parasite eggs images, respectively: visceral worm, hookworm, whipworms and pinworm.

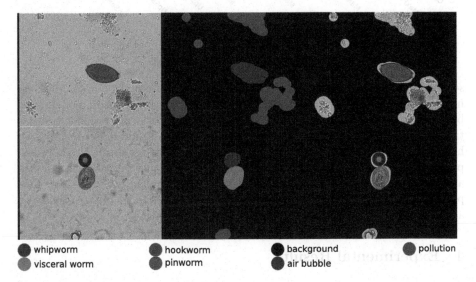

| ● whipworm | ● hookworm | ● background | ● pollution |
| ● visceral worm | ● pinworm | ● air bubble | |

Fig. 3. Training dataset sample. The first column is the training image, the second is a pixel labelled segmentation mask, and the last is the intersection between the image and the mask.

representation and then use three blocks of upsampling and convolution layers to construct segmentation masks (Fig. 4). Encoding layers are a fragment of VGG16 [17] model structure but without the pre-trained weights of the original model. The presented model does not have a fully connected layer that might mix spatial information from the entire image space. The fully convolutional network more effectively preserve local feature information from the input to the output of the model. It is especially important in a segmentation application where pixel classification is performed taking into account its neighbourhood.

3.3 Data Augmentation

The fact that our dataset is small caused that the direct use for training resulted in overfitting the model. Thus, we add the augmentation process to generate additional bath samples for training. We used Keras fit generator that provides

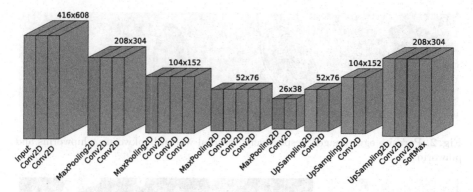

Fig. 4. Fully convolutional network model used in the paper.

sets of randomly changed images from the original dataset. In our solution, we need to generate sets of images that will gradually cover the entire model input by trained classes. For this purpose, our generator performs random translation, rotation, and flip on the dataset images. We do not add noise. Instead, we have images with different microscope focus setting. The generator also does not perform any image scaling, as that is unnecessary because microscopic samples are always examined in a constant perspective with similar magnification. This process provides randomly distributed classes on the model input, effectively augmenting the training dataset and preventing overfitting.

4   Experimental Results

For the experimental purposes, we implemented our model in Python language with the Keras library using TensorFlows 1.3 endpoint. We performed experiments on a single Nvidia GTX 1080 GPU that significantly accelerated the learning process compared to earlier CPU tests.

In the beginning, we trained the model without the dataset augmentation described in Sect. 3.3. We divided the set of 465 samples image into batches of 10 samples and set 50 epochs to learn. After the training, the model indicated that is overfitted. It was particularly evident by predicted shapes of masks that irregularly marked the contours of the objects in a similar way as it is in the training segmentation images (Fig. 5).

To overcome this problem, we add fit generator that on-demand generates randomly changed training subset. The generator provides a unique batch of training data for each epoch during classifier learning. With this dataset augmentation, we trained the model for 200 epochs. Finally, the trained model obtained better results in segmentation that were close to parasites shells (Fig. 7). The obtained results became more precise than the ground truth parasite egg segmentation, and this fact decreased the IOU metrics to about 0.5 of predicted segmentation. Our model properly detects any of the learned species of parasites

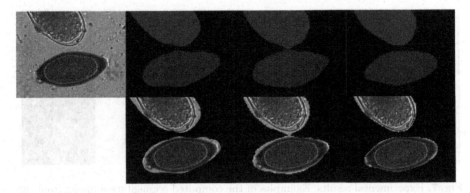

Fig. 5. Segmentation masks and the intersection with the input image. The second column presents ground truth segmentation from the training set, the second column shows segmentation before augmentation, and the fourth column presents the final segmentation and classification results.

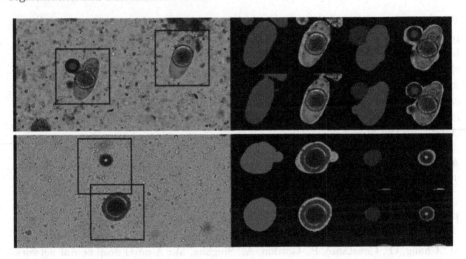

Fig. 6. Classification and segmentation results in comparison to the ground truth segmentation masks. In each example, the upper images present the ground truth masks with intersection image. The lower images present resulting predicted mask.

eggs (Fig. 6). In the case of close adjoined objects, the method might deform predicted segmentation but in our evaluation, it always properly marked the species. In the case of other classes like air bubble or pollution, some of these objects are classified as the background because in the training set most of them are labelled by default to the background class (black).

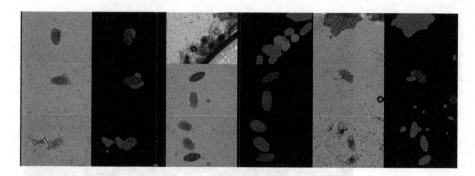

Fig. 7. Experimental results. Examples of the computed segmentation masks from the test dataset.

5   Conclusion

We presented a fully convolutional neural network for parasite microscopic sample segmentation and classification. In conclusion to experiments, the FCN model is an effective tool to microscopic sample segmentation. Comparing to models that contain fully connected layers, the presented FCN fits properly to the mutual spatial distribution of the pattern. This is especially important in the case of microscopic image prediction where pattern fragments are very similar and transparent. Only combining nearby local pattern of the image allows classifying the object correctly.

Acknowledgments. This work was supported by the Polish National Science Centre under grant no. 2017/27/B/ST6/02852.

References

1. Chang, O., Constante, P., Gordon, A., Singana, M.: A novel deep neural network that uses space-time features for tracking and recognizing a moving object. J. Artif. Intell. Soft Comput. Res. **7**(2), 125–136 (2017)
2. de Souza, G.B., da Silva Santos, D.F., Pires, R.G., Marananil, A.N., Papa, J.P.: Deep features extraction for robust fingerprint spoofing attack detection. J. Artif. Intell. Soft Comput. Res. **9**(1), 41–49 (2019)
3. Girshick, R.: Fast R-CNN. In: Proceedings of the IEEE International Conference on Computer Vision, pp. 1440–1448 (2015)
4. He, K., Gkioxari, G., Dollár, P., Girshick, R.: Mask R-CNN. In: Proceedings of the IEEE International Conference on Computer Vision, pp. 2961–2969 (2017)
5. Kamimura, R.: Supposed maximum mutual information for improving generalization and interpretation of multi-layered neural networks. J. Artif. Intell. Soft Comput. Res. **9**(2), 123–147 (2019)
6. Kirillov, A., He, K., Girshick, R., Rother, C., Dollár, P.: Panoptic segmentation. arXiv preprint arXiv:1801.00868 (2018)

7. Krizhevsky, A., Sutskever, I., Hinton, G.E.: ImageNet classification with deep convolutional neural networks. In: Advances in Neural Information Processing Systems, pp. 1097–1105 (2012)
8. Lin, T.-Y., et al.: Microsoft COCO: common objects in context. In: Fleet, D., Pajdla, T., Schiele, B., Tuytelaars, T. (eds.) ECCV 2014. LNCS, vol. 8693, pp. 740–755. Springer, Cham (2014). https://doi.org/10.1007/978-3-319-10602-1_48
9. Long, J., Shelhamer, E., Darrell, T.: Fully convolutional networks for semantic segmentation. In: Proceedings of the IEEE Conference on Computer Vision and Pattern Recognition, pp. 3431–3440 (2015)
10. Najgebauer, P., Rutkowski, L., Scherer, R.: Interest point localization based on edge detection according to gestalt laws. In: 2017 2nd IEEE International Conference on Computational Intelligence and Applications (ICCIA), pp. 349–353, September 2017
11. Najgebauer, P., Rutkowski, L., Scherer, R.: Novel method for joining missing line fragments for medical image analysis. In: 2017 22nd International Conference on Methods and Models in Automation and Robotics (MMAR), pp. 861–866, August 2017
12. Noh, H., Hong, S., Han, B.: Learning deconvolution network for semantic segmentation. In: Proceedings of the IEEE International Conference on Computer Vision, pp. 1520–1528 (2015)
13. Notomista, G., Botsch, M.: A machine learning approach for the segmentation of driving maneuvers and its application in autonomous parking. J. Artif. Intell. Soft Comput. Res. **7**(4), 243–255 (2017)
14. Pinheiro, P.O., Collobert, R., Dollár, P.: Learning to segment object candidates. In: Advances in Neural Information Processing Systems, pp. 1990–1998 (2015)
15. Ren, S., He, K., Girshick, R., Sun, J.: Faster R-CNN: towards real-time object detection with region proposal networks. In: Advances in Neural Information Processing Systems, pp. 91–99 (2015)
16. Russakovsky, O., et al.: ImageNet large scale visual recognition challenge. Int. J. Comput. Vision (IJCV) **115**(3), 211–252 (2015)
17. Simonyan, K., Zisserman, A.: Very deep convolutional networks for large-scale image recognition. arXiv preprint arXiv:1409.1556 (2014)

Application of Spiking Neural Networks to Fashion Classification

Piotr Opiełka[1]([✉]), Janusz T. Starczewski[1], Michał Wróbel[1], Katarzyna Nieszporek[1], and Alina Marchlewska[2,3]

[1] Institute of Computational Intelligence, Czestochowa University of Technology, Czestochowa, Poland
piotr.opielka@iisi.pcz.pl
[2] Information Technology Institute, University of Social Sciences, Lodz, Poland
[3] Clark University, Worcester, MA 01610, USA

Abstract. In this paper, a model of spiking neural networks is studied. Such networks are commonly called as the third generation of artificial neural networks. The main difference between them and previous generation networks is that they are based on spiking neurons. This approach leads us to the need of using specific ways of coding inputs and outputs as well as original methods of learning. The paper considers evaluation of such a network with a Fashion-MNIST dataset that contains labeled images. The results of this experiment and its conclusion are also described in the paper.

1 Introduction

Neural networks are widely used in the modern world (e.g. [9,11,13]). Most of them are based on the second generation model of a neuron that uses various activation functions. Spiking neural networks represent a class of artificial neural networks where neurons communicate by so-called trains of spikes. This is very similar to the behavior of real biological neurons so that it can be applied to an unlimited class of problems (eg. [1,5]). Because of the simplicity of neuron models used, such networks can be very simple introduced into modern low-energy hardware like for example Loihi from Intel [4]. Spiking neural networks can be applied to solve many problems that traditional neural networks solve and also others, what can be found in [14]. One of such problem could be a classification of images from a Fashion-MNIST dataset that is considered in a further part of this paper.

2 Spiking Neuron Models

Spiking neurons, similarly to biological neurons, communicate by generating and propagating pulses called spikes. Generally, all spiking neuron models share a few properties [15]:

© Springer Nature Switzerland AG 2019
L. Rutkowski et al. (Eds.): ICAISC 2019, LNAI 11508, pp. 172–180, 2019.
https://doi.org/10.1007/978-3-030-20912-4_17

- processing information from many inputs and producing a single spiking output signal,
- a probability of generating a spike depends on excitatory and inhibitory inputs,
- reaching a certain state of at least one dynamic variable leads to generate of one or more spikes

2.1 Izhikevich Neuron Model

The basic mathematical model that can be used in spiking neural networks was introduced by Izhikevich [10]:

$$v' = 0.04v^2 + 5v + 140 - u + I$$

$$u' = a(bv - u)$$

and after-spike resetting:

$$if\ v \geq 30\,mV, then \begin{cases} v \leftarrow c \\ u \leftarrow u + d \end{cases}$$

Here v is a neural membrane potential and u represents membrane recovery variable. When the membrane potential reaches $+30\,mV$, variables are reset. Variable I represents currents injected by synapses. This model can reproduce a pattern of spikes recorded from rat's motor cortex. It needs to be noticed that this model needs only 13 flops per neuron update and that makes it very computation efficient [2].

2.2 Leaky Integrate Fire Neuron Model (LIF)

This kind of spiking neuron is very popular among researchers. Its dynamics is described by the following formula:

$$C\frac{du}{dt}(t) = -\frac{1}{R}u(t) + (i_0(t) + \sum w_j i_j(t))$$

Here $u(t)$ is neural membrane potential, C is a membrane capacitance, R is an input resistance, $i_0(t)$ is an external current driving the neural state, $i_j(t)$ is the input current from j-th synaptic input and w_j represents a strength of the j-th synapse. The behavior of such neuron model is shown on the figure (Fig. 1) [15].

3   Methods of Encoding

One of the differences between a spiking neural network and a typical neural network is a type of input that is provided to neurons. There are no numerical

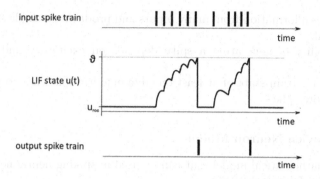

Fig. 1. Visualization of LIF neuron state while stimulating by input spikes.

data but spikes. Therefore, we have to provide methods that encode numerical data into spikes in input and the same to interpret the output. There is a discussion between two main approaches to the problem of coding: rate coding and temporal coding. It is being considered for example in [16]. The first is based on the frequency of spikes incoming to a neuron. It characterizes tolerant to disturbances but low information density. The second one – temporal coding – enables a higher level of information density. Simon Thorpe proved that human needs only 150 ms to recognize animals in photographs. The conclusion was that the first method could not be applied to the brain, so the first spikes contain most of the information [17]. However, both methods are used by researchers depending on the problem that they solve. In this paper, we use three methods of encoding (Single spike coding, Bernoulli distributed coding and Poisson distributed coding). Single spike encoding means that a time of occurrence of single input spike depends on an intensity of the input. If the input intensity is higher, a spike occurs earlier. This method comes from temporal coding. The next method used in this paper also is a temporal method and makes a dependency between an intensity of the input and probability of spike occurrence based on Bernoulli distribution. The last method is the typical rate coding method. Poisson distributed encoding combines the intensity of the input and frequency of spikes over time.

4   Methods of Learning

Without learning algorithms, we cannot make use of any neural network. In such algorithms, we modify the weights of connections between neurons. A similar situation exists in spiking neural networks. There are unsupervised and supervised methods that are widely described in [6]. From the first group, we can use Long Term Depression, Long Term Potentiation and Spike-Timing Dependent Plasticity. In the case of supervised method researchers consider Spike-Based Supervised Hebbian Learning and methods based on gradient evaluation like in [8]. Kasiński and Ponulak in [12] proposed another supervised method called *ReSuMe* that was proved to be highly accurate in producing desired spike sequences in response to a given input spike train. In this paper, we make extensive use of the back-propagation algorithm in connection with gradient evaluation.

5   Experiments and Observations

5.1   Network Architecture

The network was made of the 784-node input layer and the 10-node output layer. Connections between nodes were all-to-all (Fig. 2). Training of the network was conducted by using an approximated stochastic gradient descent algorithm. Predictions were calculated based on the activity of the output layer nodes. During learning, every neuron from the output layer has been connected with one class from a chosen dataset. The input layer was based on real-input nodes that provided spike trains into the next layer. These spike trains were encoded using single-spike encoding, Bernoulli distributed encoding and Poisson distributed encoding. Time of spike occurrence or distribution of spikes was dependent on the intensity of real values. An output layer was constructed either of (depending on a phase of experiments) Leaky Integrate and Fire or Izhikevich neurons.

5.2   Fashion-MNIST Dataset

In our research, we have used the Fashion-MNIST dataset which is considered to be a replacement for an MNIST dataset [19]. This dataset was introduced in 2017 by Zalando's researchers. In order to create a set of data that would be more challenging for neural network models than conventional MNIST and had its advantages. It contains 70 000 unique gray-scale images in the size of 28×28 pixels (Fig. 3). Images are labeled into 10 groups: t-shirt, trouser, pullover, dress, coat, sandals, shirt, sneaker, bag, ankle boots. The training dataset contains 6 000 examples from each class. The testing dataset is built from 10 000 randomly selected examples. Results obtained by authors of this dataset showed that typical SGD classifier (similar to classifier used in this paper) achieves about 81% of classification accuracy. Best results were achieved by Support Vector Machine and Gradient Boosting Classifier – 88–89% of test accuracy.

5.3   Learning Process and Results

Experiments, that we conducted, were performed by using a novel spiking neural networks environment BindsNET [7]. Although its development is at a very early stage, it is very powerful. This library is based on the PyTorch library and adds features known from third-generation neural networks. One of its most helpful advantages is flexibility and user-friendly interface. These features allowed us to test a few different configurations without making everything from scratch. Figures (Figs. 4, 5 and 6) show examples of a learning process. On the first image, we can see spikes that are propagated into an output layer. The second

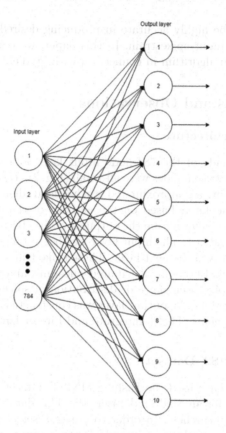

Fig. 2. Architecture of spiking neural network being considered.

image presents spikes going from the output layer. The last image shows a weight matrix in the network. The network was evaluated for each of the 500 samples from the data set. Our goal was to investigate, how different parameters have an impact on the accuracy of the network. We tried to use different types of neuron models (LIF model and Izhikevich model) and input encoding types (single spike coding, Bernoulli distributed coding and Poisson distributed coding). We were also curious about what will change a different count of time steps of simulation. In the beginning, we used 15 time steps. Then we changed it into 45 time steps. The last test consisted of 100 time steps for every sample. For every case, we checked also a time of evaluation of the network by the testing dataset. A simulation was conducted on a computer with an Intel Core i5-8300H CPU @ 2.30 GHz with 16 GB RAM (Table 1).

Results of our survey for different simulation parameters, are presented in tables (Table 2, 3 and 4).

Our experiment confirmed that the LIF neuron model is generally faster in computation. However, there is no big difference in the accuracy percentage between both neuron models. From the encoding point of view, the Single encod-

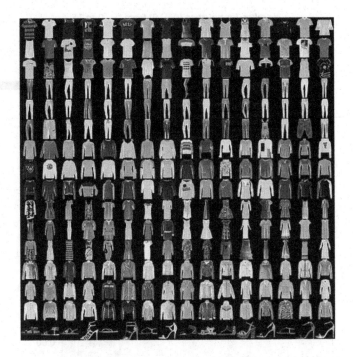

Fig. 3. Examples from a Fashion-MNIST dataset.

Table 1. Parameters of neuron models used in the observations

	Izhikevich	LIF
Spike threshold voltage	45 mV	-52 mV
Resting membrane voltage	-65 mV	-65 mV
Refractory period of the neuron	n/a	5 time steps
Lower bound of the voltage	None	None
Percent of excitatory (vs. inhibitory) neurons in the layer	100%	n/a

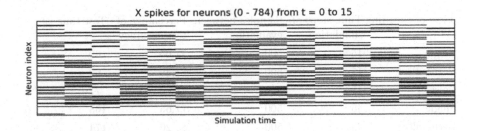

Fig. 4. Input spikes train sample.

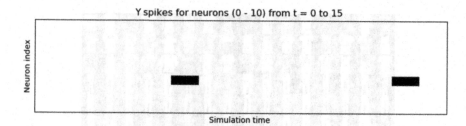

Fig. 5. Output spikes train sample.

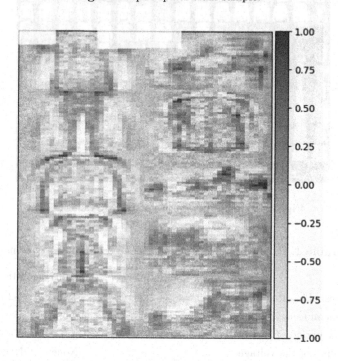

Fig. 6. Weights in the network.

Table 2. Results of simulation for Izhikevich neuron model

Type of encoding	Time steps of simulation	Samples between evaluation	Percentage of test accuracy	Test time [s]
Single	15	500	77,65	60
Bernoulli	15	500	81,46	60
Poisson	15	500	77,06	77
Single	45	500	77,65	168
Bernoulli	45	500	82,26	174
Poisson	45	500	81,48	220

Table 3. Results of simulation for LIF neuron model

Type of encoding	Time steps of simulation	Samples between evaluation	Percentage of test accuracy	Test time [s]
Single	15	500	77,18	51
Bernoulli	15	500	81,59	51
Poisson	15	500	77,21	63
Single	45	500	77,18	140
Bernoulli	45	500	82,47	151
Poisson	45	500	81,36	191

Table 4. Simulation for LIF neuron model with 100 time steps of the simulation

Type of encoding	Time steps of simulation	Samples between evaluation	Percentage of test accuracy	Test time [s]
Bernoulli	100	500	82,21	357
Poisson	100	500	81,48	447

ing had the worst results while Bernoulli encoding was the most efficient. An interesting feature that was observed was a little correlation between time steps and accuracy score. Results of the experiment were also similar to results from [10] for an SGD classifier.

6   Conclusions

This work described a concept of spiking neural networks and their properties. Such networks use spiking neurons and various methods of encoding input data into spike trains. A few methods of learning were also shortly described and examined. A simple network model was proposed and evaluated by the Fashion-MNIST dataset. The BindsNET library seemed to be very helpful in cases of implementation and evaluation of spiking neural networks. Results of learning of the network demonstrated that connection of LIF neuron model and Bernoulli distributed spike trains with a simple back-propagation algorithm allows obtaining results of accuracy about 82%; however, this result is not sufficient. Therefore further research on optimization of the learning process is needed as well as work on parallel implementation (as in [3]) of such neural networks into hardware like FPGA devices or into a memristive architecture (e.g. [18]).

References

1. Bartczuk, L., Przybyl, A., Cpalka, K.: A new approach to nonlinear modelling of dynamic systems based on fuzzy rules. Appl. Math. Comput. Sci. **26**(3), 603–621 (2016)
2. Bawane, P., Gadariye, S., Chaturvedi, S., Khurshid, A.: Object and character recognition using spiking neural network. Mater. Today Proc. **5**, 360–366 (2018)
3. Bilski, J., Smolag, J.: Parallel architectures for learning the RTRN and Elman dynamic neural networks. IEEE Trans. Parallel Distrib. Syst. **26**(9), 2561–2570 (2015)
4. Davies, M., et al.: Loihi: a neuromorphic manycore processor with on-chip learning. IEEE Micro **38**(1), 82–99 (2018)
5. Gabryel, M.: Data analysis algorithm for click fraud recognition. In: Damaševičius, R., Vasiljevienė, G. (eds.) ICIST 2018. CCIS, vol. 920, pp. 437–446. Springer, Cham (2018). https://doi.org/10.1007/978-3-319-99972-2_36
6. Gavrilov, A.V., Panchenko, K.O.: Methods of learning for spiking neural networks. a survey. In: 2016 13th International Scientific-Technical Conference on Actual Problems of Electronics Instrument Engineering (APEIE), vol. 02, pp. 455–460, October 2016
7. Hazan, H., Saunders, D.J., Khan, H., Patel, D., Sanghavi, D.T., Siegelmann, H.T., Kozma, R.: BindsNET: a machine learning-oriented spiking neural networks library in Python. Front. Neuroinf. **12**, 89 (2018)
8. Huh, D., Sejnowski, T.J.: Gradient Descent for Spiking Neural Networks, July 2017
9. Isokawa, T., Yamamoto, H., Nishimura, H., Yumoto, T., Kamiura, N., Matsui, N.: Complex-valued associative memories with projection and iterative learning rules. J. Artif. Intell. Soft Comput. Res. **8**(3), 237–249 (2018)
10. Izhikevich, E.M.: Simple model of spiking neurons. IEEE Trans. Neural Netw. **14**(6), 1569–1572 (2003)
11. Wang, S., Javaid, M., Liu, J.-B., Zhao, J., Cao, J.: On the topological properties of the certain neural networks. J. Artif. Intell. Soft Comput. Res. **8**(4), 257–268 (2018)
12. Kasinski, A., Ponulak, F.: Comparison of supervised learning methods for spike time coding in spiking neural networks. Int. J. Appl. Math. Comput. Sci. **16**, 101–113 (2006)
13. Ke, Y., Hagiwara, M.: An English neural network that learns texts, finds hidden knowledge, and answers questions. J. Artif. Intell. Soft Comput. Res. **7**(4), 229–242 (2017)
14. Maass, W.: Networks of spiking neurons: the third generation of neural network models. Neural Netw. **10**, 1659–1671 (1997)
15. Ponulak, F., Kasinski, A.J.: Introduction to spiking neural networks: information processing, learning and applications. Acta Neurobiologiae Experimentalis **71**(4), 409–433 (2011)
16. Pregowska, A., Szczepanski, J., Wajnryb, E.: Temporal code versus rate code for binary information sources. Neurocomputing **216**, 756–762 (2016)
17. Thorpe, S.: Spike arrival times: a highly efficient coding scheme for neural networks. In: Parallel Processing in Neural Systems and Computers, p. 91, January 1990
18. Wei, R., Cao, J.: Synchronization analysis of inertial memristive neural networks with time-varying delays. J. Artif. Intell. Soft Comput. Res. **8**(4), 269–282 (2018)
19. Xiao, H., Rasul, K., Vollgraf, R.: Fashion-MNIST: A Novel Image Dataset for Benchmarking Machine Learning Algorithms (2017)

Text Language Identification Using Attention-Based Recurrent Neural Networks

Michał Perełkiewicz[(✉)] and Rafał Poświata

National Information Processing Institute, Warsaw, Poland
{mperelkiewicz,rposwiata}@opi.org.pl

Abstract. The main purpose of this work is to explore the use of Attention-based Recurrent Neural Networks for text language identification. The most common, statistical language identification approaches are effective but need a long text to perform well. To address this problem, we propose the neural model based on the Long Short-Term Memory Neural Network augmented with the Attention Mechanism. The evaluation of the proposed method incorporates tests on texts written in disparate styles and tests on the Twitter posts corpus which comprises short and noisy texts. As a baseline, we apply a widely used statistical method based on a frequency of occurrences of n-grams. Additionally, we investigate the impact of an Attention Mechanism in the proposed method by comparing the results with the outcome of the model without an Attention Mechanism. As a result, the proposed model outperforms the baseline and achieves 97,98% accuracy on the test corpus covering 36 languages and keeps the accuracy also for the Twitter corpus achieving 91,6% accuracy.

1 Introduction

A text language identification problem (language ID) refers to the process of determining language based on a text structure under a given classification system. Language ID is often found as the first step in commonly used applications like text translators, web search engines, or Twitter (used in data stream tagging with appropriate language), affecting further outcomes significantly.

The main purpose of this study is to investigate the predictive performance of an Attention-based Recurrent Neural Network (ARNN) in comparison with a standard Recurrent Neural Network (RNN) and a statistical, n-gram-based approach, in a language identification problem. The use of a Bidirectional Long Short-Term Memory Neural Network (BiLSTM) model augmented with an Attention Mechanism is motivated by employing this approach successfully in other NLP tasks, such as text classification [5], language translation [12], and relation classification [15]. LSTM neural networks are capable of handling long-term dependencies in a sequential type of data. Such a type of neural networks is designed to avoid long-term dependency problems, like vanishing gradient [7].

© Springer Nature Switzerland AG 2019
L. Rutkowski et al. (Eds.): ICAISC 2019, LNAI 11508, pp. 181–190, 2019.
https://doi.org/10.1007/978-3-030-20912-4_18

Thus, this model is suitable for working with sequential text data to extract relations occurred in data.

The most problematic issues for text language identification systems are working with short texts, texts with unconventional spelling and written in an informal style, with grammatical and syntax errors and closely related language pairs. We show that the proposed method performs well for this kind of troublesome texts, even with learning only on readily available, well-formatted corpora.

The remainder of the paper is structured as follows. In Sect. 2, we review related work about language identification. Section 3 presents the proposed Attention-based BiLSTM model in detail. In Sect. 4, we describe datasets used to train and validate the model and present the results of the proposed method and two baseline methods. Finally, conclusions are included in Sect. 5.

2 Previous Work

In the past, many different methods have been used to address the problem of text language identification. Cavnar and Trenkle [2] employed a statistical, character-based n-gram model built upon the most frequent 1 to 5-grams in a text. Variants on this approach incorporate Bayesian models (for example CLD2[1] - the language identification tool created by Google in 2013), dot products of word frequency vectors [4], different measures of document similarity and the distance between n-gram profiles [1,14]. Other statistical approaches applied in language identification base on Markov models [11], kernels methods in SVMs [10]. Grefenstette [6] used a word and a part of speech (POS) correlation to determine if two text samples were written in the same or different languages. These methods are widely used in many NLP programming libraries, like Cybozu Labs Language-Detection library[2], Optimize Language Detection[3] for Java and langid.py[4] for Python. The main drawback of these statistical methods is a low efficiency in working with short texts. Other disadvantages of these language identification approaches are a high impact of foreign words occurred in the analysed text and tendency to predict errors when working with noisy text. Statistical methods based on n-grams ignore long-term relationships between characters occurring in a text.

One of the first uses of Neural Networks to address the language identification problem was presented by Chang and Lin [3]. This approach, employing a RNN and skipgram word embedding, outperformed the top results for English-Spanish and English-Nepal language pairs identification competition in the EMNLP 2014 Language Identification in Code-Switched Data[5]. Other approach based on a neural architecture [8] exploits the model build of two main components. The first is a Convolutional Neural Network (CNN) to delimit a whitespace word's

---

[1] https://github.com/CLD2Owners/cld2.

[2] https://github.com/chbrown/language-detection.

[3] https://github.com/optimaize/language-detector.

[4] https://github.com/saffsd/langid.py.

[5] http://emnlp2014.org/.

Unicode character sequence. The second is a BiLSTM recurrent neural network that maps a sequence of word vectors to a language label. Kocmi and Bojar [9] used BiLSTM Recurrent Neural Network to operate on a window of 200 Unicode characters of the input text. This model outperformed statistical models for language identification based on a short text. These neural approaches can be predictive mistake-prone for unseen text structures or text containing foreign words. Adding an Attention Mechanism to the RNN model is a potential solution to these problems.

3 Proposed Method

We adapt the BiLSTM recurrent neural architecture proposed by [9] with some changes. Firstly, the model we propose is built upon the 2-layer BiLSTM Neural Network instead of the 1-layer Bidirectional Gated Recurrent Units (GRUs) model. Secondly, we add the soft Attention Mechanism on top of the BiLSTM layers.

As input, the model takes a vector of a Unicode's character sequence[6]. We use one-hot embedding for character sequences, so if C is the set of unique characters in a dataset, then we let the size of the character embedding be $d = |C|$. For given input sequence, the embedded input vector A is defined as $A = [x_0, x_1, ..., x_T]$, where T is the sentence length. Each vector element x_t represents one Unicode character in the input sentence. The responsibility of the 2-layer BiLSTM Neural Network is to learn a sequential relationship between characters for each of given languages by optimising the weights in a hidden layer h_t at time step t. The hidden layer h_t is calculated based on the current input layer x_t and the previous state of the hidden layer h_{t-1}, according to the definition:

$$h_t = tanh(W x_t + V h_{t-1} + b_1), \tag{1}$$

where W, V are the weight vectors connected to the input vector and the previous hidden state vector respectively, and b_1 is the bias vector. The output is calculated according to the formula:

$$y_t = f(U h_t + b_2), \tag{2}$$

where U is the matrix of weights connected to the hidden state vector, b_2 is the bias vector, and f is an activation function.

In case of a bidirectional LSTMs network (BiLSTM), not only the previous hidden state h_{t-1} is taken into account during calculating the hidden state h_t, but also the next hidden state h_{t+1} which is calculated by reading the input also from the end by the bidirectional layer. The BiLSTM model contains two hidden states, $\overrightarrow{h_t}$ and $\overleftarrow{h_t}$, for each neural cell. Therefore, we extend previous calculations as follows:

$$\overrightarrow{h_t} = tanh(\overrightarrow{W} x_t + \overrightarrow{V} h_{t-1} + \overrightarrow{b_1}) \tag{3}$$

$$\overleftarrow{h_t} = tanh(\overleftarrow{W} x_t + \overleftarrow{V} h_{t+1} + \overleftarrow{b_1}) \tag{4}$$

---

[6] The input vector we use contains 100 characters.

$$y_t = f(\overrightarrow{U}\overrightarrow{h_t} + \overleftarrow{U}\overleftarrow{h_t} + b_2), \tag{5}$$

where the left and the right arrows indicate the reading direction of the input vector A. The output is calculated on the basis of the weighted sum of the $\overrightarrow{h_t}$ and $\overleftarrow{h_t}$ hidden states and $\overrightarrow{U}$ is the matrix of weights connected to the hidden state vector $\overrightarrow{h_t}$ and $\overleftarrow{U}$ is the matrix of weights connected to the hidden state vector $\overleftarrow{h_t}$.

After the deep BiLSTM neural model processing, the attention mechanism is responsible for deciding which characters and relations in the given sentence context indicate the output language to a greater or lesser extent.

Let H be a matrix consisting of output vectors $Y = [y_1, y_2, ..., y_T]$ that the BiLSTM layer produced, where T is the sentence length. For given vector Y, an attention-based model computes a *context* vector c_t as the weighted mean of the state sequence Y as follows [13]:

$$c_t = \sum_{j=1}^{T} \alpha_{tj} y_j \tag{6}$$

where α_{tj} is a weight computed at each time step t for each state y_j. Then, the context vectors are used to compute a new state sequence s, where s_t depends on s_{t-1}, c_t and the model's output at $t-1$. The weightings α_{tj} are then computed as follows [13]:

$$e_{tj} = a(s_{t-1}, y_j), \alpha_{tj} = \frac{exp(e_{tj})}{\sum_{k=1}^{k=T} exp(e_{tk})}, \tag{7}$$

where a is a learned function, which can be thought of as computing a scalar importance value for given y_j and the previous state s_{t-1}.

As the output, we use a dense neural layer with the softmax activation function. The output is the vector of probabilities over all languages classes. Let $R = [r_0, r_1, ..., r_t]$ be the output vector, where $T = |R|$ and $\sum_{i=0}^{i=T} r_i = 1$. As a result, we choose the language with the highest probability. The model is depicted in the Fig. 1.

4   Experimental Studies

4.1   Datasets

Text is characterised by many features, including the formality of used vocabulary, grammatical and stylistic correctness, grammatical structures, length, and so on. Building a suitable, multilingual text corpus which covers many text types is the crucial step in a learning and evaluating process. For this purpose, we focused on finding multilingual and diverse text corpora. The data set we used to learn and evaluate the model comprises 6 text corpora:

1. Subtitles — the collection of translated movie subtitles,
2. Wikipedia — the collection of articles from Wikipedia,

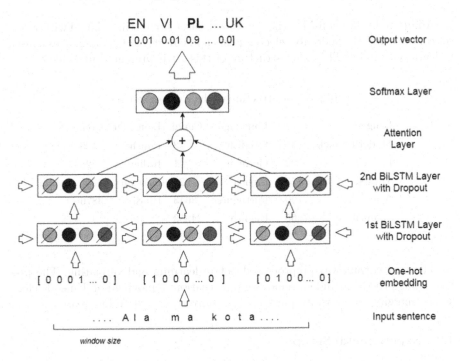

Fig. 1. The illustration of the proposed model

3. Web pages — the set of sentences crawled from randomly selected web pages,
4. News — the set of sentences crawled from news websites, like bbc.com, cnn.com.
5. EuroParl — the parallel corpus extracted from the European Parliament website,
6. Tatoeba — the set of simple sentences, created by foreign language learners.

All described corpora were mixed, keeping only languages they have in common and for which at least 400,000 sentences have been collected, taking a maximum of 100,000 sentences from each corpus. It results in the data set composed of text written in 36 languages as follows: Tatar, Maltese, Norwegian, Marathi, Hindi, Vietnamese, Croatian, Hindi, Icelandic, Czech, Arabic, Latvian, Esperanto, Macedonian, Slovenian, Ukrainian, Estonian, Slovak, Romanian, Lithuanian, Turkish, Bulgarian, Modern Greek, Swedish, Danish, Russian, Dutch, Finnish, Polish, German, English, Spanish, French, Hungarian, Italian and Portuguese. All remaining languages were rejected because of too small number of sentences in their corpus. For the final dataset, we randomly chose 200,000 sentences for each language mentioned above what results in the text corpus comprising 7,200,000 sentences in 36 languages. For testing and validation purposes 30% of data were selected and remaining 70% of the corpus served as the training set.

Additionally, we consider the Twitter dataset for testing. The Twitter test set contains 46,715 randomly selected posts and covers 14 of 36 languages chosen to learn our model. The exact structure of this set is presented in Table 1.

Table 1. The structure of the Twitter test set

Language	Count	Language	Count	Language	Count
Modern Greek	48	Swedish	73	Polish	129
Dutch	232	German	241	Italian	426
Turkish	873	French	1221	Russian	1245
Arabic	2790	Portuguese	3643	Hindi	3876
Spanish	7665	English	24253		

The text corpus was preprocessed before learning and validating. The preprocessing process included: removing punctuation, removing non Unicode characters, merging many whitespaces as one, converting text to lowercase.

4.2   Experimental Setup

The model was trained using early stopping based on the validation set. To reduce the learning time and avoid settling the learning algorithm on an error minimum, we use ADAM optimization algorithm with batch size equal to 64. As a loss function, we use cross-entropy. The best accuracy result (97,99%) for the validation set was attained after the eleventh learning epoch. The model achieved 97,98%[7] accuracy on the test set. Dropout regularization of 0.2 was used after each BiLSTM cell. Experiments included sentences between 5 and 100 characters long. Already for sentences consisting of 5 characters, accuracy reached about 73% and exceeded 95% for the sentences containing at least 14 characters.

We used Keras neural network library with the Tensorflow backend and utilized two Tesla P100 graphic cards to learn the model. The learning phase lasted about 70 hours.

4.3   Results

In addition to the described model, we used two other models for testing on the Twitter data set: a statistical, Naive Bayes model based on the frequency of occurrences of a n-gram model[8] and a 2-layer BiLSTM model without an Attention layer (the structure and the learning process were the same as in the

---

[7] Different cell sizes were used during experimentation, including 50, 150, 200, 500 dimensional hidden layers, one and two BiLSTM layers. The best results were achieved for 2 layers, each for 200 neurons.

[8] https://github.com/chbrown/language-detection.

Table 2. Accuracy measure for the baselines and the proposed model

Model	Accuracy
n-gram model	74.64%
BiLSTM without Attention	89.69%
BiLSTM with Attention	**91.60%**

case of the proposed model). Table 2 shows accuracy achieved by these models. The best result, 91.60%, achieves the BiLSTM model with Attention Mechanism. The difference between the neural models and the statistical model is significant (about 15% and 17%) but the difference among the neural models is less than 2%. The detailed results are depicted in the Fig. 2a.

Figure 2b outlines the n-gram, the BiLSTM without Attention and the proposed BiLSTM with Attention models evaluation on the Twitter test set. The gap between accuracy scored for short text for the neural networks and the statistical approaches is substantial. For posts consisting at least 24 characters, the neural models achieve about 90% accuracy and keep accuracy between the 90% and 98% for longer posts, whereas the model with Attention Mechanism attains slightly better accuracy for almost all sentence lengths. The statistical model achieves values between 80% and 94% for posts longer than 38 characters.

A more thorough analysis shows that classification mistakes occur more often in the case of the languages pair belonging to the same language family. The most common misclassified pair of languages is Spanish and Portuguese (164 of 7665 posts in Spanish were classified as Portuguese and vice versa 66 of 3643 posts in Portuguese were classified as Spanish). For Spanish, the second most common wrong language prediction is Italian (58 of 7665 posts in Spanish were classified as Italian). For Hindi, the most common misclassified language is Turkish (31 of 3876 posts in Hindi were classified as Turkish).

Except for similarity of languages pair, common reasons for classification mistakes were:

1. short posts or posts build upon proper nouns only, like *oh ok, detroit, ha ok, lady gaga, katy perry, nicki minaj, iiiiiiiiiiidc rihanna*, which occur in many languages
2. posts containing many words written in non formal way, like *retweetonly-ifyouwantnewfollowers, adorooooo ooooooooo, qqqqquuuuuuuuuuuueeeeeee noooo-jooooodaaaaaa mdkcmskck, prettttyyyyyyy huuurrrrrrrrtssssss, can u rt this gt please is my dream thanks, puedes dar rt al enlace por favor es mi sue*

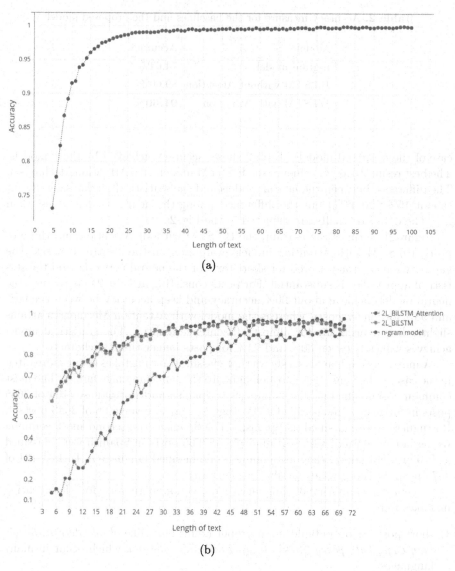

Fig. 2. (a) Accuracy in terms of a sentence length for the test set (b) Accuracy in terms of a length of sentence for the Twitter test set

5   Conclusion

We have presented the 2-layer BiLSTM neural network with the Attention Mechanism. The network was applied to language identification and achieved 91.60% accuracy on the Twitter posts corpus. The neural model performed better (17% better accuracy) than the statistical baseline model based on a frequency of occurrence of n-grams. The proposed model performs well for short and noisy text and keeps the high performance for longer text. The Attention Mechanism boosts the accuracy of language identification for the examined case.

An improvement over statistical approaches is the effect of basing the inference not on the number of occurrences of the particular letters or n-grams, but on the relations occurring between the letters in a sentence. It turns out that Recurrent Neural Networks are able to learn such characteristic relationships and correctly predict the language of text for short texts. Such relationships are characterized by greater predictive ability than the number of occurrences of specific letters or n-grams for short texts, as demonstrated by our research.

At this point, we think that further improvement can be achieved by increasing the diversity of a training text corpus and adding more advanced embedding layer, like a Convolutional layer, which could be well suited to extend a character embedding with a n-grams embedding.

References

1. Aslam, J.A., Frost, M.: An information-theoretic measure for document similarity. In: Proceedings of the 26th Annual International ACM SIGIR Conference on Research and Development in Informaion Retrieval, SIGIR 2003, pp. 449–450. ACM, New York (2003). https://doi.org/10.1145/860435.860545

2. Cavnar, W.B., Trenkle, J.M.: N-gram-based text categorization. In: Proceedings of SDAIR-94, 3rd Annual Symposium on Document Analysis and Information Retrieval, pp. 161–175 (1994)

3. Chang, J.C., Lin, C.: Recurrent-neural-network for language detection on twitter code-switching corpus. CoRR abs/1412.4314 (2014). http://arxiv.org/abs/1412.4314

4. Damashek, M.: Gauging similarity with n-grams: Language-independent categorization of text. Science **267**(5199), 843–849 (1995). http://gnowledge.sourceforge.net/damashek-ngrams.pdf

5. Du, C., H.L.: Text classification research with attention-based recurrent neural networks. Int. J. Comput. **13**(1) (2018). https://doi.org/10.15837/ijccc.2018.1.3142

6. Grefenstette, G.: Comparing two language identification schemes. In: 3rd International Conference on Statistical Analysis of Textual Data (1995)

7. Hochreiter, S., Schmidhuber, J.: Long short-term memory. Neural Comput. **9**(8), 1735–1780 (1997). https://doi.org/10.1162/neco.1997.9.8.1735

8. Kim, Y., Jernite, Y., Sontag, D., Rush, A.M.: Character-aware neural language models. In: Proceedings of the Thirtieth AAAI Conference on Artificial Intelligence, AAAI 2016, pp. 2741–2749. AAAI Press (2016)

9. Kocmi, T., Bojar, O.: LanideNN: multilingual language identification on character window. CoRR abs/1701.03338 (2017). http://arxiv.org/abs/1701.03338

10. Kruengkrai, C., Srichaivattana, P., Sornlertlamvanich, V., Isahara, H.: Language Identification Based On String Kernels, pp. 926–929, November 2005. https://doi.org/10.1109/ISCIT.2005.1567018

11. Lodhi, H., Saunders, C., Shawe-Taylor, J., Cristianini, N., Watkins, C.: Text classification using string kernels. J. Mach. Learn. Res. **2**, 419–444 (2002). https://doi.org/10.1162/153244302760200687

12. Luong, T., Pham, H., Manning, C.D.: Effective approaches to attention-based neural machine translation. In: Proceedings of the 2015 Conference on Empirical Methods in Natural Language Processing, pp. 1412–1421. Association for Computational Linguistics (2015). https://doi.org/10.18653/v1/D15-1166, http://aclweb.org/anthology/D15-1166
13. Raffel, C., Ellis, D.P.W.: Feed-forward networks with attention can solve some long-term memory problems. CoRR abs/1512.08756 (2015). http://arxiv.org/abs/1512.08756
14. Selamat, A.: Improved N-grams approach for web page language identification. In: Nguyen, N.T. (ed.) Transactions on Computational Collective Intelligence V. LNCS, vol. 6910, pp. 1–26. Springer, Heidelberg (2011). https://doi.org/10.1007/978-3-642-24016-4_1
15. Zhou, P., Shi, W., Tian, J., Qi, Z., Li, B., Hao, H., Xu, B.: Attention-based bidirectional long short-term memory networks for relation classification. In: ACL (2016)

Filter Pruning for Efficient Transfer Learning in Deep Convolutional Neural Networks

Caique Reinhold$^{(\boxtimes)}$ and Mauro Roisenberg$^{(\boxtimes)}$

Federal University of Santa Catarina, Florianopolis, Brazil
`caique.reinhold@posgrad.ufsc.br`, `mauro.roisenberg@ufsc.br`

Abstract. Convolutional Neural Networks are extensively used in computer vision applications. Many convolutional models became famous after being widely adopted in a variety of computer vision tasks because o their high accuracy and great generality. Trough Transfer Learning, pre-trained versions of these models can be applied to a large number of different tasks and datasets without the need to train an entire large convolutional model. We aim at finding methods to prune convolutional filters from these pre-trained models in order to make inference more efficient for the new task. To achieve this we propose a genetic algorithms based method for pruning convolutional filters of pre-trained models applied to a different dataset than the one they were trained for. After transferring knowledge from an already trained model to a new task, genetic algorithms are used to find good solutions to the filter pruning problem through natural selection. We then evaluate the results of the proposed methods and compare with state-of-the-art pruning strategies for convolutional neural networks. Obtained experimental results show that the method is able to maintain network accuracy while producing networks with a significant reduction in Floating Point Operations (FLOPs).

Keywords: Transfer learning · Filter pruning ·
Convolutional Neural Networks

1 Introduction

Transfer Learning aims to transfer knowledge from a source to a target domain or from a source to a target task [17]. In image recognition, transfer learning is typically applied to overcome a deficit of training data, to help with different data distributions such as lighting or background variations or to speed up model deployment as training is the most time-consuming task of building a CNN model [16]. It has been successfully applied to many tasks including image classification, scene classification, and object localization.

Some recent work has been done in applying transfer learning in a variety of tasks. In [23], the authors applied the AlexNet model pre-trained on ImageNet to the caltech-101 [5] and caltech-256 [6] datasets, training only the last layer.

© Springer Nature Switzerland AG 2019
L. Rutkowski et al. (Eds.): ICAISC 2019, LNAI 11508, pp. 191–202, 2019.
https://doi.org/10.1007/978-3-030-20912-4_19

Results are currently one of the highest accuracies for both datasets. Transfer learning have also been successfully applied in [12] where the author use pre-trained AlexNet [10], VGG [20] and GoogLeNet [21] models to the task of semantic segmentation of images, improving state-of-the-art results on the PASCAL VOC [4] dataset.

One observed trend in state of the art Convolutional Neural Networks (CNN) models is that they tend to be increasingly larger and deeper, as larger and in deeper models results in better accuracy. But this comes with a cost, as these large models are very memory and computationally consuming. This makes training of these models harder as special hardware is needed such as huge amounts of memory, high-performing Graphical Processing Units (GPU) or large scale distributed clusters [3]. The inference costs on these models also make their use prohibitive for some use cases, especially on limited hardware.

Authors in [19] show that although the capacity of a neural network to absorb information is limited by its number of parameters, not all parameters contribute in the same manner to the final network accuracy. We go further to show that for more limited applications, unused parameters can be removed while keeping the overall network accuracy.

In this work, we investigate how to prune convolutional layers from transferred weights in order to have just the necessary image feature representations for the target task, maintaining accuracy and reducing memory footprint and computation time. Although CNN models have a variety of different layers types and computations, inference run time is extensively dominated by the convolutional layers because of the computational complexity of the convolution operation [14]. Thus, pruning of the convolutional layers has a big effect on model run time as a whole.

Our approach to this problem is divided into three steps. First, we transfer the knowledge from the source to the target task. Then, evolutionary methods are used to find pruning candidates through random selection and evolution. This is done is a data-driven way, in order to find a set of weights that best suits the target task. Finally, when pruning candidates are chosen the unnecessary parts of the network are removed and the whole model is fine-tuned.

The remainder of this paper is organized as follows. In Sect. 2, a summary of related works is presented. Section 3 describes the proposed method. The results of the experiments are presented and compared in Sect. 4. Finally, conclusions are given in Sect. 5.

2   Related Work

Pruning methods for convolutional layers in CNNs can work at several granularities. In [1], authors use particle filtering to find pruning candidates. This method creates random filters of particles to simulate several connections combinations. The trained network is used as an observation function and the classification error rate for each particle is calculated. Several iterations of particle filters are applied to each layer of the network and the connections that have the lowest effect on the classification error rate are pruned. This method drops weights at an intra-kernel level, that is, some less important values inside the convolution kernel are replaced by zero, introducing sparsity to the kernel. Another method for intra-kernel pruning is proposed by Han et al. [7]. The method consists of training a network with a strong L2 regularization to force less relevant connections to have small values. Then, all values below a defined threshold are pruned.

Both of the previous methods are very effective for network compression. However, this compression does not directly translate to faster inference. As intra-kernel level pruning is performed, it introduces sparsity to network connections. Modern hardware exploits regularities in the computation for high throughput, making sparse networks need specially designed software to handle the sparsity. Even with sparse libraries, cache misses and memory access issues of sparse networks make the practical acceleration very limited [22].

Many works address this problem by performing a filter level pruning of CNNs, as no sparsity is added to the network connectivity. A convolutional layer is composed of 3D filters $F_i \in \mathbb{R}^{n \times k \times k}$, where n is the number of input feature maps and i is the ith filter in the convolutional layer. Each filter F_i outputs one feature map and is composed of n 2D kernels of height and width k. In filter level pruning, an entire filter is removed and all kernels of the next layer that maps the removed filter are removed as well, dropping weights but keeping the convolutional layer structure as is.

The work of Li et al. [11] proposed a method to prune convolutional filters based on the absolute sum of the filter weights. The authors argue that filters with small values tend to produce feature maps with weak activations compared to other filters in that layer. The method calculates the sum each layer at a time, dropping the filters and moving to the next layer. When all layers are pruned the network is fine-tuned. In experiments using the VGG-16 model trained for the CIFAR-10 [9] dataset authors report a 34.2% drop in FLOPs. While this method provides a great speed up in model inference while maintaining model accuracy, it doesn't address the transfer of pruned weights to a new domain. As the training step is usually the most time consuming part in building a neural network, pruning of pre-trained models would result in a faster way to deploy high accuracy efficient models.

In [13], authors use statistics about layer $i+1$ to guide pruning of layer i. If a feature map c in the input of layer $i+1$ produces little effect on the output of this layer then the filter that produces this feature map c in layer i can be removed. A measure of the correlation between layer $i+1$ input and output is calculated given a validation dataset and the feature maps that contributes less to layer $i+1$ are pruned from layer i. Experiments show a 59% drop in Floating Point Operations (FLOPs) for the VGG-16 model trained on ImageNet. Given the data-driven nature of the method, it could easily be applied to transfer learning models. However, because pruning is done one layer at a time, it may fall in pitfalls common to greedy strategies as filters already pruned in earlier layers may affect pruning in later layers.

To overcome the deficiencies pointed in the methods above we propose a method that is both data-driven and global. In real-world scenarios tasks are usually domain specific, thus, characteristics from the target dataset may help further optimize the network which data-driven approaches can exploit. On top of that, global pruning approach do not suffer from per layer sensitivity which may help find better solutions. To achieve this we propose a evolutionary method to prune filters from transfer learning models. In our research, we couldn't find related works applying filter pruning to transfer learning models using evolutionary methods.

3   Proposed Method

The proposed method for pruning convolutional filters consists of the following three steps: (1) Given a pre-trained network, train until convergence on the new target task; (2) Find pruning candidates and remove the selected filters; (3) Fine-tune the whole network.

In CNN models, transfer learning is carried by using a network trained on a base dataset for a base task and then transfer those learned features to a new network to be trained on a target dataset and task. This is done by copying the first n layers of the base network to the first n layers of the target network. The remaining layers in the target network are then trained with the target dataset for the target task. Although copied layers are usually fine-tuned for better accuracy in transfer learning, we find it to be irrelevant in this step as most of the weights will be further pruned.

Filter pruning can be seen as a combinatorial optimization problem, as it consists of finding the minimum subset of kernel filters that maximize network accuracy. Most filter pruning methods use greedy strategies guided by heuristics [11,13,14]. Although greedy strategies can find good solutions, they are most often sub-optimal. A well-known strategy for finding decent solutions to combinatorial optimization problems is based on genetic algorithms. The meta-heuristic search based on probabilistic selection and mutation operations of genetic algorithms would be able to reach solutions that greedy strategies would not be able to reach due to the limitation of greedy choices.

The proposed genetic algorithm to find pruning candidates works by randomly initializing a population of P individuals at first. Each individual is represented by an array L, and each element L_i of this array represents a flag of whether the ith filter (filters are all put together by the order of the layers they appear in) of the model is active or have been dropped. Once the first population is initialized each individual drops the filters represented in L and trains the model for a few epochs, evaluating the network accuracy after training. After the initial population has been initialized T tournaments take place. In each tournament, two individuals are chosen at random and their fitness is compared. The winning individual is kept as is and the losing individual is randomly mutated and needs to be trained again. The mutation operation is implemented by assigning a random value to M filters in the individual. The number M of filters mutated is chosen at random by a uniform distribution.

The optimization process has to take into account both model accuracy and pruning rate, which characterizes a multi-objective optimization problem. A simple and well-known approach to solve multi-objective optimization problems with genetic algorithms is to provide a weighted sum of each objective function as a fitness value so that the problem can be converted to a single objective function with a scalar value [8]. As both model accuracy and pruning rate are equally important to the filter pruning optimization problem we assign the same weights for both. Thus, the fitness of the individual becomes a simple mean of model accuracy and filter drop rate.

Since the genetic algorithm will try to optimize the solution with the highest fitness value, some over pruned individuals may appear in the final population since a too high drop rate can push the mean up. To choose between the population of pruning candidates a limit δ from the original model accuracy is set. The individual with the highest drop rate whose accuracy is within this defined limit is finally chosen.

When the less important filters are chosen the model is pruned. After pruning the filters, the performance degradation should be compensated by retraining the network. Fine-tuning is a necessary step to recover the generalization ability damaged by filter pruning. So, as a final step, we need to fine-tune the whole model until the original accuracy is reached.

4   Experimental Results

We empirically study the performance of the proposed method in this section. The AlexNet and VGG-16 models are used to evaluate the method. Both models are pre-trained on the ILSCVR [18] dataset and their weights are transferred and pruned for the Caltech-256 and Flower-102 [15] datasets.

During the experiments, we measure the reduction in computation by FLOPs, which is a common practice for filter pruning as it directly relates to a reduction in processing time and it's platform agnostic. Although removing a filter from a convolutional layer will reduce the overall inference time, the number of FLOPs reduced from inference time depends on the particular implementation of convolution operator. Therefore, throughout the rest of this paper, to compute the number of FLOPs, we assume convolution is implemented as a sliding window and that the nonlinearity function is computed for free. In this way, to compute the number of FLOPs in a convolutional layer we have:

$$F = 2HW(C_{in}K^2 + 1)C_{out} \tag{1}$$

where H, W and C_{in} are height, width and number of channels of the input feature map, K is the kernel width and height, C_{out} is the number of output channels, and F is the number of FLOPs. For the fully-connected layers FLOPs computation is calculated as follows:

$$F = (2I - 1)O \tag{2}$$

Where I is the number of input features and O is the number of output features.

To evaluate the method we use the Caltech-256 and Flower-102 datasets. Both datasets are used as benchmarks for evaluation on various image object classification methods [2,10,14,20]. Due to the limited number of training examples, training large models on both datasets usually depends on transfer learning to achieve acceptable results.

The Caltech-256 dataset is composed of 256 object categories containing a total of 30607 images. The domain of categories is varied, including categories from many application domains such as plants, animals or transportation. Each category contains a minimum of 80 examples and may vary to a maximum of 800. Because of the high disparity in the number of examples for each category, authors in [6] propose randomly selecting N from each category for evaluation on the dataset. Common choices of N_train are 20, 25, 30 or 40 for the training split and N_test is usually set to 25 for the test split.

The Flower-102 dataset is a more domain-specific dataset composed only of flowers commonly occurring in the United Kingdom. The dataset is composed of a total of 9818 images divided into 102 categories. Each category contains from 40 to 250 image examples. One peculiarity of the dataset is that its default test split is quite larger than the train split. The dataset is divided into 1020 images for the train and validation splits, being 10 of each category, and 6129 for the test set.

4.1 Setup

To evaluate the pruning method we use two models trained on the ILSCVR dataset and apply them to two different tasks, the Caltech-256 and Flower-102 datasets. We begin this section by explaining a bit more about how the experiments were set up at each step.

In the first step of our method, the network needs to be trained for the target dataset. In this step we copy the weights learned from ILSCVR dataset for both models and train only the last layer of the model, leaving the other weights frozen. The model is trained using Stochastic Gradient Descent (SGD) with a learning rate of 10^{-3}. Training stops when the accuracy of the model evaluated on the validation set does not improve for over 10 epochs or if training reaches a maximum of 60 epochs.

For the second step, we prune both networks on each dataset using the proposed evolutionary method. A population of 10 individuals is initiated and each individual is trained for 10 epochs after pruning to evaluate its accuracy using SGD with 10^{-3} learning rate. After the population is initialized 40 tournaments are run. For each individual mutated, a mutation rate between 20% and 50% is chosen at random and the correspondent number of flags are randomly replaced. When the tournaments are finished the individual with the highest drop rate whose validation accuracy is at most 2% below original accuracy is chosen.

In the third step, networks are pruned and need to be fine-tuned. For our tests all network layers were fine-tuned using SGD with a 10^{-4} learning rate. Training stops if validation accuracy does not improve for 10 epochs or if training reaches a maximum of 40 epochs.

Due to the small number of training examples in the datasets, a dropout rate of 40% on the fully-connected layers is used during training in all stages of the method.

4.2 Results

We report the results obtained from tests with AlexNet and VGG-16 models using our pruning method. For each test, we present the original number of filters and the number of filters left after pruning for each layer of the model. As with the number of filters, we also present their computation cost measured in FLOPs.

In Table 1 we see the results for pruning the AlexNet model on Flower-102 dataset. The accuracy rate of the model before pruning was of 70.02% with the test set. Evolutionary pruning was able to prune 43.02% of the FLOPs during model inference time. The final accuracy of the pruned network was 71.18%. Even when pruned the model outperforms the original model due to fine-tuning with a smaller learning rate. This smaller learning rate during the final step of pruning enables the model to finely adjust its weights in order to repair damaged connections caused by the pruning.

Table 1. Pruning results for AlexNet with Flower-102.

Layer	Original		After pruning	
	Filters	FLOPs	Filters	FLOPs
conv1	96	3.60×10^9	54	2.03×10^9
conv2	256	8.96×10^8	149	5.22×10^8
conv3	384	2.99×10^8	226	1.76×10^8
conv4	384	4.49×10^8	208	2.43×10^8
conv5	256	2.99×10^8	147	1.72×10^8
fc6	4096	7.55×10^7	0	7.55×10^7
fc7	4096	3.36×10^7	0	3.36×10^7
fc8	102	8.35×10^5	0	8.35×10^5
Total	1376	5.65×10^9	784	3.25×10^9

Results for the pruning of AlexNet model on Caltech-256 are shown in Table 2. Accuracy rate before pruning the model was of 67.87%. The pruning method was able to prune 34.14% of network FLOPs on inference time. After pruning of filters the achieved accuracy rate was of 66.31%. While in this task the original model accuracy could not be achieved, the drop in accuracy is only marginal if the amount of weights pruned is taken into consideration.

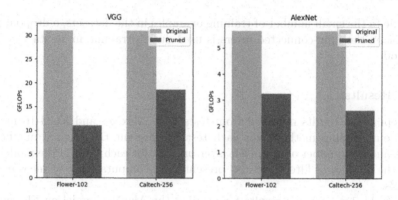

Fig. 1. Performance of original and pruned models on each dataset in GFLOPs (one billion FLOPs).

Table 2. Pruning results for AlexNet with Caltech-256.

Layer	Original		After pruning	
	Filters	FLOPs	Filters	FLOPs
conv1	96	3.60×10^9	43	1.61×10^9
conv2	256	8.96×10^8	113	3.96×10^8
conv3	384	2.99×10^8	174	1.36×10^8
conv4	384	4.49×10^8	190	2.22×10^8
conv5	256	2.99×10^8	62	1.34×10^8
fc6	0	7.55×10^7	0	7.55×10^7
fc7	0	3.36×10^7	0	3.36×10^7
fc8	0	8.35×10^5	0	8.35×10^7
Total	1376	5.65×10^9	635	2.61×10^9

In Table 3 we present the test results for pruning the VGG-16 model on Flower-102 dataset. The accuracy rate achieved before pruning was of 70.04%. While pruning the model we were able to remove 64.4% of FLOPs from inference time. The final accuracy rate after pruning was of 75.86%.

Finally, in Table 4 the results for the pruning of the VGG-16 model for the Caltech-256 dataset are presented. The initial accuracy rate for the model on the Caltech-256 was of 76.98%, while after pruning we achieved an accuracy rate of 77.06%, maintaining network accuracy even after pruning. The method was able to prune away 39.9% of FLOPs from VGG-16 inference time. In Fig. 1 we can visualize the number of FLOPs from original and pruned networks on each dataset.

Results presented in this section show a high pruning rate, comparable with many of the related work on filter pruning. In [11], authors report a 34.2% pruning rate for the VGG-16 model on CIFAR-10. Even though the Caltech-265 and Flower-102 datasets have far more object classes than the CIFAR-10,

Table 3. Pruning results for VGG-16 with Flower-102.

Layer	Original		After pruning	
	Filters	FLOPs	Filters	FLOPs
conv1	64	1.8×10^8	23	6.46×10^7
conv2	64	3.71×10^9	22	1.27×10^9
conv3	128	1.85×10^9	46	6.66×10^8
conv4	128	3.7×10^9	58	1.39×10^9
conv5	256	1.85×10^9	87	6.29×10^8
conv6	256	3.7×10^9	107	1.55×10^9
conv7	256	3.7×10^9	70	1.01×10^9
conv8	512	1.85×10^9	195	7.05×10^8
conv9	512	3.7×10^9	178	1.29×10^9
conv10	512	3.7×10^9	166	1.20×10^9
conv11	512	9.25×10^8	177	3.20×10^8
conv12	512	9.25×10^8	192	2.47×10^8
conv13	512	9.25×10^8	182	3.29×10^8
fc14	0	2.06×10^8	0	2.06×10^8
fc15	0	3.36×10^7	0	3.36×10^7
fc16	0	8.35×10^5	0	8.35×10^5
Total	4224	3.1×10^{10}	1493	1.1×10^{10}

our tests still showed a higher pruning rate, with the exception of Caltech-256 on Alexnet which is slightly above. When comparing with the results obtained in [13], which was able to achieve a pruning rate of 59% with the VGG-16 on ImageNet, with our result on the VGG-16 model with Flower-102, of 64.4% pruning rate, could indicate that a more specific domain is able to achieve a higher pruning rate.

Although one of the models had a marginal drop accuracy rate, the overall results can show that, while pruning the network, the proposed method is still able to maintain network accuracy at a reasonable level.

The perceived difference in pruning rates for the VGG-16 model on the Caltech-256 and Flower-102 datasets also indicates that the method is able to achieve higher pruning rates for datasets with a more specific domain, as the Flower-102 has fewer classes and more closely related characteristics. While this observation holds untrue for the AlexNet case, this could be explained by the fewer number of filters on the final layers, which are more prone to identify higher levels of abstraction.

Table 4. Pruning results for VGG-16 with Caltech-256.

Layer	Original		After pruning	
	Filters	FLOPs	Filters	FLOPs
conv1	64	1.8×10^8	35	9.83×10^7
conv2	64	3.71×10^9	36	2.08×10^9
conv3	128	1.85×10^9	76	1.1×10^9
conv4	128	3.7×10^9	80	2.31×10^9
conv5	256	1.85×10^9	160	1.16×10^9
conv6	256	3.7×10^9	147	2.13×10^9
conv7	256	3.7×10^9	160	2.31×10^9
conv8	512	1.85×10^9	303	1.1×10^9
conv9	512	3.7×10^9	304	2.2×10^9
conv10	512	3.7×10^9	311	2.25×10^9
conv11	512	9.25×10^8	306	5.53×10^8
conv12	512	9.25×10^8	292	5.28×10^8
conv13	512	9.25×10^8	305	5.51×10^8
fc14	0	2.06×10^8	0	2.06×10^8
fc15	0	3.36×10^7	0	3.36×10^7
fc16	0	8.35×10^5	0	8.35×10^5
Total	4224	3.1×10^{10}	2515	1.86×10^{10}

5   Conclusion

This paper presents an evolutionary method for pruning filters in convolutional neural networks in order to enable fast deploy of efficient convolutional models. Our method works in three steps. At first, a model trained on a large dataset is chosen and its weights are transferred and trained to a new target task. Then we use genetic algorithms to chose pruning candidates for the final network. The genetic algorithm works by randomly selecting individuals for tournaments where the losing individual is randomly mutated. The final step consists of pruning the filters deemed unnecessary by the genetic algorithm and fine-tuning the network repair accuracy rate. The advantage of this approach to other pruning methods is the use of genetic algorithms to prune weights in the network level, avoiding pitfalls commonly encountered with greedy approaches that prune one layer at a time. As pruning is done in a data-driven way, the method is able to use the target task characteristics to efficiently guide pruning to every task. Thus, enabling its use with transfer learning.

Experimental results show that the method provides a pruning rate comparable with state-of-the-art pruning strategies while maintaining network accuracy. It enables convolutional models which are more efficient for a given dataset with none or very small loss in the overall accuracy rate. These features make the method promising for fast deployment of convolutional models on resource-limited devices.

Acknowledgments. This work was partially supported under grant no. 5850.0105377.17.9 by Petrobras S.A.

References

1. Anwar, S., Hwang, K., Sung, W.: Structured pruning of deep convolutional neural networks. ArXiv e-prints, December 2015
2. Chai, Y., Lempitsky, V., Zisserman, A.: BiCoS: a bi-level co-segmentation method for image classification. In: IEEE International Conference on Computer Vision, pp. 2579–2586. IEEE (2011)
3. Dean, J., et al.: Large scale distributed deep networks. In: Advances in Neural Information Processing Systems, pp. 1223–1231 (2012)
4. Everingham, M., Eslami, S.M.A., Van Gool, L., Williams, C.K.I., Winn, J., Zisserman, A.: The pascal visual object classes challenge: a retrospective. Int. J. Comput. Vis. **111**(1), 98–136 (2015)
5. Fei-Fei, L., Fergus, R., Perona, P.: Learning generative visual models from few training examples: an incremental bayesian approach tested on 101 object categories. Comput. Vis. Image Underst. **106**(1), 59–70 (2007)
6. Griffin, G., Holub, A., Perona, P.: Caltech-256 object category dataset (2007)
7. Han, S., Pool, J., Tran, J., Dally, W.: Learning both weights and connections for efficient neural network. In: Advances in Neural Information Processing Systems, pp. 1135–1143 (2015)
8. Konak, A., Coit, D.W., Smith, A.E.: Multi-objective optimization using genetic algorithms: a tutorial. Reliab. Eng. Syst. Saf. **91**(9), 992–1007 (2006)
9. Krizhevsky, A., Hinton, G.: Learning multiple layers of features from tiny images. Technical report, Citeseer (2009)
10. Krizhevsky, A., Sutskever, I., Hinton, G.E.: ImageNet classification with deep convolutional neural networks. In: Advances in Neural Information Processing Systems, pp. 1097–1105 (2012)
11. Li, H., Kadav, A., Durdanovic, I., Samet, H., Graf, H.P.: Pruning filters for efficient convnets. arXiv preprint arXiv:1608.08710 (2016)
12. Long, J., Shelhamer, E., Darrell, T.: Fully convolutional networks for semantic segmentation. In: Proceedings of the IEEE Conference on Computer Vision and Pattern Recognition, pp. 3431–3440 (2015)
13. Luo, J.H., Wu, J., Lin, W.: ThiNet: a filter level pruning method for deep neural network compression. arXiv preprint arXiv:1707.06342 (2017)
14. Molchanov, P., Tyree, S., Karras, T., Aila, T., Kautz, J.: Pruning convolutional neural networks for resource efficient transfer learning. CoRR abs/1611.06440 (2016), http://arxiv.org/abs/1611.06440
15. Nilsback, M.E., Zisserman, A.: Automated flower classification over a large number of classes. In: 2008 Sixth Indian Conference on Computer Vision, Graphics & Image Processing, ICVGIP 2008, pp. 722–729. IEEE (2008)
16. Oquab, M., Bottou, L., Laptev, I., Sivic, J.: Learning and transferring mid-level image representations using convolutional neural networks. In: 2014 IEEE Conference on Computer Vision and Pattern Recognition (CVPR), pp. 1717–1724. IEEE (2014)

17. Pan, S.J., Yang, Q.: A survey on transfer learning. IEEE Trans. Knowl. Data Eng. **22**(10), 1345–1359 (2010)
18. Russakovsky, O., et al.: ImageNet large scale visual recognition challenge. Int. J. Comput. Vis. **115**(3), 211–252 (2015)
19. Shazeer, N., et al.: Outrageously large neural networks: the sparsely-gated mixture-of-experts layer. arXiv preprint arXiv:1701.06538 (2017)
20. Simonyan, K., Zisserman, A.: Very deep convolutional networks for large-scale image recognition. arXiv preprint arXiv:1409.1556 (2014)
21. Szegedy, C., et al.: Going deeper with convolutions. In: CVPR (2015)
22. Wen, W., Wu, C., Wang, Y., Chen, Y., Li, H.: Learning structured sparsity in deep neural networks. In: Advances in Neural Information Processing Systems, pp. 2074–2082 (2016)
23. Zeiler, M.D., Fergus, R.: Visualizing and understanding convolutional networks. In: Fleet, D., Pajdla, T., Schiele, B., Tuytelaars, T. (eds.) ECCV 2014. LNCS, vol. 8689, pp. 818–833. Springer, Cham (2014). https://doi.org/10.1007/978-3-319-10590-1_53

Regularized Learning of Neural Network with Application to Sparse PCA

Jan Rodziewicz-Bielewicz, Jacek Klimaszewski[✉], and Marcin Korzeń

Faculty of Computer Science and Information Technology, West Pomeranian University of Technology in Szczecin, Żołnierska 49 street, 71-210 Szczecin, Poland
{jrodziewicz,jklimaszewski,mkorzen}@wi.zut.edu.pl

Abstract. The paper presents an implementation of the regularized two-layer neural network and its application to finding sparse components. The main part of the paper concerns the learning of the sparse regularized neural network and its use as auto-encoder. A process of learning of the neural network with non-convex optimization criterion is reduced to convex optimization with constraints in an extended domain. This approach is compared with the dictionary learning procedure. The experimental part presents the comparison of our implementation and the SparsePCA procedure from the Scikit-learn package on different data sets. As a quality of the solution during experiments we take into account: the time of learning, sparsity, and quality of reconstruction. The experiments show that our approach can be competitive when a higher sparsity is needed, and in the case of a large number of attributes relative to the number of instances.

Keywords: Neural network · Sparsity · ℓ^1 penalty · Sparse PCA · Auto-encoder

1 Introduction and Motivation

Principal Component Analysis (PCA) is a well-known technique of the dimensionality reduction of the data. The common PCA technique is not free of some disadvantages. For example, minimization of a variance of components is dependent on outliers [3]. In the standard approach most of variables have an influence on each principal component and its direct interpretation is difficult.

Opposite to this approach are sparse procedures that produce components which depend only on a small subset of input variables. The sparsity can be attractive from many points of view. Especially using the sparse representation of components one can save the memory space and decrease the time of computation. In the case of special types of signals with a certain structure of dependence like images, sounds or chemometric data, such an approach provides solutions

This work was financed by the National Science Centre, Poland. Research project no.: 2016/21/B/ST6/01495.

that have often natural meaning. As the solution, one can obtain separate regions in data, e.g. the mouth and eyes in the case of face images.

The sparsity is typically understood as the number of zero coefficients in the solution or as the relative number of zero coefficients in relation to the size of data. The sparsity of the solution is ensured by adding the ℓ^1-norm penalty term on coefficients to the common fitting criterion [4,13]. There are many different techniques to ensure a sparsity of components, including use Kullback-Leiber divergence as penalty term [10] or semi-definite programming [3]. Dictionary learning is another popular technique that is for example used in the **sklearn** package [5,9].

2   Proposed Solution

A special case approach to produce sparse components is to use the two-layer neural network (as in Fig. 1) and use it as an auto-encoder—the structure that is fitted to reproduce the input patterns on the output [1,10].

2.1   Neural Network with Sparse Weights

We consider a supervised learning task with the following notations: n is the number of observations and d is the number of attributes, $\mathbf{X}_{d \times n} = \{\mathbf{x}_1, \ldots, \mathbf{x}_n\}$ is an input part of the dataset and $\mathbf{Y}_{d \times n} = \{\mathbf{y}_1, \ldots, \mathbf{y}_n\}$ is the output. Let consider the positive part function:

$$(a_i)_+ = \max(a_i, 0) = \begin{cases} a_i, & \text{for } a_i > 0 \\ 0, & \text{otherwise} \end{cases},$$

the negative part function: $(a_i)_- = (-a_i)_+$, and similarly for the vector $\mathbf{a} = [a_1, \ldots, a_d]$, we use notation: $\mathbf{a}_+ = [(a_1)_+, \ldots, (a_d)_+]$ and $\mathbf{a}_- = [(a_1)_-, \ldots, (a_d)_-]$. We have $\mathbf{a} = \mathbf{a}_+ - \mathbf{a}_-$, and note that both negative and positive parts are non-negative.

We consider a two-layer neural network with p hidden units, as shown in the Fig. 1. The hidden layer output is given by:

$$\tilde{\mathbf{v}}(\mathbf{x}) = \sigma(\mathbf{W}^1 \cdot \mathbf{x} + \mathbf{b}^1), \tag{1}$$

and the network output is given by:

$$\tilde{\mathbf{y}}(\mathbf{x}) = \sigma(\mathbf{W}^2 \cdot \mathbf{V} + \mathbf{b}^2) = \sigma(\mathbf{W}^2 \cdot \sigma(\mathbf{W}^1 \cdot \mathbf{x} + \mathbf{b}^1) + \mathbf{b}^2), \tag{2}$$

where $\sigma(\cdot)$ is the activation function, and $\mathbf{W}^1_{p \times d}$, $\mathbf{b}^1_{p \times 1}$, $\mathbf{W}^2_{d \times p}$ and $\mathbf{b}^2_{d \times 1}$ are weights and biases for the first and the second layer respectively.

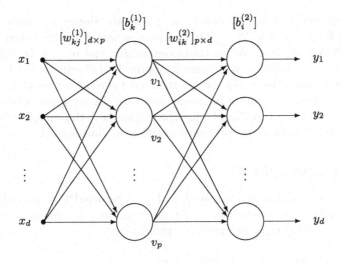

Fig. 1. Two-layer neural network.

Learning Procedure. The goal of fitting the network is to find minimum:

$$\underset{\mathbf{W}^1, \mathbf{b}^1, \mathbf{W}^2, \mathbf{b}^2}{\arg \min} \frac{1}{2n} \sum_{i=1}^{n} \| \sigma \left(\mathbf{W}^2 \sigma \left(\mathbf{W}^1 \mathbf{x}_i + \mathbf{b}^1 \right) + \mathbf{b}^2 \right) - \mathbf{y}_i \|_2^2 + \alpha \cdot \left(\| \mathbf{W}^1 \|_1 + \| \mathbf{W}^2 \|_1 \right),$$
(3)

where α is a regularization parameter. Due to non-differentiability of the ℓ^1-norm $\| \cdot \|_1$, we reformulate (3) into the equivalent bound-constrained smooth optimization problem, using the identity $|x| \equiv x_+ - x_-$ for $x_+, x_- \geqslant 0$:

$$\underset{\mathbf{W}_+^1, \mathbf{W}_-^1, \mathbf{b}^1, \mathbf{W}_+^2, \mathbf{W}_-^2, \mathbf{b}^2}{\arg \min} \frac{1}{2n} \sum_{i=1}^{n} \| \sigma \left(\mathbf{W}_*^2 \cdot \sigma \left(\mathbf{W}_*^1 \mathbf{x}_i + \mathbf{b}^1 \right) + \mathbf{b}^2 \right) - \mathbf{y}_i \|_2^2 +$$
$$+ \alpha \cdot \left(\mathbf{1}^T \mathbf{W}_+^1 \mathbf{1} + \mathbf{1}^T \mathbf{W}_-^1 \mathbf{1} + \mathbf{1}^T \mathbf{W}_+^2 \mathbf{1} + \mathbf{1}^T \mathbf{W}_-^2 \mathbf{1} \right),$$
$$\mathbf{W}_+^1 \geqslant 0, \mathbf{W}_-^1 \geqslant 0, \mathbf{W}_+^2 \geqslant 0, \mathbf{W}_-^2 \geqslant 0,$$
(4)

where $\mathbf{W}_*^1 = \mathbf{W}_+^1 - \mathbf{W}_-^1$, $\mathbf{W}_*^2 = \mathbf{W}_+^2 - \mathbf{W}_-^2$. Operator '$\geqslant$' is applied element-wise. To solve (4), L-BFGS-B [14] procedure may be used. A similar approach was considered e.g. in [8,12] in the case of learning ℓ^1-penalized logistic regression.

The network can be fitted at once, or we can use the following expand procedure. Starting from one hidden unit ($p = 1$) the neural network is trained, then we expand the current solution by adding another unit—this operation inserts a new row in the matrix $\mathbf{W}_+^1$ and a new column in the matrix $\mathbf{W}_+^2$, and a new element in the vector $\mathbf{b}^1$. The same happens to matrices $\mathbf{W}_-^1$ and $\mathbf{W}_-^2$. New values are chosen randomly. After insertion, the training procedure is repeated.

Initial neural network weights can be set randomly. However, a more advantageous way is to initialize $\mathbf{W}^1$ with the transformation matrix taken from the ordinary PCA procedure, $\mathbf{W}^2$ as transpose matrix, and $\mathbf{b}^1 = 0$, $\mathbf{b}^2 = 0$.

The presented solution is a general approach that can be used to fitting general sparse neural networks. To use such a network as auto-encoder we set σ as identity (a linear activation function), and take the input part of data as the target. The k-th row of $\mathbf{W}^1$ can be interpreted as the k-th principal component, and $\mathbf{W}^2$ is the matrix of inverse transformation to dimension d.

2.2 Sklearn SparsePCA

The presented solution is compared with the **SparsePCA** procedure from **scikit-learn**. In this procedure, a dictionary learning approach [5,9] is used, and it solves the following optimization problem:

$$
(\mathbf{U}^*, \mathbf{V}^*) = \arg \min_{U,V} \frac{1}{2} \|\mathbf{X} - \mathbf{V}\mathbf{U}\|_2^2 + \alpha \|\mathbf{V}\|_1
$$

$$
\text{subject to } \|U_k\|_2 = 1 \text{ for all } 0 \le k < p_{components}
$$

(5)

Looking at (3) we have $\|\mathbf{X} - \mathbf{W}^2\mathbf{W}^1\mathbf{X}\|_2^2$, with $\mathbf{W}^2$ corresponding to $\mathbf{V}$ and $\mathbf{W}^1\mathbf{X}$ corresponding to $\mathbf{U}$. In the auto-encoder both weight matrices are sparse and a more natural is use $\mathbf{W}^1$ as the transformation matrix and $\mathbf{W}^2$ as inverse transformation.

3   Experiments

All experiments were conducted in the **Python/sklearn** environment. In experiments we compare two methods: (1) **SparsePCA**, from **Python**'s package scikit-learn [11] and (2) our regularized two-layer neural network (**neural_network**) with linear activation function, implemented in **C++**.

Data sets Following data sets were compared (details are shown in Table 1):

- Gasoline dataset—this dataset is taken from the R package **pls** [6] and contains 60 near-infrared spectra signals for gasoline sample, described by 401 attributes, corresponding to wavelengths from 900 nm to 1700 nm.
- MNIST—MNIST dataset [7] is a large dataset of handwritten digits, that contains 60 000 training and 10 000 testing images on matrices 28×28, which results in 784 attributes.
- The Olivetti faces—this dataset [2] from **scikit-learn** package [11] contains a set of 400 face images - 10 different images per each distinct subject. Images are on matrices 64×64, which results in 4096 attributes. Images were taken at different times, varying the lighting, facial expressions and facial details (presence of glasses).

Table 1. Information about data sets.

Data set	Samples	Features	Range of attributes
Gasoline	60	401	[-0.084, 1.33]
MNIST	60000	784	[0, 255]
Olivetti faces	400	4096	[0, 1]

For all models, the separate test set was used. For MNIST the testing set is provided. Remaining datasets were not split into the learning and testing part, therefore the learning and testing part was chosen randomly using train_test_split function in a proportion 1:1. The number of iterations and tolerance for learning algorithms was set arbitrarily as 1000 for iterations and a tolerance 10^{-3}.

We also set biases $\mathbf{b}^1$ and $\mathbf{b}^2$ in the **neural_network** to zeros, therefore the data is not centered by features medians, like in the **SparsePCA**.

In the experiment, we compared the time of computations and quality of algorithms for different regularization parameter α. In this experiment, the number of fitted components was set to 50 for faces and MNIST, and 10 for gasoline. Both solutions are fitted in the same conditions in the one-thread model. The only parallel part was the n-fold cross-validation with one thread per fold. The experiments were performed on the machine with Xeon E5-2699 v4 2.20 GHz CPU and 128GB RAM. The following fitting-testing procedure was used:

```
for trial_num in [1, ..., number_of_trials]:
    x_train, x_test = train_test_split(X, test_size=0.5)
    for model in [SparsePCA, neural_network]:
        for alpha in list_of_alphas:
            model.fit(x_train)
            mse_train[trial_num] = score(model, x_train)
            mse_test[trial_num] = score(model, x_test)
score_train = mean(mse_train)
score_test = mean(mse_test)
```

Two compared solutions use a bit different optimization criteria and it results in a bit different meaning of the regularization parameter α. In order to provide comparable and similar conditions of the experiment, we present the quality measures with respect to the sparsity of solutions. This means that two models with the same sparsity were compared in time computations and the quality of reconstruction. As the measure of quality, a standard mean squared error of reconstruction (mse) is used. *Sparsity* means an average number of zero coefficients per component.

Table 2. A detailed comparison of our approach (**neural_network**) with **sklearn** procedure **SparsePCA** and ordinary **PCA** procedure. *Sparsity* means an average number of zero coeficients per component.

Data	Neural network					Sklearn SparsePCA					PCA		
	α	MSE train	MSE test	Time	Sparsity	α	MSE train	MSE test	Time	Sparsity	MSE train	MSE test	Time
Gasoline	1.4e−5	4.4e−6	7.3e−6	0.073	0.09	2.3e−4	1.2e−6	1.1e−5	10.57	65.65	0.016	0.016	0.064
	2.7e−5	4.5e−6	7.3e−6	0.071	0.62	5.2e−4	1.3e−6	1.2e−5	11.08	86.63			
	5.2e−5	7.4e−6	1.2e−5	0.469	115.1	0.001	1.6e−6	1.3e−5	7.915	121.3			
	1.0e−4	1.7e−5	2.4e−5	1.205	339.7	0.003	2.4e−6	1.4e−5	8.058	174.5			
	1.9e−4	2.3e−5	3.0e−5	1.268	374.8	0.006	4.6e−6	2.1e−5	7.459	225.9			
Olivetti faces	1.0e−4	2.0e−3	3.8e−3	392.6	564.8	0.014	2.0e−3	3.9e−3	163.5	344.0	6.4e−3	8.2e−3	2.118
	3.7e−4	2.0e−3	3.9e−3	281.5	2212	0.032	2.3e−3	3.8e−3	2699	1332			
	7.2e−4	2.1e−3	4.0e−3	268.3	2927	0.072	2.8e−3	3.9e−3	1542	2190			
	1.4e−3	2.3e−3	4.1e−3	248.4	3371	0.164	3.3e−3	4.2e−3	485.4	2817			
	2.7e−3	2.9e−3	4.4e−3	228.9	3375	0.373	4.3e−3	5.2e−3	180.5	3347			
MNIST	0.019	766.1	770.9	2969	204.4	5.179	766.1	771.0	46.83	191.2	778.9	783.7	0.864
	2.683	766.3	771.0	1271	362.5	13.89	766.3	771.1	46.08	230.7			
	19.31	769.2	773.7	1264	521.9	100.0	775.7	780.3	85.00	351.9			
	138.9	825.9	829.5	1268	746.1	268.3	831.7	835.2	755.6	616.8			
	372.8	901.9	904.4	1250	770.7	1931	1118	1119	127.7	762.6			

A detailed comparison of our approach (**neural_network**) with **sklearn** procedure **SparsePCA** and an ordinary **PCA** procedure are presented in Table 2. In Fig. 2 times of computations, quality of reconstruction and the regularization parameter α relative to given sparsity are presented.

As one can see in Fig. 2, despite the fact that **SparsePCA** is quite faster for larger sparsity, the proposed solution (**neural_network**) holds on the accuracy of reconstruction for a larger sparsity on both train and test set.

The comparison of components on the faces dataset are shown in Fig. 7. Different colors mean negative and positive coefficients, and white is exact zero. Additionally, for comparison, we present results for ordinary PCA procedure and covariance matrices for components. Orthogonality of components for ordinary PCA is theoretically guaranteed. Looking at covariance matrices we see that components found by the **neural_network** are nearly orthogonal, more than those found by the **SparsePCA**. Similar results for MNIST and gasoline are presented in Figs. 3 and 8.

The quality of reconstruction of images is shown in Figs. 5 and 6 (50 components), and reconstruction for the spectra data gasoline (10 components) is shown in Fig. 4. As one can see even for a such number of components the quality is quite good. For very similar sparsity our approach gives a better quality of reconstruction in contrast to the **SparsePCA**. For faces, one can observe a bit clearer details like glasses or moustaches. For gasoline with the same sparsity (about 80% i.e. 320 zero coefficients) quality of our **neural_network** approach is much better. For datasets gasoline and faces, where there were relatively few samples the quality of reconstruction of both sparse methods is much better then for the common **PCA** procedure.

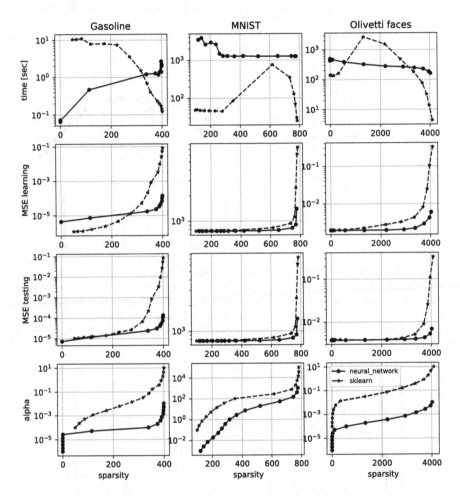

Fig. 2. The comparison of our **neural_network** approach with the **SparsePCA/sklearn** procedure. The *Sparsity* means an average number of zero coefficients per component, α (*alpha*) is the regularization parameter.

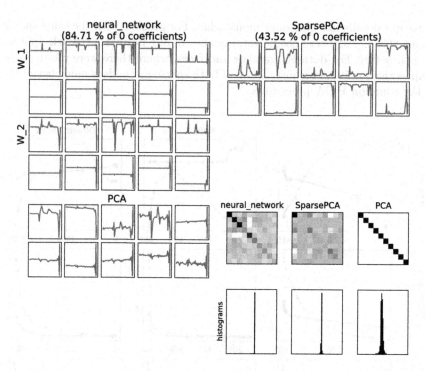

Fig. 3. The comparison of 10 components on gasoline dataset. Blue colors are components and red colors are vectors used to the reconstruction (output layer weights $\mathbf{W}^2$). Below for comparison we present results of the ordinary **PCA** procedure. In the bottom right there are presented covariance matrices for components and histograms of models' coefficients. Sparsity: **neural_network** (93.47%),**sklearn/SparsePCA** (56.33%), **PCA** (0%).

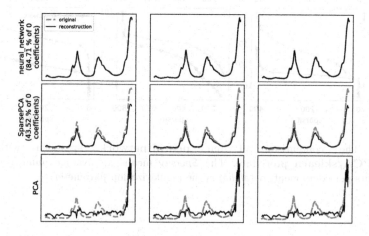

Fig. 4. The quality of reconstruction on the gasoline dataset for **neural_network**, **SparsePCA**and ordinary **PCA** respectively. Original signals are dashed, reconstructions are a solid lines.

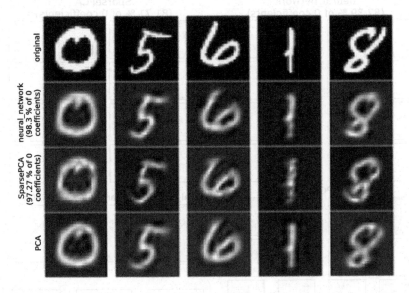

Fig. 5. The quality of reconstruction on the MNIST dataset. In the first row there are original images and below there is reconstruction using **neural_network**, **SparsePCA** and ordinary **PCA** respectively.

Fig. 6. The quality of reconstruction on the faces dataset. In the first row there are original images and below there is reconstruction using **neural_network**, **SparsePCA** and ordinary **PCA** respectively.

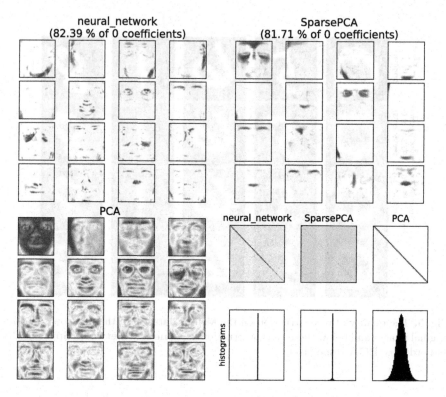

Fig. 7. The comparison of 16 components (of all 50) on faces dataset. Red colors are negative, blue are positive and white is exact zero. Bottom left: the results of the ordinary **PCA** procedure, and in bottom right: covariance matrices for components and histograms of models coefficients are presented. Sparsity: **neural_network** (82.39%),**sklearn/SparsePCA** (81.71%), **PCA**(0%).

4   Summary

In the paper, the procedure for learning sparse neural networks was presented. Such structure can be adopted as auto-encoder and effectively used to learning sparse components. In experimental part comparison with SparsePCA procedure from **scikit-learn** was presented. As one can observe our solution is time attractive at least for certain areas of sparsity especially for data with a small number of samples relative to the number of attributes. For a larger number of examples SparsePCA procedure is a bit faster. However, our solution holds on accuracy in the wider scope of sparsity, also for larger sparsity (when our solution is a bit slower). The quality of reconstruction in both sparse procedures is quite similar and it is better than those obtained by the ordinary PCA procedure. However, using our approach we could get a better sparsity with the same accuracy than in SparsePCA. Orthogonality of components is also better for our approach than in the SparsePCA procedure.

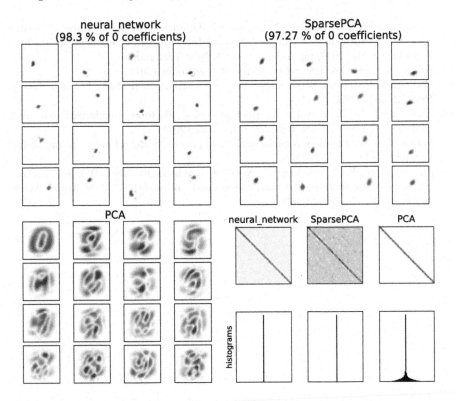

Fig. 8. The comparison of 16 components on the MNIST dataset. Red colors are negative, blue are positive and white is exact zero. Below for comparison we present results of the ordinary PCA procedure, and in the bottom right there are presented covariance matrices for components.**neural_network** (98.3% of 0 coefficients) approach with **sklearn** procedure **SparsePCA** (97.27% of 0 coefficients).

References

1. Bourlard, H., Kamp, Y.: Auto-association by multilayer perceptrons and singular value decomposition. Biol. Cybern. **59**(4), 291–294 (1988)
2. AT&T Laboratories Cambridge. The database of faces (1994)
3. d'Aspremont, A., Ghaoui, L.E., Jordan, M., Lanckriet, G.: A direct formulation for sparse PCA using semidefinite programming. CoRR, cs.CE/0406021, July 2004
4. Hastie, T., Tibshirani, R., Friedman, J.: The Elements of Statistical Learning. SSS. Springer, New York (2009). https://doi.org/10.1007/978-0-387-84858-7
5. Jenatton, R., Obozinski, G., Bach, F.: Structured Sparse Principal Component Analysis (2009)
6. Kalivas, J.H.: Two data sets of near infrared spectra. Chemometr. Intell. Lab. Syst. **37**, 255–259 (1997)
7. LeCun, Y., Cortes, C.: MNIST Handwritten Digit Database (2010)
8. Lin, C.-J., Weng, R.C., Sathiya Keerthi, S.: Trust region Newton method for logistic regression. J. Mach. Learn. Res. **9**, 627–650 (2008)

9. Mairal, J., Bach, F., Ponce, J., Sapiro, G.: Online dictionary learning for sparse coding. In: Proceedings of the 26th Annual International Conference on Machine Learning, ICML 2009, pp. 689–696. ACM, New York (2009)
10. Ng, A.: CS294A Lecture Notes: Sparse Autoencoder (2019)
11. Pedregosa, F., et al.: Scikit-learn: machine learning in python. J. Mach. Learn. Res. **12**, 2825–2830 (2011)
12. Shalev-Shwartz, S., Tewari, A.: Stochastic methods for ℓ_1-regularized loss minimization. J. Mach. Learn. Res. **12**, 1865–1892 (2011)
13. Williams, P.M.: Bayesian regularization and pruning using a Laplace prior. Neural Comput. **7**, 117–143 (1995)
14. Zhu, C., Byrd, R.H., Peihuang, L., Nocedal, J.: Algorithm 778: L-BFGS-B: Fortran subroutines for large-scale bound-constrained optimization. ACM Trans. Math. Softw. **23**(4), 550–560 (1997)

Trimmed Robust Loss Function for Training Deep Neural Networks with Label Noise

Andrzej Rusiecki[✉][iD]

Department of Computer Engineering, Wroclaw University of Science
and Technology, Wybrzeże Wyspiańskiego 27, Wrocław, Poland
andrzej.rusiecki@pwr.edu.pl

Abstract. Deep neural networks obtain nowadays outstanding results
on many vision, speech recognition and natural language processing-
related tasks. Such deep structures need to be trained on very large
datasets, what makes annotating the data for supervised learning, particularly difficult and time-consuming task. In the supervised datasets
label noise may occur, which makes the whole training process less reliable. In this paper we present a novel robust loss function based on categorical cross-entropy. We demonstrate its robustness for several amounts
of noisy labels, on popular MNIST and CIFAR-10 datasets.

Keywords: Neural networks · Deep learning · Robust learning ·
Label noise · Categorical cross-entropy

1 Introduction

In many sophisticated machine learning tasks such as computer vision, speech
recognition, or natural language processing, deep neural networks have demonstrated impressive results, very often outperforming existing, state-of-the-art
results [2]. By training deep networks on large supervised datasets, deep learning
algorithms are able to establish models that can potentially represent high-level
abstractions [3,22]. One of the reasons for deep learning popularity and success
is clearly the fact that nowadays many well-annotated large data collections are
publicly available [25].

Similarly to shallow multilayer feedforward neural networks, deep structures
are usually considered as reliable and easy-to-use tools. However, in such data-
driven approaches, quality of models strongly depends on the quality of their
training data [1,14]. To train deeper networks, usually very large annotated
datasets are required, which makes the process of preparing training data expensive and relatively time-consuming. Moreover, annotating data by many different
human annotators, search engines, or data mining algorithms analyzing social
media websites, is followed by rather obvious side effect, namely: label noise. In
this paper, we describe in details a new approach introduced in [21], combining well-known cross-entropy loss with an idea of trimmed robust estimators, to
obtain robust learning in the presence of label noise.

© Springer Nature Switzerland AG 2019
L. Rutkowski et al. (Eds.): ICAISC 2019, LNAI 11508, pp. 215–222, 2019.
https://doi.org/10.1007/978-3-030-20912-4_21

2   Robust Learning and Label Noise

Learning from noisy data has been studied previously in two main fields. The first one is learning in the presence of outliers, defined as observations distant from the bulk of the data. Such data points can be results of long-tailed noise, but also of measurement errors, or human mistakes. The quantity of outliers may range from 1% up to even 10% [9]. Typically, the problem of outlying data has been investigated for regression-like tasks, where dependent variables are continuous. However, in the case of corrupted input patterns (leverage points) one may consider classification problems as well.

The latter field of study is learning from noisy labels for classification tasks. In this domain also two basic current exists: cleaning data by removing or correcting noisy patterns, and robust learning from noisy data.

2.1   Dealing with Outliers

Multilayer neural networks minimizing mean squared error (MSE) loss, typical for regression tasks, try to match training patterns as close as possible, incorporating into their model also potential outlying data points. This is why many robust learning algorithms have been proposed [1,4,6,14,19,20]. The basic idea of such approaches is to replace MSE by another loss function, so they are often based on robust error measures. Hence, the robustness to outliers is achieved by reducing the impact of large training residuals, potentially caused by gross errors or outliers. Good review of such methods can be found in [11].

Another group of approaches are instance selection algorithms. They can be applied also to classification problems. These algorithms fall into two categories: compression methods and noise filters. Compression methods such as the CNN (Condensed Nearest Neighbor) algorithm [28] are designed to remove instances too similar to its neighbors. An example of noise filter is the ENN (Edited Nearest Neighbor) algorithm [28]. This method removes instances that are too different from the rest of the data. A large survey of instance selection algorithms for classification tasks appeared in [23].

2.2   Learning from Noisy Labels

Noisy labels are not identical with outliers, however there exist many similarities in dealing with such problems. In the case of training neural networks in the presence of label noise, the methods also can be divided into two groups.

There are many, recently proposed, approaches in the literature that aim to learn directly from noisy labels [8,10,15,18,26]. The authors usually focus on designing robust learning algorithms or even try to use large, weakly-labeled data collections, slightly modifying training process in hope that the resulting model can be acceptably accurate. In the second group of approaches, efforts are directed to clean data by removing or correcting erroneous labels. In some models the label noise is considered as conditionally independent from the input [16,24], while the others propose image-conditional models [27,29].

Approaches using modified or corrected losses were presented in [7] and [17]. In this paper we describe and evolve a new loss function based on categorical cross-entropy, robust to label noise [21].

3 New Robust Loss Function

To introduce a new robust loss function, we start with derivation of Least Trimmed Absolute Value (LTA) criterion proposed in our previous work [20]. Such modified error function was experimentally proved to be an effective tool to make the whole training algorithm more robust to outlying data points.

3.1 LTA Error Criterion

Based on the Least Trimmed Absolute value estimator, a new error criterion was proposed in [20], as a training loss robust to outliers and leverage points. We assume that the training set consists of N pairs:
$\{(x_1, t_1), (x_2, t_2), \ldots, (x_N, t_N)\}$, where $x_i \in R^\gamma$ denotes the γ-dimensional ith input vector, $t_i \in R^C$ the corresponding C-dimensional network target, and $y_i \in R^C$ its output. Robust LTA error criterion can be defined as:

$$E_{LTA} = \sum_{i=1}^{h} (|r|)_{i:N}, \tag{1}$$

where $(|r|)_{1:N} \leq \cdots \leq (|r|)_{N:N}$ are ordered absolute network output residuals written as:

$$r_i = \sum_{c=1}^{C} |(y_{ic} - t_{ic})|. \tag{2}$$

As one may notice, the error function given by Eq. (1) excludes from the training process patterns causing largest errors in a given epoch. If the estimated amount of outliers in the training data is known, then scaling factor h can be set empirically. Otherwise it can be is estimated based on the median of all absolute deviations from the median (MAD):

$$\text{MAD} (r_i) = 1.483 \text{ median}|r_i - median(r_i)|, \tag{3}$$

and the trimming parameter can be fixed or calculated as [20]:

$$h = \|\{r_i : |r_i| < 3 * \text{MAD}(|r_i|), i = 1 \ldots N\}\|. \tag{4}$$

3.2 Categorical Cross-Entropy

As one may notice, the LTA loss (like MSE) doesn't seem to be a proper choice for classification problems. As a matter of fact, neural networks cab be trained on classification taks with these error measures but their expected performance is poorer than in case of using binary or categorical cross-entropy loss.

Categorical cross-entropy loss (CCE) can be technically written as:

$$E_{CC} = -\frac{1}{N} \sum_{i=1}^{N} \sum_{c=1}^{C} (p_{ic} \log(y_{ic})), \tag{5}$$

where p_{ic} is a binary indicator function that detects whether the ith training pattern belongs to cth category. In other terms, one may interpret p_{ic} (target) as true, and y_{ic} (output) as predicted probability distribution for ith observation belonging to cth class.

3.3   Trimmed Categorical Cross-Entropy

In order to combine the advantages of using CCE loss and robustness to outlying data points obtained by the LTA error, we decided to propose new function to be minimized during network training [21]. Trimmed categorical cross-entropy loss is then defined as:

$$E_{TCC} = -\frac{1}{h} \sum_{i=1}^{h} q_{i:N}, \tag{6}$$

where $q_{1:N} \leq \cdots \leq q_{N:N}$ are ordered losses for each observation:

$$q_i = \sum_{c=1}^{C} (p_{ic} \log(y_{ic})). \tag{7}$$

The trimming parameter h can be set *a priori* based on the expected amount of label noise.

4   Experimental Results

To test the novel approach, we decided to use two well-known classification datasets, namely MNIST [13] and CIFAR-10 [12]. The performance of two variants of trimmed CCE was compared to results obtained by two other popular training losses, used to train deep neural networks in the presence of label noise. Similar preliminary results, obtained for networks trained without dropout regularization we presented in [21]. In this paper, however, we analyse the case of training with regularization, which should make the whole method less sensitive to label noise.

4.1   Testing Methodology

In our simulations we used deep convolutional neural networks (CNN) implemented with Python 3.6 in TesorFlow environment under Ubuntu 16.04. To speed up network training all the simulations were run on GTX 1080Ti GPU. We followed network architectures provided in [7] for both datasets. The details of hidden layers architectures were gathered in Table 1. However, top accuracies obtained in our experiments are slightly different from those described in [7], probably due to algorithm hyperparameters.

Table 1. Network architectures and dataset characteristic

Dataset	Deep architecture
MNIST (Input 28 × 28, 10 classes, 60k/10k training/test)	Convolution → max pooling (dropout 0.25) → fully connected 1024 neurons (dropout 0.25) → fully connected 1024 neurons (dropout 0.5)
CIFAR-10 (Input 32 × 32 × 3, 10 classes, 50k/10k training/test)	2 Convolutional layers → max pooling (dropout 0.2) → 2 Convolutional layers → max pooling (dropout 0.2) → fully connected 512 neurons (dropout 0.5)

Label Noise. To simulate label noise we applied so-called uniform noise model. In this case, for each training pattern, its label is correct with probability $1 - \mu$ and with probability μ it is uniformly sampled within the set of all available incorrect labels. To simulate different levels of noise we varied μ from $\mu = 0$ up to $\mu = 0.6$, which is equivalent to about 60% of incorrect labels in the training data.

Training Algorithm. Deep neural nets were trained with Adam algorithm that is shown to be robust against noisy gradients [5]. The training parameters were set to: learning rate $lr = 0.001$, $\beta_1 = 0.9$ and $\beta_2 = 0.999$, and the networks were trained for 250 epochs. We examined trimmed CCE with two values of trimming constant: $h = 0.9$ and $h = 0.7$. Test accuracies were averaged over 6 runs of simulations (one training took approximately 25 min on 1080Ti GPU).

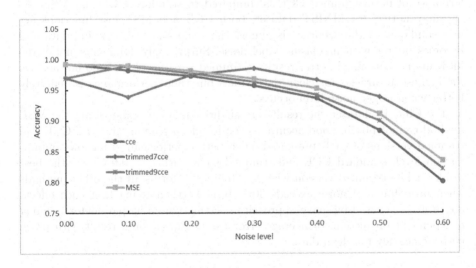

Fig. 1. Averaged test accuracy for several levels of label noise for MNIST dataset: *cce* -CCE, *trimmed7cce* - trimmed CCE with $h = 0.7$, *trimmed9cce* - trimmed CCE with $h = 0.9$, and *MSE* - MSE.

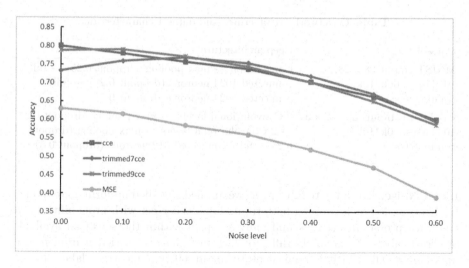

Fig. 2. Averaged test accuracy for several levels of label noise for CIFAR-10 dataset: *cce* -CCE, *trimmed7cce* - trimmed CCE with $h = 0.7$, *trimmed9cce* - trimmed CCE with $h = 0.9$, and *MSE* - MSE.

4.2   Simulation Results

In the Figs. 1 and 2 averaged results of training deep neural networks on datasets with several levels of contamination in training labels are presented. The performance of novel trimmed CCE is compared to standard CCE and MSE. As one may notice, for MNIST dataset, both CCE and MSE loss functions act in a similar way: the accuracy is almost the same for clean training data and becomes poorer with increasing label noise. Surprisingly, for higher noise, the MSE method obtained better results. Trimmed versions of CCE do not achieve the highest accuracies for clean data labels but their performance is definitely better when larger noise level occurs.

For Cifar-10 dataset the results are slightly different. First of all, the MSE method cannot obtain good accuracy even for clean training dataset. CCE and trimmed versions of CCE presented much better performance: for low contamination level, standard CCE and trimmed CCE with $h = 0.9$ obtain the best results, while trimmed version with $h = 0.7$ outperforms all the other methods when probability of noise exceeds 30%. It is worth noticing that such effects are probably caused by naive approach in setting trimming parameter. Making h dependent on median or average error (as in Eq. 4) could result with much better efficiency for clean data.

5 Conclusions

In this paper we presented a novel approach to training deep neural networks in the presence of label noise. As simulation experiments revealed, our new trimmed CCE loss, resulted in increased performance for contaminated training data labels. The trimmed CCE outperforms other algorithms especially for higher amounts of incorrect labels. The preliminary results obtained for the robust trimmed CCE loss are very promising, so the efforts should be now directed at verifying its behavior for more datasets and network architectures. Also designing an algorithm to calculate the trimming parameter automatically (e.g. making it a function of current errors) could help in improving its performance for clean datasets.

References

1. Chen, D., Jain, R.: A robust backpropagation learning algorithm for function approximation. IEEE Trans. Neural Netw. **5**(3), 467–479 (1994)
2. Erhan, D., et al.: Why does unsupervised pre-training help deep learning? J. Mach. Learn. Res. **11**, 560–625 (2010)
3. Bengio, Y., et al.: Greedy layer-wise training of deep networks. In: Advances in Neural Information Processing Systems, vol. 19, pp. 153–160. MIT Press (2007)
4. Chuang, C.C., Su, S.F., Hsiao, C.C.: The annealing robust backpropagation (ARBP) learning algorithm. IEEE Trans. Neural Netw. **11**(5), 1067–1077 (2000)
5. Kingma, D., Ba, J.: Adam: A method for stochastic optimization. arXiv preprint arXiv:1412.6980 (2014)
6. El-Melegy, M., Essai, M., Ali, A.: Robust training of artificial feedforward neural networks. In: Hassanien, A.E., Abraham, A., Vasilakos, A., Pedrycz, W. (eds.) Foundations of Computational, Intelligence Volume 1, Studies in Computational Intelligence, vol. 201, pp. 217–242. Springer, Heidelberg (2009). https://doi.org/10.1007/978-3-642-01082-8_9
7. Ghosh, A., Kumar, H., Sastry, P.S.: Robust Loss Functions under Label Noise for Deep Neural Networks, arXiv:1712.09482v1 (2017)
8. Guan, M.Y., Gulshan, V., Dai, A.M., Hinton, G.E.: Who said what: Modeling individual labelers improves classification. arXiv:1703.08774 (2017)
9. Hampel, F.R., Ronchetti, E.M., Rousseeuw, P.J., Stahel, W.A.: Robust Statistics: The Approach Based on Influence Functions. (Wiley Series in Probability and Statistics). Wiley-Interscience, New York (2005)
10. Joulin, A., van der Maaten, L., Jabri, A., Vasilache, N.: Learning visual features from large weakly supervised data. In: Leibe, B., Matas, J., Sebe, N., Welling, M. (eds.) ECCV 2016. LNCS, vol. 9911, pp. 67–84. Springer, Cham (2016). https://doi.org/10.1007/978-3-319-46478-7_5
11. Korodos, M., Rusiecki, A.: Reducing noise impact on MLP training. Soft Comput. **20**(1), 49–65 (2016)
12. Krizhevsky, A.: Learning Multiple Layers of Features from Tiny Images, Technical report (2009)
13. LeCun, Y., Cortes, C.: MNIST handwritten digit database. http://yann.lecun.com/exdb/mnist/
14. Liano, K.: Robust error measure for supervised neural network learning with outliers. IEEE Trans. Neural Netw. **7**(1), 246–250 (1996)

15. Misra, I., Lawrence, C.Z., Mitchell, M., Girshick, R.: Seeing through the human reporting bias: visual classifiers from noisy human-centric labels. In: Computer Vision and Pattern Recognition (CVPR) (2016)

16. Natarajan, N., Inderjit, S.D., Ravikumar, P.K., Tewari, A.: Learning with noisy labels. In: Advances in Neural Information Processing Systems (NIPS) (2013)

17. Patrini, G., Rozza, A., Menon, A, Nock, R., Qu, L.: Making neural networks robust to label noise: a loss correction approach. In: Computer Vision and Pattern Recognition (2017)

18. Reed, S., Lee, H., Anguelov, D., Szegedy, C., Erhan, D., Rabinovich, A.: Training deep neural networks on noisy labels with boot- strapping. arXiv preprint arXiv:1412.6596 (2014)

19. Rusiecki, A.: Robust learning algorithm based on iterative least median of squares. Neural Process. Lett. **36**(2), 145–160 (2012)

20. Rusiecki, A.: Robust learning algorithm based on LTA estimator. Neurocomputing **120**, 624–632 (2013)

21. Rusiecki, A.: Trimmed categorical cross-entropy for deep learning with label noise. Electron. Lett. **55**(6), 319–320 (2019)

22. Salakhutdinov, R., Hinton, G.E.: Semantic hashing. In: Proceedings of the 2007 Workshop on Information Retrieval and Applications of Graphical Models (SIGIR 2007). Elsevier, Amsterdam (2007)

23. Salvador, G., Derrac, J., Ramon, C.: Prototype selection for nearest neighbor classification: taxonomy and empirical study. IEEE Trans. Pattern Anal. Mach. Intell. **34**, 417–435 (2012)

24. Sukhbaatar, S., Bruna, J., Paluri, M., Bourdev, L., Fergus, R.: Training convolutional networks with noisy labels. arXiv preprint arXiv:1406.2080 (2014)

25. Vahdat, A.: Toward robustness against label noise in training deep discriminative neural networks. In: Neural Information Processing Systems (NIPS) (2017)

26. Van Horn, G., et al.: Building a bird recognition app and large scale dataset with citizen scientists: the fine print in fine-grained dataset collection. In: Computer Vision and Pattern Recognition (CVPR) (2015)

27. Veit, A., Alldrin, N., Chechik, G., Krasin, I., Gupta, A., Belongie, S.: Learning from noisy large-scale datasets with minimal supervision. In: Computer Vision and Pattern Recognition (CVPR) (2017)

28. Wilson, D.L.: Asymptotic properties of nearest neighbor rules using edited data. IEEE Trans. Syst. Man Cybern. **3**, 408–421 (1972). SMC-2

29. Xiao, T., Xia, T., Yang, Y., Huang, C., Wang, X.: Learning from massive noisy labeled data for image classification. In: Proceedings of the IEEE Conference on Computer Vision and Pattern Recognition (CVPR), pp. 2691–2699 (2015)

On Proper Designing of Deep Structures for Image Classification

Piotr Woldan[1]([⊠]) [iD], Paweł Staszewski[1] [iD], Leszek Rutkowski[1] [iD],
and Konrad Grzanek[2,3]

[1] Institute of Computational Intelligence, Czestochowa University of Technology,
Al. Armii Krajowej 36, 42-200 Czestochowa, Poland
`piotr.woldan@iisi.pcz.pl`
[2] Information Technology Institute University of Social Sciences,
Sienkiewicza 9, 90-113 Lodz, Poland
[3] Clark University, Worcester, MA, USA
`http://iisi.pcz.pl/`

Abstract. In this paper, we present several approaches to configuration of deep convolutional neural networks for image classification. A common problem when creating deep structures is their proper designing and configuration. This paper shows the learning of the baseline model for image classification and its variations with different structures based on the baseline model. Each of them has different configurations related to downsampling, pooling and filters dilatation. The paper is intended as a guideline for proper designing of deep structures based on experiences resulting from the modifications of deep models configurations.

Keywords: Convolutional neural network · Deep structure ·
Deep learning · Downsampling · Pooling · Filter dilatation

1 Introduction

When designing a deep structure intended to classify objects in an image, we usually have a lot of questions. There are several factors that must be taken while selecting a proper structure. How many layers should our model have? How to configure the entire structure? Which parameters to set during learning? Often, structures are designed in an experimental way. Of course, some of the indicators suggest when we have a problem with overfitting of the model to the training set [14] or with the vanishing gradient [16]. At the moment when we notice such a problem, depending on the situation, we are able to modify our model or learning parameters to prevent this kind of situations. Unfortunately, all modifications that we make in our structure are performed experimentally, based on very general information about a given problem.

A very popular approach to structure design is the use one of many existing models (see e.g. Fig. 1). In many articles, it can be seen that for solving a given problem, researchers reach for models that have already confirmed their effectiveness while solving other issues [5,8,9,12,22,24]. In order to use the existing

L. Rutkowski et al. (Eds.): ICAISC 2019, LNAI 11508, pp. 223–235, 2019.
https://doi.org/10.1007/978-3-030-20912-4_22

model for our research, it should work effectively on an issue of a similar complexity to our problem. However, we usually have only a few possibilities due to the limited number of verified structures. A problem arises when our issue is completely different from the most popular ones, which makes it impossible to find an existing model. Such a situation usually happens during the implementation of business projects, where most projects are unique in their field.

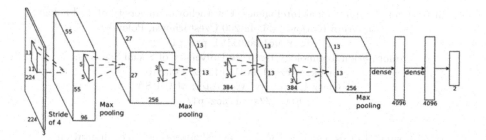

Fig. 1. An example of Deep Convolutional Neural Network (DCNN).

At the moment when our issue is very unique and we can not find the structure which is appropriate for us, then we have to design our own or modify an already existing one [23]. A very popular solution is to modify the existing structure to resolve our problem. This approach is called transfer learning. The problem then is choosing the right model and its modification. To select the most suitable structure, first we need to examine the complexity of our problem and choose a model that solves a problem similar to our (usually model is larger and solves more complex problems). The next step is the appropriate modification of this structure. Of course, some modifications cause the phenomenon of overfitting or vanishing gradient, which we have to resolve by the appropriate changing parameters of configurations.

Despite all these propositions, it sometimes turns out that such an approach is not enough. In this situation, we have only one solution, which is to create from scratch our own structure dedicated to aimed goals [15]. In this case, the task is very difficult. To create a perfect model for our problem, we must have a big experience in configuring deep structures from the very beginning. We need to know each configuration of parameters perfectly and understand how it affects the operation of our structure. Unfortunately, despite the extensive experience and many hours spent on various configuration variations, we often do not achieve satisfactory results. Of course, in the literature, we can find many different approaches to designing deep structures see e.g. [2,3,6,21]. However, this problem is very common, and deep neural networks are used for many different projects and we do not always find perfect configurations. Many of these applications require the design of our own model and each case has the problem of proper parameter configuration. Unfortunately, before our skills in designing structures will be high enough, we need to gain the right knowledge by practicing many modifications to understand how the changes affected the structure performance.

Motivated by this fact, in this paper we describe the basic structure for image classification, modifications of its configurations and explain how it influenced the processing inside the model. Obviously, the experience in designing deep structures is very valuable. For example, a good approach is designing a basic structure for classifying images and in the next step changing configuration parameters and analyzing how they affect the performance and efficiency. It is also good to pay attention not only to the depth but also to the dimensions of the propagated signal, which also can change during the experiments, e.g. a number of channels, changing stride configurations, changing pooling parameters. The number of such modifications is very large, so a proper guideline would decrease the search area to find the best configuration model.

The rest of this paper is organized as follows. Section 2 presents the dataset and architectures used for simulations. Section 3 describes commonly used methods of designing the structures and techniques of deep learning. Section 4 presents the experimental results with several changes in the configuration of the base structure, and the conclusions are drawn in Sect. 5.

2   Dataset and Architectures

2.1   Tiny ImageNet Dataset

The results presented in this article show the effectiveness of the images classification contained in the Tiny ImageNet database [11]. This dataset contains 100,000 training images divided into 200 categories (each class includes 500 images), 10,000 validation images and 10,000 test images. The size of each image in the database is 64×64 RGB pixels (see Fig. 2). This database is a fragment of scaled images from the ImageNet database [19].

Fig. 2. Sample images from the Tiny ImageNet database. (Color figure online)

2.2 Pre-processing

The original set of images (size 64 × 64 pixels) is expanded using one of the simple data augmentation techniques, which consist of image rotation. Each image from the training base is rotated by an angle of 30° to the left and to the right, thanks to which the original data set is tripled. In addition, for each of the original images, the horizontal and mirror transformation of the image has been done. These operations allow for a better generalization of the learning process. They also broaden the range of feature values of the classified objects, thanks to which the knowledge contained in the structure is much larger. The augmentation methods allow us to significantly reduce the vulnerability of our model to overfitting. Each pixel of images given at the input of structures shown in this article is normalized to $[-1, 1]$. It is also worth noting that the images were reduced by 4 pixels on each side because usually on the edge of the pictures there are not very important features. In this way, images with a size of 56 × 56 pixels are inputted to the neural network.

2.3 Baseline Architecture

The base structure (see Table 1) has been designed in such a way that it successfully copes with the problem of classification of the Tiny ImageNet, taking into account the short training time. The configuration of this structure has also been selected in such a way that it can be easily modified for simulation purposes. The base structure was created on the foundation of two cascades of convolutional layers. Each of the cascades consists of two layers of convolutions, followed by max pooling. The classifier in the model has three layers of fully connected neurons, each of which is supported in the training process by regularizing with the help of the Dropout method with the dropout rate = 0.5. In the basic structure, ELU type activation functions have been used, which largely eliminate the defects of ReLU type functions.

2.4 Modifications of the Baseline Architecture

In order to present the differences between various baseline model configurations, the modifications contain changes for pooling, downsampling and filters dilatation (see Table 1). By analyzing the learning process and the effectiveness presented during the simulation, we can verify how each of the changes affects its operation and the model performance.

3   Methods

3.1   Objective Function

To achieve good classification results, our model is learned by the classic stochastic gradient descent (SGD) method [4], although as an alternative approach various evolutionary techniques can be applied [1,7]. As a function of the cost,

Table 1. The configuration of the baseline model comparative to 5 models with modified configurations.

Configuration	Baseline	A	B	C	D	E
Layer	Conv	Conv	Conv	Conv	Conv	Conv
Channels	64	64	64	64	64	64
Kernel	5 × 5	5 × 5	5 × 5	5 × 5	5 × 5	5 ×5
Reg L2 (scale)	0.001	0.001	0.001	0.001	0.001	0.01
Stride	2 × 2	2 × 2	2 × 2	2 × 2	1 × 1	1 × 1
Activation	ELU	ELU	ELU	ELU	ELU	ELU
Zero padding	✓	✓	✓	✓	✓	✓
Layer	Conv	Conv	Conv	Conv	Conv	Conv
Channels	64	64	64	64	64	64
Kernel	3 × 3	3 × 3	3 × 3	3 × 3	3 × 3	3 × 3
Reg L2 (scale)	0.001	0.001	0.001	0.001	0.001	0.01
Stride	1 × 1	1 × 1	1 × 1	1 × 1	1 × 1	1 × 1
Dilation	1 × 1	1 × 1	2 × 2	2 × 2	1 × 1	1 × 1
Activation	ELU	ELU	ELU	ELU	ELU	ELU
Zero padding	✓	✓	✓	✓	✓	✓
Layer	Pool	Pool	Pool	Pool	Pool	Pool
Type	Max	Avg	Max	Avg	Max	Max
Size	2 × 2	2 × 2	2 × 2	2 × 2	2 × 2	2 × 2
Stride	2 × 2	2 × 2	2 × 2	2 × 2	2 × 2	2 × 2
Layer	Conv	Conv	Conv	Conv	Conv	Conv
Channels	64	64	64	64	64	64
Kernel	3 × 3	3 × 3	3 × 3	3 × 3	3 × 3	3 × 3
Reg L2 (scale)	0.001	0.001	0.001	0.001	0.001	0.01
Stride	1 × 1	1 × 1	1 × 1	1 × 1	1 × 1	1 × 1
Dilation	1 × 1	1 × 1	2 × 2	2 × 2	1 × 1	1 × 1
Activation	ELU	ELU	ELU	ELU	ELU	ELU
Zero padding	✓	✓	✓	✓	✓	✓
Layer	Conv	Conv	Conv	Conv	Conv	Conv
Channels	64	64	64	64	64	64
Kernel	3 × 3	3 × 3	3 × 3	3 × 3	3 × 3	3 × 3
Reg L2 (scale)	0.001	0.001	0.001	0.001	0.001	0.01
Stride	1 × 1	1 × 1	1 × 1	1 × 1	1 × 1	1 × 1
Dilation	1 × 1	1 × 1	2 × 2	2 × 2	1 × 1	1 × 1
Activation	ELU	ELU	ELU	ELU	ELU	ELU
Zero padding	✓	✓	✓	✓	✓	✓

Table 1. (*continued*)

Configuration	Baseline	A	B	C	D	E
Layer	Pool	Pool	Pool	Pool	Pool	Pool
Type	**Max**	**Avg**	**Max**	**Avg**	**Max**	**Max**
Size	2 × 2	2 × 2	2 × 2	2 × 2	2 × 2	2 × 2
Stride	2 × 2	2 × 2	2 × 2	2 × 2	2 × 2	2 × 2
Layer	FC	FC	FC	FC	FC	FC
Neurons	1024	1024	1024	1024	1024	1024
Reg L2 (scale)	**0.001**	**0.001**	**0.001**	**0.001**	**0.001**	**0.01**
Activation	ELU	ELU	ELU	ELU	ELU	ELU
Layer	Dropout	Dropout	Dropout	Dropout	Dropout	Dropout
Dropout rate	0.5	0.5	0.5	0.5	0.5	0.5
Layer	FC	FC	FC	FC	FC	FC
Neurons	1024	1024	1024	1024	1024	1024
Reg L2 (scale)	**0.001**	**0.001**	**0.001**	**0.001**	**0.001**	**0.01**
Activation	ELU	ELU	ELU	ELU	ELU	ELU
Layer	Dropout	Dropout	Dropout	Dropout	Dropout	Dropout
Dropout rate	0.5	0.5	0.5	0.5	0.5	0.5
Layer	FC	FC	FC	FC	FC	FC
Neurons	200	200	200	200	200	200
Reg L2 (scale)	**0.001**	**0.001**	**0.001**	**0.001**	**0.001**	**0.01**
Activation	Softmax	Softmax	Softmax	Softmax	Softmax	Softmax

we used the Cross-Entropy calculated from the Softmax activation. The L2 regularization was also used during learning, which significantly improves the generalization of the entire model [18].

3.2 Weight Initialization

A very important aspect of the basic initialization of the model is the correct selection of the weights. The weights in the deep neural network are usually chosen in a random way. It turns out that this is not the best approach because the weights randomly selected are not proportional to the strength of their corrections determined based on the backpropagation algorithm. In many cases, the weights values are disproportionately matched with the gradient values. In order for weights to be randomly selected in a manner proportional to the gradient, a good method is to initialize them using the Xavier method [10].

We chose Xavier initialization based on the normal distribution with the standard deviation calculated according to the following formula:

$$[H]\sigma = \sqrt{2}\sqrt{\frac{2}{n_{inputs} + n_{outputs}}} \tag{1}$$

The weights are randomly selected from the normal Gaussian distribution with the center at point 0. The Gaussian distribution parameters are selected in relation to the number of inputs (n_{inputs}) and outputs ($n_{outputs}$) of neurons in individual layers.

3.3   Optimization Algorithm

An additional element supporting the learning of our models is the use of the momentum optimizer in the learning process. It was proposed by Nesterov [17]. By using this method, the model learns to generalize the problem much better. Network learning using the Nesterov algorithm is almost always faster than the standard version of the algorithm that uses the momentum element. The main feature of the algorithm is to measure the gradient of the cost function not in the local position, but slightly forward in the direction of the momentum. The Nesterov algorithm significantly limits oscillations during learning, which are caused by the addition of the momentum element. Thanks to this, the model achieves convergence faster.

3.4   Network Regularization

In order to prevent overfitting of structures to training samples, in this article we use the dropout method [20]. This method consists of randomly switching off individual neurons, based on the probability set as the layer configuration parameter. Excluding individual neurons, the network learns to solve the problem of classification and reduces the risk of overfitting of the model to the training set. We must remember that the probability for the dropout layer cannot be very high, because it can cause a large loss of relevant information, leading to the problems with learning of our structure.

The second element of the structure regularization is the batch normalization method [13]. This method effectively eliminates the vanishing gradient by normalizing the signal flowing between specific layers of the model. The vanishing gradient appears when there is an excessive loss of error in the back propagation of the signal. The batch normalization layer scales the signal processed in the structure, accelerating the learning significantly.

3.5   Learning Configuration

At the input of the neural network, images with dimensions of 56×56, are given. This is the result of performing a clipping operation on original 64×64

images. Each of the structures mentioned in this article is trained through 30 epochs using the SGD algorithm. The size of the minibatch is 256. The training of the structures runs with a constant learning coefficient = 0.01, along with the momentum element = 0.9 and the Nesterov optimization. The process of learning layers of fully connected neurons is supported by the regularization, by applying the dropout method with the parameter of abandonment = 0.5. Each of the layers with weights was initiated using the Xavier method. It is worth noting that weights were initiated with the same random seed size. This means that each of the structures has an identical set of weights before learning. We also used the L2 regularization with scale = 0.001. This significantly prevents overtraining the network. At the output of each of the structures, the Softmax function was used. The cost function is the cross entropy.

4   Experimental Results

To present the differences between the baseline model and other models with modified configuration, we depicted the learning charts for all structures listed in Table 1. Two charts were generated for each model, showing the decrease of the error and effectiveness in relation to 30 learning epochs. The error was measured by MAE. The decrease of the loss function value is determined for the training and validation sets. The value of the cost function consists of the sum of costs resulting from the use of cross entropy and the cost calculated based on the L2 regularization. In the case of performance charts, they show the accuracy in individual epochs in relation to the training TOP-1 results and validation set for TOP-1 and TOP-5 results.

The analysis of the training and validation parameters on the charts from individual structures allows gaining a lot of interesting information about modifications introduced in the models. The first chart shows the baseline model learning process and we can see that the structure in this configuration reaches the accuracy on validation set equal to 39.42% for TOP-1 and 65.72% for TOP-5 (see Fig. 3). In the chart for the baseline model, it is worth to notice that during learning the error and accuracy for the training set increase significantly after several epochs in relation to the validation set. This indicates the overfitting problem. Charts generated for subsequent models present:

- **Model A** - By changing the type of pooling from MAX to AVG, the overfitting problem still occurs, but the error is slightly smaller. This proves a better generalization of the entire model (see Fig. 4).
- **Model B** - Including dilatation for filters in convolutional layers, it is worth to notice that the changes are very similar to the results achieved for model A. Changing the type of pooling or filter dilation setting, only reduces the error during the training of our structure (see Fig. 5).
- **Model C** - The modification of this model is a combination of changes contained in model A and B. This model improves the generalization of the classification of the entire validation set which represents almost the highest efficiency contained in Table 3 (see Fig. 6).

- **Model D** - In model D, the stride in the convolutional layers was changed to (1, 1). It turns out that this modification increases strengthens overfitting, which can be seen already after a few training epochs (see Fig. 7). Turning off downsampling in convolutional layer increases the number of connections between the second pooling layer and the first fully connected layer from 7 × 7 × 64 × 1024 to 14 × 14 × 64 × 1024 inputs.
- **Model E** - The configuration of model E is essentially the same as in the case of model D. However, in this modification of the structure D, we increase the scale factor for the L2 regularization from 0.001 to 0.01, which reduces overfitting (see Fig. 8), but significantly lengthens the process of the structure learning.

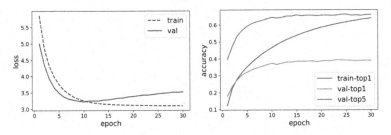

(a) Training and validation loss   (b) Training and validation accuracy

Fig. 3. Baseline model (downsampling, MAX-pooling, lack of dilations in convolutional layers)

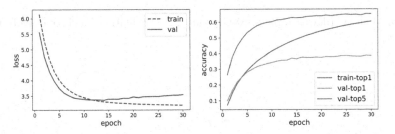

(a) Training and validation loss   (b) Training and validation accuracy

Fig. 4. Model A (downsampling, AVG-pooling, lack of dilations in convolutional layers)

Despite the fact that the modification of the structure E configuration largely reduced the problem of overfitting, its effectiveness significantly decreased. We can assume that the vanishing gradient or the low learning rate may be the reason. The possible problem may be caused by a too high factor of L2 regularization. Model configuration E is a very good fundament for further examinations to increase the effectiveness of the learning process.

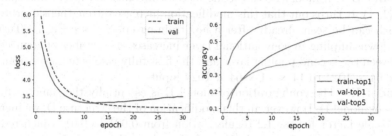

(a) Training and validation loss   (b) Training and validation accuracy

Fig. 5. Model B (downsampling, MAX-pooling, 2×2 dilations in three convolutional layers)

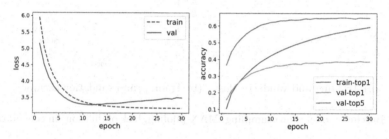

(a) Training and validation loss   (b) Training and validation accuracy

Fig. 6. Model C (downsampling, AVG-pooling, 2×2 dilations in three convolutional layers)

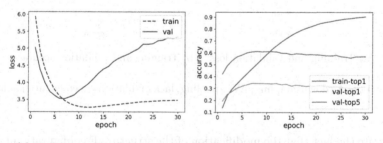

(a) Training and validation loss   (b) Training and validation accuracy

Fig. 7. Model D (without downsampling, MAX-pooling, 2×2 dilations in three convolutional layers, L2 regularization scale $= 0.001$)

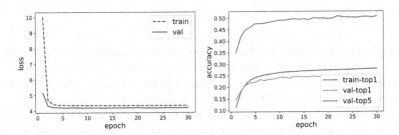

(a) Training and validation loss   (b) Training and validation accuracy

Fig. 8. Model E (the same as D but L2 regularization scale = 0.01)

When analyzing Table 2 we can check how the modifications of configurations affect the decrease of the error and the learning time depending on the number of particular epochs. The average training time of one epoch reflects the time in seconds. "Best epoch number" indicates the number of the epoch at which Top-1 validation accuracy was the highest. Top-1 accuracy measured on the training set was shown in the last row.

Table 2. Information about the best epoch at which Top-1 accuracy on the validation data was the highest, the average training time of one epoch in seconds and TOP-1 accuracy on training data.

Model	Baseline	A	B	C	D	E
Average training time	237.09	219.074	256.36	261.67	379.36	378.08
Best epoch number	23	29	29	28	7	24
TOP-1 accuracy (best epoch)	0.606	0.600	0.592	0.584	0.466	0.276

Table 3 shows the results for each of the analyzed structures. We can check how the modifications of the baseline model parameters affect its performance.

Table 3. The accuracy and other performance metrics on the validation set: the baseline model comparative to 5 models with modified configurations.

Model	Baseline	A	B	C	D	E
TOP-1 accuracy	0.394	0.387	0.390	0.389	0.344	0.255
TOP-5 accuracy	0.657	0.653	0.644	0.650	0.609	0.504
Precision	0.399	0.393	0.391	0.392	0.346	0.255
Recall	0.394	0.387	0.390	0.389	0.344	0.258
F1 score	0.386	0.379	0.381	0.380	0.329	0.236

5   Conclusions

The simulations presented in this article show the learning process in relation to different configurations of the individual structures. The main goal of our work was to learn the differences that result from individual changes and how they affect the process of deep learning. By gaining practical experience through modifying various structures, we learn how to design them better for our own use. There are different learning techniques in the field of deep neural networks as well as various ways of the configuration of structures. In order to obtain satisfying results we have to understand the changes caused by modifying structure parameters. Thanks to the presented simulations, we learn how changes in individual configuration parameters affect the operation of various deep structures.

Acknowledgment. This work was supported by the Polish National Science Center under Grant 2017/27/B/ST6/02852.

References

1. Abdelbari, H., Shafi, K.: Learning structures of conceptual models from observed dynamics using evolutionary echo state networks. J. Artif. Intell. Soft Comput. Res. **8**(2), 133–154 (2018). https://doi.org/10.1515/jaiscr-2018-0010
2. Barnes, Z., Cipollone, F., Romero, T.: Techniques for image classification on tiny-imagenet
3. Bologna, G., Hayashi, Y.: Characterization of symbolic rules embedded in deep DIMLP networks: a challenge to transparency of deep learning. J. Artif. Intell. Soft Comput. Res. **7**(4), 265–286 (2017)
4. Bottou, L.: Large-scale machine learning with stochastic gradient descent. In: Lechevallier, Y., Saporta, G. (eds.) Proceedings of COMPSTAT'2010, pp. 177–186. Springer, Heidelberg (2010). https://doi.org/10.1007/978-3-7908-2604-3_16
5. Chan, T.H., Jia, K., Gao, S., Lu, J., Zeng, Z., Ma, Y.: PCANet: a simple deep learning baseline for image classification? IEEE Trans. Image Process. **24**(12), 5017–5032 (2015)
6. Chang, O., Constante, P., Gordon, A., Singana, M.: A novel deep neural network that uses space-time features for tracking and recognizing a moving object. J. Artif. Intell. Soft Comput. Res. **7**(2), 125–136 (2017)
7. Dawar, D., Ludwig, S.A.: Effect of strategy adaptation on differential evolution in presence and absence of parameter adaptation: an investigation. J. Artif. Intell. Soft Comput. Res. **8**(3), 211–235 (2018). https://doi.org/10.1515/jaiscr-2018-0014
8. Deng, F., Pu, S., Chen, X., Shi, Y., Yuan, T., Pu, S.: Hyperspectral image classification with capsule network using limited training samples. Sensors **18**(9), 3153 (2018)
9. Girshick, R.: Fast R-CNN. In: Proceedings of the IEEE International Conference on Computer Vision, pp. 1440–1448 (2015)
10. Glorot, X., Bengio, Y.: Understanding the difficulty of training deep feedforward neural networks. In: Proceedings of the Thirteenth International Conference on Artificial Intelligence and Statistics, pp. 249–256 (2010)
11. Hansen, L.: Tiny imagenet challenge submission. CS 231N (2015)

12. He, K., Zhang, X., Ren, S., Sun, J.: Deep residual learning for image recognition. In: Proceedings of the IEEE Conference on Computer Vision and Pattern Recognition, pp. 770–778 (2016)
13. Ioffe, S., Szegedy, C.: Batch normalization: accelerating deep network training by reducing internal covariate shift. arXiv preprint arXiv:1502.03167 (2015)
14. Krizhevsky, A., Sutskever, I., Hinton, G.E.: Imagenet classification with deep convolutional neural networks. In: Advances in Neural Information Processing Systems, pp. 1097–1105 (2012)
15. Marmanis, D., Datcu, M., Esch, T., Stilla, U.: Deep learning earth observation classification using imagenet pretrained networks. IEEE Geosci. Remote Sens. Lett. **13**(1), 105–109 (2016)
16. Mou, L., Ghamisi, P., Zhu, X.X.: Deep recurrent neural networks for hyperspectral image classification. IEEE Trans. Geosci. Remote Sens. **55**(7), 3639–3655 (2017)
17. Nesterov, Y.: A method for unconstrained convex minimization problem with the rate of convergence o $(1/k^2)$. In: Doklady AN USSR, vol. 269, pp. 543–547 (1983)
18. Ng, A.Y.: Feature selection, l 1 vs. l 2 regularization, and rotational invariance. In: Proceedings of the Twenty-First International Conference on Machine Learning, p. 78. ACM (2004)
19. Russakovsky, O., et al.: ImageNet large scale visual recognition challenge. Int. J. Comput. Vision (IJCV) **115**(3), 211–252 (2015). https://doi.org/10.1007/s11263-015-0816-y
20. Srivastava, N., Hinton, G., Krizhevsky, A., Sutskever, I., Salakhutdinov, R.: Dropout: a simple way to prevent neural networks from overfitting. J. Mach. Learn. Res. **15**(1), 1929–1958 (2014)
21. Villmann, T., Bohnsack, A., Kaden, M.: Can learning vector quantization be an alternative to SVM and deep learning? - Recent trends and advanced variants of learning vector quantization for classification learning. J. Artif. Intell. Soft Comput. Res. **7**(1), 65–81 (2017). https://doi.org/10.1515/jaiscr-2017-0005
22. Wang, F., et al.: Residual attention network for image classification. In: Proceedings of the IEEE Conference on Computer Vision and Pattern Recognition, pp. 3156–3164 (2017)
23. Yu, H.: Deep convolutional neural networks for tiny imagenet classification
24. Zhang, C., et al.: A hybrid MLP-CNN classifier for very fine resolution remotely sensed image classification. ISPRS J. Photogramm. Remote Sens. **140**, 133–144 (2018)

Constructive Cascade Learning Algorithm for Fully Connected Networks

Xing Wu[1], Pawel Rozycki[2(✉)], Janusz Kolbusz[2], and Bogdan M. Wilamowski[1]

[1] Auburn University, Auburn, AL 36849-5201, USA
xzw0015@tigermail.auburn.edu, wilambm@auburn.edu
[2] University of Information Technology and Management in Rzeszow,
Sucharskiego 2, 35-225 Rzeszow, Poland
{prozycki,jkolbusz}@wsiz.rzeszow.pl
http://wsiz.rzeszow.pl

Abstract. The Fully Connected Cascade Networks (FCCN) were originally proposed along with the Cascade Correlation (CasCor) learning algorithm that having three main advantages over the Multilayer Perceptron (MLP): the structure of the network could be determined dynamically; they were more powerful for complex feature representation; the training was efficient by optimizing newly added neuron only in every stage. However, at the same time, they were criticized that the freezing strategy usually resulted in an overlarge network with the architecture much deeper than necessary. To overcome the disadvantage, in this paper, a new hybrid constructive learning (HCL) algorithm is proposed to build a FCCN as compact as possible. The proposed HCL algorithm is compared with the CasCor algorithm and some other algorithms on several popular regression benchmarks.

Keywords: Fully Connected Cascade Networks (FCCN) ·
Hybrid Constructive Learning (HCL) algorithm ·
Particle Swarm Optimization (PSO) ·
Levenberg Marquardt (LM) algorithm · Least Square (LS) method

1 Introduction

The Feedforward Neural Networks (FNN) are widely investigated in the machine learning community, like classification, regression, etc. The first step of FNN learning is to determine the connection topology of the model. There are two main types of the FNN topology: Multilayer Perceptron (MLP) and Fully Connected Cascade Networks (FCCN). Then based on the selected topology as a *priori*, structure learning is performed to search both the best size of the network and the optimal set of the parameters (the weights).

This work was partially supported by the National Science Centre, Cracow, Poland under Grant No. 2015/17/B/ST6/01880.

© Springer Nature Switzerland AG 2019
L. Rutkowski et al. (Eds.): ICAISC 2019, LNAI 11508, pp. 236–247, 2019.
https://doi.org/10.1007/978-3-030-20912-4_23

The MLP is the oldest and most popularly used topology of FNN. The neurons are arranged layer by layer. The outputs of each layer are fed into the adjacent next layer as inputs. With a long history, a lot of learning algorithms for the MLP had been proposed, like error backpropagation (EBP) [1], quickprop [2], Rprop [3], Levenberg-Marquardt (LM) algorithm [4], Broyden-Fletcher-Golfarb-Shanno (BFGS) algorithm [5], etc. However, most of these learning algorithms only focused on the parameters tuning of a fixed-size network. The other important task of the structure learning, to determine the best network size, still remains to be difficult. The trial and error approach had been used to determine the network size. However, since the MLP has too many possible structures that one has to determined how many layers (the depth) and how many neurons in each layer (the width), many trials are needed, which leads to a lot of training time. There were also some constructive and pruning algorithms for the structure learning of the MLP. However, most of the them only focused on the Single Layer Feedforward Neural networks (SLFN), the simplest MLP with only one hidden layer [6,9,16,17].

The FCCN topology was originally proposed by Fahlman and Lebiere in 1990 together with the Cascade Correlation (CasCor) algorithm [10]. The FCCN with the CasCor learning algorithm is summarized with the following advantages over the MLP topology:

1. Each hidden layer of the FCCN has only one neuron. Instead of searching for the optimal depth and width of the network as the MLP, one only needs to care the number of neurons. The CasCor algorithm is quite straightforward to construct the FCCN incrementally.
2. Each hidden neuron of the FCCN receives connections from all the inputs and all the previously installed hidden neurons, which makes it more powerful to represent high order nonlinear features.
3. The CasCor algorithm trains each neuron only once and then freezes their incoming parameters. This strategy improves the training efficiency dramatically.

Because of these advantages, the FCCN are widely used in different application fields [7,8]. However, at the same time, the freezing strategy of the CasCor algorithm was criticized to be hardly to achieve a compact solution [11]. In consequence, the result FCCN is usually much deeper than required, which makes it easy to overfit the data and also leads to some extra time for signal propagation [12].

In order to achieve a more compact FCCN and improve the generalization, many other learning algorithms were proposed for the FCCN construction. These algorithms can generally be classified into two main categories. The first is based on the CasCor algorithm and kept the freezing strategy [13,14]. The other, dropped the freezing strategy and searched the optimal structure in an exhaustive way [15]. Each time after adding the new neuron, all the parameters are fully tuned. With the fully tuning strategy, a much more compact FCCN can be achieved. For example, it was shown that the *two-spiral* problem could be solved by a FCCN with 7 neurons by tuning all the parameters using the NBN algorithm [24] while the CasCor algorithm needed the FCCN with at least 12 hidden neurons [10].

In this paper, we proposed a new Hybrid Constructive Learning (HCL) algorithm, which belongs to the second category. In every stage adding a new neuron, the initial parameters of the new neuron are searched with the Particle Swarm Optimization (PSO) by maximizing the total error reduction [16]. Then starting from the combination of the previous training results and the initialized parameters of the new neuron, a hybrid algorithm [17] based on the LM algorithm and the LS method is used to tune all the parameters iteratively. Though the fully tuning strategy slows down the training process, since the FCCN is searched in an exhaustive way, the training efficiency can still benefit from the compact structure.

2   The Cascade Neural Networks and the Learning Algorithms

In this section, the basic computation of the FCCN and some common notations will be given. In this paper, we mainly investigate the structure learning of the FCCN for function approximation problems. For simplicity, we only consider a single function to be mapped from the multi-dimensional inputs. For the problem with multiple outputs, one can split it into several independent single output approximation problems.

Assume the training data set is given as $\{(\mathbf{x}_p, y_p)|\mathbf{x}_p \in R^D, y_p \in R, p = 1, 2, ..., P\}$, in which there are P training patterns with D-dimension input and scalar output, $(\mathbf{x}_p, y_p)$ denotes the p_{th} input and output. Once given the training data set, structure learning is performed to seek the optimal network size and parameters set to minimize the approximation error on the training data, where the sum squared error (SSE) is popularly used.

$$\text{SSE} = \|\mathbf{y} - \tilde{\mathbf{y}}\|^2 = (\mathbf{y} - \tilde{\mathbf{y}})^T (\mathbf{y} - \tilde{\mathbf{y}}) \tag{1}$$

in which, $\mathbf{y}$ are the desired outputs for the training data, $\tilde{\mathbf{y}}$ are the actual outputs of the model. Nevertheless, the goal of the learning is to generalize well on the unseen data.

Different from the traditional MLP, the FCCN architecture has the forward connections between every two nodes. Each hidden neuron is a single layer and receives signals from all the inputs and the pre-existing neurons, as shown in Fig. 1. While, in general, each hidden neuron can have different activation function [10], in this paper, we only consider the sigmoid activation function for all the hidden neurons.

Assume the input weights $\mathbf{w}_k = [w_{k0}, w_{k1}, ..., w_{kD}, ..., w_{k(D+k-1)}]^T \in R^{D+k}$ where w_{ki} is the weight connecting the i_{th} node to the k_{th} hidden neuron. Here, the "node" is a generalized node, including the bias ($i = 0$), all the inputs ($i = 1, ..., D$) and all the hidden neurons ($i = D+1, ..., D+k-1$). The output of this hidden neuron for the p_{th} pattern is given by, $h_{p,k} = \frac{1}{1+\exp(-net_{p,k})}$

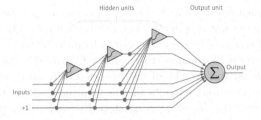

Fig. 1. FCCN architecture

in which, the *net* value $net_{p,k} = \mathbf{in}_{p,k}\mathbf{w}_k$, is the weighted summation of all the incoming signals. $\mathbf{in}_{p,k} = [1, \mathbf{x}_p, h_{p,1}, ..., h_{p,k-1}]$ are all the incoming signals of the k_{th} neuron. Denote the net values of the k_{th} hidden neuron for all the training patterns as vector $\mathbf{net}_k = [net_{1,k}, ..., net_{P,k}]^T$, their outputs as vector $\mathbf{h}_k = [h_{1,k}, ..., h_{P,k}]^T$.

For a FCCN with k hidden neurons, *signal matrix* $\mathbf{H}_k = [\mathbf{1}, \mathbf{X}, \mathbf{h}_1, ..., \mathbf{h}_k] \in R^{P \times (D+k+1)}$ can be defined, where $\mathbf{1}$ is a vector with all 1s representing the bias, $\mathbf{X}$ is the input matrix. As new hidden neuron is added during the construction, the *signal matrix* is expanding with extra column at the same time. While usually the sigmoid function is used as the output neuron for the classification problems, we simply use a linear summator for a better approximation to the analog output values, as shown in Fig. 1. Denote the weights of the output neuron are $\boldsymbol{\theta}_k \in R^{D+k+1}$, then the outputs of the FCCN for the training set are computed as, $\tilde{\mathbf{y}} = \mathbf{H}_k\boldsymbol{\theta}_k$.

2.1   Popular Learning Algorithms

The first proposed algorithm for FCCN architecture was CasCor [10]. The only parameter is the number of hidden neurons, which is much simpler compared to the depth and width of the MLP. Benefit from this, the CasCor algorithm starts with a FCCN with no hidden neurons and constructs it by simply adding neurons one by one. Each time adding the new neuron, the CasCor algorithm has two steps: *Input training* and *Output training*. In the *Input training* step, several candidates of the hidden parameters of the new neuron are randomly generated. Each candidate is independently optimized by gradient ascent methods or quickprop [2] to maximize the covariance between the outputs of this candidate neuron and the residual errors of the previous FCCN. The candidate with the maximum trained covariance is appended to the FCCN. Then in the *Output training* step, all the output weights are tuned to minimize the SSE in (1). For the architecture we investigated in this paper, since all the output weights are linear related, one can do the *Output training* with the LS method as shown below,

$$\hat{\boldsymbol{\theta}} = (\mathbf{H}^T\mathbf{H})^{-1}\mathbf{H}^T\mathbf{y} \tag{2}$$

While the CasCor algorithm worked well on many classification problems, like the *two-spiral* problem and the *parity-N* problem [10], it was argued that the covariance measurement for each hidden neuron's selection tended to make it saturate, which was not suitable for smooth regression problems [18]. For this reason, a second version of learning algorithm from the original author had been investigated in several literatures [13], namely Cascade2, which optimized the input weights and output weight of each candidate neuron by minimizing the error between the weighted outputs of this neuron and the previous FCCN's residual error during the *Input training* step. Recently, Huang *et al.* [14] used the error reduction contribution defined in Orthogonal Least Square (OLS) as the selection criterion and proposed an OLSCN algorithm, which improved the learning performance a lot.

Benefit from the freezing strategy, all the above learning algorithms worked efficiently. However, at the same time, it is likely to produce a FCCN with more hidden neurons than required, which could easily overfit the data set. To overcome this problem, Treadgold and Gedeon dropped the freezing strategy and proposed a Casper algorithm, which employed a Simulated Annealing Rprop (SARPROP) algorithm [23] to tune all the parameters in each stage [15]. Their experiments demonstrated that the fully tuning strategy could achieve a better generalization performance with much less hidden neurons. However, while the first order Rprop algorithm was used, it cost much training time. The second-order LM algorithm had been investigated for the fixed size FCCN learning [19,20], which worked more efficiently. However, the optimal network size had to be searched by a trial and error approach.

3   The Hybrid Constructive Learning Algorithm

In this section, we will introduce the proposed HCL algorithm in details. Like other constructive algorithms, the HCL starts with a minimal FCCN with no hidden neurons and adds the hidden neurons one by one. Each time adding the new hidden neuron, the learning is also divided into two steps: *Initialization* and *Fully tuning*.

3.1   Initialization

After the previous training stage, if the results are not satisfied, the learning could easily escape from the previous local minima by introducing a new hidden neuron. In the HCL algorithm, all the training results of the previous FCCN are reused as the starting points for the *Fully tuning* step. The *Initialization* mainly focused on newly added neuron.

Different from the covariance measurement of the CasCor algorithm, which was argued to force the neuron to saturate, the HCL initialize the parameters of the new neuron with the reformulated OLS criterion [16]. Consider the FCCN with k hidden neurons, whose *signal matrix* is $\mathbf{H}_k$, the residual errors after previous *Fully tuning* are $\mathbf{e}_k = \mathbf{y} - \tilde{\mathbf{y}}$. Now adding a new neuron which outputs are $\mathbf{h}_{k+1}$. Do a temporary regression with the current FCCN to the target $\mathbf{h}_{k+1}$, denote the optimal coefficients and residual errors are $\boldsymbol{\theta}_t$ and $\mathbf{e}_t$,

$$\boldsymbol{\theta}_t = (\mathbf{H}_k^T \mathbf{H}_k)^{-1} \mathbf{H}_k^T \mathbf{h}_{k+1} \tag{3}$$

$$\mathbf{e}_t = \mathbf{h}_{k+1} - \mathbf{H}_k \boldsymbol{\theta}_t \tag{4}$$

then, the error reduction contribution of this new neuron to the entire FCCN will be [16],

$$[err]_{k+1} = \frac{(\mathbf{h}_{k+1}^T \mathbf{e}_k)^2}{\mathbf{h}_{k+1}^T \mathbf{e}_t} \tag{5}$$

This objective function represents the SSE reduction after adding the new neuron while keeping the output weights always to be LS optimal. One needs to search the optimal parameters of the new neuron to maximize the objective function in (5). As shown in [16], the objective function shown in (5) is a complex multimodal function. Huang *et al.* [14] proposed a modified Newton's method to optimize a similar function. Since the local search capability of the Newton's method, several candidates were required to find the global maxima. Same as [16], the proposed HCL use the PSO to seek the optimal initialization of the new neuron. Proposed PSO algorithm is based on technique developed by Kennedy and Eberhart [21] and is described in details in [16].

3.2   Fully Tuning

After the new neuron is well initialized, it is appended to the previous FCCN directly. Then all the parameters of the new FCCN are further tuned starting from their current values. In the HCL algorithm, a second-order hybrid algorithm based on the LM algorithm and the LS method is used for this optimization task. The hybrid algorithm was previously proposed for the SLFN construction [17] and we extend it here for the FCCN learning.

The basic idea of presented algorithm is to combine the conventional LM algorithm and the LS method. The parameters of the FCCN are divided into two groups: nonlinear parameters (input weights of each hidden neuron); linear parameters (output weights). By converting the linear parameters into dependent variables of the nonlinear parameters with the LS method, one can only optimize those nonlinear parameters with the LM algorithm.

The only difference between the SLFN and the FCCN is the calculation of the $\mathbf{J}_n$ and the $\mathbf{Q}$. Compared with the SLFN, it is more complex to calculate the Jacobian matrix for the FCCN, since every neuron collects the backpropagated signals from all the following neurons. Assume current FCCN has k hidden neurons, then there are $r = (D+1) + (D+2) + ... + (D+k) = kD + \frac{k(k+1)}{2}$ nonlinear parameters. So the nonlinear Jacobian matrix $\mathbf{J}_n$ has r columns,

$$\mathbf{J}_n = [\frac{\partial \tilde{\mathbf{y}}}{\partial w_{10}}, ..., \frac{\partial \tilde{\mathbf{y}}}{\partial w_{1D}}, ..., ..., \frac{\partial \tilde{\mathbf{y}}}{\partial w_{k0}}, ..., \frac{\partial \tilde{\mathbf{y}}}{\partial w_{k(D+k-1)}}] \tag{6}$$

The sparse matrix $\mathbf{Q} \in R^{(k+D+1) \times r}$ becomes a blockwise lower triangular matrix with the first $D+1$ rows to be all zeros.

The backpropagation process according to the differential chain rule is quite complex in the FCCN case. Wilamowski and Yu provided an efficient forward-only method by using dynamic programming (DP) [20]. In this paper, we used this technique to calculate the matrix $\mathbf{J}_n$ and $\mathbf{Q}$.

Table 1. Vector version of the δ table

neuron #	1	2	3	$\cdots$	k	o
1	$\frac{\partial h_1}{\partial net_1}$					
2	$\frac{\partial h_2}{\partial net_1}$	$\frac{\partial h_2}{\partial net_2}$				
3	$\frac{\partial h_3}{\partial net_1}$	$\frac{\partial h_3}{\partial net_2}$	$\frac{\partial h_3}{\partial net_3}$			
$\vdots$	$\vdots$	$\vdots$	$\vdots$	$\ddots$		
k	$\frac{\partial h_k}{\partial net_1}$	$\frac{\partial h_k}{\partial net_2}$	$\frac{\partial h_k}{\partial net_3}$	$\cdots$	$\frac{\partial h_k}{\partial net_k}$	
o	$\frac{\partial \tilde{y}}{\partial net_1}$	$\frac{\partial \tilde{y}}{\partial net_2}$	$\frac{\partial \tilde{y}}{\partial net_3}$	$\cdots$	$\frac{\partial \tilde{y}}{\partial net_k}$	1

* All the partial derivatives are pointwise

The forward-only method removed the backpropagation process and created a lower triangular δ table to store every desired values through the forward computation. Here, we created a vector version of the δ table to store all desired values for calculating $\mathbf{J}_n$ and $\mathbf{Q}$, as shown in Table 1. The neuron number is from 1 to k in the order of installation. "o" represents the linear output neuron. The vector in the cell (i, j) is the derivative of the i_{th} neuron's output over the j_{th} neuron's net value for all the training patterns, denote as $\boldsymbol{\delta}_{i,j}$ (The partial derivatives shown in the table are all pointwise).

$$\boldsymbol{\delta}_{i,j} = \frac{\partial \mathbf{h}_i}{\partial \mathbf{net}_j} = [\frac{\partial h_{1,i}}{\partial net_{1,j}}, \frac{\partial h_{2,i}}{\partial net_{2,j}}, ..., \frac{\partial h_{P,i}}{\partial net_{P,j}}]^T \tag{7}$$

The values on the diagonal are directly the slopes of each single neuron. The other values are computed according to all the above values in the same column.

$$\boldsymbol{\delta}_{i,j} = \boldsymbol{\delta}_{i,i} \circ \sum_{m=j}^{i-1} \boldsymbol{\delta}_{m,j} w_{m \to i} \tag{8}$$

where $w_{m \to i}$ is the weight connecting the m_{th} neuron to the i_{th} neuron, $\circ$ represents pointwise product of two vectors.

After going through the forward computation, with the vectors stored in the δ table, one can calculate the $\mathbf{Q}$ matrix with the first k rows and compute the $\mathbf{J}_n$ matrix with the last row. For example, with the vector $\frac{\partial \mathbf{h}_i}{\partial \mathbf{net}_j}$ ($k \geq i \geq j \geq 1$), one can calculate the corresponding differential term in matrix $\mathbf{Q}$ as,

$$\frac{\partial \mathbf{h}_i}{\partial w_{jm}} = \frac{\partial \mathbf{h}_i}{\partial \mathbf{net}_j} \circ \mathbf{H}(:,m) \quad m = 0, 1, ..., D+j-1 \tag{9}$$

in which, $\mathbf{H}(:,m)$ is the m_{th} column of the *signal matrix* $\mathbf{H}$. Also given the vector $\frac{\partial \tilde{y}}{\partial \mathbf{net}_i}$ in the last row, one can calculate the corresponding column in the nonlinear Jacobian matrix $\mathbf{J}_n$ as,

$$\frac{\partial \tilde{y}}{\partial w_{im}} = \frac{\partial \tilde{y}}{\partial \mathbf{net}_i} \circ \mathbf{H}(:,m) \quad m = 0, 1, ..., D+i-1 \tag{10}$$

In fact, while using the conventional LM algorithm as in [20], only the last row of the δ table is finally used and the rest values are dropped, like most DP problems. However, the hybrid algorithm used all the values in the table, which may be more suitable to employ the forward-only method.

Same as [17], we introduce a regularizer λ to the hybrid algorithm, which constrains the search of the output weights in a trust region. The LS solution of the output weights becomes (11) instead of (2).

$$\theta = (\mathbf{H}^T\mathbf{H} + \lambda\mathbf{I})^{-1}\mathbf{H}^T\mathbf{y} \tag{11}$$

This regularization avoids the risk of ill conditioning, it also tends to generate a model with a better generalization. The result update formula after adding the regularization is shown in (12).

$$\Delta\mathbf{W}_v = (\mathbf{J}_n^T\mathbf{J}_n - \mathbf{J}_n^T\mathbf{H}(\mathbf{H}^T\mathbf{H} + \lambda\mathbf{I})^{-1}\mathbf{H}^T\mathbf{J}_n + \mathbf{Q}^T(\mathbf{H}^T\mathbf{H} + \lambda\mathbf{I})^{-1}\mathbf{Q} + \mu\mathbf{I})^{-1}\mathbf{J}_n^T\mathbf{e} \tag{12}$$

The *Fully tuning* step will proceed until reaching the maximum iteration T set by the user or being detected to entrap into the local minima, as described as following,

$$\left|\frac{\mathrm{SSE}(t) - \mathrm{SSE}(t - N)}{\mathrm{SSE}(t)}\right| < \eta \tag{13}$$

in which, $\mathrm{SSE}(t), \mathrm{SSE}(t - N)$ are the approximation error at the t_{th} and the $(t - N)_{th}$ iteration. N is the iteration latency. η is the decreasing threshold. Both N and η are preset by the user. When the local minima is detected, the further training is not necessary and we can stop and proceed to the *Initialization* of the next neuron.

With the *Initialization* and *Fully tuning*, the HCL constructs the FCCN in an exhaustive way. The construction process should terminate when one of the following conditions is satisfied,

1. After the *Fully tuning* step, the SSE arrives the desired value ϵ set by the user.
2. The number of hidden neurons arrives the maximum number K set by the user.
3. The construction saturates, that the construction couldn't obtain much decrease on the SSE by adding more neurons. The saturation is detected as following,

$$\left|\frac{\mathrm{SSE}_{k-L} - \mathrm{SSE}_k}{\mathrm{SSE}_{k-L}}\right| < \sigma \tag{14}$$

in which, $\mathrm{SSE}_{k-L}, \mathrm{SSE}_k$ are the SSE after the *Fully tuning* step while adding the $(k-L)_{th}$ and the k_{th} hidden neuron. L and σ are the stopping parameters set by the user.

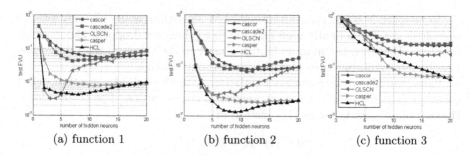

(a) function 1   (b) function 2   (c) function 3

Fig. 2. Averaged testing FVU comparison while approximating 2D functions

4   Experiment

In this section, the proposed HCL algorithm is used for the FCCN construction on three classic 2D function approximation benchmarks [6, 22]. The results are compared with other learning algorithms described in Sect. 2.1: CasCor algorithm [10], cascade2 algorithm [13], OLSCN algorithm [14], Casper algorithm [15]. Since the convergence rate of different algorithms while adding hidden neurons is different, in the experiments, we only used the stopping criterion (2) mentioned in previous section to evaluate the performance of each algorithm.

All the three functions are ranged in $[0, 1]^2$. The description of the used functions are shown as below,

1. Simple interaction function:
   $$f^{(1)}(x_1, x_2) = 10.391((x_1 - 0.4)(x_2 - 0.6) + 0.36)$$
2. Radial function:
   $$f^{(2)}(x_1, x_2) = 24.234(r^2(0.75 - r^2))$$
   in which, $r^2 = (x_1 - 0.5)^2 + (x_2 - 0.5)^2$
3. Harmonic function:
   $$f^{(3)}(x_1, x_2) = 42.659(0.1 + \tilde{x}_1(0.05 + \tilde{x}_1^4 - 10\tilde{x}_1^2\tilde{x}_2^2 + 5\tilde{x}_2^4))$$
   in which, $\tilde{x}_1 = x_1 - 0.5$ and $\tilde{x}_2 = x_2 - 0.5$.

The setup for training data and testing data are the same for all the three functions. The training data set has 225 patterns, which are generated randomly by the uniform distribution $U[0, 1]^2$. All the training data are added independently and identically distributed (i.i.d.) Gaussian noise with mean zero and standard deviation 0.25. The testing data set consists of 100×100 patterns generated from a regularly spaced grid in the range $[0, 1]^2$.

In this experiment, all the algorithms constructed the FCCN by adding hidden neurons from 0 to 20 while the other stopping criteria were not used. For the CasCor and Cascade2, quickprop was used to search the optimal input weights of each new hidden neuron while the maximum iteration was set as 100. In each stage, 8 candidates were trained independently to search the global optimal solution. For the OLSCN algorithm, in which a modified Newton's method was used to train each new neuron's input weights, the maximum iteration was set as 20. The

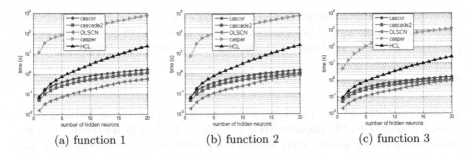

Fig. 3. Averaged training time comparison while approximating 2D functions

number of candidates was also set as 8. For the Casper algorithm, the SARPROP algorithm [23] was used to tune all the parameters in each stage. All the parameter settings were the same as in [15]. The maximum iteration was set as 1000 and the fully training stopped while the root means squared error (RMSE) decreased less than 1% in 200 continuous iterations. For the proposed HCL algorithm, in the *Initialization* step, the maximum iteration and the population size of the PSO were both set as 20; In the *Fully tuning* step, the maximum iteration were set as 200 and the parameters in (13) were set as $N = 70, \eta = 0.01$. The regularizer in (11) (12) was set as $\lambda = 0.001$. All the parameter settings were the same while approximating all the three functions.

The generalization performance of each algorithm is evaluated by the fraction of variance unexplained (FVU)[22] on the testing data, which is actually proportional to the SSE defined in (1),

$$FVU = \frac{(\mathbf{y} - \tilde{\mathbf{y}})^T (\mathbf{y} - \tilde{\mathbf{y}})}{\sum_{p=1}^{P}(y_p - \bar{y})^2} \tag{15}$$

in which, $\mathbf{y} = [y_1, y_2, ..., y_P]^T \in R^P$ are the desired outputs for the testing patterns. $\tilde{\mathbf{y}}$ are the actual outputs with the trained FCCN. $\bar{y}$ is the average value of the desired outputs for all the testing patterns.

$$\bar{y} = \frac{1}{P} \sum_{p=1}^{P} y_p \tag{16}$$

Since all the algorithms started from randomly initialized parameters, the construction with each algorithm was repeated 20 times. The averaged testing FVU and training time of each algorithm while approximating the three functions were shown in Figs. 4 and 5. From the testing FVU comparison, one can observe that the Casper algorithm and the proposed HCL algorithm could always achieved better generalization than the CasCor and Cascade2 algorithms. Though the OLSCN converged fast, it tended to overfit the data as the number of hidden neuron increased. The HCL algorithm performed similar to the Casper algorithm. However, benefit from the efficient second-order hybrid algorithm while fully tuning all the parameters, which required much fewer iterations to converge, the HCL saved much training time compared to the Casper algorithm.

5   Conclusion

In this paper, the FCCN topology is investigated for regression learning problems. Compared to the popular MLP topology, the FCCN has bridge connections, which could achieve more complex representations to the data set; And the structure parameter is only the number of hidden neurons, which is much simpler to perform construction. However, most structure learning algorithms of the FCCN used the freezing strategy, which usually obtain a FCCN much deeper than required. In order to solve this problem, we propose a Hybrid Constructive Learning (HCL) algorithm. The HCL starts from a minimal FCCN and adds the hidden neurons one by one. There are two steps in each stage of adding a new neuron: *Initialization* and *Fully tuning*. In the *Initialization* step, PSO is used to search the optimal starting point for the parameters of the new neuron. Then in the *Fully tuning* step, starting from a combination of the previous training results and the initialized new neuron, the entire FCCN is tuned by a second-order hybrid algorithm based on the LM algorithm and the LS method. The experiments shown that the HCL algorithm could construct a compact FCCN with good generalization ability.

References

1. Rumelhart, D.E., Hinton, G.E., Williams, R.J.: Learning representations by back-propagating errors. Nature **323**, 533–536 (1986)
2. Fahlman, S.E.: Fast learning variations on back-propagation: an empirical study. In: Touretzky, D., Hinton, G., Sejnowski, T. (eds.) Proceedings of the 1988 Connectionist Models Summer School (Pittsburgh, 1988), pp. 38–51. Morgan Kaufmann, San Mateo (1989)
3. Riedmiller, M., Braun, H.: A direct adaptive method for faster backpropagation learning: the RPROP algorithm. In: Ruspini, H. (ed.) Proceeding of the IEEE International Conference on Neural Networks (ICNN), San Francisco, pp. 586–591 (1993)
4. Hagan, M.T., Menhaj, M.: Training feedforward networks with the Marquardt algorithm. IEEE Trans. Neural Networks **5**, 989–993 (1994)
5. Battiti, R., Masulli, F.: BFGS optimization for faster automated supervised learning. In: International Neural-Network Conference, vol. 2, pp. 757–760 (1990)
6. Kwok, T.Y., Yeung, D.Y.: Objective functions for training new hidden units in constructive neural networks. IEEE Trans. Neural Networks **8**(5), 1131–1148 (1997)
7. Hussain, S., Mokhtar, M., Howe, J.M.: Sensor failure detection, identification, and accommodation using fully connected cascade neural network. IEEE Trans. Industr. Electron. **62**(3), 1683–1692 (2015)
8. Deshpande, G., Wang, P., Rangaprakash, D., Wilamowski, B.M.: Fully connected cascade artificial neural network architecture for attention deficit hyperactivity disorder classification from functional magnetic resonance imaging data. IEEE Trans. Cybern. **45**(12), 2668–2679 (2015)

9. Huang, G.-B., Chen, L., Siew, C.-K.: Universal approximation using incremental constructive feedforward networks with random hidden nodes. IEEE Trans. Neural Networks **17**(4), 879–892 (2006)

10. Fahlman, S.E., Lebiere, C.: The cascade-correlation learning architecture. In: Touretzky, D.S. (ed.) Advances in Neural Information Processing Systems, vol. 2, pp. 524–532. Morgan Kaufmann, San Mateo (1990)

11. Kwok, T.K., Young, D.Y.: Experimental analysis of input weight freezing in constructive neural networks. In: Proceedings of IEEE International Conference Neural Networks, San Francisco, pp. 511–516 (1993)

12. Baluja, S., Fahlman, S.: Reducing network depth in the cascade-correlation learning architecture, Technical report, Carnegie Mellon University, Pittsburgh

13. Prechelt, L.: Investigating the cascor family of learning algorithms. Neural Networks **10**(5), 885–896 (1997)

14. Huang, G.-B., Chen, L.: Orthogonal least squares algorithm for training cascade neural networks. IEEE Trans. Circuits Syst. I Regul. Pap. **59**(11), 2629–2637 (2012)

15. Treadgold, N.K., Gedeon, T.D.: A cascade network algorithm employing progressive RPROP. In: Mira, J., Moreno-Díaz, R., Cabestany, J. (eds.) IWANN 1997. LNCS, vol. 1240, pp. 733–742. Springer, Heidelberg (1997). https://doi.org/10.1007/BFb0032532

16. Wu, X., Rozycki, P., Wilamowski, B.M.: Single layer feedforward networks construction based on orthogonal least square and particle swarm optimization. In: Rutkowski, L., Korytkowski, M., Scherer, R., Tadeusiewicz, R., Zadeh, L.A., Zurada, J.M. (eds.) ICAISC 2016. LNCS (LNAI), vol. 9692, pp. 158–169. Springer, Cham (2016). https://doi.org/10.1007/978-3-319-39378-0_15

17. Wu, X., Rozycki, P., Wilamowski, B.M.: A hybrid constructive algorithm for single layer feedforward networks learning. IEEE Trans Neural Networks Learn. Syst. **26**(8), 1659–1668 (2015)

18. Hwang, J.N., You, S.S., Lay, S.R., Jou, I.C.: The cascade-correlation learning: a projection pursuit learning perspective. IEEE Trans. Neural Networks **7**, 278–289 (1996)

19. Wilamowski, B.M., Yu, H.: Improved computation for Levenberg-Marquardt training. IEEE Trans. Neural Networks **21**(6), 930–937 (2010)

20. Wilamowski, B.M., Yu, H.: Neural network learning without backpropagation. IEEE Trans. Neural Networks **21**(11), 1793–1803 (2010)

21. Kennedy, J., Eberhart, R.C.: Particle swarm optimization. In: Proceedings of IEEE International Conference on Neural Network, Perth, Australia, pp. 1942–1948 (1995)

22. Hwang, J.N., Lay, S.R., Maechler, M., Martin, D., Schimert, J.: Regression modeling in backpropagation and projection pursuit learning. IEEE Trans. Neural Networks **5**, 342–353 (1994)

23. Treadgold, N.K., Gedeon, T.D.: Simulated annealing and weigh decay in adaptive learning: the SARPROP algorithm. IEEE Trans. Neural Networks **9**, 662–668 (1998)

24. Hunter, D., Yu, H., Pukish, M.S., Kolbusz, J., Wilamowski, B.M.: Selection of proper neural network sizes and architectures-a comparative study. IEEE Trans. Industr. Inf. **8**(2), 228–240 (2012)

Generative Adversarial Networks: Recent Developments

Maciej Zamorski[1,2]([✉]), Adrian Zdobylak[1], Maciej Zięba[1,2], and Jerzy Świątek[1]

[1] Wrocław University of Science and Technology, Wrocław, Poland
maciej.zamorski@pwr.edu.pl
[2] Tooploox Ltd., Wrocław, Poland

Abstract. In traditional generative modeling, good data representation is very often a base for a good machine learning model. It can be linked to good representations encoding more explanatory factors that are hidden in the original data. With the invention of Generative Adversarial Networks (GANs), a subclass of generative models that are able to learn representations in an unsupervised and semi-supervised fashion, we are now able to adversarially learn good mappings from a simple prior distribution to a target data distribution. This paper presents an overview of recent developments in GANs with a focus on learning latent space representations.

Keywords: Machine learning · Generative Adversarial Networks · Representation learning · Overview

1 Introduction

Generative Adversarial Networks (GANs) [19] are a class of generative models that can transform vectors of generated noise into synthetic samples resembling data gathered in the training set. GANs have been successfully applied to image generation [6,25,38], semi-supervised learning [36,47,54], domain adaptation [12, 26,50,51], generation controlled by attention [49] and compression [2]. Currently, together with variational autoencoders (VAEs) [8,17,27,32,45,48], GANs are one of the most popular and researched topic in generative modelling [14,18,28]. However, correct evaluation of the GANs has been proven to be particularly difficult due to no consistent metric and inability to compute the generator probability of arbitrary samples [31]. In this work, we provide an overview of existing GAN models, starting from the basic architectures and finishing with the complex approaches focused on particular generative tasks.

2 Generative Adversarial Networks

Generative Adversarial Models (GANs) [19] in the last years have become a frequent choice for a task of approximating data distribution.

© Springer Nature Switzerland AG 2019
L. Rutkowski et al. (Eds.): ICAISC 2019, LNAI 11508, pp. 248–258, 2019.
https://doi.org/10.1007/978-3-030-20912-4_24

The basic concept of the model is taken from the game theory and assumes two competing networks, a discriminator D and a generator G.

The role of the discriminator D is to distinguish between true samples taken from data and fake samples generated by generator G. While the network D continually improves on differentiating, the generator network G learns to produce better and better samples.

In practical applications, the problem is solved by updating the parameters of discriminator and generator in alternating steps. Formally, the problem can be defined as a following min-max game:

$$\min_{G} \max_{D} V(G, D) = \mathbb{E}_{\mathbf{x} \sim p_x}[\log D(x)] + \mathbb{E}_{\mathbf{z} \sim p_z}[\log(1 - D(G(z)))] \qquad (1)$$

In early steps of learning procedures G might generate poor samples. In such scenario, D is expected to recognise majority of samples generated by G, what might lead to $log(1 - D(G(z)))$ saturation. Thus, when $1 - D(G(z))$ converges to 0 it cause generator gradient to vanish. To overcome this issue, it is advised to instead maximize $D(G(z))$, what motivates equation:

$$\max_{G} \max_{D} V(G, D) = \mathbb{E}_{\mathbf{x} \sim p_x}[\log D(x)] + \mathbb{E}_{\mathbf{z} \sim p_z}[\log(D(G(z)))] \qquad (2)$$

Despite the unquestionable potential, GANs have had few limitations, such as being unstable to train and difficult to scale. In recent years, convolutional neural networks (CNNs) have proved to be a very powerful tool for image processing. State of the art CNNs architectures consists of dozens of hidden layers, but such deep architectures did not work well with GANs. In [38] authors proposed a set of good practices for Deep Convolutional GANs training. It is advised to: avoid fully connected layers in deeper architectures, use batch normalization in generator and discriminator networks, replace pooling layers with strided convolutions for discriminator and with fractional-strided convolutions for a generator. As activation function, ReLU should be used in a generator for almost all layers except last one, where $tanh(\cdot)$ is proposed. In discriminator, on the other hand, *LeakyReLU* is worth considering. Described recommendations by no means should be treated as fixed rules, but instead might be a good starting point. Further enhancements were proposed and evaluated in [41]. To avoid generator network mode collapse, instead of optimizing expected value with a focus on discriminator's output, authors optimize it on discriminator's intermediate layer representing hidden features. By using a feature layer, a generator is believed to generate data with respect to the distribution of real data more accurately.

In vanilla GAN, a discriminator is being trained on each example independently. The second idea is to allow discriminator to look at multiple examples, in order to let a generator create more diverse examples. Feature vector $f(x_i) \in \mathbb{R}^A$ of an input x_i is multiplied by transformation tensor $T \in \mathbb{R}^{A \times B \times C}$ aggregating weights for similarity learning, which results in is matrix $M_i \in \mathbb{R}^{B \times C}$. Every row in M_i is then compared to corresponding rows in other matrices M_j by calculating the distance based on L_1 norm. This operation creates n vectors

$o_i(x_i) \in \mathbb{R}^B$, which are afterwards concatenated with input $f(x_i)$ and fed to next discriminator layer. The concept is called *minibatch discrimination*.

3   Conditional Generation

So far, no information about class or label has been regarded. The only distinction made was related to distribution the data came from. Not all problems shall be resolved by one-to-one mapping, for some of them (e.g., tagging images with keywords) more natural way is to create a one-to-many mapping. GANs can be extended by conditioning both networks G and D on some auxiliary information y [34]:

$$\max_G \max_D V(G, D) = \mathbb{E}_{\mathbf{x} \sim p_x}[\log D(x|y)] + \mathbb{E}_{\mathbf{z} \sim p_z}[\log(D(G(z|y)))] \quad (3)$$

In comparison to Conditional GAN, in AC-GAN [37] discriminator does not utilize information about the class directly. Apart from the noise $z \sim p_z$ every sample has knowledge about the class $c \sim p_c$. For image X let us denote S as a source (data or generated distribution) and C as a class label. The discriminator output is a modeled probability not only of $P(S|X)$ (like in vanilla GAN) but also of $P(C|X)$.

D is trained to optimize $L_C + L_S$ (as presented in Eqs. 4 and 5) and G is trained to optimize $L_C - L_S$. AC-GAN is capable of splitting dataset by classes and training G and D accordingly to subsets, as well as performing semi-supervised learning by ignoring loss component from class labels.

$$L_S = \mathbb{E}_{\mathbf{x} \sim p_x}[\log D(x)] + \mathbb{E}_{\mathbf{z} \sim p_z}[\log(D(G(z)))] \quad (4)$$

$$L_C = \mathbb{E}_{\mathbf{x,c} \sim p_{x,c}}[\log D(c|x)] + \mathbb{E}_{\mathbf{z,c} \sim p_{z,c}}[\log(D(G(c|z)))] \quad (5)$$

The improvement in numerical measures does not always go along with the improvement in human perception. The statement is particularly applicable in the case of image generation. Superresolution GAN [29] is designed to upscale low resolution (LR) images to high-resolution (HR) by a scale factor of 4, with the utmost care for details. Authors introduce deep ResNet adapted to GAN concept and then propose using novel loss function to increase image fidelity. To create a training set, a Gaussian filter is applied to every high-resolution image I^{HR}, and then the image is downsampled to low-resolution image I^{LR}. Generator network G is trained as a supervised deep Residual Network to estimate for given LR image an HR one. The proposed perceptual loss is defined on the activation layer of pretrained VGG19 network [43]. Final results are evaluated with a peak signal-to-noise ratio (PSNR) and structural similarity index (SSIM) as well as mean opinion score (MOS) - to quantify results with the help of human raters. Even though PSNR and SSIM scores are lower in every (out of three) conducted experiments, obtained MOS scores are respectively 6.2%, 24.8%, and 55.5% higher, what proves that mentioned numerical metrics are not sufficient to evaluate generated images.

Conditional GANs are providing additional information (class, domain-specific image) to the generator and obtain the particular type of generated images. Moreover, there are approaches, like *InfoGAN* [11], that aims at discovering some important latent components that have an influence on a generated image in purely unsupervised mode. Practically, it means that among space z in the generator we can distinguish some key features that have a significant influence on particular characteristics of generated objects, like shape, rotation or category. This goal is achieved by incorporating into adversarial training an additional term, that aims in increasing the mutual information between particular features delivered on the input of the discriminator and the generated image. After training the model, we are capable of controlling the generative process (shape, color rotation of the generated objects) by manipulating of the latent factors that were used to increase the mutual information.

4   Image to Image Translation

GAN-based models are successively applied to image-to-image translation tasks. For this particular problem, we aim at transferring some properties of the images from so-called target domain $\mathcal{X}$ to some target domain $\mathcal{Y}$ characterized by some particular features. Image-to-image translation models can be applied to transfer a segmented image to real good-looking scenery, can be utilized to transfer street views to the maps or used to create real images from hand-drawn sketches.

We can distinguish two approaches to the problem in terms of data availability used for training. In the first group we assume that models are trained using pairwise data, what practically means that we have access to the pairs of images, $\mathcal{D} = \{x_n, y_n\}$, from the two domains, $\mathcal{X}$ and $\mathcal{Y}$, where $x_n \in \mathcal{X}$ and $y_n \in \mathcal{Y}$. For the second group of approaches, we have only the access to unpaired sets of images from the domains, $X = \{x_n\}$ and $Y = \{y_n\}$.

One of the most promising generative models that utilizes pairwise data for image-to-image translation is *Pix2Pix* [24]. The main idea of this approach is based on conditional GAN model [34] where additional conditioning unit is included on the input of the generator to sample more specific objects. For this particular case generator (G) takes the example x_n from domain $\mathcal{X}$ and tries to generate the corresponding image from domain $\mathcal{Y}$. The discriminator is trained to distinguish between synthetic samples generated from that domain $\mathcal{Y}$ and the corresponding samples from the domain $\mathcal{X}$ used for conditioning in generative part of training. To keep the consistency between generated and true examples in a target domain $\mathcal{Y}$, we utilize $L1$ reconstruction loss to force generated $G(x_n)$ and corresponding true samples y_n to be close in data space.

Pix2Pix model operates on paired data from the domains. Here we present the architecture of CycleGAN [52] that operates on unpaired images from the domains. The structure of that model is composed of four neural networks: two domain-specific discriminators, D_X, and D_Y, and two generative networks, G that generates objects from domain $\mathcal{X}$ to domain $\mathcal{Y}$, and F, that transfers objects from $\mathcal{Y}$ to $\mathcal{X}$. The role of the discriminator D_Y is to distinguish between true database samples from domain $\mathcal{Y}$ and those generated by model G. The role of the generator G is to create images indistinguishable by D_Y. The analogical adversarial training is performed between discriminator D_X and generator F in the $\mathcal{X}$ domain. To obtain the cycle consistency between generated images from various domains two additional $L1$ reconstruction losses are incorporated into the training framework. The first lost is minimizing the distance between image x and corresponding reconstruction $F(G(x))$. The second loss aim at minimizing distance in $\mathcal{Y}$ domain, between $G(F(y))$ and y.

5   Feature Extraction via Learning Hidden Representation

In their original form, Generative Adversarial Networks (GANs) [19] provide only a framework to generate data based on latent feature vector. A natural question comes to mind: "how can we obtain the latent representation that may be used to generate specified images?" If there is a way to produce a mapping from latent distribution to data distribution, there should be a way to perform an 'inverse' operation. That would allow GANs to be used in an unsupervised manner to learn rich distributions about arbitrary data. However, the original model does not have a way to do that mapping.

For this purpose Bidirectional GANs (BiGANs) [15]/Adversarially Learned Inference (ALI) [16] were created. In addition to the existing Generator G the BiGAN model proposes a novelty that comes from equipping the architecture with the Encoder E, which maps the data distribution $\mathbf{x}$ to its latent representation $\mathbf{z}$. Thus the Discriminator D in BiGAN now has to discriminate not only in the data space ($\mathbf{x}$ vs $G(\mathbf{z})$ but also in the feature space ($E(\mathbf{x})$ vs $\mathbf{z}$).

The optimization problem is now $\min_{G,E} \max_D V(D, E, G)$, where training objective $V(G, D, E)$ is given as:

$$V(G, D, E) = \mathbb{E}_{\mathbf{x} \sim p_x}[\mathbb{E}_{\mathbf{z} \sim p_E(\cdot|x)}[\log D(x, z)]] + \mathbb{E}_{\mathbf{z} \sim p_z}[\mathbb{E}_{\mathbf{x} \sim p_G(\cdot|z)}[\log(1 - D(x, z))]] \tag{6}$$

The objective is optimized in a similar way to the original GAN approach, but with a key difference: there is no more 'real' and 'generated' data, as the Encoder E and Generator G now works together to fool the Discriminator D. However, the Encoder E and the Generator G do not see each other outputs. Their gradients come purely from the Discriminator decisions. However, as authors [15] point out, that in order to fool the Discriminator, the Encoder and the Generator must learn to invert each other.

Metric learning is a task of learning the function of a distance between two given objects. It's objective is to model such mapping from data distribution $p(\mathbf{x})$ to latent distribution $p(\mathbf{z})$ that for two objects $x_1, x_2 \sim p(\mathbf{x})$, the metric returns small values for similar objects and high values for dissimilar ones. It is used in situations, where defining explicit distance function is impossible, due to a low amount, high-dimensionality or complexity of the data.

One of the first machine learning models that performed distance calculation used a type of neural networks, also called Siamese Networks [7] or its variants

[13,21]. Siamese Network operated on the pair of the images and had training objective that favored small distances for objects belonging to the same group and large distance when they belong to different groups. Due to the lack of providing the context for image pair, the representations learned by the network give poor results, when used to other tasks, such as classification.

A solution to this problem was provided in Triplet Networks [23]. The authors propose a simple method to add context to presented images by providing as an input to the networks three objects denoted as x, x^+ and x^-, where x and x^+ were labeled as belonging to the same class while x and x^- were labeled as different classes. Now, denoting the features inferred from the model T from the object x as $T(x)$, the learning objective can be formulated as

$$L(d_+, d_-) = \|(d_+, d_- - 1)\|_2^2, \tag{7}$$

with d_+ and d_- defined as

$$d_\pm = \frac{\exp(\|T(x) - T(x^\pm)\|_2)}{\exp(\|T(x) - T(x^+)\|_2) + \exp(\|T(x) - T(x^-)\|_2)} \tag{8}$$

Authors use the model to solve the task of approximating data similarity [10]. For this purpose, the data already comes in the form of triplets that describe semantic closeness of samples in the dataset. Also, by giving the context, the triplet network can accurately compose a metric that is able to infer representation to be used in classification and retrieval tasks.

In [36,41] authors present an approach to train GANs in a semi-supervised manner due to a strong ability presented by GANs to capture descriptive features [15,38]. Inspired by that, [54] proposes an alternative method for a triplet metric training, called Triplet GAN, based on adapting GANs to perform not only feature extraction but also metric learning.

The main idea behind this approach is to repurpose the discriminator D from classification to a distance learning task, which results in good feature representations during the unsupervised, generative part and supervised, discriminative part of the training process.

To incorporate triplet training into GAN framework, authors propose a modified version of a loss function for a model, specified in Eq. 9, with $L(d_+, d_-)$ given as in Eq. 7.

$$L = -V(D, G) - \mathbb{E}_{\mathbf{x}_q, \mathbf{x}_+, \mathbf{x}_- \sim p_{data}(\mathbf{x}_q, \mathbf{x}_+, \mathbf{x}_-)}[\log(L(d_+, d_-)] \tag{9}$$

This approach allows improving results in metric learning tasks by allowing to use not only a labeled part of the dataset but by also learn general information about the structure of the data with unsupervised learning on an unlabeled portion of the dataset.

However, learning metric on the discriminative module of the GAN comes with limitations, of which the main one is an inability to perform sampling from the generated representation. Models presented in [15,16] present an extension to the GAN framework, by adding a module, that performs inference on a given data to a latent space representation. A natural question arises: are GANs able to perform latent space embedding that is both regularized by its ability to reconstruct the input and by metric learning approach?

Based on previously presented BiGAN [15,16] model the authors in [47] address this issue with a presentation of Triplet BiGAN. It combines approaches of BiGAN and Triplet Network [23] with a joint training objective for Encoder E that is trained with both BiGAN and triplet loss. This allows the model to not only learn features from data, but also regularize them with two constraints: the hidden layer encoding tend to be normally distributed (to match the distribution passed to Generator G), and embedding of close samples are close to each other in latent space. Representation learned by the Encoder E can be further used in tasks such as retrieval and classification. Triplet BiGAN model is trained in a semi-supervised manner, although it needs as little as 16 labeled samples per class.

Other works worth mentioning are (a) on training efficient binary feature representation - *Binary GAN* (BGAN) [44], *Binary Regularization Entropy GAN* (BRE-GAN) [9], *Binary GAN* (BinGAN) [53], (b) on domain adaptation *ARDA* [42], (c) on learning representation for 3D pointclouds - *3-D GAN* [46], *l-WGAN* [1] and *Point Cloud GAN* [30].

6   Regularized Learning of the Discriminator

In the original paper [19] the authors proposed training objective for GANs expressed as a min-max game (Eq. 1). It has been shown, that this approach resulted in highly unstable training [19] and authors recommended using an alternative objective instead (Eq. 2). However, even with the modified version, the Generator training often led to vanishing gradients once some of the generated samples were good enough to fool the Discriminator every time, resulting in mode collapse of the Generator. It may be caused by the improper definition of training objective [3,5,33], where the Generator is rewarded for creating samples indistinguishable from the ones in the training set and not for trying to match the whole distribution of the data.

In [3] authors propose a new framework for training GANs called *Wasserstein GAN*. The main improvement over the original framework comes from applying different loss function for the Generator called Wasserstein or Earth-mover distance (Eq. 10).

$$\text{EMD}(P_r, P_\theta) = \inf_{\gamma \in \Pi} \mathbb{E}_{(x,y) \sim \gamma} \|x - y\|, \tag{10}$$

where γ is a joined probability distribution between the one modeled by the Generator (P_θ) and the real data distribution P_r and Π is the set of all such distributions. The Discriminator's (in context of Wasserstein GAN called as the Critic) role in this scenario is to output a scalar of how real the generated image is, rather than a probability. In practice, the sigmoid activation usually put at the end of the Discriminator (Critic) model is in this scenario omitted.

As the version of the loss presented in Eq. 10 is intractable and thus, impossible to use in this scenario, another formulation, using Kantorovich-Rubinstein duality [3,40] is used, as specified in Eq. 11.

$$W(P_r, P_\theta) = \sup_{\|f\|_L \le 1} \mathbb{E}_{x \sim P_r}[f(x)] - \mathbb{E}_{x \sim P_\theta}[f(x)], \tag{11}$$

In order for this approach to be effective the function that the Generator G optimizes, must be the n-Lipschitz function [22], for $n = 1$, i.e. fulfill the constraint given by the Eq. 12.

$$\frac{|G(x_1) - G(x_2)|}{|x_1 - x_2|} \le 1, \tag{12}$$

To satisfy this constraint, the authors of [3] suggest clipping weights of the Generator model to the range $[-c, c]$ with the suggested value of the hyperparameter $c = 0.01$. However, this method often results in weights distributed near the border values of the range. In [20] authors present a new method for satisfying Lipschitz condition, called *gradientpenalty*. This method, instead of applying clipping, penalizes the model if the Discriminator (Critic) gradient norm moves away from its target norm value 1.

The Wasserstein GAN framework assumes one iteration update for the Generator weights for five updates of the Critic weights as a way to maintain the stability of the training procedure, but the ratio can be application-specific [4]. The *Boundary Equilibrium GAN* [5] method introduces a procedure to balance the training by the way of maintaining the equilibrium $\mathbb{E}[\mathcal{L}[(G(z))] = \gamma \mathbb{E}[\mathcal{L}(x)]$. It is achieved by the additional parameter k that scales the losses of the Generator $\mathcal{L}_G$ and the Discriminator $\mathcal{L}_D$ as shown in the Eq. 13.

$$\mathcal{L}_D = \mathcal{L}(x) - k_t \mathcal{L}(G(z_D)) \tag{13}$$

$$\mathcal{L}_G = \mathcal{L}(G(z_G))$$

$$k_{t+1} = k_t + \lambda_k(\gamma \mathcal{L}(x) - \mathcal{L}(G(z_G))),$$

where k is a proportion between the Generator and the Discriminator loss at iteration t (with $k_0 = 0$), λ_k is the proportional gain for k.

Other approaches regularizing training procedure of GAN worth mentioning are *Least Squares GANs* [33] (applying least squares difference between discriminator loss and the expected outcome), *Spectral Normalization GANs* [35] (constraining spectral norm of each layer's weights) and *Regularized GANs* [39] (adding noise as a regularizer).

7   Conclusion

In this work, we present recent developments in Generative Adversarial Networks research. We explore several selected fields of current research, focusing on the most important milestones, notably in the fields of semi-supervised learning, unsupervised style translation, and representation learning.

References

1. Achlioptas, P., Diamanti, O., Mitliagkas, I., Guibas, L.: Learning representations and generative models for 3D point clouds. In: International Conference on Machine Learning, pp. 40–49 (2018)
2. Agustsson, E., Tschannen, M., Mentzer, F., Timofte, R., Van Gool, L.: Generative adversarial networks for extreme learned image compression. arXiv preprint arXiv:1804.02958 (2018)
3. Arjovsky, M., Chintala, S., Bottou, L.: Wasserstein generative adversarial networks. In: International Conference on Machine Learning, pp. 214–223 (2017)
4. Arora, S., Ge, R., Liang, Y., Ma, T., Zhang, Y.: Generalization and equilibrium in generative adversarial nets (GANS). arXiv preprint arXiv:1703.00573 (2017)
5. Berthelot, D., Schumm, T., Metz, L.: Began: boundary equilibrium generative adversarial networks. arXiv preprint arXiv:1703.10717 (2017)
6. Brock, A., Donahue, J., Simonyan, K.: Large scale GAN training for high fidelity natural image synthesis. arXiv preprint arXiv:1809.11096 (2018)
7. Bromley, J., Guyon, I., LeCun, Y., Säckinger, E., Shah, R.: Signature verification using a "siamese" time delay neural network. In: Advances in Neural Information Processing Systems, pp. 737–744 (1994)
8. Burda, Y., Grosse, R., Salakhutdinov, R.: Importance weighted autoencoders. arXiv preprint arXiv:1509.00519 (2015)
9. Cao, Y., Ding, G.W., Lui, K.Y.C., Huang, R.: Improving GAN training via binarized representation entropy (bre) regularization. CoRR abs/1805.03644 (2018)
10. Chechik, G., Sharma, V., Shalit, U., Bengio, S.: Large scale online learning of image similarity through ranking. J. Mach. Learn. Res. **11**, 1109–1135 (2010)
11. Chen, X., Duan, Y., Houthooft, R., Schulman, J., Sutskever, I., Abbeel, P.: InfoGAN: interpretable representation learning by information maximizing generative adversarial nets. In: Advances in Neural Information Processing Systems, pp. 2172–2180 (2016)
12. Choi, Y., Choi, M., Kim, M., Ha, J.W., Kim, S., Choo, J.: StarGAN: Unified generative adversarial networks for multi-domain image-to-image translation. arXiv preprint 1711 (2017)
13. Chopra, S., Hadsell, R., LeCun, Y.: Learning a similarity metric discriminatively, with application to face verification. In: IEEE Computer Society Conference on Computer Vision and Pattern Recognition CVPR 2005, vol. 1, pp. 539–546. IEEE (2005)
14. Creswell, A., White, T., Dumoulin, V., Arulkumaran, K., Sengupta, B., Bharath, A.A.: Generative adversarial networks: an overview. IEEE Signal Process. Mag. **35**(1), 53–65 (2018)
15. Donahue, J., Krähenbühl, P., Darrell, T.: Adversarial feature learning. arXiv preprint arXiv:1605.09782 (2016)
16. Dumoulin, V., et al.: Adversarially learned inference. arXiv preprint arXiv:1606.00704 (2016)
17. Fabius, O., van Amersfoort, J.R.: Variational recurrent auto-encoders. arXiv preprint arXiv:1412.6581 (2014)
18. Goodfellow, I., Bengio, Y., Courville, A., Bengio, Y.: Deep Learning, vol. 1. MIT press, Cambridge (2016)
19. Goodfellow, I., et al.: Generative adversarial nets. In: Advances in Neural Information Processing Systems, pp. 2672–2680 (2014)

20. Gulrajani, I., Ahmed, F., Arjovsky, M., Dumoulin, V., Courville, A.C.: Improved training of wasserstein GANs. In: Advances in Neural Information Processing Systems, pp. 5767–5777 (2017)
21. Hadsell, R., Chopra, S., LeCun, Y.: Dimensionality reduction by learning an invariant mapping. In: 2006 IEEE Computer Society Conference on Computer Vision and Pattern Recognition (CVPR 2006), pp. 1735–1742. IEEE (2006)
22. Hanin, L.G.: Kantorovich-rubinstein norm and its application in the theory of lipschitz spaces. Proc. Am. Math. Soc. **115**(2), 345–352 (1992)
23. Hoffer, E., Ailon, N.: Deep metric learning using triplet network. In: Feragen, A., Pelillo, M., Loog, M. (eds.) SIMBAD 2015. LNCS, vol. 9370, pp. 84–92. Springer, Cham (2015). https://doi.org/10.1007/978-3-319-24261-3_7
24. Isola, P., Zhu, J.Y., Zhou, T., Efros, A.A.: Image-to-image translation with conditional adversarial networks. arXiv preprint (2017)
25. Karras, T., Aila, T., Laine, S., Lehtinen, J.: Progressive growing of GANs for improved quality, stability, and variation. arXiv preprint arXiv:1710.10196 (2017)
26. Kim, T., Cha, M., Kim, H., Lee, J.K., Kim, J.: Learning to discover cross-domain relations with generative adversarial networks. arXiv preprint arXiv:1703.05192 (2017)
27. Kingma, D.P., Welling, M.: Auto-encoding variational bayes. arXiv preprint arXiv:1312.6114 (2013)
28. Kurach, K., Lucic, M., Zhai, X., Michalski, M., Gelly, S.: The GAN landscape: Losses, architectures, regularization, and normalization. arXiv preprint arXiv:1807.04720 (2018)
29. Ledig, C., et al.: Photo-realistic single image super-resolution using a generative adversarial network. In: CVPR, vol. 2, p. 4 (2017)
30. Li, C.L., Zaheer, M., Zhang, Y., Poczos, B., Salakhutdinov, R.: Point cloud GAN. arXiv preprint arXiv:1810.05795 (2018)
31. Lucic, M., Kurach, K., Michalski, M., Gelly, S., Bousquet, O.: Are GANs created equal? a large-scale study. arXiv preprint arXiv:1711.10337 (2017)
32. Makhzani, A., Shlens, J., Jaitly, N., Goodfellow, I., Frey, B.: Adversarial autoencoders. arXiv preprint arXiv:1511.05644 (2015)
33. Mao, X., Li, Q., Xie, H., Lau, R.Y., Wang, Z., Smolley, S.P.: Least squares generative adversarial networks. In: 2017 IEEE International Conference on Computer Vision (ICCV), pp. 2813–2821. IEEE (2017)
34. Mirza, M., Osindero, S.: Conditional generative adversarial nets. arXiv preprint arXiv:1411.1784 (2014)
35. Miyato, T., Kataoka, T., Koyama, M., Yoshida, Y.: Spectral normalization for generative adversarial networks. arXiv preprint arXiv:1802.05957 (2018)
36. Odena, A.: Semi-supervised learning with generative adversarial networks. arXiv preprint arXiv:1606.01583 (2016)
37. Odena, A., Olah, C., Shlens, J.: Conditional image synthesis with auxiliary classifier GANs. arXiv preprint arXiv:1610.09585 (2016)
38. Radford, A., Metz, L., Chintala, S.: Unsupervised representation learning with deep convolutional generative adversarial networks. arXiv preprint arXiv:1511.06434 (2015)
39. Roth, K., Lucchi, A., Nowozin, S., Hofmann, T.: Stabilizing training of generative adversarial networks through regularization. In: Advances in Neural Information Processing Systems, pp. 2018–2028 (2017)
40. Rachev, S.T., Shortt, R.M.: Duality theorems for Kantorovich-Rubinstein and Wasserstein functionals. Mathematical Institute of Polish Academy of Sciences (1990). http://eudml.org/doc/268473

41. Salimans, T., Goodfellow, I., Zaremba, W., Cheung, V., Radford, A., Chen, X.: Improved techniques for training GANs. In: Advances in Neural Information Processing Systems, pp. 2234–2242 (2016)

42. Shen, J., Qu, Y., Zhang, W., Yu, Y.: Adversarial representation learning for domain adaptation. arXiv preprint arXiv:1707.01217 (2017)

43. Simonyan, K., Zisserman, A.: Very deep convolutional networks for large-scale image recognition. arXiv:1409.1556v6 (2015)

44. Song, J.: Binary generative adversarial networks for image retrieval. arXiv preprint arXiv:1708.04150 (2017)

45. Tolstikhin, I., Bousquet, O., Gelly, S., Schoelkopf, B.: Wasserstein auto-encoders. arXiv preprint arXiv:1711.01558 (2017)

46. Wu, J., Zhang, C., Xue, T., Freeman, B., Tenenbaum, J.: Learning a probabilistic latent space of object shapes via 3D generative-adversarial modeling. In: Advances in Neural Information Processing Systems, pp. 82–90 (2016)

47. Zamorski, M., Zieba, M.: Semi-supervised learning with bidirectional GANs. arXiv preprint arXiv:1812.11426 (2018)

48. Zamorski, M., Zięba, M., Nowak, R., Stokowiec, W., Trzciński, T.: Adversarial autoencoders for generating 3D point clouds. arXiv preprint arXiv:1811.07605 (2018)

49. Zhang, H., Goodfellow, I., Metaxas, D., Odena, A.: Self-attention generative adversarial networks. arXiv preprint arXiv:1805.08318 (2018)

50. Zhang, H., et al.: StackGAN: Text to photo-realistic image synthesis with stacked generative adversarial networks. arXiv preprint (2017)

51. Zhang, H., et al.: Stackgan++: Realistic image synthesis with stacked generative adversarial networks. arXiv preprint arXiv:1710.10916 (2017)

52. Zhu, J.Y., Park, T., Isola, P., Efros, A.A.: Unpaired image-to-image translation using cycle-consistent adversarial networks. arXiv preprint (2017)

53. Zieba, M., Semberecki, P., El-Gaaly, T., Trzcinski, T.: BinGAN: Learning compact binary descriptors with a regularized GAN. arXiv preprint arXiv:1806.06778 (2018)

54. Zieba, M., Wang, L.: Training triplet networks with GAN. arXiv preprint arXiv:1704.02227 (2017)

Fuzzy Systems and Their Applications

Fuzzy Modeling in the Task of Control Cartographic Visualization

Stanislav Belyakov[1] , Alexander Bozhenyuk[1](✉) , Janusz Kacprzyk[2] ,
and Margarita Knyazeva[1]

[1] Southern Federal University, Nekrasovskiy Str., 44, 347928 Taganrog, Russia
beliacov@yandex.ru, avb002@yandex.ru, margarita.knyazeva@gmail.com
[2] Systems Research Institute Polish Academy of Sciences,
Newelska 6, 01-447 Warsaw, Poland
janusz.kacprzyk@ibspan.waw.pl

Abstract. Visual analysis of maps, charts and plans plays an important role in decision-making on the basis of spatial data. One of the difficulties in applying visual analysis is the redundancy of the cartographic data flow that occurs when the user interacts with the geographic information system (GIS). The redundancy reduces the dynamics of dialog worsens the perception of visualized data and negatively affects the quality of decision making. This paper considers the problem of cartographic visualization control, the purpose of which is to construct the most useful images for decision making. The fuzzy representation of visual analysis experience by images is analyzed. The image includes the center and the region of its permissible transformations. The comparison of images is modeled as the classification of situations of the relative locations of the centers, the region of permissible transformations of each image and the region of their intersection. The concept of fuzzy utility function of the cartographic image is introduced. The problem of choosing useful fuzzy images of cartographic images is considered. The logic of decision making is described in the fact of comparison of fuzzy images. The method for specifying the space topology of the utility estimation is proposed. This method allows carrying out the transfer of experience in estimating the utility of images. The invariant of transfer of experience is investigated. Principles of transformation of images of precedents are formulated.

Keywords: Fuzzy control · Cartographic visualization ·
Fuzzy utility function · Decision making

1 Introduction

Visual analysis of cartographic expression traditionally is an efficient mean for problem solving that requires spatial data for their implementation. Maps, schemes and plans, that store geoinformation systems (GIS), are familiar in many applied

This work has been supported by the Ministry of Education and Science of the Russian Federation under Project "Methods and means of decision making on base of dynamic geographic information models" (Project part, State task 2.918.2017).

© Springer Nature Switzerland AG 2019
L. Rutkowski et al. (Eds.): ICAISC 2019, LNAI 11508, pp. 261–272, 2019.
https://doi.org/10.1007/978-3-030-20912-4_25

areas. In these area specialists solve informal tasks in conditions of uncertainty. The modern network of GIS is considered as big data systems [1, 2], continuously accumulating information about the outside world. The value of the accumulated data is implemented by its use for decision making, therefore GIS should be equipped with an interactive visualization mechanism that will provide the user-analyst with intelligent support in the construction of the analysis area. The selected geodata should be the most useful for searching and making decisions. The difficulty of constructing this mechanism is available for uncertainty which directly affects the definition and understanding of the utility of visualization. In this paper, we propose a method for controlling cartographic visualization, using fuzzy representation of the utility function of cartographic image.

2   The Overview of Known Solutions

Cartographic visualization is the basis of modern methods of visualization of spatial data in GIS [3]. The specificity of cartographic visualization is determined by the use of cartographic projections and standards for displaying map objects, as well as a special dialogue with the user that concentrates on the properties of maps and cartographic objects. Each visualization operation allows only manual configuration, which creates obvious difficulties in achievement of the required dialogue speed. The optimization task of the dialogue is not considered.

The problem of semantic content of not redundant data of analysis' workspace that forms holistic view of an object or situation, is traditionally solved by the repeated use of maps created by expert-cartographers [3]. It is noted in [4] that such maps are essential patterns of knowledge that are used to solve similar tasks. Researches are focused on building families of instances of the workspace in the given context. In the researches of this area, little attention is paid to the use of knowledge for the dynamic formation of workspaces.

Researches of user's interaction with GIS have been carried out in geoinformatics for many years [5]. The subject of research is the perception of cartographic images, which is limited by the speed of image construction and their complexity. In earlier works visualization problems were considered with hard limit of the speed and visualization system's memory capacity; the modern research concentrates on flow control of information on the network [6] and extraction of knowledge from the visual data. Control of the utility of visual representation of objects based on an assessment of their perception by the user in these works is not considered.

The separate area of research focus of visualization of geospatial data is the semantic classification of observable objects. In [7], for example, the real-time classification problem was investigated, granulation of data was set, representation point-of-interest was proposed, data-driven and theory-informed approach were proposed for the interactive analysis of the state of a modern city. This area of research does not affect the control of the dialogue, while paying the greatest attention to subjective interpretation of cartographic data in conditions of uncertainty.

The possibility of a holistic provision of cartographic information through impact on all human senses is investigated by cybercartography [8]. The research of authors concentrates mainly on the integration of geospatial data and models of representing heterogeneous knowledge in cartographic form. Dialogue methods in the process of using maps containing inaccurate and not completely defined objects remain less investigated.

The problems of visualization are affected by the research of analytical systems for big data. In particular, the subject of research is the behavior of the user-analyst in the process of image manipulation. An example is the work [9], in which the effect of the implementation of the functions of image manipulation ZOOM IN, ZOOM OUT, PANNED on the efficiency of the analysis of user-generated content was experimentally investigated. In these researches, user behavior is described in a deterministic manner, i.e. with the use of simplifications that worsen the quality of the results.

The interactive visual analysis is the subject of intensive research in psychology. The example is the work [10] that analyzes the role of visual analysis in the modern sense of "digital creativity" in the analysis of big data. The authors, in particular, note the importance of constructing the mental image of the problem on the basis of the cyclic return from viewing images to understanding the statement of the problem. The search for technical realization of the process of purposeful formation of the mental image is the continuation of these researches.

The approach to cartographic visualization based on the special representation of the structure of the workspace of analysis and the use of knowledge to construct informative cartographic images are developed in works [11,12]. The proposed model can be developed for the case of fuzzy description of the utility function, which will improve the quality of visualization.

Finally, we can conclude that the currently known approaches to visualization of cartographic data do not consider it as an integral process of constructing and modifying the workspace of analysis in the user's session with GIS. Intellectual support for the utility maximization function of the studied workspace remains less studied. The subjectivity and uncertainty in assessment of the content of the workspace make it necessary to search for new models for representing the utility function of cartographic images.

3   Fuzzy Image Model of the Utility Function

To solve applied problem, the analyst constructs the workspace w. Denote $I(w)$ as the utility function of the workspace w. From our point of view, the utility function is determined by the level of professional perception of the cartographic image of the workspace. Perception is an integral property that affects the quality of the mental image of the analyst's mind. The perception in the process of interactive visual analysis perception plays a crucial role, it is consistent with modern ideas about the impact of visualization on creativity [10]. Therefore, we will assume that the argument of the utility function is the number of graphic objects $N = |w|$. It increases worsens perception due to physiological limitations of vision, but the same effect is observed when it is reduced due to loss of meaningful image. A full perception corresponds to the number of image elements that is subjectively defined by the user as some "best" value $|w_{siml}| < N^* < |w_{complex}|$. Here the value $|w_{siml}|$ is the number of objects in the non-informative by subjective sensation of the user of the working area, the value $|w_{complex}|$ is the number of objects that are "very complicated" image. The fact that the parameter $N = |w|$ is available for measurement makes its use in the visualization quality control loop attractive.

Let's consider function $\tilde{I}(N)$ that is given by the form of a fuzzy set:

$$\tilde{I} = \{< \mu_{\tilde{I}}(n, i), (n, i) > | (n, i) \in N \times I\},$$
$$N \in [0, N_{\max}], I \in [0, 1], \mu_{\tilde{I}} : N \times I \to [0, 1].$$

Here, the value is the number of cartographic objects so that this number is as much as it is possible to percept. For a wide range of users, the evaluation of utility is unreliable. However, the presentation of images utility of the studied made by a professional group of specialists is quite stable and sufficiently coordinated. The membership function $\mu_{\tilde{I}}$ of any pair (n_k, i_k) adequately characterizes the expert's confidence in the utility i_k of the image consisting of objects n_k.

A comparison of utility $\tilde{I}(L)$ and $\tilde{I}(R)$ of two cartographic images with the number of objects L and R is the comparison of two values of membership function of inequalities:

$$\mu_{I(L)>I(R)} = \min_{I_n(L), I_m(R) \in \tilde{I}, I_n(L)>I_m(R)} \max\{\mu_{\tilde{I}} < L, I_n(L) >, \mu_{\tilde{I}} < R, I_m(R) >\},$$

and

$$\mu_{I(L)\leq I(R)} = \min_{I_n(L), I_m(R) \in \tilde{I}, I_n(L)\leq I_m(R)} \max\{\mu_{\tilde{I}} < L, I_n(L) >, \mu_{\tilde{I}} < R, I_m(R) >\},$$

Therefore, the logical conclusion about the utility ratio is determined by the truth of one of the rules:

$$\begin{aligned} \mu_{I(L)>I(R)} > \mu_{I(L)\leq I(R)} &\implies I(L) > I(R), \\ \mu_{I(L)>I(R)} \leq \mu_{I(L)\leq I(R)} &\implies I(R) > I(L). \end{aligned} \tag{1}$$

The main difficulty of practical application of such a model is that the function $\tilde{I}$ is partially defined and multivalued. The reason is the laboriousness of constructing its complete description. Typically, there are a limited number of precedents for $\tilde{I}$ values that have been obtained empirically. Therefore, it is necessary to search the way to use incomplete knowledge about this function. A possible option is to use a image representation of the utility function.

Using a continuous membership function $\mu_{\tilde{I}}$ for discrete pairs (n_k, i_k) we can apply an image description of knowledge. The image includes two components:

1. the concrete value that was observed experimentally. We call it "the center of the image";
2. the region of permissible transformations of the center, which do not change the meaning of the observed phenomenon.

An image that has the utility of I_i and consists of N_i objects generates an image:

$$J = <c, H(c)>, c = <n_i, i_i>, H(c) \subseteq N \times I,$$

where area $H(c)$ is given by a figure in the coordinate system (N, I).

This area displays the deep analytical knowledge of the expert. The shape and dimensions of the domain are an invariant meaning, which is embedded in the concept of utility of a particular seen and studied image. Graphical image simulates the natural process of thinking by creative human [13]. Figure 1 shows an example of the image description that was formed when studying an image with the number of elements $N_i = 100$ whose utility was estimated as $I_i = 0.7$. Expressive graphics in this case allowed to display the in-depth knowledge of the expert by an asymmetric display of the area of the permissible image transformation.

A fuzzy image is called object:

$$\tilde{J} = \{<\mu_{\tilde{j}}(H(c)), H(c)> | H(c) \subseteq N \times I\}, \mu_{\tilde{j}} : H(c) \rightarrow [0, 1]. \qquad (2)$$

Figure 2 shows the image from the previous example as a fuzzy view. This representation is an important way to indicate the connection between the center of the image and its permissible transformations with the remaining points in space. The membership function $\mu_{\tilde{j}}$ reflects the expert's confidence that an image with a number of elements n_m has utility i_i despite the fact that $<n_m, i_i> \notin H(c), c = <n_n, i_i>, n_m \neq n_n$.

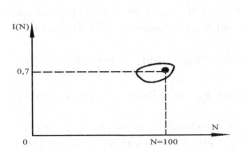

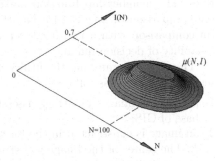

Fig. 1. Example of image description

Fig. 2. Example of representing an image with the membership function

Representation (2) provides the way to model imaginative thinking through pattern matching [13]. The matching mechanism is realized as a classification of the variants of the relative location for the elements of the images to be compared. This takes into account:

1. the size of the intersection between the regions of permissible transformations;
2. positioning of the image centers relative to the intersection area;
3. positioning of the image centers relative to each other's transformation areas.

For example, let's consider classification rules when two classes K_1 and K_2 are used. A class K_1 is regarded as a class of similar images, and the class K_2 is considered as a class of images that are far from each other. Suppose that the images are considered close if their areas of permissible transformations have common transformations and the centers of the images are in this area. Substantially this means that the permissible (inessential in the considered sense) transformations of one precedent of experience lead to another precedent. Since image centers are experimental data, it can be concluded that the existence of general transformations has been confirmed practically. It serves as a basis for concluding that the images are similar. Then the rule of assigning two matched images $\tilde{J}_1$ and $\tilde{J}_2$ to the class K_1 can be written in the form:

$$\min_{x>0,x\in H_1(c_1)\cap H_2(c_2)} \{\mu_{\tilde{J}_1}(x), \mu_{\tilde{J}_2}(x), \mu_{\tilde{J}_1}(c_2), \mu_{\tilde{J}_2}(c_1)\} > \mu_{K_1},$$

where μ_{K_1} is the minimum level of belonging to the class K_1.

The inclusion of at least one center in the region of general transformations indicates a non-commutative transformation of one center into another, which can also be considered meaningfully as the proximity of the images. The classification rule for this case is as follows:

$$\min_{x>0,x\in H_1(c_1)\cap H_2(c_2)} \{\mu_{\tilde{J}_1}(x), \mu_{\tilde{J}_2}(x), \mu_{\tilde{J}_2}(c_1)\} > \mu_{K_1},$$

All situations belong to the class K_2 if they do not satisfy the assignment rule to the class K_1. The image representation makes it possible to display the subjectivity of the evaluation of utility by introducing more classes and classification rules. The membership function makes it possible to control the reliability of the comparison of images in a larger part of the space of emergent situations (in comparison with a non-fuzzy representation of images). This increases the reliability of decision-making.

The task of comparing the utility of two images using an imaginative representation is solved as follows:

1. precedents images of utility assessment are introduced into the knowledge base of GIS;
2. an image is constructed in the form of a rectangular region for a given value L. The center of the image is a straight line $N = L$. The width of the range of permissible transformations is given by the value ΔL that is determined in the context of image analysis;
3. the constructed image is compared with known images of precedents. In this case, the utility is evaluated by some value which is set by default. Otherwise, the fuzzy value $\tilde{I}(L)$ is fixed;
4. paragraphs 2 and 3 are satisfied for the value R. The fuzzy value $\tilde{I}(R)$ is fixed;
5. the decision about the image utility is made based on the truth of the rules (1).

Analyzing the described procedure, we state the following: by reusing the precedents of experience in the form of images, the pattern matching mechanism does not allow to make a decision in the absence of experience in the analyzed area. To solve this problem, the described mechanism should be extended to the possibility of transferring experience.

4   Transformation of Experience

The difficulty of transforming the experience of estimating a certain parameter in other conditions is caused by the appearance of a semantic mismatch between the original and transformed precedents. The notion of "semantic mismatch" means the loss or distortion of the important relationships between the precedent situation and the objects of the space in which the transformation is performed. To solve the problem of transferring experience, we define the topology of space and the transformation invariant. The displaying of the situation into a given region of space is formally described by expression:

$$< \bar{c}, h_1(\bar{c}), ..., h_M(\bar{c}) >= F_{TR}(< c, h_1(c), h_2(c), ..., h_M(c) >),$$

which is interpreted as follows: a new situation $\bar{c}$, which is modelled on the basis of the known precedent of the situation c, is equivalent to it if it allows the same transformations $h_i(\bar{c}) \neq \emptyset, i = \overline{1, M}$ as the initial situation.

Let's consider the way the area topology of utility estimates is constructed. The analysis of the structure of cartographic images and the construction procedure allows us to distinguish three areas R_1, R_2, and R_3. The location of these areas is schematically shown in Fig. 3.

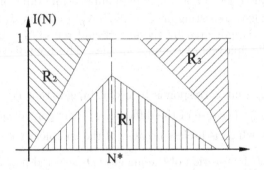

Fig. 3. Structure of the value area of the utility function

The area $R_1 \subset N \times I$ includes such low utility estimates that can't be met in practice, even if the complexity of the image is close to the value N^*. The area is bounded by a curve $I_{R_1}(N)$ on the interval $[N_{R_1}^{(1)}, N_{R_2}^{(2)}]$, and the value $N^* \in [N_{R_1}^{(1)}, N_{R_2}^{(2)}]$. For all real images, the following inequality holds: $I(N) > I_{R_1}(N)$.

The expert indicates a border $I_{R_1}(N)$. The boundary of the area should pass through the points:

- $I_{R_1}(N^*) \neq 0$, which corresponds to the minimum possible utility of a well-perceived cartographic image;
- $I_{R_1}(N_{R_1}^{(1)}) \approx 0$, which is useless because of the small number of cartographic objects in the image;

– $I_{R_1}(N_{R_1}^{(2)}) \approx 0$, which corresponds to a useless cartographic image that is not adequately perceived due to the large number of objects.

The area $R_2 \subset N \times I$ includes unattainable utility estimates caused by the low information content of simple images. The region is bounded by curves $I_{R_2}(N)$ and $I(N) = 1$ on the interval $[N_{R_2}^{(1)}, N_{R_2}^{(2)}]$, $N_{R_2}^{(1)} < N^*$. The utility of images with the number of objects $N \in [N_{R_2}^{(1)}, N_{R_2}^{(2)}]$ can't be estimated higher than it is determined by the boundary R_2: $I(N) < I_{R_2}(N)$.

The boundary $I_{R_2}(N)$ is also set by the expert. The boundary of area R_2 should cover the points:

– $I(0) = 0$;
– $I_{R_2}(N_{R_2}^{(1)}) \approx 0$, which corresponds to useless simple images from a small number of objects;
– $I_{R_2}(N_{R_2}^{(2)}) \approx 1$, which corresponds to the most useful images that can't be obtained when $N < N_{R_2}^{(2)}$.

The area $R_3 \subset N \times I$ includes unattainable in reality high utility scores due to the deterioration of the perception of complex images. The area is bounded by curves $I_{R_3}(N)$ and $I(N) = 1$ on the interval $[N_{R_3}^{(1)}, N_{R_3}^{(2)}]$, $N_{R_3}^{(1)} < N^*$. The boundary of the area determines the maximum possible value of utility that can be reached by images consisting of $N \in [N_{R_3}^{(1)}, N_{R_3}^{(2)}]$ objects: $I(N) < I_{R_3}(N)$.

The boundary is indicated by the expert and reflects his knowledge about uselessness for the analysis of complex images. The boundary of the area R_3 covers the points:

– $I_{R_2}(N_{R_3}^{(1)}) \approx 1$, that corresponds to useful images that can't be built from objects $N > N_{R_3}^{(1)}$ because of the difficulty of their perception;
– $I_{R_3}(N_{R_3}^{(2)}) \approx 0$, which is useless because of the complexity of the image.

As an invariant of the position of the images (D) selected pair of numbers $D = <d_1, d_2>$, where d_1 is a distance from the center of the image to the nearest point of the boundary of the area R_2 if $N < N^*$, or the area R_3 if $N > N^*$; d_2 is the distance from the image center to the nearest point of the boundary of the area R_1. The choice is made due to the following:

1. the value D unambiguously characterizes the class of images, the change in the number of elements and the level of utility of which is limited and determined by their position in the assessment space;
2. remoteness from the areas boundaries R_1, R_2, R_3 reflects the intuitive representation of the expert about how far the indicated utility level is far from the limit values;
3. images with the same possibilities for modification of complexity and the same levels of utility can be considered equivalent.

The boundary of permissible changes in the image includes points whose position must correspond to the invariant as well. The transformation of the domain of permissible changes is realized by the points of its boundary.

We describe the procedure for transferring experience in case of fuzzy representation of the boundaries of regions and distances between them:

1. the expert forms areas R_1, R_2, and R_3 with fuzzy boundaries $\tilde{I}_{R_1}(N)$, $\tilde{I}_{R_2}(N)$, $\tilde{I}_{R_3}(N)$, in the assessment space;
2. the expert represents existing precedent of experience as an image with a center $c =< n_c, i_c >$ and an area of permissible transformations with a boundary $\tilde{H}(c)$;
3. the point $< n_k, i_k >$ of transfer of the use case image is determined;
4. the fuzzy value of $\tilde{D}_k =< \tilde{d}_1^{(k)}, \tilde{d}_2^{(k)} >$ invariant is estimated, which includes fuzzy distances to the areas R_1, R_2, and R_3;
5. the fuzzy value of $\tilde{D}_c =< \tilde{d}_1^{(c)}, \tilde{d}_2^{(c)} >$ invariant is defined for the image center of precedent;
6. equality $\tilde{D}_c = \tilde{D}_k$ is estimated at a given level of membership;
7. if the fuzzy invariants coincide, then the domain of admissible transformations is constructed with a fuzzy boundary for $< N_k, I_k >$. Otherwise it is considered that the transformation of the source image of the precedent into a given point is impossible.

5   Experimental Study of Visualization Method

The effectiveness of the visualization method was evaluated by the reaction of corporate GIS users. To achieve this, a software layout of the visualization system was developed. It was proposed to a group of users to evaluate the quality of the dialogue with GIS. The layout was developed in the AutoCad Map environment in AutoLisp. The training of the intelligent visualization system was carried out on the information base of the corporate GIS, which includes about 10^6 objects. The volume of external data sources from cameras and sensors of technological systems is estimated as 2 TBites.

The corporate GIS users solved the following tasks:

- accounting the material resources and planning the territorial development of the enterprise. The subject of the analysis is the territorial location of equipment, internal layout of premises, the cost of reconstruction of buildings and structures;
- maintenance of enterprise engineering networks. Here, spatial distributions of terrestrial and underground communications are analyzed; decisions are taken on outages in emergency situations;
- the enterprise safety. The purpose of the analysis is both the impact of natural and man-made factors on the production process, and the analysis of hazards arising from the work of staff;
- implementing the logistics of the enterprise. The subject of the analysis is the relocation and storage of raw materials and products on the enterprise territory, planning of logistics operations;

– managing the supply and distribution of energy within the enterprise. This analysis is necessary for the distribution of energy consumption quotas, making decisions about the redistribution of energy flows in case of emergency.

Five contexts, "Administration", "Security department", "Department of Energy Supply", "Engineering Communication", and "Logistics Department" were formed in accordance with the described modes of using GIS. A knowledge base was created to manage visualization for each context. As the practice of applying the layout has shown, the average value of the number of objects of the working area N^* set by users when configuring the system ranges from several tens to hundreds of copies.

The work area redundancy level indicator (k) was estimated by the ratio of the number of objects in the source area (a) to the number of objects in the area after optimization (b): $k = \frac{a}{b}$.

An experiment was conducted for the contexts mentioned above. Table 1 shows the data set of context "Administration", which were obtained programmatically by redundancy factor (k) values and expert utility estimates (R). Evaluations of usefulness were obtained by polling users.

Average values of the indicators were calculated based on the experimental data set. Table 2 shows the names of the contexts and the average values of the redundancy reduction coefficients for each context.

We analyzed the received data and claimed that the visualization control subsystem reduced redundancy in all contexts. The difference in values k indicates the different quality of knowledge embedded in the experimental model of the system. We also show the integral mean values of the utility evaluation of the system for decision-making (R), which were obtained by the users survey.

Table 1. Redundancy reduction coefficients and values of the utility evaluation for context "Administration".

User1		User2		User3		User4	
k	R	k	R	k	R	k	R
2.1	6	1.2	4	2.4	8	2.0	5
1.5	6	1.0	4	1.5	4	2.0	6
2.5	7	2.8	6	2.3	9	2.0	6
1.9	6	2.1	7	1.7	4	1.0	2
2.0	7	4.0	7	2.4	8	1.0	5
1.8	5	1.2	4	2.4	8	2.5	8
1.6	6	2.5	7	1.5	4	1.4	3
2.3	8	1.3	5	1.5	3	1.0	3
1.8	6	2.5	7	2.1	6	1.0	4
1.8	6	2.5	7	1.5	4	2.0	6

We compared the utility estimates from Table 2 and the degree of reduction in redundancy. A statistically significant relationship was found between the reduction in redundancy and the increase in the evaluation of the quality of the decisions made. The correlation coefficient is 0.357. Thus, the result of the experiment indicates the feasibility of applying the proposed method of visualization.

Table 2. Average values of the redundancy reduction coefficients and integral mean values of the utility evaluation.

Context	k	R
Administration	1.9	6
Security Department	2.1	8
Department of Energy Supply	3.3	7
Engineering Communications Department	4	9
Logistics Department	10	8

6 Conclusion

Geoinformation systems are the main application area of the proposed method of visualization management. The main effect of the proposed method is the improvement of the quality of decision-making by providing the user-analyst with not excessive and complete cartographic images. The effect is achieved by the use of knowledge. The fuzzy model of figurative representation and the use of experience that were suggested in this work allowed performing an important point that is the estimation of utility of images. The procedure for transferring the experience of solving problems based on topology was built. Further studies are planned in the direction of automatic adaptation of GIS to changes in the cartographic database. The real world is changing, so new classes of relationships and objects are added to the GIS database. Therefore, the work of the visualization system will lose its effectiveness without the knowledge that corresponds to the new cartographic entities. It seems, that machine learning methods may solve the problem as well. That is a promising direction for our future research.

References

1. Raad, M.: Discusses geospatial big data: the next big trend in analytics (2015). https://www.geospatialworld.net/article/mansour-raad-discusses-geospatial-bigdata-the-next-big-trend-in-analytics/?utm_content=buffer3709f&utm_medium=social&utm_source=linkedin.com&utm_campaign=buffer
2. Lee, J., Kang, M.: Geospatial big data: challenges and opportunities. Big Data Res. **2**, 74–81 (2015)
3. Longley, P., Goodchild, M., Maguire, D., Rhind, D.: Geographic Information Systems and Science, 537 p. Wiley, Barcelona (2005)

4. Pangbourne, K., Alvanides, S.: Towards intelligent transport geography. J. Transp. Geogr. **34**, 231–232 (2014)
5. Lindholm, M., Sarjakovski, T.: Designing a visualization user interface. In: Modern Cartography Series, vol. 2, pp. 167–184 (1994)
6. Cranley, N., Perry, P., Murphy, L.: Dynamic content-based adaptation of streamed multimedia. J. Netw. Comput. Appl. **30**, 983–1006 (2007)
7. McKenzie, G., Janowicz, K., Gao, S., Yanget, J.: POI pulse: a multi-granular, semantic signature-based information observatory for the interactive visualization of big geosocial data. Cartographica Int. J. Geogr. Inf. Geovisualization **50**(2), 71–85 (2015)
8. Taylor, D., Lauriault, T.: Conclusion and the future of cybercartography, developments in the theory and practice of cybercartography. In: Applications and Indigenous Mapping, vol. 5, pp. 343–350 (2014)
9. Liu, Y., Wang, H., Li, G., Gao, J., Hua, H., Li, W.: ELAN: an efficient location-aware analytics system. Big Data Res. **5**, 16–21 (2016)
10. Cybulski, J., Keller, S., Nguyen, L., Saundage, D.: Creative problem solving in digital space using visual analytics. Comput. Hum. Behav. **42**, 20–35 (2015)
11. Belyakov, S., Bozhenyuk, A., Belykova, M., Rozenberg, I.: Model of intellectual visualization of geoinformation service. In: Proceedings of the 28th European Conference on Modelling and Simulation ECMS, pp. 326–333 (2014)
12. Belyakov, S., Rozenberg, I., Belykova, M.: Approach to real-time mapping, using a fuzzy information function. In: Geo-Informatics in Resource Management and Sustainable Ecosystem, Part I, pp. 510–521 (2013)
13. Kuznetsov, O.: Cognitive semantics and artificial intelligence. Sci. Techn. Inf. Process. **40**(5), 269–276 (2013)

Method for Generalization of Fuzzy Sets

Dmitry Frolov[1(✉)], Boris Mirkin[1,2], Susana Nascimento[3], and Trevor Fenner[2]

[1] Department of Data Analysis and Artificial Intelligence, National Research University "Higher School of Economics", Moscow, Russian Federation
dfrolov@hse.ru
[2] Department of Computer Science and Information Systems, Birkbeck University of London, London, UK
[3] Department of Computer Science and NOVA LINCS, Universidade Nova de Lisboa, Caparica, Portugal

Abstract. We define and find a most specific generalization of a fuzzy set of topics assigned to leaves of the rooted tree of a taxonomy. This generalization lifts the set to a "head subject" in the higher ranks of the taxonomy, that is supposed to "tightly" cover the query set, possibly bringing in some errors, both "gaps" and "offshoots". The method globally minimizes a penalty combining head subjects and gaps and offshoots. We apply this to extract research tendencies from a collection of about 18000 research papers published in Springer journals on data science. We consider a taxonomy of Data Science based on the Association for Computing Machinery Classification of Computing System 2012 (ACM-CCS). We find fuzzy clusters of leaf topics over the text collection and use thematic clusters' head subjects to make some comments on the tendencies of research.

Keywords: Recurrence · Generalization · Fuzzy cluster ·
Spectral clustering · Annotated Suffix Tree

1 Introduction

The issue of automation of structurization and interpretation of digital text collections is of ever-growing importance because of both practical needs and theoretical necessity. This paper concerns an aspect of this, the issue of generalization as a unique feature of human cognitive abilities. The existing approaches to computational analysis of structure of text collections usually involve no generalization as a specific aim. The most popular tools for structuring text collections are cluster analysis and topic modelling. Both involve features of the same level of granularity as individual words or short phrases in the texts, thus no generalization as an explicitly stated goal.

Nevertheless, the hierarchical nature of the universe of meanings is reflected in the flow of publications on text analysis. We can distinguish between at least three directions at which the matter of generalization is addressed. First of all, one should mention activities related to developing taxonomies, especially those

© Springer Nature Switzerland AG 2019
L. Rutkowski et al. (Eds.): ICAISC 2019, LNAI 11508, pp. 273–286, 2019.
https://doi.org/10.1007/978-3-030-20912-4_26

involving hyponymic/hypernymic relations (see, for example, [15,18], and references therein). A recent paper [16] should be mentioned here too, as that devoted to supplementing a taxonomy with newly emerging research topics.

Another direction is part of conventional activities in text summarization. Usually, summaries are created using a rather mechanistic approach of sentence extraction. There is, however, also an approach for building summaries as abstractions of texts by combining some templates such as subject-verb-object (SVO) triplets (see, for example, [8]).

Yet one more field of activities is what can be referred to as operational generalization. In this direction, the authors use generalized case descriptions involving taxonomic relations between generalized states and their parts to achieve a tangible goal such as improving characteristics of text retrieval (see, for example, [12] and [17].)

This paper falls in neither of these approaches, as we do not attempt to change any taxonomy. We rather try to use a taxonomy for straightforwardly implementing the idea of generalization. According to the Merriam-Webster dictionary, the term "generalization" refers to deriving a general conception from particulars. We assume that a most straightforward medium for such a derivation, a taxonomy of the field, is given to us. The situation of our concern is a case at which we are to generalize a fuzzy set of taxonomy leaves representing the essence of some empirically observed phenomenon. The most popular Computer Science taxonomy is manually developed by the world-wide Association for Computing Machinery, a most representative body in the domain; the latest release of the taxonomy has been published in 2012 as the ACM Computing Classification System (ACM-CCS) [1]. We take its part related to Data Science, as presented in a slightly modified form by adding a few leaves in [11]. We add a few more leaves to better reflect the research papers being analyzed [4].

The rest of the paper is organized accordingly. Section 2 presents a mathematical formalization of the generalization problem as of parsimoniously lifting of a given query fuzzy leaf set to higher ranks of the taxonomy and provides a recursive algorithm leading to a globally optimal solution to the problem. Section 3 describes an application of this approach to deriving tendencies in development of the data science, that can be discerned from a set of about 18000 research papers published by the Springer Publishers in 17 journals related to data science for the past 20 years. Its subsections describe our approach to finding and generalizing fuzzy clusters of research topics. The results are followed by our comments on the tendencies in the development of the corresponding parts of Data Science drawn from the lifting results. Section 3.6 concludes the paper.

2   Parsimoniously Lifting a Fuzzy Thematic Cluster in a Taxonomy: Model and Method

Mathematically, a taxonomy is a rooted tree whose nodes are annotated by taxonomy topics. We consider the following problem. Given a fuzzy set S of taxonomy leaves, find a node $t(S)$ of higher rank in the taxonomy, that covers

the set S as tight as possible. Such a "lifting" problem is a mathematical expli-
cation of the human facility for generalization, that is, "the process of forming
a conceptual form" of a phenomenon represented, in this case, by a fuzzy leaf
subset.

The problem is not as simple as it may seem to be. Consider, for the sake
of simplicity, a hard set S shown with five black leaf boxes on a fragment of a
tree in Fig. 1. Figure 2 illustrates the situation at which the set of black boxes is
lifted to the root, which is shown by blackening the root box, and its offspring,
too. If we accept that set S may be generalized by the root, this would lead to
a number, four, white boxes to be covered by the root and, thus, in this way,
falling in the same concept as S even as they do not belong in S. Such a situation
will be referred to as a gap. Lifting with gaps should be penalized. Altogether,
the number of conceptual elements introduced to generalize S here is 1 head
subject, that is, the root to which we have assigned S, and the 4 gaps occurred
just because of the topology of the tree, which imposes this penalty. Another
lifting decision is illustrated in Fig. 3: here the set is lifted just to the root of
the left branch of the tree. We can see that the number of gaps has drastically
decreased, to just 1. However, another oddity emerged: a black box on the right,
belonging to S but not covered by the root of the left branch at which the set S
is mapped. This type of error will be referred to as an offshoot. At this lifting,
three new items emerge: one head subject, one offshoot, and one gap. This is
less than the number of items emerged at lifting the set to the root (one head
subject and four gaps, that is, five), which makes it more preferable. Of course,
this conclusion holds only if the relative weight of an offshoot is less than the
total relative weight of three gaps.

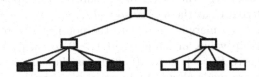

Fig. 1. A crisp query set, shown by black boxes, to be conceptualized in the taxonomy.

We are interested to see whether a fuzzy set S can be generalized by a
node t from higher ranks of the taxonomy, so that S can be thought of as falling
within the framework covered by the node t. The goal of finding an interpretable
pigeon-hole for S within the taxonomy can be formalized as that of finding one
or more "head subjects" t to cover S with the minimum number of all the
elements introduced at the generalization: head subjects, gaps, and offshoots.
This goal realizes the principle of Maximum Parsimony (MP) in describing the
phenomenon in question.

Consider a rooted tree T representing a hierarchical taxonomy so that its
nodes are annotated with key phrases signifying various concepts. We denote
the set of its *leaves* by I. The relationship between nodes in the hierarchy is

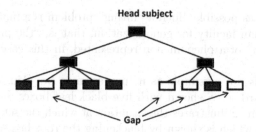

Head subject

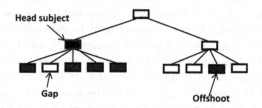

Gap

Fig. 2. Generalization of the query set from Fig. 1 by mapping it to the root, with the price of four gaps emerged at the lift.

Head subject

Gap   Offshoot

Fig. 3. Generalization of the query set from Fig. 1 by mapping it to the root of the left branch, with the price of one gap and one offshoot emerged at this lift.

conventionally expressed using genealogical terms: each node $t \in T$ is said to be the *parent* of the nodes immediately descending from t in T, its *children*. We use $\chi(t)$ to denote the set of children of t. Each *interior* node $t \in T - I$ is assumed to correspond to a concept that generalizes the topics corresponding to the leaves $I(t)$ descending from t, viz. the leaves of the subtree $T(t)$ rooted at t, which is conventionally referred to as the *leaf cluster of t*.

A *fuzzy set* on I is a mapping u of I to the non-negative real numbers that assigns a membership value, or support, $u(i) \geq 0$ to each $i \in I$. We refer to the set $S_u \subset I$, where $S_u = \{i \in I : u(i) > 0\}$, as the *base* of u. In general, no other assumptions are made about the function u, other than, for convenience, commonly limiting it to not exceed unity. Conventional, or *crisp*, sets correspond to binary membership functions u such that $u(i) = 1$ if $i \in S_u$ and $u(i) = 0$ otherwise.

Given a fuzzy query set u defined on the leaves I of the tree T, one can consider u to be a (possibly noisy) projection of a higher rank concept, u's "head subject", onto the corresponding leaf cluster. Under this assumption, there should exist a head subject node h among the interior nodes of the tree T such that its leaf cluster $I(h)$ more or less coincides (up to small errors) with S_u. This head subject is the generalization of u to be found. The two types of possible errors associated with the head subject if it does not cover the base precisely, are false positives and false negatives, referred to in this paper, as *gaps* and *offshoots*, respectively, are illustrated in Figs. 2 and 3. Altogether, the total number of head subjects, gaps, and offshoots has to be as small as possible.

A node $t \in T$ is referred to as *u-irrelevant* if its leaf-cluster $I(t)$ is disjoint from the base S_u. Consider a candidate node h in T and its meaning relative to fuzzy set u. An *h-gap* is a node g of $T(h)$, other than h, at which a *loss* of the meaning has occurred, that is, g is a maximal u-irrelevant node in the sense that its parent is not u-irrelevant. Conversely, establishing a node h as a head subject can be considered as a *gain* of the meaning of u at the node. The set of all h-gaps will be denoted by $G(h)$. Obviously, if a node is u-irrelevant, all of its descendants are also u-irrelevant.

A gap is less significant if its parent's membership value is smaller. Therefore, a measure $v(g)$ of "gap importance" should also be defined, to be reflected in the penalty function. We suggest defining the *gap importance* as $v(g) = u(par(g))$, where $par(g)$ is the parent of g. An alternative definition would be to scale these values by dividing them by the number of children of $par(g)$. However, we note that the algorithm ParGenFS below works for any definition of gap importance. Also, we define a summary gap importance: $V(t) = \sum_{g \in G(t)} v(g)$.

An *h-offshoot* is a leaf $i \in S_u$ which is not covered by h, i.e., $i \notin I(h)$. The set of all h-offshoots is $S_u - I(h)$. Given a fuzzy topic set u over I, a set of nodes H will be referred to as a *u-cover* if: (a) H covers S_u, that is, $S_u \subseteq \bigcup_{h \in H} I(h)$, and (b) the nodes in H are unrelated, i.e. $I(h) \cap I(h') = \emptyset$ for all $h, h' \in H$ such that $h \neq h'$. The interior nodes of H will be referred to as *head subjects* and the leaf nodes as *offshoots*, so the set of offshoots in H is $H \cap I$. The set of *gaps* in H is the union of $G(h)$ over all head subjects $h \in H - I$.

We define the penalty function $p(H)$ for a u-cover H as:

$$p(H) = \sum_{h \in H - I} u(h) + \sum_{h \in H - I} \sum_{g \in G(h)} \lambda v(g) + \sum_{h \in H \cap I} \gamma u(h). \qquad (1)$$

The problem we address is to find a u-cover H that globally minimizes the penalty $p(H)$. Such a u-cover will be the parsimonious generalization of the query set u.

Before applying an algorithm to minimize the total penalty, one needs to execute a preliminary transformation of the tree by pruning it from all the non-maximal u-irrelevant nodes, i.e. descendants of gaps. Simultaneously, the sets of gaps $G(t)$ and the internal summary gap importance $V(t) = \sum_{g \in G(t)} v(g)$ in Eq. (1) can be computed for each interior node t. We note that the elements of S_u are in the leaf set of the pruned tree, and the other leaves of the pruned tree are precisely the gaps. After this, our lifting algorithm ParGenFS applies. For each node t, the algorithm ParGenFS computes two sets, $H(t)$ and $L(t)$, containing those nodes in $T(t)$ at which respectively gains and losses of head subjects occur (including offshoots). The associated penalty is computed as $p(t)$ described below.

An assumption of the algorithm is that no gain can happen after a loss. Therefore, $H(t)$ and $L(t)$ are defined assuming that the head subject has not been gained (nor therefore lost) at any of t's ancestors. The algorithm ParGenFS recursively computes $H(t)$, $L(t)$ and $p(t)$ from the corresponding values for the child nodes in $\chi(t)$.

Specifically, for each leaf node that is not in S_u, we set both $L(\cdot)$ and $H(\cdot)$ to be empty and the penalty to be zero. For each leaf node that is in S_u, $L(\cdot)$ is set to be empty, whereas $H(\cdot)$, to contain just the leaf node, and the penalty is defined as its membership value multiplied by the offshoot penalty weight γ. To compute $L(t)$ and $H(t)$ for any interior node t, we analyze two possible cases: (a) when the head subject has been gained at t and (b) when the head subject has not been gained at t.

In case (a), the sets $H(\cdot)$ and $L(\cdot)$ at its children are not needed. In this case, $H(t)$, $L(t)$ and $p(t)$ are defined by:

$$H(t) = \{t\}; \quad L(t) = G(t); \quad p(t) = u(t) + \lambda V(t). \tag{2}$$

In case (b), the sets $H(t)$ and $L(t)$ are just the unions of those of its children, and $p(t)$ is the sum of their penalties:

$$H(t) = \bigcup_{w \in \chi(t)} H(w); \quad L(t) = \bigcup_{w \in \chi(t)} L(w); \quad p(t) = \sum_{w \in \chi(t)} p(w). \tag{3}$$

To obtain a parsimonious lift, whichever case gives the smaller value of $p(t)$ is chosen.

When both cases give the same values for $p(t)$, we may choose, say, (a). The output of the algorithm consists of the values at the root, namely, H – the set of head subjects and offshoots, L – the set of gaps, and p – the associated penalty.

We have proven that the algorithm ParGenFS leads to an optimal lifting indeed [4].

3   Structuring and Generalizing a Collection of Research Papers

Here are main steps of our approach:

– preparing a scholarly text collection;
– preparing a taxonomy of the domain under consideration;
– developing a matrix of relevance values between taxonomy leaf topics and research publications from the collection;
– finding fuzzy clusters according to the structure of relevance values;
– lifting the clusters over the taxonomy to conceptualize them via generalization;
– making conclusions from the generalizations.

Each of the items is covered in a separate subsection further on.

3.1   Scholarly Text Collection

Because of a generous offer from the Springer Publisher, we were able to download a collection of 17685 research papers together with their abstracts published in 17 journals related to Data Science, in our opinion, for 20 years from 1998–2017. We take the abstracts to these papers as a representative collection.

3.2 DST Taxonomy

Taxonomy is a form of knowledge engineering which is getting more and more popular. Most known are taxonomies within the bioinformatics Genome Ontology project (GO) [5], health and medicine SNOMED CT project [7] and the like. Mathematically, a taxonomy is a rooted tree, a hierarchy, whose all nodes are labeled by main concepts of a domain. The hierarchy corresponds to a relation of inclusion: the fact that node A is the parent of B means that B is part, or a special case, of A.

The subdomain of our choice is Data Science, comprising such areas as machine learning, data mining, data analysis, etc. We take that part of the ACM-CCS 2012 taxonomy, which is related to Data Science, and add a few leaves related to more recent Data Science developments. A major extract from the taxonomy of Data Science is published in [11]. The higher ranks of the taxonomy are presented in Table 1 and its full version in [4].

Table 1. ACM Computing Classification System (ACM-CCS) 2012 higher rank subjects related to Data Science.

Subject index	Subject name
1.	Theory of computation
1.1.	Theory and algorithms for application domains
2.	Mathematics of computing
2.1.	Probability and statistics
3.	Information systems
3.1.	Data management systems
3.2.	Information systems applications
3.3.	World Wide Web
3.4.	Information retrieval
4.	Human-centered computing
4.1.	Visualization
5.	Computing methodologies
5.1.	Artificial intelligence
5.2.	Machine learning

3.3 Evaluation of Relevance Between Texts and Key Phrases

Most popular and well established approaches to scoring keyphrase-to-document relevance include the so-called vector-space approach [14] and probabilistic text model approach [2]. These, however, rely on individual words and text preprocessing. We utilize a method [3,13], which requires no manual work.

An Annotated Suffix Tree (AST) is a weighted rooted tree used for storing text fragments and their frequencies. To build an AST for a text string, all suffixes from this string are extracted. A k-suffix of a string $x = x_1x_2 \ldots x_N$ of length N is a continuous end fragment $x_k = x_{N-k+1}x_{N-k+2} \ldots x_N$. For example, a 3-suffix of string $INFORMATION$ is substring ION, and a 5-suffix, $ATION$. Each AST node is assigned a symbol and the so-called annotation (frequency of the substring corresponding to the path from the root to the node including the symbol at the node). The root node of AST has no symbol or annotation. An algorithm for building an AST for any given string $x = x_1x_2 \ldots x_N$ is described below.

1. Initialize an AST to consist of a single node, the root: T.
2. Find all the suffixes of the given string: $\{x^k = x_{N-k+1}x_{N-k+2} \ldots x_N | k = 1, 2, \ldots, N\}$.
3. For each suffix x^k find its maximal overlap, that is, a path from the root in T coinciding with its beginning fragment $x^{k_{max}}$. At each node of the path for $x^{k_{max}}$ add 1 to the annotation. If the length of the overlap $x^{k_{max}}$ is less than k, the path is extended by adding new nodes corresponding to symbols from the remaining part of this suffix. Annotations of all the new nodes are set to be 1.

To accelerate the working of the method, one should use efficient versions of algorithms utilising suffix trees and suffix arrays (see, for example, [6]).

Having an AST T built, we can score the string-to-document relevance over the AST. To do this, we follow [10] by computing the conditional probability of node u in T:

$$p(u) = \frac{f(u)}{f(parent(u))}. \tag{4}$$

For all the immediate offspring of the root (R), formula has the following form:

$$p(u) = \frac{f(u)}{\sum\limits_{v \in T : parent(v) = R} f(v)}, \tag{5}$$

where $f(u)$ is the frequency annotation of the node u. Using the formula above, one can calculate the probability of node u relative to all its siblings. For each suffix x_k of string x the relevance score $s(x_k, T)$ is defined as:

$$s(x_k, T) = \frac{1}{k_{max}} \sum\limits_{i=1}^{k_{max}} p(x_i^k). \tag{6}$$

The AST relevance score of string x and text T is defined as the mean of all the suffix scores:

$$S(x, T) = \frac{1}{N} \sum\limits_{k=1}^{N} s(x_k, T). \tag{7}$$

In practical computations, we split any document into a set of strings (usually consisting of 2–3 consecutive words), create an empty AST for the document and add these strings in the AST in sequence, by using the algorithm above.

To lessen the effects of frequently occurring general terms, the scoring function is modified by five-fold decreasing the weight of stop-words. The list of stop-words includes: "learning, analysis, data, method" and a few postfixes: "s/es, ing, tion". After an AST for a document has been built, the time complexity of calculating the string-to-document relevance score is $O(m^2)$ where m is the length of the query string. This does not depend on the document length, in contrast to the popular Levenshtein-distance based approaches.

3.4   Defining and Computing Fuzzy Clusters of Taxonomy Topics

Clusters of topics should reflect co-occurrence of topics: the greater the number of texts to which both topics t and t' are relevant, the greater the interrelation between t and t', the greater the chance for topics t and t' to fall in the same cluster. We have tried several popular clustering algorithms. Unfortunately, no satisfactory results have been found. Therefore, we present here results obtained with the FADDIS algorithm from [10] developed specifically for finding thematic clusters. This algorithm implements assumptions that are relevant to the task:

LN Laplacian Normalization: Similarity data transformation modeling – to an extent – heat distribution and, in this way, making the cluster structure sharper.

AA Additivity: Thematic clusters behind the texts are additive so that similarity values are sums of contributions by different hidden themes.

AN Non-Completeness: Clusters do not necessarily cover all the key phrases available as the text collection under consideration may be irrelevant to some of them.

Co-relevance Topic-to-Topic Similarity Score. Given a keyphrase-to-document matrix R of relevance scores, it is converted to a keyphrase-to-keyphrase similarity matrix A or scoring the "co-relevance" of keyphrases according to the text collection structure. The similarity score $a_{tt'}$ between topics t and t' can be computed as the inner product of vectors of scores $r_t = (r_{tv})$ and $r_{t'} = (r_{t'v})$ where $v = 1, 2, \ldots, V = 17685$. The inner product is moderated by a natural weighting factor assigned to texts in the collection. The weight of text v is defined as the ratio of the number of topics n_v relevant to it and n_{max}, the maximum n_v over all v = 1, 2, ..., V. A topic is considered relevant to v if its relevance score is greater than 0.2 (a threshold found experimentally, see [3]).

Additive Fuzzy Spectral Clustering. Let us denote the total set of leaf topics by T and assume that a fuzzy cluster over T is represented by a fuzzy membership vector $\boldsymbol{u} = (u_t)$, $t \in T$, such that $0 \le u_t \le 1$ for all $t \in T$, and an intensity $\mu > 0$, a scale coefficient to relate the membership scores to the similarity scores. For T being a set of research topics and $\boldsymbol{u} = (u_t)$, $t \in T$, a membership values vector representing the a semantic substructure of a corpus of research papers under consideration, the product $(\mu u_t)(\mu u_{t'}) = \mu^2 u_t u_{t'}$ can be considered as the contribution by the research direction represented by the cluster under consideration to the total similarity score $a_{tt'}$ between topics t and t'. The additive fuzzy clustering model in [10] states that the entries in the topic-to-topic similarity matrix A can be considered as resulting from additive contributions of K fuzzy clusters, up to small errors to be minimized:

$$a_{tt'} = \sum_{k=1}^{K} \mu_k^2 u_{kt} u_{kt'} + e_{tt'}, \tag{8}$$

where $\boldsymbol{u}_k = (u_{kt})$ is the membership vector of cluster k, and μ_k its intensity. These assumptions require that clusters are extracted according to an additive model. A method developed in [10], FADDIS, finds clusters in (8) one-by-one, which accords with the assumptions above. Paper [10] provides some theoretical and experimental computation results to demonstrate that FADDIS is competitive over other fuzzy clustering approaches.

To make the hidden cluster structure in similarity data sharper, we apply the so-called Laplacian normalization [9].

FADDIS Thematic Clusters. After computing the 317×317 topic-to-topic co-relevance matrix, converting in to a topic-to-topic Lapin transformed similarity matrix, and applying FADDIS clustering, we sequentially obtained 6 clusters, of which three clusters seem especially homogeneous. We denote them using letters L, for 'Learning'; R, for 'Retrieval'; and C, for 'Clustering'. These clusters are presented in Table 2.

Table 2. Clusters L, R, C: topics with largest membership values.

Cluster L		Cluster R		Cluster C	
$u(t)$	Topic	$u(t)$	Topic	$u(t)$	Topic
0.300	Rule learning	0.211	Query representation	0.327	Biclustering
0.282	Batch learning	0.207	Image representations	0.286	Fuzzy clustering
0.276	Learning to rank	0.194	Shape representations	0.248	Consensus clustering
0.217	Query learning	0.194	Tensor representation	0.220	Conceptual clustering
0.216	Apprenticeship learning	0.191	Fuzzy representation	0.192	Spectral clustering
0.213	Models of learning	0.187	Data provenance	0.187	Massive data clustering
0.203	Adversarial learning	0.173	Equational models	0.159	Graph based conceptual clustering

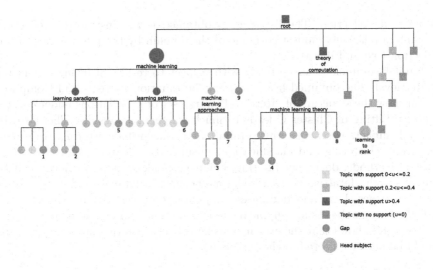

Fig. 4. Lifting results for Cluster L: Learning. Gaps are numbered, see Table 3.

3.5 Results of Lifting Clusters L, R, and C Within DST

All obtained clusters are lifted in the DST taxonomy using ParGenFS algorithm with the gap penalty $\lambda = 0.1$ and off-shoot penalty $\gamma = 0.9$.

The results of lifting Cluster L are shown in Fig. 4. The cluster has received three head subjects: machine learning, machine learning theory, and learning to rank. These represent the structure of the general concept "Learning" according

Table 3. Gaps at the lifting of Cluster L

Number	Topics
1	Ranking, supervised learning by classification, structured outputs
2	Sequential decision making in practice, inverse reinforcement learning in practice
3	Statistical relational learning
4	Sequential decision making, inverse reinforcement learning
5	Unsupervised learning
6	Learning from demonstrations, kernel approach
7	Classification and regression trees, kernel methods, neural networks, learning in probabilistic graphical models, learning linear models, factorization methods, markov decision processes, stochastic games, learning latent representations, multiresolution, support vector machines
8	Sample complexity and generalization bounds, Boolean function learning, kernel methods, boosting, bayesian analysis, inductive inference, structured prediction, markov decision processes, regret bounds
9	Machine learning algorithms

to our text collection. The list of gaps obtained is less instructive, reflecting probably a relatively modest coverage of the domain by the publications in the collection (see in Table 3).

Similar comments can be made with respect to results of lifting of Cluster R: Retrieval. The obtained head subjects: Information Systems and Computer Vision show the structure of "Retrieval" in the set of publications under considerations. Lifting of Cluster C leads to much fragmentary results. There are 16 (!) head subjects here: clustering, graph based conceptual clustering, trajectory clustering, clustering and classification, unsupervised learning and clustering, spectral methods, document filtering, language models, music retrieval, collaborative search, database views, stream management, database recovery, mapreduce languages, logic and databases, language resources. As one can see, the core clustering subjects are supplemented by methods and environments in the cluster – this shows that the ever increasing role of clustering activities perhaps should be better reflected in the taxonomy.

3.6   Making Conclusions

We can see that the topic clusters found with the text collection do highlight areas of soon-to-be developments. Three clusters under consideration closely relate, in respect, to the following processes:

- theoretical and methodical research in learning, as well as merging the subject of learning to rank within the mainstream;
- representation of various types of data for information retrieval, and merging that with visual data and their semantics; and
- various types of clustering in different branches of the taxonomy related to various applications and instruments.

In particular, one can see from the "Learning" head subjects (see Fig. 4 and comments to it) that main work here still concentrates on theory and method rather than applications. A good news is that the field of learning, formerly focused mostly on tasks of learning subsets and partitions, is expanding currently towards learning of ranks and rankings. Of course, there remain many sub-areas to be covered: these can be seen in and around the list of gaps in Table 3.

Moving to the lifting results for the information retrieval cluster R, we can clearly see the tendencies of the contemporary stage of the process. Rather than relating the term "information" to texts only, as it was in the previous stages of the process of digitalization, visuals are becoming parts of the concept of information. There is a catch, however. Unlike the multilevel granularity of meanings in texts, developed during millennia of the process of communication via languages in the humankind, there is no comparable hierarchy of meanings for images. One may only guess that the elements of the R cluster related to segmentation of images and videos, as well as those related to data management systems, are those that are going to be put in the base of a future multilevel system of meanings for images and videos.

Regarding the "clustering" cluster C with its 16 (!) head subjects, one may conclude that, perhaps, a time moment has come or is to come real soon, when the subject of clustering must be raised to a higher level in the taxonomy to embrace all these "heads". At the beginning of the Data Science era, a few decades ago, clustering was usually considered a more-or-less auxiliary part of machine learning, the unsupervised learning. Perhaps, soon we are going to see a new taxonomy of Data Science, in which clustering is not just an auxiliary instrument but rather a model of empirical classification, a big part of the knowledge engineering. When discussing the role of classification as a knowledge engineering phenomenon, one encounters three conventional aspects of classification:

- structuring the phenomena;
- relating different aspects of phenomena to each other;
- shaping and keeping knowledge of phenomena.

Each of them can make a separate direction of research in knowledge engineering.

References

1. The 2012 ACM Computing Classification System. http://www.acm.org/about/class/2012. Accessed 30 Apr 2018
2. Blei, D.: Probabilistic topic models. Commun. ACM **55**(4), 77–84 (2012)
3. Chernyak, E.: An approach to the problem of annotation of research publications. In: Proceedings of the Eighth ACM International Conference on Web Search and Data Mining, pp. 429–434. ACM (2015)
4. Frolov, D., Mirkin, B., Nascimento, S., Fenner, T.: Finding an appropriate generalization for a fuzzy thematic set in taxonomy. Working paper WP7/2018/04, Moscow, Higher School of Economics Publ. House (2018)
5. Gene Ontology Consortium: Gene ontology consortium: going forward. Nucleic Acids Res. **43**, D1049–D1056 (2015)
6. Grossi, R., Vitter, J.S.: Compressed suffix arrays and suffix trees with applications to text indexing and string matching. SIAM J. Comput. **35**(2), 378–407 (2005)
7. Lee, D., Cornet, R., Lau, F., De Keizer, N.: A survey of SNOMED CT implementations. J. Biomed. Inform. **46**(1), 87–96 (2013)
8. Lloret, E., Boldrini, E., Vodolazova, T., MartÃnez-Barco, P., Munoz, R., Palomar, M.: A novel concept-level approach for ultra-concise opinion summarization. Expert Syst. Appl. **42**(20), 7148–7156 (2015)
9. Mirkin, B., Nascimento, S.: Additive spectral method for fuzzy cluster analysis of similarity data including community structure and affinity matrices. Inf. Sci. **183**(1), 16–34 (2012)
10. Mirkin, B.: Clustering: A Data Recovery Approach. Chapman and Hall/CRC Press, Boca Raton (2012)
11. Mirkin, B., Orlov, M.: Three aspects of the research impact by a scientist: measurement methods and an empirical evaluation. In: Migdalas, A., Karakitsiou, A. (eds.) Optimization, Control, and Applications in the Information Age. PROMS, vol. 130, pp. 233–259. Springer, Cham (2015). https://doi.org/10.1007/978-3-319-18567-5_12
12. Mueller, G., Bergmann, R.: Generalization of workflows in process-oriented case-based reasoning. In: FLAIRS Conference, pp. 391–396 (2015)

13. Pampapathi, R., Mirkin, B., Levene, M.: A suffix tree approach to anti-spam email filtering. Mach. Learn. **65**(1), 309–338 (2006)
14. Salton, G., Buckley, C.: Term-weighting approaches in automatic text retrieval. Inf. Process. Manage. **25**(5), 513–523 (1998)
15. Song, Y., Liu, S., Wang, H., Wang, Z., Li, H.: Automatic taxonomy construction from keywords. U.S. Patent No. 9,501,569. U.S. Patent and Trademark Office, Washington, D.C. (2016)
16. Vedula, N., Nicholson, P.K., Ajwani, D., Dutta, S., Sala, A., Parthasarathy, S.: Enriching taxonomies with functional domain knowledge. In: The 41st International ACM SIGIR Conference on Research & Development in Information Retrieval, pp. 745–754. ACM (2018)
17. Waitelonis, J., Exeler, C., Sack, H.: Linked data enabled generalized vector space model to improve document retrieval. In: Proceedings of NLP & DBpedia 2015 Workshop in Conjunction with 14th International Semantic Web Conference (ISWC), vol. 1486. CEUR-WS (2015)
18. Wang, C., He, X., Zhou, A.: A short survey on taxonomy learning from text corpora: issues, resources and recent advances. In: Proceedings of the 2017 Conference on Empirical Methods in Natural Language Processing, pp. 1190–1203 (2017)

The 2-Additive Choquet Integral of Bi-capacities

Jabbar Abbas[✉]

Department of Applied Sciences, University of Technology, Baghdad, Iraq
100033@uotechnology.edu.iq

Abstract. In this paper, we propose the expression of a 2-additive Choquet integral of bi-capacities by using a bipolar Möbius transform based on ternary-element sets. This expression is equivalent to the expressions which are defined by Grabisch and Labreuche [12], and defined by Mayag et al. [13].

Keywords: Bi-capacities · The bipolar Möbius transform ·
The bipolar Choquet integral · 2-additivity

1 Introduction

The Choquet integral has been widely applied as an aggregation operator in multiple criteria decision making problems. Recently, the concept of bi-capacity has been proposed by Grabisch and Labreuche [11] as a generalization of capacity [6] (fuzzy measure [3,4,14,15] or non-additive measure [8]), who consider the case where scores are expressed on a bipolar scale, i.e. having a central neutral level, usually 0. The bipolar Choquet integral with respect to bi-capacities has been introduced by Grabisch and Labreuche [12] as a generalization of the Choquet integral. Other remarkable works on bi-capacities include the one of Fujimoto and Murofushi [9], who defined the Möbius transform of bi-capacities under the name of bipolar Möbius transform.

In [1,2], a new framework for studying the bipolar Choquet integral has been proposed by introducing a concept of ternary-element sets. This framework allows a simple way to prove new results on bi-capacity and bipolar Choquet integral as it was done for capacity. In this paper, we introduce the bipolar Möbius transform based on ternary-element sets. Then, we propose the expression of a 2-additive Choquet integral of bi-capacities based on the idea of ternary-element sets. This expression is equivalent of the expressions which are defined by Grabisch and Labreuche [12], and defined by Mayag et al. [13].

The organization of the paper is as follows. The next section recalls the basic concepts of bi-capacities based on the idea of ternary-element sets. Section 3 presents the bipolar Möbius transform based on ter-element sets. In Sects. 4 and 5, we first introduce the k-additivity of bi-capacities based on ter-element sets, then we propose the expression of a 2-additive Choquet integral of bi-capacities. The paper finishes with some conclusions.

© Springer Nature Switzerland AG 2019
L. Rutkowski et al. (Eds.): ICAISC 2019, LNAI 11508, pp. 287–295, 2019.
https://doi.org/10.1007/978-3-030-20912-4_27

2   Bi-capacities

In this section, we begin by recalling basic concepts of bi-capacities based on ter-element sets (for more details, see [1,2]).

2.1   Bi-capacities Based on Ter-Element Sets

In multi-criteria decision making problem, we shall represent the criterion i as i^+ whenever i is positively important, as i^- whenever i is negatively important, and as i^0 whenever i is neutral, and we call this element a *ternary-element* (or simply *ter-element*). A ter-element set A is the set of the form $A := \{\tau_1, \ldots, \tau_n\}$ where $\tau_i = i^+$, i^-, or i^0 $\forall\, i = 1, \ldots, n$. Hence, we consider the set of all possible combinations of ter-elements of n criteria given by

$$\mathcal{T} := \{\{\tau_1, \cdots, \tau_n\} \mid \tau_i \in \{i^+, i^-, i^0\}, \ \forall\, i = 1, \cdots, n\},$$

which corresponds to $\mathcal{Q}$ in the notation of classical bi-capacities [11].

The order relation $\sqsubseteq$ between ter-element sets on $\mathcal{T}$ is given by the following definition.

Definition 1. *Suppose A and B are ter-element sets of $\mathcal{T}$. Then, $A \sqsubseteq B$ iff $\forall\, i = 1, \ldots, n$,*

$$\text{``if } i^+ \in A \text{ implies } i^+ \in B\text{''}, \text{ and ``if } i^0 \in A \text{ implies } i^+ \text{ or } i^0 \in B\text{''}. \tag{1}$$

Using the concept of ter-element sets, we define an equivalent definition of bi-capacity as follows.

Definition 2. *A set function $\nu : \mathcal{T} \to [-1, 1]$, is called bi-capacity if it satisfies the following conditions:*

(1) $\nu(X^+) = \nu(\{1^+, \cdots, n^+\}) = 1$, $\nu(X^0) = \nu(\{1^0, \cdots, n^0\}) = 0$, and $\nu(X^-) = \nu(\{1^-, \cdots, n^-\}) = -1$,
(2) $\forall\, A, B \in \mathcal{T}$, $A \sqsubseteq B$ implies $\nu(A) \leq \nu(B)$.

A bi-capacity is also said to be additive if the following relation holds:

$$\forall\, A \in \mathcal{T}, \quad \nu(A) = \sum_{i^+ \in A} \nu(i^+) + \sum_{i^- \in A} \nu(i^-). \tag{2}$$

2.2   The Order Relation $\subseteq$ on $\mathcal{T}$

Bi-capacity is set function defined on the structure of the underlying partially ordered set [7]. We can introduce an order on the structure $\mathcal{T}$ different from the order ($\sqsubseteq$) described in Definition 1. Thus, we adopt the following definition of an order ($\subseteq$) on the structure $\mathcal{T}$ which is equivalent to Bilbao order on bi-cooperative game [5].

Definition 3. *Suppose A and B are ter-element sets of T. Then, $A \subseteq B$ iff $\forall\, i = 1, \ldots, n$,*

$$\text{``if } i^+ \in A \text{ implies } i^+ \in B\text{''} \quad \text{and} \quad \text{``if } i^- \in A \text{ implies } i^- \in B\text{''}. \tag{3}$$

In this order:

- the number of positively important elements i^+ of the ter-element set $A \in T$, denoted by a^+, is defined as $a^+ = \sum\limits_{i=1}^{n} \chi_A(i^+)$, where,

$$\chi_A(i^+) = \begin{cases} 1 \text{ if } i^+ \in A, \\ 0 \text{ if } i^+ \notin A. \end{cases}$$

- the number of negatively important elements i^- of the ter-element set $A \in T$, denoted by a^-, is defined as $a^- = \sum\limits_{i=1}^{n} \chi_A(i^-)$, where,

$$\chi_A(i^-) = \begin{cases} 1 \text{ if } i^- \in A, \\ 0 \text{ if } i^- \notin A. \end{cases}$$

- the cardinality of the ter-element set $A \in T$ is

$$a = |A| = a^+ + a^-. \tag{4}$$

- Unanimity games can be generalized to *bi-unanimity* games for this order as the following form: for all $A \in T$,

$$u_A(B) = \begin{cases} 1 \text{ iff } B \supseteq A, \\ 0 \text{ iff otherwise.} \end{cases} \tag{5}$$

3   The Bipolar Möbius Transforms

The Möbius transform is an important concept for capacities since the Möbius transform represents the coordinates of capacities in the basis of unanimity game. Moreover, the Choquet integral has a very simple expression when the Möbius transform is used. In [11], Grabisch M. and Labreuche Ch. have been defined the Möbius transform for bi-capacity. Another equivalent representation of bi-capacity has been proposed, by Fujimoto and Murofushi [9] who called the bipolar Möbius transform. In this section, we define the equivalent expression of bipolar Möbius transform for bi-capacity.

We define the bipolar Möbius transform for bi-capacities based on ternary-element sets of the order relation $\subseteq$ on T as follows.

Definition 4. *To any bi-capacity ν on T, another function $b_\nu : T \longrightarrow \mathcal{R}$ can be associated by*

$$\nu(A) = \sum_{B \subseteq A} b_\nu(B), \quad \forall A \in T. \tag{6}$$

The function b_ν is called the bipolar Möbius transform of ν, and is given by the following proposition.

Proposition 1. *Let* $\nu : \mathcal{T} \longrightarrow \mathcal{R}$ *be a bi-capacity and* $b_\nu : \mathcal{T} \longrightarrow \mathcal{R}$ *the bipolar Möbius transform of* ν. *Then,*

$$b_\nu(A) = \sum_{B \subseteq A} (-1)^{a-b} \ \nu(B), \quad \forall A \in \mathcal{T}. \tag{7}$$

Proof: From Definition 4, we have $\nu(B) = \sum_{C \subseteq B} b_\nu(C), \quad \forall B \in \mathcal{T}$. Then,

$$\sum_{B \subseteq A} (-1)^{a-b} \ \nu(B) = (-1)^a \sum_{B \subseteq A} (-1)^b \ (\sum_{C \subseteq B} b_\nu(C))$$

where, the order $\subseteq$ is defined by Eq. (3), and the cardinality of the ter-element sets is defined by Eq. (4).

$$= (-1)^a \sum_{C \subseteq A} b_\nu(C) (\sum_{B, C \subseteq B \subseteq A} (-1)^b)$$

$$= (-1)^a \sum_{C = A} b_\nu(C) (\sum_{B, C \subseteq B \subseteq A} (-1)^b) + (-1)^a \sum_{C \subset A} b_\nu(C) (\sum_{B, C \subseteq B \subseteq A} (-1)^b)$$

$$= (-1)^a \ b_\nu(A) \ (-1)^a + (-1)^a \sum_{C \subset A} b_\nu(C) \ (0)$$

$$= b_\nu(A).$$

■

4 k-Additivity of Bi-capacities Based on Ter-Element Sets

Möbius representation it has relation with the concept of k-*additivity*. The fundamental notion of k-*additivity* proposed by Grabisch and Labreuche [11] enables to reduce the number of bi-capacity coefficients. Also, Fujimoto et al. [10] have proposed the characterization of k-additivity of bi-capacities by using the bipolar Möbius transform. In this section, we define k-additivity of bi-capacities based on ter-element sets.

Definition 5. *Let* $k \in \{1, \dots, n-1\}$, *a bi-capacity based on ter-element set* ν *is said to be k-additive if it's bipolar Möbius transform* $b_\nu(A) = 0$ *whenever* $a > k$, *and there exists some* $A \in \mathcal{T}$, *such that* $a = k$ *and* $b_\nu(A) \neq 0$.

By a similar argument as in [13], we propose the following properties of a 2-additive bi-capacity based on ter-element set ν and its bipolar Möbius transform b_ν.

Property 1. Let ν be a 2-additive bi-capacity and b_ν its bipolar Möbius transform. For all i, $j \in \{1, \cdots, n\}$, $i \neq j$, and any $A \in \mathcal{T}$ we have:

$$\nu(A) = \sum_{i^+ \in A} b_\nu(\{i^+\}) + \sum_{j^- \in A} b_\nu(\{j^-\}) + \sum_{\substack{i^+ \in A \\ j^- \in A}} b_\nu(\{i^+, j^-\})$$

$$+ \sum_{\{i^+, j^+\} \subseteq A} b_\nu(\{i^+, j^+\}) + \sum_{\{i^-, j^-\} \subseteq A} b_\nu(\{i^-, j^-\}). \tag{8}$$

Proof: From Definition 4, we have $\nu(A) = \sum_{B \subseteq A} b_\nu(B)$, $\forall A \in \mathcal{T}$. Since, ν is 2-additive. Therefore, the Eq. (8) can be proofed by using the relation between ν and b_ν. ∎

Property 2. The necessary and sufficient conditions to get a 2-additive bi-capacity generated by (8) are: for any $A \in \mathcal{T}$ and $k^+ \in A$,

$$b_\nu(\{k^+\}) + \sum_{j^- \in A} b_\nu(\{k^+, j^-\}) + \sum_{i^+ \in A \setminus k^+} b_\nu(\{i^+, k^+\}) \geq 0. \tag{9}$$

$$b_\nu(\{k^-\}) + \sum_{j^+ \in A} b_\nu(\{k^-, j^+\}) + \sum_{i^- \in A \setminus k^-} b_\nu(\{i^-, k^-\}) \leq 0. \tag{10}$$

Proof: The proof is based on the expression of $\nu(A)$ given in (8) and on these equivalent monotonicity properties (which are easy to check): $\forall A \in \mathcal{T}$ and $\forall A \subseteq A'$,

(i) $\nu(A) \leq \nu(A')$ iff $\nu(A \setminus k^+) \leq \nu(A)$ $\forall k^+ \in A$,
(ii) $\nu(A') \leq \nu(A)$ iff $\nu(A) \leq \nu(A \setminus k^-)$ $\forall k^- \in A$.

∎

Property 3. For any $A \in \mathcal{T}$ and $k^+ \in A$, such that $a > 2$, the inequalities (9) and (10) can be rewritten in terms of bi-capacity ν as follows

$$\sum_{j^- \in A} \nu(\{k^+, j^-\}) + \sum_{i^+ \in A \setminus k^+} \nu(\{i^+\}) \geq (a-2)\nu(\{k^+\}) + \sum_{j^- \in A} \nu(\{j^-\}) + \sum_{i^+ \in A \setminus k^+} \nu(\{i^+\}). \tag{11}$$

$$\sum_{j^+ \in A} \nu(\{k^-, j^+\}) + \sum_{i^- \in A \setminus k^-} \nu(\{i^-\}) \leq (a-2)\nu(\{k^-\}) + \sum_{j^+ \in A} \nu(\{j^+\}) + \sum_{i^- \in A \setminus k^-} \nu(\{i^-\}). \tag{12}$$

Proof: The inequalities (11) and (12) are obtained by using the relation (6) between ν and b_ν in the inequalities (9) and (10), respectively. ∎

Thus, the properties 1, 2, and 3 show that the computation of a 2-additive bi-capacity ν can be done by knowing only the values of ν on the elements $\{i^+\}, \{i^-\}, \{i^+, j^-\}, \{i^+, j^+\}, \{i^-, j^-\}$ for all i, $j \in \{1, \cdots, n\}$, $i \neq j$ such that the inequalities (11) and (12), which correspond to the 2-additive monotonicity of a bi-capacity, are satisfied.

5   The 2-Additive Choquet Integral of Bi-capacities

Suppose that to each alternative in a multicriteria decision making problem is described by a real input vector $\mathbf{x} = (x_1, \ldots, x_i, \ldots, x_n)$, $x_i \in \mathcal{R}$ with $i \in \{1, \ldots, n\}$. Hereafter, we consider a ter-element set $X^* := \{\tau_1, \ldots, \tau_n\}$ with $\tau_i = i^+$ if $x_i > 0$, $\tau_i = i^-$ if $x_i < 0$, and $\tau_i = i^0$ if $x_i = 0$; $\forall\, i = 1, \ldots, n$. The bipolar Choquet integral of $\mathbf{x}$ in term of bi-capacity ν is given by the following definition.

Definition 6. *Let $\nu : \mathcal{T} \to [-1,\ 1]$, be a bi-capacity. Then, the bipolar Choquet integral of $\mathbf{x}$ with respect to ν is given by*

$$Ch_\nu(\mathbf{x}) = \sum_{i=1}^{n} [|x_{\pi(i)}| - |x_{\pi(i+1)}|]\, \nu(\{A_{\pi(\tau_i)}\}), \tag{13}$$

where $\tau_i \in \{i^+, i^-, i^0\}$, $A_{\pi(\tau_i)} = \{\pi(\tau_1), \cdots, \pi(\tau_i), \pi((i+1)^0), \pi((i+2)^0), \cdots\}$ is ter-element set $\subseteq X^*$, and π is a permutation on $\mathbf{x}$ so that $|x_{\pi(1)}| \geq \cdots \geq |x_{\pi(n)}|$ with the convention $x_{\pi(n+1)} := 0$.

An equivalent expression for the Eq. (13) is

$$Ch_\nu(\mathbf{x}) = \sum_{i=1}^{n} |x_{\pi(i)}|[\nu(\{A_{\pi(\tau_i)}\}) - \nu(\{A_{\pi(\tau_{(i-1)})}\})] \tag{14}$$

with the same notation above and $\nu(\{A_0\}) := 0$.

Proposition 2 [2]. *Let $\nu : \mathcal{T} \to [-1,\ 1]$, be a bi-capacity. Then, the bipolar Choquet integral of $\mathbf{x}$ with respect to ν is given by*

$$Ch_\nu(\mathbf{x}) = \sum_{i=1}^{n} [|x_{\pi(i)}| - |x_{\pi(i-1)}|]\, \nu(\{A_{\pi(\tau_i)}\}), \tag{15}$$

or as

$$Ch_\nu(\mathbf{x}) = \sum_{i=1}^{n} |x_{\pi(i)}|[\nu(\{A_{\pi(\tau_i)}\}) - \nu(\{A_{\pi(\tau_{(i+1)})}\})] \tag{16}$$

where $\tau_i \in \{i^+, i^-, i^0\}$, $A_{\pi(\tau_i)} = \{\cdots, \pi((i-2)^0), \pi((i-1)^0), \pi(\tau_i), \cdots, \pi(\tau_n)\}$ is ter-element set $\subseteq X^*$, and π is a permutation on $\mathbf{x}$ so that $|x_{\pi(1)}| \leq \cdots \leq |x_{\pi(n)}|$ with the convention $x_{\pi(0)} := 0$ and $\nu(\{A_{n+1}\}) := 0$.

The following numerical example illustrates the bipolar Choquet integral based on the ter-element sets.

Example 1: For $n = 3$, let us consider $\mathbf{x} = (4, 6, -3)$. Then, $X^* = \{1^+, 2^+, 3^-\}$. Applying the bipolar Choquet integral with respect to bi-capacity based on the ter-element sets (Formula (10)) we obtain $Ch_\nu(4, 6, -3) = (6 - 4)\,\nu(\{2^+, 1^0, 3^0\}) + (4 - 3)\,\nu(\{2^+, 1^+, 3^0\}) + (3 - 0)\nu(\{2^+, 1^+, 3^-\}) = 2\,\nu(\{2^+, 1^0, 3^0\}) + \nu(\{2^+, 1^+, 3^0\}) + 3\,\nu(\{2^+, 1^+, 3^-\})$.

The expression of bipolar Choquet integral in terms of the bipolar Möbius transform was suggested by Fujimoto and Murofushi [9]. In this section, we propose bipolar Choquet integral in terms of the bipolar Möbius transform based on the ter-element sets of real input **x**.

Similarly to the bipolar Choquet integral based on the ter-element sets, we also consider a ter-element set $X^* := \{\tau_1, \ldots, \tau_n\}$ with $\tau_i = i^+$ if $x_i > 0$, $\tau_i = i^-$ if $x_i < 0$, and $\tau_i = i^0$ if $x_i = 0$; $\forall\ i = 1, \ldots, n$. Each input value of x_i is expressed by

$$x_i^+ = x_i \text{ if } x_i > 0, \quad x_i^- = -x_i \text{ if } x_i < 0,$$
$$x_i^+ = 0 \text{ if } x_i \leq 0; \quad and \quad x_i^- = 0 \quad \text{ if } x_i \geq 0.$$

Thus, the following proposition gives alternative expression of bipolar Choquet integral in terms of the bipolar Möbius transform.

Proposition 3. *Let $\nu : \mathcal{T} \rightarrow \mathcal{R}$, be a bi-capacity. Then, bipolar Choquet integral of **x** with respect to ν can be represents as*

$$C_\nu(\mathbf{x}) = \sum_{A \subseteq X^*} b_\nu(A) \bigwedge_{\tau_i \in A} |x_i|, \quad \tau_i \in \{i^+, i^-\},\ i = 1, \ldots, n.$$

$$= \sum_{A \in \mathcal{T}} b_\nu(A)\ (\bigwedge_{i^+ \in A} x_i^+ \wedge \bigwedge_{i^- \in A} x_i^-), \quad i = 1, \ldots, n. \tag{17}$$

Proof: Using the equivalent expression of bipolar Choquet integral based on ter-element set (Proposition 2, Formula (16)), we have

$$Ch_\nu(\mathbf{x}) = \sum_{i=1}^{n} |x_{\pi(i)}|[\nu(\{A_{\pi(\tau_i)}\}) - \nu(\{A_{\pi(\tau_{(i+1)})}\})]$$

Then, we take the bi-unanimity game u_A (Formula (5)) for any $A \in \mathcal{T}$, and denote by j the leftmost index in the ordered sequence $\{\pi(i), \tau_i \in A\}$, we get

$$C_{u_A}(\mathbf{x}) = \sum_{\tau_i \in A} |x_i|\ [u_A(\{B_{(\tau_i)}\}) - u_A(\{B_{(\tau_{i+1})}\})]$$

$$= |x_j|$$

$$= \bigwedge_{\tau_i \in A} |x_i|$$

Hence by linearity of the integral with respect to the bi-capacities and decomposition of any ν in the basis of bi-unanimity game, we obtain

$$C_\nu(\mathbf{x}) = \sum_{A \subseteq X^*} b_\nu(A) \bigwedge_{\tau_i \in A} |x_i|$$

Note that, the order $\subseteq$ is defined by Eq. (3). Thus

$$= \sum_{A \in \mathcal{T}} b_\nu(A)\ (\bigwedge_{i^+ \in A} x_i^+ \wedge \bigwedge_{i^- \in A} x_i^-), \quad i = 1, \ldots, n.$$

■

Therefore, for all i, $j \in \{1, \cdots, n\}$, $i \neq j$, and any $A \in \mathcal{T}$, the Choquet integral of $\mathbf{x}$ with respect to a 2-additive bi-capacity ν is given by:

$$C_\nu(\mathbf{x}) = \sum_{i=1}^{n} b_\nu(\{i^+\}) \, x_i^+ + \sum_{i=1}^{n} b_\nu(\{i^-\}) \, x_i^- + \sum_{i,j=1}^{n} b_\nu(\{i^+,j^-\}) \, (x_i^+ \wedge x_j^-)$$

$$+ \sum_{\{i^+,j^+\} \subseteq X^*} b_\nu(\{i^+,j^+\}) \, (x_i^+ \wedge x_j^+) + \sum_{\{i^-,j^-\} \subseteq X^*} b_\nu(\{i^-,j^-\}) \, (x_i^- \wedge x_j^-). \qquad (18)$$

We illustrate the expression of bipolar Choquet integral in terms of the bipolar Möbius transform by the following numerical example.

Example 2 [Example 1 continued]: We apply the expression of bipolar Choquet integral in terms of the bipolar Möbius transform (Eq. (17)) for $\mathbf{x} = (4, 6, -3)$ we have,
$C_\nu(4, 6, -3) = 4 \, b_\nu(\{1^+, 2^\phi, 3^\phi\}) + 6 \, b_\nu(\{1^\phi, 2^+, 3^\phi\}) + 3 \, b_\nu(\{1^\phi, 2^+, 3^-\}) + 4 \, b_\nu(\{1^+, 2^+, 3^\phi\}) + 3 \, b_\nu(\{1^+, 2^\phi, 3^-\}) + 3 \, b_\nu(\{1^\phi, 2^+, 3^-\}) + 3 \, b_\nu(\{1^+, 2^+, 3^-\})$.
From Eq. (7), we get
$\quad = 2 \, \nu(\{1^\phi, 2^+, 3^\phi\}) + \nu(\{1^+, 2^+, 3^\phi\}) + 3 \, \nu(\{1^+, 2^+, 3^-\})$.

6   Conclusions

The definition of bi-capacity based on ter-element set satisfies properties similar to the classical definition of bi-capacity [11]. According to this definition and introducing and other order relation equivalent to Bilbao order on bi-cooperative game [5], the expression of a 2-additive Choquet integral of bi-capacity is appropriately proposed. The proposed result is consistent as a generalization of the expression of a 2-additive Choquet integral for capacity.

References

1. Abbas, J.: Bipolar Choquet integral of fuzzy events. In: IEEE Conference on Computational Intelligence in Multi-Criteria Decision-Making, pp. 116–123 (2014)
2. Abbas, J.: The bipolar Choquet integrals based on ternary-element sets. J. Artif. Intell. Soft Comput. Res. **6**(1), 13–21 (2016)
3. Abbas, J.: Logical twofold integral. Eng. Techol. J. **28**(3), 477–483 (2010)
4. Abbas, J., Abhang, R.: A logical method to estimate reliability of quantum communication channels. Al-Nahrain Univ. J. Sci. **14**(1), 142–149 (2011)
5. Bilbao, J.M., Fernandez, J.R., Jimenez Losada, A., Lebron, E.: Bicooperative games. In: First World Congress of the Game Theory Society (Games 2000), Bilbao, Spain, 24–28 July 2000
6. Choquet, G.: Theory of capacities. Ann. Inst. Fourier **5**, 131–295 (1953)
7. Davey, B.A., Priestley, H.A.: Introduction to Lattices and Orders. Cambridge University Press, Cambridge (1990)

8. Denneberg, D.: Non-additive Measure and Integral. Kluwer Academic Publisher, Dordrecht (1994)
9. Fujimoto, K., Murofushi, T.: Some characterizations of k-monotonicity through the bipolar Möbius transform in bi-capacities. J. Adv. Comput. Intell. Intell. Inform. **9**(5), 484–495 (2005)
10. Fujimoto, K., et al.: k-Additivity and C-decomposability of bi-capacities and its integral. Fuzzy Sets Syst. **158**, 1698–1712 (2007)
11. Grabisch, M., Labreuche, C.: Bi-capacities I: definition, Mobius transform and interaction. Fuzzy Sets Syst. **151**, 211–236 (2005)
12. Grabisch, M., Labreuche, C.: Bi-capacities II: the Choquet integral. Fuzzy Sets Syst. **151**, 237–259 (2005)
13. Mayag, B., Rolland, A., Ah-Pine, J.: Elicitation of a 2-additive bi-capacity through cardinal information on trinary actions. In: Greco, S., Bouchon-Meunier, B., Coletti, G., Fedrizzi, M., Matarazzo, B., Yager, R.R. (eds.) IPMU 2012. CCIS, vol. 300, pp. 238–247. Springer, Heidelberg (2012). https://doi.org/10.1007/978-3-642-31724-8_25
14. Sugeno, M.: Theory of fuzzy integrals and its applications. Ph.D. Thesis, Tokyo Institute of Technology (1974)
15. Wang, Z., Klir, G.J.: Fuzzy Measure Theory. Plenum Press, New York (1992)

A New Class of Uninorm Aggregation Operations for Fuzzy Theory

Sándor Jenei[✉]

University of Pécs, Pécs, Hungary
jenei@ttk.pte.hu
http://jenei.ttk.pte.hu/home.html

Abstract. Uninorms play a prominent role both in the theory and applications of Aggregations, Fuzzy Theory, and of Mathematical Fuzzy Logic. In this paper the class of group-like uninorms is introduced. First, two variants of a construction method – called partial-lexicographic product – will be recalled; it constructs a large subclass of group-like FL_e-algebras. Then two specific ways of applying the partial-lexicographic product construction to construct uninorms will be presented. The first one constructs starting from $\mathbb{R}$ and modifying it in some way by $\mathbb{Z}$'s, what we call basic group-like uninorms, whereas with the second one may extend group-like uninorms by using $\mathbb{Z}$ and a basic uninorm to obtain further group-like uninorms. All group-like uninorms obtained this way have finitely many idempotents. On the other hand, we assert that the only way to construct group-like uninorms which have finitely many idempotents is to apply this extension (by a basic group-like uninorm) consecutively, starting from a basic group-like uninorm. In this way a complete characterization for group-like uninorms which possess finitely many idempotents is given. The obtained uninorm class can be candidate for the aggregation operation of several applications. The paper is illustrated with several 3D plots.

Keywords: Uninorm · Construction · Characterization

1 Introduction

Aggregation operations are crucial in numerous pure and applied fields of mathematics. Fuzzy Theory is another large field, involving both pure mathematics and impressive range of applications. Mathematical fuzzy logics have been introduced in [10], and the topic is a rapidly growing field ever since. In all these fields (and the list in far from being exhaustive) a crucial role is played by t-norms, t-conorms, and uninorms [13].

A *uninorm U* (as introduced in [20]) is a function of type $[0,1] \times [0,1] \to [0,1]$, that is, binary operations over the closed real unit interval $[0,1]$, such that the following axioms are satisfied.

This work was supported by the GINOP 2.3.2-15-2016-00022 grant.

L. Rutkowski et al. (Eds.): ICAISC 2019, LNAI 11508, pp. 296–303, 2019.
https://doi.org/10.1007/978-3-030-20912-4_28

- $U(x,y) = U(y,x)$ (Symmetry)
- if $y \leq z$ then $U(x,y) \leq U(x,z)$ (Monotonicity)
- $U(U(x,y),z) = U(x,U(y,z))$ (Associativity)
- there exists $t \in]0,1[$ such that $U(x,t) = x$ (Unit Element)

Establishing the structure theory of uninorms seems to be quite difficult. Several authors have characterized particular subclasses of them, see e.g., [2–5,7,11,14, 15,18,19]. Not only uninorms are interesting for a structural description purpose, but also different generalizations of them play a central role in many studies, see [1,6] for example.

Group-like uninorms play a similar role among uninorms then the Łukasiewicz t-norm, or in general the class of IMTL-algebras do in the class of t-norms. In this paper we shall characterize a new subclass of uninorms, namely, the class of group-like uninorms which have finitely many idempotent elements.

To this end, first a few notions follow here:

Residuation is a crucial property in Mathematical Fuzzy Logics, and in Substructural Logics, in general [8,16]. A uninorm is residuated if there exists a function I_U of type $[0,1] \times [0,1] \to [0,1]$, that is, a binary operation on $[0,1]$, such that the following is satisfied: $U(x,y) \leq z$ if and only if $I_U(x,z) \geq y$. Frequently one uses the infix notation for a uninorms, too, and writes $x \circledast y$ in stead of $U(x,y)$, and $x \to_\circledast y$ instead of $I_T(x,y)$.

A generalization of residuated t-norms and uninorms is the notion of FL_e-algebras. This generalization is done by replacing $[0,1]$ by an arbitrary lattice, possibly without top and bottom elements: An FL_e-algebra[1] is a structure $(X,\wedge,\vee,\circledast,\to_\circledast,t,f)$ such that $(X,\wedge,\vee)$ is a lattice, $(X,\leq,\circledast,t)$ is a commutative, residuated[2] monoid, and f is an arbitrary constant. One defines $x' = x \to_\circledast f$ and calls an FL_e-algebra *involutive* if $(x')' = x$ holds. Call an FL_e-algebra *group-like* or *odd* if it is involutive and $t = f$. For a group-like FL_e-algebra $\mathbf{X}$, let $gr(X)$ be the set of invertible elements of $\mathbf{X}$. It turns out that there is a subalgebra of $\mathbf{X}$ on $gr(X)$, denote it by $\mathbf{X_{gr}}$ and call it the group part of $\mathbf{X}$.

Speaking in algebraic terms, t-norms and uninorms are the monoidal operations of commutative totally ordered monoids over $[0,1]$. Likewise, residuated t-norms and uninorms are just the monoidal operations of FL_e-algebras over $[0,1]$. According to the terminology above, the class of involutive t-norms constitutes the Łukasiewicz t-norm, and all IMTL-algebras on $[0,1]$, in general. Also according to the terminology above, we call a uninorm group-like if it is residuated, involutive, and $t = f$ holds, where $x' = x \to_\circledast t$. For group-like uninorms (and also for bounded group-like FL_e-algebras, in general) we know more about

---

[1] Other terminologies for FL_e-algebras are: pointed commutative residuated lattices or pointed commutative residuated lattice-ordered monoids.

[2] That is, there exists a binary operation $\to_\circledast$ such that $x \circledast y \leq z$ if and only if $x \to_\circledast z \geq y$; this equivalence is called residuation condition or adjointness condition, $(\circledast, \to_\circledast)$ is called an adjoint pair. Equivalently, for any x,z, the set $\{v \mid x \circledast v \leq z\}$ has its greatest element, and $x \to_\circledast z$ is defined as this element: $x \to_\circledast z := \max\{v \mid x \circledast v \leq z\}$.

their behaviour in the boundary, as it holds true that

$$U(x,y) = \begin{cases} \in]0,1[& \text{if } x,y \in]0,1[\\ 0 & \text{if } \min(x,y) = 0 \\ 1 & \text{if } x,y > 0 \text{ and } \max(x,y) = 1 \end{cases}.$$

Therefore, values of a group-like uninorm U in the open unit square $]0,1[^2$ fully determine U. As a consequence, one can view a group-like uninorm U as a binary operation on $]0,1[$. Because of these observations, throughout the paper we shall use the term *group-like uninorm* is a slightly different manner: Instead of requiring the underlying universe to be $[0,1]$, we only require that the underlying universe is order isomorphic to the open unit interval $]0,1[$. This way, for example the usual addition of real numbers, that is letting $V(x,y) = x + y$, becomes a group-like uninorm in our terminology. This is witnessed by any order-isomorphism from $]0,1[$ to $\mathbb{R}$, take for instance $\varphi(x) = \tan(\pi x - \frac{\pi}{2})$. Using φ, any group-like uninorm (on $\mathbb{R}$, for example) can be carried over to $[0,1]$ by letting, in our example,

$$U(x,y) = \begin{cases} \varphi^{-1}(V(\varphi(x),\varphi(y))) & \text{if } x,y \in]0,1[\\ 0 & \text{if } \min(x,y) = 0 \\ 1 & \text{if } x,y \neq 0 \text{ and } \max(x,y) = 1 \end{cases}.$$

As said above, group-like FL_e-chains are involutive FL_e-chains satisfying the condition that the unit of the monoidal operation coincides with the constant that defines the order-reversing involution $'$; in notation $t = f$. Since for any involutive FL_e-chain $t' = f$ holds, one extremal situation is the integral case, that is, when t is the top element of the universe and hence f is its bottom one, and the other extremal situation is the group-like case when the two constants coincide. Prominent examples of group-like FL_e-algebras are lattice-ordered abelian groups and odd Sugihara algebras, the latter constitute an algebraic semantics of a logic at the intersection of relevance logic and fuzzy logic [9]. These two examples are extremal in the sense that lattice-ordered abelian groups have a single idempotent element, namely the unit element, whereas all elements of any odd Sugihara algebra are idempotent. In order to narrow the gap between the two extremal classes mentioned above, in [12] a deeper knowledge have been gained about the class of group-like FL_e-chains, including a Hahn-type embedding theorem and a representation theorem by means of totally-ordered abelian groups and a there-introduced construction, called partial-lexicographic product. Although not cited here in its explicit form, the representation theorem has a crucial role in showing the main result of this paper.

First, we adopt the partial-lexicographic product construction (Definition 2) to the setting of group-like uninorms by introducing two specific ways of applying it; the construction of basic group-like uninorms in Definition 3 and an extension method by a group-like uninorm in (2). With these one can construct group-like uninorms which have finitely many idempotent elements. Our main result asserts that the only way to construct such uninorms is to apply these: Starting from a group-like uninorm and extending it consecutively by group-like uninorms

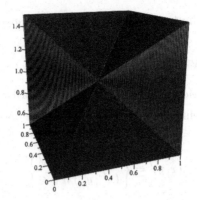

Fig. 1. Visualization: The only odd Sugihara algebra over $]0,1[$.

(Theorem 2). In this way a complete characterization for group-like uninorms which possess finitely many idempotents is given, similar to the well-known characterization of continuous t-norms [17].

In this paper we shall describe the necessary theory behind this result, and shall also present several examples by means of plots, see Figs. 1, 2 and 3 for some examples.

2   Partial Lex-Products, Basic Group-Like Uninorms, and Structural Description

Let us start with a few notations and definitions.

Definition 1. For a chain (a linearly ordered set) $(X, \leq)$ and for $x \in X$ define the predecessor $x_\downarrow$ of x to be the maximal element of the set of elements which are smaller than x, if it exists, define $x_\downarrow = x$ otherwise. Define the successor $x_\uparrow$ of x dually. We say for $Z \subseteq X$ that Z is *discretely embedded* into X if for $x \in Z$ it holds true that $x \notin \{x_\uparrow, x_\downarrow\} \subseteq Z$. If $\mathbf{H}$ is subalgebra of an odd FL_e-algebra $\mathbf{X}$, and H is discretely embedded into X then we denote it by $\mathbf{H} \leq_d \mathbf{X}$. We denote by $\mathbb{R}$ and $\mathbb{Z}$ the odd FL_e-chain of the reals and the integers, respectively.

Crucial for our purposes will be the so-called *partial lexicographic product* construction. Denote the lexicographic product by $\overleftarrow{\times}$.

Definition 2 [12]. Let $\mathbf{X} = (X, \wedge_X, \vee_X, *, \rightarrow_*, t_X, f_X)$ be an odd FL_e-algebra and $\mathbf{Y} = (Y, \wedge_Y, \vee_Y, \star, \rightarrow_\star, t_Y, f_Y)$ be an involutive FL_e-algebra, with residual complement $'$ and $'$, respectively.

A. Add a new element $\top$ to Y as a top element and annihilator (for $\star$), then add a new element $\bot$ to $Y \cup \{\top\}$ as a bottom element and annihilator. Extend $'$ by $\bot' = \top$ and $\top' = \bot$. Let $\mathbf{V} \leq \mathbf{X_{gr}}$. Let

$$X_V \overleftarrow{\times} Y = (V \times (Y \cup \{\top, \bot\})) \cup ((X \setminus V) \times \{\bot\}),$$

and let $\mathbf{X_V} \overset{\leftarrow}{\times} \mathbf{Y}$, the *type I partial lexicographic product* of $\mathbf{X}, \mathbf{V}$ and $\mathbf{Y}$ be given by

$$\mathbf{X_V} \overset{\leftarrow}{\times} \mathbf{Y} = \left(X_V \overset{\leftarrow}{\times} Y, \leq, \circledast, \rightarrow_\circledast, (t_X, t_Y), (f_X, f_Y) \right),$$

where $\leq$ is the restriction of the lexicographical order of $\leq_X$ and $\leq_{Y \cup \{\top, \bot\}}$ to $X_V \overset{\leftarrow}{\times} Y$, $\circledast$ is defined coordinatewise, and the operation $\rightarrow_\circledast$ is given by $(x_1, y_1) \rightarrow_\circledast (x_2, y_2) = ((x_1, y_1) \circledast (x_2, y_2)')'$, where

$$(x, y)' = \begin{cases} (x^{\vec{\ast}}, \bot) & \text{if } x \notin V \\ (x^{\vec{\ast}}, y^{\vec{\ast}}) & \text{if } x \in V \end{cases}.$$

B. Assume that X_{gr} is discretely embedded into X. Add a new element $\top$ to Y as a top element and annihilator. Let

$$X \overset{\leftarrow}{\times} Y = (X \times \{\top\}) \cup (X_{gr} \times Y)$$

and let $\mathbf{X} \overset{\leftarrow}{\times} \mathbf{Y}$, the *type II partial lexicographic product* of $\mathbf{X}$ and $\mathbf{Y}$ be given by

$$\mathbf{X} \overset{\leftarrow}{\times} \mathbf{Y} = \left(X \overset{\leftarrow}{\times} Y, \leq, \circledast, \rightarrow_\circledast, (t_X, t_Y), (f_X, f_Y) \right),$$

where $\leq$ is the restriction of the lexicographical order of $\leq_X$ and $\leq_{Y \cup \{\top\}}$ to $X \overset{\leftarrow}{\times} Y$, $\circledast$ is defined coordinatewise, and the operation $\rightarrow_\circledast$ is given by $(x_1, y_1) \rightarrow_\circledast (x_2, y_2) = ((x_1, y_1) \circledast (x_2, y_2)')'$, where $'$ is defined coordinatewise[3] by

$$(x, y)' = \begin{cases} (x^{\vec{\ast}}, \top) & \text{if } x \notin X_{gr} \text{ and } y = \top \\ ((x^{\vec{\ast}})_\downarrow, \top) & \text{if } x \in X_{gr} \text{ and } y = \top. \\ (x^{\vec{\ast}}, y^{\vec{\ast}}) & \text{if } x \in X_{gr} \text{ and } y \in Y \end{cases} \tag{1}$$

Theorem 1 [12]. *Adapt the notation of Definition 2.* $\mathbf{X_V} \overset{\leftarrow}{\times} \mathbf{Y}$ *and* $\mathbf{X} \overset{\leftarrow}{\times} \mathbf{Y}$ *are involutive* FL_e-*algebras with the same rank[4] as that of* $\mathbf{Y}$. *In particular, if* $\mathbf{Y}$ *is odd then so are* $\mathbf{X_V} \overset{\leftarrow}{\times} \mathbf{Y}$ *and* $\mathbf{X} \overset{\leftarrow}{\times} \mathbf{Y}$.

Definition 3 (Basic group-like uninorms). Let $\mathbb{U}_0 = \mathbb{R}$ and for $n \in \mathbb{N}$ let $\mathbb{U}_{n+1} = \mathbb{Z} \overset{\leftarrow}{\times} \mathbb{U}_n$. The operation $\overset{\leftarrow}{\times}$ can be proved to be associative, so it can equivalently be written without brackets as

$$\mathbb{U}_n = \underbrace{\mathbb{Z} \overset{\leftarrow}{\times} \ldots \overset{\leftarrow}{\times} \mathbb{Z}}_{n} \overset{\leftarrow}{\times} \mathbb{R}.$$

---

[3] Note that intuitively it would make up for a coordinatewise definition, too, in the second line of (1) to define it as $(x^{\vec{\ast}}, \bot)$. But $\bot$ is not amongst the set of possible second coordinates. However, since X_{gr} is discretely embedded into X, if $(x^{\vec{\ast}}, \bot)$ would be an element of the algebra then it would be equal to $((x^{\vec{\ast}})_\downarrow, \top)$.

[4] The rank of an involutive FL_e-algebra is positive if $t > f$, negative if $t < f$, and 0 if $t = f$.

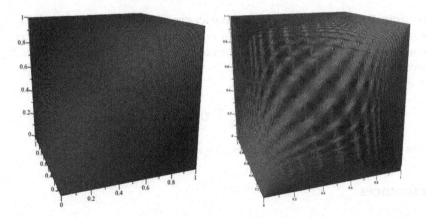

Fig. 2. Visualization: Two basic group-like uninorms, $\mathbb{U}_0 = \mathbb{R}$ and $\mathbb{U}_1 = \mathbb{Z} \overleftarrow{\times} \mathbb{R}$ shrank into $]0, 1[$. One can describe $\mathbb{U}_1$ as infinitely many $\mathbb{U}_0$ components. Imagine $\mathbb{U}_2$ in the same way: as infinitely many $\mathbb{U}_1$ components, etc.

Having defined all necessary notions, we are ready to state the main theorem: a representation theorem for those group-like uninorms which has finitely many idempotent elements, by means of basic group-like uninorms and an extension method. Alternatively, one may view Theorem 2 as a representation theorem for those group-like uninorms which has finitely many idempotent elements, by means of $\mathbb{Z}$ and $\mathbb{R}$ and the type I and type II partial-lexicographic product constructions (see Figs. 2 and 3 for some examples).

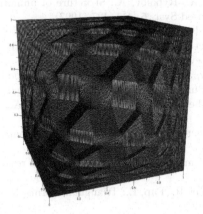

Fig. 3. Visualization: An example for the first type extension, $\mathbb{R}_Z \overleftarrow{\times} \mathbb{R}$ shrank into $]0, 1[$

Theorem 2 (Representation by basic group-like uninorms). *If* $\mathbf{U}$ *is a group-like uninorm, which has finitely many* $(m \in \mathbf{N}, m \geq 1)$ *idempotents in its negative cone*[5] *then there exists a sequence* $k \in \mathbf{N}^{\{1,\ldots,m\}}$ *such that* $\mathbf{U} \simeq \mathbf{U}_m$, *where for* $i \in \{1,\ldots,m\}$,

$$\mathbf{U}_i = \begin{cases} \mathbb{U}_{k_1} & \text{if } i = 1 \\ \mathbf{U}_{i-1_{\mathbf{H}_{i-1}}} \overset{\leftarrow}{\times} \mathbb{U}_{k_i} & \text{if } 2 \leq i \leq m \end{cases}, \tag{2}$$

where for $2 < i \leq m$, $\mathbf{H}_{i-1}$ *is a countable subgroup of* $(\mathbf{U}_{i-1})_{\mathbf{gr}}$.

References

1. Akella, P.: Structure of n-uninorms. Fuzzy Sets Syst. **158**(15), 1631–1651 (2007)
2. De Baets, B.: Idempotent uninorms. Eur. J. Oper. Res. **118**(3), 631–642 (1999)
3. Fodor, J.C.: On rational uninorms. In: Proceedings of the First Slovakian-Hungarian Joint Symposium on Applied Machine Intelligence, Herlany, Slovakia, pp. 139–147 (2003)
4. De Baets, B., Fodor, J.C.: On the structure of uninorms and their residual implicators. In: Gottwald, S., Klement, E.P. (eds.) 18th Linz Seminar on Fuzzy Set Theory: Enriched Lattice Structures for Many-Valued and Fuzzy Logics, Johannes Kepler Universitt, Linz, Austria, 25 February–1 March 1997, pp. 81–87 (1997)
5. Drygas, P.: On the structure of continuous uninorms. Kibernetika **43**(2), 183–196 (2007)
6. Drygas, P.: On the structure of uninorms on L*. In: Magdalena, L., Ojeda-Aciego, M., Verdegay, J.L. (eds.) Proceedings of IPMU2008, Torremolinos, Malaga, pp. 1795–1800 (2004)
7. Fodor, J.C., Yager, R., Rybalov, A.: Structure of uninorms. Int. J. Uncertainty Fuzziness Knowl. Based Syst. **5**, 411–427 (1997)
8. Galatos, N., Jipsen, P., Kowalski, T., Ono, H.: Residuated Lattices: An Algebraic Glimpse at Substructural Logics. Studies in Logic and the Foundations of Mathematics, vol. 151. Elsevier, Amsterdam (2007)
9. Galatos, N., Raftery, J.G.: A category equivalence for odd Sugihara monoids and its applications. J. Pure Appl. Algebra **216**, 2177–2192 (2012)
10. Hájek, P.: Metamathematics of Fuzzy Logic. Kluwer Academic Publishers, Dordrecht (1998)
11. Jenei, S.: On the structure of rotation-invariant semigroups. Arch. Math. Logic **42**, 489–514 (2003)
12. Jenei, S.: The Hahn embedding theorem for a class of residuated semigroups (submitted)
13. Klement, E.P., Mesiar, R., Pap, E.: Triangular Norms. Kluwer Academic Publishers, Dordrecht (2000)
14. Mesiarová-Zemánková, A.: Characterization of uninorms with continuous underlying t-norm and t-conorm by their set of discontinuity points. IEEE Trans. Fuzzy Syst. **28**(2), 705–714 (2018)
15. Mesiarová-Zemánková, A.: Characterizing set-valued functions of uninorms with continuous underlying t-norm and t-conorm. Fuzzy Sets Syst. **334**, 83–93 (2018)

---

[5] The negative cone consists of the elements which are smaller or equal to t.

16. Metcalfe, G., Montagna, F.: Substructural fuzzy logics. J. Symb. Logic **72**(3), 834–864 (2007)
17. Mostert, P.S., Shields, A.L.: On the structure of semigroups on a compact manifold with boundary. Ann. Math. **65**, 117–143 (1957)
18. Petrik, M., Mesiar, R.: On the structure of special classes of uninorms. Fuzzy Sets Syst. **240**, 22–38 (2014)
19. Su, Y., Zong, W., Drygas, P.: Properties of uninorms with the underlying operation given as ordinal sums. Fuzzy Sets Syst. https://doi.org/10.1016/j.fss.2018.04.011
20. Yager, R.R., Rybalov, A.: Uninorm aggregation operators. Fuzzy Sets Syst. **80**, 111–120 (1996)

Different Forms of Generalized Hypothetical Syllogism with Regard to R-Implications

Katarzyna Miś⬤ and Michał Baczyński[✉]⬤

Institute of Mathematics, University of Silesia in Katowice,
Bankowa 14, 40-007 Katowice, Poland
{kmis,michal.baczynski}@us.edu.pl

Abstract. In this paper we investigate the generalized hypothetical syllogism (GHS). We present few versions of the well known GHS equation. We focus our attention on R-implications and give some results concerning left-continuous t-norms. We show some solutions of GHS equations based on the compositional rule of inference and Bandler-Kohout subproduct. Also we sketch the idea of new possible functional equations coming from the GHS.

Keywords: Generalized hypothetical syllogism ·
Composition rule of inference · Bandler-Kohout subproduct ·
Fuzzy implications · Fuzzy conjunction · t-norm

1 Introduction

Fuzzy inference schemas (FIS) play a key role in approximate reasoning (AR) based on fuzzy sets. Here we are focused on IF-THEN fuzzy rules of the form

$$\text{IF } x \text{ is } A, \text{ THEN } y \text{ is } B,$$

where the antecedent fuzzy set $A \in \mathcal{F}(X)$ and the consequent fuzzy set $B \in \mathcal{F}(Y)$ represent some properties (in our paper $\mathcal{F}(X)$ denotes all fuzzy sets on the universe X). Then for a given fuzzy observation x is A', a corresponding output fuzzy set $B' \in \mathcal{F}(Y)$, which means that y is B', is deduced using some inference mechanism.

In general we can consider a system of IF-THEN fuzzy rules of the form

$$\text{IF } x \text{ is } A_i, \text{ THEN } y \text{ is } B_i, \qquad i \in \{1, \ldots, n\}, \tag{1}$$

for fuzzy sets $A_i \in \mathcal{F}(X), B_i \in \mathcal{F}(Y)$ and some $n \in \mathbb{N}$. Usually such IF-THEN fuzzy rules can be represented as a fuzzy relation R. The most often applied representations of R are the following (cf. [15]):

This work was supported by the National Science Centre, Poland, through research Project Number 2015/19/B/ST6/03259.

L. Rutkowski et al. (Eds.): ICAISC 2019, LNAI 11508, pp. 304–313, 2019.
https://doi.org/10.1007/978-3-030-20912-4_29

1. $\check{R}(x,y) = \max_{i \in \{1,\ldots n\}} C(A_i(x), B_i(y))$, where C is a fuzzy conjunction, mostly a t-norm (this approach was introduced by Mamdani and Assilian [12]).
2. $\hat{R}(x,y) = \min_{i \in \{1,\ldots n\}} I(A_i(x), B_i(y))$ where I is a fuzzy implication (standard conditional approach).

We will concentrate our attention on the case when $n = 1$. In general the inferred output y is B' is obtained as a composition of A' and R as follows (see [15])

$$B' = A'@R,$$

where @ is a fuzzy relational composition that involves several fuzzy logic operations. Moreover, we can consider different types of composition @. One of the most important and widely used is the compositional rule of inference (CRI), which was introduced by Zadeh [16]. It can written in the following way

$$B' = A' \circ R. \qquad (2)$$

We understand it as: "from the fact that 'x is A'' we can infer 'y is B''" because of the composition of A' and R. In details, Eq. (2) can be written as

$$B'(y) = \sup_{x \in X} C(A'(x), R(x,y)), \qquad y \in Y,$$

where C is again a t-norm (or some other operation which generalizes classical conjunction).

Another well known composition @ is the Bandler-Kohout subproduct [3,13]. This one can be seen as follows

$$B' = A' \triangleleft R, \qquad (3)$$

which can be extended to the form

$$B'(y) = \inf_{x \in X} I(A'(x), R(x,y)), \qquad y \in Y,$$

where I is a fuzzy implication. We only want to point out that it was shown by Štěpnička and Jayaram [15] that BK-subproduct satisfies the same important properties as the CRI does and it is as effective as CRI. Hence it can be used in FIS.

Having chosen fuzzy relation R and the composition @ we define a fuzzy function. Its domain is the family of all fuzzy sets on the universe X, i.e. $\mathcal{F}(X)$. Namely, $f_R^@ : \mathcal{F}(X) \to \mathcal{F}(Y)$ given by $f_R^@(A) = A@R$, $A \in \mathcal{F}(X)$ (see [15]). For the correctness and ability of application of FIS it is crucial to take fuzzy relation R which allows to obtain some meaningful results. Here we require the property of interpolativity. A fuzzy function $f_R^@$ has this property, if $f_R^@(A_i) = B_i$ (for a given fuzzy rule like in a system (1)). This property is equivalent to the following scheme of Modus Ponens:

IF x is A_i, THEN y is B_i
IF x is A_i
_____
y is B_i

In this paper we investigate the following scheme known as a generalized hypothetical syllogism (GHS):

RULE:	IF x is A, THEN z is B	
RULE:	IF z is B, THEN y is C	(4)
CONCLUSION:	IF x is A, THEN y is C	

where fuzzy sets $A \in \mathcal{F}(X), B \in \mathcal{F}(Y), C \in \mathcal{F}(Z)$ represent some properties. These conditional statements are usually used when AR is involved. In this paper we are focused on one functional equation connected with (GHS). Using introduced notation it can be written as follows

$$R_3(x,y) = R_1(x,z)@R_2(z,y), \qquad (5)$$

where R_1, R_2 and R_3 are fuzzy relations defined on $X \times Z$, $Z \times Y$ and $X \times Y$, respectively. Equation (5) corresponds to the scheme (4). In the next sections we will discuss some particular versions of this equation for different compositions @. Firstly, it Sect. 2 we recall some basic definitions and facts regarding fuzzy connectives including R-implications. This family of fuzzy implications provides a good example to show the solutions of GHS equations. Section 3 contains main results. Finally some ideas for future work are given.

2   Preliminaries

We assume that the reader is familiar with the classical results concerning basic fuzzy connectives, but to make this work more self-contained, we place some of them here.

Definition 2.1 ([5]). *A function $C \colon [0,1]^2 \to [0,1]$ is called a fuzzy conjunction if it satisfies the following conditions:*

(C1) *is non-decreasing with respect to both variables,*
(C2) $C(0,0) = C(0,1) = C(1,0) = 0, \qquad C(1,1) = 1.$

Another important fuzzy connective is a semicopula.

Definition 2.2 ([4]). *A function $S \colon [0,1]^2 \to [0,1]$ is called a semicopula, if it satisfies the following conditions:*

(S1) $S(x,1) = S(1,x) = x, \qquad x \in [0,1],$
(S2) *S is non-decreasing with respect to both variables.*

Definition 2.3 (see [6,9]). *A function $T \colon [0,1]^2 \to [0,1]$ is called a **triangular norm** (**t-norm** in short), if it satisfies the following conditions, for all $x, y, z \in [0,1]$,*

(T1) $T(x,y) = T(y,x),$
(T2) $T(x, T(y,z)) = T(T(x,y), z),$

(T3) T *is non-decreasing with respect to both variables,*
(T4) $T(x,1) = x.$

Now, we recall the definition and some important properties of fuzzy implications.

Definition 2.4 (see [1,6]**).** *A function* $I\colon [0,1]^2 \to [0,1]$ *is called a **fuzzy implication**, if it satisfies the following conditions:*

(I1) I *is non-increasing with respect to the first variable,*
(I2) I *is non-decreasing with respect to the second variable,*
(I3) $I(0,0) = I(1,1) = 1$ *and* $I(1,0) = 0.$

Definition 2.5 (see [1]**).** *We say that a fuzzy implication* I *satisfies*

*(i) the **identity principle**, if*

$$I(x,x) = 1, \qquad x \in [0,1], \tag{IP}$$

*(ii) the **left neutrality property**, if*

$$I(1,y) = y, \qquad y \in [0,1], \tag{NP}$$

*(iii) the **ordering property**, if*

$$x \le y \iff I(x,y) = 1, \qquad x,y \in [0,1]. \tag{OP}$$

As we mentioned in Introduction we want to present some results for one particular family of fuzzy implications.

Definition 2.6 ([1, **Definition 2.5.1**]**).** *A function* $I\colon [0,1]^2 \to [0,1]$ *is called an R-implication if there exists a t-norm* T *such that*

$$I(x,y) = \sup\{t \in [0,1] \mid T(x,t) \le y\}, \qquad x,y \in [0,1]. \tag{6}$$

If I *is generated from a t-norm* T, *then it will be denoted by* I_T.

Note that it is possible to generate an R-implication from just a fuzzy conjunction with specific properties (see [11]). Moreover, we will use the following useful characterization of some subclass of all R-implications.

Theorem 2.7 ([1, **Proposition 2.5.2**]**).** *Let* T *be a t-norm. Then the following statements are equivalent:*

1. T *is left-continuous.*
2. *A pair* (T, I_T) *satisfies a residual principle*

$$T(x,z) \le y \iff I_T(x,y) \ge z, \qquad x,y,z \in [0,1], \tag{RP}$$

3. *The supremum in* (6) *is the maximum, i.e.,*

$$I_T(x,y) = \max\{t \in [0,1] \mid T(x,t) \le y\}, \qquad x,y \in [0,1].$$

3 Types of Generalized Hypothetical Syllogism Equations

The first type of GHS equation which we investigate is the one come from (2) when $R = \hat{R}$. If we substitute fuzzy sets by unit intervals, we obtain the following equation.

$$\sup_{z \in [0,1]} (T(I(x,z), I(z,y))) = I(x,y), \qquad x,y \in [0,1]. \qquad \text{(CRI-GHS)}$$

This equation is the most known when GHS is discussed. It appeared in [10], later in [14]. It was also the main topic of the paper [2]. Let us recall the most important result from that paper. The main question posed there was the following.

Let T be a t-norm. Does always a pair (T, I_T) satisfy (CRI-GHS)?

The answer is *No* (see [2, Example 4.7]). It turned out it is true only for left-continuous t-norms (cf. [8] and [2, Corollary 4.11]). Also the following important result has been obtained earlier.

Theorem 3.1 ([2, **Theorem 4.12**]). *Let T^* be a t-norm and T be a left-continuous t-norm. Then the following statements are equivalent:*

(i) The pair (T^*, I_T) satisfies (CRI-GHS).
(ii) $T^* \leq T$.

The next question is the following.

Is satisfying (CRI-GHS) by a pair (T, I_T) equivalent to the left-continuity of T?

The answer is *Yes*. We show this fact in the next result.

Theorem 3.2. *Let T be a t-norm. Then the following statements are equivalent:*

(i) T is left-continuous.
(ii) (T, I_T) satisfies (CRI-GHS).

Proof. By Theorem 3.1 it is enough to show $(ii) \Rightarrow (i)$. Let T be a t-norm. Suppose that the pair (T, I_T) satisfies (CRI-GHS) but T is not left-continuous. From Theorem 2.7 it means (T, I_T) does not satisfy (RP). Also note that the following implication (which is a part of (RP)) is true for any t-norm T^* and all $x, y, z \in [0,1]$,

$$T^*(x,z) \leq y \Rightarrow I_{T^*}(x,y) \geq z,$$

because for fixed $x, y, z \in [0,1]$, if $z \in \{t \in [0,1] \mid T^*(x,t) \leq y\}$, then $z \leq \sup\{t \in [0,1] \mid T^*(x,t) \leq y\} = I_{T^*}(x,y)$. Hence, if T is not left-continuous, then there exist $x_0, y_0, z_0 \in [0,1]$ such that $I_T(x_0, y_0) \geq z_0$ and $T(x_0, z_0) > y_0$. Therefore using (CRI-GHS) we have

$$y_0 < T(x_0, z_0) \leq T(x_0, I_T(x_0, y_0)) = T(I_T(1, x_0), I_T(x_0, y_0))$$
$$\leq \sup_{t \in [0,1]} T(I_T(1,t), I_T(t,y)) = I_T(1,y) = y;$$

a contradiction.   □

Furthermore, another question is interesting.

Is left-continuity sufficient condition for a fuzzy conjunction C to a pair (C, I_C) satisfy (CRI-GHS)?

It seems no (based on the proof of the previous theorem and [8, Theorem 6]). However, we know that such pair (C, I_C) might satisfy (RP) (see [11]).

The next equation comes from BK-subproduct and $R = \check{R}$ in Eq. (3). In this case, we obtain the GHS equation of the form

$$\inf_{z \in [0,1]} I_1(C(x,z), C(z,y)) = I_2(x,y), \qquad x,y \in [0,1], \qquad \text{(BK-GHS)}$$

where I_1, I_2 are fuzzy implications and C is a semicopula. Here, if these functions will be a solution of (BK-GHS), we will say that the triplet (C, I_1, I_2) satisfies (BK-GHS).

Firstly, observe some general facts.

Remark 3.3. Let C be a semicopula, I_1 be a fuzzy implication and $I_2 \colon [0,1]^2 \to [0,1]$ be any function. Next, let (C, I_1, I_2) satisfy (BK-GHS). Then the following statements are equivalent:

(i) I_2 is a fuzzy implication.
(ii) I_1 satisfies (IP).

Moreover, note that with very less assumptions regarding C, I_1 and I_2 we have the following result.

Proposition 3.4. *Let $C, I_1, I_2 \colon [0,1] \to [0,1]$, C have a neutral element 1 and let $I_2(1,1) = 1$. If (C, I_1, I_2) satisfies (BK-GHS), then I_1 satisfies (IP).*

Proof. It is enough to notice that if (C, I_1, I_2) satisfies (BK-GHS), then

$$1 = I_2(1,1) = \inf_{z \in [0,1]} I_1(C(1,z), C(z,1)) = \inf_{z \in [0,1]} I_1(z,z).$$

Hence $1 = I_1(z,z)$ for all $z \in [0,1]$. $\qquad\square$

For the further investigations we will need the following fact where, in contrast to assumptions given in [7], the left-continuity of T is not necessary.

Theorem 3.5 (cf. [7, cf. Proposition 1.5]). *If T is a t-norm, then*

$$I_T(x,y) \le I_T(T(x,z), T(z,y)), \qquad x,y,z \in [0,1].$$

Proof. Let us take $x, y, z, t \in [0,1]$. If $T(x,t) \le y$, then from commutativity and associativity of T we obtain

$$T(T(x,z),t) = T(T(z,x),t) = T(z,T(x,t)) \le T(z,y).$$

Hence

$$\{t \in [0,1] \mid T(x,t) \le y\} \subset \{t \in [0,1] \mid T(T(x,z),t) \le T(z,y)\},$$
$$\sup\{t \in [0,1] \mid T(x,t) \le y\} \le \sup\{t \in [0,1] \mid T(T(x,z),t) \le T(z,y)\},$$

and using (6) we obtain $I_T(x,y) \le I_T(T(x,z), T(z,y))$. $\qquad\square$

Also, we will use this simple fact.

Lemma 3.6. *Let $F, G\colon [0,1]^2 \to [0,1]$. Then for any $x, y, z \in [0,1]$ we have*

$$F(x,y) \leq F(G(x,z), G(z,y)) \iff F(x,y) \leq \inf_{t \in [0,1]} F(G(x,t), G(t,y)).$$

Proof. Let us show the proof of $(\Rightarrow)$ (the opposite one is clear). Assume that for any $x, y, z \in [0,1]$ we have $F(x,y) \leq F(G(x,z), G(z,y))$ and suppose there exist $x_0, y_0 \in [0,1]$ such that $F(x_0, y_0) > \inf_{t \in [0,1]} F(G(x_0,t), G(t,y_0))$. However then there must exist $z_0 \in [0,1]$ such that $F(x_0, y_0) > F(G(x_0, z_0), G(z_0, y_0))$ which is a contradiction with the assumptions. □

Now we can present the following result.

Theorem 3.7. *Let $F, G\colon [0,1]^2 \to [0,1]$, G be a semicopula and let (F, G) satisfy the inequality*

$$F(x,y) \leq F(G(x,z), G(z,y)).$$

Then (G, F, F) satisfies (BK-GHS).

Proof. From Lemma 3.6 we know that it is enough to show the following inequality

$$I_2(x,y) \geq \inf_{z \in [0,1]} I_1(C(x,z), C(z,y)), \qquad x, y \in [0,1].$$

We obtain

$$\inf_{z \in [0,1]} F(G(x,z), G(z,y)) \leq F(G(x,1), G(1,y)) = F(x,y),$$

for all $x, y \in [0,1]$. Therefore (G, F, F) satisfies (BK-GHS). □

Now, we can easily formulate the following corollary using Theorem 3.7 and Lemma 3.6.

Corollary 3.8. *If T is a t-norm, then the triplet (T, I_T, I_T) satisfies* (BK-GHS).

In the family of all fuzzy implications we can consider the partial order induced from the unit interval $[0,1]$.

Corollary 3.9. *Let T be a t-norm and I_1 be a fuzzy implication. If the triplet (T, I_1, I_T) satisfies* (BK-GHS), *then $I_1 \geq I_T$.*

Proof. If (T, I_1, I_T) satisfies (BK-GHS), then for arbitrary $x, y \in [0,1]$ we have

$$I_T(x,y) = \inf_{z \in [0,1]} I_1(T(x,z), T(z,y)) \leq I_1(T(x,1), T(1,y)) = I_1(x,y).$$

□

The inverse implication is not true as we show below.

Example 3.10. Let us take the Łukasiewicz t-norm

$$T_{\mathbf{LK}}(x,y) = \max\{0, x + y - 1\}, \qquad x, y \in [0,1].$$

Of course

$$I_{T_{\mathbf{LK}}}(x,y) = I_{\mathbf{LK}}(x,y) = \min\{1, 1 - x + y\}, \qquad x, y \in [0,1],$$

is the Łukasiewicz implication. Next, let I_1 be the Weber implication given by

$$I_1(x,y) = I_{\mathbf{WB}}(x,y) = \begin{cases} 1, & x < 1, \\ y, & x = 1, \end{cases} \qquad x, y \in [0,1].$$

Of course $I_{\mathbf{LK}} \leq I_{\mathbf{WB}}$. We show that the triplet $(T_{\mathbf{LK}}, I_{\mathbf{WB}}, I_{\mathbf{LK}})$ does not satisfy (BK-GHS). Indeed, let us take $x = \frac{1}{2}$ and $y = \frac{1}{3}$. For any $z \in [0,1]$ we have $T_{\mathbf{LK}}(\frac{1}{2}, z) < 1$, thus from the definition of $I_{\mathbf{WB}}$ we obtain

$$\inf_{z \in [0,1]} I_{\mathbf{WB}}\left(T_{\mathbf{LK}}\left(\frac{1}{2}, z\right), T_{\mathbf{LK}}\left(z, \frac{1}{3}\right)\right) = 1,$$

but $I_{\mathbf{LK}}(x,y) = I_{\mathbf{LK}}\left(\frac{1}{2}, \frac{1}{3}\right) = \frac{5}{6}$. Therefore the triplet $(T_{\mathbf{LK}}, I_{\mathbf{WB}}, I_{\mathbf{LK}})$ does not satisfy (BK-GHS).

Now, we could think if it is possible to consider other different GHS equations. Namely, for two given types of this equation we could replace $\check{R}$ and $\hat{R}$. Hence, we would obtain such equations

$$I(x,y) = \sup_{z \in [0,1]} C(C(x,z), C(z,y)), \qquad x, y \in [0,1],$$

$$I_2(x,y) = \inf_{z \in [0,1]} I_1(I_2(x,z), I_2(z,y)), \qquad x, y \in [0,1], \qquad (7)$$

where I, I_1, I_2 are fuzzy implications and C is a semicopula. It is easy to see these equations do not have any solutions. Indeed, for example suppose there exist fuzzy implications I_1, I_2 satisfying (7). Then we have

$$1 = I_2(0,0) = \inf_{z \in [0,1]} I_1(I_2(0,z), I_2(z,0)) = \inf_{z \in [0,1]} I_1(1, I_2(z,0))$$

$$= I_1(1, I_2(1,0)) = I_1(1,0) = 0,$$

Another interesting equations arise if we consider "mixed" versions of already examined Eqs. (CRI-GHS) and (BK-GHS). Here, we would like to mention about two types of such equations, namely

$$\inf_{z \in [0,1]} I_1(C(x,z), I_2(z,y)) = I_3(x,y), \qquad x, y \in [0,1], \qquad (8)$$

where I_1, I_2, I_3 are fuzzy implications and C is a semicopula. In general we can have here 3 different fuzzy implications. Hence, we will write (C, I_1, I_2, I_3) satisfies (8), if these functions will form its solution. In our future work we will consider some particular cases for the above equation. One simple fact is the following.

Proposition 3.11. *Let I_1, I_2 be fuzzy implications and C be a semicopula. If I_2 satisfies (NP), then (C, I_1, I_2, I_1) satisfies (8).*

Proof. Firstly, note that for any $x, y, z \in [0, 1]$ we have

$$I_1(C(x, z), I_2(z, y)) \geq I_1(C(x, 1), I_2(z, y)) \geq I_1(C(x, 1), I_2(1, y)).$$

Thus $\inf_{t \in [0,1]} I_1(C(x, t), I_2(t, y)) = I_1(C(x, 1), I_2(1, y))$. If I_2 satisfies (NP), then $I_1(C(x, 1), I_2(1, y)) = I_1(x, y)$.   □

In the future we also investigate the following equation.

$$\inf_{z \in [0,1]} I_1(I_2(x, z), C(z, y)) = S(x, y), \qquad x, y \in [0, 1], \tag{9}$$

where I_1, I_2 are fuzzy implications, C semicopula and S some aggregation function. Here it is also good to start working with R-implications because we can find some solutions of (9) among them.

4   Conclusions

In this paper we have presented different approaches to the generalized hypothetical syllogism. This leaded us to some new functional equations. Also we shown some new results for the most known versions of GHS equations. We indicated the family of R-implications as a rich of solutions of (CRI-GHS) and (BK-GHS) equations. We outlined the idea of another versions of GHS equations.

Acknowledgment. This work was supported by the National Science Centre, Poland, through research Project Number 2015/19/B/ST6/03259. The authors would like to thank Professor Balasubramaniam Jayaram for the inspiring discussion during his stay in Katowice and his constructive suggestions which contributed to the development of this research topic.

References

1. Baczyński, M., Jayaram, B.: Fuzzy Implications, Studies in Fuzziness and Soft Computing, vol. 231. Springer, Heidelberg (2008). https://doi.org/10.1007/978-3-540-69082-5
2. Baczyński, M., Miś, K.: Selected properties of generalized hypothetical syllogism including the case of R-implications. In: Medina, J., et al. (eds.) IPMU 2018. CCIS, vol. 853, pp. 673–684. Springer, Cham (2018). https://doi.org/10.1007/978-3-319-91473-2_57
3. Bandler, W., Kohout, L.J.: Semantics of implication operators and fuzzy relational products. Int. J. Man Mach. Stud. **12**, 89–116 (1980)
4. Durante, F., Sempi, C.: Semicopulae. Kybernetika **41**(3), 315–328 (2005)
5. Fodor, J., Keresztfalvi, T.: Nonstandard conjunctions and implications in fuzzy logic. Int. J. Approx. Reason. **12**(2), 69–84 (1995)
6. Fodor, J., Roubens, M.: Fuzzy Preference Modelling and Multicriteria Decision Support. Kluwer Academic Publishers, Dordrecht (1994)

7. Gottwald, S.: Fuzzy Sets and Fuzzy Logic: The Foundations of Application – from a Mathematical Point of View. Vieweg+Teubner Verlag, Wiesbaden (1993). https://doi.org/10.1007/978-3-322-86812-1

8. Igel, C., Temme, K.H.: The chaining syllogism in fuzzy logic. IEEE Trans. Fuzzy Syst. **12**, 849–853 (2004)

9. Klement, E.P., Mesiar, R., Pap, E.: Triangular Norms. Kluwer Academic Publishers, Dordrecht (2000)

10. Klir, G.J., Yuan, B.: Fuzzy Sets and Fuzzy Logic: Theory and Applications. Prentice Hall, Upper Saddle River (1995)

11. Król, A.: Dependencies between fuzzy conjunctions and implications. In: Galichet, S., Montero, J., Mauris, G. (eds.) Proceedings of the 7th Conference of the European Society for Fuzzy Logic and Technology (EUSFLAT-2011) and LFA-2011. Advances in Intelligent Systems Research, vol. 1, pp. 230–237. Atlantis Press (2011)

12. Mamdani, E.H., Assilian, S.: An experiment in linguistic synthesis with a fuzzy logic controller. Int. J. Man Mach. Stud. **7**, 1–13 (1975)

13. Pedrycz, W.: Applications of fuzzy relational equations for methods of reasoning in presence of fuzzy data. Fuzzy Sets Syst. **16**, 163–175 (1985)

14. Vemuri, N.R.: Investigations of fuzzy implications satisfying generalized hypothetical syllogism. Fuzzy Sets Syst. **323**, 117–137 (2017)

15. Štěpnička, M., Jayaram, B.: On the suitability of the Bandler-Kohout subproduct as an inference mechanism. IEEE Trans. Fuzzy Syst. **18**(2), 285–298 (2010)

16. Zadeh, L.A.: Outline of a new approach to the analysis of complex systems and decision processes. IEEE Trans. Syst. Man Cybern. **3**, 28–44 (1973)

A Fuzzy-Dynamic Bayesian Network Approach for Inference Filtering

Munyque Mittelmann[1(✉)], Jerusa Marchi[2], and Aldo von Wangenheim[2]

[1] IRIT - University of Toulouse, 31000 Toulouse, France
munyquee@gmail.com
[2] Federal University of Santa Catarina, Florianópolis, SC 88040-900, Brazil
{jerusa.marchi,aldo.vw}@ufsc.br

Abstract. Bayesian Networks (BN) are used for representing and inferring over variables with aleatory uncertainty. Dynamic Bayesian Networks (DBN) extend this concept by introducing temporal dependencies that catch dynamic behaviors from the domain variables. Effective and efficient modeling through BN demands data discretization on categories. However, these categories may have vagueness uncertainty, once are used labels not defined by exact numerical thresholds. Fuzzy Theory provides a framework for modeling vagueness uncertainty. Although hybrid theories to integrate Fuzzy Theory and BN inference process have been proposed, there are still limitations on using fuzzy evidence on DBN. The related works restrict the evidence modeling to the overlapping of only two fuzzy membership functions. Thereby, this work proposes a method for Dynamic Fuzzy-Bayesian inference over non-dichotomic variables. To evaluate the proposal, the model is applied as a classifier on the Detection Occupancy Dataset and compared with other approaches. In the experiments, the model obtained Accuracy 97% and Recall 92%.

Keywords: Dynamic Bayesian Network · Fuzzy Theory ·
Fuzzy-Bayesian inference

1 Introduction

Many computational problems require inference over incomplete or uncertain sensory data. Probabilistic Models, as Bayesian Networks (BN), allow to represent and infer on variables with aleatory uncertainty, which derives from natural variability of the physical world [6]. Using the knowledge extracted from observations, BN allows inferring, for example, the probability of heavy rain given the information of a high thermometer temperature. Another problem using sensory data is temporal pattern recognition [12]. When data has sequential characteristic, as temporal series data or data generated from dynamic systems.

This study was financed by the Coordination for the Improvement of Higher Education Personnel - Brazil (CAPES) - Finance Code 001. Munyque Mitttelmann acknowledges the support of the ANR project AGAGE ANR-18-CE23-0013.

L. Rutkowski et al. (Eds.): ICAISC 2019, LNAI 11508, pp. 314–323, 2019.
https://doi.org/10.1007/978-3-030-20912-4_30

BN can be extended to Dynamic Bayesian Networks (DBN) to introduce temporal dependencies that catch dynamic behaviors from the domain variables.

Despite sensory measurements usually admit continuous values (e.g. real numbers), there's a practical limitation for applying BN, once most software and algorithms do not allow continuous variables [16]. Thereby, effective and efficient BN modeling demand data discretization on categories, frequently done through of expert specifications.

However, the linguistic labels used by expert humans frequently have vagueness uncertainty, once they cannot be defined by exact numerical thresholds [10]. For example, the temperature can be classified in vague linguistic terms like cold, warm and hot. Fuzzy Theory provides a framework for modeling vagueness uncertainty. We divide the research works in Fuzzy-Dynamic Bayesian Networks into three groups depending on the point where Fuzzy Theory is included: (i) before (pre-processing), (ii) after (post-processing) and (iii) during the inference of the DBN.

On the pre-processing stage, Fuzzy Theory is used for providing DBN parameters, like presented in [7,11,19]. On the other hand, researches using Fuzzy Theory on DBN post-processing apply Fuzzy Inference Systems over the probability distribution from the DBN, as can be seen in [8,17].

When estimating conditional and *posteriori* probabilities, pre-processing and post-processing approaches do not consider the vagueness present in the evidence variables when they are defined by fuzzy states. Models integrating Fuzzy and DBN during the inference process, i.e. by allowing fuzzy states in the evidence variables are proposed with the objective of fullfill tasks like (i) prediction as presented by Teixeira and Zaverucha [18] and by Zhang and Li [20]; (ii) filtering as presented by Naderpour et al. [14] and Di Tomaso and Baldwin [6] and/or (iii) most probable explanation as presented by Naderpour et al. [15] and Di Tomaso and Baldwin [6]. However, these works limit the evidence modeling in fuzzy partitioning with just two membership functions, i.e. dichotomic states[1] and there are cases where dichotomic modeling cannot express properly the semantic relationships among concepts. Consider, for instance, the BN reasoning support to children and adolescents metabolic risk diagnose, presented in [1], where the terms *overweight, obese, severe obese* are quite related. A patient diagnosed as *overweight* can be in an increasing process of becoming *obese* or even *severe obese* and can be useful to the BN inference to have this relation properly represented. In this case, having non-dichotomic modeling of the obese measurement can bring this relation highlighted.

Brignoli et al. [1] present a BN model for inference on overlapping states. But they do not consider temporal dependency among the network variables, like data from temporal series or dynamic systems. In this paper, we extend Brignoli's approach to dynamic domains by introducing a Fuzzy-Dynamic Bayesian inference model for filtering task that considers non-dichotomic evidence.

The work is organized as follows: Sect. 2 presents the Fuzzy-Bayesian inference process proposed in [1]. Section 3 introduces Dynamic Bayesian Networks.

---

[1] A dichotomic variable can be split only in two states.

In Sect. 4 we present our proposal. Section 5 presents some preliminary experiments performed using the proposed model and the results are presented and discussed. Section 6 concludes the paper, bringing final considerations and future works.

2   Fuzzy-Bayesian Inference

In order to incorporate fuzzy aspects into the inference process of Bayesian models, it is necessary to adapt these models to deal with fuzzy evidence. In [1] is presented a hybrid Fuzzy-Bayesian approach (Fuzzy-BN) that allows the inclusion of non-dychotomic fuzzy variables into the Bayesian inference process. In that work, the probability $\mathcal{P}$ over fuzzy evidence is defined by:

$$\mathcal{P}(H_i|E_j) = \frac{P(H_i)\prod_{j=1}^{m}\sum_{k=1}^{u}(P_{x_k}(E_j|H_i).\mu_{x_k}(E_j))}{\sum_{l=1}^{n}P(H_l)\prod_{j=1}^{m}\sum_{k=1}^{u}(P_{x_k}(E_j|H_l).\mu_{x_k}(E_j))} \tag{1}$$

where n are the hypothesis states; m are the evidence; u are the evidence states; H_i is the hypothesis array, with $1 \leq i \leq n$; E_j is the evidence array, with $1 \leq j \leq m$; $P_{x_k}(E_j|H_i)$ is the conditional probability of the state x_k of evidence E_j given H_i, with $1 \leq k \leq u$; $P(H_i)$ is the probability *a priori* over H_i; and $\mu_{x_k}(E_j)$ represents the membership degree of the state x_k of the evidence E_j with relation to the fuzzy membership function.

Therefore, $\mathcal{P}(H_i|E_j)$ is the conditional probability of H_i adapted by the imprecision over the evidence variables E_j.

3   Dynamic Bayesian Networks and Filtering

DBN is a way to extend BN for modeling probability distributions over semi-infinite collections of random variables [13]. In DBN, each time slice t can have any amount of unobservable variables X^t and observable (or evidence) variables E^t. The notation adopted in this work uses $X^{a:b}$ for representing the corresponding set of variables from X^a to X^b, where a and b are natural numbers.

DBN model needs the definition of three probability distributions: (i) the prior distribution of the unobservable variables at the initial time $P(X^0)$; (ii) the transition model $P(X^t|X^{t-1})$; and (iii) the sensor model or observation model $P(E^t|X^t)$[12]. The transition model $P(X^t|X^{t-1})$ describes how the unobservable variables X^t are affected by the states of the unobservable variables on the previous time. The sensor model $P(E^t|X^t)$ defines how the evidence variables (sensors) are affected by the real world state.

Assuming the world state is caused by a stationary process, transition and sensor models are the same in any time t. Whether we assume that DBN describes a first order Markov process, for any finite t, the joint distribution over all variables is defined by [12]:

$$P(X^0, X^1, ..., X^t, E^1, ..., E^t) = P(X^0)\prod_{i=1}^{t}P(X^i|X^{i-1})P(E^i|X^i) \tag{2}$$

The main inference tasks in DBN are (i) filtering, that estimates $P(X^t|e^{1:t})$; (ii) prediction, that estimates $P(X^{t+k}|e^{1:t})$, for some $k > 0$; (iii) smoothing, that $P(X^k|e^{1:t})$, for some $0 \leq k < t$; and (iv) the most probable explanation, that estimates $argmax_{x^{1:t}} P(x^{1:t}|e^{1:t})$ [12].

In this research, we explore filtering inference, in which an observation set is used to estimated *a posterior* distributions over the current state. Considering the First Order Markov hypothesis over observable and non-observable variables, the estimation of $P(X^{t+1}|e^{1:t+1})$ is defined by [13]:

$$P(X^{t+1}|e^{1:t+1}) = \alpha P(e^{t+1}|X^{t+1}) \sum_{x^t} P(X^{t+1}|X^t)P(x^t|e^{1:t}) \qquad (3)$$

where $P(e^{1:t+1}|X^{t+1})$ can be directly obtained through the sensor model. In the sum, $P(X^{t+1}|X^t)$ is the transition model and $P(x^t|e^{1:t})$ is the current state distribution. α is a normalizing constant to ensure that the inputs sum of $P(X^{t+1}|e^{1:t+1})$ results 1.

The recursive resolution of $\sum_{x^t} P(X^{t+1}|X^t)P(x^t|e^{1:t})$ is called forward propagation and projects the probability distribution of the states X from time t to $t+1$.

Next section we introduce our inference model considering filtering inference in Dynamic Bayesian Networks and the Fuzzy-Bayesian model introduced in Sect. 2.

4   Fuzzy-Dynamic Bayesian Inference

This work aims to propose filtering in DBN over observable variables whose states are defined by fuzzy membership functions. In order to allow the multiple state overlapping, the adopted strategy is based on the Fuzzy-BN from Brignoli et al. [1].

Following, it will be presented the inference equation induction filtering over fuzzy evidence. Resuming Eq. 3, that assumes the First Order Markov hypothesis, we have:

$$P(x_i^{t+1}|e^{1:t+1}) = \alpha P(e^{t+1}|x_i^{t+1}) \sum_{l=1}^{n} P(x_i^{t+1}|x_l^t)P(x_l^t|e^{1:t}) \qquad (4)$$

where i represents the ith state from the unobservable variable and n is the total amount of unobservable variable states. Taking the normalizing constant α as $\frac{1}{P(e^{1:t+1})}$, we have:

$$P(x_i^{t+1}|e^{1:t+1}) = \frac{P(e^{t+1}|x_i^{t+1}) \sum_{l=1}^{n} P(x_i^{t+1}|x_l^t)P(x_l^t|e^{1:t})}{P(e^{1:t+1})} \qquad (5)$$

If the sample space Ω^{t+1} could be divided in a finite amount of n mutually exclusive events x_j^{t+1}, where $\sum_{j=1}^{n} x_j^{t+1} = \Omega^{t+1}$ and if $P(e^{1:t+1}) > 0$, then it is possible to define $P(e^{1:t+1})$ as [9]:

$$P(e^{1:t+1}) = \sum_{j=1}^{n} (P(e^{t+1}|x_j^{t+1})P(x_j^{t+1})) \tag{6}$$

Considering that in DBN filtering the distribution of the states x_j from t to $t+1$ is projected by the forward propagation $\sum_{l=1}^{n} P(x_i^{t+1}|x_l^t)P(x_l^t|e^{1:t})$ (see Sect. 3), so we can define $P(e^{1:t+1})$ as:

$$P(e^{1:t+1}) = \sum_{j=1}^{n} (P(e^{t+1}|x_j^{t+1}) \sum_{l=1}^{n} P(x_i^{t+1}|x_l^t)P(x_l^t|e^{1:t})) \tag{7}$$

Thus, using Eq. 7 in Eq. 5, the filtering inference can be described by:

$$P(x_i^{t+1}|e^{1:t+1}) = \frac{P(e^{t+1}|x_i^{t+1}) \sum_{l=1}^{n} P(x_i^{t+1}|x_l^t)P(x_l^t|e^{1:t})}{\sum_{j=1}^{n}(P(e^{t+1}|x_j^{t+1}) \sum_{l=1}^{n} P(x_i^{t+1}|x_l^t)P(x_l^t|e^{1:t}))} \tag{8}$$

Considering the existence of k combined evidence, represented by $e_1^{1:t+1}$, ..., $e_k^{1:t+1}$ denoted by $E^{1:t+1}$ and assuming the evidence independence given x_i^{t+1}, it is possible to apply the conditional independence property [3]. Thereby, the filtering is defined as:

$$P(x_i^{t+1}|E^{1:t+1}) = \frac{\sum_{l=1}^{n} P(x_i^{t+1}|x_l^t)P(x_l^t|E^{1:t}) \prod_{m=1}^{k} P(e_m^{t+1}|x_i^{t+1})}{\sum_{j=1}^{n}(\sum_{l=1}^{n} P(x_i^{t+1}|x_l^t)P(x_l^t|E^{1:t}) \prod_{m=1}^{k} P(e_m^{t+1}|x_j^{t+1}))} \tag{9}$$

The proposed inference model considers the representation of Fuzzy-Dynamic Bayesian Networks (Fuzzy-DBN) with k evidence variables (E^{t+1}) and one unobservable variable (hypothesis x^{t+1}). Each e_j^{t+1} can have multiple discrete or continuous states. Continuous states of e_j^{t+1} are classified through a fuzzy qualifier, such that $e_j^{t+1}s_w$ is the evidence e_j^{t+1} observed on the fuzzy state s_w. Lastly, $\mu_{s_w}(e_j^{t+1})$ represents the membership degree of e_j^{t+1} to the state s_w.

Inspired in Brignoli et al. [1], we define the conditional possibility $\tilde{P}$ of e_j^{t+1} given x_i^{t+1} as:

$$\tilde{P}(e_j^{t+1}|x_i^{t+1}) = \sum_{w=1}^{u} P_{s_w}(e_j^{t+1}|x_i^{t+1}).(\mu_{s_w}(e_j^{t+1})) \tag{10}$$

where u are the fuzzy states from the evidence variable e_j^{t+1}.

Using Eq. (10) for considering the fuzzy states s_w from the variable e_j^{t+1} in Eq. (9), we have the probability $\mathcal{P}$ of x_i^{t+1} given the fuzzy evidence $E^{1:t+1}$ defined as:

$$\mathcal{P}(x_i^{t+1}|E^{1:t+1}) = \frac{\sum_{l=1}^{n} P(x_i^{t+1}|x_l^t)\mathcal{P}(x_l^t|E^{1:t}) \prod_{m=1}^{k} \tilde{P}(e_m^{t+1}|x_i^{t+1})}{\sum_{j=1}^{n}(\sum_{l=1}^{n} P(x_j^{t+1}|x_l^t)\mathcal{P}(x_l^t|E^{1:t}) \prod_{m=1}^{k} \tilde{P}(e_m^{t+1}|x_j^{t+1}))} \tag{11}$$

or, considering the right side of Eq. 10:

$$\mathcal{P}(x_i^{t+1}|E^{1:t+1}) = \frac{\sum_{l=1}^{n} P(x_i^{t+1}|x_l^t)\mathcal{P}(x_l^t|E^{1:t})\prod_{m=1}^{k}\sum_{w=1}^{u}P_{s_w}(e_i^{t+1}|x^{t+1})(\mu_{s_w}(e_j^{t+1}))}{\sum_{j=1}^{n}(\sum_{l=1}^{n}P(x_j^{t+1}|x_l^t)\mathcal{P}(x_l^t|E^{1:t})\prod_{m=1}^{k}\sum_{w=1}^{u}P_{s_w}(e_j^{t+1}|x^{t+1})(\mu_{s_w}(e_j^{t+1})))}$$

(12)

Equation 12 defines the proposed mathematics formulation for supporting filtering inference in Fuzzy-DBN with multiple evidence and multiple states.

5   Model Evaluation

In order to evaluate our proposal, we present a classification experiment with fuzzy evidence with overlapping states using the Occupancy Detection dataset [2] from the UCI Repository [5]. The dataset is composed by 20560 instances of sequential and experimental data for binary classification for room occupancy. The Data set has 21.23% of occupied class instances and the remaining in the not occupied class. We used the following attributes as observable variables: Temperature (in Celsius), Relative Humidity (in %), Light (in Lux) and CO_2 (in ppm). The unobservable variable is Occupancy and assumes the values true or false representing the occupied status of the room.

The fuzzy modeling was obtained from the observation of the interval and distribution from each variable values. The fuzzy parameters were refined after some preliminary tests. The observable variables was categorized in linguistic concepts (*low, medium, high*) and modeled using Fuzzy Sets. Figure 1 shows the fuzzy modeling used for each observable variable: (a) Light, (b) CO_2, (c) Humidity e (d) Temperature. The observable variables have overlapping states and their membership values are not necessarily complementary. For example, a measurement of $19,5\,°C$ has the membership degree equal to $0,755$ for the *low* state, $0,325$ for the *medium* state and $0,186$ for the *high*.

Both the proposal and the compared works were implemented using the same fuzzy modeling. In order to enable the network parameters learning, the observable variables were pre-classified by the fuzzy modeling, where each observed value was categorized in the class with the highest membership degree.

The data set was randomly divided into two subsets: 70% for training and 30% for evaluation. In order to obtain the *priori* distribution of the unobservable variable at the initial time, the transition model and the sensor model, we applied the Expectation Maximization Algorithm [4] on the training subset.

After these procedures, the proposal was applied to the evaluation subset. First, the evidence values was fuzzified, such to obtain the membership of each evidence e_j^t to each state s_w, that is: $\mu_{s_w}(e_j^t)$.

The proposal was used as a classifier, where the unobservable variable in the current time with the biggest probability was considered the predicted class. The network inputs are the observable evidence E^1 to E^T, where T denotes the current time slice.

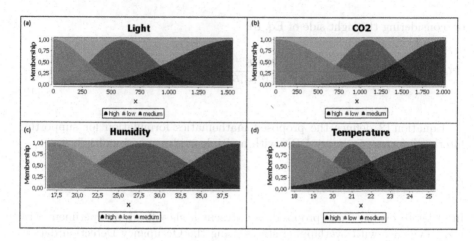

Fig. 1. Fuzzy modeling for the observable variables

After the rule inference application, according to Eq. 12, the model produces the probability of the unobservable variable x_i^T for all $1 \le i \le n$, with n representing the variable states x^T. As a classifier, the output is the state x_i^T with the highest probability value.

The fuzzy evidence modeling limitation in [6,14,15,18,20] prevents their use on situations with non-dichotomic variables. Thereby, our proposal is compared to the DBN filtering inference and with the Fuzzy-BN approach from Brignoli et al. [1], as presented in the next section.

5.1   Result Analysis

For the experiments, we used four-time slices in the Fuzzy-DBN (our proposal). Figure 2 presents the Fuzzy-DBN topology.

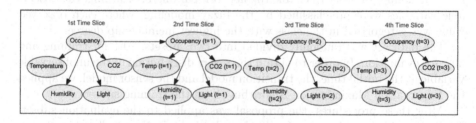

Fig. 2. Fuzzy-DBN topology with four-time slices

The Confusion Matrix summarizes the amount of correct and incorrect predictions by the Fuzzy-DBN (Table 1). The Fuzzy-DBN classification is compared with DBN and Fuzzy-BN classification in Table 2.

Table 1. Confusion matrix for the unobservable variable occupancy

		True class	
		Yes	No
Predicted class	Yes	474	33
	No	39	1896

In comparison with Fuzzy-BN, the proposed Fuzzy-DBN obtained an Accuracy improvement of $1,369\%$. This means that, by adding time slices on the Fuzzy-BN, the proposed inference increased the correct predictions in the classification. The Recall value shows an improvement of the correct classification of samples as positive occupancy when the room is actually occupied. F_1-score suggests the improvement in Recall was more meaningful for the classification quality than the decrease in Precision.

Table 2. Classification measurements for Fuzzy-BN, DBN and Fuzzy-DBN

Measurement	Fuzzy-BN	DBN	Fuzzy-DBN
Accuracy	0,957412	0,967240	0,970516
Recall	0,849903	0,879159	0,923977
Inverse Recall	0,986003	0,994121	0,982893
Precision	0,941685	0,978558	0,934911
Inverse Precision	0,961091	0,964230	0,979845
F_1-score	0,893443	0,926199	0,929412

The inclusion of fuzzy evidence on the DBN results in an Accuracy improvement of $0,339\%$. Fuzzy-DBN also obtained better results in Recall, Inverse Precision and F_1-score. These metrics show that the proposal improves the network ability to correctly classify the instances when the room is occupied. As a disadvantage, the decrease in precision shows a growth in the false positives cases. Despite this, the F_1-score suggests that the true positive increase overcome the false positive in the Fuzzy-DBN classification.

Figure 3 presents the Receiver Operating Characteristic (ROC) Curve for the positive classification of occupancy. Fuzzy-BN and Fuzzy-DBN obtained similar results. However, the DBN ROC Curve shows that the False Positive Rate had a faster increase according to the threshold variation, in comparison with another two approaches.

Both the time slices inclusion in the Fuzzy-BN and the fuzzy evidence inclusion in the DBN, provide improvements when using the Fuzzy-DBN, as can be mainly observed in the obtained Accuracy and F_1-score.

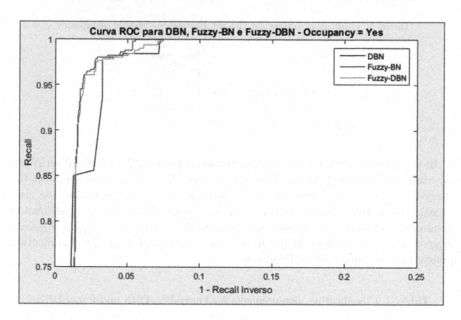

Fig. 3. ROC Curve for DBN, Fuzzy-BN and Fuzzy-DBN for the positive classification of occupancy

6   Conclusion

Existing approaches to infer in Dynamic Bayesian Networks over vagueness data restrict the overlapping and modeling of evidence states to only two fuzzy states. Thereby, in order to allow the overlapping of multiple states and to consider them in the inference process, this work proposed a model for Dynamic Fuzzy-Bayesian inference over non-dichotomic variables.

The proposed model is inspired by a fuzzy-BN model, where the membership degree is used to define the conditional possibility of the fuzzy evidence. We present a generic model, in the sense that it allows multiple evidence, multiple fuzzy states, and multiple time slices.

The model was applied as a classifier on the Detection Occupancy Dataset, where our proposal obtained Accuracy 97%, F_1-score 92% and Recall 92%. The compared Fuzzy-BN can be equivalent to our approach if and only if no time slices are considered. Thus, Fuzzy-DBN shows better classification results when adding time slices to the Bayesian inference. In another hand, the comparison of the proposal with the DBN, suggests that the use of fuzzy evidence increase the classification quality.

As future works, it is possible to extend the proposal for other inference tasks, like prediction, most probable explanation and smoothing. Besides that, it is important to investigate methods for optimizing the decision about how much time slices could be considered, in order to achieve a better relationship between computational cost and classification performance.

References

1. Brignoli, J.T., Pires, M.M., Nassar, S.M., Sell, D.: A fuzzy-Bayesian model based on the superposition of states applied to the clinical reasoning support. In: IntelliSys 2015 - Proceedings of 2015 SAI Intelligent Systems Conference, pp. 210–219 (2015)
2. Candanedo, L.M., Feldheim, V.: Accurate occupancy detection of an office room from light, temperature, humidity and $CO2$ measurements using statistical learning models. Energy Build. **112**, 28–39 (2016)
3. Dawid, A.P.: Conditional independence in statistical theory. J. R. Stat. Soc. Ser. B (Methodol.) **41**(1), 1–31 (1979)
4. Dempster, A.P., Laird, N.M., Rubin, D.B.: Maximum likelihood from incomplete data via the EM algorithm. J. R. Stat. Soc. Ser. B (Methodol.) **39**(1), 1–38 (1977)
5. Dheeru, D., Karra Taniskidou, E.: (UCI) Machine Learning Repository (2017). http://archive.ics.uci.edu/ml
6. Di Tomaso, E., Baldwin, J.F.: An approach to hybrid probabilistic models. Int. J. Approx. Reason. **47**(2), 202–218 (2008)
7. Feng, Y., Jia, Q., Chu, M., Wei, W.: Engagement evaluation for autism intervention by robots based on dynamic Bayesian network and expert elicitation. IEEE Access **5**, 19494–19504 (2017)
8. Khalid, A.J., Wang, J., Nurudeen, M.: A new fault classification model for prognosis and diagnosis in CNC machine. In: 2013 25th Chinese Control and Decision Conference, CCDC 2013, pp. 3538–3543 (2013)
9. Kolmogorov, A.N.: Foundations of the Theory of Probability (1956)
10. Li, Y., Chen, J., Feng, L.: Dealing with uncertainty: a survey of theories and practices. IEEE Trans. Knowl. Data Eng. **25**, 2463–2482 (2013)
11. Li, J., Gao, X.: Fuzzy variable structure dynamic Bayesian network applying target recognition. In: 2016 First IEEE International Conference on Computer Communication and the Internet (ICCCI), pp. 434–438 (2016)
12. Mihajlovic, V., Petkovic, M.: Dynamic Bayesian networks: a state of the art. CTIT Tech. Rep. Ser. **34**, 1–37 (2001)
13. Murphy, K.P.: Dynamic Bayesian networks: representation, inference and learning. Ph.D. thesis, University Of California, Berkeley (2002)
14. Naderpour, M., Lu, J., Zhang, G.: A fuzzy dynamic Bayesian network-based situation assessment approach. In: 2013 IEEE International Conference on Fuzzy Systems (FUZZ-IEEE), pp. 1–8 (2013)
15. Naderpour, M., Lu, J., Zhang, G.: An intelligent situation awareness support system for safety-critical environments. Decis. Support. Syst. **59**(1), 325–340 (2014)
16. Nojavan, F.A., Qian, S.S., Stow, C.A.: Comparative analysis of discretization methods in Bayesian networks. Environ. Model. Softw. **87**, 64–71 (2017)
17. Sykes, E.R.: Preliminary findings of visualization of the interruptible moment. In: Mewhort, D.J.K., Cann, N.M., Slater, G.W., Naughton, T.J. (eds.) HPCS 2009. LNCS, vol. 5976, pp. 215–229. Springer, Heidelberg (2010). https://doi.org/10.1007/978-3-642-12659-8_16
18. Teixeira, M.A., Zaverucha, G.: A partitioning method for fuzzy probabilistic predictors. In: Neural Information Processing, pp. 929–934 (2004)
19. Yao, J.Y., Li, J., Li, H., Wang, X.: Modeling system based on fuzzy dynamic bayesian network for fault diagnosis and reliability prediction (2015)
20. Zhang, H., Li, R.: Emotional nonverbal communication based on fuzzy dynamic Bayesian network. In: 9th International Conference on Control, Automation, Robotics and Vision, ICARCV 2006 (2006)

The Estimation of Uncertain Gates: An Application to Educational Indicators

Guillaume Petiot[✉]

Catholic Institute of Toulouse, 31000 Toulouse, France
guillaume.petiot@ict-toulouse.fr
http://www.ict-toulouse.fr

Abstract. Uncertain gates in possibility theory correspond to noisy gates in probability theory. They allow us to reduce the number of parameters which must be elicited to define conditional possibility tables in possibilistic networks. Usually the choice of the connector and its parameters is made by experts but sometimes if there is an existing CPT or if data are available, it can be interesting to perform an estimation of uncertain connectors. This estimation allows us to better understand how information is combined. Furthermore, it is possible to match one of three sorts of behaviour (indulgent, compromise, severe) with the corresponding information. This point is important for knowledge engineering. If the data are available, the estimation can also be useful to verify if the uncertain connector fits with the data, because expert knowledge is often imprecise and uncertain. In this paper, we will show how to perform the estimation of uncertain gates and we will illustrate our approach with several examples of results in the domain of education.

Keywords: Uncertain gates · Possibility theory ·
Knowledge engineering · Estimation · Uncertainty

1 Introduction

The knowledge of a human expert is often imprecise and uncertain. Possibility theory, presented in [14], provides a solution to these drawbacks which take into account the imprecision and the uncertainty of knowledge. If knowledge can be modelled by a Directional Acyclic Graph, it is possible to use a possibilistic network for the propagation of new information. Possibilistic networks [1,3] in possibility theory are an analogy of Bayesian networks [11,12] in probability theory. The main difficulty in possibilistic networks is to elicit Conditional Possibility Tables. The parameters to elicit grow exponentially with the number of parents of the variable leading to a too large number of parameters to define. One solution to this problem is to use a function of the parents of the variable for the computation of the CPT. This solution is proposed by noisy gates in probability theory. Thus, the number of parameters is considerably reduced. Noisy gates provide another advantage which is the modelling of noise. Moreover, in

© Springer Nature Switzerland AG 2019
L. Rutkowski et al. (Eds.): ICAISC 2019, LNAI 11508, pp. 324–334, 2019.
https://doi.org/10.1007/978-3-030-20912-4_31

complex systems it is difficult to have a perfect model of knowledge. We often forget variables which involve bad predictions of the models. The use of a special variable, called leakage variable, to represent the unknown knowledge gives birth to a second kind of model. In possibility theory, uncertain gates offer the same advantages as noisy gates. Another benefit of uncertain gates is the possibility to define connectors with behaviours indulgent, compromise or severe. So the use of uncertain gates makes easier knowledge engineering.

There are many applications of possibilistic networks with CPTs. It is also possible to have data in addition to expert knowledge. It can be interesting to know which uncertain connector is the best to fit with the data. Moreover, if we have already defined an uncertain gate based only on knowledge, it can be more reassuring to compare the one estimated from the data and the one defined by experts.

This paper deals with the estimation of uncertain gates from CPTs and from data. In the first part, we will present possibility theory and in the second part uncertain gates. Then we will focus on the estimation of uncertain gates. And finally, we will propose an example of the estimation of uncertain gates in the domain of educational indicators.

2   Possibility Theory

Uncertain gates are an analogy of noisy gates in possibility theory [14], which allows us to model imprecise and uncertain knowledge by a possibility distribution. For example, if V is a variable and π_V its possibility distribution defined from the referential Ω to $[0, 1]$, then we can say that if $\pi_V(v) = 0$ then $V = v$ is not possible, if $\pi_V(v) = 1$ then $V = v$ is possible or fully plausible and finally if $\pi_V(v) = \alpha$ then $V = v$ is plausible with the degree α. If we have a subset A of Ω, then we can define the possibility measure Π and the necessity measure N as in [6]. The possibility measure is a function defined from the set of all subsets of Ω noted $P(\Omega)$ to $[0, 1]$:

$$\forall A \in P(\Omega), \Pi(A) = \sup_{x \in A} \pi(x). \tag{1}$$

The necessity measure is a function from $P(\Omega)$ to $[0, 1]$:

$$\forall A \in P(\Omega), N(A) = 1 - \Pi(\neg A) = \inf_{x \notin A} 1 - \pi(x) \tag{2}$$

The main property of possibility theory is:

$$\forall A \in P(\Omega), \forall B \in P(V), \Pi(A \cup B) = \max(\Pi(A), \Pi(B)). \tag{3}$$

We can see in the above formula that possibility theory is not additive but maxitive.

3 Uncertain Gates

The possibilistic networks [1,2] can be defined by using the factoring property. The factoring property is established from the joint possibility distribution $\Pi(V)$ for a DAG $G = (V, A)$, where V is the set of variables and A the set of edges between the variables. $\Pi(V)$ can be factorized as follows:

$$\Pi(V) = \bigotimes_{X \in V} \Pi(X/Pa(X)). \tag{4}$$

With Pa the parents of the variable X and $\bigotimes$ the function minimum.

Noisy gates in probability theory are defined by using the Independence of Causal Influence [4,8,16]. In fact, there is a set of causal variables $X_1, ..., X_n$ which influence the result of an effect variable Y. To take into account uncertainty, we can add variables Z_i between each X_is. So we obtain the equation $Y = f(Z_1, ..., Z_n)$ where f is a deterministic function. Expert descriptions of complex systems are often incomplete because the more the system is complex, the less the link between the variables is easy to analyse. This problem leads us to exclude the unknown knowledge of the model during the knowledge discovering phase. The solution proposed by the authors in [4] is to use a leakage variable Z_l to model the unknown knowledge. So we can propose a new leaky ICI model derived from the previous noisy model. The following figure presents the leaky ICI model (Fig. 1):

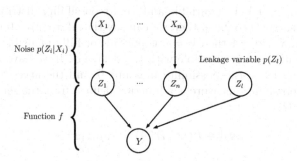

Fig. 1. Leaky ICI model.

If there is no causal interaction in the effects of the variables X_i on the variable Y, then we can perform a marginalization as follows:

$$P(y|x_1, ..., x_n) = \sum_{z_1,...,z_n} P(y|z_1, ..., z_n) \times P(z_1, ..., z_n|x_1, ..., x_n) \tag{5}$$

$$P(y|x_1, ..., x_n) = \sum_{z_1,...,z_n} P(y|z_1, ..., z_n) \times \prod_{i=1}^{n} P(z_i|x_i) \tag{6}$$

$$\text{where } P(y|z_1, ..., z_n) = \begin{cases} 1 \text{ if } y = f(z_1, ..., z_n) \\ 0 \text{ else} \end{cases} \tag{7}$$

As a result, we obtain the following formula in probability theory:

$$P(y|x_1, ..., x_n) = \sum_{z_1,...,z_n : y = f(z_1,...,z_n)} \prod_{i=1}^{n} P(z_i|x_i) \tag{8}$$

In possibility theory, there is the following formula demonstrated by the authors of [5]:

$$\pi(y|x_1, ..., x_n) = \max_{z_1,...,z_n : y = f(z_1,...,z_n)} \otimes_{i=1}^{n} \pi(z_i|x_i) \tag{9}$$

The $\otimes$ is the minimum. The CPT is obtained by the calculation of the above formula. For Boolean variables, the possibility table between the variables X_i and Z_i is the following (Table 1):

Table 1. Possibility table for Boolean variables.

$\pi(Z_i|X_i)$	x_i	$\neg x_i$
z_i	1	s_i
$\neg z_i$	κ_i	1

In the previous table, the κ can be interpreted as the possibility that an inhibitor exists if the cause is met. On the other hand, s_i can be seen as the possibility that a substitute exists when the cause is not met.

If the modalities of a variable are ordered, we can encode the modality by an intensity level as in [5]. For example, in our experimentation there are three levels of intensity such as low, medium and high, and we will encode the modalities with values 0 for low, 1 for medium and 2 for high. So we obtain (Table 2):

Table 2. Possibility table for multivalued variables.

$\pi(Z_i|X_i)$	$x_i = 2$	$x_i = 1$	$x_i = 0$
$z_i = 2$	1	$s_i^{2,1}$	$s_i^{2,0}$
$z_i = 1$	$\kappa_i^{1,2}$	1	$s_i^{1,0}$
$z_i = 0$	$\kappa_i^{0,2}$	$\kappa_i^{0,1}$	1

If we consider as in [5] that a cause of weak intensity cannot produce a strong effect, then all $s_i = 0$. In our application, these parameters are greater than 0. So there are 6 parameters per variable. If we add a leakage variable Z_l in the previous model, we obtain the following equation:

$$\pi(y|x_1, ..., x_n) = \max_{z_1, ..., z_n, z_l : y = f(z_1, ..., z_n, z_l)} \otimes_{i=1}^{n} \pi(z_i|x_i) \otimes \pi(z_l) \qquad (10)$$

Several uncertain gates have already been presented by replacing the function f by logical functions AND, OR or their generalizations MIN and MAX. The authors of [5] have defined these operators. It is also possible to use a weighted average function, or the operator OWA [13], as described in our previous study [10]. For this experimentation we will use the connectors uncertain MIN, uncertain MAX and uncertain weighted average (WAVG).

4   Estimation

In possibilistic networks, the number of parameters of the CPTs is growing exponentially when the number of parents of a variable is growing. As a result, the task of knowledge elicitation is more and more difficult. This leads to several problems in knowledge engineering [15]. For example, if a variable has 10 parents and each variable has 2 modalities, then we have $2^{11} = 2048$ parameters to elicit. If the data are available, the solution can be to perform an estimation of the CPT but often it is difficult to have the data to estimate all parameters. So one solution can be to try to use uncertain gates to compute CPTs. With uncertain gates, the number of parameters is greatly reduced. In fact, we have only to define the parameters of uncertain gates. Another problem is knowing which uncertain gates to use. Several uncertain gates exist among behaviours severe, compromise or indulgent. If the CPT already exists, it can be helpful to replace the CPT by an uncertain gate, but to do this, we have to perform an estimation of the parameters and to select one connector among all which exist.

More generally, there are two cases to distinguish for the computation of uncertain gates. The first one is the simple case where we would like to perform an estimation of uncertain gates from an existing CPT. To do this, we have to compare the CPT generated by an uncertain gate and an existing CPT. This leads to an optimisation problem which consists in estimating the parameters of the uncertain gate. In fact, we look for the closest CPT compared to a reference CPT. If we have to compare CPTs, we need to use a measure of distance between the CPTs. Several distances can be used [7] such as Euclidean, Skew divergence, Kullback-Leibler Divergence, Cosine, L_1,... So we present below some of these distance measures for two conditional possibilities π_i and π_f of a variable Y and ∂_Y the domain of Y. If $X_1, ..., X_n$ are the parents of the variable Y and $\partial_{X_1}, ..., \partial_{X_n}$ the domains of these variables, we obtain $(y, x_1, ..., x_n)$ an instanced vector in the Cartesian product $\Delta = \partial_Y \times \partial_{X_1} \times ... \times \partial_{X_n}$. We propose the following distances for the CPTs (Table 3):

Table 3. Existing distance measures between the CPTs.

Distance	Formula
Euclidean (E)	$\sqrt{\displaystyle\sum_{(y,x_1,\ldots,x_n)\in\Delta}(\pi_i(y|x_1,\ldots,x_n)-\pi_f(y|x_1,\ldots,x_n))^2}$
KL Div. (KL)	$\displaystyle\sum_{(y,x_1,\ldots,x_n)\in\Delta}\pi_i(y|x_1,\ldots,x_n)(\log\pi_i(y|x_1,\ldots,x_n)-\log\pi_f(y|x_1,\ldots,x_n))$
Skew Div. (SD_α)	$KL(\pi_i(y|x_1,\ldots,x_n),\alpha\pi_i(y|x_1,\ldots,x_n)+(1-\alpha)\pi_f(y|x_1,\ldots,x_n))$
Cosine (C)	$\dfrac{\displaystyle\sum_{(y,x_1,\ldots,x_n)\in\Delta}\pi_i(y|x_1,\ldots,x_n)\pi_f(y|x_1,\ldots,x_n)}{\sqrt{\displaystyle\sum_{(y,x_1,\ldots,x_n)\in\Delta}\pi_i(y|x_1,\ldots,x_n)^2}\displaystyle\sum_{(y,x_1,\ldots,x_n)\in\Delta}\pi_f(y|x_1,\ldots,x_n)^2}$
L_1	$\displaystyle\sum_{(y,x_1,\ldots,x_n)\in\Delta}|\pi_i(y|x_1,\ldots,x_n)-\pi_f(y|x_1,\ldots,x_n)|$

For our first experimentation we propose to use the Euclidean distance. We will compare 4 estimation methods: gradient descent, simulated annealing, tabu research, and genetic algorithm. If we consider the example of the gradient descent, we have at first initialized all parameters of the uncertain gates to a random value in $[0,1]$. Then we generate the CPT and we calculate the initial distance. Next, we evaluate all neighbours of the parameters by adding and subtracting a step. We consider only the smallest distance for the CPTs generated by the neighbours. Its parameters become our temporary solution. We reiterate this until the distance is lower than a constant, or a maximum number of iterations is reached. As an example, we present below the algorithm for the estimation of the parameters of the Uncertain MIN with a gradient descent:

Algorithm 1. Estimation of the parameters of the uncertain MIN.

Input : Y a variable; $X_1,\ldots,X_n$ the n parents of Y; $\pi(Y|X_1,\ldots,X_n)$ the initial CPT; *step* a constant.
Output: The result is $\pi(Z_i|X_i)$.

```
1  begin
2  |   iteration ⟵ 0; error ⟵ +∞; CError ⟵ +∞
3  |   Initialize(π(Zᵢ|Xᵢ))
4  |   while iteration < max and error > ε do
5  |   |   π′(Zᵢ|Xᵢ) ⟵ π(Zᵢ|Xᵢ); CError ⟵ error
6  |   |   forall the π*(Zᵢ|Xᵢ) ∈ GenerateNeighbour(π(Zᵢ|Xᵢ), step) do
7  |   |   |   π*(Y|X₁,...,Xₙ) ⟵ UncertainMIN(Y,X₁,...,Xₙ,π*(Zᵢ|Xᵢ))
8  |   |   |   if E(π*(Y|X₁,...,Xₙ),π(Y|X₁,...,Xₙ)) < CError then
9  |   |   |   |   CError ⟵ E(π*(Y|X₁,...,Xₙ),π(Y|X₁,...,Xₙ))
10 |   |   |   |_  π′(Zᵢ|Xᵢ) ⟵ π*(Zᵢ|Xᵢ)
11 |   |   if CError < error then
12 |   |   |   error ⟵ CError
13 |   |   |_  π(Zᵢ|Xᵢ) ⟵ π′(Zᵢ|Xᵢ)
```

The second case is the estimation of the CPT from data. If the data are stored in a database β, then we propose to perform an estimation of the conditional possibility tables before applying an estimation algorithm. To perform the estimation of the conditional possibility tables, we used an adaptation of the Maximum Likelihood to possibility theory. The formula of the conditional possibility estimation is as follows:

$$\pi(X_i = x_k | pa(X_i) = x_j) = \frac{\alpha_{i,j,k}}{\max_k \alpha_{i,j,k}} \tag{11}$$

Where $\alpha_{i,j,k}$ is the number of record in β for which the variable X_i has the value x_k and its parents the configuration x_j.

5 Experimentation

In this section, we propose to perform the estimation of several connectors from an existing CPT in order to choose the best one. This choice allows us to better understand how the variables are combined. This is also a solution to reduce the disk space or the memory used by a CPT. For our experimentation we consider the data of our previous study [9] performed to improve the monitoring of our students by using the e-learning platform Moodle. The first example concerns the CPT of the indicator of dropout, which is an educational indicator. The following table has been elicited by experts (Table 4):

Table 4. CPT of the indicator of dropout.

	Absence			Low			Medium			High		
	No participation	Low	Medium	High	Low	Medium	High	Low	Medium	High		
Indicator of dropout	Low	1.0	1.0		0.6	1.0	0.4		0.3	0.4	0.3	0.2
	Medium	0.6	7.0		1.0	0.5	1.0		1.0	1.0	0.7	0.5
	High	0.1	0.2		0.3	0.3	0.5		0.5	0.6	1.0	1.0

So the goal of our experimentation is to replace the above table by an uncertain connector. We consider only three uncertain connectors: the uncertain MIN, the uncertain MAX and the uncertain WAVG. We present below the minimal distance obtained during the parameter estimation by using the Gradient Descent (GD), Simulated Annealing (SA), Tabu Research (TR) and Genetic Algorithm (GA) (Table 5).

Table 5. Final distance for the parameters estimation after 20000 iterations.

	GD	SA	TR	GA
Uncertain MIN	1.02	0.92	0.92	0.92
Uncertain MAX	1.37	1.28	1.48	1.27
Uncertain WAVG	0.70	0.33	**0.32**	0.43

In the following figure, we can see that the gradient descent is converging rapidly to the results for all connectors. Nevertheless, the best estimation of the parameters is performed by tabu research in Fig. 2c. In Fig. 2d we can see that the connector uncertain WAVG is the one that fits the best with the target CPT.

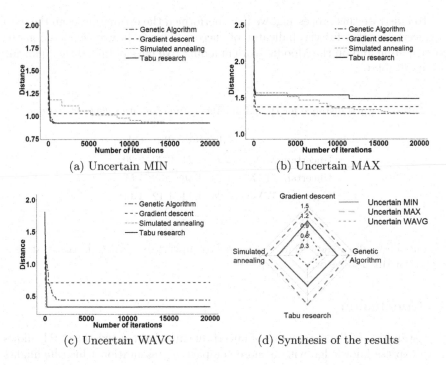

(a) Uncertain MIN

(b) Uncertain MAX

(c) Uncertain WAVG

(d) Synthesis of the results

Fig. 2. Comparison of three parameter estimations for the uncertain gates.

Another problem is how to estimate uncertain gates from data. The quality of the estimation depends on the data. We consider that we already have the DAG of the possibilistic network. The first processing will be the estimation of the conditional possibility table from the data. Then we can perform the estimation of the parameters for several uncertain gates connectors before selecting the best connector. This can be resumed in the following Fig. 3:

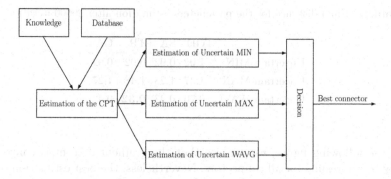

Fig. 3. Selection of the best uncertain gates.

To illustrate this processing, we have performed the estimation from the data of uncertain gates for the indicator of success. This indicator depends on the participation and on the Moodle score in a quiz. We have obtained the following results (Table 6):

Table 6. Final distance for the parameters estimation after 20000 iterations.

	GD	SA	TR	GA
Uncertain MIN	2.24	2.21	2.20	2.20
Uncertain MAX	1.75	1.56	1.58	1.57
Uncertain WAVG	1.24	1.14	1.12	**1.09**

The above data show that the connector uncertain WAVG is the best connector for this indicator.

6   Conclusion

The estimation of the parameters of uncertain gates from an existing CPT allows us to express knowledge with a more compact representation which highlights the behaviour of the information combination. To do this we used an algorithm of optimization which measures at each iteration the distance between the current CPT and the target CPT in order to find the CPT which fits the best with the target CPT. In the first example, we compared the estimation of the uncertain gates parameters for the CPT of the educational indicator of dropout. To do this we used several estimation methods for three uncertain connectors. As a result, we proposed a solution to select the best connector: the one which fits the best with the target CPT and for which the distance is the minimum. Then we suggested a solution for the selection of the uncertain connector from the data in case no CPT is available. We proposed the second example which illustrates this approach. This study is a basis for our next research which will consist in converting an existing possibilistic network into a possibilistic network with uncertain gates. This implies replacing all CPTs by uncertain gates. We would like to better evaluate our manner of estimating uncertain gates parameters from data. Finally, we need to better analyse the case where uncertain gates can be estimated from an existing CPT given by an expert and estimated also from new available data.

References

1. Benferhat, S., Dubois, D., Garcia, L., Prade, H.: Possibilistic logic bases and possibilistic graphs. In: Proceedings of the Conference on Uncertainty in Artificial Intelligence, pp. 57–64 (1999)
2. Borgelt, C., Gebhardt, J., Kruse, R.: Possibilistic graphical models. In: Della Riccia, G., Kruse, R., Lenz, H.-J. (eds.) Computational Intelligence in Data Mining. ICMS, vol. 408, pp. 51–67. Springer, Vienna (2000). https://doi.org/10.1007/978-3-7091-2588-5_3
3. Benferhat, S., Smaoui, S.: Représentation hybride des réseaux causaux possibilistes, pp. 43–50. Rencontres francophones sur la Logique Floue et ses Applications, Cépadués Editions, Nantes (2004)
4. Dìez, F., Drudzel, M.: Canonical probabilistic models for knowledge engineering. Technical report CISIAD-06-01 (2007)
5. Dubois, D., Fusco, G., Prade, H., Tettamanzi, A.: Uncertain logical gates in possibilistic networks. an application to human geography. In: Beierle, C., Dekhtyar, A. (eds.) SUM 2015. LNCS (LNAI), vol. 9310, pp. 249–263. Springer, Cham (2015). https://doi.org/10.1007/978-3-319-23540-0_17
6. Dubois, D., Prade, H.: Possibility Theory: An Approach to Computerized Processing of Uncertainty. Plenum Press, New York (1988)
7. Lee, L.: On the effectiveness of the skew divergence for statistical language analysis. In: Proceedings of Artificial Intelligence and Statistics (AISTATS), pp. 65–72 (2001)
8. Heckerman, D., Breese, J.: A new look at causal independence. In: Proceedings of the Tenth Annual Conference on Uncertainty in Artificial Intelligence (UAI-94), Morgan Kaufmann Publishers, San Francisco, CA, USA, pp. 286–292 (1994)
9. Petiot, G.: Calcul d'indicateurs pédagogiques par des réseaux possibilistes. LFA 2016, Cépadués Editions, La Rochelle, pp. 195–202 (2016)
10. Petiot, G.: Merging information using uncertain gates: an application to educational indicators. In: Medina, J., et al. (eds.) IPMU 2018. CCIS, vol. 853, pp. 183–194. Springer, Cham (2018). https://doi.org/10.1007/978-3-319-91473-2_16
11. Neapolitan, R.E.: Probabilistic Reasoning in Expert Systems: Theory and Algorithms. Wiley, New York (1990)
12. Pearl, J.: Probabilistic Reasoning in Intelligent Systems: Networks of Plausible Inference, 2nd edn. Morgan Kaufman Publishers Inc., San Mateo (1988)
13. Yager, R.R.: On ordered weighted averaging aggregation operators in multi-criteria decision making. IEEE Trans. Syst. Man Cybern. 18, 183–190 (1988)
14. Zadeh, L.A.: Fuzzy sets as a basis for a theory of possibility. Fuzzy Sets Syst. 1, 3–28 (1978)

15. Zagorecki, A., Druzdzel, M.J.: Knowledge engineering for Bayesian networks: how common are noisy-MAX distributions in practice? IEEE Trans. Syst. Man Cybern.: Syst. **43**(1), 186–195 (2013)
16. Zagorecki, A., Druzdzel, M.J.: Probabilistic independence of causal influences. In: Probabilistic Graphical Models, pp. 325–332 (2006)

Fuzzy Reasoning in Control and Diagnostics of a Turbine Engine – A Case Study

Wojciech Rafajłowicz$^{(\boxtimes)}$ [iD], Wojciech Domski [iD], Andrzej Jabłoński [iD], Adam Ratajczak [iD], Wojciech Tarnawski [iD], and Zbigniew Zajda [iD]

Faculty of Electronics, Wrocław University of Science and Technology, Wrocław, Poland
wojciech.rafajlowicz@pwr.edu.pl

Abstract. The article presents selected cases of application of fuzzy-logic techniques in technological process control. It presents the possibilities of supporting manufacturers of road machines for road drying with innovative solutions in the field of artificial intelligence. It presents an algorithmic approach to determine the quality (welfare) of the device, taking into account important process parameters, processed with the use of fuzzy-logic technique. The methodology for controlling the rotation of the turbine engine in the initial phase of its start-up is presented, using rules based on fuzzy logic. The results of the calculations are presented in a graphical form, friendly to interpretation by users and machine manufacturer. The article discusses the technical aspects of the TORGOS road machine control system, indicating the multifunctionality of the authors' controller and its software.

Keywords: Soft computing · Fuzzy-logic · Industrial application

1 Introduction

In recent years there have been some failures in the industrial use of fuzzy logic. Industrial fuzzy logic controllers have disappeared almost completely in the offers of many global manufacturers. At the same time, however, there has been a very dynamic growth of solutions based on various methods of artificial intelligence. The authors of this paper have decided to use the fuzzy logic technique [6], as one of the methods of artificial intelligence, in the specific process of controlling turbine engine rotation in the initial stage of its start-up. Operating experience, based on manual and intuitive fuel dosing in the machine, closely related to various temperatures of air, fuel and turbine, inspired the development of dedicated algorithms based on the fuzzy logic technique. Analysis of numerous bibliographic sources confirmed the principle that fuzzy logic-based control or inference brought very good results in specific process/objects – where conventional

The authors would like to thank PHU CEMAR Import-Export for kind permission to publish joint research results.

L. Rutkowski et al. (Eds.): ICAISC 2019, LNAI 11508, pp. 335–345, 2019.
https://doi.org/10.1007/978-3-030-20912-4_32

algorithms did not give satisfactory results. The control problem presented here belongs to such a class of issues in which the unconventional approach proved to be effective. An additional, positive circumstance, which influenced the decision on the method of solving the problem, was the possibility of free shaping the software in the machine controller and sufficient computing power of the applied microcontrollers. It should be emphasized that the so-called expert knowledge about the desired behaviour of the turbine engine in various combinations of the three (above-mentioned) temperatures was obtained from the users of TORGOS machines. Another important prerequisite for the application of the fuzzy logic technique was the automatic evaluation of the condition of the machine. On the basis of the obtained data, the authors developed algorithms evaluating the so-called welfare of the machine.

Recent research [4,5,7] shows that the fuzzy logic technique could be successfully applied to the diagnostics and to build up fault tolerant systems. Fuzzy logic was also used in other industrial applications [1,3,9,13,18].

For a convenient interpretation of the obtained results, 3D graphic forms were used. The obtained results are essential for the manufacturer and users of TORGOS machines.

2   Road Dryer

TORGOS 35 is an industrial road dryer (Fig. 1) for professional use. It is used for drying wet road sections (e.g., motorways) on which horizontal markings are to be applied. The machine does not have its own drive. The source of hot air is a high-speed turbine engine powered by diesel oil. Due to the high temperature of the blown out air, the machine should be in motion in order to not damage the road surface. To start the turbine engine, a battery-powered DC motor is enrolled as a starter. Other systems and components, such as a glow plug, valves and pumps, are also powered from the battery. Both procedures, for starting and stopping of the turbine engine are complicated, as well as the control during the functional operation of the engine. That is why the engine's operation is controlled by a microcomputer driver equipped with a real-time operating system. The machine controller implements advanced control algorithms (e.g., fuzzy logic methodology), diagnostics (Fourier analysis), communication, geographical location and others.

Torgos 35 is currently the most innovative road dryer, mass-produced in Poland.

3   Control Hardware and Software

A proprietary controller fulfills two main functions. The first of these is to control the machine functions such as start, normal work and cooling. The second function is gathering data regarding machine work in those states. For technical reasons the control system in the machine is divided into two, separate parts equipped with independent microcontrollers (MAIN – master controller

Fig. 1. Torgos 35 road drying machine [8].

module and HMI – operator interface module). The main controller module is located close to the turbine, and the user interface driver is mounted at the top of the machine, allowing easy operator access. The use of digital communication between modules limits the number of cables needed to support all additional modules. The human–machine interface part is responsible for communication with a cloud–based server and with the user of the machine. The part called MAIN controls directly high–current devices in the machine and runs control loops. The general overview of the system can be seen in Fig. 3.

The data are gathered by the MAIN section and sent via the HMI part into a cloud–based storage, see Fig. 2.

The array of data is quite large and consists of 20 variables. Additionally, during the start-up process, an acoustic sample is acquired and its Fourier transform is calculated. Thus, the control of the start-up process is based on fusion of data from different sources.

The data are sent via GPRS to the cloud-based server. Additionally also geolocation data are sent, the web-based application allows for viewing of those data as well as management of machine maintenance and repair. Those functions are outside of the scope of this paper.

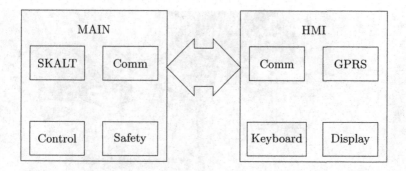

Fig. 2. General overview of the control system.

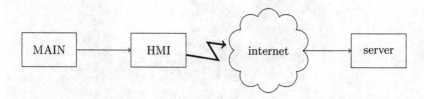

Fig. 3. Physical division of the control system.

4   The Use of Fuzzy Logic in Assessing the Machine State

The assessment of the machine's mechanical state is crucial from the preventive maintenance point of view. As described in the previous section, process data are transferred to the web server.

Two main factors used in determining machine conditions are the highest amplitude of the sound spectrum and power/resulting rpm ratio.

The amplitude factor is relatively obvious. When the condition of the machine deteriorates[1] it starts to makes a louder noise. The literature regarding the exact frequency is well known see [17] and [16], but it requires exact knowledge of the current rotational speed. The use of simple $\max A_i$ helps in cases when the frequency varies somewhat.

In Fig. 5 we can see how inputs are fuzzified. Parametrization is self-descripting in that case and can be seen in Fig. 6. The result is calculated in a typical way by assigning weights to each fuzzy input and calculating weight-center.

The result is displayed as an estimation of the machine state in the form of a bar graph.

---

[1] Mostly high-speed ball bearing.

5   The Use of Fuzzy Logic in Control of the Machine

The measurement of external temperature is an important factor which greatly influences the working of the road dryer both in its starting stage and during normal operation. Based on gathered experience during operation of the TORGOS machine in the winter season when the temperature is below 0 °C and in autumn when the ambient temperature is positive, it can be concluded that this temperature has a significant impact on the starting stage. This, in turn, requires each machine parameter to be tuned accordingly. This process is relatively time consuming and the obtained results are not always optimal. This situation can

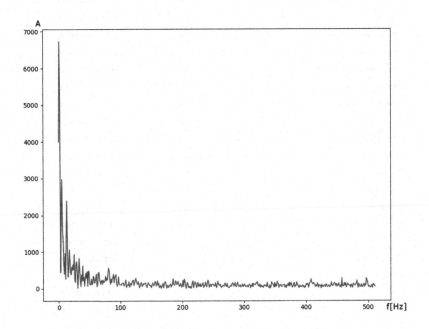

Fig. 4. Example of the spectral diagram for the machine.

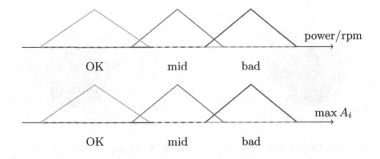

Fig. 5. Fuzzification and defuzzification in case of machine state.

Name	Value	Last change date
IDParametr1	1	2017-11-20 22:53:47
IDParametrskalt_ok_start	0	2017-10-14 20:48:06
IDParametrskalt_ok_end	10000	2017-10-14 20:48:43
IDParametrskalt_mid_start	9000	2017-10-14 20:49:23
IDParametrskalt_mid_end	20000	2017-10-14 20:50:00
IDParametrskalt_bad_start	19000	2017-10-14 20:50:28
IDParametrskalt_bad_end	100000	2017-10-14 20:50:46
IDParametrratio_ok_start	0	2017-10-14 20:51:08
IDParametrratio_ok_end	150	2017-10-14 20:51:22
IDParametrratio_mid_start	140	2017-10-14 20:51:40
IDParametrratio_mid_end	180	2017-10-14 20:51:52
IDParametrratio_bad_start	170	2017-10-14 20:52:12
IDParametrratio_bad_end	250	2017-10-14 20:52:24
IDParametrt11	100	2017-10-14 20:54:09
IDParametrt21	75	2017-10-14 20:54:19
IDParametrt31	20	2017-10-14 20:54:29
IDParametrt12	75	2017-10-14 20:54:38
IDParametrt22	50	2017-10-14 20:54:48
IDParametrt32	20	2017-10-14 20:54:57
IDParametrt13	20	2017-10-14 20:55:16
IDParametrt23	20	2017-10-14 20:55:28
IDParametrt33	0	2017-10-14 20:55:36
additional	0	2017-10-14 20:57:34

Fig. 6. Self descriptive parameters for fuzzyfication and defuzzification.

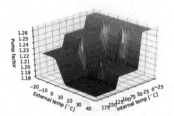

Fig. 7. Pump coefficient for -20 [°C] fuel temperature

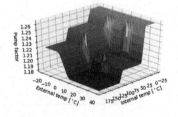

Fig. 8. Pump coefficient for -10 [°C] fuel temperature

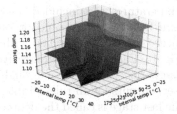

Fig. 9. Pump coefficient for 0 [°C] fuel temperature

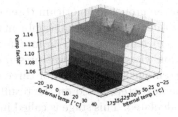

Fig. 10. Pump coefficient for +10 [°C] fuel temperature

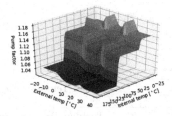

Fig. 11. Pump coefficient for +20 [°C] fuel temperature

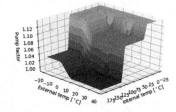

Fig. 12. Pump coefficient for +30 [°C] fuel temperature

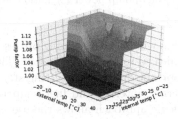

Fig. 13. Pump coefficient for +40 [°C] fuel temperature

be improved by making the starting algorithm dependent on external temperature by using the fuzzy logic controller. The fuzzy logic controller allows the use of gathered expert know–how during machine tuning. This knowledge can be introduced into an algorithm as a set of rules. Those rules have a direct influence on the control quality (Fig. 4).

An important aspect is the direct external temperature measurement. Because of the main controller PCB placement, in close proximity to the turbine, the measurement cannot be conducted directly. The measurement of ambient temperature is done by the HMI board which is not in close proximity to the turbine. This removes the temperature disturbance from the turbine work. After successful measurement the data is sent to the main controller PCB where it is used in the proposed algorithm.

In the proposed algorithm three different temperatures were included. Those temperatures are: external (ambient) temperature, fuel temperature and internal (turbine) temperature. The measured temperature values are fuzzyfied with a function whose example was presented in the Fig. 14. Each temperature receives a percentage share in each of three quality classes: "lo", "average" and "high". In the next step, based on the resulting fuzzy set, outputs for all rules (Table 1) are calculated. This stage is called inference. The last stage is called the defuzzy-fication where numerical values (desired pump power coefficient) are calculated instead of qualitative terms as in the fuzzyfication stage. This step was presented in the Fig. 15.

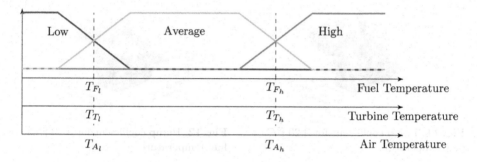

Fig. 14. Fuzzy sets for fuel pump power regulation (fuzzyfication stage).

The presented algorithm will influence tuning process of the fuel pump based on three temperatures which were mentioned before. The tuned fuel pomp effi-ciency is particularly important during the starting stage. Because of the direct dependency between external, internal and fuel temperature is difficult to cal-culate. The use of fuzzy logic approach allows the use of expert knowledge and use it directly in the control algorithm.

Table 1 of rules was implemented in the fuzzy controller. It contains a num-ber of rules that describe the desired pump efficiency in certain temperature conditions.

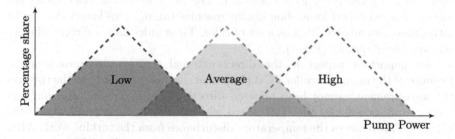

Fig. 15. Fuel pump power regulation (defuzzyfication stage).

Rules in the form of Table 1 were implemented inside the fuzzy controller. Using this information a set of figures was generated (Figs. 7, 8, 9, 10, 11, 12 and 13). The figures show a surface of fuel pump efficiency in certain temperature conditions. Due to three dimensions the range of plots was presented where each plot shows certain fuel temperature.

6   Summary

In this paper two applications of relatively basic fuzzy logic-based methods were shown. One of them provides information for the owner of the machine and for

Table 1. Fuzzy rules for controlling pump efficiency

No.	Fuel temperature	Turbine temperature	Air temperature	Pump power
1	low	low	low	**high**
2	low	low	average	**high**
3	low	low	high	**high**
4	low	average	low	**high**
5	low	average	average	**high**
6	low	average	high	**high**
7	low	high	low	**average**
8	low	high	average	**average**
9	low	high	high	**average**
10	average	low	low	**high**
11	average	low	average	**average**
12	average	low	high	**average**
13	average	average	low	**average**
14	average	average	average	**average**
15	average	average	high	**average**
16	average	high	low	**low**
17	average	high	average	**low**
18	average	high	high	**low**
19	high	low	low	**average**
20	high	low	average	**average**
21	high	low	high	**average**
22	high	average	low	**low**
23	high	average	average	**low**
24	high	average	high	**low**
25	high	high	low	**low**
26	high	high	average	**low**
27	high	high	high	**low**

the company servicing them. The other is directly integrated into the control system. The rather unusual method of multiplier for existing parameters is a direct requirement coming from the customer, who intended to keep as much of current the system as possible in order to simplify maintenance.

Overall it is difficult to estimate how the machine state estimation is used by customers without a large survey.

On the other hand a fuzzy-based adaptation of parameters to the environment and previous machine state allowed for widening the market for road drying machines to places with much harsher climates and this is deemed important by the customer.

One may try to increase the performance of the control system by applying the neuro-fuzzy approach (see [2,14,15]).

An alternative approach to diagnostics can be computer vision as in [12]. Also other methods can be used, both classical [10] or neural-network based [11].

References

1. Beg, I., Rashid, T.: Modelling uncertainties in multi-criteria decision making using distance measure and topsis for hesitant fuzzy sets. J. Artif. Intell. Soft Comput. Res. **7**(2), 103–109 (2017). https://content.sciendo.com/view/journals/jaiscr/7/2/article-p103.xml

2. Cpalka, K., Rutkowski, L.: Flexible Takagi-Sugeno fuzzy systems. In: Proceedings of IEEE International Joint Conference on Neural Networks, IJCNN 2005, vol. 3, pp. 1764–1769. IEEE (2005)

3. Dâ^{TM} Aniello, G., Gaeta, M., Loia, F., Reformat, M., Toti, D.: An environment for collective perception based on fuzzy and semantic approaches. J. Artif. Intell. Soft Comput. Res. **8**(3), 191–210 (2018). https://content.sciendo.com/view/journals/jaiscr/8/3/article-p191.xml

4. Ferdaus, M.M., Anavatti, S.G., Garratt, M.A., Pratama, M.: Development of c-means clustering based adaptive fuzzy controller for a flapping wing micro air vehicle. J. Artif. Intell. Soft Comput. Res. **9**(2), 99–109 (2019). https://content.sciendo.com/view/journals/jaiscr/9/2/article-p99.xml

5. Huang, Y.C., Sun, H.C.: Dissolved gas analysis of mineral oil for power transformer fault diagnosis using fuzzy logic. IEEE Trans. Dielectr. Electr. Insul. **20**(3), 974–981 (2013)

6. Kacprzyk, J.: Multistage Fuzzy Control: A Prescriptive Approach. Wiley, New York (1997)

7. Liu, M., Cao, X., Shi, P.: Fault estimation and tolerant control for fuzzy stochastic systems. IEEE Trans. Fuzzy Syst. **21**(2), 221–229 (2013)

8. PHU Cemar Import-Export: Webpage (2019). http://cemar.pro/

9. Prasad, M., Liu, Y.T., Li, D.L., Lin, C.T., Shah, R.R., Kaiwartya, O.P.: A new mechanism for data visualization with TSK-type preprocessed collaborative fuzzy rule based system. J. Artif. Intell. Soft Comput. Res. **7**(1), 33–46 (2017). https://content.sciendo.com/view/journals/jaiscr/7/1/article-p33.xml

10. Rafajlowicz, E.: Optimal experiment design for identification of linear distributed-parameter systems: frequency domain approach. IEEE Trans. Autom. Control **28**(7), 806–808 (1983)

11. Rafajłowicz, E., Skubalska-Rafajłowicz, E.: RBF nets for approximating an object's boundary by image random sampling. Nonlinear Anal. Theor. Methods Appl. **71**(12), e1247–e1254 (2009)

12. Rafajłowicz, E., Wietrzych, J., Rafajłowicz, W.: A computer vision system for evaluation of high temperature corrosion damages in steam boilers. In: Korbicz, J., Kowal, M. (eds.) Intelligent Systems in Technical and Medical Diagnostics. AISC, vol. 230, pp. 391–402. Springer, Heidelberg (2014). https://doi.org/10.1007/978-3-642-39881-0_33

13. Riid, A., Preden, J.S.: Design of fuzzy rule-based classifiers through granulation and consolidation. J. Artif. Intell. Soft Comput. Res. **7**(2), 137–147 (2017). https://content.sciendo.com/view/journals/jaiscr/7/2/article-p137.xml

14. Rutkowski, L., Cpałka, K.: A neuro-fuzzy controller with a compromise fuzzy reasoning. Control Cybern. **31**(2), 297–308 (2002)

15. Rutkowski, L.: Flexible Neuro-fuzzy Systems: Structures, Learning and Performance Evaluation, vol. 771. Springer, New York (2006). https://doi.org/10.1007/b115533

16. Rzeszuciński, P., Orman, M., Pinto, C., Krishnamoorthi, K.: Wykrywanie uszkodzeń łożysk tocznych z wykorzystaniem sygnałów akustycznych rejestrowanych telefonem komórkowym. Maszyny Elektryczne - Zeszyty Problemowe **2**(110), 163–168 (2016)

17. Starczyński, J., Sułowicz, M.: Wykrywanie uszkodzeń w silnikach indukcyjnych w oparciu o sygnały akustyczne. Maszyny Elektryczne - Zeszyty Problemowe **4**(108), 149–156 (2015)

18. Zhao, Y., Liu, Q.: A continuous-time distributed algorithm for solving a class of decomposable nonconvex quadratic programming. J. Artif. Intell. Soft Comput. Res. **8**(4), 283–291 (2018). https://content.sciendo.com/view/journals/jaiscr/8/4/article-p283.xml

Application of Type-2 Fuzzy Sets for Analyzing Production Processes

Anton Romanov$^{(\boxtimes)}$ ⓘ, Aleksey Filippov ⓘ,
and Nadezhda Yarushkina ⓘ

Ulyanovsk State Technical University, Ulyanovsk, Russia
romanov73@gmail.com

Abstract. The manufacturing processes of the aircraft factory are analyzed to improve the quality of management decisions. Production processes models based on time series models are proposed. The applying of fuzzy smoothing of time series is considered. A new technique for extracting fuzzy trends for forecasting time series proposed. The use of type-2 fuzzy sets for making new models of time series with the aim of improving the quality of the forecast considered. An information system is being built to calculate the production capacity using these models. The system implements the algorithms for the calculation of production capacity based on a methodology approved in the industry. The information extracted from the production processes is supposed to be used as a component of the models. An experiment with checking the quality of smoothing of time series is described. The experiment shows the possibility and advantages of modeling time series using type-2 fuzzy sets.

Keywords: Time series · Type-2 fuzzy sets · Production capacity · Aircraft factory

1 Introduction

The technological preparation of complex production at large enterprise requires the analysis of production capacities. The aim is to increase the efficiency of the use of material, technical and human resources [1]. The calculation of a production capacity based on a methodology approved in the industry has many disadvantages, like not enough precision because of averaging and troubles with adaptation to the concrete factory. The proposed new models and algorithms allow you to adapt the methodology to increase the efficiency of management at the expense of the increasing precision of forecast of production processes.

The goal requires solving the next tasks:

- input data definition;
- the creation of models reflecting the state of production processes;
- development algorithms for calculation of production capacity.

© Springer Nature Switzerland AG 2019
L. Rutkowski et al. (Eds.): ICAISC 2019, LNAI 11508, pp. 346–357, 2019.
https://doi.org/10.1007/978-3-030-20912-4_33

The solution of these tasks allows building a unified information environment for technological support of production. The task is to balance the production capacity of an aircraft factory. The current approach of management is based on using a common methodology for a few factories approved in the industry. Methodology contains algorithms and coefficients, accumulated from the statistic of production. The main disadvantage of this approach is a strong discrepancy between the real production indicators and the collected statistical data on the concrete factory [2].

Limitations of methodology application:

- the long extraction time of statistical coefficients from production indicators;
- the impossibility of dynamic adaptation of calculations into separate periods shorter than the forecast horizon;
- the methodology does not provide for adaptation to a specific production.

By analyzing this methodology it was found out that the coefficients (staff time, staff performance, equipment performance and depreciation of equipment) are aggregated and averaged information from the indicators of production processes. These processes are easily represented by discrete time series. Using a fuzzy approach allows creating models with more options such as improving quality because of applying knowledge about time series [5, 6, 15]. Also by analyzing production processes, it was found that this discrete interval is the one month - the minimum forecast horizon, and the time interval in which the indicators are unchanged.

2   Types of Extracted Time Series of Factory

The task is to extract changes in the values of production processes indicators. Time series models are used for tracking these changes. The methodology for calculating the balance of power capacity uses some coefficients, defined above. But these coefficients not always must be given by an expert or a method. Each of them can be extracted in the factory. As an example, staff time can be tracked for each factory unit; depreciation of equipment can be calculated based on summarizing volumes of completed works.

By analysis factory data was extracted the following types of time series:

- staff work time fund (fluctuating time series);
- tool work time fund (fluctuating time series);
- performance ratio (growing time series);
- area usage (growing time series);
- depreciation of equipment (growing time series).

These types of time series may be different for different factory units. For all types of processes can be identified as monthly indicator values. Very important to find the following characteristics of time series: seasonality, local and global tendencies. The proposition is to use several models for smoothing, extracting and forecasting tendencies and values of the time series of production processes.

3 Using F-Transform for Smoothing of Time Series

Using F-transform for smoothing of time series has advantages over other smoothing methods, like exponential smoothing [10], because of possibilities to include knowledge information about time series. Smoothed time series gives a better tendency forecast. Generally, the F-transform of the function $f : P \to \mathbb{R}$ is a vector whose components can be considered as weighted local mean values of f. This paper assumes $\mathbb{R}$ is the set of real numbers, $[a, b] \subseteq \mathbb{R}$ and $P = \{p_1, \ldots, p_l\}, n < l$, is a finite set of points such that $P \subseteq [a, b]$. Function $f : P \to \mathbb{R}$ defined on the set P is called discrete.

Below basic facts about the F-transform as they were presented in [3].

The first step in the definition of the F-transform of f is a selection of a fuzzy partition of the interval $[a, b]$ by the finite number $n \geq 3$ of fuzzy sets $A_1, \ldots, A_n$. According to the original definition, there are five axioms which characterize a fuzzy partition: normality, locality, continuity, unimodality, and orthogonality (the Ruspini condition) [3].

A fuzzy partition is called uniform if the fuzzy sets $A_2, \ldots, A_{n-1}$ are shifted copies of the symmetrized A_1. The membership functions $A_1, \ldots, A_n$ in the fuzzy partition are called basic functions. The basic function A_k covers a point p_j if $A_k(p_j) > 0$.

Figure 1 shows a uniform fuzzy partition of an interval $[a, b]$ by fuzzy sets $A_1, \ldots, A_n, n \geq 3$, with triangular membership functions. The formal expressions of these functions are given below where $h = \frac{b-a}{n-1}$.

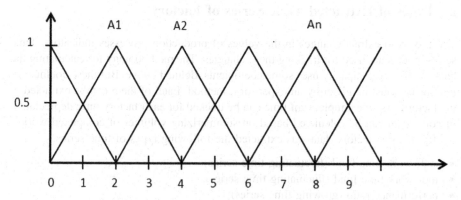

Fig. 1. An example of a uniform fuzzy partition by triangular membership functions.

$$A_1(x) = \begin{cases} 1 - \frac{x-a}{h}, & x \in [a, x_2], \\ 0, & otherwise, \end{cases}$$

$$A_1(x) = \begin{cases} \frac{|x-x_k|}{h}, & x \in [x_{k-1}, x_{k+1}], \\ 0, & otherwise, \end{cases}$$

$$A_1(x) = \begin{cases} \frac{x - x_n}{h}, & x \in [x_{n-1}, b], \\ 0, & \text{otherwise} \end{cases}$$

In the subsequent text fix the interval $[a, b]$, a finite set of points $P \subseteq [a, b]$ and relaxed fuzzy partition $A_1, \ldots, A_n$ of $[a, b]$. Denote $a_{kj} = A_k(p_j)$ and consider $n \times l$ matrix A with elements a_{kj}. A is a partition matrix of P. Below, a matrix of a special uniform partition is presented.

Assume that the points $p_1, \ldots, p_l \in [a, b]$ are equidistant so that $a = p_1, b = p_l$, $p_{i+1} = p_i + h, i = 1, \ldots, l - 1$, and $h > 0$ is a real number. Let $A_1, \ldots, A_n$ be a uniform partition $[a, b]$ such that each basic function A_k has a triangular shape and covers fixed number of points, say N. Moreover, let nodes $x_0, x_1, \ldots, x_{n\_n}, x_{n+1}$ be among the points $p_1, \ldots, p_l$ so that $x_0 = p_1, x_{n+1} = p_l$. If N is an odd number, say $N = 2r - 1$, then $l = (n + 1)r - 1$. In this particular case, the basic function A_k covers the points $p_{(k-1)r+1}, \ldots, p_{(k+1)r-1}$, so that

$$A_k\left(p_{(k-1)r+1}\right) = \tfrac{1}{r}, \ldots, A_k(p_{kr-1}) = \tfrac{r-1}{r}, A_k(p_{kr}) = 1,$$
$$A_k(p_{kr+1}) = \tfrac{r-1}{r}, \ldots, A_k\left(p_{(k+1)r-1}\right) = \tfrac{1}{r}.$$

Thus, the partition matrix A has a fixed structure; it depends on one parameter r and does not require the computation of $A_k(p_j)$ at each point p_j.

4 Discrete F-Transform

Once the basic functions $A_1, \ldots, A_n$ are selected, define (see [4]) the (direct) F-transform of a discrete function $f : P \to \mathbb{R}$ as a vector $(F_1, \ldots, F_n)$ where the k-th component F_k is equal to

$$F_k = \frac{\sum_{j=1}^{l} f\left(p_j\right) * A_{k(p_j)}}{\sum_{j=1}^{l} A_{k(p_j)}}, k = 1, \ldots, n. \tag{1}$$

In order to stress that the F-transform components $F_1, \ldots, F_n$ depend on $A_1, \ldots, A_n$ the F-transform is taken with respect to $A_1, \ldots, A_n$.

Let us identify the function $f : P \to \mathbb{R}$ with the vector-column $\$f = (f_1, \ldots, f_l)^T$ of its values on P so that $f_j = f(p_j)$, $\$j = 1, \ldots, l$. Moreover, let partition $\$A_1, \ldots, A_n$ be represented by the matrix A. The vector $(F_1, \ldots, F_n)$ is the F-transform of f determined by A if

$$(F_1, \ldots, F_n) = \left(\frac{(Af)_1}{a_1}, \ldots, \frac{(Af)_n}{a_n} \right) \tag{2}$$

where $(Af)_k$ is the k-th component of the product Af, $a_k = \sum_{j=1}^{l} a_{kj}, k = 1, \ldots, n$. Expression (2) is a matrix form of the F-transform of f. It will be denoted by $F_n(f)$.

Obviously, the computation on the basis of (2) is less complex than that one based on (1). The reason is in the unified representation of the partition matrix A which does not include a computation of each A_k at every point p_j.

5 Forecasting Time Series Based on Fuzzy Trends

The fuzzy elementary trend modeling method [7, 8, 14] is used to predict numerical values and fuzzy trends in the state of process indicators.

The forecast uses hypothesis testing:

- Hypothesis 1. The hypothesis of conservation of trend. The Forecast is constructed on base the previous period. The formula for the predicted value

$$\tau_{t+1} = \tau_t + \tau_p,$$

where τ_{t+1} – forecast for the next period of time; τ_t – real value at time t; τ_p – the value of the trend over the previous period of time.

- Hypothesis 2. The hypothesis of stability of the trend. The moving average is used to predict

$$\tau_{t+1} = \tau_t + G\tau_p,$$

where $G\tau_p$ – importance of a dominant fuzzy trend. Consider the trend of the previously selected period. Select the predominant cluster of trends. The forecast for the above formula is calculated. The trend is built. Optimistic forecast for some number of occurrences of trends used. The highest average trend is selected.

- Hypothesis 3. Forecasting for a given period on the basis of fuzzy elementary trends. Stages of the prediction algorithm for the period based on trends: the expert sets the number of considered trends for the previous period. For example, for half a year - a set of trends A. Either he sets the pattern set of trends. The presumed trend following this set is known.

$$\{\tau_{t_{n-m}}, \ldots, \tau_{t_{n-1}}, \tau_{t_n}\}$$

Search for a set of trends A in all other previous periods.

$$\left\{\tau'_{t_{n-l-k}}, \ldots, \tau'_{t_{n-l-(k-1)}}, \tau'_{t_{n-l}}\right\}$$

If such a set of B is found in which the C trend is located after this found set B then trend c is considered into account. The forecast equal to the trend C is constructed.

$$\tau_{t+1} = \tau_t + \tau'_{t_{n-l+1}}$$

If the set B, which would coincide with the set A, was not found then the search for the set is repeated, but it is already not looking for its complete coincidence. Select new pattern A is shorter into one trend. This is repeated until a suitable set of trends B [10]. To select the best hypothesis, an entropy time series is additionally introduced [11].

6 Definition of Type-2 Fuzzy Sets to Use in Time Series Models

The tasks of time series modeling are solved by a large number of methods. These methods have a different mathematical basis, are divided according to application possibilities (that is, they may have particular applicability conditions depending on the type of problem being solved and the nature of the time series), they may require constant or temporary use of the analyst directly during the modeling process. An important condition for the application of methods is the focus on obtaining short-term forecasts. It follows from the recent features of the processes for which time series models are applied.

The nature of fuzzy time series due to the use of expert estimates, the inherent uncertainty of which belongs to the class of fuzziness. Unlike stochastic uncertainty, fuzziness hinders or even excludes the use of statistical methods and models, but can be used to make subject-oriented decisions based on approximate human reasoning. The formalization of intellectual operations that simulate human fuzzy statements about the state and behavior of complex phenomena, forms today an independent area of applied research, called "fuzzy modeling" [3].

This direction includes a complex of problems, the methodology for solving which is based on the theory of fuzzy sets, fuzzy logic, fuzzy models (systems) and granular calculations.

In 1975, Lotfi Zadeh presented fuzzy sets of the second order (type-2) and fuzzy sets of higher orders, to eliminate the disadvantages of type-1 fuzzy sets. These disadvantages can be attributed to the problem that membership functions are mapped to exact real numbers. This is not a serious problem for many applications, but in cases where it is known that these systems are uncertain.

The solution to the above problem can be the use of type-2 fuzzy sets, in which the boundaries of the membership areas themselves are fuzzy [9].

It can be concluded that this function represents a fuzzy set of type-2, which is three-dimensional, and the third dimension itself adds a new degree of freedom to handle uncertainties. In [9] Mendel defines and differentiates two types of uncertainties, random and linguistic. The first type is characteristic, for example, for the processing of statistical signals, and the characteristic of linguistic uncertainties is contained in systems with inaccuracies based on data determined, for example, through expert statements.

To illustrate, note the main differences between type-1 fuzzy sets and type-2 fuzzy sets. Let us turn to Fig. 2, which illustrates a simple triangular membership function.

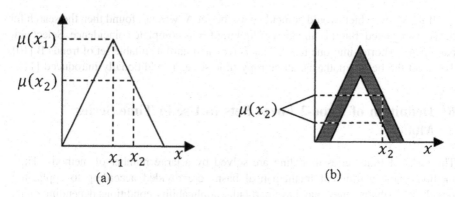

Fig. 2. The type of fuzzy sets of the 1st (a) and the 2nd (b) types.

Figure 2(a) shows a clear assignment of the degree of membership. In this case, to any value of x, there corresponds only one point value of the membership function. If you use a fuzzy membership function of the second type, you can graphically generate its designation as an area called the footprints of uncertainty (FOU). In contrast to the use of the membership function with clear boundaries, the values of the membership function of type-2 are themselves fuzzy functions.

This approach gave the advantage of approximating a fuzzy model to a verbal one. People can have different estimates of the same uncertainty. Especially it concerns estimated expressions. Therefore, it became necessary to exclude a unique comparison of the obtained value of the degree of the membership function. Thus, when an expert assigns membership degrees, the risk of error accumulation is reduced because of the non-inclusion of points located near the boundaries of the function and under doubt.

7 Time Series Model Based on Type-2 Fuzzy Sets

Time series modeling based on type-2 fuzzy sets allows to build the model reflecting the uncertainty of the choice of values of coefficients or values of indicators determined by an expert. Choose an interval time series as the type of time series for the object of modeling. For our subject area, previously selected time series of indicators are easily represented by the proposed type of time series: most time series have a rare change in values. Can mark stability of intervals. For interval time series, an algorithm for constructing a model is described in [12].

The formal model of the time series:

$$TS = \{ts_i\}, \ i \in N,$$

where $ts_i = [t_i, B_{ti}]$ is an element of the time series at the moment of time t_i and a value in the form of a type-2 fuzzy set B_{ti}. For the entire time series, the universe of type-2 fuzzy sets is defined as $U = (B_1, \ldots, B_l), B_i \in U, l \in N$, l - the number of fuzzy sets in the universe. A set B_{ti} is a type-2 fuzzy set, therefore, a type-1 fuzzy set is assigned to it as a value. For interval time series, a prerequisite for creating type-1 sets is a part separated from the source series, limited, for example, by a time interval of 1 day, 1 month or 1 year. For the selected interval, a universe of type-1 fuzzy sets is defined.

The algorithm for constructing a model will be used the same as described in [12] except for the moment of choice of intervals: they will be determined based not on the time characteristic, but on the boundaries of the initially formed type-2 sets.

The form of fuzzy sets is proposed to use a triangular due to the small computational complexity when conducting experiments.

8 Algorithms Calculation Production Capacity of Information System

The developed information system implements the next functions:

- performs the calculation of production capacities;
- reveals a deficit and forms recommendations for balancing capacities by determining;
- the possibility of redistribution of the volumes of the same type of work;
- identifies the need to enter additional production areas and equipment;
- identifies the need for recruitment and redeployment of staff.

The basic input data is the production program. The list of products are given and the scope of work for their creation, distributed by a period. the amount of work can be redistributed between time periods based on current indicators of production processes, their dynamics at the factory.

Three types of resources exist human, material and production area. For calculation production capacity the following steps are required:

- Identify the units for which calculate production capacity.
- For each unit, calculate the current capacity for each of the three types of resources.
- For each unit define the free capacity for each of the three types of resources.

So, the next steps depend on the resource type. For human resources need to set the following possibilities for calculation production capacity: transfer between units and hiring new workers. Limiting factors are the skills of specific employees in the transfer and the delayed start of the work of the employee in hiring.

Append calculation production capacity algorithm by next steps:

- If there are free human resources and a transfer of workers between factory units is possible, then fulfill it.
- Otherwise, hire new workers.

These steps show the priority that used at the factory.

Material resources, such as equipment and machines, are difficult to transfer between departments. If there are no available resources, then the only option is to purchase new equipment.

The current implementation of the information system is based on average values of indicators throughout the year. Proposed to use new models to analyze the time series of indicators at more frequent intervals. To do this, an important role will be determined by the accumulated information in the enterprise information systems.

9   Smoothing and Forecasting Time Series Algorithm

The operation of the algorithm is closely related to the nature of the time series. Modeling using type ~ 2 fuzzy sets was chosen based on the interval nature of the time series. For other types of time series, smoothing and prediction are allowed, but no experiments have been performed.

The work of the algorithm can be represented as a sequence of the following steps:

Step1. Determine the universe of observations.

Step 2. Determine the type and number of type 1 fuzzy sets for a time series.

Step 3. Averaging over time intervals. For the time series of the aircraft factory, this interval equals one month. This value will represent the point of the time series for fuzzification by type 1 fuzzy sets. For each of these intervals, parts of the original time series are extracted.

Step 4. Fuzzify a time series of averaged points with type 1 fuzzy sets.

Step 5. Match each fuzzy value of type 1 to three fuzzy values of type 2: a fuzzy minimum, maximum and average value of a segment of the time series.

Step 6. Establish relations for type 1 fuzzy sets.

Step 7. Calculate the prediction for type 1 fuzzy sets.

Step 8. Calculate the prediction for type 2 fuzzy sets.

Step 9. Evaluate errors.

For best results, the prediction step should include trend analysis [7, 8, 14].

10   Experiment

The experiment plan implies the construction of time series models and the assessment of their quality. For experiments, time series have been generated.

The forecasting process at this stage will not be carried out; therefore, an internal measure of the quality of the model will be assessed using the SMAPE criterion [13]:

$$SMAPE = \frac{100\%}{n} \sum_{t=1}^{n} \frac{|F_t - A_t|}{(|A_t| + |F_t|)/2}$$

Consider the process of smoothing the coefficient. The original time series has 60 points. For comparison, the graph of Fig. 3 shows the smoothing of the time series by the F-transform method [4].

For smoothing, a set of 15 type-2 fuzzy sets and 5 sets of type-1 was selected. As can be seen from Fig. 4, 5 points of a smooth series were obtained. SMAPE score for both types of smoothing:

- for F-transform - 2.01%,
- for type-2 fuzzy sets - 0.65%.

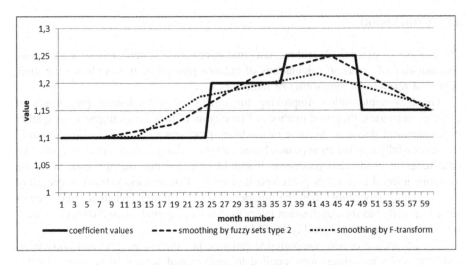

Fig. 3. Smoothing the time series of the coefficient

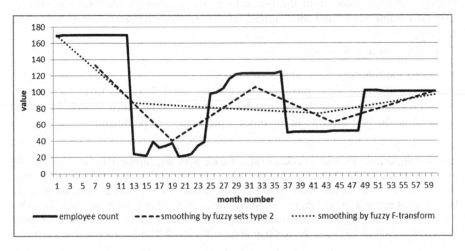

Fig. 4. Smoothing the time series of employee count

Next smooth employee count time series, Fig. 4. For smoothing, a set of 15 type-2 fuzzy sets and 5 sets of type-1 was chosen. For the time series, 5 points of a smoothed series were also obtained. SMAPE score for both types of smoothing:

- for F-transform - 47.54%,
- for type-2 fuzzy sets - 13.23%.

It was also a comparison of the internal measures of the quality of the model for SMAPE with simple exponential smoothing. The estimates showed the best by 0.1% smoothing quality by the method proposed using type-2 fuzzy sets.

11 Conclusion

The analysis of existing algorithms, data and information systems has shown a strong accumulation of errors in calculations of balance enterprise. It was shown the great impact of operational monitoring of indicators.

These principles allow improving the quality of technological preparation of complex industries. Proposed methods of prediction of time series improve the quality of management decisions because of modeling processes in the information system.

Successfully applied an approach based on type-2 fuzzy sets, to create a model of a time series of production processes. It should be noted that the approach based on modeling interval time series gives a positive result. This moment is fixed as a result of the smoothing procedure when the number of selected points and their values are as close as possible to the stabilization intervals. Smoothing model based on type-2 fuzzy sets shows better internal quality by SMAPE criterion.

The integration of soft computing techniques, i.e., the F-transform and fuzzy trend and time series modeling, were applied to analyze and forecast time series. In this contribution, is described as a new software system that was elaborated using the proposed theory. Aside from the F-transform, the technology platform includes an analysis of time series and their trends, which are characterized in terms of natural language.

Further research areas are:

- extract the rule base from time series models;
- creation of a time series prediction mechanism based on type-2 fuzzy sets;
- development of a modeling system based on fuzzy time series models for calculation production capacity in the process preparation of production.

Acknowledgments. The authors acknowledge that the work was supported by the framework of the state task of the Ministry of Education and Science of the Russian Federation No. 2.1182.2017/4.6 "Development of methods and means for automating the production and technological preparation of aggregate-assembly aircraft production in the conditions of a multi-product production program". The reported study was funded by RFBR and the government of Ulyanovsk region according to the research projects No 18-47-730022 and No 18-47-732016.

References

1. Yarushkina, N.G., et al.: Modeling the process of technological preparation of production based on ontological engineering. Autom. Manag. Process. **4**, 4–100 (2017). (in Russian)
2. Yarushkina, N.G., et al.: Integration of design diagrams and ontologies in the objective of the balancing of the capacity of the aviation-building enterprise. Autom. Manag. Process. **4**, 85–93 (2017). (in Russian)
3. Perlieva, I., Yarushkina, N., Afanasieva, T., Romanov, A.: Time series analysis using soft computing methods. Int. J. Gen. Syst. **42**(6), 687–705 (2013)
4. Perlieva, I.: Fuzzy transforms: theory and applications. Fuzzy Sets Syst. **157**, 993–1023 (2006)

5. Sarkar, M.: Ruggedness measures of medical time series using fuzzy-rough sets and fractals. Pattern Recognit. Lett. Arch. **27**, 447–454 (2006)

6. Hwang, J.R., Chen, S.M., Lee, C.H.: Handling forecasting problems using fuzzy time series. Fuzzy Sets Syst. **100**, 217–228 (1998)

7. Herbst, G., Bocklish, S.F.: Online recognition of fuzzy time series patterns. In: 2009 International Fuzzy Systems Association World Congress and 2009 European Society for Fuzzy (2009)

8. Kacprzyk, J., Wilbik, A.: Using Fuzzy Linguistic summaries for the comparison of time series. In: 2009 International Fuzzy Systems Association World Congress and 2009 European Society for Fuzzy Logic (2009)

9. Mendel, J.M., John, R.I.B.: Type-2 fuzzy sets made simple. IEEE Trans. Fuzzy Syst. **10**(2), 117–127 (2002)

10. Gardner Jr., E.S.: Exponential smoothing: the state of the art. J. Forecast. **4**, 1–38 (1989)

11. Yarushkina, N.G., Timina, I.A., Egov, E.N.: Measure of entropy in software quality VII Russian scientific-practical conference. Fuzzy Syst. Soft Comput. Intell. Technol. **2**, 201–208 (2017). (in Russian)

12. Bajestani, N.S., Zare, A.: Forecasting TAIEX using improved type 2 fuzzy time series. Expert Syst. Appl. **38–5**, 5816–5821 (2011)

13. SMAPE criterion by Computational Intelligence in Forecasting (CIF). http://irafm.osu.cz/cif/main.php

14. Pedrycz, W., Chen, S.M. (eds.): Time Series Analysis, Modeling and Applications: A Computational Intelligence Perspective (e-book Google). Intelligent Systems Reference Library, vol. 47, p. 404 (2013). https://doi.org/10.1007/978-3-642-33439-9

15. Novak, V.: Mining information from time series in the form of sentences of natural language. Int. J. Approx. Reason. **78**, 1119–1125 (2016)

On Explainable Recommender Systems Based on Fuzzy Rule Generation Techniques

Tomasz Rutkowski[1,3], Krystian Łapa[2(✉)], Robert Nowicki[2], Radosław Nielek[3], and Konrad Grzanek[4,5]

[1] Senfino, 1412 Broadway 21st floor, New York City, NY 10018, USA
XAI@senfino.com
[2] Institute of Computational Intelligence,
Czestochowa University of Technology, Częstochowa, Poland
{krystian.lapa,robert.nowicki}@iisi.pcz.pl
[3] Polish-Japanese Academy of Information Technology,
Koszykowa 86, 02-008 Warsaw, Poland
nielek@pjatk.edu.pl
[4] Information Technology Institute, University of Social Sciences,
90-113 Łódź, Poland
kgrzanek@san.edu.pl
[5] Clark University, Worcester, MA 01610, USA

Abstract. This paper presents an application of the Zero-Order Takagi-Sugeno-Kang method to explainable recommender systems. The method is based on the Wang-Mendel and the Nozaki-Ishibuchi-Tanaka techniques for the generation of fuzzy rules, and it is best suited to predict users' ratings. The model can be optimized using the Grey Wolf Optimizer without affecting the interpretability. The performance of the methods has been shown using the MovieLens 10M dataset.

Keywords: Explainable AI · Recommender systems ·
Wang-Mendel and Nozaki-Ishibuchi-Tanaka methods ·
Grey Wolf Optimizer · Interpretability

1 Introduction

In recent years, there have been many attempts to add explainability and transparency to machine learning models [1,5]. However, not so many papers have been published regarding explainability in recommender systems.

A recommender (or recommendation) system is any system that offers items in a personalized way to a specific user or guides him to the product best suited to his profile. There are three general types of recommender systems - collaborative filtering, content-based and hybrid approach [2,13,19].

Collaborative filtering systems recommend items by identifying other users with similar taste disregarding attributes of considered objects. Content-based

© Springer Nature Switzerland AG 2019
L. Rutkowski et al. (Eds.): ICAISC 2019, LNAI 11508, pp. 358–372, 2019.
https://doi.org/10.1007/978-3-030-20912-4_34

recommender systems analyze the attributes of considered objects, therefore they do not need any information about other users' preferences. Hybrid approach combines many different recommendation methods. For the purpose of this paper, we focus on content-based recommender systems. Collaborative filtering uses similarity to other people and has two downsides. One is that it requires many ratings from different users, otherwise, the algorithm would face so-called cold-start problem. The other problem is that from the explainability perspective it is not enough to say that a recommender system recommends something because other people like it too. With the content-based approach, the challenge is to analyze items that user rated before, prepare the profile of preferences and recommend new items based on this knowledge. The goal of our research is to provide not only recommendations but also explanations. We believe that to achieve truly explainable system it has to be interpretable and transparent [9].

As presented in previous work [17], it is possible to use rule-based [10,14] recommender systems to achieve explainability without losing too much accuracy. Such a system is usually based on fuzzy logic [3,16]. As rules are by definition interpretable by humans, they can be used to generate explanations. However, it is not trivial to generate rules from examples, reduce them and optimize [15]. In this paper, we propose a new method derived from Wang-Mendel and Nozaki-Ishibuchi-Tanaka methods, combined with the Zero-Order Takagi-Sugeno-Kang fuzzy system. It allows to deal with singleton outputs, which can be further optimized using Wolf Grey Optimizer. All experiments use the MovieLens 10M dataset.

Structure of the paper is as follows: Sect. 2 contains a description of rule generation methods, Sect. 3 presents a proposed approach, Sect. 4 shows the simulation results and the conclusions are drawn in Sect. 5.

2   Rule Generation Methods

In this section, the basic methods of generating fuzzy rules from data have been presented.

2.1   Wang-Mendel Method

In the Wang-Mendel method fuzzy rules are created as follows:

$$R_j : \text{IF } x_1 \text{ IS } A_{1,inp_{j,1}} \text{ AND ... AND} \atop x_n \text{ IS } A_{n,inp_{j,n}} \text{ THEN } y \text{ IS } B_{out_j} , \tag{1}$$

where R_j stands for j-th fuzzy rule, j is fuzzy rule index ($j = 1, ..., M$), M is the number of fuzzy rules (initial number of fuzzy rules is equal to the number of data set samples), x_i stands for fuzzy system inputs ($i = 1, ..., n$), n is the number of fuzzy system inputs, y is fuzzy system output, $A_{i,l}$ stand for input fuzzy sets where i indicates the index of system input and l indicates the index of fuzzy set in i-th input ($l = 1, ..., m$), m is the number of fuzzy partitions,

B_l stands for output fuzzy sets, and indexes $inp_{j,i}$ and out_j indicates the fuzzy sets from corresponding inputs and outputs, which are selected as follows:

$$\mu_{A_{i,inp_{j,i}}}(\bar{x}_{j,i}) = \max_{l=1,...,m}\left\{\mu_{A_{i,l}}(\bar{x}_{j,i})\right\}, \tag{2}$$

$$\mu_{B_{out_j}}(\bar{y}_j) = \max_{l=1,...,m}\left\{\mu_{B_l}(\bar{y}_j)\right\}, \tag{3}$$

where $\bar{x}_{j,i}$ stands for data set input values, $\bar{y}_j$ stand for data set output values, $\mu_A(\cdot)$ and $\mu_B(\cdot)$ are membership functions of corresponding fuzzy sets.

The initial fuzzy rule base in form of (1) is subject to reduction. For this process for each j-th fuzzy rule an importance degree is calculated:

$$\lambda_j(\bar{x}_j, \bar{y}_j) = T\left\{\mu_{B_{out_j}}(\bar{y}_j), \mu_{A_{1,inp_{j,1}}}(\bar{x}_{j,1}), ..., \mu_{A_{n,inp_{j,n}}}(\bar{x}_{j,n})\right\}, \tag{4}$$

where T stands for algebraic t-norm operator. The final rule base is obtained by reducing conflicting rules (with equal values of $inp_{j,i}$ and different values of out_j) and identical rules (with equal values of $inp_{j,i}$ and out_j). During the reduction, only rules with the highest value of (4) are kept and thus the final rule base contain K fuzzy rules ($K \le M$).

2.2 Nozaki-Ishibuchi-Tanaka Method

In the Nozaki-Ishibuchi-Tanaka method fuzzy rules also have form of (1). However, instead of calculating out_j indexes by Eq. (3) for each fuzzy rule singletons s_j are calculated as follows:

$$s_j = \frac{\sum_{j=1}^{M} \tau_j(\bar{x}_j)^\alpha \cdot y_j}{\sum_{j=1}^{M} \tau_j(\bar{x}_j)^\alpha}, \tag{5}$$

where $\alpha > 0$ is a parameter of the method (in this its value its selected as 1) and the $\tau_j(\bar{x}_j)$ is the activation level of j-th fuzzy rule calculated as follows:

$$\tau_j(\bar{x}_j) = T\left\{\mu_{A_{1,inp_{j,1}}}(\bar{x}_{j,1}), ..., \mu_{A_{n,inp_{j,n}}}(\bar{x}_{j,n})\right\}. \tag{6}$$

The final rule base is obtained by reducing fuzzy rules with identical inputs (with equal values of $inp_{j,i}$ and s_k) after which K fuzzy rules remain ($K \le M$). Finally, the out_k indexes are selected as follows:

$$\mu_{B_{out_k}}(s_k) = \max_{l=1,...,m}\left\{\mu_{B_l}(s_k)\right\}. \tag{7}$$

3 Proposed Method Description

The proposed method is based on the fuzzy rule generation methods with equally (uniform) spaced partitions. Such an approach allows to obtain clear and readable fuzzy sets (see e.g. Fig. 1). The two methods are considered as a base methods: Wang-Mendel (WM) and Nozaki-Ishibuchi-Tanaka (NIT). On the basis of WM and NIT methods, Mamdani fuzzy systems can be efficiently created.

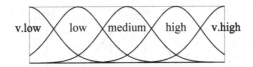

Fig. 1. Example of equally spaced partitions

3.1   Zero-Order Takagi-Sugeno-Kang Fuzzy System

In this paper, we propose to use fuzzy system resulting from WM and NIT methods in the form of Zero-Order Takagi-Sugeno-Kang (ZO-TSK) fuzzy system. In such a system the output is calculated as follows:

$$y\left(\bar{\mathbf{x}}\right) = \frac{\sum_{k=1}^{K} v_k \cdot \tau_k\left(\bar{\mathbf{x}}\right)}{\sum_{k=1}^{K} \tau_k\left(\bar{\mathbf{x}}\right)}, \tag{8}$$

v_k are singleton positions $(k = 1, ..., K)$, K stands for the number of fuzzy rules, $\mu_k(\cdot)$ stands for rule activation level calculated as in Eq. (6). The singletons are numeric values as opposed to output fuzzy sets. Such an approach changes the form of fuzzy rules to the following:

$$R_k : \text{IF } x_1 \text{ IS } A_{1,inp_{k,1}} \text{ AND ... AND} \\ x_n \text{ IS } A_{n,inp_{k,n}} \text{ THEN } y = v_k \tag{9}$$

The use of numerical values in a fuzzy rule changes the way they can be interpreted. However, the authors think that this is beneficial for a recommendation systems in which the output value of the system is usually a numerical value (e.g. movie rate).

In this paper, three ways to create a ZO-TSK system were used: WM-T (where the singleton values are set as centers of output fuzzy sets of corresponding rules from WM Mamdani type fuzzy system), NIT-T (where the singleton values are set as centers of output fuzzy sets of corresponding rules from NIT Mamdani type fuzzy system) and NIT-S (where the values of singletons as set directly to s_k values from NIT method) - see Fig. 2. Without any further optimization, the WM-T system will behave identically to WM, and the NIT-T system to NIT. In this paper, further modifications are considered, which is why the names of these systems are distinguished.

3.2   System Optimization

The core of this paper is the assumption that singleton values can be optimized without loss of the system interpretation. In order to get it, the ranges of singletons for each fuzzy rule are limited individually. The limitation results from

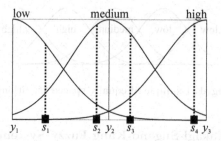

Fig. 2. Example of **s** values generated by NIT method that are used as singletons values in NIT-S case and **y** values (centers of output fuzzy sets) used as singletons in NIT-T case.

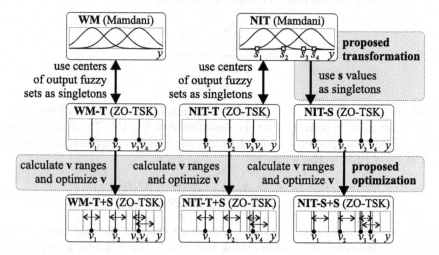

Fig. 3. Idea of the method proposed in this paper. It is worth noting that from one output fuzzy set a different number of singletons can be created (equal to the number of rules that are connected to a given set), double-sided arrows indicate the calculated ranges $< v_{k,min}; v_{k,max} >$ in which singletons can be optimized. The systems WM-T and NIT-T are identical without further modifications of systems WM and NIT.

data set outputs of data set samples for which the highest activation level for a specified fuzzy rule was achieved. The limitations are calculated as follows:

$$v_{k,min} = \min_{\left\{ j \in \{1,...,M\}: \mu_k(\bar{\mathbf{x}}_z) = \max\limits_{l=1,...,K} \left\{ \mu_{R_l}(\bar{\mathbf{x}}_j) \right\} \right\}} \left\{ \bar{y}_j \right\}, \qquad (10)$$

$$v_{k,max} = \max_{\left\{ j \in \{1,...,M\}: \mu_k(\bar{\mathbf{x}}_j) = \max\limits_{l=1,...,K} \left\{ \mu_{R_l}(\bar{\mathbf{x}}_j) \right\} \right\}} \left\{ \bar{y}_j \right\}. \qquad (11)$$

With this assumption, the ranges of values for each singleton are different ($v_{k,min}$ and $v_{k,max}$ are calculated for each k-th fuzzy rule). In addition, narrowing the ranges to values resulting from the data should not cause loss of trust in the system's prediction.

The optimization of singleton values can be performed by any optimization algorithm (see e.g. [4,18]). In this paper, a GWO is used to optimize WM-T, NIT-T, and NIT-S systems and the optimized systems will be referred accordingly as WM-T+S, NIT-T+S and NIT-S+S. The Grey Wolf Optimizer (GWO) is a meta-heuristics inspired by leadership hierarchy and hunting procedure of grey wolves in nature [11]. It has been successfully applied for solving various optimization problems (see e.g. [8,12,20]). In this algorithm, the three best individuals (wolves) are called in sequence alpha (α), beta (β) and delta (δ). The rest of the wolves are called omega (ω).

The modification (called hunting) of individuals parameters is performed only for ω wolves. It is assumed that α, β and δ wolves have better knowledge about the potential location of optimum (called prey). The hunting is performed as follows:

$$D_{\alpha/\beta/\delta} = \left| C_{\alpha/\beta/\delta} \cdot X_{\alpha/\beta/\delta} - X \right|, \tag{12}$$

$$X_{1/2/3} = X_{\alpha/\beta/\delta} - A_{1/2/3} \cdot \left(D_{\alpha/\beta/\delta} \right), \tag{13}$$

$$X\left(t+1\right) = \frac{1}{3}\left(X_1 + X_2 + X_3\right), \tag{14}$$

where X are individual parameters, $X_{\alpha/\beta/\delta}$ are respectively parameters of best wolves and $C_{\alpha/\beta/\delta}$ and $A_{\alpha/\beta/\delta}$ are calculated as follows:

$$A = 2 \cdot a \cdot r_1 - a, \tag{15}$$

$$C = 2 \cdot r_2, \tag{16}$$

where r_1 and r_2 are random vectors in $[0, 1]$ and component a linearly decreases from 2 to 0 over the course of algorithm iterations. Such a procedure allows for a smooth transition from exploration to exploitation and does not require setting any real value parameters of the actual algorithm [6].

It is also worth adding that the other elements of the fuzzy system (e.g. fuzzy sets) are not subject of optimization, which makes possible keeping the entire fuzzy system and fuzzy sets in a clear form. The idea of the method proposed in this paper is presented on Fig. 3. The proposed approach is new in the literature.

3.3   Data Set Preparation

The fuzzy systems used in this paper process the numeric parameters, however, the recommendation systems often include inputs with nominal values. Moreover, multiple nominal values can be assigned to single item attribute. To process such data, aggregation of nominal values was proposed in this paper. For each user and each attribute of rated by user items a list of unique nominal values is created. Then, the user preferences of each value are calculated as an average rate of the item that contains a particular value. Then, fuzzy system inputs for nominal attributes are calculated as an average preference of all values that occurs in a given attribute of an item (see Fig. 4).

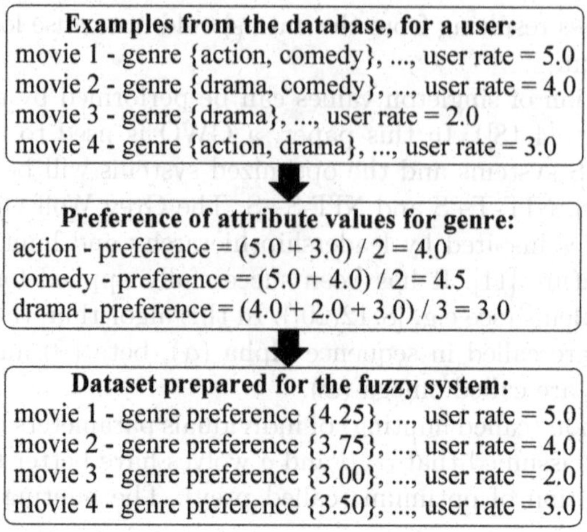

```
┌─────────────────────────────────────────────────────┐
│  Examples from the database, for a user:            │
│  movie 1 - genre {action, comedy}, ..., user rate = 5.0 │
│  movie 2 - genre {drama, comedy}, ..., user rate = 4.0  │
│  movie 3 - genre {drama}, ..., user rate = 2.0      │
│  movie 4 - genre {action, drama}, ..., user rate = 3.0  │
└─────────────────────────────────────────────────────┘
```

▼

```
┌─────────────────────────────────────────────────────┐
│  Preference of attribute values for genre:          │
│  action - preference = (5.0 + 3.0) / 2 = 4.0        │
│  comedy - preference = (5.0 + 4.0) / 2 = 4.5        │
│  drama - preference = (4.0 + 2.0 + 3.0) / 3 = 3.0   │
└─────────────────────────────────────────────────────┘
```

▼

```
┌─────────────────────────────────────────────────────┐
│  Dataset prepared for the fuzzy system:             │
│  movie 1 - genre preference {4.25}, ..., user rate = 5.0 │
│  movie 2 - genre preference {3.75}, ..., user rate = 4.0 │
│  movie 3 - genre preference {3.00}, ..., user rate = 2.0 │
│  movie 4 - genre preference {3.50}, ..., user rate = 3.0 │
└─────────────────────────────────────────────────────┘
```

Fig. 4. Example of a dataset preparation for a user

It is worth to mention that the user's rate of an item may result from preferences of various attributes, and therefore the values of specific system inputs will not always be consistent with the rate of an item as is shown in Fig. 4. Moreover, the proposed aggregation may result in the loss of some information (the user may provide ratings based on attributes not included in the database and also it is not possible to accurately detect the preferences of specific combinations of values). Nevertheless, the proposed approach allows for the creation of fuzzy rules detecting dependencies between preferences of attributes and also provides very clear fuzzy rules (due to, among others, the low number of system inputs created).

3.4 Summary of the Proposed Method

The proposed method: (a) can be based on fuzzy rules generation methods with equally (uniform) spaced partitions, which allows obtaining clear and readable fuzzy sets, (b) it is based on transforming fuzzy systems into Zero-Order Takagi-Sugeno-Kang type, that are simple in interpretation, (c) it allows keeping trust of system prediction optimizing only singleton values in limited ranges of values calculated for each rule, (d) it uses recent and almost parameter-less optimization algorithm, which allows getting good results, and (e) a data set preparation method is used to create numeric inputs for the fuzzy system from nominal values.

4 Simulations

In the simulations the following system were tested: WM-T, NIT-T, NIT-S, WM-T+S, NIT-T+S, NIT-S+S. Moreover, a different numbers of fuzzy partitions

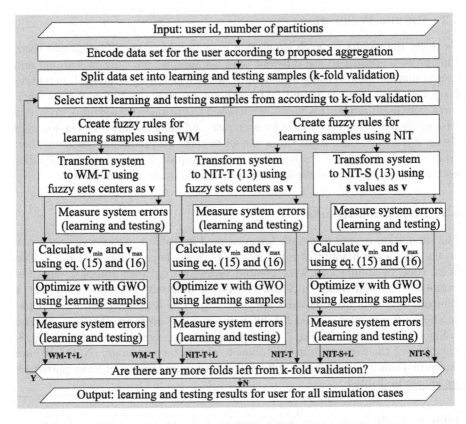

Fig. 5. Diagram showing the proposed methods and process of performed simulations for a single user.

were compared $m = \{3,5\}$. A larger number of partitions would force to use more linguistic variables (e.g. very very low) and thus significantly reduce the transparency of fuzzy rules. In spite of this, only exemplary additional tests were made to show the possibilities of the proposed approach with larger number of partitions. The process of performed simulations for single user is presented in Fig. 5.

The following parameters was set for all systems: triangular norms = algebraic, fuzzy sets = Gaussian type. The following parameters of GWO were set: population size = 16, number of iterations = 100.

4.1   Data Set

For the simulations, a MovieLens 10m database is used [7], and three inputs are prepared: genre preference (multiple nominal values), year (numeric values), keywords preference (multiple nominal values). Moreover, a data sets were prepared for first 100 users that rated more than 30 movies from the database.

4.2 Results Verification

To verify the results for each simulation case 10-fold cross-validation was used. This process applied to use different data set samples not only in learning and testing phases but also using 90% of data samples (learning samples) for creating fuzzy rule base using WM and NIT methods. Moreover, a different error measures were used: *rmse* (this measure was used to optimize the system), *accuracy* (the predicted value was round to user rate and thus 10 different classes were obtained), *yesno* (the output value was set to class 1 if prediction was lower than average rate and to class 2 otherwise - such an approach is used e.g. in [17]). For both *accuracy* and *yesno* typical classification accuracy were measured.

4.3 Simulation Results

The simulation results in details are presented in Table 1. An overview of *rmse* depending on the amount of rated movies by users is presented in Table 2. The fuzzy rules in simulations were created basing on data set samples, thus the number of created fuzzy rules differ only for different users (for each user a different data sets are created - see Sect. 3.3). The dependencies between the number of fuzzy rules created for different groups of users are shown in average in Fig. 6 and in details in Fig. 7. The optimization process is presented in Fig. 8. Examples of the fuzzy system that allow to obtain best accuracy (NIT-S+S) are shown in Table 3. Exemplary results of using a higher number of fuzzy partitions are shown in Table 4.

Table 1. Simulation results in details, average stands for average results obtained for all users, st. dev stands for standard deviation, lrn stands for learning samples, tst stands for testing samples

m	system	rmse				accuracy				yesno			
		average		st. dev.		average		st. dev.		average		st. dev.	
		lrn	tst	lrn	tst	lrn	tst	lrn	tst	lrn	tst	lrn	tst
3	WM−T	0.368	0.424	0.057	0.182	55.38	50.89	7.03	10.76	94.78	93.12	3.31	8.49
	NIT−T	0.317	0.376	0.028	0.160	59.29	54.53	4.95	10.45	96.19	94.61	2.37	7.10
	NIT−S	0.350	0.438	0.018	0.167	53.92	45.74	4.66	10.21	96.54	93.23	1.39	8.25
	WM−T+S	0.275	0.354	0.022	0.149	64.27	56.62	5.61	10.12	98.94	96.87	0.63	4.53
	NIT−T+S	0.271	**0.351**	0.021	0.148	64.79	**56.96**	5.27	**10.02**	99.03	**96.97**	0.57	**4.48**
	NIT−S+S	**0.263**	0.357	**0.017**	0.148	**66.85**	56.52	**4.55**	10.31	**99.06**	96.25	**0.49**	5.42
5	WM−T	0.206	0.327	0.016	0.151	79.53	65.23	3.96	9.55	98.68	96.93	0.60	4.54
	NIT−T	0.202	0.323	0.014	0.153	80.55	66.22	3.55	9.56	98.91	97.11	0.47	4.45
	NIT−S	0.174	0.321	0.011	0.157	84.92	66.14	2.40	9.38	99.42	96.94	0.26	4.60
	WM−T+S	0.144	0.289	0.011	0.149	89.19	**71.30**	2.08	**9.14**	99.74	97.96	0.17	3.22
	NIT−T+S	0.142	0.288	0.010	**0.149**	89.46	71.28	2.14	9.21	99.77	**97.99**	0.17	**3.16**
	NIT−S+S	**0.132**	**0.288**	**0.010**	0.150	**90.68**	70.85	**1.73**	9.18	**99.79**	97.97	**0.10**	3.19

Table 2. *rmse* results in details with the division of users by the number of rated movies (*o*)

m	system	learning samples					testing samples				
		$o < 50$	$50 \leq o < 100$	$100 \leq o < 200$	$200 \leq o < 400$	$o \geq 400$	$o < 50$	$50 \leq o < 100$	$100 \leq o < 200$	$200 \leq o < 400$	$o \geq 400$
3	WM-T	0.352	0.350	0.377	0.418	0.406	0.463	0.409	0.415	0.435	0.419
	NIT-T	0.327	0.296	0.323	0.346	0.353	0.429	0.365	0.363	0.360	0.368
	NIT-S	0.289	0.328	0.377	0.425	0.480	0.442	0.435	0.427	0.452	0.504
	WM-T+S	0.266	0.253	0.294	0.303	0.330	0.402	0.347	0.344	0.323	0.352
	NIT-T+S	0.260	0.250	0.290	0.300	0.324	0.398	0.345	0.340	0.320	0.349
	NIT-S+S	0.230	0.240	0.289	0.310	0.345	0.394	0.354	0.344	0.337	0.370
5	WM-T	0.159	0.184	0.237	0.258	0.302	0.349	0.327	0.322	0.302	0.330
	NIT-T	0.157	0.178	0.233	0.258	0.297	0.347	0.323	0.315	0.303	0.323
	NIT-S	0.099	0.156	0.213	0.234	0.289	0.339	0.327	0.313	0.291	0.326
	WM-T+S	0.092	0.126	0.178	0.193	0.225	0.321	0.294	0.279	**0.251**	0.267
	NIT-T+S	0.092	0.124	0.175	0.188	0.219	0.322	**0.292**	0.277	0.251	**0.260**
	NIT-S+S	**0.070**	**0.114**	**0.168**	**0.186**	**0.222**	**0.317**	0.295	**0.277**	0.252	0.266

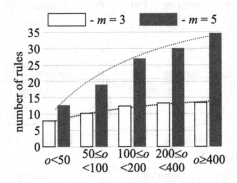

Fig. 6. A number of fuzzy rules created with the division of users by the number of rated movies (*o*)

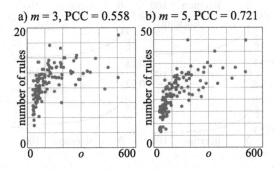

Fig. 7. Correlation between a number of rated movies (*o*) and a number of fuzzy rules created on prepared data sets, PCC stands for the Pearson Correlation Coefficient

4.4   Simulation Conclusions

The optimization of singleton parameters in specified ranges allow obtaining another increase in system accuracy (see WM-T+S, NIT-T+S, and NIT-S+S systems in Table 1).

The best *rmse*, *accuracy* and *yesno* were obtained for NIT-S+S system, where initial singleton positions resulted from the values s_k calculated by NIT method (see NIT-S+S system in Table 1).

The proposed solution allowed to achieve very high *yesno* recommendation accuracy (at level of 98% for testing data samples) and high classification accuracy of predicting exact user rate of the movie (72%) - see Table 1. In the latter, the increase in accuracy comparing to standard WM-T and NIT-T methods is higher than 5% (see Table 1).

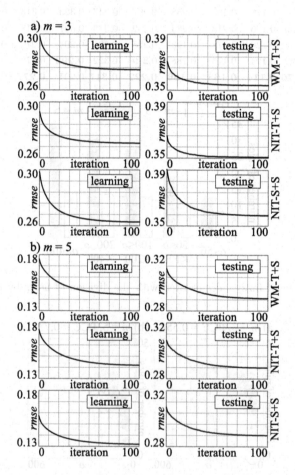

Fig. 8. Average *rmse* improvement during iterations of GWO

Table 3. Example of fuzzy system for NIT-S+S obtained for user 127 that rated 192 movies for $m = 3$ (left part of table) $m = 5$ (right part of table).

	fuzzy sets				fuzzy sets			

low medium high   v.low low medium high v.high
genre preference   genre preference

low medium high   v.low low medium high v.high
year   year

low medium high   v.low low medium high v.high
keywords preference   keywords preference

fuzzy rules					fuzzy rules			
	IF		THEN		IF		THEN	
k	genre preference	year	keywords preference	user rate	k	genre preference	year	keywords preference	user rate
		IS		=			IS		=
1	low	medium	low	2.01	1	v.low	medium	v.low	2.01
2	medium	high	medium	2.85	2	high	v.low	high	3.99
3	high	low	medium	3.85	3	high	medium	medium	2.99
4	high	medium	medium	3.21	4	high	high	low	2.86
5	high	high	low	2.00	5	high	high	medium	3.02
6	high	high	medium	3.66	6	high	high	high	4.15
7	high	high	high	5.00	7	high	v.high	low	2.85
					8	high	v.high	medium	3.45
					9	high	v.high	high	4.15
					10	v.high	low	medium	3.07
					11	v.high	medium	low	2.93
					12	v.high	medium	medium	2.92
					13	v.high	medium	high	5.00
					14	v.high	high	medium	3.00
					15	v.high	high	high	4.61
					16	v.high	high	v.high	5.00
					17	v.high	v.high	low	2.32
					18	v.high	v.high	medium	3.03
					19	v.high	v.high	high	4.65
					20	v.high	v.high	v.high	5.00
detailed results for selected user					**detailed results for selected user**				
$rmse = 0.29234$ (lrn), 0.30583 (tst)					$rmse = 0.17194$ (lrn), 0.21830 (tst)				
$accuracy = 58.8\%$ (lrn), 56.4% (tst)					$accuracy = 87.9\%$ (lrn), 84.3% (tst)				
$yesno = 98.6\%$ (lrn), 97.1% (tst)					$yesno = 100.0\%$ (lrn), 99.3% (tst)				

The use of more partitions ($m = 5$) allowed to increase the accuracy of the system in every case (see Table 1), thus the number of created fuzzy rules increased (see Fig. 6).

The use of a higher number of partitions does not give a significant improvement of testing $rmse$, $accuracy$ and $yesno$, especially if $m > 7$ (see Table 4). However, this results in more rules and the need to differentiate between more

Table 4. Additional comparison of results for NIT-S+S system with a higher number of fuzzy partitions.

m	rmse				accuracy				yesno				rules
	average		st. dev.		average		st. dev.		average		st. dev.		
	learn.	test.	learn.	test.	learn.	test.	learn.	test.	learn.	test.	learn.	test.	
3	0.263	0.357	0.017	0.148	66.85	56.52	4.55	10.31	99.06	96.25	0.49	5.42	10.87
5	0.132	0.288	0.010	0.150	90.68	70.85	1.73	9.18	99.79	97.97	0.10	3.19	21.78
7	0.081	0.273	0.009	0.168	95.54	74.05	0.91	8.73	99.88	97.43	0.03	4.03	29.14
9	0.051	0.270	0.006	0.178	97.98	75.72	0.43	8.11	99.92	97.18	0.02	4.45	35.20
11	0.039	0.273	0.005	0.188	98.62	75.68	0.34	8.26	99.97	97.13	0.01	4.41	38.79
13	0.029	0.272	0.005	0.191	98.96	76.36	0.27	7.80	99.98	97.23	0.01	4.34	41.86

linguistic labels of fuzzy sets, which significantly reduces the interpretability and readability of the system.

The $rmse$ error calculated for learning samples increases simultaneously with the number of rated movies (see Table 2). This may be due to many factors: ratings based on attributes not included in the inputs, contradictions included in the user's ratings, use of proposed data set preparation method, etc.

The $rmse$ calculated for unknown data samples (testing samples) is optimal in the case of 100–400 rated movies (in particular if $m = 5$ - see Table 2). This shows that the optimal number of rated movies for which there is no loss of information is contained in this range. Too many rated movies cause that the system has a too weak structure and would require to increase m or use of additional system inputs. Too few rated movies make it difficult to predict the correct recommendation for testing samples (see Table 2).

The number of fuzzy rules increases logarithmically along with the number of rated movies (see Fig. 6). The average number of fuzzy rules for $m = 3$ is close to 12, such a number may allow interpretation of the operation of the entire system. In the case of $m = 5$ average number of fuzzy rules is close to 28 and thus the interpretation of the operation of the entire system may be more difficult, which does not exclude the possibility of the interpretation of specific recommendations.

The correlation between the number of rated movies (o) and the number of created fuzzy rules according to the Pearson Correlation Coefficient is moderate in case of $m = 3$ and strong in case of $m = 5$ (see Fig. 7).

In simulation studies, the phenomenon of overfitting was not observed (see Fig. 8). Moreover, learning $rmse$ usually decreased to the same extent as testing $rmse$ (see Fig. 8).

It can be concluded that the exemplary fuzzy systems presented seem to be clear and interpretable at the same time ensuring high accuracy of operation (see Table 3).

Sample interpretations that can be drawn from the fuzzy rules presented in Table 3 are as follows: the user prefer older movies in some cases (see user rate for $k = 3$ and $k = 4$), the genre preference is less important for the user than keywords preference (see user rate for $k = 1$ and $k = 5$ vs $k = 6$), the keywords preference does not affect the result linearly (see user rate for $k = 5$, $k = 6$ and $k = 7$), etc.

Authors want to draw attention to the fact that interpreting results is much harder in the case of $m = 5$. It is worth noting, that the interpretations do not matter from the point of view of the explanation of specific recommendations and are given here as an example. In the case of specific recommendations, the user should only analyze these fuzzy rules that have influenced the result of the recommendation. Such solutions will be considered and analyzed in future work.

5   Conclusions

The proposed approach allows achieving high accuracy with a reasonable number of interpretable fuzzy rules. The use of ZO-TSK and optimization of singletons has allowed a significant improvement in results.

Conducted experiments proved that applying the Grey Wolf Optimizer to train the model gives better accuracy without losing interpretability of the system. The Zero-Order Takagi-Sugeno-Kang fuzzy system can be effectively used as a content-based recommender system that provides accurate results with intepretability, transparency, and explainability.

Acknowledgment. This research was supported by the Polish National Science Center grants 2015/19/B/ST6/03179.

References

1. Bologna, G., Hayashi, Y.: Characterization of symbolic rules embedded in deep DIMLP networks: a challenge to transparency of deep learning. J. Artif. Intell. Soft Comput. Res. **7**(4), 265–286 (2017)
2. Burke, R.: Hybrid recommender systems: survey and experiments. User Model. User-Adap. Inter. **12**(4), 331–370 (2002)
3. D'Aniello, G., Gaeta, M., Loia, F., Reformat, M., Toti, D.: An environment for collective perception based on fuzzy and semantic approaches. J. Artif. Intell. Soft Comput. Res. **8**(3), 191–210 (2018)
4. Dawar, D., Ludwig, S.A.: Effect of strategy adaptation on differential evolution in presence and absence of parameter adaptation: an investigation. J. Artif. Intell. Soft Comput. Res. **8**(3), 211–235 (2018)
5. Doran, D., Schulz, S., Besold, T.R.: What does explainable AI really mean? A new conceptualization of perspectives. CoRR, abs/1710.00794 (2017)
6. Faris, H., et al.: Grey wolf optimizer: a review of recent variants and applications. Neural Comput. Appl. **30**(2), 413–435 (2018)
7. Harper, F.M., Konstan, J.A.: The MovieLens datasets: history and context. ACM Trans. Interact. Intell. Syst. (TiiS) **5**(4), 19 (2016)

8. Jayabarathi, T., et al.: Economic dispatch using hybrid grey wolf optimizer. Energy **111**, 630–641 (2016)
9. Lipton, Z.C.: The mythos of model interpretability. Commun. ACM **61**, 36–43 (2018)
10. Liu, H., Gegov, A., Cocea, M.: Rule based networks: an efficient and interpretable representation of computational models. J. Artif. Intell. Soft Comput. Res. **7**(2), 111–123 (2017)
11. Mirjalili, S., Mirjalili, S.M., Lewis, A.: Grey wolf optimizer. Adv. Eng. Softw. **69**, 46–61 (2014)
12. Mittal, N., Singh, U., Sohi, B.S.: Modified grey wolf optimizer for global engineering optimization. Appl. Comput. Intell. Soft Comput. **2016**, 8 (2016)
13. Pazzani, M.J., Billsus, D.: Content-based recommendation systems. In: Brusilovsky, P., Kobsa, A., Nejdl, W. (eds.) The Adaptive Web. LNCS, vol. 4321, pp. 325–341. Springer, Heidelberg (2007). https://doi.org/10.1007/978-3-540-72079-9_10
14. Prasad, M., Liu, Y.-T., Li, D.-L., Lin, C.-T., Shah, R.R., Kaiwartya, O.P.: A new mechanism for data visualization with Tsk-type preprocessed collaborative fuzzy rule based system. J. Artif. Intell. Soft Comput. Res. **7**(1), 33–46 (2017)
15. Riid, A., Preden, J.-S.: Design of fuzzy rule-based classifiers through granulation and consolidation. J. Artif. Intell. Soft Comput. Res. **7**(2), 137–147 (2017)
16. Rutkowski, L.: Computational Intelligence: Methods and Techniques. Springer, Heidelberg (2008). https://doi.org/10.1007/978-3-540-76288-1
17. Rutkowski, T., et al.: A content-based recommendation system using neuro-fuzzy approach. In: 2018 IEEE International Conference on Fuzzy Systems (FUZZ-IEEE). IEEE (2018)
18. Sadiqbatcha, S., Jafarzadeh, S., Ampatzidis, Y.: Particle swarm optimization for solving a class of type-1 and type-2 fuzzy nonlinear equations. J. Artif. Intell. Soft Comput. Res. **8**(2), 103–110 (2018)
19. Schafer, J.B., Frankowski, D., Herlocker, J., Sen, S.: Collaborative filtering recommender systems. In: Brusilovsky, P., Kobsa, A., Nejdl, W. (eds.) The Adaptive Web. LNCS, vol. 4321, pp. 291–324. Springer, Heidelberg (2007). https://doi.org/10.1007/978-3-540-72079-9_9
20. Song, X., et al.: Grey Wolf Optimizer for parameter estimation in surface waves. Soil Dyn. Earthq. Eng. **75**, 147–157 (2015)

Different Aggregation Modes Applications Within the Framework of Weights Uncertainty

Anna Tikhonenko-Kędziak[1] and Mirosław Kurkowski[2(✉)]

[1] Millennium Bank SA, S. Żaryna 2A, Warsaw, Poland
anna.tikhonenko@gmail.com
[2] Institute of Computer Science,
Cardinal St. Wyszynski University, Warsaw, Poland
m.kurkowski@uksw.edu.pl

Abstract. The main aim of the work is an investigation of different aggregation modes applications within the framework of weights uncertainty. There are many aggregation modes using for decision making, which can be described using not only real numbers. Some precise aggregation modes, under the condition of uncertainty, requires operation of exponentiation with uncertainty power and we proposed the easy and clarity method to its calculation. Therefore, the specific aim of the work is the development of methods for modifying values of fuzzy weights in order to be able to use any aggregation modes for decision-making problems.

Keywords: Fuzzy weights · Weights uncertainty · Aggregation modes

1 Introduction

It is known that different variants of the aggregation of local criteria give rise to different results. This situation follows from the fact that the validity of the stage of formulation of a global criterion as an aggregation of local criteria is dominant. It is obvious that the evaluation of the validity of the criteria is not essential in some optimization processes and sometimes all local criteria have the same validity (weight) for decision-makers. In addition, the weights definition by using real numbers sometimes is not possible.

For example, using the real numbers is rather difficult for the specification of linguistic terms of local criteria validity. It follows from the paper [34] that if you propose to a group of specialists to assess the well-known objects, linguistic terms usually will be almost the same, because these people have studied using the same textbooks, reading the same articles, and they work in the same field. However, if you manage them to use numeric estimators for evaluating, it usually will be more difficult and no consensus there will be [34] because the numeric results are associated with a high personal responsibility, which each person tries to avoid. The problem lies in the fact that, as has been proven by psychologists, the process of human thinking is based on a verbal presentation of knowledge. Therefore, this fact is a cause of confusion with the use of numeric ratings even in the case of experts who have long been working together in specific fields.

© Springer Nature Switzerland AG 2019
L. Rutkowski et al. (Eds.): ICAISC 2019, LNAI 11508, pp. 373–384, 2019.
https://doi.org/10.1007/978-3-030-20912-4_35

Hence, the more accurate is using the transformation of verbal terms to interval or fuzzy values, applied to various types of aggregation modes. There are many aggregation modes using for decision making, which can be described using not only real numbers [2–9, 20, 21–23, 26, 27, 29], but the uncertainty of the weights is no less important for consideration [27–30].

Fuzzy weight also may be used for issues related to time comparisons for computationally intensive problems [3] or fuzzy neural networks [4] to assess, inter alia, the critical non-linear factors.

The majority of the publications deal with additive aggregation mode which mode has the form of the weighted sum, but this approach does not provoke controversy due to the specific determination of the operation on fuzzy sets. The disadvantage of this method is that the results obtained are not precise [12]. As shown in [12], the aggregation based on the "principle of maximal pessimism" is much more precise. The main problem associated with the use of a particular method of aggregation in terms of uncertainty weights is the complexity of the exponentiation methods with fuzzy power [new]. In [15] representation of fuzzy numbers by using the interval sum for creating a final ranking in the framework of the TOPSIS method, is proposed. The use of this method, together with a direct interval extension method [14], allows us to convert the fuzzy power into an interval form and solves, thus, the problem of exponentiation with fuzzy power.

The rest of the paper is set up as follows. In Sect. 2, we analyze the aggregation modes and show a situation in which the aggregation of aggregation modes is necessary. In Sect. 3 we present the aggregation modes under the condition of interval weight uncertainty and propose the use of conventional methods of interval analysis. Section 4 is devoted to the aggregation modes in the framework of fuzzy weight uncertainty extended by the method proposed in Sect. 3. In Sect. 5 we show an aggregation of aggregation modes based on synthesis methods of the fuzzy sets of type 2 and level 2 theory. In Sect. 6 we present an illustrative numerical example. Section 7 contains some concluding remarks.

2   Aggregation Modes

Let be given a continuous set of alternatives X with n equivalent local criteria presented by the respective membership functions $\mu_1(x), \ldots, \mu_n(x)$. In practice, most decision-making problems require the introduction of relative coefficients for criteria weights. So, we can use the following methods of aggregation:

(1) the aggregation based on the "principle of maximal pessimism" - D_1,
(2) additive aggregation - D_2,
(3) multiplicative aggregation - D_3.

Having regard to the weights $w_i(i = 1, \ldots, n)$ calculated on the basis of the pair comparison matrix or given by an expert:

$$D_1 = \min\{\mu_1(X)^{w_1}, \ldots, \mu_n(X)^{w_n}\}, \tag{1}$$

$$D_2 = \prod_{i=1}^{n} \mu_i(X)^{w_i}, \tag{2}$$

$$D_3 = \sum_{i=1}^{n} \mu_i w_i(X), \tag{3}$$

where $X = (x_1, x_2, \ldots, x_n)$ is the vector of quality parameters.

Of course, other methods of aggregation exist, but usually, in practice, we use the mentioned before methods (1)–(3) and their combinations [12]. Many works (see [1, 10, 18, 19]) indicate the additive aggregation mode as best from local criteria. However, using this method not always get reliable results. It may be concluded from [12] that using the strategy based on the D_1 expression we obtain the best option for alternatives assessment and optimizations tasks in the case of describing the criteria by membership functions. As it was proved in [16], strategy optimization on the basis of the minimum operation, i.e. the aggregation based on the "principle of maximal pessimism" in finding the best alternatives among the worst, is the approach which guarantees reliable results in line with our intuition only.

In our situation, it means that the realization degree of the criteria in optimum point shall be not less than one of the least important criterion. The appropriate solution to the optimization task is Pareto-optimal. The main problem associated with the use of a particular method of aggregation in terms of uncertainty weights is the lack of definition of the exponentiation with fuzzy power. In [15] representation of fuzzy numbers by using the interval sum for creating a final ranking in the framework of the TOPSIS method, is proposed. The use of this method, together with a direct interval extension method [14], allows us to convert the fuzzy power into an interval form and solves, thus, the problem of exponentiation with fuzzy power.

However, it should be noted that in many cases, the most justified aggregation mode D_1 (1) does not correspond to the experience and intuition of decision makers in assessing alternatives and optimization [11]. Therefore, in the case of complex tasks with a large number of local criteria and restrictions, after receiving the guaranteed ratings based on D_1 aggregations (1), it makes sense to apply some other additive and multiplicative modes to build a global criterion. If the results obtained by all used modes of aggregation are similar (at least, at the level of quality), it makes us conclude that obtained results are adequate.

Therefore, in the next section, we consider the abovementioned modes of aggregation under a condition of interval weight uncertainty.

3 Aggregation Modes Under Condition of Interval Weight Uncertainty

In this section, we present and analyze the most often used aggregation modes of local criteria under a condition of interval weight uncertainty.

Let be given a continuous set of alternatives X with n equivalent local criteria presented by the respective membership functions $\mu_1(x), \mu_2(x), \ldots, \mu_n(x)$ and $W = \{[w_1^L, w_1^U], [w_2^L, w_2^U], \ldots, [w_n^L, w_n^U]\}$ be the vector of local criteria weights.

It is easy to see that the expressions of D_1, D_2, D_3 in the case of interval weight uncertainty can be written as follows:

$$D_1' = min\left\{\mu_1(X)^{[w_1^L, w_1^U]}, \ldots, \mu_n(X)^{[w_n^L, w_n^U]}\right\}, \tag{4}$$

$$D_2' = \prod_{i=1}^{n} \mu_i(X)^{[w_i^L, w_i^U]}, \tag{5}$$

$$D_3' = \sum_{i=1}^{n} [w_i^L, w_i^U] \cdot \mu_i(X). \tag{6}$$

In accordance with interval arithmetic we have:

$$x^{[\underline{a}, \bar{a}]} = \left[min\left\{x^{w^L}, x^{w^U}\right\}, max\left\{x^{w^L}, x^{w^U}\right\}\right], \tag{7}$$

$$x \cdot [\underline{a}, \bar{a}] = \left[min\{x \cdot w^L, x \cdot w^U\}, max\{x \cdot w^L, x \cdot w^U\}\right]. \tag{8}$$

Indeed, if we substitute the last two formulas $\left(x^{[\underline{a}, \bar{a}]}, \text{and} \, x \cdot [\underline{a}, \bar{a}]\right)$ to the previous expressions (D_1', D_2', D_3'), we get:

$$D_1'' = min\left[min\left\{\mu_1(X)^{[w_1^L, w_1^U]}\right\}, max\left\{\mu_1(X)^{[w_1^L, w_1^U]}\right\}\right], \\ \ldots, \left[min\left\{\mu_n(X)^{[w_n^L, w_n^U]}\right\}, max\left\{\mu_n(X)^{[w_n^L, w_n^U]}\right\}\right]\right\}, \tag{9}$$

$$D_2'' = \prod_{i=1}^{n} \left[min\left\{\mu_i(X)^{w_i^L}, \mu_i(X)^{w_i^U}\right\}, max\left\{\mu_i(X)^{w_i^L}, \mu_i(X)^{w_i^U}\right\}\right], \tag{10}$$

$$D_3'' = \sum_{i=1}^{n} \left[min\{w_i^L \cdot \mu_i(X), w_i^U \cdot \mu_i(X)\}, max\{w_i^L \cdot \mu_i(X), w_i^U \cdot \mu_i(X)\}\right]. \tag{11}$$

We can see that in D_1'' (9) we deal with the comparison of the interval value. For this purpose, we use the method proposed in [12]. This method is based on interval subtraction and the determination of the measure to designate the largest or the smallest range. Therefore, for intervals $B = [\underline{b}, \bar{b}]$ and $A = [\underline{a}, \bar{a}]$, a value that allows us to measure the distance between the intervals and to indicate is this interval is larger or smaller, can be presented in the following form [12]:

$$\Delta_{A-B} = \frac{1}{2}\left((a^L - b^U) + (a^U - b^L)\right). \tag{12}$$

4 Aggregation Modes in Framework of Fuzzy Weight Uncertainty

Now we strictly formulate our problem. Let be given a continuous set of alternatives X with n equivalent local criteria presented by the respective membership functions $\mu_1(x), \mu_2(x), \ldots, \mu_n(x)$, and $W = \left\{ \left[w_1^L, w_1^M, w_1^U \right], \left[w_2^L, w_2^M, w_2^U \right], \ldots, \left[w_n^L, w_n^M, w_n^U \right] \right\}$, be the vector of weights of local criteria, where $\left[w_i^L, w_i^M, w_i^U \right]$ is fuzzy weight of i-th local criterion.

Thus we see that expressions of D_1, D_2, D_3, in the case of fuzzy weight uncertainty, can be rewritten as follows:

$$D_1''' = min\left\{ \mu_1(X)^{\left[w_1^L, w_1^M, w_1^U \right]}, \ldots, \mu_n(X)^{\left[w_n^L, w_n^M, w_n^U \right]} \right\}, \tag{13}$$

$$D_2''' = \prod_{i=1}^{n} \mu_i(X)^{\left[w_i^L, w_i^M, w_i^U \right]}, \tag{14}$$

$$D_3''' = \sum_{i=1}^{n} \left[w_i^L, w_i^M, w_i^U \right] \cdot \mu_i(X). \tag{15}$$

It is obvious that as far there is no problem with D_3 calculation (see D_3'''), in the case of aggregation modes D_1 (1) and D_2 (2) we have a problem with exponentiation with fuzzy power.

Now we present a representation of fuzzy values with use α-cut. To calculate the fuzzy value D_1''', D_2''', D_3''' (13)–(15) we use α-cut representations of fuzzy values. This allows us to avoid the restrictions related to the triangular form of fuzzy numbers. Of course, if we deal with regular triangular or trapezoidal forms, MCDM problem can be solved by using the highest and lowest α-cuts without loss of important information. Let us recall the basic definitions of fuzzy arithmetic based on the α-cut representation [15, 29, 33].

If $\tilde{A}$ is fuzzy value, then $\tilde{A} = \sum_\alpha \alpha A_\alpha$, where αA_α is α-cut of fuzzy set A in X composed of the elements of interval $A_\alpha = \{x \in X, \mu_A \geq \alpha\}$, which degrees of membership to A must be not less than α.

It was proved in [17] that if A and B are fuzzy values, then all arithmetical operations on them can be presented as operations on the sets of crisp intervals corresponding to their α-cuts: $(A \otimes B)_\alpha = A_\alpha \otimes B_\alpha$, where $\otimes \in \{ +, -, \cdot, / \}$.

Then, the procedure of exponentiation with fuzzy power we can define as follows:
$x^{\tilde{A}} = x^{(\sum_\alpha \alpha A_\alpha)/\alpha}$, where αA_α is a fuzzy subset. Given that A is the interval value, the expression (17) can be presented in the following form:

$$x^{\tilde{A}} = x^{\frac{\sum_\alpha \alpha [A_\alpha^L, A_\alpha^U]}{\alpha}} = \left[min\left\{ x^{\frac{\sum_\alpha \alpha \cdot A_\alpha^L}{\alpha}}, x^{\frac{\sum_\alpha \alpha \cdot A_\alpha^U}{\alpha}} \right\}, max\left\{ x^{\frac{\sum_\alpha \alpha \cdot A_\alpha^L}{\alpha}}, x^{\frac{\sum_\alpha \alpha \cdot A_\alpha^U}{\alpha}} \right\} \right]. \tag{16}$$

Therefore, in the case of fuzzy weight uncertainty, the aggregation modes D_1, D_2 and D_3, with regard to the distinction on α-cut, can be written as follows:

$$D_1^4 = min\left\{\mu_1(X)^{\frac{\sum_\alpha \alpha \cdot \left[w_{1\alpha}^L, w_{1\alpha}^U\right]}{\alpha}}, \ldots, \mu_n(X)^{\frac{\sum_\alpha \alpha \cdot \left[w_{n\alpha}^L, w_{n\alpha}^U\right]}{\alpha}}\right\}, \tag{17}$$

$$D_2^4 = \prod_{i=1}^n \mu_i(X)^{\frac{\sum_\alpha \alpha \cdot \left[w_{i\alpha}^L, w_{i\alpha}^U\right]}{\alpha}}, \tag{18}$$

$$D_3^4 = \sum_{i=1}^n \frac{\sum_\alpha \alpha \cdot \left[w_{i\alpha}^L, w_{i\alpha}^U\right]}{\alpha} \cdot \mu_i(X). \tag{19}$$

Indeed, the last expressions can be presented in the following form:

$$D_1^4 = min\{[min\{\delta_1^L, \delta_1^U\}, max\{\delta_1^L, \delta_1^U\}], \ldots, [min\{\delta_n^L, \delta_n^U\}, max\{\delta_n^L, \delta_n^U\}]\}, \tag{20}$$

where $\delta_i^L = \mu_i(X) \cdot \frac{\sum_\alpha \alpha \cdot w_{i\alpha}^L}{\alpha}$, $\delta_i^U = \mu_i(X) \cdot \frac{\sum_\alpha \alpha \cdot w_{i\alpha}^U}{\alpha}$ for $i = 1, \ldots, n$.

$$D_2^4 = \prod_{i=1}^n \left[min\{\tilde{\delta}_i^L, \tilde{\delta}_i^U\}, max\{\tilde{\delta}_i^L, \tilde{\delta}_i^U\}\right], \tag{21}$$

where $\tilde{\delta}_i^L = \mu_i(X)^{\frac{\sum_\alpha \alpha w_{i\alpha}^L}{\alpha}}$, $\tilde{\delta}_i^U = \mu_i(X)^{\frac{\sum_\alpha \alpha w_{i\alpha}^U}{\alpha}}$ for $i = 1, \ldots, n$.

$$D_3^4 = \sum_{i=1}^n min\left[\left\{\frac{\sum_\alpha \alpha w_{i\alpha}^L}{\alpha} \cdot \mu_i(X), \frac{\sum_\alpha \alpha w_{i\alpha}^U}{\alpha} \cdot \mu_i(X)\right\}, \right.$$
$$\left. max\left\{\frac{\sum_\alpha \alpha w_{i\alpha}^L}{\alpha} \cdot \mu_i(X), \frac{\sum_\alpha \alpha w_{i\alpha}^U}{\alpha} \cdot \mu_i(X)\right\}\right]. \tag{22}$$

5   Aggregation of Aggregation Modes

It was shown in [12] that the main disadvantage of the additive aggregation is the possibility of partial compensation of small values by large values of the other criteria. It is possible even in situations when the most important local criterion is completely false, but the aggregation mode D_3 (3) delivers pretty good results. Therefore, in some areas (ex. in modeling ecological processes [25]), the use of additive aggregation is strongly prohibited.

If the results obtained using different methods of aggregation are similar, it indicates the confirmation of their optimality. Otherwise, we must carry out a detailed analysis of local criteria and their weights or apply an aggregation of aggregation modes. This method was developed in [12, 24] and based on synthesis methods of the fuzzy sets of type 2 and level 2 theory.

Type 2 fuzzy sets were introduced by Zadeh in [31, 32] within the framework of mathematical linguistic terms formalization. In essence, these sets are an extension of the ordinary fuzzy sets (type 1) in the case when membership function is presented by another fuzzy set.

Let A is a type 2 fuzzy set on X. Then, for every $x \in X$ a fuzzy set on Y and corresponding membership function exist and can be presented in the following form [10]:

$$\mu_A(x) = \left\{ \frac{f_x(y_i)}{y_i} \right\}, \tag{23}$$

for $i = 1, ..., n$, where a fuzzy set on Y is characterized by membership function $f_x(y)$. Completion of the type 2 fuzzy set can be represented by the relation

$$\mu_{\bar{A}}(x) = \left\{ \frac{f_x(y_i)}{1 - y_i} \right\}, \tag{24}$$

for $i = 1, ..., n$.

If A and B are type 2 fuzzy sets and

$$\mu_A(x) = \left\{ \frac{f_x(y_i)}{y_i} \right\}, \ \mu_B(x) = \left\{ \frac{g_x(z_j)}{z_j} \right\}, \tag{25}$$

where $i = 1, ..., n, j = 1, ..., m$, then membership function of set $D = A \cup B$ takes the following form:

$$\mu_D(x) = \left\{ \frac{min\left(f_x(y_i), g_x(z_j)\right)}{max\left(y_i, z_j\right)} \right\}, \ i = 1, \ldots, n, j = 1, \ldots, m, \tag{26}$$

Similarly, for intersection we have

$$C = A \cap B \text{ we have } \mu_C(x) = \left\{ \frac{min\left(f_x(y_i), g_x(z_j)\right)}{min\left(y_i, z_j\right)} \right\}. \tag{27}$$

For simplicity, we don't use the generalized presentation of operations on fuzzy sets by the t-norm and s-norms. We shall describe briefly the level 2 fuzzy sets. If elements $x \in X$ are fuzzy sets of different set Z, then, in discretization situation, level 2 fuzzy set A can be represented as follows [33]:

$$A = \left\{ \frac{\mu_A(x_i)}{x_i} \right\}, \ x_i = \left\{ \frac{h_i(z_j)}{z_j} \right\}, \tag{28}$$

$$A = \left\{ \frac{max_i[\mu_A(x_i)h_i(z_j)]}{z_j} \right\}, \tag{29}$$

$i = 1, ..., n, j = 1, ..., m,$

The last expression shows that the degree of membership z_j to A can be presented by the following expression

$$\mu_A(z_j) = max_i[\mu_A(x_i)h_i(z_j)] \ i = 1,\ldots,n. \tag{30}$$

Aforementioned elements of the theory of type 2 and level 2 fuzzy sets are applied to the generalizations of aggregation modes in order to obtain some kind of generalized terms within the framework of a considered problem. It is worth noting that, in the context of the proposed approach avoids the application of the minimum operation, multiplication and sum witch aggregations of aggregation modes, because using them leads inevitably to a sequence of unlimited aggregation problems.

Let we have K variants of aggregation modes and M selected local criteria, and let $\mu(D^i)$, $i = 1, \ldots, K$, be a membership function represented the subjective opinions of decision-makers with a degree of "closeness" of specific i-th aggregation mode to the ideal (the best from all viewpoints D_{ideal} aggregation that satisfies all conditions, even not explicitly formulated at the verbal level).

It is worth noting that $\mu(D^i)$ may be presented by the experts in the linguistic form and then $\mu(D^i)$ can be modified to the fuzzy sets form. Therefore, such idealized global criterion can be expressed as a type 2 fuzzy set [12] $D_{ideal} = \frac{\mu(D^i)}{D^i}$, where D^i is an aggregation mode using in the special case, i.e. D_1, D_2, D_3.

On the other hand, each D^i can be represented as a fuzzy set based on an ordinary set of considered alternatives. Then, we have:

$$D^j = \left\{\frac{D^i(z_j)}{z_j}\right\}, j = 1,\ldots,M, \tag{31}$$

where z_j are alternatives and $D^i(z_j)$ is a degree of adequacy of an alternative z_j to the criterion of D^i type.

The result of the substitution of the last two expression is the mathematical structure which is a type 2 and level 2 fuzzy set [10]:

$$D_{ideal} = \left\{\frac{\mu_{ideal}(z_j)}{z_j}\right\} j = 1,\ldots,M, \tag{32}$$

where $\mu_{ideal}(z_j) = max_i[\mu(D_i) \cdot D^i(z_j)] \ j = 1,\ldots,M$. Of course, the best alternative z_j has the largest value of the function $\mu_{ideal}(z_j)$.

6 Numerical Examples

Suppose that the alternatives in decision-making problem are presented by objective assessments, while the weight of local criteria is specified in subjective assessments by linguistic terms "very high", "high", "medium high", "medium", "low", "very low" [26]. It was shown in [12] that linguistic terms are usually presented by triangular form fuzzy numbers. Average results of experiments obtained during many analyses of the alternatives and the local criteria weights are presented in Tables 1 and 2. In order to simplify the example, the values shown in Table 1 are normalized.

Table 1. Normalized assessment of alternatives according to the four criteria.

	C_1	C_2	C_3	C_4
A_1	0.125	0.375	0.1667	0.3636
A_2	0.25	0.5	0.5	0.4545
A_3	0.625	0.125	0.3333	0.1818

Table 2. Experts assessments of criteria weights.

Criterion	Numerical assessment	Verbal term
C_1	[0.1, 0.4, 0.9]	MH
C_2	[0.1, 0.3, 0.4]	M
C_3	[0.2, 0.25, 0.3]	L
C_4	[0.2, 0.6, 0.8]	H

Then, using the approach described above and the TOPSIS method [5, 14, 15], we obtain the rankings for D_1, D_2, D_3 presented in Tables 3, 4 and 5, respectively.

Table 3. The rating obtained by aggregation with "principle of max. pessimism".

	Numerical assessment	Evaluation	Rating
A_1	[0.5656, 0.7236]	0.6446	2
A_2	[0.6839, 0.8060]	0.7450	1
A_3	[0.5701, 0.6634]	0.6167	3

Table 4. The rating obtained by multiplicative aggregation.

	Numerical assessment	Evaluation	Rating
A_1	[0.2719, 0.4083]	0.3401	3
A_2	[0.4292, 0.5653]	0.4972	1
A_3	[0.3076, 0.4219]	0.3647	2

Table 5. The rating obtained by additive aggregation.

	Numerical assessment	Evaluation	Rating
A_1	[0.1717, 0.2380]	0.2049	3
A_2	[0.2673, 0.3669]	0.3171	1
A_3	[0.1952, 0.2960]	0.2456	2

It is easy to see that the assessment designated by aggregation based on the "principle of maximal pessimism" slightly differ from two another modes, so aggregation of aggregation modes is necessary in this case [12, 13].

Pair comparison matrix obtained as a result of the analysis of the accuracy of each mode [12] is shown in Table 6.

Table 6. Pair comparison matrix for aggregation modes.

Aggregation mode	D_1	D_2	D_3
D_1	1	3	9
D_2	$\frac{1}{3}$	1	9
D_3	$\frac{1}{9}$	$\frac{1}{9}$	1

The final result of an aggregation of aggregation modes is shown in Table 7. After comparing the received values, we conclude that A_2 is the best alternative.

Table 7. Rating obtained by aggregation of aggregation modes.

Alternatives	Evaluation	Rating
A_1	0.4512	2
A_2	0.5215	1
A_3	0.4317	3

The final rating is $A_3 < A_1 < A_2$. As part of our approach based on aggregation of aggregation modes, we get "compromise" ranking, which is similar to the ranking obtained by aggregation based on "principle of maximal pessimism" (see Table 6). Such effect we obtain thanks to setting large weights to aggregation mode based on the "principle of maximal pessimism".

7 Conclusion

A new approach to the solution of exponentiation with fuzzy power problem is proposed. This method gives the ability to use much more aggregation modes under the condition of fuzzy weight uncertainty in an easy way. In this work, we propose to use other types of aggregation modes and show uses of their aggregation in the framework of fuzzy weight uncertainty. The benefits of the proposed method are simplicity and clarity. Using the aggregation of aggregation modes, we obtain "compromise" ranking, which is similar to the ranking obtained by aggregation based on "the principle of maximal pessimism". Such effect we obtain thanks to setting large weights to aggregation mode based on the "principle of maximal pessimism", because of its precision.

The study is cofounded by the European Union from resources of the European Social Fund. **Project** POKL "Information technologies: Research and their interdisciplinary applications", Agreement UDA-POKL.04.01.01-00-051/10-00.

References

1. Bana e Costa, C.A., Vansnick, J.S.: MACBETH—an interactive path towards the construction of cardinal value functions. Int. Trans. Oper. Res. **1**(4), 489–500 (1994)
2. Boran, F.E., Cenc, S., Kurt, M., Akay, D.: A multi-criteria untuitionistic fuzzy group decision making for supplier selection with TOPSIS method. Expert Syst. Appl. **36**, 11363–11368 (2009)
3. Botzheimab, J., Földesic, P.: Novel calculation of fuzzy exponent in the sigmoid functions for fuzzy neural networks. Neurocomputing **129**, 458–466 (2014)
4. Botzheimab, J., Földesic, P.: Parametric approximation of fuzzy exponent for computationally intensive problems. Int. J. Innov. Comput. Inf. Control **8**, 5725–5744 (2012)
5. Chen, C.T.: Extension of the TOPSIS for group decision-making under fuzzy environment. J. Fuzzy Sets Syst. **114**(1), 1–9 (2000)
6. Chen, S.J., Hwang, C.L.: Fuzzy Multiple Attribute Decision Making. Lecture Notes in Economics and Mathematical System Series, vol. 375. Springer, New York (1992). https://doi.org/10.1007/978-3-642-46768-4
7. Chen, M.F., Tzeng, G.H., Ding, C.G.: Fuzzy MCDM approach to select service provider. In: IEEE International Conference on Fuzzy Systems, pp. 572–577 (2003)
8. Chu, T.C., Lin, Y.C.: A fuzzy TOPSIS method for robot selection. Int. J. Manuf. Technol. **21**, 284–290 (2003)
9. Deng, H., Yeh, C.H., Willis, R.J.: Inter-company comparison using modified TOPSIS with objective weights. Comput. Oper. Res. **27**, 963–973 (2000)
10. Dias, L.C., Climaco, J.N.: Additive aggregation with variable interdependent parameters: the VIP analysis software. J. Oper. Res. Soc. **51**(9), 1070–1082 (2000)
11. Dubois, D., Koenig, J.L.: Social choice axioms for fuzzy set aggregation. Fuzzy Sets Syst. **43**, 257–274 (1991)
12. Dymowa, L.: Soft Computing in Economics and Finance. Springer, Heidelberg (2010). https://doi.org/10.1007/978-3-642-17719-4
13. Dymova, L., Sevastjanov, P.: The operations on intuitionistic fuzzy values in the framework of Dempster-Shafer theory. Knowl. Based Syst. **35**, 132–143 (2012)
14. Dymova, L., Sevastjanov, P., Tikhonenko, A.: A direct interval extension of TOPSIS method. Expert Syst. Appl. **40**, 4841–4847 (2013)
15. Dymova, L., Sevastjanov, P., Tikhonenko, A.: An approach to generalization of fuzzy TOPSIS method. Inf. Sci. **238**, 149–162 (2013)
16. Germejer, J.: Introduction in the Theory of Operational Researches, Moscow, Science, p. 220 (1971)
17. Kaufmann, A., Gupta, M.M.: Introduction to Fuzzy Arithmetic Theory and Applications. Nostrand Reinhold, New York (1985)
18. Liu, P.: An extended TOPSIS method for multiple attribute group decision making based on generalized interval-valued trapezoidal fuzzy numbers. J. Informatica **35**, 185–196 (2011)
19. Lou, J.S., Szarko, J.M., Xu, T., Luping, Y., Marks, T.J., Chen, L.X.: Effects of additives on the morphology of solution phase aggregates formed by active layer components of high-efficiency organic solar cells. J. Am. Chem. Soc. **133**(51), 20661–20663 (2011)

20. Nieto-Morote, A., Ruz-Vila, F.: A fuzzy AHP multi-criteria decision-making approach applied to combined cooling, heating and power production systems. Int. J. Inf. Technol. Decis. Making 10(3), 497–517 (2011)
21. Nurnadiah, Z., Lazim, A., Suzuri, M.H., Maizura, N.M.N., Ahmad, J.: A novel hybrid fuzzy weighted average for MCDM with interval triangular type-2 fuzzy sets. WSEAS Trans. Syst. 12(4), 212–228 (2013)
22. Nurnadiah, Z., Lazim, A.: Weight of interval type-2 fuzzy Rasch model in decision making approach: ranking causes lead of road accident occurrence. Int. J. Soft Comput. 7(1), 1–11 (2012)
23. Park, K.S., Kim, S.H.: A note on the fuzzy weighted additive rule. J. Fuzzy Sets Syst. 77, 315–320 (1996)
24. Sewastianow, P., Lymanow, N.: Wielokryterialna identyfikacja i optymalizacja procesów technologicznych, p. 224. Nauka i Technika, Mińsk (1990)
25. Silvert, W.: Ecological impact classification with fuzzy sets. Ecological Modelling 96, 1–10 (1997)
26. Wang, T.C., Lee, H.-D.: Developing a fuzzy TOPSIS approach based on subjective weights and objective weights. Expert Syst. Appl. 36, 8980–8985 (2009)
27. Wang, T.C., Lee, H.-D., Wu, C.-C.: A fuzzy TOPSIS approach with subjective weights and objective weights. In: Proceedings of the 6th WSEAS International Conference on Applied Computer Science, Hangzhou, China, 15–17 April 2007
28. Weber, E.U.: From subjective probabilities to decision weights: the effect of asymmetric loss function on the evaluation of uncertain outcomes and events. Psychol. Bull. 115(2), 228–242 (1994)
29. Yue, Z.: A method for group decision making based on determining weights of decision makers using TOPSIS. J. Appl. Math. Modell. 35, 1926–1936 (2011)
30. Yue, Z.: An extended TOPSIS for determining weights of decision makers with interval numbers. J. Knowl. Based Syst. 24, 146–153 (2011)
31. Zadeh, L.A.: Fuzzy sets. Inf. Control 8, 338–353 (1965)
32. Zadeh, L.A.: The concept of linguistic variable and its application to approximate reasoning —I. Inf. Sci. 8, 199–249 (1975)
33. Zadeh, L.A.: Quantitative fuzzy semantics. Inf. Sci. 3, 177–200 (1971)
34. Zollo, G., Iandoli, L., Cannavacciuolo, A.: The performance requirements analysis with fuzzy logic. Fuzzy Econ. Rev. 4, 35–69 (1999)

Fuzzy Clustering High-Dimensional Data Using Information Weighting

Yevgeniy V. Bodyanskiy[1] , Oleksii K. Tyshchenko[2]([⊠]) ,
and Sergii V. Mashtalir[3]

[1] Control Systems Research Laboratory, Kharkiv National University of Radio
Electronics, 14 Nauky Ave, Kharkiv 61166, Ukraine
yevgeniy.bodyanskiy@nure.ua
[2] Institute for Research and Applications of Fuzzy Modeling,
CE IT4Innovations, University of Ostrava, 30. dubna 22,
701 03 Ostrava, Czech Republic
lehatish@gmail.com
[3] Department of Informatics, Kharkiv National University of Radio Electronics,
14 Nauky Ave, Kharkiv 61166, Ukraine
sergii.mashtalir@nure.ua

Abstract. The fuzzy clustering algorithm for high-dimensional data is proposed in this paper. An objective function which is insensitive to the "concentration of norms" phenomenon is also introduced. We recommend using a weighted parameter in the objective function. The proposed fuzzy clustering algorithm is compared with FCM in the experimental part. Dependence of the clustering algorithm's results on the weighted parameter changes has also been investigated and tested.

Keywords: Fuzzy clustering · Distance metric · High-dimensional data · Computational intelligence · Membership function

1 Introduction

Multidimensional data clustering is an essential part of modern Data Mining which aims at finding in some sense homogeneous groups (clusters or classes) of observations in analyzed data arrays [1–4]. A traditional approach designed for solving this problem assumes that each vector of observations may be attributed only to a single class, though there's a more common case when any feature vector belongs simultaneously to several clusters with some degree. Such a claim is a subject of the fuzzy clustering analysis [5–14]. There's an assumption that classes of homogeneous data cannot be separated from each other, but they can overlap each other, i.e., each observation belongs to clusters with some degree or membership. This membership degree varies in an interval [0, 1].

Initial information for fuzzy clustering consists of a data sample which is formed of N $(n \times 1)$-dimensional feature vectors (images) $X = \{x_1, x_2, \ldots, x_k, \ldots, x_N\} \subset R^n$ where $k = 1, 2, \ldots, N$ is a number of a particular observation from the data array.

L. Rutkowski et al. (Eds.): ICAISC 2019, LNAI 11508, pp. 385–395, 2019.
https://doi.org/10.1007/978-3-030-20912-4_36

A result of clustering is a partition of X into m overlapping classes with some degree of membership $U_q(k)$ of the k-th feature vector x_k to the q-th cluster, $q = 1, 2, \ldots, m$.

Initial data are usually centered and preliminarily normalized concerning all components so that all the observations belong to the hypercube $[-1, 1]^n$. Thus, the initial data acquire a form of $\tilde{X} = \{\tilde{x}_1, \tilde{x}_2, \ldots, \tilde{x}_N\} \subset R^n$, $\tilde{x}_k = (\tilde{x}_{k1}, \tilde{x}_{k2}, \ldots, \tilde{x}_{kn})^T$, $-1 \leq x_{ki} \leq 1$, $1 < m < N$, $1 \leq q \leq m$, $1 \leq i \leq n$, $1 \leq k \leq N$. In addition to that, it can be noticed that this data transformation is not the only possible one. For instance, a transformation $\|\tilde{x}_k\|^2 = 1$ is used in self-organizing maps by Kohonen [15].

Although there are many fuzzy clustering algorithms, every method has its advantages and drawbacks, all of them have the same undesired effect which has been recently noticed by Klawonn [16]. This shortcoming which is typical for the most of fuzzy clustering algorithms under high-dimensional conditions is that possibilities of using fuzzy clustering techniques are somewhat limited due to the "concentration of norms" phenomenon that makes membership degrees of observation be proportionally distributed between all clusters. To overcome this effect, unique distance metrics may be used which provide an opportunity of overlapping clusters' division more effectively in high-dimensional spaces.

Therefore, the task of developing a fuzzy clustering approach to processing high-dimensional data is considered in this paper. To overcome the "concentration of norms" effect, it is required to apply distances of a particular type. Some in-depth analysis was performed for θ value in order to find out how this parameter influences the whole behavior of a clustering system in some real-world test cases.

Some theoretical aspects of fuzzy clustering procedures are covered in Sect. 2. In Sect. 3, the introduced fuzzy clustering procedures are presented in details. Section 4 discusses the application of the developed methods to a set of test cases and the analysis of their performance. In Sect. 5, the conclusion is drawn, and some further research in this area is proposed.

2   Fuzzy Clustering Algorithms

Fuzzy clustering procedures based on objective functions are considered to be rather strict from a mathematical point of view [17], and they can solve an optimization problem under some a priori assumptions. Here, the probabilistic approach is the most widely-used one, and it is based on minimization of the objective function

$$
E(U_q(k), w_q) = \sum_{k=1}^{N} \sum_{q=1}^{m} U_q^\beta(k) D(\tilde{x}_k, w_q) = \sum_{k=1}^{N} \sum_{q=1}^{m} U_q^\beta(k) \|\tilde{x}_k - w_q\|^2
$$

$$
= \sum_{k=1}^{N} \sum_{q=1}^{m} U_q^\beta(k) \sum_{i=1}^{n} (\tilde{x}_{ki} - w_{qi})^2 \tag{1}
$$

under constraints

$$\sum_{q=1}^{m} U_q(k) = 1, \tag{2}$$

$$0 \le \sum_{k=1}^{N} U_q(k) \le N \tag{3}$$

where $U_q(k) \in [0, 1]$ is a membership degree of a vector $\tilde{x}_k$ to the q-th class, w_q is a centroid (prototype) of the q-th cluster, β is a nonnegative fuzzification parameter (a fuzzifier) that specifies overlapping borders between groups of points, $k = 1, 2, \ldots, N$. An $(N \times m)$-matrix $U = \{U_q(k)\}$ (a fuzzy partition matrix) is obtained as a result of clustering.

Introducing the Lagrange function

$$L(U_q(k), w_q, \rho(k)) = \sum_{k=1}^{N} \sum_{q=1}^{m} U_q^{\beta}(k) \|\tilde{x}_k - w_q\|^2 + \sum_{k=1}^{N} \rho(k) (\sum_{q=1}^{m} U_q(k) - 1)$$

($\rho(k)$ are indefinite Lagrange multipliers) and solving the Karush-Kuhn-Tucker system of equations

$$\begin{cases} \dfrac{\partial L(U_q(k), w_q, \rho(k))}{\partial U_q(k)} = 0, \\ \nabla_{w_q} L(U_q(k), w_q, \rho(k)) = \vec{0}, \\ \dfrac{\partial L(U_q(k), w_q, \rho(k))}{\partial \rho(k)} = 0, \end{cases}$$

the following solution is obtained

$$\begin{cases} U_q(k) = \dfrac{(\|\tilde{x}_k - w_q\|^2)^{\frac{1}{1-\beta}}}{\sum\limits_{l=1}^{m} (\|\tilde{x}_k - w_q\|^2)^{\frac{1}{1-\beta}}}, \\ w_q = \dfrac{\sum\limits_{k=1}^{N} U_q^{\beta}(k) \tilde{x}_k}{\sum\limits_{k=1}^{N} U_q^{\beta}(k)} \end{cases} \tag{4}$$

which coincides with the popular fuzzy C-means algorithm (FCM) if $\beta = 2$ [18]

$$\begin{cases} U_q(k) = \dfrac{(\|\tilde{x}_k - w_q\|^2)^{-1}}{\sum\limits_{l=1}^{m} (\|\tilde{x}_k - w_q\|^2)^{-1}}, \\ w_q = \dfrac{\sum\limits_{k=1}^{N} U_q^{2}(k) \tilde{x}_k}{\sum\limits_{k=1}^{N} U_q^{2}(k)}. \end{cases} \tag{5}$$

Fuzzy clustering algorithms of the type (4) are very popular because they differ from each other in a kind of $D(\tilde{x}_k, w_q)$ metrics used in the criterion (1): Minkowski, Mahalanobis, etc. Under these circumstances, the influence of vectors' dimensionality under processing has not been considered as obtained results.

Using a particular type of the objective function for fuzzy clustering, it was offered in [19], and it was studied in [16] concerning high-dimensional problems:

$$E(U_q(k), w_q) = \sum_{k=1}^{N} \sum_{q=1}^{m} (\theta U_q^2(k) + (1-\theta)U_q(k)) \left\| \tilde{x}_{ki} - w_{qi} \right\|^2 \quad (6)$$

and its corresponding Lagrange function

$$L(U_q(k), w_q, \rho(k)) = \sum_{k=1}^{N} \sum_{q=1}^{m} (\theta U_q^2(k) + (1-\theta)U_q(k)) \left\| \tilde{x}_k - w_q \right\|^2 + \sum_{k=1}^{N} \rho(k) \left(\sum_{q=1}^{m} U_q(k) - 1 \right).$$

Solving the Karush-Kuhn-Tucker system of equations, it leads to

$$\begin{cases} U_q(k) = -\frac{1-\theta}{2\theta} + \dfrac{1 + m\frac{1-\theta}{2\theta}}{\sum_{l=1}^{m} \frac{\|\tilde{x}_k - w_q\|^2}{\|\tilde{x}_k - w_l\|^2}}, \\[3ex] w_q = \dfrac{\sum_{k=1}^{N} (\theta U_q^2(k) + (1-\theta)U_q(k))\tilde{x}_k}{\sum_{k=1}^{N} (\theta U_q^2(k) + (1-\theta)U_q(k))} \end{cases} \quad (7)$$

that coincides with the conventional FCM (5) for $\theta = 1$, and when $\theta \to 0$ it matches the hard k-means clustering procedure (HKM). The algorithm (7) is the so-called fuzzy C-means method with a polynomial fuzzifier (PFCM) [20]. In terms of properties, the algorithm (6) is closer to a crisp clustering procedure for small θ values that works stable in high-dimensional problems.

There's one more approach to fuzzy clustering high-dimensional data which was proposed by Klawonn [21], and it has to do with weighting individual components $\tilde{x}_{ki}$ of an n-dimensional feature vector $\tilde{x}_k$.

3 The Proposed Clustering Algorithms

The following expression is used as an objective function

$$E(U_q(k), w_q) = \sum_{k=1}^{N} \sum_{q=1}^{m} U_q^\beta(k) \sum_{i=1}^{n} \gamma_{qi}^t (\tilde{x}_{ki} - w_{qi})^2 = \sum_{k=1}^{N} \sum_{q=1}^{m} U_q^\beta(k) D(\tilde{x}_k, w_q) \quad (8)$$

with constraints

$$\sum_{q=1}^{m} U_q(k) = 1 \tag{9}$$

and

$$\sum_{i=1}^{n} \gamma_{qi} = 1 \, \forall q = 1, 2, \ldots, m \tag{10}$$

where γ_{qi} is a weight value of the i-th attribute in the q-th cluster, $t > 1$ is similar to a fuzzifier β.

Optimizing the objective function (8) under the constraints (9)–(10), it leads to the following fuzzy clustering algorithm:

$$
\begin{cases}
\gamma_{qi} = \dfrac{1}{\displaystyle\sum_{h=1}^{n} \left(\dfrac{\displaystyle\sum_{k=1}^{N} U_q^{\beta}(k)(\tilde{x}_{ki}-w_{qi})^2}{\displaystyle\sum_{k=1}^{N} U_q^{\beta}(k)(\tilde{x}_{kh}-w_{qi})^2} \right)^{\frac{1}{t-1}}}, \\[4ex]
U_q(k) = \dfrac{(\displaystyle\sum_{i=1}^{n} \gamma_{qi}^{t}(\tilde{x}_{ki}-w_{qi})^2)^{\frac{1}{1-\beta}}}{\displaystyle\sum_{l=1}^{m} (\displaystyle\sum_{i=1}^{n} \gamma_{li}^{t}(\tilde{x}_{ki}-w_{li})^2)^{\frac{1}{1-\beta}}}, \\[4ex]
w_{qi} = \dfrac{\displaystyle\sum_{k=1}^{N} U_q^{\beta}(k)\tilde{x}_{ki}}{\displaystyle\sum_{k=1}^{N} U_q^{\beta}(k)}
\end{cases} \tag{11}
$$

which is insensitive to the "concentration of norms" phenomenon [16].

The following expression is advised as an objective function for fuzzy clustering:

$$
E(U_q(k), w_q) = \sum_{k=1}^{N} \sum_{q=1}^{m} U_q^{\beta}(k)(\theta \sum_{i=1}^{n} (\tilde{x}_{ki} - w_{qi}))^2 + (1 - \theta) \sum_{i=1}^{n} \gamma_{qi}^{t}(\tilde{x}_{ki} - w_{qi})^2) =
$$

$$
= \sum_{k=1}^{N} \sum_{q=1}^{m} U_q^{\beta}(k) D^K(\tilde{x}_k, w_q) \tag{12}
$$

under the constraints (9)–(10).

To solve this problem, let's consider the Lagrange function which takes the constraints (10) into account

$$
L(U_q(k), w_q, \lambda_q, \gamma_{qi}) = \sum_{k=1}^{N} \sum_{q=1}^{m} U_q^{\beta}(k)(\theta \sum_{i=1}^{n} (\tilde{x}_{ki} - w_{qi})^2 + (1 - \theta) \sum_{i=1}^{n} \gamma_{qi}^{t}(\tilde{x}_{ki} - w_{qi})^2) + \sum_{q=1}^{m} \lambda_q(\sum_{i=1}^{n} \gamma_{qi} - 1) \tag{13}
$$

(λ_q are indefinite Lagrange multipliers) and its corresponding Karush-Kuhn-Tucker system of equations:

$$
\begin{cases}
\frac{\partial L(U_q(k),w_q,\lambda_q,\gamma_{qi})}{\partial \gamma_{qi}} = \sum_{k=1}^{N} U_q^{\beta}(k)(1-\theta)t\gamma_{qi}^{t-1}(\tilde{x}_{ki}-w_{qi})^2 + \lambda_q = 0, \\
\frac{\partial L(U_q(k),w_q,\lambda_q,\gamma_{qi})}{\partial \lambda_q} = \sum_{i=1}^{n} \gamma_{qi} - 1 = 0.
\end{cases}
\tag{14}
$$

Carrying out the following chain of manipulations similar to Klawonn [21],

$$
\lambda_q = (1-\theta)t\gamma_{qi}^{t-1} \sum_{k=1}^{N} U_q^{\beta}(k)(\tilde{x}_{ki}-w_{qi})^2,
$$

$$
\gamma_{qi} = \left(\frac{\lambda_q}{(1-\theta)t \sum_{k=1}^{N} U_q^{\beta}(k)(\tilde{x}_{ki}-w_{qi})^2} \right)^{\frac{1}{t-1}},
$$

$$
1 = \sum_{i=1}^{n} \left(\frac{\lambda_q}{(1-\theta)t \sum_{k=1}^{N} U_q^{\beta}(k)(\tilde{x}_{ki}-w_{qi})^2} \right)^{\frac{1}{t-1}}
$$

$$
= \left(\frac{\lambda_q}{(1-\theta)t} \right)^{\frac{1}{t-1}} \sum_{i=1}^{n} \left(\frac{1}{\sum_{k=1}^{N} U_q^{\beta}(k)(\tilde{x}_{ki}-w_{qi})^2} \right)^{\frac{1}{t-1}},
$$

$$
\lambda_q = \frac{(1-\theta)t}{\left(\sum_{k=1}^{n} \left(\frac{1}{\sum_{k=1}^{N} U_q^{\beta}(k)(\tilde{x}_{ki}-w_{qi})^2} \right)^{\frac{1}{t-1}} \right)^{t-1}},
$$

the comparison is obtained:

$$
\gamma_{qi} = \frac{1}{\sum_{h=1}^{n} \left(\frac{\sum_{k=1}^{N} U_q^{\beta}(k)(\tilde{x}_{ki}-w_{qi})^2}{\sum_{k=1}^{N} U_q^{\beta}(k)(\tilde{x}_{kh}-w_{qi})^2} \right)^{\frac{1}{t-1}}},
$$

i.e., γ_{qi} does not depend on the θ parameter in this case.

Completing the system (14) with the third equation

$$\frac{\partial L(U_q(k), w_q, \lambda_q, \gamma_{qi})}{\partial w_{qi}} = 0 = -2\sum_{k=1}^{N} U_q^{\beta}(k)(\theta(\tilde{x}_{ki} - w_{qi}) + (1-\theta)\gamma_{qi}^t(\tilde{x}_{ki} - w_{qi})),$$

it follows that

$$\sum_{k=1}^{N} U_q^{\beta}(k)(\theta\tilde{x}_{ki} + (1-\theta)\gamma_{qi}^t\tilde{x}_{ki}) = \sum_{k=1}^{N} U_q^{\beta}(k)(\theta w_{qi}(k) + (1-\theta)\gamma_{qi}^t w_{qi})$$

and

$$w_{qi} = \frac{\sum_{k=1}^{N} U_q^{\beta}(k)\tilde{x}_{ki}(\theta + (1-\theta)\gamma_{qi}^t)}{\sum_{k=1}^{N} U_q^{\beta}(k)(\theta + (1-\theta)\gamma_{qi}^t)} = \frac{\sum_{k=1}^{N} U_q^{\beta}(k)\tilde{x}_{ki}}{\sum_{k=1}^{N} U_q^{\beta}(k)}.$$

The weighting parameters γ_{qi} and the centroids w_{qi} are found after optimization of the Lagrange function (13).

In addition to the Lagrange function (13), let's introduce the Lagrange function that takes the constraints (9) from the function (12) in the form

$$L(U_q(k), w_q, \rho(k)) = \sum_{k=1}^{N}\sum_{q=1}^{m} U_q^{\beta}(k)D^K(\tilde{x}_k, w_q) + \sum_{k=1}^{N}\rho(k)(\sum_{q=1}^{m} U_q(k) - 1). \quad (15)$$

From the system of equations

$$\begin{cases} \frac{\partial L(U_q(k), w_q, \rho(k))}{\partial U_q(k)} = \beta U_q^{\beta-1}(k)D^K(\tilde{x}_k, w_q) + \rho(k) = 0, \\ \frac{\partial L(U_q(k), w_q, \rho(k))}{\partial \rho(k)} = \sum_{q=1}^{m} U_q(k) = 1 \end{cases}$$

it follows that

$$U_q(k) = \frac{(D^K(\tilde{x}_k, w_q))^{\frac{1}{1-\beta}}}{\sum_{l=1}^{m}(D^K(\tilde{x}_k, w_l))^{\frac{1}{1-\beta}}}.$$

The final result of the optimization method (12) under the constraints (9), (10) is

$$
\begin{cases}
\gamma_{qi} = \dfrac{1}{\displaystyle\sum_{h=1}^{n} \left(\dfrac{\displaystyle\sum_{k=1}^{N} U_q^\beta(k)(\tilde{x}_{ki}-w_{qi})^2}{\displaystyle\sum_{k=1}^{N} U_q^\beta(k)(\tilde{x}_{kh}-w_{qi})^2} \right)^{\frac{1}{t-1}}}, \\[4mm]
U_q(k) = \dfrac{(\theta \displaystyle\sum_{i=1}^{n} (\tilde{x}_{ki}-w_{qi})^2 + (1-\theta) \displaystyle\sum_{i=1}^{n} \gamma_{qi}^t(\tilde{x}_{ki}-w_{qi})^2)^{\frac{1}{1-\beta}}}{\displaystyle\sum_{l=1}^{m} (\theta \displaystyle\sum_{i=1}^{n} (\tilde{x}_{ki}-w_{li})^2 + (1-\theta) \displaystyle\sum_{i=1}^{n} \gamma_{li}^t(\tilde{x}_{ki}-w_{li})^2)^{\frac{1}{1-\beta}}}, \\[4mm]
w_{qi} = \dfrac{\displaystyle\sum_{k=1}^{N} U_q^\beta(k)\tilde{x}_{ki}}{\displaystyle\sum_{k=1}^{N} U_q^\beta(k)}.
\end{cases}
\tag{16}
$$

Considering $\beta = t = 2$, similarly to FCM, the optimization procedure which is based on a metric of type $D^K(\tilde{x}_k, w_q)$ can be obtained from (12):

$$
\begin{cases}
\gamma_{qi} = \left(\displaystyle\sum_{h=1}^{n} \left(\dfrac{\displaystyle\sum_{k=1}^{N} U_q^2(k)(\tilde{x}_{ki}-w_{qi})^2}{\displaystyle\sum_{k=1}^{N} U_q^2(k)(\tilde{x}_{kh}-w_{qi})^2} \right) \right)^{-1}, \\[4mm]
U_q(k) = \dfrac{(\theta \displaystyle\sum_{i=1}^{n} (\tilde{x}_{ki}-w_{qi})^2 + (1-\theta) \displaystyle\sum_{i=1}^{n} \gamma_{qi}^2(\tilde{x}_{ki}-w_{qi})^2)^{-1}}{\displaystyle\sum_{l=1}^{m} (\theta \displaystyle\sum_{i=1}^{n} (\tilde{x}_{ki}-w_{li})^2 + (1-\theta) \displaystyle\sum_{i=1}^{n} \gamma_{li}^2(\tilde{x}_{ki}-w_{li})^2)^{-1}}, \\[4mm]
w_{qi} = \dfrac{\displaystyle\sum_{k=1}^{N} U_q^2(k)\tilde{x}_{ki}}{\displaystyle\sum_{k=1}^{N} U_q^2(k)}.
\end{cases}
$$

4   Experimental Results

To find out how well the proposed approach performs in comparison with well-known methods (with the conventional FCM notably), we conducted an experiment with the help of the R software. In this experimental research, an artificially generated data set was used for the schematic description of the realm under research. In our opinion, this example makes it possible to depict the algorithm's functioning in the simplest case schematically. The basic point of the practical part of the work had to do with discovering how and in which way precisely the value θ influences the general performance of the procedure.

The comparison results can be seen in Fig. 1. It can be seen from these results that the proposed approach (Fig. 1a) correctly defined centers of two clusters in the initial data set (a black circle and a square with a cross), some elements of the group 2 were erroneously attributed to group 1 (a circle with a cross) during the FCM at a similar generation stage of input data. However, given the fact that the experiments were not conducted on the same data set, and data can't be generated identical with absolute certainty that the initial data don't affect the obtained results in a given case.

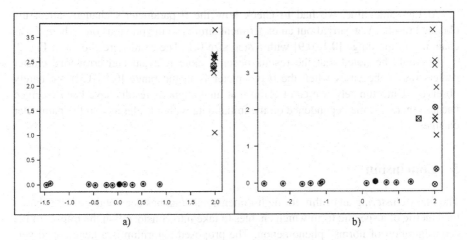

Fig. 1. Comparison results. The proposed method and FCM.

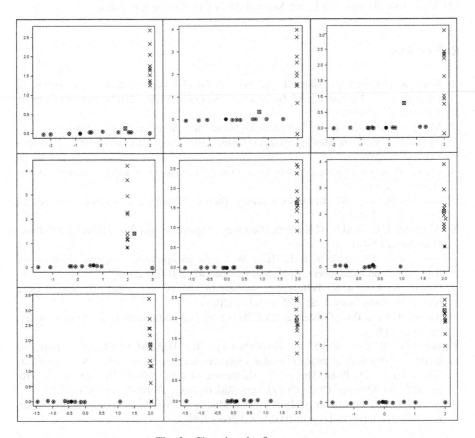

Fig. 2. Changing the θ parameter.

At the same time, we had to check how the θ parameter's changes affect the obtained results. We carried out an experiment similar to the previous one where θ was changing in the range [0.1; 0.9] with a step size 0.1. The results are shown in Fig. 2.

It should be noted that the results become more relevant and erroneous cluster centers (as in the cases when the θ parameter is in the range [0.1; 0.3]) are barely observed. Unfortunately, we can't claim that unambiguous results have been received because there's some dependence on the initial data without reference to the parameter changes.

5 Conclusion

The fuzzy clustering algorithm for high-dimensional data has been obtained. It is based on a metric of a specific form which enables to take into consideration the impact of the "concentration of norms" phenomenon. The proposed algorithm is a generalized version of several fuzzy clustering procedures.

Acknowledgment. Oleksii K. Tyshchenko carried out his investigation within the project TAČR TL01000351 provided by the National Agency of the Czech Republic.

References

1. Kruse, R., Borgelt, C., Klawonn, F., Moewes, C., Steinbrecher, M., Held, P.: Computational Intelligence. A Methodological Introduction. Springer, Berlin (2013). https://doi.org/10.1007/978-1-4471-5013-8
2. Mumford, C.L., Jain, L.C.: Computational Intelligence. Springer, Berlin (2009)
3. Aggarwal, C.C.: Data Mining. Springer, Cham (2015). https://doi.org/10.1007/978-3-319-14142-8
4. Larose, D.T.: Discovering Knowledge in Data: An Introduction to Data Mining. Wiley, Hoboken (2014)
5. Gan, G., Ma, Ch., Wu, J.: Data Clustering: Theory, Algorithms, and Application. SIAM, Philadelphia (2007)
6. Aggarwal, C.C., Reddy, C.K.: Data Clustering: Algorithms and Applications. CRC Press, Boca Raton (2014)
7. Yang, M.-S., Chang-Chien, S.-J., Hung, W.-L.: An unsupervised clustering algorithm for data on the unit hypersphere. Appl. Soft Comput. **42**, 290–313 (2016)
8. Gosain, A., Dahiya, S.: Performance analysis of various fuzzy clustering algorithms: a review. Procedia Comput. Sci. **79**, 100–111 (2016)
9. Xu, R., Wunsch, D.C.: Clustering. IEEE Press Series on Computational Intelligence. Wiley, Hoboken (2009)
10. Babichev, S., Lytvynenko, V., Korobchynskyi, M., Taiff, M.A.: Objective clustering inductive technology of gene expression sequences features. In: Kozielski, S., Mrozek, D., Kasprowski, P., Małysiak-Mrozek, B., Kostrzewa, D. (eds.) BDAS 2017. CCIS, vol. 716, pp. 359–372. Springer, Cham (2017). https://doi.org/10.1007/978-3-319-58274-0_29
11. Abonyi, J., Feil, B.: Cluster Analysis for Data Mining and System Identification. Birkhauser, Basel (2007). https://doi.org/10.1007/978-3-7643-7988-9

12. Hu, Z., Bodyanskiy, Ye.V., Tyshchenko, O.K.: A cascade deep neuro-fuzzy system for high-dimensional online possibilistic fuzzy clustering. In: Proceedings of the 11th International Scientific and Technical Conference "Computer Sciences and Information Technologies", CSIT 2016, Lviv, pp. 119–122 (2016)

13. Hu, Z., Bodyanskiy, Ye.V., Tyshchenko, O.K., Boiko, O.O.: A neuro-fuzzy Kohonen network for data stream possibilistic clustering and its online self-learning procedure. Appl. Soft Comput. J. **68**, 710–718 (2018)

14. Bodyanskiy, Ye.V., Tyshchenko, O.K., Kopaliani, D.S.: An evolving connectionist system for data stream fuzzy clustering and its online learning. Neurocomputing **262**, 41–56 (2017)

15. Kohonen, T.: Self-Organizing Maps. Springer, Berlin (1995). https://doi.org/10.1007/978-3-642-97610-0

16. Klawonn, F.: What can fuzzy cluster analysis contribute to clustering of high-dimensional data? In: Masulli, F., Pasi, G., Yager, R. (eds.) WILF 2013. LNCS (LNAI), vol. 8256, pp. 1–14. Springer, Cham (2013). https://doi.org/10.1007/978-3-319-03200-9_1

17. Bezdek, J.C.: Pattern Recognition with Fuzzy Objective Function Algorithms. Plenum Press, New York (1981)

18. Hoeppner, F., Klawonn, F., Kruse, R., Runkler, T.: Fuzzy Clustering Analysis: Methods for Classification, Data Analysis, and Image Recognition. Wiley, Chichester (1999)

19. Klawonn, F., Höppner, F.: What is fuzzy about fuzzy clustering? Understanding and improving the concept of the fuzzifier. In: R. Berthold, M., Lenz, H.-J., Bradley, E., Kruse, R., Borgelt, C. (eds.) IDA 2003. LNCS, vol. 2810, pp. 254–264. Springer, Heidelberg (2003). https://doi.org/10.1007/978-3-540-45231-7_24

20. Bezdek, J.C., Keller, J., Krishnapuram, R., Pal, N.R.: Fuzzy Models and Algorithms for Pattern Recognition and Image Processing. Springer, New York (2005)

21. Keller, A., Klawonn, F.: Fuzzy clustering with a weighting of data variables. Int. J. Uncertainty Fuzziness Knowl. Based Syst. **8**(6), 735–746 (2000)

Evolutionary Algorithms and Their Applications

Solving the Software Project Scheduling Problem with Hyper-heuristics

Joaquim de Andrade$^{(\boxtimes)}$, Leila Silva, André Britto, and Rodrigo Amaral

Federal University of Sergipe, Sao Cristovao, Sergipe, Brazil
{jjaneto,leila,andre}@dcomp.ufs.br, rodrigoamaral@gmail.com

Abstract. Search-based Software Engineering applies meta-heuristics to solve problems in the Software Engineering domain. However, to configure a meta-heuristic can be tricky and may lead to suboptimal results. We propose a hyper-heuristic (HH), GE-SPSP, to configure the Speed-Constrained Particle Swarm Optimization (SMPSO) meta-heuristic based on Grammatical Evolution (GE) to solve the Software Project Scheduling Problem. A grammar describes several parameters types and values to configure the SMPSO and the HH use it to return the best configuration set found during the search. The results are compared to conventional meta-heuristics and suggest that GE-SPSP can achieve statistically equal or better results than to the compared meta-heuristics.

Keywords: Search-based software engineering · Scheduling · Hyper-heuristic

1 Introduction

Software Engineering problems usually involve conflicting trade-off goals, such as project costs and duration. These problems may have a large number of solutions, and to explore the search space of all possible solutions is a complex task. Search-based Software Engineering (SBSE) [9] is the field of study that applies optimization algorithms to find optimal or near-optimal solutions to software engineering problems. SBSE techniques have been applied in many software engineering domains and [10] is a relevant survey about this area.

Related to the area, the Software Project Scheduling Problem (SPSP) [1] is a management problem that aims to assign employees to tasks in order to minimize project duration and costs. The scheduling task is an essential activity when establishing project planning, as bad planning is pointed out to be responsible for project failure [20].

Since SPSP optimizes two criteria, it can be modeled as a multi-objective optimization problem. For this kind of problem, SBSE techniques,

This work was financed by COPES-UFS, by CAPES - Brasil, finance code 001, and by CNPq, project number 425861/2016-3.

L. Rutkowski et al. (Eds.): ICAISC 2019, LNAI 11508, pp. 399–411, 2019.
https://doi.org/10.1007/978-3-030-20912-4_37

like meta-heuristics, can be applied in order to find feasible solutions. Vega-Velázquez *et al.* [22] present a survey showing that SPSP is mostly solved with multi-objective meta-heuristics based on Genetic Algorithm, Ant Colony Optimization, and other variants of evolutionary algorithms. The Speed-Constrained Multi-objective Swarm Particle Optimization (SMPSO) [18] is a variant of the Particle Swarm Optimization (PSO) [12] that includes, among several improvements, an external archive to store non-dominated solutions found during the search process. The SMPSO meta-heuristic has good results in many problems [5]. Despite that, we are not aware of any work that uses SMPSO for SPSP solving.

Meta-heuristics, however, are sensitive to the configuration set that is defined before its execution. The configuration set could change accordingly with the problem or the instance of the problem, and thus the software engineering must select the configuration set that maximizes the results. Nevertheless, most of the configuration sets are defined through empirical tests, but this is an exhaustive task since it consumes time for tests and computational resources.

In this direction, Hyper-heuristics (HH) [21] appears as a solution to this drawback because they can select configuration sets for SPSP solving. HH is a more general heuristics that can generate or select low-level heuristics based on some objective functions. The decision procedure is made by learning and can be categorized into two forms: online and offline. The former is done during the search, while the latter is done first in a set with training instances and its result is applied for real instances. Although SBSE is a promising field to apply HH, few approaches are addressing this research direction [8].

This work proposes an offline HH named Grammatical Evolution Hyper-Heuristic for the Software Project Scheduling Problem (GE-SPSP) for training variants of SMPSO algorithm in order to solve the SPSP. Furthermore, this paper presents an experimental set comparing the results achieved against the results of the Nondominated Sorting Genetic Algorithm II (NSGA-II) [6], the Nondominated Sorting Chemical Reaction Optimization (NCRO) [3] and the standard SMPSO.

The HH used is based on the Grammatical Evolution (GE) [19] method. This method uses a grammar to generate programs, in the context of Genetic Programming (GP) [13]. In this work, the program is the SMPSO algorithm, and the grammar defines the parameters to be used by the algorithm, like swarm size, archive type, mutation operator, among others.

We propose nine experiments to validate the proposal. To that end, the NSGA-II, the NCRO and the standard SMPSO meta-heuristics are used to confront their solutions with HH's. The NSGA-II was chosen because it is one of the most used meta-heuristics in the optimization literature and NCRO because in previous work achieved better solutions than NSGA-II for the SPSP. The results are evaluated considering the hypervolume (HV) metric [4], the Kruskal-Wallis statistical test and the Bonferroni post-hoc method and suggest that the use of hyper-heuristics is promising for generating good solutions for the SPSP.

The remainder of this paper is as follows: Sect. 2 briefly presents related works. Section 3 describes the hyper-heuristics and how they can generate SMPSO instances to find solutions for the SPSP. Section 4 details the experiments and its two phases (training and testing). Finally, Sect. 5 gives some final considerations and directions for future research.

2   Related Work

Hyper-heuristics have been used in many fields of optimization [4]. Nevertheless, in the context of SBSE, hyper-heuristics are addressed in a few works. Guizzo *et al.* [7] propose an online hyper-heuristic to solve the Integration and Test Order Problem. Their hyper-heuristic uses two different functions, the Choice Function (CF) and Multi-armed Bandit (MAB), to select the best low-level heuristic throughout the evolutionary search. To perform the selection, the authors proposed a new quality measure that takes into account the dominance concept and the number of matings in the search.

As online search has a higher computational cost, Mariani *et al.* [16] propose an offline hyper-heuristic to solve the same problem. This hyper-heuristic is based on Grammatical Evolution and achieved better results than Guizzo et al. [7].

Basgalupp *et al.* [2] designed a hyper-heuristic to produce an effort prediction tree and use instances from the real world. Their work concludes that hyper-heuristics are capable of generating decision-trees that outperform the traditional methods in the field of effort decisions.

Jia *et al.* [11] use an online hyper-heuristic to generate instances of Simulated Annealing (SA) meta-heuristic in order to solve the Combinatorial Interactional Testing (CIT). Whenever the set of tests changes, their hyper-heuristics learns the changes and creates different SA instances. Their results showed that is possible to outperform the existing results by using hyper-heuristics.

In order to obtain a good software modular structure, Kumari *et al.* [14] propose a genetic algorithm based on hyper-heuristic that selects one heuristic from a set of twelve low-level heuristics to solve the problem. The heuristics are combinations of mutation, selection and crossover operators. Their outcomes suggest that the hyper-heuristics can be used in order to achieve software with high cohesion and low coupling.

Grammatical Evolution is also used in other fields of optimization. Sabar *et al.* [21] show that, for Combinatorial Optimization Problems, GE outperforms the traditional hyper-heuristics. In this work, we show that it is also possible to achieve statistically equal or better solutions to the SPSP using hyper-heuristics that generate SMPSO instances. The results suggest that SBSE is a field that can be explored with the techniques found in the literature on hyper-heuristics.

3   Grammatical Evolution for SPSP Algorithm

Grammatical Evolution Hyper-Heuristic for the Software Project Scheduling Problem, GE-SPSP, works by generating variants of the SMPSO meta-heuristic to solve the SPSP. We propose a grammar, in BNF's form [17], that describes parameters types and values of a configuration set for the SMPSO. To produce a configuration set itself, the GE method decodes a given solution according to the grammar. The HH works by applying the evolutionary operators to the solutions, generating different configuration sets, and returning the best configuration set found during the search.

3.1   Speed-Constrained Multi-objective Particle Swarm Optimization

The SMPSO is a variant of the Multi-Objective Particle Swarm Optimization (MOPSO) meta-heuristic, proposed in Nebro et al. [18], and it is inspired on the social behavior of birds when searching for food in a group. In SMPSO, each solution is called a particle and the entire population is called a swarm. This characteristic forces the search to be influenced by the local best or the global best. In order to assure the convergence of the algorithm, SMPSO uses a velocity operator that moves each particle in the search space. However, once the velocity may become too high and cause erratic movements, SMPSO introduces a velocity restriction that prevents this event. An archive is used to maintain every non-dominated solution found during the search. The archive is bound and it is necessary to define the archive type and size. Also, SMPSO applies a mutation procedure to avoid fast convergence. In the end, the algorithm returns a set of non-dominated solutions. Thus, to configure SMPSO, four main parameters must be configured: swarm size, mutation operator, archive size and type.

3.2   The Grammar

The proposed algorithm explores the different configurations of the parameters discussed above. To do so, the combination of these parameters is written in grammar in BNF's form. Figure 1 presents the grammar of our problem. The first production, denoted by $< SMPSO >$, defines the parameters to be explored by the hyper-heuristic: swarm size, mutation operator, archive size and type.

Here, we consider swarm sizes of 50, 75, 100 and 125 as these are the most used values in the literature. The mutation operators comprise the choice of a mutation and its probability. We consider three kinds of mutations: polynomial mutation (PM), uniform (UM) and simple random (SR). As mutation can severely affect the evolutionary search, we gave the hyper-heuristic the capacity to be wider whenever good results are found; hence we defined 11 choices of probability, where N is the number of variables of the problem. The initialization rule defines whether the generated meta-heuristic will create a fully random population or will follow a parallel diversified strategy.

An archive is defined as a set that stores the best non-dominated solutions found during the search. In our grammar, its size can vary from 0, $swarmSize$, $1.5 * swarmSize$, and to $2 * swarmSize$. When the archive is full, new solutions may replace bad ones based on an established criteria. In our proposal, we have defined two strategies to maintain the solutions inside the archive: by ranking and by diversity. The ranking strategy uses information about the Pareto dominance of a solution in relation to another one (Dominance Rank, Strength or Depth) or by its fitness value. The diversity strategy establishes which solution is ordered first while the latter by its contribution to diversity when compared to the others. In case of a tie, the archive considers which one contributes more to a diversity strategy by using the crowding distance (CD), k-th nearest neighbor (KNN), adaptive grid (AG) or hypervolume contribution (HC).

```
⟨SMPSO⟩ ::= ⟨swarmSize⟩ ⟨mutationOperatorsPSO⟩ ⟨archive⟩ ⟨initialization⟩

⟨swarmSize⟩ ::= 50 | 75 | 100 | 125

⟨mutationOperatorsPSO⟩ ::= ⟨mutationOperator⟩ ⟨mutationProbability⟩

⟨mutationOperator⟩ ::= Polynomial Mutation
              | Uniform Mutation
              | Simple Random Mutation

⟨mutationProbability⟩ ::= 0.01 | 0.02 | 0.05 | 0.1 | 0.2
              | 0.5 | 0.7 | 0.8 | 0.9 | 1.0 | 1.0 / N

⟨archive⟩ ::= ⟨fitnessAssignment⟩ ⟨archiveSize⟩

⟨archiveSize⟩ ::= 0 | swarmSize | swarmSize * 1.5 | swamrSize * 2

⟨fitnessAssignment⟩ ::= ⟨rankingStrategy⟩ ⟨diversityStrategy⟩

⟨rankingStrategy⟩ ::= null | Dominance Rank | Dominance Strength
              | Dominance Depth | Raw Fitness

⟨diversityStrategy⟩ ::= null | Crowding Distance | K-th Nearest Neighbor
              | Adaptive Grid | Hypervolume Contribution

⟨initialization⟩ ::= Random | Parallel Diversified Initialization
```

Fig. 1. Grammar used in this work.

3.3   GE-SPSP Algorithm

The GE-SPSP template is shown in Algorithm 1. The GE is a Genetic Programming (GP) variant procedure that uses the grammar in Fig. 1 to guide the evolutionary search of the HH. This is done by mapping each individual X of the HH into a fully configured SMPSO. In GE, the individual X is a chromosome, which is usually represented as an integer array. To reach a fully configured SMPSO, GE keeps decoding the genes by selecting and transforming an abstract value, $i.e$ a rule, into a concrete value, a terminal. A terminal can be a parameter value or a parameter type. Every individual belonging to S is then converted to an SMPSO variant and solves the SPSP. The SPSP result is assigned to the SMPSO instance according to some metric. These are the steps executed in lines $1-3$ in Algorithm 1. Next, the HH selects the best individuals of S and apply evolutionary steps (*crossover, mutation, prune* and *duplication*) in order to generate new individuals (descendants) from the previous individuals that will lead to new SMPSO configurations. The initial steps are repeated in lines 7 and 8, and S is updated with the best individuals generated at each iteration until reaching the stopping criterion. In the end, the HH returns the configuration set that reached the best value according to the metric used.

4   Experiments

The experiments were divided into two parts. The first one is the training phase, where we executed GE-SPSP nine times in order to get nine different SMPSO configuration sets. Executing GE-SPSP more than once is necessary to create a substantial sample for the statistical validation. Since our computational resources are limited, we fixed nine executions as the maximum.

Algorithm 1. Template of the hyper-heuristic

Data: Grammar
Result: The best meta-heuristic found
1 Let S be the set of the initial population;
2 Map each individual X of S to a parameter set by using the grammar;
3 Evaluate each meta-heuristic configured according each X to the problem;
4 **while** *Stopping Criteria **not** Achieved* **do**
5   X = Select the Bests Individuals of S;
6   Apply operators in X, in the order: *crossover, mutation, prune* and *duplication*;
7   Map each individual X of S to a parameter set;
8   Evaluate each meta-heuristic configured according each X to the problem;
9   Update S with individuals of X;
10 **end**

Next, in the testing phase, each one of the nine configuration sets executed the SPSP thirty times, comparing the obtained results against each other to see the best configuration set. To validate our hypothesis, we compare the achieved results against the ones obtained by NCRO, NSGA-II and the standard SMPSO. We use the Kruskal-Wallis test to assert if there is a statistical difference between the results and the Bonferroni post-hoc test to see which groups differ. Before the training, however, we defined the SPSP instance and the metric to evaluate the meta-heuristics.

4.1   Algorithms and Parameters

The parameters for GE-SPSP were defined after empirical evaluations and are presented in Table 1. We fixed the population size to 70 individuals and the stopping criterion to 10, 000 evaluations. The other parameters were chosen to respect the characteristics of the solution. Since the individuals of the GE-SPSP are represented as integer arrays, the mutation and crossover operators must be able to work with such representations. The pruning and duplication operators are responsible for the length of the individual, by decreasing or increasing the array size, respectively. Finally, we selected the binary tournament operator for the selecting phase.

The NCRO and NSGA-II are both bio-inspired meta-heuristics. NCRO simulates the interactions and transformations of molecules inside a chemical reaction, while NSGA-II mimics the genetic mechanism. They have the same algorithm scheme with differences in the details. NCRO updates its population with four different operations and does not have a selection operator; NSGA-II uses three operators to modify the population, but both meta-heuristics use a nondominated sorting to maintain the best individuals during the search. In our experiments, both algorithms have a population of 100 individuals and stop their execution after $100,000$ evaluations. They also have the same parameters for mutation and crossover: PM $(p = 1/L)$ and simulated binary crossover (SBX), respectively. For the selection operator, NSGA-II also uses the binary tournament operator. SMPSO also have a population size of 100 individuals, a stop criterion of 250 evaluations and the CD archive with 100 individuals.

Table 1. Configuration set of GE-SPSP, NCRO and NSGA-II used in the experiments.

Parameter	GE-SPSP	NSGA-II	SMPSO	NCRO
Population	70	100	100	100
Stop criterion	$10,000$	$100,000$	250	$100,000$
Mutation	Integer, $p = 0.01$	PM, $p = 1/L$	PM, $p = 1/L$	PM, $p = 1/L$
Crossover	Single point	SBX, $p = 0.9, \lambda = 20$	–	SBX, $p = 0.9, \lambda = 20$
Selection	Binary tournament	Binary tournament	–	–
Pruning	$p = 0.01$, $index = 10$	–	–	–
Duplication	$p = 0.01$	–	–	–
Kinect energy	–	–	–	$10,000$
Collision type	–	–	–	0.5
Kinect energy loss	–	–	–	0.2
Synthesis thres.	–	–	–	0.0
Decomp. thres.	–	–	–	0.0
Archive type/Size	–	–	CD, 100	–

4.2 SPSP Instance

The SPSP instance represents one possible scenario in a software project. In summary, an instance contains a set of employees and a set of tasks, as described in [1]. Luna *et al.* [15] present several instances for SPSP. We select the one having sixteen tasks and eight employees. This choice was influenced by our computational resources, as the running time is influenced by the size of the set of employees/tasks.

4.3 Metrics

To assert the quality of the solutions generated by each multi-objective meta-heuristic, we used the hypervolume quality indicator [4]. This metric considers both convergence and diversity of the Pareto front (PF) returned by the algorithm in relation to a reference point in the objective space. As the SPSP have two objectives function within the interval $[0, 1]$, our nadir point is $(1, 1)$.

4.4 Training Phase

After running GE-SPSP nine times, nine different configuration sets were formed. To return the best configuration set found during the search, GE-SPSP tested 10,000 other configuration sets. The best configuration set of each execution is presented in Table 2. By analyzing them, we can see that they do not have many differences from each other; moreover, GE-SPSP converges at the end of each execution. It might be that these combination sets and its variations can actually be the best configurations for the SPSP. The differences are concentrated in the swarm size, iterations, mutation, and initialization. The major difference between the archive types is that all configuration sets from ALG_0 to ALG_7 use the AG archive, while the CD archive is used in ALG_8.

Table 2. Configuration set generated at each execution of the training.

Instance	Population	Iterations	Mutation	Archive	Initialization
ALG_0	125	200	PM, $p = 0.1$	AG, 125	Aleatory
ALG_1	125	200	SR, $p = 0.5$	AG, 150	Aleatory
ALG_2	100	250	PM, $p = 0.05$	AG, 120	Parallel diversified
ALG_3	100	250	UM, $p = 0.1$	AG, 120	Aleatory
ALG_4	125	200	PM, $p = 0.7$	AG, 150	Aleatory
ALG_5	125	200	PM, $p = 0.1$	AG, 150	Aleatory
ALG_6	100	250	PM, $p = 0.1$	AG, 100	Aleatory
ALG_7	125	200	PM, $p = 0.01$	AG, 120	Parallel diversified
ALG_8	100	250	PM, $p = 1/L$	CD, 125	Aleatory

4.5 Testing Phase

In the testing phase, each meta-heuristic used in this work was independently executed thirty times. We obtained one Pareto front for each execution for each meta-heuristic. In the end, each meta-heuristic had its thirty fronts merged, and the repeated points or the dominated ones were excluded. Therefore, a front of a meta-heuristic is composed of the bests points found throughout the search and it is called PF_{know}. The true Pareto front for the SPSP is not known.

Due to legibility reasons, in Fig. 2 we present only the PF_{know} of ALG_8 and ALG_4, the best and worse SMPSO generated, respectively. In addition, we also include the PF_{know} of NCRO, NSGA-II and the original SMPSO. The PF_{know} is in the form of a Cartesian plane since the objectives are represented in each axis. Since SPSP is a minimization problem, solutions that are closer to the origin of the axes are classified as the best ones.

The PF_{know} of ALG_8 is the one with more diversification in its solutions, in terms of the project cost. It achieves solutions with the project cost varying between $[1.59 \times 10^6, 1.75 \times 10^6]$. On the other hand, ALG_4 could not generate solutions with project cost less than 1.63×10^6. Its PF_{know} is composed of fewer points than the others in the graphic. We can observe that ALG_8 is indeed the best metaheuristic, in terms of the hypervolume. Such result is presented in Table 3b, showing that ALG_8 achieved a HV value of 0.923, while the others generated metaheuristics varied within the interval $[0.65, 0.70]$. The biggest difference between the configuration sets is the archive type. ALG_8 uses the Crowding Archive, that has the property of maintaining the divergence between the solutions. This single difference enhances the performance, maximizing the HV value.

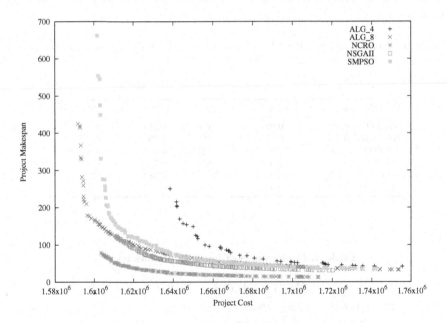

Fig. 2. PF_{know} generated by ALG_4, ALG_8, NCRO, NSGA-II and SMPSO.

4.6   Comparison Against Other Meta-Heuristics

When comparing with the other meta-heuristics, we observe that NCRO and NSGA-II have more success on minimizing the project makespan. Considering

Fig. 2, we can see that their performance was similar, and this is related to both capability of convergence. The PF_{know} of NCRO does not have any solution with makespan above 100, dominating almost all PF_{know} of ALG_4, for example. Specifically to NCRO, our choice of configuration favored the mutation operator, and thus this has implied in a better exploitation of the local space. Coello *et al.* [5] details the reasons for the convergence of NSGA-II. Table 3b shows that NCRO and NSGA-II achieved a HV of 0.885 and 0.817, respectively.

The SMPSO had a similar performance in relation to ALG_8, although did not achieve the same spreadness. The former achieves a HV of 0.830 while the last a HV of 0.923. By analyzing the PF_{know} of SMPSO and ALG_8, it is difficult to see differences within the region of project cost between the interval $[1.64 \times 10^6; 1.74 \times 10^6]$, but as the cost is minimized, ALG_8 shows more ability to explore the search area. The differences between these two metaheuristics are in the details. ALG_8 can handle better the mutation and thus can generate solutions with lower costs. It also has a maximum archive capacity. The SMPSO has a maximum of 100 solutions, while ALG_8 can store 125 solutions. The fact that these two metaheuristics achieve the bests results in the experiments raises the hypothesis that, at least using the proposed grammar in this work, the configuration set of ALG_8 is the one that probably generates more nondominated solutions.

Table 3. Average and Standard Deviation achieved by each algorithm in the experiments.

(a)			(b)		
Algorithm	Average	Standard Deviation	Algorithm	Average	Standard Deviation
NCRO	0.885	0.02	ALG_3	0.680	0.05
NSGA-II	0.817	0.02	ALG_4	0.650	0.05
SMPSO	0.830	0.04	ALG_5	0.661	0.05
ALG_0	0.677	0.05	ALG_6	0.704	0.04
ALG_1	0.68	0.05	ALG_7	0.684	0.54
ALG_2	0.691	0.04	ALG_8	0.923	0.02

Table 4. Bonferroni post-hoc test p-values results.

	ALG_4	ALG_8	NCRO	NSGA-II
ALG_8	$< 2e-16$	–	–	–
NCRO	$< 2e-16$	$7.7e-06$	–	–
NSGA-II	$2.1e-14$	$< 2e-16$	$< 2e-16$	–
SMPSO	$< 2e-16$	$< 2e-16$	$8.5e-11$	0.26

To validate our work, we perform the Kruskal-Wallis test. With a significance level of 0.05, the test stated that there is a significant difference between the metaheuristics results. We also performed the Bonferroni post-hoc test (Table 4) to assess if there are differences between the metaheuristics of Fig. 2. Indeed, ALG_8 produced a statistical difference and better PF_{know} than the others meta-heuristics.

There are some points to consider about GE-SPSP. It takes eight executions to generate a configuration set as ALG_8, that outperforms the results from conventional meta-heuristics as NSGA-II and NCRO. Sometimes, GE-SPSP produced bad configurations as ALG_4 and ALG_5 when compared in the same scenario. In the real world, it could be the scenario where the software engineer might urgently need a solution and the GE-SPSP would return a bad configuration set. Another point to consider is the execution time. GE-SPSP was implemented in Java programming language and required, on average, 20 h of execution to give a result with a computer configured with 16 GB of DDR3 RAM and Intel Xeon Silver 4108 processor over an Ubuntu 16.08. This is a drawback, as this time could not be available to the project manager. However, we believe that this required time can be reduced with improvements in code and design optimizations. Nevertheless, GE-SPSP is still a viable approach, once that ALG_8 outperforms the results and even the worst solutions are not strictly dominated by any other meta-heuristic used in this experiments.

The SPSP execution time for a single run of NCRO, NSGA-II and SMPSO required, on average, no more than one minute. Thus, to execute all 30 runs, we had an average of 30 min per meta-heuristic. All meta-heuristics were also implemented in Java programming language using the jMetal framework[1].

5   Conclusions

This work investigated the SPSP problem by using a GE hyper-heuristic that generates SMPSOs configuration sets that are applied to solve the SPSP. We have compared these solutions with solutions of NCRO, NSGA-II, and the standard SMPSO heuristics. The results show that the hyper-heuristic can generate configurations that it is statistically equal or better than the compared ones.

The results highlighted the impact that the configuration set can have on the performance of the meta-heuristic. The SMPSOs variants generated by the hyper-heuristic are similar in several aspects. However, the main differential of the configuration that outperforms the existing results is the archive type. Hence, these experiments suggest that archives play a central role in the final result and thus, must be selected carefully.

As future work, we intend to improve the GE-SPSP in order to reduce the execution time. We also intend to model GE-SPSP as a framework in order to work with any kind of meta-heuristic, such as PAES or NSGA-II. We expect that this approach would increase the variability of the results. An immediate future

---

[1] jMetal is a Java-based framework for multi-objective optimization and it is available in https://github.com/jMetal/jMetal.

work is to investigate more SPSP instances in order to consolidate these preliminary results. The grammar could also be expanded, adding more parameters such as different type of archives to be searched.

References

1. Alba, E., Chicano, F.: Software project management with gas. Inf. Sci. **177**, 2380–2401 (2007)
2. Basgalupp, M.P., Barros, R.C., da Silva, T.S., de Carvalho, A.C.: Software effort prediction: a hyper-heuristic decision-tree based approach. In: Proceedings of the 28th Annual ACM Symposium on Applied Computing, pp. 1109–1116. ACM (2013)
3. Bechikh, S., Chaabani, A., Said, L.B.: An efficient chemical reaction optimization algorithm for multiobjective optimization. IEEE Trans. Evol. Comput. **45**(10), 2051–2064 (2015)
4. Burke, E.K., et al.: Hyper-heuristics: a survey of the state of the art. J. Oper. Res. Soc. **64**(12), 1695–1724 (2013)
5. Coello, C.A.C., Lamont, G.B., Veldhuizen, D.A.V.: Evolutionary Algorithms for Solving Multi-Objective Problems. Genetic and Evolutionary Computation, 2nd edn. Springer, US (2007). https://doi.org/10.1007/978-0-387-36797-2
6. Deb, K., Pratap, A., Argawal, S., Meyarivan, T.: A fast and elitist multiobjective genetic algorithm: NSGA-II. IEEE Trans. Evol. Comput. **6**(2), 182–197 (2002)
7. Guizzo, G., Fritsche, G.M., Vergilio, S.R., Pozo, A.T.R.: A hyper-heuristic for the multi-objective integration and test order problem. In: Proceedings of the 2015 Annual Conference on Genetic and Evolutionary Computation, pp. 1343–1350. ACM (2015)
8. Harman, M., Burke, E., Clark, J., Yao, X.: Dynamic adaptive search based software engineering. In: Proceedings of the ACM-IEEE International Symposium on Empirical Software Engineering and Measurement, pp. 1–8. ACM (2012)
9. Harman, M., Jones, B.F.: Search-based software engineering. Inf. Softw. Technol. **43**(14), 833–839 (2001)
10. Harman, M., Mansouri, S.A., Zhang, Y.: Search-based software engineering: trends, techniques and applications. ACM Comput. Surv. (CSUR) **45**(1), 11 (2012)
11. Jia, Y., Cohen, M.B., Harman, M., Petke, J.: Learning combinatorial interaction test generation strategies using hyperheuristic search. In: Proceedings of the 37th International Conference on Software Engineering, vol. 1, pp. 540–550. IEEE Press (2015)
12. Kennedy, J., Eberhart, R.: Particle swarm optimization. In: Neural Networks, 1995. Proceedings., IEEE International Conference on Neural Networks, vol. 6, December 1995
13. Koza, J.: Genetic Programming: On the Programming of Computers by Means of Natural Selection. Complex Adaptive Systems, 1st edn. A Bradford Book, Massachusetts (1992)
14. Kumari, A.C., Srinivas, K., Gupta, M.: Software module clustering using a hyper-heuristic based multi-objective genetic algorithm. In: Advance Computing Conference (IACC), 2013 IEEE 3rd International, pp. 813–818. IEEE (2013)
15. Luna, F., González-Álvarez, D.L., Chicano, F., Vega-Rodríguez, M.A.: The software project scheduling problem: a scalability analysis of multi-objective metaheuristics. Appl. Soft Comput. J. **15**, 136–148 (2014)

16. Mariani, T., Guizzo, G., Vergilio, S.R., Pozo, A.T.: Grammatical evolution for the multi-objective integration and test order problem. In: Proceedings of the Genetic and Evolutionary Computation Conference 2016, pp. 1069–1076. ACM (2016)

17. Naur, P., et al.: Revised report on the algorithmic language Algol 60. In: O'Hearn, P.W., Tennent, R.D. (eds.) ALGOL-like Languages. Progress in Theoretical Computer Science, pp. 19–49. Springer, Boston (1997). https://doi.org/10.1007/978-1-4612-4118-8_2

18. Nebro, A.J., Durillo, J.J., Garcia-Nieto, J., Coello, C.C., Luna, F., Alba, E.: SMPSO: a new PSO-based metaheuristic for multi-objective optimization. In: 2009 IEEE Symposium on Computational Intelligence in Multi-Criteria Decision-Making(MCDM), pp. 66–73. IEEE (2009)

19. O'Neill, M., Ryan, C.: Grammatical evolution. IEEE Trans. Evol. Comput. **5**(4), 349–358 (2001)

20. Project Management Institute: Pulse of the Profession (2017). Report

21. Sabar, N.R., Ayob, M., Kendall, G., Qu, R.: Grammatical evolution hyper-heuristic for combinatorial optimization problems. Strategies **3**, 4 (2012)

22. Vega-Velázquez, M.Á., García-Nájera, A., Cervantes, H.: A survey on the software project scheduling problem. Int. J. Prod. Econ. **202**, 145–161 (2018)

Influence of Social Coefficient
on Swarm Motion

Bożena Borowska[(✉)]

Institute of Information Technology, Lodz University of Technology,
Wólczańska 215, 90-924 Łódź, Poland
bozena.borowska@p.lodz.pl

Abstract. This paper presents an improved effective particle swarm optimization algorithm named SCPSO. In SCPSO, in order to overcome disadvantages connected with premature convergence, a new approach associated with the social coefficient is included. Instead of random selected social coefficients, the author has proposed dynamically changing coefficients affected by experience of particles. The presented method was tested on a set of benchmark functions and the results were compared with those obtained through MPSO-TVAC, standard PSO (SPSO) and DPSO. The simulation results indicate that SCPSO is an effective optimization method.

Keywords: Optimization · Particle swarm optimization ·
Acceleration coefficient · Improved particle swarm optimization

1 Introduction

Particle swarm optimization (PSO) is a method modeled on the behavior of the swarm of insects in their natural environment. It was developed by Kennedy and Eberhart in 1995 [1–3] and nowadays has been successfully applied in many areas of science and engineering connected with optimization [4–10]. However, likewise other evolutionary optimization methods, PSO can experience some problems related to the convergence speed and escaping from a local optima [11]. Important parameters that affect the effectiveness of PSO are acceleration coefficients called cognitive and social coefficients. The cognitive coefficient affects local search [12] whereas the social coefficient maintains the right velocity and direction of global search. A fine tuning social coefficient can help overcome disadvantages connected with premature convergence and improve the efficiency of PSO.

Many various approaches at the right choice of coefficients have been studied. Eberhart and Kenedy [13] recommended a fixed value of the acceleration coefficient. In their opinion, both social and cognitive coefficients should be the same and equal to 2.0. Ozcan [14] and Clerc [15] in their research agreed that the coefficients should be the same but proved they should rather be equal to 1.494 what results in faster convergence. According to Venter and Sobieszczański [16], the algorithm performs better when coefficients are different and propose to applied a small cognitive coefficient ($c_1 = 1.5$) and a large social coefficient ($c_2 = 2.5$). A different approach has been proposed by Ratnaweera et al. [17]. The authors examined the efficiency of a self-organizing PSO

© Springer Nature Switzerland AG 2019
L. Rutkowski et al. (Eds.): ICAISC 2019, LNAI 11508, pp. 412–420, 2019.
https://doi.org/10.1007/978-3-030-20912-4_38

with time-varying acceleration coefficients. They concluded that the PSO performance can be greatly improved by using a simultaneously decreasing cognitive coefficient and an increasing social coefficient. Hierarchical PSO with jumping time-varying acceleration coefficients for real-world optimization was proposed by Ghasemi et al. [18]. The particle swarm optimization with time varying acceleration coefficients were also explored in [19–22]. A different approach based on the nonlinear acceleration coefficient affected by the algorithm performance was recommended by Borowska [23]. According to Mehmod et al. [24] algorithm PSO performs faster with fitness-based acceleration coefficients. PSO based on self-adaptation acceleration coefficient strategy was suggested by Guo and Chen [25]. A new model on social coefficient was presented by Cai et al. [26]. In order not to lose some useful information inside the swarm, they proposed to use the dispersed social coefficient with an information index about the differences of particles. Additionally, to provide a diversity of the particles, a mutation strategy was also introduced. A novel particle swarm concept based on the idea of two types of agents in the swarm with adaptive acceleration coefficients were considered by Ardizzon et al. [27].

This paper presents an improved effective particle swarm optimization algorithm named SCPSO. In SCPSO, a new approach connected with the social coefficient is proposed in order to better determine the velocity value and search direction of the particles and, consequently, to improve the convergence speed as well as to find a better solution. The presented method was tested on a set of benchmark functions and the results were compared with those obtained through MPSO-TVAC with a time-varying acceleration coefficient [17], the standard PSO (SPSO) and DPSO with the dispersed strategy [26]. The simulation results indicate that SCPSO is an effective optimization method.

2 The Standard PSO Method

In the PSO method, the optimization process is based on the behavior of the swarm of individuals. In practice, a swarm represents a set of particles each of which is a point in the coordinate system that possess a position represented by a vector $X_i = (x_{i1}, x_{i2}, ..., x_{iD})$ and a velocity represented by a vector $V_i = (v_{i1}, v_{i2}, ..., v_{iD})$. In the first step of the algorithm, both the position and velocity of each particle are randomly generated. In subsequent iterations, their positions and velocities in the search space are updated according to the formula:

$$V_i = wV_i + c_1 r_1 (pbest_i - X_i) + c_2 r_2 (gbest - X_i) \tag{1}$$

$$X_i = X_i + V_i \tag{2}$$

where the inertia weight w controls the impact of previously found velocity of particle on its current velocity. Factors c_1 and c_2 are cognitive and social acceleration coefficients, respectively. They decide how much the particles are influenced by their best found positions (*pbest*) as well as by the best position found by the swarm (*gbest*). The variables r_1 and r_2 are random real numbers selected between 0 and 1. In each iteration, the locations of the particles are evaluated based on the objective function. The equation of the objective function depends on an optimization problem. Based on the assessment, each particle keeps its knowledge about the best position that has found so far and the highest quality particle is selected and recorded in the swarm. This knowledge is updated in each step of the algorithm. In this way particles move in the search space towards the optimum.

3 The SCPSO Strategy

The proposed SCPSO is a new variant of the PSO algorithm in which the new approach connected with the social acceleration coefficient has been introduced. In the original PSO, to find an optimal value, particles follow two best values: the best position found by the particle itself and the best value achieved by the swarm. The direction and rate of particle speed are affected by the acceleration coefficients, that are the real numbers, the same in a whole swarm and randomly selected between 0 and 1. It implies that some information connected with swarm behaviours can be lost or not taken into account. Owing to this, a new approach for calculating the social coefficient has been introduced. The value of this coefficient is not constant but is changing dynamically as a function of the maximal and minimal fitness of the particles. It also depends on the current and total numbers of iterations. In each iteration, a different social coefficient is established. The equations describing this relationship are as follows:

$$c_2 = c_2 + ((f_{min}/f_{max})k^{-1})/iter_{max} \tag{3}$$

$$V_i = wV_i + c_1r_1(pbest_i - X_i) + c_2r_2(gbest - X_i) \tag{4}$$

where a parameter k determines the current number of iterations, f_{min} and f_{max} are the values of maximal and minimal fitness in the current iteration, respectively, $iter_{max}$ describes the maximal number of iterations. To secure the diversity of the particles and help omit local optima, the mutation operator is applied. The proposed approach helps maintain the right velocity values and search direction of the particles and improves the convergence speed.

4 Simulation Results

The presented SCPSO method was tested on the benchmark functions described in Table 1. The results of these tests were compared with the simulation results of the dispersed particle swarm optimization (DPSO) [17], the standard PSO and the modified version (MPSO-TVAC) with a time-varying accelerator coefficient [26].

For all tested functions, the applied population consisted of 100 particles with four different dimension sizes $D = 30, 50, 100$ and 200, respectively. The inertia weight was linearly decreasing from 0.9 to 0.4. All settings (the acceleration coefficients and their values) regarding the MPSO-TVAC and DPSO were adopted from Ratnawera [17] and Cai [26], respectively. For the modified MPSO-TVAC, c_1 coefficient is decreasing from 2.5 to 0.5. The value of c_2 coefficient is increasing from 0.5 to 2.5. In the DPSO algorithm, c_1 and c_{up} coefficients are equal to 2.0 while the value of c_{low} coefficient is set to 1.0. Detailed settings of the parameter values of all tested methods were collected in Table 2. The details of MPSO-TVAC and DPSO used for comparison can be found in [17] and [26], respectively. For each case, the simulations were run 20 times. The maximum number of iterations depends on the dimension and was equal to 1500 for 30 dimensions, 2500 for 50 dimensions, 5000 for 100 dimensions, and 10000 for 200 dimensions, respectively.

Table 1. Optimization test functions

Function	Formula	Minimum	Range of x
Sphere	$f_1 = \sum_{i=1}^{n} x_i^2$	0	$(-100, 100)$
Schwefel	$f_3 = \sum_{i=1}^{n} -x_i \sin\left(\sqrt{|x_i|}\right)$	420.9687	$(-500, 500)$
Ackley	$f_4 = -20\exp\left(-0.2\sqrt{\frac{1}{n}\sum_{i=1}^{n} x_i^2}\right) - \exp\left(\frac{1}{n}\sum_{i=1}^{n}\cos(2\pi x_i)\right) + 20 + e$	0	$(-32, 32)$
Rastrigin	$f_5 = \sum_{i=1}^{n} \left(x_i^2 - 10\cos(2\pi x_i) + 10\right)$	0	$(-5.12, 5.12)$
Brown	$f_6 = \sum_{i=1}^{n-1} \left[\left(x_i^2\right)^{\left(x_{i+1}^2 + 1\right)} + \left(x_{i+1}^2\right)^{\left(x_i^2 + 1\right)} \right]$	0	$(-1, 4)$
Zakharov	$f_7 = -\sum_{i=1}^{n} x_i + \left(\sum_{i=1}^{n}\frac{i}{2}x_i\right)^2 + \left(\sum_{i=1}^{n}\frac{i}{2}x_i\right)^4$	0	$(-10, 10)$
Penalized	$f_8 = \frac{\pi}{n}\left\{10\sin^2(\pi x_1) + \sum_{i=1}^{n-1}(x_i - 1)^2[1 + 10\sin^2(\pi x_{i+1})]\right.$ $\left. + (x_n - 1)^2\right\} + \sum_{i=1}^{n} u(x_i, 10, 100, 4),$ $u(z, a, k, m) = \begin{cases} k(z-a)^m, & z > a, \\ 0, & -a \leq z \leq a, \\ k(-z-a)^m, & z < -a. \end{cases}$	0	$(-50, 50)$

The exemplary results of the simulations are shown in Tables 3, 4, 5, 6 and 7. The presented values have been averaged over 20 trials.

The results of the performed simulations show that the SCPSO algorithm with the proposed approach achieves superior optimization performance over the remaining tested algorithms. In almost all considered cases, the average function values found by the SCPSO algorithm were lower than those achieved by the remaining tested methods. The mean values of Rastrigin, Brown and Schwefel problems achieved by the SCPSO are lower, despite higher (in most cases) standard deviations. For Ackley function, in almost all cases (except the case with 30 dimension) the mean values achieved by SCPSO were lower than those achieved by the other algorithms. The standard deviations were also lower, which indicates greater stability of SCPSO. For 30 dimensions, the outcomes found by SCPSO were a bit worse than the mean values found by MPSO-TVAC but better than the results achieved by DPSO and SPSO.

The proposed approach extends the adaptive capability of the particles and improves their search direction. The mutation strategy helps SCPSO maintain diversity between particles in the search space and facilitates the avoidance of the overcome premature convergence problem.

The increase in the number of particles (with the same dimension) resulted in faster convergence of the algorithms and allowed to find better optimal values. In turn, the decrease in the number of particles in the swarm caused the increase in dispersion of the results, and deterioration of the results.

Table 2. Parameter values of algorithms.

Parameter	SPSO	MPSO-TVAC	DPSO	SCPSO
w	0.9-0.4	0.9-0.4	0.9-0.4	0.6-0.4
c_1	2.0	2.5-0.5	2.0	1.7
c_2	2.0	0.5-2.5	–	Dynamically changing
c_{up}	–	–	2.0	–
c_{low}	–	–	1.0	–
r_1	[0, 1]	[0, 1]	[0, 1]	[0, 1]
r_2	[0, 1]	[0, 1]	[0, 1]	[0, 1]
D	30, 50, 100, 200	30, 50, 100, 200	30, 50, 100, 200	30, 50, 100, 200

Table 3. Performance of the MPSO-TVAC, DPSO, SPSO and SCWPSO algorithms for Schwefel 2.26 function.

Dimension	Algorithm	Mean value	Standard dev.
30	SPSO	−6.72E+003	1.02E+003
	MPSO-TVAC	−6.62E+003	6.15E+002
	DPSO	−8.58E+003	4.63E+002
	SCPSO	**−8.61E+003**	4.55e+002
50	SPSO	−1.01E+004	1.32E+003
	MPSO-TVAC	−9.77E+003	7.92E+002
	DPSO	−1.38E+004	7.35E+002
	SCPSO	**−9.76E+005**	7.43E+002
100	SPSO	−1.81E+004	2.20E+003
	MPSO-TVAC	−1.79E+004	1.51E+003
	DPSO	−2.72E+004	1.19E+003
	SCPSO	**−3.01E+004**	1.32E+003
200	SPSO	−3.13E+004	4.21E+003
	MPSO-TVAC	−4.02E+004	4.36E+003
	DPSO	−5.51E+004	1.99E+003
	SCPSO	**−5.62E+004**	2.47E+003

Table 4. Performance of the MPSO-TVAC, DPSO, SPSO and SCPSO algorithms for Rastrigin function.

Dimension	Algorithm	Mean value	Standard dev.
30	SPSO	1.99E+001	5.17E+000
	MPSO-TVAC	1.60E+001	4.06E+000
	DPSO	6.40E+000	5.07E+000
	SCPSO	**6.08E+000**	5.13E+000
50	SPSO	3.99E+001	7.93E+000
	MPSO-TVAC	3.64E+001	6.52E+000
	DPSO	1.53E+001	5.58E+000
	SCPSO	**1.37E+001**	6.32E+000
100	SPSO	9.37E+001	9.96E+000
	MPSO-TVAC	8.81E+001	9.12E+000
	DPSO	**4.14E+001**	7.33E+000
	SCPSO	4.20E+001	7.86E+000
200	SPSO	2.23E+002	1.74E+001
	MPSO-TVAC	1.94E+002	3.08E+001
	DPSO	9.98E+001	1.14E+001
	SCPSO	**9.96E+001**	1.57E+001

Table 5. Performance of the MPSO-TVAC, DPSO, SPSO and SCPSO algorithms for Ackley function.

Dimension	Algorithm	Mean value	Standard dev.
30	SPSO	7.59E–006	1.04E–005
	MPSO-TVAC	**6.51E–014**	8.53E–014
	DPSO	4.78E–011	9.15E–011
	SCPSO	4.25E–012	7.89E–012
50	SPSO	1.70E–004	1.28E–004
	MPSO-TVAC	9.95E–005	1.73E–004
	DPSO	1.58E–008	1.78E–008
	SCPSO	**1.18E–009**	1.64E–008
100	SPSO	3.31E–001	5.01E–001
	MPSO-TVAC	4.69E–001	1.91E–001
	DPSO	3.68E–007	1.63E–007
	SCPSO	**3.27E–008**	1.85E–007
200	SPSO	2.13E–000	2.19E–001
	MPSO-TVAC	6.94E–001	4.08E–001
	DPSO	9.49E–007	4.07E–007
	SCPSO	**9.22E–008**	4.63E–007

Table 6. Performance of the MPSO-TVAC, DPSO, SPSO and SCPSO algorithms for Brown function.

Dimension	Algorithm	Mean value	Standard dev.
30	SPSO	8.79E+010	2.96E+005
	MPSO-TVAC	1.60E+001	4.06E+000
	DPSO	6.40E+000	5.07E+000
	SCPSO	**6.08E+000**	5.13E+000
50	SPSO	1.06E+004	1.03E+002
	MPSO-TVAC	3.64E+001	6.52E+000
	DPSO	1.53E+001	5.58E+000
	SCPSO	**1.37E+001**	6.32E+000
100	SPSO	6.14E+007	2.48E+003
	MPSO-TVAC	7.34E+005	9.12E+000
	DPSO	4.51E+003	7.33E+000
	SCPSO	**4.23E+002**	7.86E+000
200	SPSO	8.73E+012	1.74E+010
	MPSO-TVAC	6.91E+010	3.26E+009
	DPSO	5.34E+009	2.14E+007
	SCPSO	**4.89E+009**	3.48E+007

Table 7. Performance of the MPSO-TVAC, DPSO, SPSO and SCPSO algorithms for Zakharov function.

Dimension	Algorithm	Mean value	Standard dev.
30	SPSO	5.42E+002	1.04E–005
	MPSO-TVAC	5.03E–004	3.67E–003
	DPSO	4.11E–005	3.45E–003
	SCPSO	**3.75E–005**	3.09E–003
50	SPSO	1.53E+003	3.91E+001
	MPSO-TVAC	7.32E–001	8.57E–002
	DPSO	6.59E–002	7.88E–003
	SCPSO	**6.17E–002**	5.69E–003
100	SPSO	7.48E+004	2.73E+002
	MPSO-TVAC	6.65E+003	5.26E+002
	DPSO	5.73E+002	3.84E+002
	SCPSO	**4.51E+002**	2.77E+002
200	SPSO	7.19E+005	8.47E+003
	MPSO-TVAC	6.84E+004	4.53E+002
	DPSO	7.16E+003	5.02E+002
	SCPSO	**6.03E+003**	4.54E+002

5 Summary

In this paper, a novel version of particle swarm optimization algorithm called SCPSO has been implemented. The changes are connected with social cooperation and movement of the particles in the search space and has been introduced to improve the convergence speed and to find a better quality solution. The influence of the introduced changes on a swarm motion and performance of the SCPSO algorithm was studied on a set of known benchmark functions.

The results of the described investigations were compared with those obtained through MPSO-TVAC with time-varying accelerator coefficient, the standard PSO and the dispersed particle swarm optimization (DPSO). The proposed strategy improved the algorithm performance. The new algorithm was more effective over MPSO-TVAC, SPSO and DPSO in almost all cases.

References

1. Kennedy, J., Eberhart, R.C.: Particle swarm optimization. In: IEEE International Conference on Neural Networks, Perth, Australia, pp. 1942–1948 (1995)
2. Kennedy, J., Eberhart, R.C., Shi, Y.: Swarm Intelligence. Morgan Kaufmann Publishers, San Francisco (2001)
3. Robinson, J., Rahmat-Samii, Y.: Particle swarm optimization in electromagnetics. IEEE Trans. Antennas Propag. **52**, 397–407 (2004)
4. Guedria, N.B.: Improved accelerated PSO algorithm for mechanical engineering optimization problems. Appl. Soft Comput. **40**, 455–467 (2016)
5. Dolatshahi-Zand, A., Khalili-Damghani, K.: Design of SCADA water resource management control center by a bi-objective redundancy allocation problem and particle swarm optimization. Reliab. Eng. Syst. Saf. **133**, 11–21 (2015)
6. Mazhoud, I., Hadj-Hamou, K., Bigeon, J., Joyeux, P.: Particle swarm optimization for solving engineering problems: a new constraint-handling mechanism. Eng. Appl. Artif. Intell. **26**, 1263–1273 (2013)
7. Yildiz, A.R., Solanki, K.N.: Multi-objective optimization of vehicle crashworthiness using a new particle swarm based approach. Int. J. Adv. Manuf. Technol. **59**, 367–376 (2012)
8. Hajforoosh, S., Masoum, M.A.S., Islam, S.M.: Real-time charging coordination of plug-in electric vehicles based on hybrid fuzzy discrete particle swarm optimization. Electr. Power Syst. Res. **128**, 19–29 (2015)
9. Yadav, R.D.S., Gupta, H.P.: Optimization studies of fuel loading pattern for a typical Pressurized Water Reactor (PWR) using particle swarm method. Ann. Nucl. Energy **38**, 2086–2095 (2011)
10. Puchala D., Stokfiszewski K., Yatsymirskyy M., Szczepaniak B.: Effectiveness of fast Fourier transform implementations on GPU and CPU. In: Proceedings of the 16th International Conference on Computational Problems of Electrical Engineering (CPEE), Ukraine, pp. 162–164 (2015)
11. Shi, Y., Eberhart, R.C.: Empirical study of particle swarm optimization. In: Proceedings of the Congress on Evolutionary Computation, vol. 3, pp. 1945–1950 (1999)
12. Shi, Y., Eberhart, R.C.: Parameter selection in particle swarm optimization. In: Porto, V.W., Saravanan, N., Waagen, D., Eiben, A.E. (eds.) EP 1998. LNCS, vol. 1447, pp. 591–600. Springer, Heidelberg (1998). https://doi.org/10.1007/BFb0040810

13. Eberhart, R.C., Kennedy, J.: A new optimizer using particle swarm theory. In: Proceedings of the 6th International Symposium on Micro Machine and Human Science, Japan, pp. 39–43 (1995)
14. Ozcan, E., Mohan, C.K.: Particle swarm optimization: surfing the waves. In: Proceedings of IEEE Congress on Evolutionary Computation, pp. 1944–1999 (1999)
15. Clerc, M.: The swarm and the queen: towards a deterministic and adaptive particle swarm optimization. In: Proceedings of ICEC, Washington, DC, pp. 1951–1957 (1999)
16. Venter, G., Sobieszczanski-Sobieski, J.: Particle swarm optimization. In: Proceedings of 43rd AIAA/ASME/ASCE/AHS/ASC Structure, Structure Dynamics and Materials Conference, pp. 22–25 (2002)
17. Ratnaweera, A., Halgamuge, S.K., Watson, H.C.: Self-organizing hierarchical particle swarm optimizer with time-varying acceleration coefficients. IEEE Trans. Evol. Comput. 8(3), 240–255 (2004)
18. Ghasemi, M., Aghaei, J., Hadipour, M.: New self-organising hierarchical PSO with jumping time-varying acceleration coefficients. Electron. Lett. 53, 1360–1362 (2017)
19. Chaturvedi, K.T., Pandit, M., Srivastava, L.: Particle swarm optimization with time varying acceleration coefficients for non-convex economic power dispatch. Electr. Power Energy Syst. 31, 249–257 (2009)
20. Mohammadi-Ivatloo, B., Moradi-Dalvand, M., Rabiee, A.: Combined heat and power economic dispatch problem solution using particle swarm optimization with time varying acceleration coefficients. Electr. Power Syst. Res. 95, 9–18 (2013)
21. Jordehi, A.R.: Time Varying Acceleration Coefficients Particle Swarm Optimization (TVACPSO): a new optimization algorithm for estimating parameters of PV cells and modules. Energy Convers. Manag. 129, 262–274 (2016)
22. Beigvand, S.D., Abdi, H., Scala, M.: Optimal operation of multicarrier energy systems using time varying acceleration coefficient gravitational search algorithm. Energy 114, 253–265 (2016)
23. Borowska, B.: Social strategy of particles in optimization problems. In: Advances in Intelligent Systems and Computing. Springer (2019, in Press)
24. Mehmood, Y., Sadiq, M., Shahzad, W.: Fitness-based acceleration coefficients to enhance the convergence speed of novel binary particle swarm optimization. In: Proceedings of International Conference on Frontiers of Information Technology (FIT), pp. 355–360 (2018)
25. Guo, L., Chen, X.: A novel particle swarm optimization based on the self-adaptation strategy of acceleration coefficients. In: Proceedings of International Conference on Computational Intelligence and Security, pp. 277–281. IEEE (2009)
26. Cai, X., Cui, Z., Zeng, J., Tan, Y.: Dispersed particle swarm optimization. Inf. Process. Lett. 105, 231–235 (2008)
27. Ardizzon, G., Cavazzini, G., Pavesi, G.: Adaptive acceleration coefficients for a new search diversification strategy in particle swarm optimization algorithms. Inf. Sci. 299, 337–378 (2015)

An Evaluative Study of Adaptive Control of Population Size in Differential Evolution

Petr Bujok[✉][iD]

University of Ostrava, 30. dubna 22, 70103 Ostrava, Czech Republic
petr.bujok@osu.cz

Abstract. In this paper, a newly proposed setting of a diversity-based adaptive mechanism of population size setting in differential evolution (DE) is experimentally studied. Seven state-of-the-art adaptive DE variants and classic DE are used in the experiments where 22 real-world problems are solved. The obtained results are assessed by statistical tests. The diversity-based approach often performs substantially better compared with the original fixed population size setting or linearly decreasing population size. A newly proposed setting of the control parameter performs at least the same or better than the original setting.

Keywords: Differential evolution · Population diversity ·
Acceptable interval · Experimental comparison · Real-world problems

1 Introduction

Differential evolution (DE) introduced by Storn and Price in [10] is an evolutionary algorithm primarily proposed for real-parameter optimisation problems. A population P is represented by a set of real parameters vectors (points) x_i, $x_i = (x_1, \ldots, x_D)$, $i = 1, \ldots, N$, where D is the dimension of the problem to be solved and N is the population size. An initial population P is generated randomly, uniformly distributed in the boundary constrained search space $\Omega = \prod_{j=1}^{D}[a_j, b_j]$, $a_j < b_j$. The objective function $f(x)$ is defined in all $x \in \Omega$ and the point x^* fulfilling the condition $f(x^*) \leq f(x)$, $\forall x \in \Omega$ is the solution of the global optimisation problem.

The population is developed by application of evolutionary operators as mutation, crossover, and selection. A new trial point y_i is created from a mutant point v_i generated by using a kind of a mutation strategy and from the current point x_i of the population by the application of the crossover. If $f(y_i) \leq f(x_i)$, the better individual y_i replaces the current vector in the successive generation.

The performance of the DE algorithm is strongly dependent on the control parameters setting appropriate for the problem to be solved. The proper setting is possible to be found by the trial-and-error method but this is time-consuming. There are many adaptive variants of DE [3,5]. However, most of the proposed

© Springer Nature Switzerland AG 2019
L. Rutkowski et al. (Eds.): ICAISC 2019, LNAI 11508, pp. 421–431, 2019.
https://doi.org/10.1007/978-3-030-20912-4_39

adaptive DE variants modify the values of F and CR, change the DE strategy but use a fixed population size. A fixed population size is also often used in real applications. Only a few papers deal with the adaptation of the population size in spite of the fact that the population size is also a very important parameter of DE which influences the efficiency of the search. The latter DE with population size adaptation is used in a very popular jSO algorithm [1].

In our recent experiments [8,9], a new mechanism for control of the population size was applied in several well-known algorithms. The mechanism uses a current diversity of the population, and our results show that the real diversity level differs from the required one. This is the main reason for enhancing this mechanism.

In this study, a recently proposed method of the population-size adaptation is enhanced to increase its efficiency. The method is based on monitoring of the population diversity in each generation and increasing or decreasing of the population size to keep the population diversity near the value which is expected desirable for convergence.

The rest of the paper is organised as follows. The known methods of population-size adaptation and recently proposed diversity-control mechanism are surveyed in Sect. 2. New ideas for better control of population diversity are proposed in Sect. 2.1. Experimental settings and the results of experiments are presented in Sects. 3 and 4, and Sect. 5 conclude the paper.

2   Mechanism Controlling Diversity of Population

Teo introduced a self-adaptive approach to change the size of the population in DE [12]. The initial size is set to $10 \times D$, and it is self-adapted at the end of each generation. There are distinguished two kinds of the proposed method where both use a specific mutation strategy.

Brest et al. proposed a dynamic approach to adapt the population size in DE [2]. The idea is based on the reduction of the population size in several ($pmax = 4$) stages. It means that the overall search process is divided into four parts, distinguished by $pmax - 1$ reductions. In each reduction, half of the individuals are removed from the population and then $N/2$ individuals survive for the next generations. A better individual with a smaller function value from each pair ($\{x_i, x_{i+1}\}$, $i = 1, 3, 5, \ldots, N - 1$) is selected to the next stage.

Probably the most well-known approach of population size control is applied in L-SHADE variant [11]. Tanabe and Fukunaga proposed a simple and efficient idea. At first, a very big population size is set to prefer the exploration phase. During the search process, the population size is linearly reduced to achieve the least value $N = 4$ at the end of the run. The population size is controlled by removing the worst individual (evaluated by cost function). The efficiency of L-SHADE algorithm was confirmed by the first position at CEC 2014 symposium. The same 'L' approach was also used in another DE variants typically derived from L-SHADE algorithm.

A comprehensive review of the population size setting in the DE algorithm is provided by Piotrowski in [7]. Several different approaches are compared on two sets of problems. As supposed, the lower D, the lower the population size, and the higher D, the higher the population size performs better. Better results are provided by DE when N is set in accordance to D (i.e. $N = 3 \times D$ or $N = 5 \times D$). The best results are often achieved when an adaptive approach of the population size setting is applied.

In the aforementioned approaches, only the function value of individuals plays the role of decision criteria. In our recently proposed mechanism, the population diversity is used to adapt population size in DE [9]. The estimate of the diversity is based on a root square of an average square of the distance of individuals from the centroid of the population (1).

$$div = \sqrt{\frac{1}{N} \sum_{i=1}^{N} \sum_{j=1}^{D} (x_{ij} - \bar{x}_j)^2}, \tag{1}$$

where $\bar{x}_j$ is the mean of jth coordinate of the points in the current generation of population P, N is the current size of population,

$$\bar{x}_j = \frac{1}{N} \sum_{i=1}^{N} x_{ij}. \tag{2}$$

When the initial population is created, the diversity is measured and labelled as div_{init}. Then, it is used as a reference value in the definition of relative measure div_r of the diversity in the current generation of population (3),

$$div_r = \frac{div}{div_{\text{init}}}. \tag{3}$$

Relative number of currently depleted function evaluations is defined by (4).

$$FES_r = \frac{FES}{MaxFES}, \tag{4}$$

where FES is the current number of function evaluations and $MaxFES$ is the number of function evaluations allowed for the search. The size of the population is changed depending on the current relative diversity. It is suggested to keep the relative diversity div_r near its required value $rdiv_r$ linearly decreasing from value 1 at the beginning of the search to value 0 from the last tenth of the search (see the dashed line in Fig. 1). It means to change the population size only when the current relative diversity is lower than acceptable interval (AI), i.e. $(1 - AI) \times rdiv_r$ or larger than $(1 + AI) \times rdiv_r$. This $AI \times 100\%$ acceptable interval serves to extend the area where the current relative diversity is acceptable compared with the required one (see the black solid lines in Fig. 1). In the last tenth, the zero value is strictly required.

The div_r characteristic is computed after each generation. The value of parameter AI was set to 0.1 in all previous experiments. The size of the population is increased by 1 and a random point from the search space is added when the div_r is lower than $0.9 \times rdiv_r$. The population size is decreased by 1 and the worst point is excluded when the div_r is larger than $1.1 \times rdiv_r$. There are minimal and maximal values of the population size used in the approach, N_{min} and N_{max}. The search process starts with N_{init}. $N_{min} = 8$, $N_{max} = 5 \times D$, and $N_{init} = 50$ are suggested and also used in our experiments in this paper (as in [9]).

2.1 Newly Proposed Idea for Diversity-Control Mechanism

A setting of AI value significantly changes the resulting area where the current relative diversity is accepted (see solid red lines in Fig. 1) and where the current population size remains without an update. An increase of the AI value promises a decreasing frequency of the population size update because the current relative diversity is accepted in the wider area between the solid red lines (Fig. 1). There are a lot of possible settings of the AI parameter to experimentally verify our hypothesis. For simplicity, we set this parameter to a relatively strongly different value, $AI = 0.5$. The results of the substantially different AI values (i.e. 0.1 and 0.5) demonstrate the sensitivity of the mechanism on the AI setting. If the results of two extreme AI settings are performing similarly, the values of AI from (0.1, 0.5) are also performing similarly. The proposed 50 % acceptable interval is experimentally tested and statistically compared with the original 10 % setting.

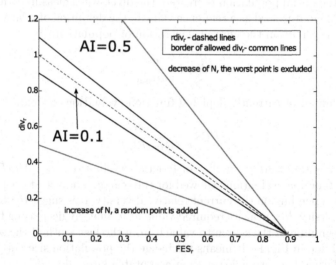

Fig. 1. Required relative diversity $rdiv_r$ and the area of allowed relative diversity (Color figure online)

3   Experimental Settings

Seven well-known adaptive DE variants (details are in survey [3]) and classical (canonical) DE are used to compare the efficiency of the previous and the new setting of the AI parameter. The most frequently used linear population size reduction is also applied. All four versions of all eight algorithms (original, linear reduction, and two diversity based variants) are applied to a set of 22 real-world problems from a competition in Special Session on Real-Parameter Numerical optimisation CEC 2011 [4]. The functions in the benchmark differ in the computational complexity and in the dimension of the search space which varies from $D = 1$ to $D = 240$, the dimensionality of most problems exceeds $D = 20$. The labels of the test problems are taken from [4]. The test functions are described in [4] in detail, including the experimental settings required for the competition. This experimental setting is also used in our experimental comparison. For each algorithm and problem, 25 independent runs were carried out. The run of the algorithm stops if the prescribed number of function evaluation $MaxFES = 150000$ is reached. Partial results of the algorithms after reaching one third and two-thirds of $MaxFES$ were also recorded. The point in the terminal population with the smallest function value is the solution of the problem found in the run.

For better orientation in the following results, the original versions of algorithms are abbreviated 'ORI', variants with a linear population-size reduction are labelled 'LIN', the proposed mechanism with $AI = 0.1$ is denoted by 'D01' and the newly proposed settings $AI = 0.5$ is marked by 'D05'.

The control parameters of the adaptive DE variants are set to the recommended values. The population size of the original algorithms is set to the same value $N = 90$. A setting of the linear population size reduction mechanism follows the original description $N_{\text{init}} = 18 \times D$ and $N_{\text{min}} = 4$. The control parameters of the proposed diversity-based mechanism are set $N_{min} = 8$, $N_{max} = 5 \times D$ (for low dimension at least 10), and $N_{init} = 50$. The classic DE algorithm used in this experiment employs strategy DE/rand/1/bin with $F = 0.8$ and $CR = 0.5$.

4   Results of Experiments

All 32 variants of DE algorithms are compared on 22 problems, and the results are assessed by statistical methods. All selected statistical tests used in this study are described in more detail in [6]. Due to the amount of the results, the basic characteristics of the algorithms are not presented. At first, the Friedman non-parametric test providing an overall insight into the comparison of the algorithms' performance. The test was carried out on medians of minimal function values at three stages of the search, namely after $FES = 50,000, 100,000$, and $150,000$ (see Table 1). The algorithms in columns are ordered from the most efficient to the worst performing, based on the mean rank values in the final stage ($FES = 150,000$).

The first three positions are for three SHADE variants with updating population size, where mean ranks of diversity-based versions are substantially lower compared with the popular L-SHADE algorithm. The order of the population-size mechanisms follows several scenarios. Variants of SHADE, EPSDE, and jDE have the best ranks for the diversity-based mechanism with newly used $AI = 0.5$.

Table 1. Mean ranks from the Friedman tests at three stages of the search.

FES/Alg	SHAD05	SHAD01	LSHADE	EPSD05	b6e6rl	EPSD01	CoBiD01	SHADE
50,000	6.1	8.4	21.2	10.3	11	11.5	13.3	8.7
100,000	7.1	8.8	18.3	10.1	10.5	10.5	12.9	10.5
150,000	7.6	7.9	9.5	11.3	11.5	11.8	12.9	12.9
FES/Alg	CoD01	CoD05	EPSDE	jDED05	IDE	jDED01	LEPSDE	b6e6D05
50,000	13.3	13.7	11.8	15.8	13.6	13.9	22.7	11.6
100,000	13.2	13	13.1	13.2	13.8	12.8	21.4	14.4
150,000	13.7	13.9	15	15.3	15.5	15.8	15.8	16
FES/Alg	CoBiD05	b6e6D01	LjDE	IDED05	CoDE	CoBiDE	LCoBiDE	Lb6e6rl
50,000	11.6	12.9	24	12.3	17	16.8	24.2	22.2
100,000	14.4	14	22.6	13.4	15.9	16.3	23.6	20.7
150,000	16	16.1	16.6	16.8	16.9	17	17.1	17.6
FES/Alg	jDE	IDED01	LCoDE	DED01	DED05	LIDE	LDE	DE
50,000	14.8	14	26.4	24.2	24.3	21.7	28.7	26.3
100,000	16	15	25.8	23.5	24.7	22	28.8	27.5
150,000	18.1	18.6	21.8	23.9	24	25.6	27.1	28.3

In CoBiDE, CoDE, and DE the best results achieves the mechanism with original $AI = 0.1$ (in abbreviations of new enhanced algorithms 'DE' or 'rl' part is omitted to keep the table compact). The original b6e6rl and IDE are better with a static population size, which is in this study set $N = 100$. Six DE variants out of eight have better results for the diversity-based mechanism with either setting of AI compared with the results of the linear-based mechanism or static N value. Notice that this test evaluates algorithms on 22 different problems and therefore some algorithms perform better in some types of problems. The results of the last stage ($FES = 150,000$) are compared statistically for all settings of N and each DE algorithm separately to show the efficiency of four different population size approaches (Fig. 2). Each line represents mean ranks from one application of the Friedman test. The first column of the plot (denoted 'none') represents mean ranks of the original DE variants. The performance of the original DE algorithms compared with three population mechanisms are very varied. The fixed population has the best results for IDE and b6e6rl variants, whereas SHADE with $N = 100$ has the worst results. The biggest difference from four N settings is observed in the classic DE, where the diversity-based mechanism with $AI = 0.1$ outperformed other three approaches. The results of the diversity-based mechanism with newly proposed $AI = 0.5$ are very similar in all eight DE variants, which generally perform rather better except for the classic DE.

Previous results provide an overall insight into algorithms' performance regarding all 22 real-world problems. A comparison of four different population settings in each DE variant and each problem is assessed by the Kruskal-Wallis non-parametric one-way ANOVA test. In Table 3, there are collected symbols for statistical significance. When the significance level is lower than 0.001, a symbol '***' is used; for the significance values lower than 0.01, a symbol '**';

Table 2. Significant wins of four population size mechanisms from the Wilcoxon rank-sum tests for all problems and algorithms.

Algorithm	ORI/LIN	ORI/D01	ORI/D05	LIN/D01	LIN/D05	D01/D05
b6e6rl	10/4	11/4	11/5	5/10	6/10	4/8
CoBiDE	6/7	6/10	5/11	2/11	1/12	3/6
CoDE	8/4	6/10	3/10	0/16	0/15	0/4
DE	6/6	1/12	1/15	3/9	2/15	3/1
EPSDE	9/3	5/9	5/10	3/11	3/12	1/2
IDE	8/0	14/1	8/3	0/13	0/14	0/8
jDE	3/14	3/7	4/4	7/10	5/11	5/5
SHADE	1/12	2/15	2/13	5/4	3/6	1/3
Total (%)	29/28.4	27.3/38.6	22.2/40.3	14.2/47.7	11.4/54	9.7/21

and similarly for the significance under 0.05, a symbol '*'. A symbol '≈' represents a situation when there is no significant difference between the population size settings. We can observe that problems T03 and T08 are solved similarly by all proposed mechanisms. These problems have dimension levels $D = 1$ and $D = 7$, and all algorithms in the comparison in all runs achieved the same function values. Nevertheless, the information from Table 3 does not provide a deeper insight into the population mechanisms individually. Therefore, non-parametric two-sample Wilcoxon rank-sum tests are applied to compare all four

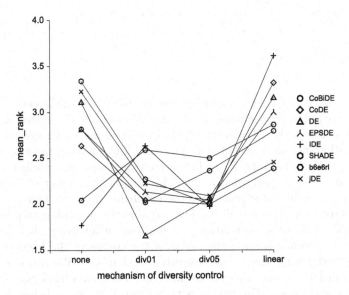

Fig. 2. Mean ranks of all versions of algorithms in the last stage from the Friedman tests.

Table 3. Significance of four different population settings from the Kruskal-Wallis tests.

Fun	D	b6e6rl	CoBiDE	CoDE	DE	EPSDE	IDE	jDE	SHADE
T01	6	***	***	***	***	***	≈	***	***
T02	30	***	***	***	***	***	***	***	***
T03	1	≈	≈	≈	≈	≈	≈	≈	≈
T04	1	***	***	≈	≈	≈	≈	***	≈
T05	30	***	***	***	***	***	***	***	***
T06	30	***	***	***	***	***	***	***	***
T07	20	***	***	***	≈	***	***	***	***
T08	7	≈	≈	≈	≈	≈	≈	≈	≈
T09	126	***	***	***	***	***	***	***	***
T10	12	**	***	***	***	≈	*	≈	≈
T11.1	120	***	***	***	***	***	***	***	*
T11.2	240	***	***	***	***	***	***	***	***
T11.3	6	***	***	≈	***	≈	≈	≈	***
T11.4	13	***	***	***	≈	***	***	**	**
T11.5	15	**	***	***	***	***	***	≈	***
T11.6	40	***	***	***	**	***	***	***	***
T11.7	140	***	***	***	***	***	***	***	***
T11.8	96	***	***	***	***	***	***	***	**
T11.9	96	***	***	***	***	***	***	***	**
T11.10	96	***	***	***	***	***	***	***	*
T13	26	***	***	***	***	***	***	**	***
T14	22	**	***	***	***	*	***	***	***

population settings for each algorithm and problem. The numbers of problems where the population mechanisms win significantly are illustrated in Table 2. The rows represent the DE algorithms, and the columns are for possible pairs of the population mechanisms. For example, 'ORI/LIN' denotes the number where the fixed population size performs better compared with the number where the linear decrease of N performs better. The remaining number of 22 problems from each cell of this table represents the problems where both approaches perform similarly. The last row of Table 2 contains the percentage representation of the total wins of the population size mechanism involving all DE variants. The three first columns state the ratios of the counts of the fixed population settings ('ORI') with three other adaptive mechanisms. We can observe that regarding all DE variants there is no difference between a fixed population size and its linear decrease. The reason is that fixed N performs better for b6e6rl, CoDE, EPSDE, and IDE, and the linear mechanism performs better for jDE and SHADE vice versa. A comparison of the diversity-based mechanism ($AI =$ 0.1) with fixed N shows the supremacy of the proposed method. Only b6e6rl and IDE perform better with fixed $N = 100$ setting. A similar situation is for the newly proposed value of $AI = 0.5$ where the ratio is even more substantial. It is interesting that this setting increases the performance of the IDE variant compared with the fixed N value.

More interesting results are obvious from a comparison between the proposed diversity-based mechanism and the linear decrease of N. The proposed approach outperforms the 'LIN' mechanism. The situation for the SHADE variant is slightly balanced for the original setting $AI = 0.1$, but the newly proposed $AI = 0.5$ outperforms the 'linear' variant. The most interesting results are in the last columns of this table where a comparison of two AI settings is represented. It is clear that the newly proposed value $AI = 0.5$ performs similarly or better compared with the original setting. The most similar results are achieved for the jDE variant. The results of the CoDE and IDE variants show the increase of the efficiency by using a higher AI value.

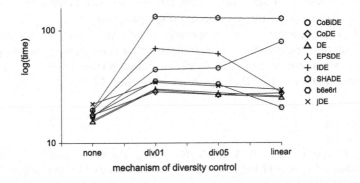

Fig. 3. Estimated time complexity of the population mechanisms.

Very important information about the efficiency of algorithms is provided by the time complexity needed for solving the problems with various dimensionality, i.e. T01, T02, and T11.2. Five independent runs for each algorithm on each of these problems are performed and the mean time in seconds at a logarithmic measure is depicted in Fig. 3. It is obvious that it is less time consuming to use a fixed population size (column 'none'). There is no substantial difference between efficiency of proposed adaptive mechanisms. In the IDE and b6e6rl algorithms, the linear approach performs faster than the diversity-based approach. The time complexity of CoBiDE with the linear population size mechanism has higher time demands than the diversity-based mechanism. The time complexity of the SHADE algorithm is high with any adaptive population size approach.

5   Conclusion

In this paper, a newly proposed setting of the control parameter of the diversity-based adaptive mechanism of population size setting is experimentally studied. In this study fixed population setting and well-known linear-decrease of population size are also applied to assess the proposed approach. All four settings are applied to seven state-of-the-art adaptive DE variants and classic DE in the experiments where 22 real-world problems are solved. The obtained results are assessed by statistical tests.

The results of the experiments show that the proposed diversity-based approach often performs substantially better than the original fixed population size setting. The proposed method outperforms even a well-known linear population size reduction approach. Adaptive variants of b6e6rl and IDE perform better with a fixed population size setting. Inefficient results of some adaptive DE versions could be caused by their adaptive mechanisms controlling population development. A more sophisticated change of some control parameters should increase the final results even of these methods. Particularly worse results of some linear population size adaptation DE variants are caused by a very big population size in problems with higher dimensionality.

The time complexity of the proposed mechanism is not worse than of the linear population size variant, which indicates that the diversity-based approach is useful in a real application. The newly proposed setting of $AI = 0.5$ performs at least the same or better than the original setting $AI = 0.1$.

References

1. Brest, J., Maučec, M.S., Bošković, B.: Single objective real-parameter optimization: algorithm jSO. In: 2017 IEEE Congress on Evolutionary Computation (CEC), pp. 1311–1318 (2017)
2. Brest, J., Sepesy Maučec, M.: Population size reduction for the differential evolution algorithm. Appl. Intell. **29**(3), 228–247 (2008)
3. Das, S., Mullick, S., Suganthan, P.: Recent advances in differential evolution-an updated survey. Swarm Evol. Comput. **27**, 1–30 (2016)
4. Das, S., Suganthan, P.N.: Problem definitions and evaluation criteria for CEC 2011 competition on testing evolutionary algorithms on real world optimization problems. Technical report, Jadavpur University, India and Nanyang Technological University, Singapore (2010)
5. Das, S., Suganthan, P.N.: Differential evolution: a survey of the state-of-the-art. IEEE Trans. Evol. Comput. **15**, 27–54 (2011)
6. Hollander, M., Wolfe, D.: Nonparametric Statistical Methods. Wiley Series in Probability and Statistics. Wiley, Hoboken (1999)
7. Piotrowski, A.P.: Review of differential evolution population size. Swarm Evol. Comput. **32**, 1–24 (2017)
8. Poláková, R., Bujok, P.: Popular optimisation algorithms with diversity-based adaptive mechanism for population size. In: Advances in Intelligent Systems and Computing (2018, in press)

9. Poláková, R., Tvrdík, J., Bujok, P.: Adaptation of population size according to current population diversity in differential evolution. In: 2017 IEEE Symposium Series on Computational Intelligence (IEEE SSCI), pp. 2627–2634 (2017)
10. Storn, R., Price, K.V.: Differential evolution - a simple and efficient heuristic for global optimization over continuous spaces. J. Glob. Optim. **11**, 341–359 (1997)
11. Tanabe, R., Fukunaga, A.S.: Improving the search performance of SHADE using linear population size reduction. In: IEEE Congress on Evolutionary Computation (CEC), pp. 1658–1665 (2014)
12. Teo, J.: Exploring dynamic self-adaptive populations in differential evolution. Soft Comput. **10**(8), 673–686 (2006)

A New Hybrid Particle Swarm Optimization and Evolutionary Algorithm

Piotr Dziwiński[1]([⊠])(iD), Łukasz Bartczuk[1]([⊠])(iD), and Piotr Goetzen[2,3]

[1] Institute of Computational Intelligence, Częstochowa University of Technology,
Częstochowa, Poland
{piotr.dziwinski,lukasz.bartczuk}@iisi.pcz.pl
[2] Information Technology Institute, University of Social Sciences,
90-113 Łódź, Poland
pgoetzen@san.edu.pl
[3] Clark University Worcester, Worcester, MA 01610, USA

Abstract. Particle swarm optimization (PSO) has proved fast convergence in many optimization problems but still has the main drawback - falling in a local minimum. This paper presents a new Hybrid Particle Swarm Optimization and Evolutionary algorithm (HPSO-E) to solve this problem by introducing a new population of children particles obtained by applying a mutation and crossover operators taken from the evolutionary algorithm. In this way, we connect the best properties of the algorithms: fast convergence of the PSO and ability to global search introduced by the evolutionary algorithm. The novel hybrid algorithm shows sufficient convergence for unimodal benchmark function and excellent convergence for selected hard multimodal benchmark functions.

Keywords: Hybrid algorithm · Particle swarm optimization ·
Evolutionary algorithm

1 Introduction

Optimization is a fundamental challenge in many practical problems, especially when constructing fuzzy systems [7,29,39,40], neuro-fuzzy systems [8,32], solving fuzzy nonlinear equations [36] or determining the parameters of the complex systems [33–35,46–50]. Traditional algorithms have difficulty determining the best global solution in the case of highly complex real-world problems (multimodal, high dimensional or containing noise). During the past decades, many different nature-inspired methods have been proposed to solve problems, that are too hard for traditional methods, e.g.: genetic algorithm [3,4,16,26], genetic programming [1,26], evolutionary algorithm [1,9,16], evolutionary strategies [1,9], differential evolution [10,19], directed evolution [31] and swarm intelligence methods [2,5,6,15,20–22,45].

One example of such a method that allows obtaining outstanding results is the Particle Swarm Optimization algorithm (PSO) [2,5,6,20,30,41,43].

© Springer Nature Switzerland AG 2019
L. Rutkowski et al. (Eds.): ICAISC 2019, LNAI 11508, pp. 432–444, 2019.
https://doi.org/10.1007/978-3-030-20912-4_40

The PSO has been proposed by Kenedy and Eberhart [15] and is inspired by the social behavior of animals like fish schooling or bird flocking. The PSO has the following features: simplicity, stochastic movement, positive feedback and ability to adapt to the changing environment and to obtain high-quality solutions in a short time. However, PSO reveals some disadvantages - it may be easily trapped in local optimum (often called premature convergence).

Despite the success of PSO in many practical applications, traditional PSO still has room for improvements in updating velocity and ensuring a balance between exploitation and exploration. From that reason, many studies have been concentrated on further improving the performance of PSO. Those methods can be classified into the following categories: inertial weight varying strategy [28,51], parameter selection and convergence analysis [38,42], swarm topology structure selection [22,23,27] and hybrid PSO combined with some evolutionary operators taken from other nature-inspired algorithms [4,11–14,17,18,24,25].

In this paper, we propose a novel Hybrid Particle Swarm Optimization and Evolutionary algorithm (HPSO-E). The algorithm is obtained by introducing a new temporal swarm (which corresponds to a population in the evolutionary algorithm), that contains particles modified by the typical mutation and crossover operators used in the evolutionary algorithms. Moreover, we propose a new strategy of replacement of particles in the base swarm.

The rest of the paper has been organized as follows. In Sect. 2 we present the base version of the PSO algorithm. We outlined our algorithm in Sect. 3. Section 4 describes the simulations and obtained results. The last section contains conclusions.

2   Particle Swarm Optimization Algorithm

The PSO algorithm is a simple method to solve optimization problems in the form:

$$\min_{\mathbf{x} \in \mathbf{R}^D} f(\mathbf{x}) \tag{1}$$

where $f(\mathbf{x})$ is an optimized objective function and $\mathbf{x}$ is a solution of the problem. In this algorithm the solution $\mathbf{x} = [x^1, \ldots, x^D]$ is described as the particle i, $i = 1 \ldots N$, that also contains information about the best local solution $\mathbf{p}_{it} = [p_{it}^1, \ldots, p_{it}^D]$ found so far, and velocity vector $\mathbf{v}_{it} = [v_{it}^1, \ldots, v_{it}^D]$ in the iteration t. Each particle of the swarm moves with the velocity $\mathbf{v}_{it}$ throughout the solution space in different directions using the best local solution $\mathbf{p}_{it}$ found by the particle so far and the best global solution $\mathbf{g}_t = [g_t^1, \ldots, g_t^D]$ of the entire swarm. A new velocity $\mathbf{v}_{i(t+1)}$ and position $\mathbf{x}_{i(t+1)}$ of each particle are computed according to Eqs. (2) and (3):

$$v_{i(t+1)}^d = v_{it}^d \cdot w + \psi_1 \cdot r_1 \cdot (p_{it}^d - x_{it}^d) + \psi_2 \cdot r_2 \cdot (g_t - x_{it}^d) \tag{2}$$

$$x_{i(t+1)}^d = x_{it}^d + v_{i(t+1)}^d. \tag{3}$$

where w is an inertia weight specifying change value of the velocity between iteration (t) and $(t+1)$, (for $w = 1$, we can obtain the base algorithm introduced by Kennedy and Eberhart [15]), ψ_1 and ψ_2 are two acceleration coefficients that scale the influence of the best local and global solutions, r_1 and r_2 are two uniform random values within the range $(0, 1]$.

The inertia weight w is used to balance between exploration and exploitation of the search space. For values close to 1, particles move fast and perform the process of exploration. For small values, for example, $(w < 0.85)$, the velocity decreases and particles perform the process of exploitation. The pseudocode of the PSO algorithm is shown below.

Algorithm 1. Algorithm of particle swarm optimization (PSO)

Data: Population size N, acceleration constant ψ_1, ψ_2, inertia weight w
Result: The best solution $\mathbf{g}_{t_{max}}$
1 Initialization;
2 **repeat**
3   Evaluate each particles $ex_{it} = f_{ob}(\mathbf{x}_{it})$;
4   Update the best local solution $\mathbf{p}_{it}$;
5   Update the best global solution $\mathbf{g}_t$;
6   **for** $i \leftarrow 1$ **to** N **do**
7   Compute $\mathbf{v}_{i(t+1)}$ according to equation (2);
8   Compute $\mathbf{x}_{i(t+1)}$ according to equation (3);
9          $t \leftarrow t + 1$;
10 **until** *Terminate condition has not been met*;

---

3   Hybrid Particle Swarm Optimization and Evolutionary Algorithm (HPSO-E)

The PSO algorithm presented in the previous section was successfully used to solve many optimization problems. However, it can be easily trapped in local optima. From that reason, in this paper, we propose a novel Hybrid Particle Swarm Optimization and Evolutionary algorithm (HPSO-E). This method combines the GPSO and evolutionary algorithms by using mutation and crossover operators for the best particles of the swarm. Moreover, a new strategy of replacement of particles in the base swarm by particles modified by evolutionary operators is proposed. The details of the new HPSO-E method are presented in Algorithm 2. Lines 1–4 of the Algorithm 2 correspond to typical initialization phase of PSO algorithm. All particles are initially set according to the following equations:

$$\mathbf{x}_{i0} = \mathbf{x}_{min} + (\mathbf{x}_{max} - \mathbf{x}_{min}) \cdot \mathbf{r}_1, \tag{4}$$

$$\mathbf{p}_{i0} = \mathbf{x}_{min} + (\mathbf{x}_{max} - \mathbf{x}_{min}) \cdot \mathbf{r}_2, \tag{5}$$

$$\mathbf{g}_0 = \mathbf{x}_{min} + (\mathbf{x}_{max} - \mathbf{x}_{min}) \cdot \mathbf{r}_3, \tag{6}$$

where: $i = 1, 2, \ldots, N$, N is particle number, $\mathbf{r}_1$, $\mathbf{r}_2$, $\mathbf{r}_3$ are the random uniform vectors taking values in $(0, 1)^D$. Next, the velocity and position of each particle is modificated in lines 6–8 according to standard PSO strategy described by Eqs. (2) and (3). Later, the base swarm $\mathbf{X}$ is evaluated, and the best local position $\mathbf{p}_{it}$ is updated according to the following equation (lines 9–10):

$$(\mathbf{p}_{it}, ep_{it}) = \begin{cases} (\mathbf{x}_{it}, ex_{it}) & \text{if } ex_{it} < ep_{it} \\ (\mathbf{p}_{it}, ep_{it}) & otherwise. \end{cases} \tag{7}$$

Algorithm 2. Hybrid particle swarm optimization evolutionary algorithm (HPSO-E)

Data: Population size $N = |\mathbf{X}|$, acceleration constant ψ_1, ψ_2, inertia weight w, evolutionary operators probability p_e, crossover probability p_c, number of crossover positions n_c, mutation probability p_m, number of mutated positions n_m and turnament size T;

Result: The best solution $\mathbf{g}_{t_{max}}$

1 Initialize the current position $\mathbf{x}_{it}$, the best local position $\mathbf{p}_{it}$ and the global best solution $\mathbf{g}_t$ according to equations (4-6) respectively, $t = 0$;

2 Evaluate each particle $ex_{it} = f_{ob}(\mathbf{x}_{it})$, $ep_{it} = f_{ob}(\mathbf{p}_{it})$, $\mathbf{x}_{it} \in \mathbf{X}_t$;

3 Update the best local solution $\mathbf{p}_{it}$, $\mathbf{p}_{it} \in \mathbf{P}_t$ according to equation (7);

4 Update the best global solution $\mathbf{g}_t$ according to equation (9);

5 **repeat**

6   **for** $i \leftarrow 1$ **to** N **do**

7   Compute $\mathbf{v}_{i(t+1)}$ according to equation (2);

8   Compute $\mathbf{x}_{i(t+1)}$ according to equation (3);

9   Evaluate each particle of the main population $ex_{it} = f_{ob}(\mathbf{x}_{it})$;

10   Update the best local solution $\mathbf{p}_{it}$ according to equation (7);

11   Set the temporal swarm of offspring as empty set $\mathbf{CH}_t = \emptyset$;

12   **for** $i \leftarrow 1$ **to** N **do**

13   **if** $(p_e > r(0,1))$ **then**

14   **if** $(p_m > r(0,1))$ **then**

15                  $(\mathbf{ch}_m, j) = \text{Tournament}(\mathbf{P}_t, T)$;

16   Mutate$(\mathbf{ch}_m, n_m)$;

17   Evaluate the particle $ech_m = f_{ob}(\mathbf{ch}_m)$;

18   Insert $(\mathbf{ch}_m, ech_m, j)$ into $\mathbf{CH}_t$;

19   **if** $(p_c > r(0,1))$ **then**

20                  $(\mathbf{ch}_{c1}, j1) = \text{Tournament}(\mathbf{P}_t, T)$;

21                  $(\mathbf{ch}_{c2}, j2) = \text{Tournament}(\mathbf{P}_t, T)$;

22   Crossover$(\mathbf{ch}_{c1}, \mathbf{ch}_{c2}, n_c)$;

23   Evaluate the particle $ech_{c1} = f_{ob}(\mathbf{ch}_{c1})$;

24   Evaluate the particle $ech_{c2} = f_{ob}(\mathbf{ch}_{c2})$;

25   Insert $(\mathbf{ch}_{c1}, ech_{c1}, j1)$ into $\mathbf{CH}_t$;

26   Insert $(\mathbf{ch}_{c2}, ech_{c2}, j2)$ into $\mathbf{CH}_t$;

27   Replacement strategy of $\mathbf{p}_{it}$ according to equation (8);

28   Update the best global solution $\mathbf{g}_t$ according to equation (9);

29      $t \leftarrow t + 1$;

30 **until** *Terminate condition has not been met*;

Lines 11–26 of Algorithm 2 describe the process of creation of temporal swarm by applying evolutionary operators mutation and crossover. Evolutionary operators are applied N times with probability p_e, where crossover and mutation are used according to probabilities p_c and p_m respectively. The evolutionary operators are applied to particles determined by the tournament selection method, where selection criterion is the best local solution $\mathbf{p}_{it}$ of the particle. The mutation operator Mutate($\mathbf{ch}_m, n_m$) changes at most n_m random mutation positions in the solution vector $\mathbf{ch}_m$. The crossover operator Crossover($\mathbf{ch}_{c1}, \mathbf{ch}_{c2}, n_c$) exchanges information between two selected particles $\mathbf{ch}_{c1}$ and $\mathbf{ch}_{c2}$ from the base swarm at most n_c random positions.

Next, particles from base swarm $\mathbf{X}$ are replaced by better particles (in the sense of fitness value) from the temporal swarm $\mathbf{CH}_t$ according to the following equation:

$$(\mathbf{x}_{it}, ep_{it}) = \begin{cases} (\mathbf{ch}, f_{ob}(\mathbf{ch})) \text{ if } (\mathbf{ch}, f_{ob}(\mathbf{ch}), j) \in \mathbf{CH}_t, \ j = i, \ f_{ob}(\mathbf{ch}) < ep_{it} \\ (\mathbf{x}_{it}, ep_{it}) \quad otherwise, \end{cases} \tag{8}$$

It should be noted that particles from the base swarm can be replaced only by solutions derived from them, furthermore during this operation only the actual position and the best local solution are changed (other data are stored in the particle - a speed and direction of movement - remains unchanged). In this way, genetic operators do not influence the range of exploitation of the PSO. The proposed replacement strategy may direct the base swarm to the new promising search regions (increasing speed and diversity of the swarm).

Finally, the best global solution $\mathbf{g}_t$ is updated according to the following equation:

$$(\mathbf{g}_t, eg_t) = \begin{cases} (\mathbf{p}_{it}, ep_{it}) \text{ if } ep_{it} < eg_t \\ (\mathbf{g}_t, eg_t) \quad otherwise. \end{cases} \tag{9}$$

4   Simulations

In order to confirm the usefulness of the proposed algorithm, a set of simulations was performed for 10 benchmark functions [44] described in Table 1. The obtained results have been compared with results of five other PSO algorithms:

- Traditional global PSO algorithms with inertia weight (GPSO) [37];
- Fully informed PSO whose velocity is calculated according to the information from all of the neighbors (FIPSO-F) [27];
- Fully informed PSO with the USquare topology (FIPSO-S) [27];
- Comprehensive learning PSO (CLPSO) [23] employs a comprehensive learning strategy to optimize every dimension of the vector and exchanges the information on the best solution between different particles;
- Particle swarm optimization using dynamic tournament topology (DT-PSO) [44] where the neighborhood of each particle is reorganized using the tournament strategy.

Table 1. Benchmark functions

Type	Function	Search range	Best value
Unimodal functions	$F_1(x) = \sum_{i=1}^{D} x_i^2$	$[-100, 100]^D$	0
	$F_2(x) = \sum_{i=1}^{D} \left(\sum_{j=1}^{i} x_j \right)^2$	$[-100, 100]^D$	0
	$F_3(x) = \sum_{i=1}^{D} i x_i^4 + \text{random}[0, 1)$	$[-1.28, 1.28]^D$	0
	$F_4(x) = \sum_{i=1}^{D} (\lfloor x_i + 0.5 \rfloor)^2$	$[-100, 100]^D$	0
Multimodal functions	$F_5(x) = \sum_{i=1}^{D-1} \left(100 \left(x_i^2 - x_{i+1} \right) + (x_i - 1)^2 \right)$	$[-2, 2]^D$	0
	$F_6(x) = -20 e^{-0.2 \sqrt{\frac{1}{D} \sum_{i=1}^{D} x_i^2}} - e^{\frac{1}{D} \sum_{i=1}^{D} \cos(2\pi x_i)} + 20 + e$	$[-32, 32]^D$	0
	$F_7(x) = \sum_{i=1}^{D} \frac{x_i^2}{4000} - \prod_{i=1}^{D} \cos(\frac{x_i}{\sqrt{i}}) + 1$	$[-600, 600]^D$	0
	$F_8(x) = \sum_{i=1}^{D} \left(x_i^2 - 10 \cos(2\pi x_i) + 10 \right)$	$[-5, 5]^D$	0
	$\begin{cases} F_9(x) = \sum_{i=1}^{D} \left(y_i^2 - 10 \cos(2\pi y_i) + 10 \right) \\ y_i = \begin{cases} x_i & \|x_i\| < \frac{1}{2} \\ \frac{\text{round}(2x_i)}{2} & \|x_i\| \geq \frac{1}{2} \end{cases} \end{cases}$	$[-5, 5]^D$	0
	$\begin{cases} F_{10}(x) = \sum_{i=1}^{D-1} \left(100(z_i^2 - z_{i+1})^2 + (z_i - 1)^2 \right) + 390 \\ z_i = x_i - o_i + 1 \end{cases}$	$[-200, 200]^D$	390

The used parameters for each algorithm are presented in Table 2. Those parameters were set on the values proposed by the authors of the corresponding algorithms. The maximum fitness evaluation is set to $ne_{max} = D * 10000$, where D is dimension number, D is set to 30. Simulations for each algorithm have been independently run 30 times in order to reduce statistical variations.

Table 2. The parameters for all evaluated algorithms

Algorithm	Functions	Parameters	Source
GPSO	F_1–F_{10}	N: 26, w: 0.75, ψ_1: 1.5, ψ_2: 1.7	[37]
FIPSO-F	F_1–F_{10}	N:26, χ: 0.7298, ψ: 4.1	[27]
FIPSO-S	F_1–F_{10}	N:26, χ: 0.7298, ψ: 4.1	[27]
CLPSO	F_1–F_{10}	N:40, w_0: 0.9, w_1: 0.4, c: 1.49445, m: 7, T: 2	[23]
DT-PSO	F_1–F_{10}	N:64, w: 1, ψ: 4.1, K: 0.1, M: 6, P: 0.05	[44]
HPSO-E	F_1–F_6	N:26, w: 0.68, ψ_1: 1.5, ψ_2: 1.75, p_e: 0.1, p_c: 0, n_c: 3, p_m: 0.9, n_m: 2, T: 9	-
HPSO-E	F_7–F_{10}	N:26, w: 0.76, ψ_1: 1.5, ψ_2: 1.75, p_e: 0.5, p_c: 0.3, n_c: 3, p_m: 0.9, n_m: 2, T: 9	-

Table 3. The results of the 30 experiments for different evaluated algorithms and different benchmark functions (D = 30).

Function		GPSO	FIPSO-F	FIPSO-S	CLPSO	DT-PSO	HPSO-E
F_1	Mean	4.28e−105	4.15e−001	1.06e+003	1.85e−030	1.24e−134	**2.26e−147**
	Std	1.87e−104	1.21e+000	3.11e+002	1.41e−030	4.46e−134	**8.52e−147**
	Best	1.15e−112	5.18e−008	6.40e+002	1.76e−031	1.46e−136	**5.07e−161**
	Worst	1.03e−103	6.29e+000	1.77e+003	5.82e−030	2.52e−133	**4.32e−146**
F_2	Mean	5.70e−010	4.52e+003	1.38e+005	7.25e+001	3.21e−006	**6.38e−020**
	Std	1.05e−009	1.64e+003	3.28e+004	2.30e+001	3.23e−006	**2.56e−019**
	Best	2.72e−011	2.02e+003	7.70e+004	2.69e+001	9.40e−008	**3.35e−024**
	Worst	4.93e−009	7.97e+003	2.12e+005	1.23e+002	1.46e−005	**1.39e−018**
F3	Mean	3.24e−003	4.46e−002	4.41e+000	4.28e−003	**9.12e−004**	4.15e−003
	Std	1.38e−003	2.17e−002	2.55e+000	1.15e−003	**5.05e−004**	2.35e−003
	Best	1.28e−003	1.19e−002	1.45e+000	1.54e−003	**2.89e−004**	8.54e−004
	Worst	5.90e−003	9.94e−002	1.23e+001	6.34e−003	**2.54e−003**	1.23e−002
F4	Mean	**0.00e+000**	4.90e+000	9.98e+002	**0.00e+000**	**0.00e+000**	**0.00e+000**
	Std	**0.00e+000**	7.77e+000	2.48e+002	**0.00e+000**	**0.00e+000**	**0.00e+000**
	Best	**0.00e+000**	0.00e+000	5.47e+002	**0.00e+000**	**0.00e+000**	**0.00e+000**
	Worst	**0.00e+000**	3.70e+001	1.59e+003	**0.00e+000**	**0.00e+000**	**0.00e+000**
F_5	Mean	1.33e+001	3.00e+001	1.10e+003	2.48e+001	1.42e+001	**1.81e+000**
	Std	2.25e+000	9.54e+000	3.18e+002	1.19e+000	**2.47e−001**	1.48e+000
	Best	7.27e+000	2.53e+001	6.06e+002	2.12e+001	1.36e+001	**7.20e−003**
	Worst	1.89e+001	8.11e+001	2.13e+003	2.60e+001	1.46e+001	**5.23e+000**
F_6	Mean	4.57e−001	6.91e−001	2.04e+001	8.14e−015	**4.00e−015**	8.52e−014
	Std	6.70e−001	5.66e−001	4.10e−001	1.61e−015	**0.00e+000**	2.90e−013
	Best	7.55e−015	1.92e−004	1.93e+001	7.55e−015	**4.00e−015**	7.55e−015
	Worst	2.12e+000	2.16e+000	2.09e+001	1.47e−014	**4.00e−015**	1.63e−012
F_7	Mean	2.16e−002	1.02e−001	9.08e+000	**4.69e−015**	2.47e−004	1.77e−002
	Std	2.35e−002	1.00e−001	2.65e+000	**2.37e−014**	1.33e−003	2.18e−002
	Best	0.00e+000	3.73e−003	5.14e+000	0.00e+000	0.00e+000	**0.00e+000**
	Worst	1.05e−001	5.23e−001	1.65e+001	**1.32e−013**	7.40e−003	7.10e−002
F_8	Mean	4.54e+001	2.41e+001	3.11e+002	8.62e−014	9.15e+000	**0.00e+000**
	Std	9.62e+000	5.17e+000	1.75e+001	4.64e−013	2.62e+000	**0.00e+000**
	Best	2.39e+001	1.30e+001	2.65e+002	0.00e+000	5.97e+000	**0.00e+000**
	Worst	7.26e+001	3.28e+001	3.40e+002	2.58e−012	1.69e+001	**0.00e+000**
F_9	Mean	2.39e+001	2.50e+001	3.07e+002	6.67e−002	1.12e+001	**1.89e−015**
	Std	7.52e+000	5.99e+000	2.20e+001	2.49e−001	3.20e+000	**1.02e−014**
	Best	1.09e+001	1.40e+001	2.55e+002	0.00e+000	4.99e+000	**0.00e+000**
	Worst	3.88e+001	4.35e+001	3.41e+002	1.00e+000	2.00e+001	**5.68e−014**
F_{10}	Mean	**4.11e+002**	6.88e+004	6.20e+011	3.84e+003	4.39e+002	4.11e+002
	Std	**3.43e+001**	2.35e+005	5.13e+011	6.27e+003	8.25e+001	3.66e+001
	Best	3.91e+002	6.16e+002	1.70e+011	7.57e+002	4.00e+002	**3.90e+002**
	Worst	5.73e+002	1.29e+006	2.04e+012	3.61e+004	7.13e+002	**5.68e+002**

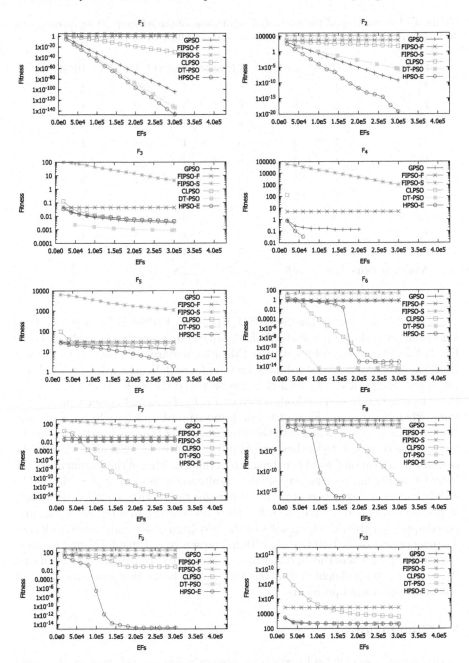

Fig. 1. The average performance of the algorithms for four unimodal functions F_1–F_4, and six multimodal functions F_5–F_{10} obtained in 30 experiments (D = 30).

Table 4. The ranking of the evaluated algorithms obtained from 30 experiments for 10 benchmark functions and 30 dimensions (the smallest value is the best).

Function	GPSO	FIPSO-F	FIPSO-S	CLPSO	DT-PSO	HPSO-E
F_1	3	5	6	4	2	1
F_2	2	5	6	4	3	1
F_3	2	5	6	4	1	3
F_4	1	2	3	1	1	1
F_5	2	5	6	4	3	1
F_6	4	5	6	2	1	3
F_7	4	5	6	1	2	3
F_8	5	4	6	2	3	1
F_9	4	5	6	2	3	1
F_{10}	1	5	6	4	3	2
Average rank	2.8	4.6	5.7	2.8	2.2	**1.7**

The obtained results for the GPSO, FIPSO-F, FIPSO-S, DT-PSO, CLPSO algorithms, and the proposed HPSO-E algorithm are presented in Tables 3, 4, and Fig. 1. Table 3 contains values of mean (Mean), standard deviation (Std), the best (Best) and the worst (Worst) obtained results for each benchmark function. From presented results, it can be seen that the proposed HPSO-E algorithm is better than the other evaluated methods tested on F_1, F_2, F_5 F_8 and F_9 benchmark functions, where F_5, F_8, and F_9 are hard multimodal problems for which the number of local optima increases fast with the dimensions. For the benchmark function F_6 the result is very close to the best one in this case of the CLPSO algorithm. In the case of F_{10} multimodal hard benchmark function (shifting of the F_5 function), the HPSO-E algorithm obtains very similar results to the two other algorithms. The significantly worse results were obtained only for F_7 function; however, the hybrid algorithm works better than the other three algorithms. In other cases, the proposed approach gives similar results as the best from other evaluated algorithms. The overall rank of the HPSO-E algorithm is presented in Table 4. Figure 1 presents the average progress of the used algorithms. From these charts, it can be seen that the proposed method achieved satisfactory results faster than other methods for half of the considered problems.

5   Conclusions

In this paper, a new hybrid particle swarm optimization evolutionary algorithm was presented. This method combined the classical GPSO method with the evolutionary algorithm. It was obtained by introducing a new temporal swarm, that contains particles modified by mutation and crossover operators. Moreover, a new strategy of replacement of particles in the base swarm was proposed. The simulations performed for 10 benchmark functions showed that our method allowed for achieving better results than other considered algorithms for half of the problems, which proves the usefulness of the proposed method.

References

1. Abdelbari, H., Shafi, K.: Learning structures of conceptual models from observed dynamics using evolutionary echo state networks. J. Artif. Intell. Soft Comput. Res. **8**(2), 133–154 (2018)
2. Alexandridis, A., Chondrodima, E., Sarimveis, H.: Cooperative learning for radial basis function networks using particle swarm optimization. Appl. Soft Comput. **49**, 485–497 (2016)
3. Ali, A.F., Tawhid, M.A.: A hybrid particle swarm optimization and genetic algorithm with population partitioning for large scale optimization problems. Ain Shams Eng. J. **8**(2), 191–206 (2017)
4. Alsumait, J., Sykulski, J., Al-Othman, A.: A hybrid GA–PS–SQP method to solve power system valve-point economic dispatch problems. Appl. Energy **87**(5), 1773–1781 (2010)
5. Behrang, M.A., Assareh, E., Noghrehabadi, A.R., Ghanbarzadeh, A.: New sunshine-based models for predicting global solar radiation using PSO (particle swarm optimization) technique. Energy **36**(5), 3036–3049 (2011)
6. Cervantes, A., Galván, I.M., Isasi, P.: AMPSO: a new particle swarm method for nearest neighborhood classification. IEEE Trans. Syst. Man Cybern. Part B (Cybern.) **39**(5), 1082–1091 (2009)
7. Cpałka, K., Rutkowski, L.: Flexible Takagi-Sugeno fuzzy systems. In: Proceedings of the International Joint Conference on Neural Networks 2005, Montreal, pp. 1764–1769 (2005)
8. Cpałka, K., Rutkowski, L.: A new method for designing and reduction of neuro-fuzzy systems. In: Proceedings of the 2006 IEEE International Conference on Fuzzy Systems (IEEE World Congress on Computational Intelligence, WCCI 2006), Vancouver, BC, Canada, pp. 8510–8516 (2006)
9. Cpałka, K., Rutkowski, L.: Evolutionary learning of flexible neuro-fuzzy systems. In: Proceedings of the 2008 IEEE International Conference on Fuzzy Systems (IEEE World Congress on Computational Intelligence, WCCI 2008), Hong Kong, CD, 1–6 June, pp. 969–975 (2008)
10. Dawar, D., Ludwig, S.A.: Effect of strategy adaptation on differential evolution in presence and absence of parameter adaptation: an investigation. J. Artif. Intell. Soft Comput. Res. **8**(3), 211–235 (2018)
11. Davoodi, E., Hagh, M.T., Zadeh, S.G.: A hybrid Improved Quantum-behaved Particle Swarm Optimization–Simplex method (IQPSOS) to solve power system load flow problems. Appl. Soft Comput. **21**, 171–179 (2014)
12. Dziwiński, P., Avedyan, E.D.: A new approach to nonlinear modeling based on significant operating points detection. In: Rutkowski, L., Korytkowski, M., Scherer, R., Tadeusiewicz, R., Zadeh, L.A.; Zurada, J.M. (eds.) ICAISC 2015. LNCS (LNAI), vol. 9120, pp. 364–378. Springer, Cham (2015). https://doi.org/10.1007/978-3-319-19369-4_33
13. Dziwiński, P., Avedyan, E.D.: A new method of the intelligent modeling of the nonlinear dynamic objects with fuzzy detection of the operating points. In: Rutkowski, L., Korytkowski, M., Scherer, R., Tadeusiewicz, R., Zadeh, L.A., Zurada, J.M. (eds.) ICAISC 2016. LNCS (LNAI), vol. 9693, pp. 293–305. Springer, Cham (2016). https://doi.org/10.1007/978-3-319-39384-1_25

14. Dziwiński, P., Bartczuk, Ł., Tingwen, H.: A method for non-linear modelling based on the capabilities of PSO and GA algorithms. In: Rutkowski, L., Korytkowski, M., Scherer, R., Tadeusiewicz, R., Zadeh, L.A., Zurada, J.M. (eds.) ICAISC 2017. LNCS (LNAI), vol. 10246, pp. 221–232. Springer, Cham (2017). https://doi.org/10.1007/978-3-319-59060-8_21

15. Eberhart, R., Kennedy, J.: A new optimizer using particle swarm theory. In: Proceedings of the Sixth International Symposium on Micro Machine and Human Science, MHS 1995, pp. 39–43 (1995)

16. Esmin, A.A.A., Lambert-Torres, G., Alvarenga, G.B.: Hybrid evolutionary algorithm based on PSO and GA mutation. In: 2006 Sixth International Conference on Hybrid Intelligent Systems (HIS 2006), p. 57. IEEE (2006)

17. Esmin, A.A., Matwin, S.: HPSOM: a hybrid particle swarm optimization algorithm with genetic mutation. Int. J. Innov. Comput. Inf. Control. 9(5), 1919–1934 (2013)

18. Fang, N., Zhou, J., Zhang, R., Liu, Y., Zhang, Y.: A hybrid of real coded genetic algorithm and artificial fish swarm algorithm for short-term optimal hydrothermal scheduling. Int. J. Electr. Power Energy Syst. 62, 617–629 (2014)

19. Gabryel, M.: The bag-of-words method with different types of image features and dictionary analysis. J. Univers. Comput. Sci. 24(4), 357–371 (2018)

20. Han, H.G., Lu, W., Hou, Y., Qiao, J.F.: An adaptive-PSO-based self-organizing RBF neural network. IEEE Trans. Neural Netw. Learn. Syst. 29(1), 104–117 (2018)

21. Kennedy, J.: Small worlds and mega-minds: effects of neighborhood topology on particle swarm performance. In: Proceedings of the 1999 Congress on Evolutionary Computation-CEC99 (Cat. No. 99TH8406), vol. 3, pp. 1931–1938. IEEE (1999)

22. Liang, J.J., Suganthan, P.N.: Dynamic multi-swarm particle swarm optimizer. In: Proceedings 2005 IEEE Swarm Intelligence Symposium, SIS, pp. 124–129. IEEE (2005)

23. Liang, J.J., Qin, A.K., Suganthan, P.N., Baskar, S.: Comprehensive learning particle swarm optimizer for global optimization of multimodal functions. IEEE Trans. Evol. Comput. 10(3), 281–295 (2006)

24. Łapa, K., Cpałka, K., Wang, L.: New method for design of fuzzy systems for nonlinear modelling using different criteria of interpretability. In: Rutkowski, L., Korytkowski, M., Scherer, R., Tadeusiewicz, R., Zadeh, L.A., Zurada, J.M. (eds.) ICAISC 2014. LNCS (LNAI), vol. 8467, pp. 217–232. Springer, Cham (2014). https://doi.org/10.1007/978-3-319-07173-2_20

25. Łapa, K., Cpałka, K., Przybył, A., Grzanek, K.: Negative space-based population initialization algorithm (NSPIA). In: Rutkowski, L., Scherer, R., Korytkowski, M., Pedrycz, W., Tadeusiewicz, R., Zurada, J.M. (eds.) ICAISC 2018. LNCS (LNAI), vol. 10841, pp. 449–461. Springer, Cham (2018). https://doi.org/10.1007/978-3-319-91253-0_42

26. Łapa, K., Cpałka, K., Przybył, A.: Genetic programming algorithm for designing of control systems. Inf. Technol. Control. 47(5), 668–683 (2018)

27. Mendes, R., Kennedy, J., Neves, J.: The fully informed particle swarm: simpler, maybe better. IEEE Trans. Evol. Comput. 8(3), 204–210 (2004)

28. Nickabadi, A., Ebadzadeh, M.M., Safabakhsh, R.: A novel particle swarm optimization algorithm with adaptive inertia weight. Appl. Soft Comput. 11(4), 3658–3670 (2011)

29. Nowicki, R.K., Starczewski, J.T.: A new method for classification of imprecise data using fuzzy rough fuzzification. Inf. Sci. 414, 33–52 (2017)

30. Ramadan, H.S., Bendary, A.F., Nagy, S.: Particle swarm optimization algorithm for capacitor allocation problem in distribution systems with wind turbine generators. Int. J. Electr. Power Energy Syst. 84, 143–152 (2017)

31. Rotar, C., Iantovics, L.B.: Directed evolution – a new metaheuristc for optimization. J. Artif. Intell. Soft Comput. Res. **7**(3), 183–200 (2017)

32. Rutkowski, L., Cpałka, K., Flexible weighted neuro-fuzzy systems. In: Proceedings of the 9th International Conference on Neural Information Processing (ICONIP 2002), Orchid Country Club, Singapore, CD, 18–22 November (2002)

33. Rutkowski, L., Cpałka, K.: Neuro-fuzzy systems derived from quasi-triangular norms. In: Proceedings of the IEEE International Conference on Fuzzy Systems, Budapest, 26–29 July, vol. 2, pp. 1031–1036 (2004)

34. Rutkowski, T., Romanowski, J., Woldan, P., Staszewski, P., Nielek, R., Rutkowski, L.: A content-based recommendation system using neuro-fuzzy approach. In: FUZZ-IEEE 2018, pp. 1–8 (2018)

35. Rutkowski, T., Romanowski, J., Woldan, P., Staszewski, P., Nielek, R.: Towards interpretability of the movie recommender based on a neuro-fuzzy approach. In: Rutkowski, L., Scherer, R., Korytkowski, M., Pedrycz, W., Tadeusiewicz, R., Zurada, J.M. (eds.) ICAISC 2018. LNCS (LNAI), vol. 10842, pp. 752–762. Springer, Cham (2018). https://doi.org/10.1007/978-3-319-91262-2_66

36. Sadiqbatcha, S., Jafarzadeh, S., Ampatzidis, Y.: Particle swarm optimization for solving a class of type-1 and type-2 fuzzy nonlinear equations. J. Artif. Intell. Soft Comput. Res. **8**(2), 103–110 (2018)

37. Shi, Y., Eberhart, R.: A modified particle swarm optimizer. In: 1998 IEEE International Conference on Evolutionary Computation Proceedings. IEEE World Congress on Computational Intelligence (Cat. No. 98TH8360), pp. 69–73. IEEE (1998)

38. Shi, Y., Eberhart, R.C.: Parameter selection in particle swarm optimization. In: Porto, V.W., Saravanan, N., Waagen, D., Eiben, A.E. (eds.) EP 1998. LNCS, vol. 1447, pp. 591–600. Springer, Heidelberg (1998). https://doi.org/10.1007/BFb0040810

39. Starczewski, J.T.: Centroid of triangular and gaussian type-2 fuzzy sets. Inf. Sci. **280**, 289–306 (2014)

40. Starczewski, J.T., Nieszporek, K., Wróbel, M., Grzanek, K.: A fuzzy SOM for understanding incomplete 3D faces. In: Rutkowski, L., Scherer, R., Korytkowski, M., Pedrycz, W., Tadeusiewicz, R., Zurada, J.M. (eds.) ICAISC 2018. LNCS (LNAI), vol. 10842, pp. 73–80. Springer, Cham (2018). https://doi.org/10.1007/978-3-319-91262-2_7

41. Tambouratzis, G.: Using particle swarm optimization to accurately identify syntactic phrases in free text. J. Artif. Intell. Soft Comput. Res. **8**(1), 63–67 (2018)

42. Trelea, I.C.: The particle swarm optimization algorithm: convergence analysis and parameter selection. Inf. Process. Lett. **85**(6), 317–325 (2003)

43. Vlachogiannis, J.G., Lee, K.Y.: A comparative study on particle swarm optimization for optimal steady-state performance of power systems. IEEE Trans. Power Syst. **21**(4), 1718–1728 (2006)

44. Wang, L., Yang, B., Orchard, J.: Particle swarm optimization using dynamic tournament topology. Appl. Soft Comput. **48**, 584–596 (2016)

45. Yang, S., Sato, Y.: Swarm intelligence algorithm based on competitive predators with dynamic virtual teams. J. Artif. Intell. Soft Comput. Res. **7**(2), 87–101 (2017)

46. Zalasiński, M., Cpałka, K.: Novel algorithm for the on-line signature verification using selected discretization points groups. In: Rutkowski, L., Korytkowski, M., Scherer, R., Tadeusiewicz, R., Zadeh, L.A., Zurada, J.M. (eds.) ICAISC 2013. LNCS (LNAI), vol. 7894, pp. 493–502. Springer, Heidelberg (2013). https://doi.org/10.1007/978-3-642-38658-9_44

47. Zalasiński, M., Cpałka, K., Er, M.J.: A new method for the dynamic signature verification based on the stable partitions of the signature. In: Rutkowski, L., Korytkowski, M., Scherer, R., Tadeusiewicz, R., Zadeh, L.A., Zurada, J.M. (eds.) ICAISC 2015. LNCS (LNAI), vol. 9120, pp. 161–174. Springer, Cham (2015). https://doi.org/10.1007/978-3-319-19369-4_16

48. Zalasiński, M., Cpałka, K., Hayashi, Y.: A new approach to the dynamic signature verification aimed at minimizing the number of global features. In: Rutkowski, L., Korytkowski, M., Scherer, R., Tadeusiewicz, R., Zadeh, L.A., Zurada, J.M. (eds.) ICAISC 2016. LNCS (LNAI), vol. 9693, pp. 218–231. Springer, Cham (2016). https://doi.org/10.1007/978-3-319-39384-1_20

49. Zalasiński, M., Cpałka, K., Rakus-Andersson, E.: An idea of the dynamic signature verification based on a hybrid approach. In: Rutkowski, L., Korytkowski, M., Scherer, R., Tadeusiewicz, R., Zadeh, L.A., Zurada, J.M. (eds.) ICAISC 2016. LNCS (LNAI), vol. 9693, pp. 232–246. Springer, Cham (2016). https://doi.org/10. 1007/978-3-319-39384-1_21

50. Zalasiński, M., Cpałka, K.: New algorithm for on-line signature verification using characteristic hybrid partitions. In: Wilimowska, Z., Borzemski, L., Grzech, A., Świątek, J. (eds.) Information Systems Architecture and Technology: Proceedings of 36th International Conference on Information Systems Architecture and Technology – ISAT 2015 – Part IV. AISC, vol. 432, pp. 147–157. Springer, Cham (2016). https://doi.org/10.1007/978-3-319-28567-2_13

51. Zhang, Y., Zhao, Y., Fu, X., Xu, J.: A feature extraction method of the particle swarm optimization algorithm based on adaptive inertia weight and chaos optimization for Brillouin scattering spectra. Opt. Commun. **376**, 56–66 (2016)

Evolutionary Algorithms Applied to a Shielding Enclosure Design

Tomas Kadavy$^{(\boxtimes)}$ ⓘ, Stanislav Kovar ⓘ, Michal Pluhacek ⓘ, Adam Viktorin ⓘ, and Roman Senkerik ⓘ

Tomas Bata University in Zlin, T.G.Masaryka 5555, 760 01 Zlin, Czech Republic
{kadavy,skovar,pluhacek,aviktorn,senkerik}@utb.cz

Abstract. Currently, electromagnetic compatibility presents a severe problem for electric and electronic devices; therefore, the demand for protection has rapidly increased in recent years. Unfortunately, the design of a high-quality shield can involve different pitfalls, and it is impossible to explore and test every possible solution. Many times, the model of an existing structure form different scientific areas have been successfully redesigned using knowledge and techniques adopted from the field of artificial intelligence. The soft computing based approach has been verified here, and selected real case study is presented in this paper.

Keywords: Shielding effectiveness · Shielding enclosure · SHADE · HCLPSO · FA · CST Microwave Studio

1 Introduction

Electromagnetic compatibility has become a severe problem for electronic and electric device design and implementation. The increase of electromagnetic interference has led to a rise in demand for electromagnetic shielding. The protection quality is given by the shielding effectiveness, that is given as a ratio of a signal received by antenna without a shield to a signal gained by a receiver with shield cover [1]. The research paper [1] also defines the term called shielding enclosure, which is a mechanical structure to protect the device against the electromagnetic fields effects.

This work was supported by the Ministry of Education, Youth and Sports of the Czech Republic within the National Sustainability Programme Project no. LO1303 (MSMT-7778/2014), further by the European Regional Development Fund under the Project CEBIA-Tech no. CZ.1.05/2.1.00/03.0089 and by Internal Grant Agency of Tomas Bata University under the Projects no. IGA/CebiaTech/2019/002. This work is also based upon support by COST (European Cooperation in Science & Technology) under Action CA15140, Improving Applicability of Nature-Inspired Optimisation by Joining Theory and Practice (ImAppNIO), and Action IC1406, High-Performance Modelling and Simulation for Big Data Applications (cHiPSet). The work was further supported by resources of A.I. Lab at the Faculty of Applied Informatics, Tomas Bata University in Zlin (ailab.fai.utb.cz).

© Springer Nature Switzerland AG 2019
L. Rutkowski et al. (Eds.): ICAISC 2019, LNAI 11508, pp. 445–455, 2019.
https://doi.org/10.1007/978-3-030-20912-4_41

This study aims at the finding of an optimal solution for shielding enclosure which is suitable for security cameras. Cameras, and especially image sensors, represent the devices with the highest level of sensitivity to electromagnetic field [2]. Therefore, it is required to provide suitable protection which is crucial for security services. The experiment pitfall is presented by a simple fact that the box should have a dense grid for a quality electromagnetic shielding; however, at the same time, the camera vision should be clear, and the grid should be sparse and as transparent as possible.

The artificial intelligence based techniques were successfully used to redesign several different structures or devices in various scientific or engineering fields [3]; for example, the design of an analog circuit [5], antennas [4] or wings for aeronautical purposes [6].

In this paper, three representatives of evolutionary computation techniques have been used to find the optimal product design, since each algorithm exhibits unique features and performance. The simulations of an evolved shielding enclosures have been carried out, tested and evaluated thanks to CST Microwave Studio simulation software [7].

This represents the clear motivation behind this paper, as we wanted to study and show applicability and performance of evolutionary computation techniques in this particular engineering case study.

The rest of the paper is structured as follows. Brief descriptions of used evolutionary and swarm algorithms are given in Sect. 2. In Sect. 3, the experiment is described in detail. The results and conclusion sections follow afterward.

2   Used Evolutionary Computation Techniques

The evolutionary computation techniques are steadily gaining popularity not only among researches interested in the field of artificial intelligence but in other scientific or engineering fields. Many times these algorithms proved their applicability and effectivity. Whenever some problem cannot be solved using some traditional methods of numerical optimization (complex multimodal problems with many local optima) or time restrictions are not allowing to test sufficient quantity of possible combination of parameters, the simple and natural choice is to use any metaheuristic algorithm. However, due to a large amount of existing metaheuristic algorithms, it could be a challenging task to select the most suitable algorithm for a specific problem. Often a researcher has to test several algorithms to pick the most promising one or to use some benchmarks which can help with the future choice.

In this paper, three different algorithms were selected either based on their promising results on widely accepted benchmark set (SHADE) or because they were previously used with promising results on similar tasks (HCLPSO and FA). The brief description of each used algorithm is given in the next subsections.

2.1   Success-History Based Adaptive Differential Evolution

The original Differential Evolution (DE) was created in 1995 by Storn and Price [8]. Since then, DE has been actively studied and changed from the original algorithm, to improve algorithm robustness. During the last few years, the Success-History based Adaptive DE (SHADE) algorithm [9] has been one of the most researched DE variants and, it or its improved versions [10,11] have performed very well in CEC single objective optimization competitions [12–14]. Therefore it becomes a promising candidate for this shield enclosure design task.

The SHADE algorithm is initialized with a random population of individuals that represent solutions of the optimization problem, additional memories for F and CR values are initialized as well. The population size NP is set by the user. In continuous optimization, each individual is composed of a vector x of length D, which is a dimensionality (number of optimized attributes) of the problem, where each vector component represents a value of the corresponding attribute, and the individual also contains the objective function value $f(x)$.

In the mutation step (1), individual $\boldsymbol{x}_{r1}$ is randomly selected from a population and $\boldsymbol{x}_{r1}$ is randomly selected from the union of the current population and the external archive of inferior solutions.

$$\boldsymbol{v}_i = \boldsymbol{x}_i + F_i \left(\boldsymbol{x}_{pbest} - \boldsymbol{x}_i \right) + F_i \left(\boldsymbol{x}_{r1} - \boldsymbol{x}_{r2} \right) \tag{1}$$

Where $\boldsymbol{x}_{pbest}$ is randomly selected from the best $NP \times p$ individuals in the current population. The p value is randomly generated for each mutation by RNG with uniform distribution from the range $[p_{min}, 0.2]$ [2], where $p_{min} = 2/NP$. The scaling factor value F_i is given by (2).

$$F_i = C\left[M_{F,r}, 0.1\right] \tag{2}$$

Where $M_{F,r}$ is a randomly selected value (by index r) from M_F memory and C stands for Cauchy distribution. In the crossover step, mutated vector v_i is combined with the original vector x_i, and they produce trial vector u_i (3).

$$u_{j,i} = \begin{cases} v_{j,i} & \text{if } U\left[0,1\right] \le CR_i \text{ or } j = j_{rand} \\ x_{j,i} & \text{otherwise} \end{cases} \tag{3}$$

Where CR_i is the used crossover rate value, and j_{rand} is an index of an attribute that has to be from the mutated vector v_i (ensures generation of a vector with at least one new component). The value CR_i is generated from the Gaussian distribution with a mean parameter value of $M_{CR,r}$, which is randomly selected from M_{CR} memory and standard deviation value of 0.1.

The final selection step ensures that the optimization progress will lead to better solutions because it allows only individuals of better or at least equal objective function value to proceed into the next generation $G+1$ (4) where G is the index of the current generation.

$$\boldsymbol{x}_{i,G+1} = \begin{cases} \boldsymbol{u}_{i,G} & \text{if } f\left(\boldsymbol{u}_{i,G}\right) \le f\left(\boldsymbol{x}_{i,G}\right) \\ \boldsymbol{x}_{i,G} & \text{otherwise} \end{cases} \tag{4}$$

More detailed information on the historical memory updates M_F and M_{CR}, as well as information on recommended values and description of the algorithm together with pseudocode, is described in the original paper [9].

2.2 Heterogeneous Comprehensive Learning Particle Swarm Optimization

The new and modern variant on classical Particle Swarm Optimization (PSO) [15] algorithm was firstly introduced in 2015 by Lynn and Suganthan [16]. This particular algorithm was used for unit commitment in power system [17], and it is still under active developed.

The main characteristic of this new algorithm, called Heterogeneous Comprehensive Learning Particle Swarm Optimization (HCLPSO), is that it contains two subpopulations. The PSO instead typically consist of only one population.

The first subpopulation is enhanced for exploration and the second one is enhanced for exploitation. Each subpopulation computes the velocity of a particle through the different formulas. The exploration-enhanced subpopulation uses the formula (5).

$$v_{ij}^{t+1}=w\cdot v_{ij}^t+c_1\cdot r_1\cdot\left(pBest_{fi(j)}-x_{ij}^t\right) \tag{5}$$

On the other hand, the exploitation-enhanced subpopulation calculates particles velocity by (6).

$$v_{ij}^{t+1}=w\cdot v_{ij}^t+c_1\cdot r_1\cdot\left(pBest_{fi(j)}-x_{ij}^t\right) + c_2\cdot r_2\cdot\left(gBest_j-x_{ij}^t\right) \tag{6}$$

Where the $t+1$ stands for actual velocity and the t is previous value. The v_{ij} is then the velocity of i-th particle in j-th dimension. The w is for inertia weight, and it can be a constant value, or it can change its value depending on the number of already computed iterations [18]. The c_1 and c_2 are the learning factors, and r_1 and r_2 are pseudo-random numbers of unimodal distribution in the range $<0, 1>$. The x_{ij} is the position of an i-th particle for j-th dimension. All these previously mentioned variables are also used in classical PSO. One exception is the $pBest_{fi(j)}$, which is the example particle generated throughout comprehensive learning (CL) strategy [19]. Where: $f_i(d) = [f_i(1), f_i(2), \ldots, f_i(D)]$ pointing i-th particle to use its own $pBest$ or the $pBest$ of another particle in particular dimension d. The D is then the dimension size of the solution search space. An update of a particle position is then calculated by a classical PSO Eq. (7).

$$x_{ij}^{t+1} = x_{ij}^t + v_{ij}^{t+1} \tag{7}$$

Thank this learning strategy, each particle can learn from all other $pBests$ of both subpopulations. With the learning probability Pc (8), the particle generates the example particle if for the m (refreshing gap) evaluations the particle's $pBest$ is not improved. The NP is the number of particles in both subpopulations.

$$Pc_i = 0.05 + 0.45\cdot\frac{e^{\frac{10(i-1)}{NP-1}} - 1}{e^{10} - 1} \tag{8}$$

The Pc defines with which probability (from 0.05 to 0.5) the i-particle select its own or other's $pBest$ for the corresponding dimension. If the particle should not choose its $pBest$, two random particles are selected, and the particle with better fitness value is chosen for the corresponding dimension.

2.3   Firefly Algorithm

The Firefly Algorithm (FA) is one of the typical representatives of swarm intelligence (SI) group. It was developed and introduced to the world by Yang in 2008 [20,21]. The FA was also successfully used for many optimization problems. For example, the design of antenna [22], job scheduling [23] and solving the traveling salesman problem [24].

The fundamental principle of this algorithm lies in simulating the mating behavior of fireflies at night when fireflies emit light to attract a suitable partner. The movement of one firefly towards another one is then defined by Eq. (9), where x_{ik}^{t+1} is a new position of firefly i for dimension k, x_{ik}^{t} is the current position of firefly i and x_{jk}^{t} is a selected brighter firefly (with better objective function value). α is a randomization parameter ($\alpha \in$ <0, 1>). The original FA use the random value drawn from the uniform distribution. Finally, $sign$ simply provides random direction -1 or 1 to ensure that the firefly could travel in both directions.

$$x_{ik}^{t+1} = x_{ik}^{t} + \beta_i \cdot \left(x_{jk}^{t} - x_{ik}^{t}\right) + \alpha \cdot sign \tag{9}$$

The brightness I_i of a firefly is computed by the Eq. (10) where $f(x_i)$ is the CF value of corresponding i-firefly, γ stands for the light absorption parameter of a media in which fireflies are and m is another user-defined coefficient and it should be set $m \geq 1$. The variable r_{ij} is the Euclidean distance (11) between the two compared fireflies (d stands for the current dimension size of the optimized problem). The firefly x_i could only fly (9) towards the x_j firefly if $I_j < I_i$.

$$I_i = \frac{f(x_i)}{1 + \gamma r_{ij}^{m}} \tag{10}$$

$$r_{ij} = \sqrt{\sum_{k=1}^{d} \left(x_{ik} - x_{jk}\right)^2} \tag{11}$$

$$\beta_i = \frac{\beta_i'}{1 + \gamma r_{ij}^{m}} \tag{12}$$

The attractiveness β_i (12) is proportional to the brightness I_i as mentioned in the rules above and, so these equations are quite similar to each other. The β_i' is the initial attractiveness defined by the user, the γ is again the light absorption parameter and the r_{ij} is once more the Euclidean distance.

3   Experiment Design

The experiment used two distinct software. The first was Wolfram Mathematica [25] that secured execution of all used metaheuristic algorithms, and the second one was CST Microwave Studio [7]. This simulation software has been used for the modeling of a shielding enclosure with a front grid and shielding effectiveness calculations. CST Studio involves particular macro which was used to model creation and subsequent calculations. This macro was created by Mathematica software which adjusted the dimensions of the optimization task (parameters), depicted in Table 1. The values of these parameters were obtained by metaheuristic algorithm. Every time a running metaheuristic algorithm required the evaluation of objective function for a particular parameter setting, the Mathematica created a macro that was sent to CST Studio, which executed a specific simulation. When this simulation was finished, the CST generated a data structure with results. These results contained the shielding effectiveness in dB for several tested frequencies. The results were then averaged to get a single number f_s (i.e., shielding quality).

The parameters that were evolutionarily tuned were used to create a front-mask grid of a shielding enclosure for cameras. The shape and size of gaps in the mask have a direct effect on the shielding quality f_s. The smaller the gaps, the better the shielding should be. However, from the camera perspective, the large the gaps are the better is the vision quality f_v. Vision quality f_v was computed as a fraction between solid and empty (holes) space. These objective functions are in contradictory. Therefore, the final objective function $f(x)$ for parameters x was defined as (13).

$$f(x) = \frac{w_1}{f_{s(x)}} - w_2 \cdot f_v(x) \tag{13}$$

Where w_1 and w_2 are weights that help transfer this multi-objective problem to single-objective. The values of these weights are strongly affecting the solution quality and were initially set for this primary research study as $w_1 = 1$ and $w_2 = 1$.

Table 1. Optimization parameter definition and ranges.

Parameter name	Description	Allowed range
Pitch	The length between the centers of gaps	$\langle 2,\ 6 \rangle$ in $\mathbb{R}$ $[mm]$
Radius	The radius of the inner circle of gaps	$\langle 1.5,\ 4 \rangle$ in $\mathbb{R}$ $[mm]$
Edge	A number of edges of designed gaps	$\langle 3,\ 12 \rangle$ in $\mathbb{N}$ $[-]$
Angle1	The angle of gaps in odd rows	$\langle 0,\ 359 \rangle$ in $\mathbb{R}$ $[°]$
Angle2	Relative angle to Angle1 of even rows	$\langle 0,\ 359 \rangle$ in $\mathbb{R}$ $[°]$
Thickness	The thickness of the front mask of the enclosure	$\langle 1,\ 3 \rangle$ in $\mathbb{R}$ $[mm]$

The shielding effectiveness f_s was measured in CST studio using simulations and test probes. One tested probe was located inside of the enclosure and another probe between model and wave plane which serves as a source of the electromagnetic waves. Probes detected the level of an electrical field which helped to calculate designed enclosure shielding effectiveness. The wave plane dimension in x and y-axes were equal to the dimensions of the model in the same axes. The example of a simulation setting with enclosure and gaps in front-mask can be seen in Fig. 1.

4 Results

Because of the stochastic nature of used optimization algorithms, it was necessary to perform many repeated evaluations of the objective function. However, to finish one simulation (i.e., one objective function evaluation) in CST studio, it took approx. 5–20 min. Therefore, it was impossible to test various settings of used algorithms (the recommended settings by Authors of each respective algorithm SHADE/HCLPSO/FA were used), and an only single run of each algorithm was carried out. This is also a reason, as to why such a set of metaheuristics algorithm has been selected. The general applicability of evolutionary techniques has been verified (even though for single and extremely time demanding execution) for state of the art competition winning classical evolutionary based SHADE algorithm, effective modern swarm-based algorithm HCLPSO and simpler FA mimicking randomized search over the objective function hyperplane. Since only a single run was performed, to maximize the reliability of comparisons, all three algorithms have used the same initialization (i.e., initial population). A maximum number of function evaluations was set to $MAXFES = 5,000$, and the population size was set to $NP = 50$. In Fig. 2, it can be seen the convergence graphs of all three compared algorithms.

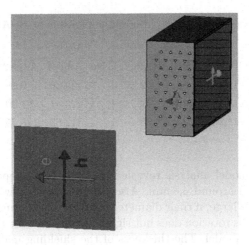

Fig. 1. Example of a designed shielding enclosure.

From the convergence plot, it can be observed that SHADE algorithm has the fastest convergence speed. Also, it achieved the best results among the compared

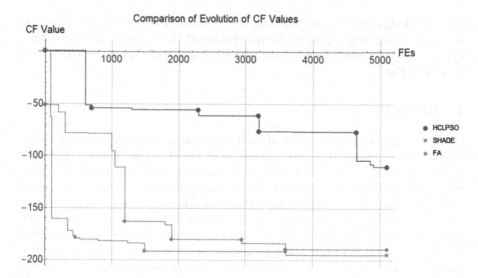

Fig. 2. Convergence graph for SHADE, HCLPSO, and FA in the task of shielding effectiveness $f(x)$ optimization.

algorithms. The second best performing algorithm is FA with slower convergence speed. The worst results were achieved by HCLPSO algorithm. Table 2 contains the final cost function value $f(x)$ achieved by each algorithm accompanied by the final values of optimized parameters.

Table 2. Final CF value and values optimized parameters for SHADE, HCLPSO, and FA.

Algorithm	CF	Pitch	Radius	Edge	Angle1	Angle2	Thickness
SHADE	−194.87	4.83	1.52	4	129.30	0.08	2.70
FA	−189.39	1.89	1.77	4	223.41	91.90	2.62
HCLPSO	−110.06	2.34	1.93	4	312.63	178.75	2.67

The obtained model analysis revealed that the best shape for apertures is square with pitches around 4.8 mm. Also, the distance between the boundary points of the gaps is large, if their diameter is taken into account. Results showed that the mutual gaps rotation does not significantly affect the resulting shielding effectiveness of the model. The thickness of the shielding material is always at approx. 2.6–2.7 mm.

Figures 3, 4 and 5 shows the shielding effectiveness calculated by CST studio for different probe positions over the tested frequencies and all three used metaheuristic algorithms.

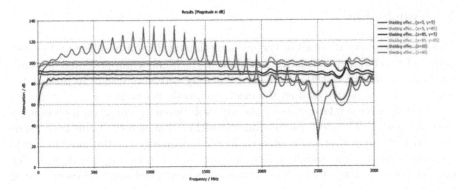

Fig. 3. Shielding effectiveness in dB calculated for FA.

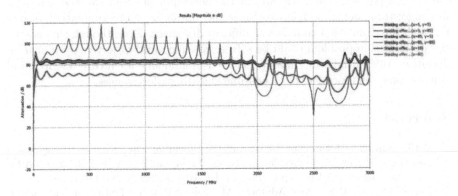

Fig. 4. Shielding effectiveness in dB calculated for HCLPSO.

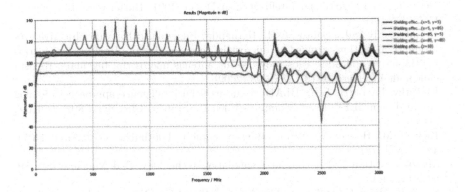

Fig. 5. Shielding effectiveness in dB calculated for SHADE.

5   Conclusion

This research paper is aimed at the investigation on the applicability and performance of selected metaheuristic algorithms in the highly computational demanding task of a finding optimal front-face shielding enclosure design to protect the sensitive camera device against the electromagnetic fields effects.

In total, three modern state of the art evolutionary computation techniques were used here. The best performing algorithm that achieved the best result was SHADE algorithm. The process focused primarily on the shielding grid dimension calculation, which is a crucial part of the shielding box design. The objective was to find an optimal balance between shielding effectiveness and camera visibility.

The results lend weight to the argument that the utilization of evolutionary computation techniques in this particular engineering design case study was beneficial. Future research will aim at the development of an effective and parallel algorithm, better weights settings and obtaining more simulation results although the simulation time is a significant drawback. Even though this particular optimization problem could be solved by some multi-objective optimization algorithm, this initial study mainly serves as a guideline for future research and to have some reference values of possible shielding effectiveness.

References

1. IEEE Standard Method for Measuring the Shielding Effectiveness of Enclosures and Boxes Having all Dimensions between 0.1 m and 2 m. IEEE Std 299.1-2013, pp. 1–96, January 2014. https://doi.org/10.1109/IEEESTD.2014.6712029
2. Pospisilik, M., Riha, M., Adamek, M., Silva, R.M.S.: DSLR camera immunity to electromagnetic fields - experiment description. WSEAS Trans. Circ. Syst. **14**, 10 (2015). http://www.wseas.org/multimedia/journals/circuits/2015/b105801-436.pdf. Accessed 01 Mar 2017
3. Gero, J.S. (ed.): Artificial Intelligence in Design 1991. Butterworth-Heinemann, Oxford (2014)
4. Brianeze, J.R., Silva-Santos, C.H., Hernández-Figueroa, H.E.: Multiobjective evolutionary algorithms applied to microstrip antennas design algoritmos evolutivos multiobjetivo aplicados a los proyectos de antenas microstrip. Ingeniare. Revista chilena de ingeniería **17**(3), 288–298 (2009)
5. El-Turky, F., Perry, E.E.: BLADES: an artificial intelligence approach to analog circuit design. IEEE Trans. Comput.-Aided Des. Integr. Circ. Syst. **8**(6), 680–692 (1989)
6. Hicks, R.M., Henne, P.A.: Wing design by numerical optimization. J. Aircr. **15**(7), 407–412 (1978)
7. Microwave Studio: CST-computer simulation technology. Bad Nuheimer Str **19**, 64289 (2008)
8. Storn, R., Price, K.: Differential Evolution-A Simple and Efficient Adaptive Scheme for Global Optimization over Continuous Spaces, vol. 3. ICSI, Berkeley (1995)
9. Tanabe, R., Fukunaga, A.: Success-history based parameter adaptation for differential evolution. In: 2013 IEEE Congress on Evolutionary Computation (CEC), pp. 71–78. IEEE, June 2013

10. Tanabe, R., Fukunaga, A. S.: Improving the search performance of SHADE using linear population size reduction. In: 2014 IEEE Congress on Evolutionary Computation (CEC), pp. 1658–1665. IEEE, July 2014

11. Viktorin, A., Pluhacek, M., Senkerik, R.: Success-history based adaptive differential evolution algorithm with multi-chaotic framework for parent selection performance on CEC 2014 benchmark set. In: 2016 IEEE Congress on Evolutionary Computation (CEC), pp. 4797–4803. IEEE, July 2016

12. Liang, J.J., Qu, B.Y., Suganthan, P.N., Hernández-Díaz, A.G.: Problem definitions and evaluation criteria for the CEC 2013 special session on real-parameter optimization, p. 201212. Zhengzhou University, Zhengzhou, China and Nanyang Technological University, Singapore, Technical Report, Computational Intelligence Laboratory (2013)

13. Liang, J.J., Qu, B.Y., Suganthan, P.N.: Problem definitions and evaluation criteria for the CEC 2014 special session and competition on single objective real-parameter numerical optimization. Zhengzhou University, Zhengzhou China and Technical Report, Nanyang Technological University, Singapore, Computational Intelligence Laboratory (2013)

14. Liang, J. J., Qu, B. Y., Suganthan, P. N., Chen, Q.: Problem definitions and evaluation criteria for the CEC 2015 competition on learning-based real-parameter single objective optimization. Technical Report 201411A, Computational Intelligence Laboratory, Zhengzhou University, Zhengzhou China and Technical Report, Nanyang Technological University, Singapore (2014)

15. Kennedy, J., Eberhart, R.: Particle swarm optimization. In: Proceedings of the IEEE International Conference on Neural Networks, pp. 1942–1948 (1995)

16. Lynn, N., Suganthan, P.N.: Heterogeneous comprehensive learning particle swarm optimization with enhanced exploration and exploitation. Swarm Evol. Comput. **24**, 11–24 (2015)

17. Lynn, N.: Heterogeneous particle swarm optimization with an application of unit commitment in power system, Singapore. Thesis. School of Electrical and Electronic Engineering. Supervisor Ponnuthurai Nagaratnam Suganthan (2016)

18. Kennedy, J.: The particle swarm: social adaptation of knowledge. In: Proceedings of the IEEE International Conference on Evolutionary Computation, pp. 303–308 (1997)

19. Liang, J.J., Qin, A.K., Suganthan, P.N., Baskar, S.: Comprehensive learning particle swarm optimizer for global optimization of multimodal functions. IEEE Trans. Evol. Comput. **10**, 281–295 (2006)

20. Yang, X.S.: Nature-Inspired Metaheuristic Algorithms, pp. 242–246. Luniver Press, Beckington (2008)

21. Yang, X.-S.: Firefly algorithms for multimodal optimization. In: Watanabe, O., Zeugmann, T. (eds.) SAGA 2009. LNCS, vol. 5792, pp. 169–178. Springer, Heidelberg (2009). https://doi.org/10.1007/978-3-642-04944-6_14

22. Zaman, M.A., et al.: Nonuniformly spaced linear antenna array design using firefly algorithm. Int. J. Microwave Sci. Technol. **2012**, 8 (2012)

23. Yousif, A., Abdullah, A.H., Nor, S.M.: Scheduling jobs on grid computing using firefly algorithm (2011)

24. Jati, G.K., Suyanto: Evolutionary discrete firefly algorithm for travelling salesman problem. In: Bouchachia, A. (ed.) ICAIS 2011. LNCS, vol. 6943, pp. 393–403. Springer, Heidelberg (2011). https://doi.org/10.1007/978-3-642-23857-4_38

25. Wolfram, S.: Mathematica. Cambridge University Press, Cambridge (1996)

Hybrid Multi-population Based Approach for Controllers Structure and Parameters Selection

Krystian Łapa[1](✉), Krzysztof Cpałka[1], and Józef Paszkowski[2,3]

[1] Institute of Computational Intelligence, Częstochowa University of Technology,
Częstochowa, Poland
{krystian.lapa,krzysztof.cpalka}@iisi.pcz.pl
[2] Information Technology Institute, University of Social Sciences, 90-113 Łodź,
Poland
[3] Clark University, Worcester, MA 01610, USA
jpaszkowski@san.edu.pl

Abstract. Population-based algorithms are used to solve optimization problems. In order to improve their efficiency, new ways of processing the population are investigated. One approach is to use many populations which operations are synchronized with each other. In this article, we propose a new approach in which specified populations are processed using different population algorithms. It has been tested for a known practical problem of selecting the structure and parameters of the controller.

Keywords: Population based algorithm · Multi-population ·
Controller · Structure selection · Parameters selection

1 Introduction

Meta-heuristics are a group of general-purpose algorithms that allows one to optimize parameters of the problem under consideration (see e.g. [4,11,14]). Such problems concern variety of issues, starting from simple function minimization problems, through more complex problems where optimal parameters have to be found, and finishing on problems where parameters of systems that can solve them are seeking (e.g. parameters of fuzzy systems [10,29,33,41,42], neural networks [6,19,22,23], self-organizing maps [16,36], controllers [3], etc.). The latter are particularly important because such systems can be used e.g. in modeling, classification or control issues and thus it applies to multiple areas like business, chemistry, economy, medicine, industrial, etc.

Most of the developed at the moment group of meta-heuristics algorithms are population-based algorithms. These algorithms operate on a group (population) of solutions (individuals) and process them with the purpose of solution improvement in each algorithm's step. Usually, each individual encodes a set

© Springer Nature Switzerland AG 2019
L. Rutkowski et al. (Eds.): ICAISC 2019, LNAI 11508, pp. 456–468, 2019.
https://doi.org/10.1007/978-3-030-20912-4_42

of solution parameters, which quality can be evaluated using fitness function defined adequately to the considered problem. The idea of processing population of individuals usually lies on using a typical schema that can be found in the literature (see e.g. mutation and crossover operators [9]).

Due to the fact that many population-based algorithms are being constantly created (see Table 1) it is not easy to choose the best one for the specified problem. This is also related to the "No Free Lunch" (NFL) theorem in search and optimization, that says that if an algorithm gains in performance on one class of problems then is necessarily loses by its performance on the other problems [40]. The development of algorithms causes that more and more ideas from nature or other areas are used as inspiration to processing populations (see Table 1). This trend is currently being criticized because it creates doubts about the originality of the papers [15]. Thus some editorial boards of magazines cease to accept papers with unconvincing analogies [35].

Table 1. List of exemplary population-based algorithms that have been recently described in the literature.

Algorithm	Inspiration	Year
Bison Behavior Optimization [21]	Bison	2018
Butterfly Optimization Algorithm [2]	Butterfly	2018
Mushroom Reproduction Optimization [5]	Mushrooms	2018
Rhinoceros Search Algorithm [12]	Rhinoceros	2018
Squirrel Search Algorithm [18]	Squirrels	2018
Volleyball Premier League Algorithm [31]	Volleyball	2018
Laying Chicken Algorithm [17]	Chickens	2017
Grasshopper Optimisation Algorithm [34]	Grasshoppers	2017
Spotted Hyena Optimizer [13]	Hyenas	2017
Thermal Exchange Optimization [20]	Thermal exchange	2017
Sonar Inspired Optimization [38]	Sonar	2017
Killer Whale Algorithm [7]	Killer whale	2017

In this paper, a different approach is proposed. A set of cooperating well-known algorithms is used, rather than introducing a new population-based algorithm that is inspired by some phenomena (e.g. from nature). Such groups of algorithms are called multi-population based, and populations in them can share or trade individuals depending on the adopted migration strategy. In the typical multi-population based algorithms all the populations are processed by one particular type of algorithm [30]. This paper proposes a hybrid approach in which different algorithms can be used. Furthermore, in simulations, a specific problem is considered that concerns the design of a control system. In the problem, two types of parameters have to be found: binary one that defines the controller structure, and a real one that defines controller parameters. This causes that the used algorithms should be modified because typical approaches allow only for the processing of real parameters.

Structure of the paper is as follows: Sect. 2 contains a description of controllers considered in the paper, Sect. 3 presents a description of hybrid multi-population based algorithm proposed in the paper, Sect. 4 shows simulation results, conclusions are drawn in Sect. 5.

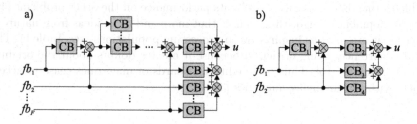

Fig. 1. Controller structure considered in this paper: (a) general structure with F feedback signals, (b) an example of structure with two feedback signals (fb_1 and fb_2).

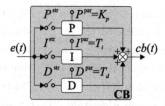

Fig. 2. Considered control block (CB) structure described by formula (1).

2 Description of Considered Controller

Control is an important issue from the scientific and practical point of view. In the literature controllers can be divided into: (a) based on linear terms P, I, and D [8,37], (b) based on computational intelligence [24,26,28], and (c) hybrid solutions that combines approaches from other groups [25,27]. In this paper the controller based on linear terms is considered. It is shown in Fig. 1. In its structure each control block (CB) contains all the P, I, and D linear terms. Moreover, to avoid redundancy, each of these terms can be excluded from operation by use of an additional binary parameters (see Fig. 2): $P^{str} \in \{0,1\}$, $I^{str} \in \{0,1\}$, and $D^{str} \in \{0,1\}$. These parameters stand for activation of P, I, and D elements: values equal to 1 stand for active elements. Thanks to this approach, the selection of the parameters of the linear terms and their corresponding binary parameters allows to adjust the controller's structure to a given simulation problem.

Furthermore, this approach ensures that this process can be automated (e.g. by using a population algorithm). The output of the CB is calculated as follows:

$$cb(t) = P^{\text{str}} \cdot P^{\text{par}} \cdot e(t) + I^{\text{str}} \cdot I^{\text{par}} \cdot \int_0^t e(t)\, dt + D^{\text{str}} \cdot D^{\text{par}} \cdot \frac{de(t)}{dt}. \qquad (1)$$

Using the proposed structure (see Figs. 1 and 2) causes that proper encoding of the parameters has to be used. In this paper the following encoding is proposed:

$$\mathbf{X}_{ch} = \left\{ \mathbf{X}_{ch}^{\text{par}}, \mathbf{X}_{ch}^{\text{str}} \right\}, \qquad (2)$$

where part $\mathbf{X}_{ch}^{\text{par}}$ encodes the real parameters of the controller and part $\mathbf{X}_{ch}^{\text{str}}$ encodes binary parameters of the controller. The part $\mathbf{X}_{ch}^{\text{par}}$ is defined as follows:

$$\mathbf{X}_{ch}^{\text{par}} = \left\{ \begin{matrix} P_{ch,1}^{\text{par}}, I_{ch,1}^{\text{par}}, D_{ch,1}^{\text{par}}, \cdots \\ P_{ch,M}^{\text{par}}, I_{ch,M}^{\text{par}}, D_{ch,M}^{\text{par}} \end{matrix} \right\} = \left\{ X_{ch,1}^{\text{par}}, \ldots, X_{ch,L^{\text{par}}}^{\text{par}} \right\}, \qquad (3)$$

where $P_{ch,m}^{\text{par}}, I_{ch,m}^{\text{par}}, D_{ch,m}^{\text{par}}$ stand for P, I, and D parameters of m-th CB ($m = 1, \ldots, M$) of the individual ch, M stands for number of CB blocks encoded in the individual ch, $L^{\text{par}} = 3 \cdot M$ stands for number of genes in part $\mathbf{X}_{ch}^{\text{par}}$. The part $\mathbf{X}_{ch}^{\text{str}}$ is defined as follows:

$$\mathbf{X}_{ch}^{\text{str}} = \left\{ \begin{matrix} P_{ch,1}^{\text{str}}, I_{ch,1}^{\text{str}}, D_{ch,1}^{\text{str}}, \cdots \\ P_{ch,M}^{\text{str}}, I_{ch,M}^{\text{str}}, D_{ch,M}^{\text{str}} \end{matrix} \right\} = \left\{ X_{ch,1}^{\text{str}}, \ldots, X_{ch,L^{\text{str}}}^{\text{str}} \right\}, \qquad (4)$$

where $L^{\text{str}} = L^{\text{par}}$ stands for number of genes in part $\mathbf{X}_{ch}^{\text{str}}$.

3   Description of Proposed Approach

In the proposed approach it is assumed that a set of different population-based algorithms $alg_1, alg_2, \ldots, alg_A$ can cooperate and thus better results can be achieved. The considered cooperation is based on migration between populations. For this purpose, every population selects individuals (e.g. by roulette

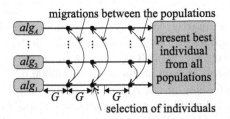

Fig. 3. The idea of the proposed approach, where: A stands for a number of algorithms and G stands for a number of what iterations will be carried out. It is assumed that each algorithm can be different and a different set of parameters can be assigned to it.

wheel method) and transfers their copies to other populations. This step is performed every G iterations of the algorithm (see Fig. 3). Because each population-based algorithm is characterized by a certain set of parameters, and their correct selection allows to adjust their operation not only to a given problem but also to ensure an appropriate compromise between the exploration and exploitation of parameters, it was assumed that each cooperating algorithm can have a separate set of parameters assigned.

Because the controller structure used is defined by both real and binary parameters, the majority of well-known population algorithms cannot be directly used to optimize it. To overcome this, additional mechanisms (operators) must be introduced to allow one to modify parameters of other types than the default. Examples of modifications for selected algorithms are shown in Table 2 and as it can be seen for grey wolf optimizer (GWO) algorithm an additional parameter that defines chance for binary mutation has to be added. Moreover, for the algorithm DE, a power of a CR is used due to the fact that CR have a usually higher value than p_m, which would result in a too chaotic modification of the controller's structure.

Table 2. Examples of hybridization of exemplary population-based algorithms that allows one to optimize both the real and binary type of parameters ($p_m \in (0, 1)$ stands for mutation probability [32], $CR \in [0, 1]$ stands for crossover constant [32], and $u(0, 1)$ stands for random number from range $\in [0, 1]$).

Parameter	Genetic Algorithm (GA)	Differential Evolution (DE)	Grey Wolf Optimizer (GWO)
Real	Crossover: default Mutation: default	Crossover: default	Hunting: default
Binary	Crossover: default Mutation: if $u(0, 1) < p_m$ $x := (x + 1)\,\%2$	Mutation: if $u(0, 1) < CR^2$ $x := (x + 1)\,\%2$	Hunting: if $u(0, 1) < 0.2$ $x := (x + 1)\,\%2$

4 Simulations

In the simulations, a quarter car active suspension control problem was considered [1]. The parameters of active suspension model (see Fig. 4) are following: unsprung mass $m_u = 48.3\,\mathrm{kg}$, sprung mass $m_s = 395.3\,\mathrm{kg}$, tire stiffness $k_t = 30010.0\,\mathrm{N/m}$, sprung stiffness $k_s = 340000.0\,\mathrm{N/m}$, sprung damping $d_s = 1450.0\,\mathrm{Ns/m}$. Meaning of the rest of the active suspension model parameters is following: z_r-road profile, z_t-tire compression, z_u-displacement of unsprung mass, z-suspension travel, z_s-displacement of sprung mass. Measured signals for the controller are following: $fb_1 = \ddot{z}_s$, $fb_2 = \ddot{z}_u$ ($F = 2$ and thus $M = 4$-see Fig. 1b). In the simulations the following parameters were set: simulation time

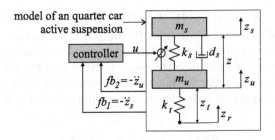

Fig. 4. Active suspension control system.

8 s, simulation time step $T = 0.1$ ms, interval between subsequent controller activations: 0.5 ms, $G \in \{\infty, 10, 20\}$ (with the assumptions $G = \infty$ no migrations are made), $A = 6$, population size: 100, number of iterations: 200, and number of repetitions: 50.

The main aim of the controller is to improve passenger comfort and car handling. Controlled object was modelled as follows:

$$\dot{\mathbf{x}} = \mathbf{A}\mathbf{x} + \mathbf{B}\mathbf{u} + \mathbf{f}, \tag{5}$$

where $\mathbf{A}$ is a state matrix in the form:

$$\mathbf{A} = \begin{bmatrix} 0 & 1 & 0 & 0 \\ -\frac{k_s}{m_s} & -\frac{d_s}{m_s} & \frac{k_s}{m_s} & \frac{d_s}{m_s} \\ 0 & 0 & 0 & 1 \\ \frac{k_s}{m_u} & \frac{d_s}{m_s} & -\frac{k_s+k_t}{m_u} & -\frac{d_s}{m_s} \end{bmatrix}, \tag{6}$$

$\mathbf{x}$ is a state vector (initial values of the state vector were set to zero) described as follows:

$$\mathbf{x} = \begin{bmatrix} x_1 & x_2 & x_3 & x_4 \end{bmatrix}^{\mathrm{T}} = \begin{bmatrix} z_s & \ddot{z}_s & z_u & \ddot{z}_u \end{bmatrix}^{\mathrm{T}}, \tag{7}$$

$\mathbf{B}$ is an input matrix represented by the formula:

$$\mathbf{B} = \begin{bmatrix} 0 & \frac{1}{m_s} & 0 & -\frac{1}{m_u} \end{bmatrix}^{\mathrm{T}}, \tag{8}$$

$\mathbf{u}$ is an input vector from the controller and $\mathbf{f}$ is input vector from kinematic extortion described by the following equation:

$$\mathbf{f} = \begin{bmatrix} 0 & 0 & 0 & -\frac{k_t}{m_u} \end{bmatrix}^{\mathrm{T}} \cdot z_r. \tag{9}$$

Controlled object was discretized with formula (5) with time step T as follows:

$$\mathbf{x}(i+1) = \mathbf{A}_d \cdot \mathbf{x}(i) + \mathbf{B}_d \cdot \mathbf{u}(i) + \mathbf{f}_d, \tag{10}$$

where $\mathbf{A}_d = \mathbf{I} + \mathbf{A} \cdot T$, $\mathbf{B}_d = \mathbf{B} \cdot T$, and $\mathbf{f}_d = \mathbf{f} \cdot T$. In order to model sensor constrains, quantization resolution for the output signal u and feedback signals (fb_1, fb_2) was set to 0.0001. In order to model actuator constrains, output signal u of the controller was limited to the range $[-1000, +1000]$ [39].

To evaluate the controller the functions presented in Table 3 were used. These functions were aggregated into a single fitness function as follows:

$$\mathrm{ff}\,(\mathbf{X}) = \sum_{n=1}^{N} w_n \cdot a_n \cdot \mathrm{ff}_n\,(\mathbf{X}), \tag{11}$$

where w_n is a weight of fitness function component ($n = 1, ..., N$, N is a number of fitness function components), a_n is a normalization factor of the fitness function component, and $\mathrm{ff}_n\,(\mathbf{X})$ is the fitness function component defined in Table 3.

Table 3. Components of fitness function (11) used for considered simulation problem of quarter car active suspension control system, where: $i = 1, \ldots, Z$ is a sample index, Z is the number of samples and it was defined as follows $Z = \frac{T}{T_s}$, and r_o are sorted by time value, minima and maxima of the regulator output signal.

n	Name	w_n	a_n	Component of the ff (X)
1	Passenger comfort	1.00	100	$\mathrm{ff}_1\,(\mathbf{X}) = \left(\frac{1}{Z} \cdot \sum_{i=1}^{Z} \ddot{z}_{s,i}^2 \right)^{0.5}$
2	Car handling	0.20	5000	$\mathrm{ff}_2\,(\mathbf{X}) = \left(\frac{1}{Z} \cdot \sum_{i=1}^{Z} z_{t,i}^2 \right)^{0.5}$
3	Suspension maximum travel	0.10	250	$\mathrm{ff}_3\,(\mathbf{X}) = \max_{z=1,\ldots,Z} \{|z_i|\}$
4	Suspension travel	0.10	100	$\mathrm{ff}_4\,(\mathbf{X}) = \left(\frac{1}{Z} \cdot \sum_{i=1}^{Z} z_i^2 \right)^{0.5}$
5	Complexity	0.10	1	$\mathrm{ff}_5\,(\mathbf{X}) = \frac{1}{3M} \sum_{m=1}^{M} \left(P_m^{str} + I_m^{str} + D_m^{str} \right)$
6	Control force	0.20	0.0025	$\mathrm{ff}_6\,(\mathbf{X}) = \left(\frac{1}{Z} \cdot \sum_{i=1}^{Z} u_i^2 \right)^{0.5}$
7	Oscillations of controller	0.20	0.0005	$\mathrm{ff}_7\,(\mathbf{X}) = \sum_{o=1}^{O-1} |r_o - r_{o+1}|$

To verify the proposed method different combinations of populations were tested (see Table 4). The controller's operation was additionally checked on a various road profile to verify if the controller can adapt to a different scenario (see z_r in Fig. 5). The detailed simulation results are presented in Table 5. An example of obtained controller structure and its performance is shown in Table 6 and Fig. 5, respectively.

Table 4. Algorithm variants tested in the simulations ($a = 1, ..., A$ stands for population index, a^h stands for maximum value of a parameter in GWO algorithm).

Simulation Case	Population used and population' parameters					
	$a = 1$	$a = 2$	$a = 3$	$a = 4$	$a = 5$	$a = 6$
GA	GA $p_c = 0.95$ $p_m = 0.20$ $m_r = 0.30$	GA $p_c = 0.90$ $p_m = 0.22$ $m_r = 0.25$	GA $p_c = 0.85$ $p_m = 0.24$ $m_r = 0.20$	GA $p_c = 0.80$ $p_m = 0.26$ $m_r = 0.15$	GA $p_c = 0.75$ $p_m = 0.28$ $m_r = 0.10$	GA $p_c = 0.70$ $p_m = 0.30$ $m_r = 0.05$
DE	DE $F = 0.60$ $CR = 0.15$	DE $F = 0.50$ $CR = 0.30$	DE $F = 0.40$ $CR = 0.45$	DE $F = 0.30$ $CR = 0.60$	DE $F = 0.2$ $CR = 0.75$	DE $F = 0.10$ $CR = 0.90$
GWO	GWO $a^h = 2.00$	GWO $a^h = 1.70$	GWO $a^h = 1.40$	GWO $a^h = 1.10$	GWO $a^h = 0.80$	GWO $a^h = 0.50$
HYB	GA $p_c = 0.95$ $p_m = 0.20$ $m_r = 0.30$	GA $p_c = 0.70$ $p_m = 0.30$ $m_r = 0.05$	DE $F = 0.60$ $CR = 0.15$	DE $F = 0.10$ $CR = 0.90$	GWO $a^h = 2.00$	GWO $a^h = 0.50$

Table 5. Averaged simulation results (fitness function value).

Simulation case	$G = \infty$	$G = 10$	$G = 20$
GA	1.16362	1.16411	1.16259
DE	1.20871	1.21744	1.22512
GWO	1.14659	**1.14533**	1.15392
HYB	**1.14481**	1.16472	**1.14257**

Table 6. Example of obtained controller (performance of such controller is shown in Fig. 5a and c, m index correspond to CB block index shown in Fig. 1b).

m	K_p	T_i	T_d
1	**22.93**	Reduced	Reduced
2	**1851.01**	Reduced	Reduced
3	Reduced	Reduced	Reduced
4	Reduced	**30230.94**	**44.52**

The simulations conclusions are as follows: (a) Using frequent migrations ($G = 10$) causes too fast convergence of the algorithm and usually worsen results (see Table 5). (b) Migrations do not always improve algorithm performance (see DE in Table 5). (c) The best results were achieved for the proposed solution with a low migration rate (see HYB and $G = 20$ in Table 5). (d) The obtained

a) trapezoidal active   b) trapezoidal passive   c) testing active   d) testing passive

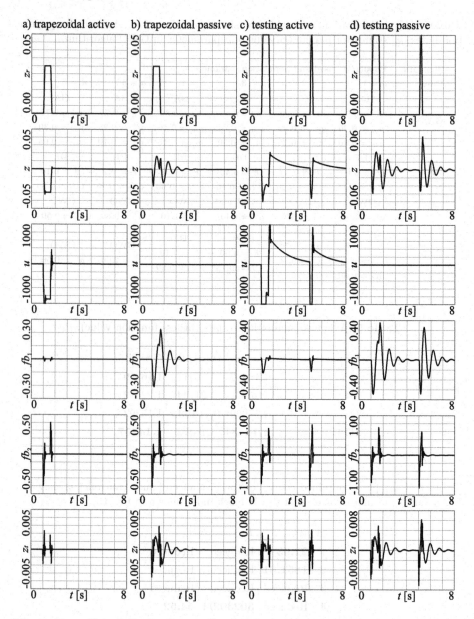

Fig. 5. Examples of obtained controllers performance and comparison with passive systems.

controller performs much better than passive system (see e.g. z and fb_1 signals in Fig. 5). (e) The obtained controller's structure is simple with more than 50% of elements reduced (see Table 6).

5   Conclusions

In this article, a new approach to optimization using a multi-population based algorithm was proposed. Its feature is that subpopulations can be processed with different algorithms and synchronized accordingly. The set of algorithm components can be freely modified and the algorithms may have different values of their own parameters. In the simulations, the quarter car active suspension control problem was considered. The proposed approach allowed us to: (a) find the structure and parameters of the controller, (b) obtain better results in terms of accuracy than in the case when the subpopulations were processed with the same algorithm.

Acknowledgment. The project was financed by the Częstochowa University of Technology-Faculty of Mechanical Engineering and Computer Scient grant for young scientists with number BS/MN 1-109-301/18/P.

References

1. Agharkakli, A., Sabet, G.S., Barouz, A.: Simulation and analysis of passive and active suspension system using quarter car model for different road profile. Int. J. Eng. Trends Technol. **3**(5), 636–644 (2012)
2. Arora, S., Singh, S.: Butterfly optimization algorithm: a novel approach for global optimization. Soft Comput. **23**(3), 715–734 (2019)
3. Ayadi, N., Derbel, N., Morette, N., Novales, C., Poisson, G.: Simulation and experimental evaluation of the EKF simultaneous localization and mapping algorithm on the wifibot mobile robot. J. Artif. Intell. Soft Comput. Res. **8**(2), 91–101 (2018)
4. Bartczuk, Ł., Dziwiński, P., Red'ko, V.G.: The concept on nonlinear modelling of dynamic objects based on state transition algorithm and genetic programming. In: Rutkowski, L., Korytkowski, M., Scherer, R., Tadeusiewicz, R., Zadeh, L.A., Zurada, J.M. (eds.) ICAISC 2017. LNCS (LNAI), vol. 10246, pp. 209–220. Springer, Cham (2017). https://doi.org/10.1007/978-3-319-59060-8_20
5. Bidar, M., Kanan, H.R., Mouhoub, M., Sadaoui, S.: Mushroom Reproduction Optimization (MRO): a novel nature-inspired evolutionary algorithm. In: IEEE Congress on Evolutionary Computation (2018)
6. Bilski, J., Kowalczyk, B., Grzanek, K.: The parallel modification to the Levenberg-Marquardt algorithm. In: Rutkowski, L., Scherer, R., Korytkowski, M., Pedrycz, W., Tadeusiewicz, R., Zurada, J.M. (eds.) ICAISC 2018. LNCS (LNAI), vol. 10841, pp. 15–24. Springer, Cham (2018). https://doi.org/10.1007/978-3-319-91253-0_2
7. Biyanto, T.R., et al.: Killer whale algorithm: an algorithm inspired by the life of killer whale. Procedia Comput. Sci. **124**, 151–157 (2017). https://doi.org/10.1016/j.procs.2017.12.141
8. Boyd, S., Hast, M., Åström, K.J.: MIMO PID tuning via iterated LMI restriction. Int. J. Robust Nonlinear Control **26**(8), 1718–1731 (2016)
9. Cpałka, K.: Design of Interpretable Fuzzy Systems. SCI, vol. 684. Springer, Cham (2017). https://doi.org/10.1007/978-3-319-52881-6
10. Cpałka, K., Rutkowski, L.: Flexible Takagi-Sugeno fuzzy systems. In: Proceedings of the International Joint Conference on Neural Networks, Montreal, pp. 1764–1769 (2005)

11. Dawar, D., Ludwig, S.A.: Effect of strategy adaptation on differential evolution in presence and absence of parameter adaptation: an investigation. J. Artif. Intell. Soft Comput. Res. **8**(3), 211–235 (2018)

12. Deb, S., Tian, Z., Fong, S., Tang, R., Wong, R, Dey, N.: Solving permutation flow-shop scheduling problem by rhinoceros search algorithm. Soft Comput. (2018). https://doi.org/10.1007/s00500-018-3075-3

13. Dhiman, G., Kumar, V.: Spotted hyena optimizer: a novel bio-inspired based metaheuristic technique for engineering applications. Adv. Eng. Softw. **114**, 48–70 (2017). https://doi.org/10.1016/j.advengsoft.2017.05.014

14. Dziwiński, P., Bartczuk, Ł., Przybyszewski, K.: A population based algorithm and fuzzy decision trees for nonlinear modeling. In: Rutkowski, L., Scherer, R., Korytkowski, M., Pedrycz, W., Tadeusiewicz, R., Zurada, J.M. (eds.) ICAISC 2018. LNCS (LNAI), vol. 10842, pp. 516–531. Springer, Cham (2018). https://doi.org/10.1007/978-3-319-91262-2_46

15. Fister Jr, I., Mlakar, U., Brest, J., Fister, I.: A new population-based nature-inspired algorithm every month: is the current era coming to the end. In: Proceedings of the 3rd Student Computer Science Research Conference, pp. 33–37. University of Primorska Press (2016)

16. Galkowski, T., Starczewski, A., Fu, X.: Improvement of the multiple-view learning based on the self-organizing maps. In: Rutkowski, L., Korytkowski, M., Scherer, R., Tadeusiewicz, R., Zadeh, L.A., Zurada, J.M. (eds.) ICAISC 2015. LNCS (LNAI), vol. 9120, pp. 3–12. Springer, Cham (2015). https://doi.org/10.1007/978-3-319-19369-4_1

17. Hosseini, E.: Laying chicken algorithm: a new meta-heuristic approach to solve continuous programming problems. J. Appl. Comput. Math. **6**(1) (2017). https://doi.org/10.4172/2168-9679.1000344

18. Jain, M., Singh, V., Rani, A.: A novel nature-inspired algorithm for optimization: squirrel search algorithm. Swarm Evol. Comput. (2018). https://doi.org/10.1016/j.swevo.2018.02.013

19. Jin, X.B., Yang, N.X., Su, T.L., Kong, J.L.: Time-series main trend analysis by adaptive dynamics model. In: 10th International Conference on Modelling, Identification and Control (ICMIC), pp. 1–5. IEEE (2018)

20. Kaveh, A., Dadras, A.: A novel meta-heuristic optimization algorithm: thermal exchange optimization. Adv. Eng. Softw. **110**, 69–84 (2017). https://doi.org/10.1016/j.advengsoft.2017.03.014

21. Kazikova, A., Pluhacek, M., Senkerik, R., Viktorin, A.: Proposal of a new swarm optimization method inspired in bison behavior. In: Matoušek, R. (ed.) MENDEL 2017. AISC, vol. 837, pp. 146–156. Springer, Cham (2019). https://doi.org/10.1007/978-3-319-97888-8_13

22. Laskowski, Ł., Laskowska, M., Jelonkiewicz, J., Boullanger, A.: Spin-glass Implementation of a Hopfield neural structure. In: Rutkowski, L., Korytkowski, M., Scherer, R., Tadeusiewicz, R., Zadeh, L.A., Zurada, J.M. (eds.) ICAISC 2014. LNCS (LNAI), vol. 8467, pp. 89–96. Springer, Cham (2014). https://doi.org/10.1007/978-3-319-07173-2_9

23. Liu, J.B., Zhao, J., Wang, S., Javaid, M., Cao, J.: On the topological properties of the certain neural networks. J. Artif. Intell. Soft Comput. Res. **8**(4), 257–268 (2018)

24. Łapa, K., Cpałka, K.: Evolutionary approach for automatic design of PID controllers. In: Gawęda, A.E., Kacprzyk, J., Rutkowski, L., Yen, G.G. (eds.) Advances in Data Analysis with Computational Intelligence Methods. SCI, vol. 738, pp. 353–373. Springer, Cham (2018). https://doi.org/10.1007/978-3-319-67946-4_16

25. Łapa, K., Cpałka, K.: Flexible fuzzy PID controller (FFPIDC) and a nature-inspired method for its construction. IEEE Trans. Industr. Inf. **14**(3), 1078–1088 (2018). https://doi.org/10.1109/TII.2017.2771953

26. Łapa, K., Cpałka, K.: On the application of a hybrid genetic-firework algorithm for controllers structure and parameters selection. In: Borzemski, L., Grzech, A., Świątek, J., Wilimowska, Z. (eds.) ISAT 2015. AISC, vol. 429, pp. 111–123. Springer, Cham (2016). https://doi.org/10.1007/978-3-319-28555-9_10

27. Łapa, K., Cpałka, K.: PID-fuzzy controllers with dynamic structure and evolutionary method for their construction. In: Borzemski, L., Świątek, J., Wilimowska, Z. (eds.) ISAT 2017. AISC, vol. 655, pp. 138–148. Springer, Cham (2018). https://doi.org/10.1007/978-3-319-67220-5_13

28. Łapa, K., Cpałka, K., Przybył, A., Saito, T.: Fuzzy PID controllers with FIR filtering and a method for their construction. In: Rutkowski, L., Korytkowski, M., Scherer, R., Tadeusiewicz, R., Zadeh, L.A., Zurada, J.M. (eds.) ICAISC 2017. LNCS (LNAI), vol. 10246, pp. 292–307. Springer, Cham (2017). https://doi.org/10.1007/978-3-319-59060-8_27

29. Łapa, K., Cpałka, K., Wang, L.: New method for design of fuzzy systems for nonlinear modelling using different criteria of interpretability. In: Rutkowski, L., Korytkowski, M., Scherer, R., Tadeusiewicz, R., Zadeh, L.A., Zurada, J.M. (eds.) ICAISC 2014. LNCS (LNAI), vol. 8467, pp. 217–232. Springer, Cham (2014). https://doi.org/10.1007/978-3-319-07173-2_20

30. Ma, H., Shen, S., Yu, M., Yang, Z., Fei, M., Zhou, H.: Multi-population techniques in nature inspired optimization algorithms: a comprehensive survey. Swarm Evol. Comput. **44**, 365–387 (2019)

31. Moghdani, R., Salimifard, K.: Volleyball premier league algorithm. Appl. Soft Comput. **64**, 161–185 (2018). https://doi.org/10.1016/j.asoc.2017.11.043

32. Rutkowski, L.: Computational Intelligence: Methods and Techniques. Springer, Heidelberg (2008). https://doi.org/10.1007/978-3-540-76288-1

33. Rutkowski, L., Cpałka, K., Flexible weighted neuro-fuzzy systems. In: Proceedings of the 9th International Conference on Neural Information Processing (ICONIP 2002), Orchid Country Club, Singapore, 18–22 November 2002

34. Saremi, S., Mirjalili, S., Lewis, A.: Grasshopper optimisation algorithm: theory and application. Adv. Eng. Softw. **105**, 30–47 (2017). https://doi.org/10.1016/j.advengsoft.2017.01.004

35. Sörensen, K.: Metaheuristics-the metaphor exposed. Int. Trans. Oper. Res. **22**(1), 3–18 (2015)

36. Starczewski, J.T., Pabiasz, S., Vladymyrska, N., Marvuglia, A., Napoli, C., Woźniak, M.: Self organizing maps for 3D face understanding. In: Rutkowski, L., Korytkowski, M., Scherer, R., Tadeusiewicz, R., Zadeh, L.A., Zurada, J.M. (eds.) ICAISC 2016. LNCS (LNAI), vol. 9693, pp. 210–217. Springer, Cham (2016). https://doi.org/10.1007/978-3-319-39384-1_19

37. Szczypta, J., Przybył, A., Cpałka, K.: Some aspects of evolutionary designing optimal controllers. In: Rutkowski, L., Korytkowski, M., Scherer, R., Tadeusiewicz, R., Zadeh, L.A., Zurada, J.M. (eds.) ICAISC 2013. LNCS (LNAI), vol. 7895, pp. 91–100. Springer, Heidelberg (2013). https://doi.org/10.1007/978-3-642-38610-7_9

38. Tzanetos, A., Dounias, G.: A new metaheuristic method for optimization: sonar inspired optimization. In: Boracchi, G., Iliadis, L., Jayne, C., Likas, A. (eds.) EANN 2017. CCIS, vol. 744, pp. 417–428. Springer, Cham (2017). https://doi.org/10.1007/978-3-319-65172-9_35

39. Van der Sande, T.P.J., Gysen, B.L.J., Besselink, I.J.M., Paulides, J.J.H., Lomonova, E.A., Nijmeijer, H.: Robust control of an electromagnetic active suspension system: simulations and measurements. Mechatronics **23**(2), 204–212 (2013)
40. Wolpert, D.H., Macready, W.G.: No free lunch theorems for optimization. IEEE Trans. Evol. Comput. **1**(1), 67–82 (1997)
41. Zalasiński, M., Cpałka, K., Hayashi, Y.: New method for dynamic signature verification based on global features. In: Rutkowski, L., Korytkowski, M., Scherer, R., Tadeusiewicz, R., Zadeh, L.A., Zurada, J.M. (eds.) ICAISC 2014. LNCS (LNAI), vol. 8468, pp. 231–245. Springer, Cham (2014). https://doi.org/10.1007/978-3-319-07176-3_21
42. Zalasiński, M., Cpałka, K.: Novel algorithm for the on-line signature verification using selected discretization points groups. In: Rutkowski, L., Korytkowski, M., Scherer, R., Tadeusiewicz, R., Zadeh, L.A., Zurada, J.M. (eds.) ICAISC 2013. LNCS (LNAI), vol. 7894, pp. 493–502. Springer, Heidelberg (2013). https://doi.org/10.1007/978-3-642-38658-9_44

Improving Population Diversity Through Gene Methylation Simulation

Michael Cilliers and Duncan A. Coulter[✉]

University of Johannesburg, Auckland Park, Johannesburg 2006, South Africa
dcoulter@uj.ac.za

Abstract. During the runtime of many evolutionary algorithms, the diversity of the population starts out high and then rapidly diminishes as the algorithm converges. The diversity will directly influence the algorithm's ability to perform effective exploration of the problem space. In most cases if exploration is required in the latter stages of the algorithm, there may be insufficient diversity to allow for this. This paper proposes an algorithm that will better maintain diversity throughout the runtime of the algorithm which will in turn allow for better exploration during the latter portion of the algorithm's run.

Keywords: Evolutionary algorithms · Population diversity ·
Exploration

1 Introduction

When working with evolutionary algorithms, one of the key factors that must be considered is the balance between exploration and exploitation [1]. If the algorithm focuses on exploration, large portions of the search space will be evaluated without thoroughly checking specific areas. A focus on exploration will thus be required to find the portions of the search space which contain good candidate solutions. Conversely, if the algorithm focuses on exploitation, small areas of the search space will be checked thoroughly. The required exploration and exploitation will be dependant on the distribution of good solutions in the search space. This distribution is often unknown prior to execution, which complicates the task of achieving a good balance. If the algorithm's exploration of the search space is inadequate, it can converge on a sub-optimal solution. A lack of sufficient exploitation can lead to the algorithm not converging at all. Ideally an algorithm will initially focus on exploration to identify the promising areas of the search space. The algorithm should then shift its focus over to exploitation in order to thoroughly check the promising areas that were identified during the initial portion of the algorithm.

With evolutionary algorithms modelled after the replication of DNA, a major contributor towards exploration is the crossover (reproduction) operation. During the crossover operation the genes from parent solutions are combined to

© Springer Nature Switzerland AG 2019
L. Rutkowski et al. (Eds.): ICAISC 2019, LNAI 11508, pp. 469–480, 2019.
https://doi.org/10.1007/978-3-030-20912-4_43

form child solutions. If the parents are dissimilar, the resulting child should differ from the contributing parents. These changes from parent to child will result in substantial jumps within the search space thereby driving exploration.

Exploitation on the other hand, is mainly driven by the mutation operation. If mutation is applied to a solution, a subset of the genes making up the solution are altered. The changes that are made to individual genes are usually small. This means that the resulting solution will be very similar to the solution pre-mutation. These small changes will result in an exploration of the local solution space. Depending on the configuration of the algorithm, it is possible for mutation to contribute towards exploration and for crossover to promote exploitation. It will however be less effective.

As mentioned above, crossover by dissimilar parents will produce children that are dissimilar from the parents. However, when two similar parents reproduce, the child will be similar to the parents. This means that genetic diversity is a requirement for effective exploration in an algorithm [1]. Most algorithms achieve the required diversity through the generation of the initial population. Solutions are distributed across the search space or pre-selected portions of the search space.

As the population starts to converge on a single solution, the diversity of the population will decrease which will in turn decrease the exploration of the algorithm [2]. This is ideal to facilitate the transition from exploration to exploitation.

When working with dynamic environments where the search space changes during the execution of the algorithm, a single transition from exploration to exploitation is not ideal. If substantial change occurs in the environment, another stage of exploration will be required to adapt to the change. If the diversity of the population has been diminished enough, the algorithm will not be able to effectively adapt to the change.

The maintaining of genetic diversity is not only required for dynamic environments. There are other situations where this is the case, for example multimodal and noisy optimisation problems. This paper will however focus on dynamic environments.

This paper aims to develop a new evolutionary algorithm based on methylation driven epigenetics to better adapt to changes in the environment. First the paper will cover some background information. Then the developed algorithm will be explained. The testing procedure will then be covered. Finally the results and the conclusion will be presented showing that the developed algorithm is able to better adapt to changes in the environment.

2   Biological Gene Coding

In biology genes can be divided into coding and non-coding genes. Coding genes will contribute towards the transcription process when RNA strands are created from the DNA template. The RNA will then be translated to form proteins. This means that non-coding genes will not affect the proteins that are created.

The ratio between coding and non-coding gene can differ drastically between different species.

The non-coding genes can in turn also be separated into two groups. The first group, while not directly used in the transcription process, will still affect it [4]. These genes will help to control which portion of the chromosome gets used and which portions do not. The second group of non-coding genes will have no impact on the transcription process. These genes will remain unused until the non-coding portions of the chromosome changes. This can happen due to mutation.

One mechanism that facilitates the determination of whether a particular genetic region is considered as coding or non-coding is DNA methylation. Some of the base pairs that make up the DNA strands allow the formation of methyl groups on the DNA molecule [5]. If this happens the transcription of the gene is suppressed. The gene will thus still form part of the DNA, but will not be used when the protein is expressed. During reproduction the offspring DNA undergoes encoding to set methylation. Methylation patterns will thus be inherited during reproduction. One attribute that gets highlighted by the above-mentioned process, is the separation between gene storage and gene expression. This separation can have a substantial effect when DNA changes. Minor changes to DNA can have a substantial effect on the eventual protein that gets expressed.

3   Current Techniques for Maintaining Exploration

3.1   Genetic Islands

One approach that has been used to try and maintain diversity in populations is that of genetic islands. Genetic islands operate by having multiple population evolve in isolation [6]. Each of the islands/populations will then independently converge on a solution and lose diversity. It is however possible that different populations may converge on different solutions. In this case there will be some diversity between the populations. The diversity can then be introduced into the individual populations by exchanging individuals between the populations.

There are some drawbacks to the genetic island technique. Firstly, it is possible that multiple of the populations can converge on the same point. It should also be noted that with enough time and individual exchange, all the population will eventually converge on a single point.

A second disadvantage is that the computational requirement for a genetic island implementation is significantly higher than that for a standard genetic algorithm. This is due to the population being duplicated multiple times and the calculations having to be repeated for each population.

Lastly it is also a disadvantage that all the diversity that is maintained through the multiple populations, are all relative to high fitness regions of the current search space. Usually this will mean that even if the populations are converging on different points, these points will be relatively close together.

One big advantage of genetic islands is that it is intrinsically parallelizable. Each of the islands can be executed on their own separate computing nodes. To scale up an algorithm, more nodes can be added to support more islands. This means that genetic islands are well suited to take advantage of cloud computing.

3.2 Gene Expression Programming

As mentioned above, in biological chromosomes there is a separation between gene storage and gene expression. Although most evolutionary algorithms do not exhibit this behavior, there are some that mimic this separation. One example of this is Gene Expression Programming. Gene Expression Programming represents the chromosome as a sequential list of genes [3]. The chromosome is then operated on using existing crossover and mutation techniques. When the fitness of an individual is calculated, the chromosome is converted into a tree structure which is then passed to the fitness function for evaluation. The structure of the produced tree can change dramatically even if just one of the genes is updated. The conversion from chromosome to tree can also result in a portion of the chromosome not affecting the resulting tree at all.

One disadvantage of gene expression programming is that it is limited to a small subset of problems. The solutions produced must also be expressible as a tree structure for gene expression programming to be usable.

3.3 Niching

Niching is a group of algorithms that try to maintain exploration and identify multiple optima in the search space. This is done by dividing the population into separate groups. Different groups are then able to identify different optima. An example of a method that has been used to achieve this, is fitness sharing. Fitness sharing works by taking solutions that are close to each other and sharing the fitness value between them. This limits the number of solutions that can group on a single point. Other groups will thus form on other optima in the search space.

3.4 Restarting

One technique that has been developed to try and overcome premature convergence is Restarting. This technique starts the evolution process, but then proceeds to restart the process before it converges on a solution. This process is repeated a number of times gathering information during each run. Finally all the gathered information is used to perform one last targeted search.

4 Proposed Algorithm

The aim of the proposed algorithm is to try and increase the population diversity during the lifetime of the algorithm over that of the standard genetic algorithm. More specifically it will aim to improve the diversity during the latter portion of the algorithm. The increased diversity should allow the algorithm to better adapt to changes in the environment by being able to switch the focus of the algorithm back to exploration. To try and achieve this goal, gene methylation will be added to the chromosome. Ideally the non-coding portion of the chromosome will act as a reservoir of genetic material that can be accessed when diversity is required.

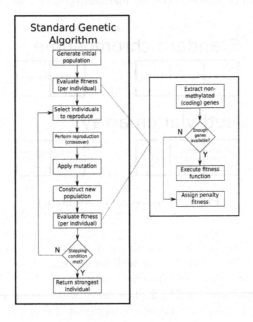

Fig. 1. Proposed algorithm

The added methylation layer will also act to separate the storage and expression of genes. As mentioned above, this can influence the expressed result of changes to genes. Small mutations can result in more significant changes in the resulting solution. It can however also affect the results of more substantial changes by dampening the effect when the genes are expressed.

A small change to the methylation information can result in the coding portions of the solution changing. The newly coding genes should not have been subject to the diminishing diversity and will thus serve as new genetic material. The resulting solution will thus be dissimilar to the majority of the population and thus diversity increases.

```
def get_expressed_genes(individual):
expressed_genes = []
for i=0 to len(individual.genes):
if individual.methylation[i] == false:
expressed_genes.append(individual.genes[i])
return expressed_genes
```

Algorithm 1. Expressing genes

The proposed algorithm will build upon the standard genetic algorithm as illustrated in Fig. 1. The representation of the chromosome will be updated to facilitate DNA methylation. The chromosome will be extended to contain more genes than the number that will be expressed and used by the fitness function. The proposed algorithm will also update the chromosome by adding in an extra component to track which of the genes are methylated and which are not.

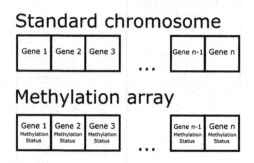

Fig. 2. Chromosome representation

To achieve the above mentioned an array is added to the existing chromosome. The length of the added array will match that of the chromosome, with each element in the newly added array corresponding to one of the genes in the chromosome as shown in Fig. 2. The array will contain methylation information indicating which of the genes are methylated and which not. The initial methylation status of each gene is randomised with a bias towards expressing the gene.

When evaluating the fitness of an individual, the genes will not serve directly as the inputs for the fitness function. The specific genes that will be used will first have to be selected and then used as the inputs for the fitness function. To do the selection, the genes in the chromosome will be iterated over in order. For each gene the methylation status will be evaluated and if the gene is methylated it will be disregarded. The number of required genes will then be taken from the resulting list of genes to serve as inputs for the fitness function. This process is shown in Algorithm 1 and Fig. 3.

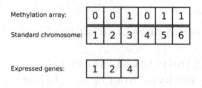

Fig. 3. Expressing genes

When crossover is applied to individuals, the methylation information will accompany the corresponding genes when they are carried over to the offspring. This will be achieved by copying the appropriate sections of the methylation array to the offspring as demonstrated in Fig. 4.

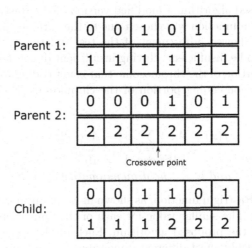

Fig. 4. Performing crossover

The methylation information of an individual will undergo mutation alongside the gene portion of the chromosome. The methylation information will however have a lower mutation rate than the gene portion. If the methylation information changes too rapidly, specific genes will not get the required time to improve sufficiently.

The mutation of the methylation array will function by taking individual values in the methylation array and inverting the methylation status of the corresponding gene as illustrated in Fig. 5. This means that if mutation is applied

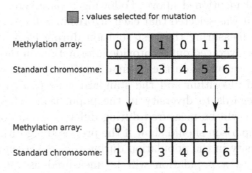

Fig. 5. Performing mutation

to a non-methylated gene, it will become methylated or if a methylated gene is acted upon it will become non-methylated.

5   Test Problem

To test the proposed algorithm a modified version of the Rastrigin function was used. The Rastrigin function was chosen due to the variable dimensionality that it provides. This allowed adjustment of the test function if the initial dimensionality proved to be insufficient. Having insufficient dimensionality would have meant that the portion of the chromosome that is not coding would end up being small or that the non-coding portion of the chromosome is disproportionately large.

$$f(x) = An + \sum_{i=1}^{n} [x_i^2 - A\cos(2\pi x_i)]$$
$$Where\ A\ =\ 10$$
$$and\ n\ =\ the\ dimensionality\ of\ x$$

(1)

The standard Rastrigin function, as shown in Eq. 1, optimizes on zero for each of the dimensions. The similar value for each of the dimensions is not desirable for the testing of the proposed algorithm. Each of the genes in the proposed algorithm can possibly affect different dimensions as the expression of the genes changes. If all the dimensions optimize on the same value, the effect of a specific gene will remain the same regardless of how it is expressed. To avoid this problem the Rastrigin function was transposed so that each of the dimensions would have different optimal values.

For the testing ten dimensions will be used. When applying the standard genetic algorithm to the problem, the chromosome will contain the 10 values being optimised. For the developed algorithm the chromosome has to be extended as mentioned above. The length of the chromosome for this test will be selected to double the number of required genes. This results in a chromosome containing 20 values of which 10 will be expressed.

To evaluate the effectiveness of the proposed algorithm it will be compared to the standard genetic algorithm. Both algorithms will be applied to the adapted Rastrigin function mentioned above. Following a parameter study of the produced prototype, it was selected that each algorithm will be executed 200 times. Each run will be measuring the best solution during each generations. These values will then be averaged out to provide information on the rate at which the specific algorithm converges on the optimal solution.

The developed algorithm and the standard genetic algorithm will also be compared with regards to diversity in the population. The average diversity for each algorithm will be measured during different points of the convergence process. This comparison should show if the proposed algorithm is successful at maintaining diversity in the population during the convergence process.

The diversity of a population will be measured as the average distance between all the individuals in the population. The distance between two individuals in the standard genetic algorithm will be calculated as the Euclidean distance between the two individuals. It should be noted that other distance measures could be used based on the specific problem.

The distance calculation used for the developed algorithm will consist of two parts. The first part will be the same as the method used for the standard genetic algorithm and will be used to calculate the distance of the coding portion of the chromosome. The second portion will measure the distance that results due to the non-coding part of the chromosome. For this portion of the chromosome, the position of a specific gene is less relevant as it could eventually express in a number of different ways depending on how the chromosome evolves. For this reason, non-coding genes are not paired based on the position in the chromosome, but rather on the smallest difference when calculating the Euclidean distance. Finally, the two values are combined by averaging them to produce the distance between the individuals.

The third portion of the testing process will attempt to validate the effectiveness of increased diversity in a population. To test this, a dynamic environment will be used. As before the transposed Rastrigin function will be used. To achieve the dynamic environment, the transposition will be updated. When the change occurs the current optimal found solution will not be accurate anymore and the algorithm will have to adjust to try and find the new optima.

The developed algorithm and the standard genetic algorithm that will be used for the testing, will be setup to match each other as close as possible. Both algorithms will use populations containing 1000 individuals. For crossover both algorithms use fitness proportionate selection. The mutation rate for the standard genetic algorithm is set to 10%. The developed algorithm matches the 10% on the gene portion of the chromosome, but uses a separate mutation rate for the methylation values for which 1% is used.

6   Results

Figure 6 shows the fitness of the best found solution during each generation. As mentioned above multiple runs were executed and the result averaged out. From the figure it can be seen that the proposed algorithm performed slightly worse than the standard genetic algorithm. This is understandable as the developed algorithm has the added methylation layer that will affect performance. Changes in the methylation of individuals can slow down convergence. This can be minimised by limiting the mutation rate of the methylation information.

Figure 7 compares the diversity of the of the developed algorithm to that of the standard genetic algorithm. Results show that the standard genetic algorithm quickly loses genetic diversity as the population converges on a solution. The developed algorithm also loses diversity during the duration of the algorithm, but does so at a much slower rate. The developed algorithm is also able to maintain a higher level of diversity once the diversity loss levels out.

Finally, Fig. 8 shows the convergence rate of the algorithms when change occurs in the environment. The large spike in fitness indicates the point where the change in the environment occurred. The developed algorithm is able to

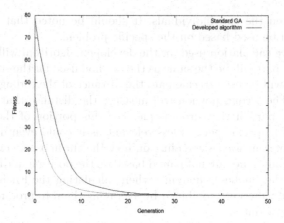

Fig. 6. Convergence rate of algorithm

recover from the change and converge on a new value, faster than the standard genetic algorithm.

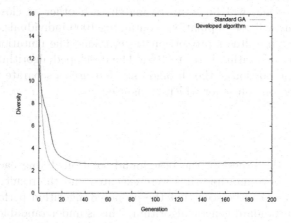

Fig. 7. Diversity of population

To test the statistical significance of the result, we will evaluate the number of generations it takes to re-optimise after the change in the environment occurs. We considered the algorithm as re-optimised when the fitness moved below 0,001. Using this method we calculated the mean number of generations for both the standard genetic algorithm and the proposed algorithm to re-converge. The mean number for the standard genetic algorithm was 140,96 while the developed algorithm did it in 99,435. The sample standard deviation for the developed algorithm runs were 17,085.

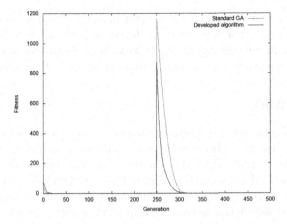

Fig. 8. Convergence after change in environment

To establish the statistical significance the null hypothesis will be that the developed algorithm is not more efficient. The probability of the observed results occurring if this is the case is then determined. If the probability is less than 0,01 then we will reject the null hypothesis and have established that the developed algorithm is more efficient.

The z-value is determined as follows:

$$z = \frac{x - \mu}{\sigma} = \frac{140.96 - 99.435}{17.085} = 2.43 \tag{2}$$

Performing a lookup of the z-value using a z-table results in a probability of 0,00755 which is less than the specified 0,01.

The null hypothesis can then be rejected and it can be stated that the developed algorithm is more efficient when re-optimising after a change over the given test function.

7   Conclusion

Based on the results produced by the tests, the developed algorithm is better at maintaining diversity in the population when comparing it to the standard genetic algorithm. The developed algorithm was able to maintain diversity slightly longer than the standard genetic algorithm and was able to maintain a higher level of diversity after the population diversity stopped diminishing.

The results also indicated the developed algorithm can effectively make use of the available diversity to adapt to changes in the search space. Figure 8 showed that the developed algorithm outperformed the standard genetic algorithm when exploration was required after the population became stagnant.

Lastly the tests showed that the above was achieved with only a slight decrease in convergence effectiveness in a static environment.

Based on the above points it can be concluded that the developed algorithm did achieve the goals that where set out. It was able to maintain better diversity than the standard genetic algorithm. It was also able to leverage the increased diversity to improve convergence when changes occur in the environment.

7.1 Future Work

The addition of gene methylation in this paper has produced positive results. The method of implementing these methylation patterns can however be expanded. One option that will be explored is the use of a probabilistic data structure to store methylation information. One option here will be the use of Bloom filters. A possible advantage that can be gained from this, is that the imperfect storage of a Bloom filter will better match the imperfect genetic process.

Another area that could be explored, is the simulation of gene-regulatory networks when expressing the methylation information. This could potentially allow the formation of gene groups that follow the same expression pattern. In turn this could lead to genes that work well together to be stored together in the non-coding portion of the chromosome. Ideally these genes could then become expressed together when the coding portion of the chromosome changes.

References

1. Črepinšek, M., Liu, S., Mernik, M.: Exploration and exploitation in evolutionary algorithms: a survey. ACM Comput. Surv. **45**, 35 (2013)
2. Eiben, A.E., Schoenauer, M.: Evolutionary computing. Inf. Process. Lett. **82**, 1–6 (2002)
3. Ferreira, C.: Gene expression programming in problem solving. In: Roy, R., Köppen, M., Ovaska, S., Furuhashi, T., Hoffmann, F. (eds.) Soft Computing and Industry, pp. 635–653. Springer, London (2002). https://doi.org/10.1007/978-1-4471-0123-9_54
4. Kornienko, A.E., Guenzl, P.M., Barlow, D.P., Pauler, F.M.: Gene regulation by the act of long non-coding RNA transcription. BMC Biol. **11**, 59 (2013)
5. Law, J.A., Jacobsen, S.E.: Establishing, maintaining and modifying DNA methylation patterns in plants and animals. Nat. Rev. Genet. **11**, 204 (2010)
6. Whitley, D., Rana, S., Heckendorn, R.B.: Island model genetic algorithms and linearly separable problems. In: Corne, D., Shapiro, J.L. (eds.) AISB EC 1997. LNCS, vol. 1305, pp. 109–125. Springer, Heidelberg (1997). https://doi.org/10.1007/BFb0027170

Strategizing Game Playing Using Evolutionary Approach

Abhinav Nagpal[1]([✉]) and Goldie Gabrani[2]

[1] School of Computer Science and Engineering, Vellore Institute of Technology,
Vellore, India
abhinavnagpal12@gmail.com
[2] Department of Computer Science and Engineering, BML Munjal University,
Gurugram, India
goldie.gabrani@bmu.edu.in

Abstract. Since the inception of evolutionary algorithms, the capabilities of genetic algorithms is showcased by games. This paper proposes the use of a genetic algorithm for the game, Tetris. An evolutionary approach is used to design a Tetris bot. The proposed approach uses a novel set of parameters to decide which move needs to be taken by the Tetris bot for each falling Tetromino. These parameters represent the various genes present in the chromosome. Each individual is being allowed to play the game once. Once the entire population has played, the population undergoes crossover and mutation. In this way, the parameters are evolved to get a better bot. The most evolved bot as per the fitness is allowed to simulate 200 rounds of Tetris during which its actions are recorded. Further, Frequent Pattern Growth algorithm, a data mining technique, is used to extract knowledge from the given stored actions. The extracted knowledge is used for mining association rules and identifying strategies used by the evolved bot to play the game.

Keywords: Tetris · Artificial Intelligence · Genetic algorithms ·
Data mining · Frequent pattern growth algorithm

1 Introduction

There are many games that pose an intellectual challenges. Such games include Poker, Go, Chess etc. As a result, Artificial Intelligence (AI) algorithms are being used for game playing, especially in the last few years. Tetris has also attracted researchers attention. Tetris, a block-matching game, was designed and programmed by a Russian game developer, Alexey Pajitnov. It consists of geometric shapes called tetrominoes. Each of the tetrominoes consists of 4 blocks. There are 7 types of tetrominoes representing the letters of the English alphabet: I, J, L, O, S, T, Z. The game has a game board that has a grid of size 10×20 cells. The objective of the game is to place the randomly falling pieces onto the game board such that it does not cross the top margin of the board. Each row filled

© Springer Nature Switzerland AG 2019
L. Rutkowski et al. (Eds.): ICAISC 2019, LNAI 11508, pp. 481–492, 2019.
https://doi.org/10.1007/978-3-030-20912-4_44

completely with tetrominoes is cleared, thus decreasing the height of the stack by one. The falling tetromino can be moved left or right and rotated by 90°. As the game proceeds, the game levels up and the speed by which the pieces fall also increases, thus making it difficult to place the tetrominoes at the right position. Even though the game appears to be simple, developing a Tetris bot is a big challenge. Since the game has a grid with 7 blocks; the game has $2^{10 \times 27} \approx 10^{60}$ states [1]. As this state space is very large, a brute force approach cannot be used and therefore there is a need to use certain optimization techniques to develop the Tetris bot. This game can be played in both offline and online mode.

Demaine et al. [2] were able to prove that the offline version of the game was NP–complete on the basis of the reduction between the 3–partition problem and Tetris. According to Burgiel [3], it is impossible to win at Tetris in the sense that one cannot play the game indefinitely. There are some sequences of pieces that will cause a player to lose the game with probability one. Tetris has been employed in testing machine learning (ML) algorithms. AI techniques such as reinforcement learning and state space search have seen success in the development of this game. Fehey [4] developed a Tetris bot by hand-tuning the parameters involved in the evaluation function. The bot was able to clear lines on 63×10^4 average. Bohm et al. [5] used genetic algorithms to allow 'smart' solutions to develop naturally. Szita et al. [6] used cross–entropy methods in Tetris. The weights of the features introduced by [4] were optimized using this algorithm and thus the game could clear $35 \times 10^4 \pm 86\%$ lines.

Langenhoven et al. [7] with the help of Particle Swarm Optimization (PSO) developed a feed-forward neural network that was used as an evaluation function. Inputs to the network are the weights of the feature functions the value of the state is the output. The bot could clear 15×10^4 lines on average. Lundgaard and McKee [8], at the University of Oklahoma used deep learning and reinforcement learning to develop an AI algorithm for Tetris. They used neural networks and Q-learning, a reinforcement learning technique, to train their AI agents. The neural network was used to define the state-action policy and the expected rewards.

Most of the authors [6,9] have worked on developing a bot that knows only the current piece and not the subsequent piece. In the case of the 'two-piece' approach, the player would be able to play a better move for the current piece by knowing the move of the next piece. The performance of height-based weighing functions was studied in [10] and the results were also compared with the non-height-based weighing functions for holes. It used the 'two-piece' approach to assist the player. Rollinson [11] used greedy-search and a depth-2 search combined with a genetic algorithm and Nelder–Mead optimization to develop a bot. The result was that the depth-2 search optimized with the Nelder–Mead algorithm performed the best and could clear 4000–5000 lines/rows.

In this paper, a genetic algorithm followed by frequent pattern growth algorithm (GAFP) is proposed. The GAFP uses features of both genetic algorithm and frequent pattern growth to find the right game strategies to be used while playing Tetris. The proposed algorithm is divided into two parts–the genetic algorithm that is used to get an evolved AI that passes the fitness limit and the frequent pattern growth algorithm that is used to extract game strategies from the evolved AI. The rest of the paper is divided into the following sections–Sect. 2 explains in detail the design of the GAFP algorithm; Sect. 3 discusses the GA part of the algorithm. It elaborates on the all the sub-methods involved in it. Section 4 describes about the frequent pattern algorithm briefly. Section 5 shows an example explaining the GA part of the algorithm along with all the processes involved by the bot in playing a move; Sect. 6 talks about the implementation, outcomes and association rules obtained using the GAFP algorithm. Finally, some concluding remarks are given in Sect. 7.

2   Design of the Proposed GAFP Algorithm

The proposed algorithm uses an evolutionary approach that is genetic algorithm (GA) followed by frequent pattern growth algorithm (FP) (hence, named GAFP) to evolve a player's gameplay and adapt better to the falling tetrominoes. The Tetris bot developed would be able to play the game with the goal of clearing as many rows as possible. A fitness function has been used to select better performing individuals and continuously evolve the bot with time. Due to time constraints, an upper limit k has been set to the fitness function. The algorithm will stop once we get a bot with a fitness value greater than the limit. The evolved bot will then be made to play 200 rounds of Tetris during which, the move (actions) it takes for each falling tetromino will be recorded. The symbols used and attributes of an action have been mentioned in Table 3 and Sect. 6 respectively. Later, we will apply the FP algorithm on these stored actions of the most evolved bot to extract the strategies used by the bot to play the game.

Table 1. Constant hyper-parameters for GAFP algorithm.

Hyper-parameter	Value
Population size n	50
Mutation step M_s	0.2
Mutation rate M_r	0.1
Number of children per generation	25
Number of individuals removed per selection	25
Maximum confidence	85%

The role of GA part of the algorithm (Algorithm 2) is to evolve a Tetris bot with the goal of clearing as many lines as possible and which meets the upper limit set on the fitness function. And the role of FP part of the algorithm is evaluating the most evolved bot and gets the techniques (rules) it uses to play the game. Figure 1 and Table 1 shows the flowchart and constant hyper–parameters for the GAFP algorithm.

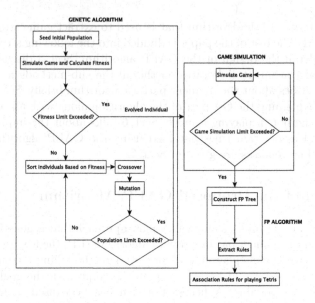

Fig. 1. Flowchart for GAFP algorithm

3   Genetic Algorithm Part of GAFP

Genetic algorithm involved in evolving the bot is carried out in a number of steps. These steps are now explained.

3.1   Initialization

In this step, an initial population of n individuals is created. Each individual is made up of certain parameters as mentioned in Table 2 that will determine its gameplay. A random approach has been used to initiate the population. This is done to ensure that the population does not have similar solutions and are diverse. It has been experimentally observed that the random solutions are the ones that makes the population better. On the other hand, heuristic initialization only affects the initial fitness of the population. Moreover, the assumptions used for deciding the heuristics could be incorrect too.

3.2   Evaluation

Each individual of a generation is then allowed to play the game once. In order to play a move, a depth–1 search algorithm has been employed which performs the search for the best move on the current tetromino as well as the next piece by performing a look ahead. This will allow the bot to drop the pieces in the best position while taking the next state into account. In the search algorithm, the action was defined as the number of rotations and the horizontal translation of the piece, assuming that the piece will be dropped from that point to get to

Table 2. Parameters and their meaning.

Parameter	Meaning
Aggregate height	Sum of the height of each column
Holes	Number of holes; a hole is an unfilled unit in the Tetris board such that all the other units around it is filled
Complete line	Number of complete lines in the board
Bumpiness	Variation in the column heights; computed by summing up the absolute differences between every adjacent columns
Relative height	Height of the highest column minus lowest column
Weighted height	Height of the highest column
Maximum hole height	Highest row that contains at least one hole

the next state. For each tetromino, the bot takes two steps to decide the best action:

- Try all moves: To generate all possible different actions that the bot can do for the given piece and a board state.
- Evaluate: To calculate the rating of each possible action and perform the best of them (Algorithm 1). The bot played the move that generated the highest rating.

Each possible move of the generated piece was rated according to a function:

$$\text{Rating of a move} = \sum (w_i \times p_i) \tag{1}$$

The individual loses if the tetromino crosses the top margin of the board. The fitness of the individual sum of all the ratings of a move. This is then calculated and stored.

$$\text{Fitness function} = \alpha = \sum (Rating\ of\ move_i) \tag{2}$$

3.3   Selection

In this step, the set of individuals that are fit for the crossover step of GA are selected from the entire population. The top 50% of the population is selected for crossover.

3.4   Crossover

Crossover, a convergence operation, is employed to pull the population towards a local minimum/maximum New individuals are created in this crossover step. This is done by firstly selecting two individuals randomly from the present population to create a new individual. The children will take up the parameter of one of the two parents. This is done to combine traits to create an individual that inherits the best traits from each of its parents. Crossover is done using the crossover rate c_r, which is the probability that two chromosomes will swap their parameters.

Table 3. Symbols and their meanings.

Symbol	Definition
α	Number of lines cleared by the ith
a_i	Fitness of be best bot of the jth generation
C_r	Crossover rate
M_r	Mutation rate
M_s	Mutation step
p_i	i^{th} parameter of the genome
x	Number of parameters in the
w	Weights employed in the game
w_i	i^{th} weight of the game
n	Number of individuals in a generation
k	Fitness limit

3.5 Mutation

Changing the value of the parameter of the genome by a small amount randomly carries out mutation of the individual. The mutation rate M_r is the probability whether the parameter will change. The mutation step M_s, is used to put a limit to how much the value can change. The rate of mutation is less than crossover as the end goal is to bring the population to convergence. It affects the members of the population by a small amount.

Algorithm 1. Pseudocode for Move Evaluation

```
1  Function Evaluate (B,I,Moves,moveTaken));
     Input   : B: N×X matrix representing individuals I: individual that needs to
               be evaluated
               Moves: List storing all possible moves
               MoveTaken: List storing moves taken
   Output: Individual fitness
2  while (game is not over) do
3    │  moves = tryMoves() moves = sort(moves) // sort moves by ratings
4    │  moveTaken = takeMove(moves)
5    │  individual.fitness = calculateFitness(moveTaken)
6  end
```

3.6 Repetion

The same procedure is now applied to the new generation of individuals. This is carried out until the terminating step is reached. A limit k was kept on the value of the fitness function. The individual stops when it reaches this limit.

Algorithm 2. Pseudocode for GA part of the algorithm

---

1 <u>Function Genetic</u> (B,K,C_r, m_r, m_s);

Input : B: $N \times X$ matrix representing individuals I: individual that needs to
            be evaluated
            K: Fitness limit
            m_r: Mutation Rate
            m_s: Mutation Step
            C_r: Crossover rate

Output: Most evolved bot

2 B = InitializeBot(B) **while** *(k¡a_i)* **do**

3   B = evaluate(B) // All individuals play the game

4   B = sort(B) // Individuals sorted based on fitness

5   B = Remove(B) // Remove bottom 50% individuals

6   B = crossover(B,c_r) // Crossover stage

7   B = mutate(B,m_r, m_s) //Mutation stage

8 **end**

---

4   Frequent Pattern Growth Algorithm Part of GAFP

FP growth algorithm is one of the fastest and most efficient algorithms for association rule mining. It is a rule-based ML technique for identifying the presence of any relationship present between the variables in a database. It is based on the construction of the FP tree. A predefined minimum support and minimum confidence are used to implement the algorithm. High minimum support [12] leads to the identification of fewer association rules while a high confidence level ensures stronger association rules. If the lift ratio is greater, greater will be the strength of the association rule. FP algorithm unlike Apriori requires only two scans of the database. It works according to the divide-and-conquer strategy. In general, associative rule mining can be divided into two parts:

- Find a variable or combination of variables that occur more than the predefined minimum support.
- Generate association rules from those combinations keeping the minimum confidence as the constraint.

The FP growth algorithm consists of two parts:

- Construction of the FP tree: The FP-tree is constructed in two scans of the database. The database is first scanned to find the support of every item present in the database. The items with support less than the minimum support is discarded. The items are then sorted based on their support values. It reads the transaction one by one and constructs a path leading to the formation of the FP–tree.
- FP tree growth: After the FP tree has constructed, the set of frequent patterns are extracted using the tree.

5   An Example Demonstrating the Working of GAFP Algorithm

Let us consider an arbitrary individual with the feature values as given in Table 2. Let the bot be at a stage as shown in Fig. 2 (Board 1). Figure 2 also shows the state space Board 1.1, Board 1.2, Board 1.3, ..., Board 1.23, Board 1.24 representing the possible positions where the blocks can be placed. For each such state of the Board, the bot will find the rating and move to the game state that has the best rating. Table 4 shows the values for w (value of the bot parameters) and p (games feature values). Using equation (1), the rating for the Board 1.1 and Board 1.24 move can be calculated as 7.25 and 7.26 respectively. Hence, the bot moves to the board state 1.24.

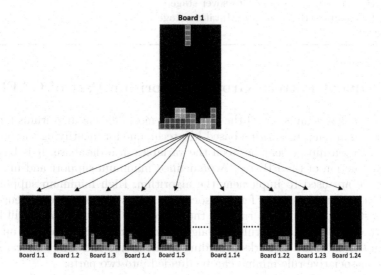

Fig. 2. Search tree generated for a tetromino

6   Implementation and Results

Once the most evolved bot was generated after implementing the GA, the most evolved bot goes through the game simulation where it is made to play 200 rounds of Tetris until it loses in each round. Its actions are recorded in a separate database. An action is the placement of the block that depends on the rating of the move. A total of 5025040 actions were stored. In order to implement the FP algorithm, 4 attributes were considered for each action taken by the bot. These attributes are:

- Type of tetromino T where t = {I, O, J, Z, L, S}
- Rotation r where r = {0, 1, 2, 3} where r = 0 means no rotation, r = 1 means 90–degree rotation and so on.

Table 4. Value of game features and parameters for board 1.1 and board 1.24.

Parameter	W_i	p (Board 1.1)	p (Board 1.24)
Holes	−0.4545	0	0
Complete lines	0.9521	0	1
Weighted height	−0.6732	5	4
Bumpiness	0.2121	15	9
Aggregate height	0.2132	32	32
Relative height	0.1231	5	3
Maximum height hole	−0.1234	0	0

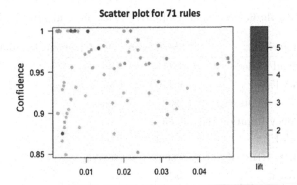

Fig. 3. Scatter plot for the all the generated rules

- N_1: Used to describe the roughness of the place where the block will fall to its right neighbour. Calculated as $X_{i+1} - X_i$ where X_i is the height of the leftmost column S occupied by the block. If height(S) > 9, N1 $= 0$.
- N_2: Used to describe the roughness of the place where the block will fall to its right neighbour. Calculated as $X_{i+1} - X_i$ where X_i is the height of the leftmost column S occupied by the block. If height(S) > 7, $N_2 = 0$.

The performance of the GAFP algorithm can be seen in Fig. 3. The confidence level was kept at 85%. The FP growth algorithm was able to find 71 rules. Figure 3 shows the scatter plot for all the generated rules and Table 5 shows the top 10 rules as per the lift ratio.

Any of the generated rules can be described as follows:

$\{Piece = L, N_1 = 2, N_2 = 1\,or\,2\,or\,3\} \Rightarrow \{R = 3\}$: If the incoming tetromino is L shaped and there is a location with $N_1 = 2$, $N_2 = \{1, 2, 3\}$ then to place the tetromino at that location, the bot will rotate the tetromino thrice.

Table 6 summarizes results of other algorithms on Tetris gameplay compared to our algorithm. As seen from the Table 6, GAFP was able to outperform many other algorithms due to the strategies learnt due to FP algorithm. The comparison shows that our method was able to outperform even the RL algorithms such as the

Table 5. Top 8 rules along with their confidence and lift ratio.

Rule	Confidence	Lift ratio
{Piece = L, N_1 = 2, N_2 = 1 or 2 or 3} ⇒ {R = 3}	1	5.72
{Piece = L, N_1 = 1, N_2 = 2} ⇒ {R = 3}	0.875	5.15
{Piece = O, N_1 = 0, N_2 = 3} ⇒ {R = 0}	1	3.27
{Piece = O, N_1 = 1, N_2 = 1} ⇒ {R = 0}	1	3.22
{Piece = T, N_1 = 1, R = 2} ⇒ {N_2 = 1}	1	3.21
{Piece = S, N_1 = 1, R = 0} ⇒ {N_2 = 1}	1	3.15
{Piece = O, N_1 = 0, N_2 = 0} ⇒ {R = 0}	0.96	3.12
{Piece = S, N_1 = 0, N_2 = 1} ⇒ {R = 0}	0.96	3.05

Table 6. Performance of GAFP with other algorithms.

Algorithm	Mean Score	Reinforcement learning
Hand Coded	621167	No
GA [5]	581106	No
LP + Bootstrap [13]	4267	Yes
Policy Iteration [14]	3383	Yes
LPSI [16]	<3000	Yes
RRL–KBR [15]	≈50	Yes
GAFP	831167	Yes

policy iteration method along with the hand-coded algorithm. Its not sensible to compare the running times as there is a linear relation between running times and score of the bot.

7   Conclusions

In this paper, GA is used to create a Tetris bot and FP algorithm is applied to find strategies used by the most evolved bot to play Tetris. The novelty of the paper is to analyse the strategy of the bot learnt during training with the help of FP algorithm. Figure 4 shows performance of the genetic algorithm. This bot exceeded the fitness limit of eliminating 150000 lines. The strategy consisted of 4 attributes (i.e. N1, N2, rotation, piece). Although it is easy to manually construct the rules that could decide the right position to place the current tetromino, it should be pointed out that the proposed bot was not fed with such rules separately. One of the advantages of using GA to train the bot was that One of the key challenges of this paper was the time constraint since simulation of a bot takes many hours. Making the bot play longer brings out better strategies. Constructing good features was another tough task because one must try to deduce what features allowed the AI to stay alive as long as possible.

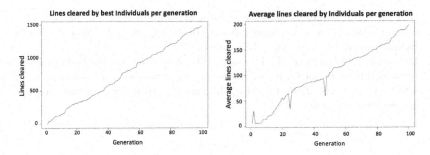

Fig. 4. Left: Graph showing the average lines cleared by individual per generation; Right: Graph showing the lines cleared by best individual per generation

References

1. Baccherini, D., Merlini, D.: Combinatorial analysis of tetris-like games. Discret. Math. **308**, 4165–4176 (2008)
2. Demaine, E.D., Hohenberger, S., Liben-Nowell, D.: Tetris is hard, even to approximate. In: Warnow, T., Zhu, B. (eds.) COCOON 2003. LNCS, vol. 2697, pp. 351–363. Springer, Heidelberg (2003). https://doi.org/10.1007/3-540-45071-8_36
3. Burgiel, H.: How to lose at tetris. Math. Gaz. **81**, 194–200 (1997)
4. Fahey, C.: Tetris AI: Computer Plays Tetris. http://www.colinfahey.com/tetris/tetris.html. Accessed 6 June 2018
5. Bohm, N., Kokai, G., Mandl, S.: Evolving a heuristic function for the game of tetris. In: LWA, pp. 118–122. Humboldt University of Berlin, Berlin (2005)
6. Szita, I., Lorincz, A.: Learning tetris using the noisy cross-entropy method. Neural Comput. **18**, 2936–2941 (2006)
7. Langenhoven, L., Van Heerden, W.S., Engelbrecht, A.P.: Swarm tetris: applying particle swarm optimization to tetris. In: IEEE Congress on Evolutionary Computation, Barcelona, pp. 1–8 (2010). https://doi.org/10.1109/CEC.2010.5586033
8. Lundgaard, N., McKee, B.: Reinforcement learning and neural networks for tetris. Technical report, University of Oklahoma, Oklahoma (2006)
9. Brzustowski, J.: Can you win at tetris? Master's thesis, University of British Columbia, Canada (1992)
10. Bergmark, M.: Tetris: a heuristic study: using height-based weighing functions and breadth-first search heuristics for playing tetris. Bachelor's thesis, KTH, School of Engineering Sciences, Stockholm, Sweden (2015)
11. Rollinson, D., Wagner, G.: Tetris AI generation using Nelder-Mead and genetic algorithms (2010)
12. Han, J., Pei, J., Yin, Y., Mao, R.: Mining frequent patterns without candidate generation: a frequent-pattern tree approach. Data Min. Knowl. Discov. **8**, 53–87 (2004)
13. Farias, V.F., Van Roy, B.: Tetris: a study of randomized constraint sampling. In: Calafiore, G., Dabbene, F. (eds.) Probabilistic and Randomized Methods for Design under Uncertainty, pp. 189–201. Springer, London (2006). https://doi.org/10.1007/1-84628-095-8_6
14. Bertsekas, D.P., Tsitsiklis, J.N.: Neuro-Dynamic Programming. Athena Scientific, Belmont (1996)

15. Ramon, J., Driessens, K.: On the numeric stability of Gaussian processes regression for relational reinforcement learning. In: ICML 2004 Workshop on Relational Reinforcement Learning, pp. 10–14 (2004)
16. Lagoudakis, M.G., Parr, R., Littman, M.L.: Least-squares methods in reinforcement learning for control. In: Vlahavas, I.P., Spyropoulos, C.D. (eds.) SETN 2002. LNCS (LNAI), vol. 2308, pp. 249–260. Springer, Heidelberg (2002). https://doi.org/10.1007/3-540-46014-4_23

Using the Evolutionary Computation Approach in the Initial Phase of Protocol Discovering

Dariusz Pałka[1(✉)] , Marcin Piekarczyk[2] , and Krzysztof Wójcik[3]

[1] Faculty of Electrical Engineering, Automatics, IT and Biomedical Engineering,
Department of Applied Computer Science, AGH University of Science and
Technology, Al. Mickiewicza 30, 30-059 Krakow, Poland
dpalka@agh.edu.pl
[2] Institute of Computer Science, Pedagogical University of Cracow, 2 Podchorazych
Ave, 30-084 Krakow, Poland
marp@up.krakow.pl
[3] Cracow University of Technology, Jana Pawła II 37 Av., 31-864 Krakow, Poland
krzysztof.wojcik@mech.pk.edu.pl

Abstract. The paper presents the method of identifying the initial pool
of request-response pairs for Active Protocol Discoverer. This method is
suitable for the bottom-up form of protocol discovering, in which the
samples of requests are generated, and the high order form (e.g. grammar) of protocol description is created on the basis of these samples.
The method is based on the evolutionary computation approach similar
to linear genetic programming, in which particular requests are treated
as individuals (programs) with different lengths.

Keywords: Protocol discovering · Evolutionary computation ·
Linear genetic programming

1 Introduction

The goal of the protocol discovering process is to find a form of protocol description using samples of conversations held by their participants. Automatic protocol discovering is particularly useful when formal protocol specification does not exist, is incomplete or outdated.

As shown in [10], protocol discovering has numerous applications, which include automated process discovery [6], inferring business protocols of web services [8], discovering models of software processes [4], workflow mining in Enterprise Resource Planning, Customer Relationship Management software, Business to Business applications [3], and discovering communication protocols used by hardware devices. Other important applications of protocol discovering are connected with detecting potential software and hardware vulnerabilities [5,17].

Another reason for the increasing demand for protocol discovering is the popularization of concepts of the Internet of Things, Wireless Sensor Networks and

© Springer Nature Switzerland AG 2019
L. Rutkowski et al. (Eds.): ICAISC 2019, LNAI 11508, pp. 493–505, 2019.
https://doi.org/10.1007/978-3-030-20912-4_45

Pervasive Computing [12,14]. In such environments various devices which use different protocols should cooperate together. Because of relatively fast changes in protocols used by particular devices, a need exists for neighbouring devices to automatically (or symptomatically) adapt to these changes [15].

Other demands for protocol discovering are connected with using legacy devices or legacy software components (e.g. web services) for which protocol specification is unavailable.

There are two main approaches to the process of discovering protocols:

- passive protocol discovering - in which a discoverer system only observes conversations between participants and does not generate any messages (neither requests nor responses) [4,5,8]. Examples of this approach include Automatic Protocol Reverse Engineering Tools [13], which requires network traces as input [9]
- active protocol discovering [10] - where the discoverer takes active part in conversations by generating requests to other participants of the conversation and - on the basis of their responses - tries to discover the protocol

In active protocol discovering generating new requests by a discoverer is an important part of the process. With no or limited knowledge about the protocol under discovery - especially at the beginning of a discovery process - the simplest and most typically used method is random brute force generation of requests. However, even in this initial phase of the discovery process the techniques based on evolutionary computation (EC), e.g. Linear Genetic Programming (LGP) [7,11], can be used and, as shown below, can be more efficient than random generation of requests.

2   The Proposed Approach

Similar to [10], in this study we will consider a bipartite protocol i.e. a protocol of communication between two participants. One of them is the unknown system (treated as the black box) whose protocol should be discovered, and the other is the Active Protocol Discoverer. It is also assumed that each conversation consists of consecutive pairs of request-response. All requests and responses will be treated as byte strings, i.e. sequences of one or more bytes[1].

The protocol discovery process can have two basic forms:

- top-down, in which the high order form of the protocol description (see below) is created, and next individual requests are generated from this form of description.
- bottom-up, in which first the requests (e.g. binary strings) are generated and next, on their basis, the generalized form (high order) of the description is created.

---

[1] The text string is a special case of a byte string.

It may be reasonable to combine these two forms of protocol discovery in one process. For example, at the beginning of a discovery process, when little is known about an unknown system, the bottom-up approach can be more efficient, and later, when we already have some model (or models) of this system, we can use the top-down approach to tune the model/s.

The protocol under consideration may be described in various (high order) forms, for example, deterministic and non-deterministic finite state machines (FSM), push-down automata, Petri nets, regular grammars, and context-free grammars. The example of the top-down approach for active protocol discovering based on Grammatical Evolution by Grammatical Evolution $(GE)^2$ is presented in paper [10].

This study proposes the method of generating requests for protocol discovering in the bottom-up manner. The method described in the paper is based on the evolutionary computation approach, specifically, on Linear Genetic Programming (LGP). In this case, individuals (which represent the requests) are treated as a linear sequence of symbols from an unknown language (protocol) which should be discovered. The goal of the proposed method is to discover as many various responses from the system with an unknown protocol (treated as the black box) as possible. As mentioned above, it is useful in the initial phase of protocol discovery of an unknown system. Request-response pairs found this way can later be used to create generalized forms of protocol description (e.g. context-free grammars), which, however, is out of scope of this paper.

3   The Process of Discovering Responses Using EC

The process of discovering responses is based on evolution of clusters of individuals.

The cluster of individuals C is 2-tuple:

$$C = (r, P) \tag{1}$$

where:

- r - the response from the system with an unknown protocol
- P - population of individuals (requests)

Each cluster C is characterized by unique response r from the system with an unknown protocol.

Two clusters $C_i = (r_i, P_i)$ and $C_j = (r_j, P_j)$ are not equal if:

$$C_i \neq C_j \iff r_i \neq r_j \tag{2}$$

On the basis of Linear Genetic Programming technique, the proposed process of the initial discovery of responses from an unknown system is as follows:

1. The initial cluster of individuals is created. Each cluster has its own population of sentences (which represent the requests) and is characterized by responses from the system with an unknown protocol. The response for the initial cluster is set as empty (i.e. no response from the system with an unknown protocol)

2. The first generation of the population of sentences (binary strings with various length) for the cluster from step 1 is randomly created. Each generated sentence represents a request which will be sent to the system with an unknown protocol (the passive participant of a conversation)
3. Generated requests are sent one by one to the system with an unknown protocol and the responses from the system are registered
   (a) If the response is the same as the one which characterizes the current cluster, fitness of an individual (request) is calculated and stored
   (b) If the response is new (never seen before), the procedure of request-response simplification is executed (see below). If the simplified response is new, a new cluster with its own population of sentences is created. The simplified request is added to this new population, and its fitness is calculated and stored in a new cluster. Each such cluster evolves independently of other clusters
   (c) If the response has been seen before, the request (and its fitness) is added to the cluster characterized by this response
4. For each cluster, on the basis of fitness values, candidates (requests) for the next generation are selected
5. The next generation of individuals is created (for each cluster separately), using genetic operations, such as crossover and mutation
6. The process loops to step 3, and co-evolution of each cluster continues until the stop condition occurs

3.1   The Procedure of Request-Response Simplification

When a new response (never seen before) from the system with an unknown protocol is observed, the procedure aimed at limiting this potentially complex response to a single one should be executed. Otherwise, the registered response may be a concatenation of two (or more) successive responses. This is the case if the generated request is treated by the system with an unknown protocol as two (or more) separate requests one after another. The procedure (see Algorithm 1) uses a bisection method for finding requests that will generate single responses.
    In brief, this algorithm works as follows:

– the initial value of integer 'step' variable is set as the length of the initial request string divided by 2
– the initial value of the final request is set as the initial request
– the temporary request is created as a substring of the initial request form the first character to the character with the number denotes the difference between the length of the request and 'step' variable.
– the temporary request is sent to the system
– if there is a response from the system, the final request is set as the temporary request and the length of the temporary request is decreased by the value of 'step' variable.
– otherwise, the final request is not modified and the length of the temporary request is increased by the value of 'step' variable.

input : A request string *request* and a response string *response*,
output: A simplified response string *finalResponse*, a request string
     for a simplified response *finalRequest*

requestStart ← 0;
requestEnd ← Len(request);
step ← Len(request) / 2;
tempRequestEnd ← requestEnd − step;
finalResponse ← response;

while step > *0* **do**
 | currentRequest ← Substring(request, requestStart,
 | tempRequestEnd);
 | // Send a request to the system and read its response
 | currentResponse ← GetResponseForRequest(currentRequest);
 | **if** Len(currentResponse) > *0* **then**
 | | requestEnd ← tempRequestEnd;
 | | finalResponse ← currentResponse;
 | | tempRequestEnd ← tempRequestEnd − step;
 | **else**
 | | tempRequestEnd ← tempRequestEnd + step;
 | **end**
 | step ← step / 2;
end
finalRequest ← Substring(request, requestStart, requestEnd);

Algorithm 1. The procedure of request-response simplification

- the new 'step' value is set as the current 'step' value divided by 2
- the while loop is repeated for as long as 'step' value is greater than 0
- the final request and the corresponding final response are the output of the algorithm

3.2   The Fitness Function

In order to select individuals (byte strings that represent requests in the protocol) which will be used to create the next generation, fitness values for each of them are calculated. The fitness function has the form:

$$fitness(request) = \begin{cases} \frac{1}{1+|request|}, \text{if the response comes from the current cluster} \\ 0, \text{otherwise} \end{cases}$$

(3)

where:

- |request| - the length of a request i.e. the number of bytes in a byte string

If the response to a request is different that the response characteristic for the current cluster, the request obtains zero as the fitness value. Otherwise, fitness is in inverse proportion to the length of the request (the shortest requests are preferred - their fitness value is greater than that of the longest ones).

3.3   Genetic Operators

The following genetic operators are used to create the next generations:

- crossover - operates on two individuals and is one-point, that is within each of two individuals a random crossover point in the chromosome is selected and particular sections of the chromosome for individuals are swapped
- mutation - operates on one individual and changes a randomly selected part of its chromosome. It can assume two forms: whole byte mutation and single bit mutation. In case of whole byte mutation, after a random selection of the position of a byte in the chromosome, this byte is replaced by a randomly selected value.
- duplication - operates on a single individual and creates an exact copy of a selected individual
- random creation - randomly generates a new individual (a whole chromosome)

3.4   Selection

Individuals used in creating the next generation are selected on the basis of their fitness values (by using genetics operations). The deterministic tournament selection is used in this process i.e. k^2 individuals are selected from a population at random, then the best one (with the greatest fitness value) is selected as the parent of the next generation of individuals, then a selected genetic operation is used to create offspring. The process is repeated until the whole next generation of the population is created.

4   Case Study

This section presents sample results of the proposed approach to preliminary protocol discovering. The case study is based on protocol discovering for Pan-Tilt-Zoom teleconference cameras. Because the protocol used by these cameras is known (it is VISCA protocol), the results obtained in the protocol discovering process can be compared with the specification provided by their manufacturer. However, the proposed approach is universal and can be applied in any bipartite protocol.

4.1   The Testing Environment

Video System Control Architecture (VISCA) protocol was the protocol to be discovered in the study. VISCA is a control protocol designed by Sony, which is used in many teleconference and surveillance Pan-Tilt-Zoom cameras. The tests were executed independently on three different VISCA cameras:

- Sony EVI-D31
- Sony EVI-D70P
- Sony EVI-D100P

---

[2] where k is tournament size.

Because VISCA uses RS-232 protocol as Data Link Layer, the PTZ cameras were linked to a computer with running Protocol Discoverer using RS-232 Terminal Server. Such solution allows for simultaneous connection of a number of cameras (in this test three) for which a protocol is being discovered.

4.2   The Parameters of the Evolutionary Process

The parameters of the process of preliminary protocol discovering used in the tests are shown in Table 1.

Table 1. Evolution parameters used in the tests

Parameter	Value
Population size for each request-response cluster	100
Tournament size	5
Crossover probability	55%
Mutation probability	15%
Duplication probability	15%
Random creation probability	15%

5   Results

The process of preliminary protocol discovering using LGP was run three times for each VISCA camera and in total 15.000 individuals (requests to camera) for each run were tested. Additionally, a test randomly generating 15.000 individuals (byte strings) was performed for each camera. The results of random generation of requests were used as comparative values for assessing efficiency of the proposed method of generating requests using LGP.

The number of unique responses identified using the proposed method for generating requests for each camera is presented in Fig. 1.

As can be seen, the numbers of unique responses identified for Sony EVI-D31 and Sony EVI-D100P cameras are similar, while the number of requests for Sony EVI-D70P camera is about 4 times lower. It might have been caused by the fact that cameras EVI-D31 and EVI-D100P are primarily dedicated for teleconferences, while the EVI-D70P is dedicated for a wider range of applications (e.g. distance learning, security systems, etc.) [16] and has to be more resistant to unexpected requests in control protocol.

Figure 3 shows a histogram of lengths of identified unique responses obtained using the proposed evolutionary approach. The distribution of the length of responses is similar for all Sony EVI cameras. The number of identified unique requests quickly decreases with an increase in the length of requests. This part of distribution is similar to exponential decay.

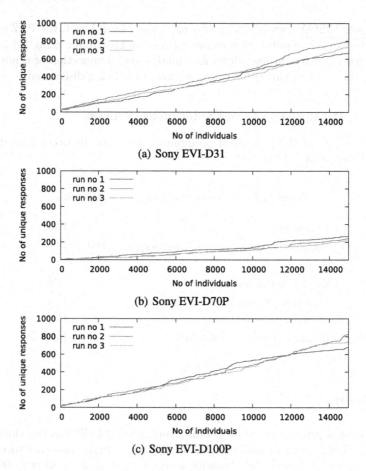

Fig. 1. The number of unique responses identified after testing a given number of individuals (requests) using the proposed method for preliminary protocol discovering.

Figure 2 shows a number of unique responses found for each camera using random generation of requests. In this approach, first, the length of the request was randomly generated in the range between 1 and 100 with uniform distribution, and next the value of each byte in the request was randomly generated.

The histograms of the lengths of the responses obtained using random generation of requests are shown in Fig. 4.

As can be noticed, the proposed method based on the evolutionary approach allows for finding a greater number of unique responses than the method which generates individuals (requests) in a random way. For EVI-D31 camera the approach using random generation of individuals found 431 unique responses, while the proposed approach based on LGP found 666, 794, 733 unique responses in runs 1, 2 and 3, respectively. For EVI-D70P camera random generation found

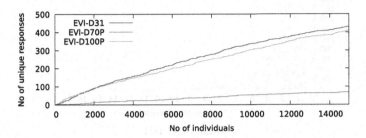

Fig. 2. The number of unique responses identified after testing a given number of individuals (requests) using the method of random generation of individuals

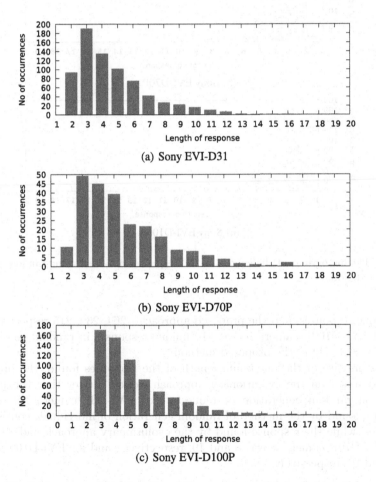

Fig. 3. The histograms of the lengths of the responses obtained using the proposed method for preliminary protocol discovering

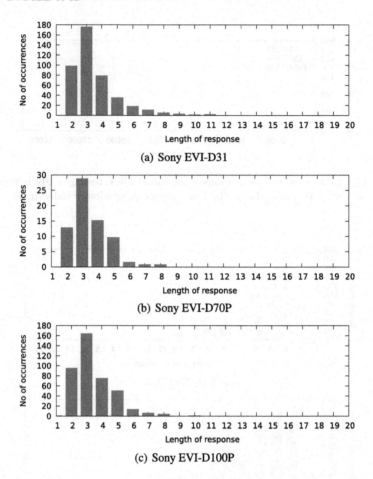

Fig. 4. The histograms of the lengths of the responses obtained using random generation of individuals

69 unique responses, and the proposed approach - 264, 239, 215 respectively. In
case of EVI-D100P camera it was 410 unique responses in random generation,
and 678, 823, 742 in the proposed method.

Also in case of the maximum length of the responses found, the proposed
method based on the evolutionary approach worked better that the method
based on random generation of requests. For EVI-D31 camera the longest
response found by the method of random generation of individuals consisted of
11 bytes, while the response found by the evolutionary approach had 19 bytes.
For EVI-D70P camera it was 8 and 19, respectively, and for EVI-D100 camera
- 10 and 19, respectively.

5.1   The Results of Request-Response Simplification

The example of request-response simplification while discovering a protocol for Sony EVI-D31 camera is a reduction of the response from: [E9, FF, D3, FF, F0, 53, 72, 36, FF, DF, 19, 05, 45, 40, FF, 83, FF, B7, 72, 39, 49, FF][3] to [E9, FF], which is a reduction in the length of the response from 22 to 2 bytes. The reduction of the request in this example was from 222 to 45 bytes. After applying the procedure of request-response simplification, all identified responses end with value FF, which is not unexpected, as it is VISCA packet terminator [1, 2]. Additionally, only 34 responses from the total number of 1353 unique responses contained more that one (in each case two) bytes with value FF. Such responses were a concatenation of two VISCA response packets (each ended with FF value). The most frequent response with two VISCA packets was: [E0, 60, 03, FF, E0, E0, 52, FF], where the first packet [E0, 60, 03, FF] was error message 'command buffer full', and the second packet [E0, 52, FF] was 'Command completion' for socket 2 (see [2]).

6   Conclusions

The approach presented in this paper is dedicated for preliminary protocol discovering by an Active Protocol Discoverer. This approach is suitable for the bottom-up form of protocol discovering i.e. the form where sample requests are generated first and then the high order form of the description of the protocol (for example, grammar) is created on the basis of this sample. The proposed method is based on the evolutionary approach, especially on Linear Genetic Programming, in which programs (in this case requests) are represented by sequences of instructions (bytes). These sequences of bytes (requests) are created using genetics operators and may have different lengths. This approach is an alternative to generating sample requests in a totally random manner, which is typically applied in the initial phase of protocol discovering where there is no knowledge about the protocol under consideration. As the example of the initial phase of discovering responses for VISCA protocol presented in this paper demonstrates, this approach is more efficient than the approach based on random generation of individuals. Two potential drawbacks of the proposed approach should be mentioned. One of them is a constant increase of the number of clusters of individuals and, consequently, the number of individuals which must be evaluated in each generation. If some clusters do not contribute to finding new request-response pairs, thus to finding new clusters, their evolution may slow down the whole process of finding new solutions (request-response pairs). Identifying such unusable clusters and optimizing searching process is a challenge which should be addressed in further studies. The second drawback is connected with the procedure of request-response simplification – the bisection approach was proposed to limit this potentially complex response to a single one. The computational complexity of this algorithm is $O(\log n)$, where n is the length of the request under

---

[3] The presented values are given in the hexadecimal system.

simplification. For long requests this computational complexity can be significant. Limiting this complexity, by, for example, using some heuristic techniques can be another challenge in further studies in this area.

References

1. Sony Color Video Camera Technical Manual. http://www.vaddio.com/library? path=d&file=tc_sony_d100_techmanual.pdf
2. Sony EVI-D30/D31 Command List. https://www.cs.rochester.edu/~nelson/ courses/vision/resources/sony_evi-d31.pdf
3. van der Aalst, W., van Dongen, B., Herbst, J., Maruster, L., Schimm, G., Weijters, A.: Workflow mining: a survey of issues and approaches. Data Knowl. Eng. **47**(2), 237–267 (2003). http://www.sciencedirect.com/science/article/pii/ S0169023X03000661
4. Cook, J.E., Wolf, A.L.: Discovering models of software processes from event-based data. ACM Trans. Softw. Eng. Methodol. **7**(3), 215–249 (1998). https://doi.org/ 10.1145/287000.287001
5. Cui, W., Kannan, J., Wang, H.J.: Discoverer: automatic protocol reverse engineering from network traces. In: Proceedings of 16th USENIX Security Symposium on USENIX Security Symposium SS 2007, pp. 14:1–14:14. USENIX Association, Berkeley, CA, USA (2007). http://dl.acm.org/citation.cfm?id=1362903.1362917
6. Leemans, S.J.J.: Automated Process Discovery, pp. 121–130. Springer, Cham (2019). https://doi.org/10.1007/978-3-319-77525-8_88
7. Brameier, M.F., Banzhaf, W.: Linear Genetic Programming (Genetic and Evolutionary Computation). Springer, New York (2007). https://doi.org/10.1007/978-0-387-31030-5
8. Motahari-Nezhad, H.R., Saint-Paul, R., Casati, F., Benatallah, B.: Deriving protocol models from imperfect service conversation logs. IEEE Trans. Knowl. Data Eng. **20**, 1683–1698 (2008). http://ieeecomputersociety.org/10.1109/TKDE.2008. 87
9. Narayan, J., Shukla, S.K., Clancy, T.C.: A survey of automatic protocol reverse engineering tools. ACM Comput. Surv. **48**(3), 40:1–40:26 (2015). https://doi.acm. org/10.1145/2840724
10. Pałka, D., Zachara, M., Wójcik, K.: Active protocol discoverer based on grammatical evolution. In: Borzemski, L., Swiatek, J., Wilimowska, Z. (eds.) ISAT 2017. AISC, vol. 655, pp. 95–106. Springer, Cham (2018). https://doi.org/10.1007/978-3-319-67220-5_9
11. Poli, R., Langdon, W.B., McPhee, N.F.: A Field Guide to Genetic Programming. Lulu Enterprises, UK Ltd (2008)
12. Qin, Y., Sheng, Q.Z.: Big Data Analysis and IoT, pp. 141–152. Springer, Cham (2019), https://doi.org/10.1007/978-3-319-77525-8_308
13. Sija, B.D., Goo, Y.H., Shim, K.S., Hasanova, H., Kim, M.S.: A survey of automatic protocol reverse engineering approaches, methods, and tools on the inputs and outputs view. Secur. Commun. Netw. **2018**, 8370341:1–8370341:17 (2018)
14. Silvis-Cividjian, N.: Pervasive Computing: Engineering Smart Systems. Undergraduate Topics in Computer Science. Springer, Heidelberg (2017). https://doi.org/10. 1007/978-3-319-51655-4

15. Son, H., Lee, D.: Towards interactive networking: runtime message inference approach for incompatible protocol updates in IOT environments. Future Gener. Comput. Syst. (2019). http://www.sciencedirect.com/science/article/pii/S0167739X18319460

16. Sony: EVI-D70/D70P(PAL) Camera. https://pro.sony/en_GR/products/ptz-network-cameras/evi-d70-d70p-pal-

17. Wang, Y., Yun, X., Zhang, Y., Chen, L., Zang, T.: Rethinking robust and accurate application protocol identification. Comput. Netw. **129**, 64–78 (2017). http://www.sciencedirect.com/science/article/pii/S1389128617303572

Population Diversity Analysis in Adaptive Differential Evolution Variants with Unconventional Randomization Schemes

Roman Senkerik[1]([⊠]) ⓘ, Adam Viktorin[1] ⓘ, Tomas Kadavy[1] ⓘ,
Michal Pluhacek[1] ⓘ, Anezka Kazikova[1] ⓘ, Quoc Bao Diep[2],
and Ivan Zelinka[2] ⓘ

[1] Faculty of Applied Informatics, Tomas Bata University in Zlin,
T. G. Masaryka 5555, 760 01 Zlin, Czech Republic
senkerik@utb.cz
[2] Faculty of Electrical Engineering and Computer Science,
Technical University of Ostrava, 17. listopadu 15, Ostrava, Czech Republic
ivan.zelinka@vsb.cz

Abstract. This research represents a detailed insight into the modern and popular hybridization of unconventional quasiperiodic/chaotic sequences and evolutionary computation. It is aimed at the influence of different randomization schemes on the population diversity, thus on the performance, of two selected adaptive Differential Evolution (DE) variants. Experiments are focused on the extensive investigation of totally ten different randomization schemes for the selection of individuals in DE algorithm driven by the default pseudo-random generator of Java environment and nine different two-dimensional discrete chaotic systems, as the unconventional chaotic pseudo-random number generators. The population diversity is recorded for 15 test functions from the CEC 2015 benchmark set in $10D$.

Keywords: Differential evolution · Complex dynamics · Deterministic chaos · Population diversity · Chaotic map

1 Introduction

Together with this persistent development of metaheuristics algorithms, chaos with its properties like ergodicity, stochasticity, self-similarity, and density of periodic orbits became a very popular and modern tool for improving the performance of various ECT's. The metaheuristics algorithm of the interest here is Differential Evolution (DE) [1], specifically its popular adaptive variants.

This research deals with the mutual intersection of the two computational intelligence fields, which are the complex sequencing and dynamics given by the selected chaotic systems, and evolutionary computation techniques (ECT's). Since the key operation in metaheuristic algorithms is the randomness, recent research in unconventional and chaotic approach for metaheuristics mostly uses straightforwardly periodic sequences or various chaotic maps in the place of pseudo-random number

© Springer Nature Switzerland AG 2019
L. Rutkowski et al. (Eds.): ICAISC 2019, LNAI 11508, pp. 506–518, 2019.
https://doi.org/10.1007/978-3-030-20912-4_46

generators (PRNG). The original chaos-based approach is tightly connected with the importance of randomization within heuristics as compensation of a limited amount of search moves. This idea has been carried out in several papers describing different techniques to modify the randomization process [2]. Also, the influence of randomization operations to parameter adaptation was profoundly experimentally tested in [3].

The basic concept of embedding chaotic dynamics into the evolutionary/swarm algorithms as chaotic pseudo-random number generator (CPRNG) is given in [4]. Firstly, the PSO algorithm with elements of chaos was introduced as CPSO [5], followed by the initial testing of chaos embedded DE [6–8]. Original inertia weight based PSO strategy driven by CPRNGs was also profoundly investigated [9]. Recently the chaos driven heuristic concept has been utilized in many swarm-based algorithms [10–12], as well as many applications with DE [13, 14].

The organization of this paper is the following: Firstly, the motivation for this research is proposed. The next sections are focused on the description of the essentials of used DE variants, the concept of embedding unconventional randomization sequences into DE, the experiment background, and results discussions.

2 Motivation and Related Research

Even though the hybridization of ECT's and unconventional randomization schemes (mostly with chaos) is becoming very popular in recent years, many research questions remain, as to why it works, why it may be beneficial to use the chaotic and other quasi-random sequences for driving the selection, mutation, crossover or other processes in particular heuristics.

This paper aims to help find the way to some answers through a detailed analysis of population dynamics through population diversity.

Moreover, current research trends in metaheuristic algorithms are focused on distance/diversity based approaches [15–17] monitoring exploration abilities of algorithms either through a distance between individuals at the search space, or keeping population diverse in critical beginning stages of the optimization process.

This research is a follow up for findings and conclusions from population diversity analyses in chaos driven DE published in [18, 19]. The motivation and the originality of the presented research can be summarized as follows:

- To present a comprehensive review of the adaptive DE driven by unconventional randomization schemes, so that the readers can easily navigate between different chaotic CPRNGs and different well known adaptive DE strategies, and to see the direct comparisons of performances and deeper insight into population dynamics.
- Here, more detailed graphical analyses supporting statements in the conclusion section are provided.
- Adaptive state of the art versions jDE and Success-History Based Adaptive Differential Evolution (SHADE) are investigated here. All previously reported research papers were mostly focused on the simplest strategies.

- Thus this reported research can be beneficial for researchers focusing on the important research related to exploration abilities of the metaheuristic algorithms and avoiding premature convergence through the population diversity analyses.

3   Differential Evolution

This section describes the basics of adaptive jDE and SHADE variants. The original DE [16] has four static control parameters – a number of generations G, population size NP, scaling factor F and crossover rate CR. In the evolutionary process of DE, these four parameters remain unchanged and depend on the initial user setting. The jDE and SHADE algorithms, on the other hand, adapts the F and CR parameters during the evolution. Moreover, SHADE is using more complex adaptive schemes and historical archive for removed inferior solutions. The concept of essential operations in jDE and SHADE algorithms is shown in following sections, for a detailed description of either original DE refer to [1, 20], or for jDE see [21], and SHADE is detailed in [22].

3.1   The jDE Algorithm

In this research, we have used jDE and chaotic C_jDE with original DE "rand/1/bin" (1) mutation strategy and binomial crossover (2). The generated ensemble of two control parameters F_i and CR_i is assigned to each i-th individual of the population and survives with the solution if an individual is transferred to the new generation. The initialization of values of F and CR is designed to be either fully random with uniform distribution for each individual in the population or can be set according to the recommended values in the literature. If the newly generated solution is not successful, i.e., the trial vector has worse fitness than the compared original active individual; the new (possibly) reinitialized control parameters values disappear together with not successful solution. The both aforementioned DE control parameters may be randomly mutated with predefined probabilities τ_1 and τ_2. If the mutation condition happens, a new random value of $CR \in [0, 1]$ is generated, possibly also a new value of F which is mutated in $[F_l, F_u]$. These new control parameters are after that stored in the new population. Input parameters are typically set to $F_l = 0.1$, $F_u = 0.9$, $\tau_1 = 0.1$, and $\tau_2 = 0.1$ as originally given in [21].

Mutation Strategies and Parent Selection

The parent indices (vectors) are selected either by standard PRNG with uniform distribution or by CPRNG in case of chaotic versions. Mutation strategy "rand/1/bin" uses three random parent vectors with indexes $r1$, $r2$ and $r3$, where $r1 = U[1, NP]$, $r2 = U[1, NP]$, $r3 = U[1, NP]$ and $r1 \neq r2 \neq r3$. Mutated vector $v_{i, G}$ is obtained from three different vectors x_{r1}, x_{r2}, x_{r3} from current generation G with the help of scaling factor F_i as follows:

$$v_{i,G} = x_{r1,G} + F_i(x_{r2,G} - x_{r3,G}) \tag{1}$$

Crossover and Selection

The trial vector $u_{i,G}$ which is compared with original vector $x_{i,G}$ is completed by crossover operation (2). CR_i value in jDE algorithm is not static.

$$u_{j,i,G} = \begin{cases} v_{j,i,G} & \text{if } U[0, 1] \leq CR_i \text{ or } j = j_{rand} \\ x_{j,i,G} & \text{otherwise} \end{cases} \qquad (2)$$

Where j_{rand} is a randomly selected index of a feature, which has to be updated ($j_{rand} = U[1, D]$), D is the dimensionality of the problem. The vector which will be placed into the next generation $G + 1$ is selected by elitism. When the objective function value of the trial vector $u_{i,G}$ is better than that of the original vector $x_{i,G}$, the trial vector will be selected for the next population. Otherwise, the original will remain (3).

$$x_{i,G+1} = \begin{cases} u_{i,G} & \text{if } f(u_{i,G}) \leq f(x_{i,G}) \\ x_{i,G} & \text{otherwise} \end{cases} \qquad (3)$$

3.2 Shade

The mutation strategy used in SHADE is "current-to-*pbest*/1/" and uses four parent vectors – current i-th vector $x_{i,G}$, vector $x_{pbest,G}$ randomly selected from the $NP \times p$ best vectors (regarding objective function value) from current generation G. The p value is randomly generated by uniform PRNG U[p_{min}, 0.2], where $p_{min} = 2/NP$. Third parent vector $x_{r1,G}$ is randomly selected from the current generation and last parent vector $x_{r2,G}$ is also randomly selected, but from the union of current generation G and external archive A. Also, vectors $x_{i,G}$, $x_{r1,G}$ and $x_{r2,G}$ has to differ, $x_{i,G} \neq x_{r1,G} \neq x_{r2,G}$. The mutated vector $v_{i,G}$ is generated by (4).

$$v_{i,G} = x_{i,G} + F_i(x_{pbest,G} - x_{i,G}) + F_i(x_{r1,G} - x_{r2,G}) \qquad (4)$$

The i-th scaling factor F_i is generated from a Cauchy distribution with the location parameter $M_{F,r}$. SHADE algorithm uses the very same crossover (2) and elitism schemes (3) as canonical DE with the following differences. CR value is not static, CR_i is generated from a normal distribution with a mean parameter value $M_{CR,r}$ And the elitism process uses the historical archive. For the archive and historical memories updates, details about the parameters $M_{F,r}$ and $M_{CR,r}$ due, to the limited space here, see [22].

4 Chaotic Systems for Pseudo-Random Generators

The general idea of CPRNG is to replace the default PRNG with the chaotic system. Following nine well known and frequently studied discrete dissipative chaotic maps were used as the CPRNGs for jDE and SHADE. Systems of the interest were: *Arnold Cat Map, Burgers Map, Delayed Logistic Map, Dissipative Standard Map, Henon Map, Ikeda Map, Lozi Map* (4), *Sinai Map* and *Tinkerbell Map*. With the typical settings and definitions as in [23], systems exhibit typical chaotic behavior. Please refer to the (5) for the examples of maps definition (popular and widely studied Lozi map). Also, Fig. 1 shows the short chaotic sequences for three selected maps. These plots support the claims that due to the presence of self-similar chaotic sequences, the heuristic is forced to neighborhood-based selection (or alternative neighborhood like communication in swarms).

$$
\begin{aligned}
X_{n+1} &= aX_n - Y_n^2 \\
Y_{n+1} &= bY_n + X_nY_n
\end{aligned}
\tag{5}
$$

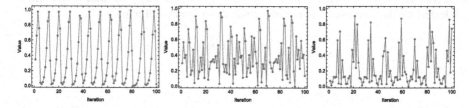

Fig. 1. Chaotic sequences normalized to the typical range of 0-1 for CPRNG, either with significant sequencing and periodicity or with patterns of self-similarity; Delayed Logistic (left), Lozi (center) and Tinkerbelt maps (right).

Once the start position of the chaotic system has been obtained (by default PRNG), the system generates the next sequence using its current position. Used approach is based on the following definition (6), where the *rndreal* represents the normalized pseudo-random value from the typical range of 0–1, *rndChaos* is the current output iteration of the chaotic map (selected *x*-axis), and *maxval* is the maximum value from generated chaotic series. This approach is causing so-called folding of the attractor around *y*-axis.

$$
rndreal = \left| \frac{rndChaos}{maxval} \right|
\tag{6}
$$

5   Experiment Design and Results

The CEC 15 benchmark suite was selected [24]. The dimension D was set to 10, which is close to real-life engineering problems. Every instance was repeated 51 times with the maximum number of objective function evaluations set to 100 000 (10,000 × D). The convergence and population diversity were recorded for all tested algorithm – original jDE/SHADE and nine versions of C_jDE/C_SHADE with different CPRNGs. All algorithms used the same set of control parameters: population size $NP = 50$, initial settings $F = 0.5$, $CR = 0.8$ (only jDE), and $H = 20$ (only SHADE). Experiments were performed in the environment of *Java*; original jDE and SHADE, therefore, have used the built-in *Java linear congruential pseudorandom number generator* representing traditional pseudorandom number generator in comparisons.

The Population Diversity (PD) measure [25] is based on the sum of deviations (8) of individual's components from their corresponding means (7), where i is the population member iterator and j is the vector component iterator.

$$\overline{x_j} = \frac{1}{NP} \sum_{i=1}^{NP} x_{ij} \tag{7}$$

$$PD = \sqrt{\frac{1}{NP} \sum_{i=1}^{NP} \sum_{j=1}^{D} \left(x_{ij} - \overline{x_j}\right)^2} \tag{8}$$

Due to the limited space and due to the simple fact, that direct benchmarking-based performance comparisons was not the main aim of this paper, the statistical comparisons in comprehensive tables containing mean, median, max/min results are not given here. Instead, we are presenting the boxplots in Figs. 2 and 3, depicting the mean value (middle line), 25–75% quantiles, upper and lower fences, outliers (black dot) and far

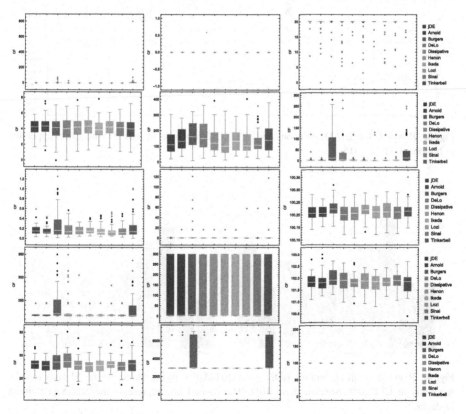

Fig. 2. Boxplots for jDE versions and all CEC15 functions in 10D, 51 runs; from upper left to bottom right: $f1$ - $f15$.

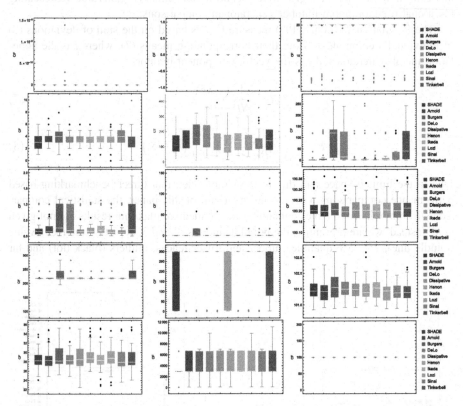

Fig. 3. Boxplots for SHADE versions and all CEC15 functions in 10D, 51 runs; from upper left to bottom right: $f1$ - $f15$.

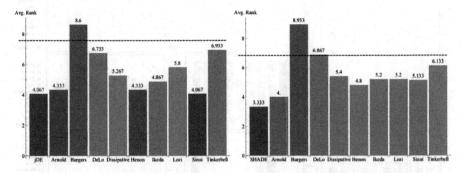

Fig. 4. Ranking of all algorithms (jDE – left, SHADE – right), based on the 51 runs and 15 functions of CEC2015 benchmark in 10D. The dashed line represents the Nemenyi Critical Distance.

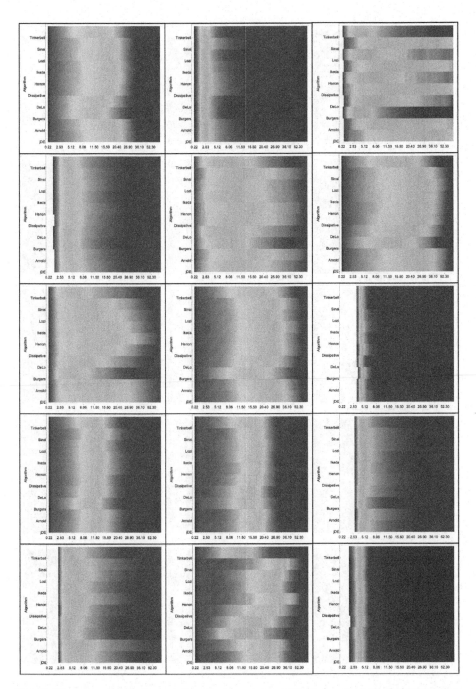

Fig. 5. Heat maps for the average diversity, ten versions of jDE algorithm, all CEC15 functions in 10D, 51 runs; from upper left to bottom right: $f1$ - $f15$. A logarithmic scale, the x-axis is showing % of MaxFES.

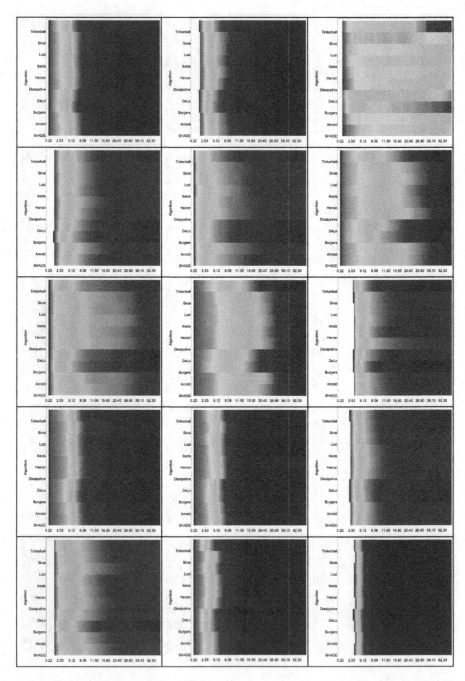

Fig. 6. Heat maps for the average diversity, ten versions of SHADE algorithm, all CEC15 functions in 10D, 51 runs; from upper left to bottom right: *f*1 - *f*15. A logarithmic scale, the *x*-axis is showing % of MaxFES.

outliers (grey dot). Further, a ranking of the algorithms, given in Fig. 4, was evaluated based on the *Friedman test with Nemenyi post hoc test*. Figures 5 and 6 depict the graphical comparisons (heat maps) of the population diversity provided for the first 1000 generations in logarithmic scale. It can be assumed that the start of the optimization process is critically sensitive to keeping the population's diversity as much as possible to ensure space exploration. The results discussion is in the next section.

6 Conclusion

The primary aim of this original work is to provide a more in-depth insight into the inner dynamics of indices selection in DE. The focus is to experimentally investigate the influence of different types of unconventional non-random (chaotic) sequences to the population diversity, and therefore, as well as to the performance of the popular modern adaptive DE variants, which are jDE and SHADE.

The research of randomization issues and insights into the inner dynamic of metaheuristic algorithms was many times addressed as essential and beneficial. The results presented here support the approach for different randomization schemes (multi-chaotic generators [26]) or ensemble systems, where we can profit from the combined/selective population diversity (i.e., exploration/exploitation) tendencies, sequencing-based either stronger or moderate progress towards the function extreme, all given by the smart combination of multi-randomization schemes. The findings can be summarized as:

- From the heat maps depicted in Figs. 5 and 6, we can clearly see the correlations between rankings (Fig. 4) and boxplots (Figs. 2 and 3). Also, we can observe several combinations of behavior for particular (clusters of) CPRNGs, that are securing maintaining of higher population diversity for a longer time (Arnold, Lozi, Sinai, Henon, and Dissipative maps), thus obtaining balanced results in comparison with original version of DE variant. Specifically, Sinai map shows very interesting characteristics in some instances, for example in the case of *f*3 the population diversity is particularly restored and it increased during the algorithm run. This map secured to keep the higher population diversity and exploration phase for a longer period. This in return is beneficial for the result of the optimization.
- Mutual comparing of rankings and box plots also reveals an interesting phenomenon. Although in most cases, there is no a significant difference between the performance of the tested versions, according to the critical distance, in some instances, the chaotic versions performed significantly worse. Such a worse performance was repeatedly observed for three chaotic maps: Delayed logistic, Burgers, and Tinkerbell. On the other hand, these maps usually secured robust progress towards function extreme (local) followed by premature population stagnation phase, thus repeatedly secured finding of minimum values (See boxplots in Figs. 2 and 3). Also from the heat maps (Figs. 5 and 6), we can see the rapid decrease of the population diversity. Overall, C_jDE and C_SHADE versions seem to be very effective in finding the min. values of the objective function (Figs. 2 and 3).

- The statistical performance comparisons (rankings) in Fig. 4 reveal the fact that original full random strategy "Rand/1/" used in jDE seems to be the conservative choice for the hybridization with unconventional randomization schemes. The SHADE variant shows the possible conflict between the attraction to the "pbest" solutions in the population and other indices selected based on the chaotic series. The quasirandom/chaotic sequencing for indices selection may be suppressed by the operations with external archive and the structure of "current-to-pbest/1" strategy. Overall, the parameter adaptation is beneficial without any doubt regarding the performance of the algorithms.

To finalize this detailed research, the graphical comparisons (heat maps), detailed statistical insights (box plots) supported by rankings, can help other researchers in developing more robust and effective metaheuristics. Since adaptive variants of DE have been used here, we can clearly see, that not only the adaptive/learning/ensemble based control parameters adjusting can be used for securing desired behavior and ideal ratio between exploration/exploitation abilities, but also unconventional chaotic/quasiperiodic sequencing have strong influence to the population diversity and may create the sub-populations (or inner neighborhood selection schemes [27]), hence the metaheuristic can benefit from the searching within those sub-populations and quasi-periodic exchanges of information between individuals.

Acknowledgement. This work was supported by the Ministry of Education, Youth and Sports of the Czech Republic within the National Sustainability Programme Project no. LO1303 (MSMT-7778/2014), further by the European Regional Development Fund under the Project CEBIA-Tech no. CZ.1.05/2.1.00/03.0089 and by Internal Grant Agency of Tomas Bata University under the Projects no. IGA/CebiaTech/2019/002. This work is also based upon support by COST (European Cooperation in Science & Technology) under Action CA15140 (ImAppNIO), and Action IC1406 (cHiPSet). The work was further supported by resources of A.I. Lab at the Faculty of Applied Informatics, Tomas Bata University in Zlin (ailab.fai.utb.cz), and by grant of SGS 2019/137, VSB-Technical University of Ostrava.

References

1. Price, K.V., Storn, R.M., Lampinen, J.A.: Differential Evolution: A Practical Approach to Global Optimization. NCS. Springer, Heidelberg (2005). https://doi.org/10.1007/3-540-31306-0
2. Weber, M., Neri, F., Tirronen, V.: A study on scale factor in distributed differential evolution. Inf. Sci. **181**(12), 2488–2511 (2011)
3. Zamuda, A., Brest, J.: Self-adaptive control parameters' randomization frequency and propagations in differential evolution. Swarm Evol. Comput. **25**, 72–99 (2015)
4. Caponetto, R., Fortuna, L., Fazzino, S., Xibilia, M.G.: Chaotic sequences to improve the performance of evolutionary algorithms. IEEE Trans. Evol. Comput. **7**(3), 289–304 (2003)
5. Coelho, L., Mariani, V.C.: A novel chaotic particle swarm optimization approach using Hénon map and implicit filtering local search for economic load dispatch. Chaos, Solitons Fractals **39**(2), 510–518 (2009)
6. Davendra, D., Zelinka, I., Senkerik, R.: Chaos driven evolutionary algorithms for the task of PID control. Comput. Math Appl. **60**(4), 1088–1104 (2010)

7. Zhenyu, G., Bo, C., Min, Y., Binggang, C.: Self-Adaptive chaos differential evolution. In: Jiao, L., Wang, L., Gao, X.-b., Liu, J., Wu, F. (eds.) ICNC 2006. LNCS, vol. 4221, pp. 972–975. Springer, Heidelberg (2006). https://doi.org/10.1007/11881070_128

8. Ozer, A.B.: CIDE: chaotically initialized differential evolution. Expert Syst. Appl. **37**(6), 4632–4641 (2010)

9. Pluhacek, M., Senkerik, R., Davendra, D.: Chaos particle swarm optimization with Eensemble of chaotic systems. Swarm Evol. Comput. **25**, 29–35 (2015)

10. Gandomi, A.H., Yang, X.S., Talatahari, S., Alavi, A.H.: Firefly algorithm with chaos. Commun. Nonlinear Sci. Numer. Simul. **18**(1), 89–98 (2013)

11. Zhang, C., Cui, G., Peng, F.: A novel hybrid chaotic ant swarm algorithm for heat exchanger networks synthesis. Appl. Therm. Eng. **104**, 707–719 (2016)

12. Wang, G.G., Deb, S., Gandomi, A.H., Zhang, Z., Alavi, A.H.: Chaotic cuckoo search. Soft. Comput. **20**(9), 3349–3362 (2016)

13. Coelho, L., Ayala, H.V.H., Mariani, V.C.: A self-adaptive chaotic differential evolution algorithm using gamma distribution for unconstrained global optimization. Appl. Math. Comput. **234**, 452–459 (2014)

14. Metlicka, M., Davendra, D.: Chaos driven discrete artificial bee algorithm for location and assignment optimisation problems. Swarm Evol. Comput. **25**, 15–28 (2015)

15. Viktorin, A., Senkerik, R., Pluhacek, M., Kadavy, T., Zamuda, A.: Distance based parameter adaptation for success-history based differential evolution. Swarm Evol. Comput. (2018)

16. Sudholt, D.: The Benefits of Population Diversity in Evolutionary Algorithms: A Survey of Rigorous Runtime Analyses. arXiv preprint arXiv:1801.10087 (2018)

17. Corus, D., Oliveto, P.S.: Standard steady state genetic algorithms can hillclimb faster than mutation-only evolutionary algorithms. IEEE Trans. Evol. Comput. **22**(5), 720–732 (2018)

18. Senkerik, R., Viktorin, A., Pluhacek, M., Kadavy, T., Zelinka, I.: How unconventional chaotic pseudo-random generators influence population diversity in differential evolution. In: Rutkowski, L., Scherer, R., Korytkowski, M., Pedrycz, W., Tadeusiewicz, R., Zurada, J.M. (eds.) ICAISC 2018. LNCS (LNAI), vol. 10841, pp. 524–535. Springer, Cham (2018). https://doi.org/10.1007/978-3-319-91253-0_49

19. Zelinka, I., et al.: Differential evolution and chaotic series. In: 2018 25th International Conference on Systems, Signals and Image Processing (IWSSIP), pp. 1–5. IEEE, June 2018

20. Das, S., Mullick, S.S., Suganthan, P.: Recent advances in differential evolution – an updated survey. Swarm Evol. Comput. **27**, 1–30 (2016)

21. Brest, J., Greiner, S., Bosković, B., Mernik, M., Zumer, V.: Self- adapting control parameters in differential evolution: a comparative study on numerical benchmark problems. IEEE Trans. Evol. Comput. **10**(6), 646–657 (2006)

22. Tanabe, R., Fukunaga, A.S.: Improving the search performance of SHADE using linear population size reduction. In: 2014 IEEE Congress on Evolutionary Computation (CEC). IEEE, pp. 1658–1665 (2014)

23. Sprott, J.C.: Chaos and Time-Series Analysis. Oxford University Press, New York (2003)

24. Chen, Q., Liu, B., Zhang, Q., Liang, J.J., Suganthan, P.N., Qu, B.Y.: Problem definition and evaluation criteria for CEC 2015 special session and competition on bound constrained single-objective computationally expensive numerical optimization. Computational Intelligence Laboratory, Zhengzhou University, China and Nanyang Technological University, Singapore, Technical report (2014)

25. Poláková, R., Tvrdík, J., Bujok, P., Matoušek, R.: Population-size adaptation through diversity-control mechanism for differential evolution. In MENDEL, 22th International Conference on Soft Computing, pp. 49–56 (2016)

26. Viktorin, A., Pluhacek, M., Senkerik, R.: Success-history based adaptive differential evolution algorithm with multi-chaotic framework for parent selection performance on CEC2014 benchmark set. In: 2016 IEEE Congress on Evolutionary Computation (CEC), pp. 4797–4803. IEEE, July 2016
27. Das, S., Abraham, A., Chakraborty, U., Konar, A.: Differential evolution using a neighborhood-based mutation operator. IEEE Trans. Evol. Comput. 13(3), 526–553 (2009)

Analyzing Control Parameters in DISH

Adam Viktorin[(✉)] [iD], Roman Senkerik [iD], Michal Pluhacek [iD],
and Tomas Kadavy [iD]

Faculty of Applied Informatics, Tomas Bata University in Zlin,
T. G. Masaryka 5555, 760 01 Zlin, Czech Republic
{aviktorin,senkerik,pluhacek,kadavy}@utb.cz

Abstract. This paper presents the analysis of the difference in control
parameter adaptation between jSO and DISH algorithms. The DISH
algorithm uses a distance based parameter adaptation and therefore, is
based on the distance between successful offspring and its parent solution
rather than on the difference in their corresponding objective function
values. The DISH algorithm outperforms the jSO algorithm on the CEC
2015 benchmark set and the adaptation behavior on functions, where the
performance is significantly different, is analyzed and commented. The
findings from this paper might be used in the future design of jSO based
single-objective optimization algorithms.

Keywords: Differential Evolution · jSO · DISH · Control parameter ·
Scaling factor · Crossover rate

1 Introduction

The Differential Evolution (DE) is a heuristic algorithm initially designed for
single-objective numerical optimization. It was proposed in 1995 by Storn and
Price [1], and since then it has been a prospering field in the heuristic optimization research. Recent variants of the DE have been quite successful in the
optimization competitions held within a Congress on Evolutionary Computation
(CEC) during the last couple of years. The common denominator of promising
DE based algorithms is an adaptive version of DE, which uses historical memories for storing successful control parameter values. This algorithm is called

This work was supported by the Ministry of Education, Youth and Sports of the Czech
Republic within the National Sustainability Programme Project no. LO1303 (MSMT-
7778/2014), further by the European Regional Development Fund under the Project
CEBIA-Tech no. CZ.1.05/2.1.00/03.0089 and by Internal Grant Agency of Tomas Bata
University under the Projects no. IGA/CebiaTech/2019/002. This work is also based
upon support by COST (European Cooperation in Science & Technology) under Action
CA15140, Improving Applicability of Nature-Inspired Optimisation by Joining The-
ory and Practice (ImAppNIO), and Action IC1406, High-Performance Modelling and
Simulation for Big Data Applications (cHiPSet). The work was further supported by
resources of A.I.Lab at the Faculty of Applied Informatics, Tomas Bata University in
Zlin (ailab.fai.utb.cz).

© Springer Nature Switzerland AG 2019
L. Rutkowski et al. (Eds.): ICAISC 2019, LNAI 11508, pp. 519–529, 2019.
https://doi.org/10.1007/978-3-030-20912-4_47

Success-History based Adaptive Differential Evolution (SHADE) and was proposed by Tanabe and Fukunaga in 2013 [2]. Over the last few years, a handful of improvements to the original SHADE have been introduced and currently, the widely used variant is jSO from 2017 by Brest et al. [3].

In 2017, a simple innovation to the SHADEs' historical memory update scheme was proposed by Viktorin et al. [4]. This innovation suggested usage of distance based parameter adaptation for scaling factor and crossover rate memories to improve algorithms exploration ability. Viktorin et al. later proposed this novel historical memory update scheme for jSO as well and titled the resulting algorithm DISH – DIstance based parameter adaptation for Success-History based Differential Evolution [5].

It is crucially important to understand how the control parameters evolve [6] and how they are affected by the novel memory update scheme. Thus, this paper provides an initial analysis of the control parameter evolution in the jSO and DISH algorithms and provides commented results with suggestions for the future use to improve the performance with the use of gained knowledge. The motivation is to not only propose novel algorithms with experimentally better performance, but to understand their inner workings, so the researchers would be able to implement the algorithm on real-world optimization problems and adapt the algorithm to the problem properties, thus improving its performance and optimization quality.

The paper is structured as follows: Next section provides a description of the DISH algorithm; Sect. 3 describes the experiment design; Sect. 4 provides results along with a commentary, and the conclusion is in Sect. 5.

2   DISH

The DISH algorithm is a direct descendant of the 1995 DE [1]. The steady progress in the DE field is apparent, and state-of-the-art DE-based algorithms are considerably different from the original DE, but they still share the same basic concept of a randomized first population of solutions, mutation, crossover and elitist selection. However, these operators evolved over the years, and new mechanisms were added into the algorithm. One of the most popular mechanisms is an adaptation of the control parameters – population size NP, scaling factor F and crossover rate CR. Adaptive DE algorithms are also among the most successful ones during annual CEC competitions on single objective optimization. DISH algorithm is no exception, and its evolution line can be described as follows:

1. DE from 1995 by Storn and Price [1].
2. JADE from 2009 [7] – algorithm created by Zhang and Sanderson proposed a novel mutation strategy – current-to-$p$best/1 with an optional archive of inferior solutions.
3. SHADE from 2013 by Tanabe and Fukunaga [2] – built on the JADE algorithm with added memories for historically successful F and CR values and

new adaptation mechanism for these parameters. This algorithm placed 3rd in the CEC 2013 competition.

4. The linear decrease of population size was introduced into SHADE and created L-SHADE algorithm [8], the winner of the CEC 2014 competition.

5. Improved L-SHADE algorithm titled iL-SHADE [9] was proposed for a CEC 2016 competition by Brest et al. This algorithm introduced changes to the historical memory update system and the initialization of the historical memories. It also proposed a new mechanism for treating F and CR parameters based on the ratio between current and maximum generation (phase of the optimization). This algorithm placed 4th in the CEC 2016 competition.

6. Distance based parameter adaptation was proposed for SHADE based algorithms by Viktorin et al. in 2017 [4]. This novel adaptation mechanism based on the distance between solutions instead of on the difference between objective function value was presented on SHADE and L-SHADE algorithms and shown its superiority over the original.

7. jSO algorithm was proposed by Brest et al. in 2017 [3]. The algorithm uses a novel current-to-$p$best-w/1 mutation strategy and slightly changes fixed values for F and CR parameters. The jSO algorithm was 2nd in the CEC 2017 bound constrained competition.

8. DISH algorithm was introduced in 2018 by Viktorin et al. [5] and it incorporates the distance based parameter adaptation into the jSO algorithm to improve its performance.

The following subsections provide the details of DISH algorithm mechanisms followed by a pseudo-code.

2.1   Initialization

First of all, the initial population P, of solutions to the optimized problem, is generated randomly. The size of the population is determined by the user via NP_{init} parameter (initial population size). Each individual solution x is a vector of length D, which is a dimension of the problem and each vector component is generated within its lower lo and upper up bounds by a uniform pseudo-random number generator (1).

$$x_{j,i} = U\left[lo_j,\ up_j\right] \text{ for } j = 1,\ \ldots,\ D; i = 1,\ \ldots,\ NP_{init} \tag{1}$$

Other parameters and variables that have to be set in the initialization phase are:

1. Final population size – NP_f.
2. Stopping criterion – a maximum number of objective function evaluations $MAXFES$ in the most common case (also in this study).
3. p_{max} and p_{min} parameters for mutation operator. $p_{max} = 0.25$ and $p_{min} = p_{max}/2 = 0.125$
4. External archive A is initialized empty. $A = \emptyset$

5. Historical memory size H. $H = 5$
6. Historical memories for scaling factor M_F (2) and crossover rate M_{CR} (3).
7. Update historical memory index k. $k = 1$.

$$M_{F,i} = 0.5 \text{ for } i = 1, \ldots, H - 1, \ M_{F,H} = 0.9 \tag{2}$$

$$M_{CR,i} = 0.8 \text{ for } i = 1, \ldots, H - 1, \ M_{CR,H} = 0.9 \tag{3}$$

The following steps – mutation, crossover and selection are repeated for each individual solution in the generation G and these generations are repeated until the stopping criterion is met.

2.2 Mutation

The mutation operator used in DISH is a jSOs' current-to-pbest-w/1, which combines a greedy approach in the first difference and the explorative factor in the second difference (4).

$$v_i = x_i + F_{w,i} \left(x_{pBest} - x_i \right) + F_i \left(x_{r1} - x_{r2} \right) \tag{4}$$

The v_i is the i-th mutated vector created from current solution vector x_i, one of the $100p\%$ best solutions in the population x_{pBest} where p is determined by (5), a random solution from the population x_{r1} and random solution from the union of the population and external archive x_{r2}. It is also important to note that all vectors are mutually different – $x_i \neq x_{pBest} \neq x_{r1} \neq x_{r2}$. The differences are scaled by two scaling factor parameters, scaling factor F_i (6) and weighted scaling factor $F_{w,i}$ (8).

$$p = FES_{ratio} * (p_{max} - p_{min}) + p_{min} \tag{5}$$

Where FES_{ratio} stands for the ratio between the current number of objective function evaluations FES and the maximum number of objective function evaluations $MAXFES$ ($FES_{ratio} = FES/MAXFES$). Therefore, parameter p increases linearly with objective function evaluations.

$$F_i = C\left[M_{F,r}, 0.1\right] \tag{6}$$

The scaling factor value F_i is generated from Cauchy distribution with the location parameter $M_{F,r}$ and scale parameter value of 0. The index r is randomly generated from the range $[1, H]$. If the generated value F_i is smaller or equal to 0, it is generated again and if it is higher than 1, it is set to 1. Also, the scaling factor F_i is influenced by the FES_{ratio} in order to truncate its value in the exploration phase of the algorithm run (7).

$$F_i = 0.7, \ FES_{ratio} < 0.6 \text{ and } F_i > 0.7 \tag{7}$$

$$F_{w,i} = \begin{cases} 0.7 * F_i, & FES_{ratio} < 0.2 \\ 0.8 * F_i, & FES_{ratio} < 0.4 \\ 1.2 * F_i, & \text{otherwise} \end{cases} \tag{8}$$

The weighted scaling factor $F_{w,i}$ is based on the optimization phase given by the FES_{ratio}.

The next step after the mutation is the crossover.

2.3   Crossover

The crossover operator in DISH algorithm is binomial and is based on the crossover rate value CR_i generated from the normal distribution (9) with a mean parameter value $M_{CR,r}$ selected from the crossover rate historical memory and standard deviation value of 0.1.

$$CR_i = N\left[M_{CR,r}, 0.1\right] \tag{9}$$

The CR_i value is also bounded between 0 and 1 and whenever it is generated outside these bounds, it is truncated to the nearest bound. The crossover rate value is also a subject to the optimization phase given by FES_{ratio} (10).

$$CR_i = \begin{cases} \max(CR_i, 0.7), & FES_{ratio} < 0.25 \\ \max(CR_i, 0.6), & FES_{ratio} < 0.5 \\ CR_i, & \text{otherwise} \end{cases} \tag{10}$$

And finally, the binomial crossover is depicted in (11).

$$u_{j,i} = \begin{cases} v_{j,i} \text{ if } U\left[0, 1\right] \le CR_i \text{ or } j = j_{rand} \\ x_{j,i} \qquad\qquad \text{otherwise} \end{cases} \tag{11}$$

Where u_i is called a trial vector and j_{rand} is an index of one component that has to be taken from the mutated vector v_i. The j_{rand} index ensures that at least one vector component of the original vector x_i will be replaced. Thus in the following selection step, the tested trial vector will provide new information.

2.4   Selection

In the selection step, a quality of the trial solution vector u_i is compared to the quality of the original solution vector x_i. The quality is given by the objective function value of these solutions. And since the selection operator is elitist, the trial solution has to have at least equal objective function value as the original solution in order to proceed into the next generation $G+1$ (12).

$$x_{i,G+1} = \begin{cases} u_{i,G} \text{ if } f\left(u_{i,G}\right) \le f\left(x_{i,G}\right) \\ x_{i,G} \qquad \text{otherwise} \end{cases} \tag{12}$$

Where $f()$ depicts the objective function value and in this case, the objective is the minimization of it.

The mutation, crossover and selection operators are repeated for each individual solution in the population, and after the population is exhausted, the algorithm proceeds to the next generation. But before processing each individual solution of the next generation, two essential mechanisms are incorporated into the algorithm – linear decrease of the population size and the update of historical memories. These two mechanisms are described in the following subsections.

2.5   Linear Decrease of the Population Size

The population size is decreased during the algorithm run in order to provide more time for exploration in the later phase of optimization. Thus, the smaller population of individual solutions will have more time to exploit promising areas of the objective function landscape.

The mechanism used in the DISH algorithm is a simple linear decrease of population size, which uses the information of current objective function evaluations to shrink the population of solutions. A new population size NP_{new} is calculated as follows (13).

$$NP_{new} = \text{round} \left(NP_{init} - FES_{ratio} * (NP_{init} - NP_f) \right) \tag{13}$$

The size of an external archive A is connected to the size of the population and therefore, after decreasing the population size, the archive size is decreased as well. Whereas when decreasing the population size, the worst individual solutions are discarded from the population, in the archive, solutions to discard are selected randomly.

2.6   Update of Historical Memory

Historical memories M_F and M_{CR} store historically successful values of scaling factors F and crossover rates CR that were helpful in the production of better trial individual solutions. Therefore, these memories have to be updated during the optimization in order to store recently used values. After each generation, one cell of both memories is updated and for that, the algorithm uses index k to remember, which cell will be updated. The index is initialized to 1 and therefore, after the first generation, the first memory cell will be updated. The index is increased by one after each update and when it overflows the memory size H, it starts from 1 again. There is one exception to the update, the last cell of both memories is never updated and still contains values 0.9 for both control parameters.

What will be stored in the k-th cell after the generation G is computed by a weighted Lehmer mean (14) of corresponding generation control parameter arrays S_F and S_{CR}. These arrays are filled during the generation by the values of control parameters when the trial solution succeeds in the selection step.

$$\text{mean}_{WL}(S) = \frac{\sum_{n=1}^{|S|} w_n \bullet S_n^2}{\sum_{n=1}^{|S|} w_n \bullet S_n} \tag{14}$$

The $\text{mean}_{WL}()$ stands for weighted Lehmer mean and the computation is equal for both S_F and S_{CR}, therefore, there is no subscript for S in the equation. The k-th memory cells of M_F and M_{CR} are then updated according to (15) and (16).

$$M_{F,k} = \begin{cases} \text{mean}_{WL}(S_F) & \text{if } S_F \neq \emptyset \text{ and } k \neq H \\ M_{F,k} & \text{otherwise} \end{cases} \tag{15}$$

$$M_{CR,k} = \begin{cases} \text{mean}_{WL}\left(\boldsymbol{S}_{CR}\right) & \text{if } \boldsymbol{S}_{CR} \neq \emptyset \text{ and } k \neq H \\ M_{CR,k} & \text{otherwise} \end{cases} \tag{16}$$

The weights for the weighted Lehmer means (14) are in the case of DISH algorithm computed as depicted in (17). This weighting was introduced as the distance based parameter adaptation [4]. It is titled like that, because in the original SHADE, L-SHADE, iL-SHADE and jSO algorithms, the weights were based on the difference between objective function values of trial individual solution $\boldsymbol{u}_i$ and its corresponding original individual solution $\boldsymbol{x}_i$, whereas in DISH, the weight is computed from the Euclidean distance between those two - $\boldsymbol{u}_i$ and $\boldsymbol{x}_i$.

$$w_n = \frac{\sqrt{\sum_{j=1}^{D}\left(\boldsymbol{u}_{n,j,G} - \boldsymbol{x}_{n,j,G}\right)^2}}{\sum_{m=1}^{|\boldsymbol{S}_{CR}|}\sqrt{\sum_{j=1}^{D}\left(\boldsymbol{u}_{m,j,G} - \boldsymbol{x}_{m,j,G}\right)^2}} \tag{17}$$

This approach promotes exploitation and tries to avoid the premature convergence of the algorithm into local optima.

Complete pseudo-code of the DISH algorithm is available in [5].

3   Experiment Setup

In this study, the CEC 2015 benchmark was used as a testbed. The CEC 2015 benchmark contains 15 test functions of various properties – unimodal, simple multimodal, hybrid and composition functions. The DISH algorithm was compared to its original version without distance based parameter adaptation – jSO. According to the benchmark rules, both algorithms were run 51 times on each of the problems in four different dimensionality settings – $D = 10, 30, 50$ and 100, and the stopping criterion was set to $10,000 \times D$.

The settings of parameters were the same for both algorithms (jSO, DISH):

1. Initial population size $NP_{init} = 25*\log(D)\sqrt{D}$.
2. Final population size $NP_f = 4$.
3. Historical memory size $H = 5$.
4. External archive size $|\boldsymbol{A}| = NP$.

The scaling factor history $\boldsymbol{M}_F$ and crossover rate history $\boldsymbol{M}_{CR}$ contents were recorded after each generation to provide a comparison in the behavior of those memories without (jSO) and with distance based parameter adaptation (DISH).

4   Results and Discussion

This section provides the results of both jSO and DISH algorithms on the CEC2015 benchmark set. Since the distance based parameter adaptation used in DISH is more suitable for higher dimensional problems [5], there were no significant differences in the performance between jSO and DISH in the 10D

experiment. Thus and due to limited space, the results are omitted from this paper.

Table 1 provides summarized results of Wilcoxon rank–sum test (significance level 5%) between the original jSO and DISH algorithms. The values reached in all 51 independent runs were used as a test data.

The scaling factor history M_F and crossover rate history M_{CR} values are reported for all cases, where there was a significant difference in performance between jSO and DISH. Individual subfigures inside Figs. 1, 2 and 3 represent the average value of each historical memory cell. The size of the memories H was set to 5, thus each memory has 5 cells. The last cell is not updated and contains a value of 0.9 for both, scaling factor memory and crossover rate memory. This creates a straight line in each subfigure at level 0.9. The rest of the memory cells (4 in this experiment) is initialized to 0.5 for scaling factor and 0.8 for crossover rate. After each generation, a single memory cell is updated, and this repeats for the whole optimization run. The reported subfigures show average content of each memory cell over 51 independent runs – red for scaling factor memory cells in jSO, blue for scaling factor memory cells in DISH, cyan for crossover rate memory cells in jSO and magenta for crossover rate memory cells in DISH.

Table 1. Summarized results of the Wilcoxon rank–sum test comparing jSO and DISH performance in varying dimensions.

Dimension	jSO wins	Draws	DISH wins
10	0	15	0
30	0	12	3
50	0	8	7
100	2	7	6

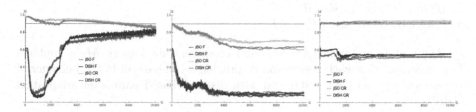

Fig. 1. The evolution of historical memories values of M_F (jSO – red, DISH – blue) and M_{CR} (jSO – cyan, DISH – magenta). CEC2015 30D, top left – $f6$, top right – $f9$ and bottom $f11$. (Color figure online)

Results in Fig. 1 show that for functions 6 and 11, the crossover rate values tend to be quite similar for both, jSO and DISH and there is a visible difference in the behavior of scaling factor memories. A complete opposite can be seen in the behavior on function 9, where only crossover rate memory evolution differs in later generations. While the difference in results is statistically significant, it can be seen in Table 1, that the difference for functions 6 and 11 is of a higher grade than in the case of function 9. Thus, it seems that the different behavior of scaling factor memory in the case of distance based parameter adaptation (DISH) helps to achieve better results on $30D$ problems.

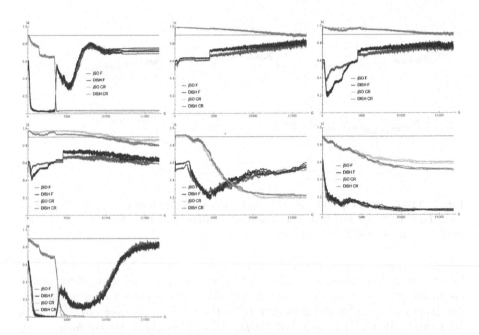

Fig. 2. The evolution of historical memories values of M_F (jSO – red, DISH – blue) and M_{CR} (jSO – cyan, DISH – magenta). CEC2015 $50D$, from top left – $f4$, $f6$, $f8$, $f10$, $f11$, $f12$ and $f13$. (Color figure online)

A very similar result to that in Fig. 1 is visible in Fig. 2, which depicts memories behavior on $50D$ functions. There, the behavior on functions with better improvement (functions 4, 6, 8, 10 and 11) is mostly visibly different for scaling factor memory, whereas the crossover rate memory behaves similarly.

Interesting results are visible in Fig. 3 ($100D$ problems), where two subfigures for functions 1 and 6 show very similar behavior of both memories, but the scaling factor memory of jSO retains smaller values than the memory in DISH. This leads to significantly better results of the jSO algorithm. On the other hand, memory evolution on functions 4 and 11, where DISH provides better results, shows that both crossover rate and scaling factor memory behavior varies for both algorithms, where on function 11 the difference is more noticeable.

Another unexpected result of this analysis is that both memories might be initialized too low. Higher values (e.g., 0.6 for scaling factor memory and 0.9

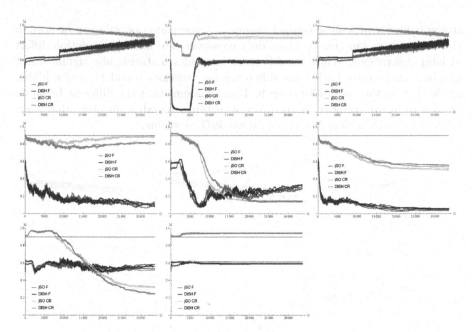

Fig. 3. The evolution of historical memories values of M_F (jSO – red, DISH – blue) and M_{CR} (jSO – cyan, DISH – magenta). CEC2015 $100D$, from top left – $f1$, $f4$, $f6$, $f9$, $f11$, $f12$, $f14$ and $f15$. (Color figure online)

for crossover rate memory) might bring a speed up in the first phase of the optimization, since there is a fast convergence towards these values in the first few generations, and sometimes even to higher values (crossover rate – $f6$ $30D$, $f6$, $f8$ and $f10$ in $50D$, $f1$ and $f6$ in $100D$). This will be studied in the future work along with possibilities of updating the distance based parameter adaptation scheme.

5 Conclusion

This paper provided an experimental analysis of the behavior of scaling factor and crossover rate memories of jSO and DISH algorithms. Those algorithms were compared on the basis of the CEC 2015 benchmark set, and it was shown that the distance based parameter adaptation used in the DISH algorithm might be useful for the improvement of the algorithms' performance. This preliminary study also showed that the scaling factor parameter has a higher impact on the overall optimization result than the crossover rate value and that both of these parameters might be initialized to more suitable values. This is also a suggestion for the future direction of research in the area of jSO or DISH based single-objective optimization algorithms along with more objective function value-free parameter adaptation schemes (as is the distance based parameter adaptation), since the greedy approach leads only to premature convergence of the algorithm (mainly in high dimensional decision spaces).

References

1. Storn, R., Price, K.: Differential evolution-a simple and efficient adaptive scheme for global optimization over continuous spaces, vol. 3. ICSI, Berkeley (1995)
2. Tanabe, R., Fukunaga, A.: Success-history based parameter adaptation for differential evolution. In: 2013 IEEE Congress on Evolutionary Computation (CEC), pp. 71–78. IEEE, June 2013
3. Brest, J., Maučec, M.S., Bošković, B.: Single objective real-parameter optimization: algorithm jSO. In: 2017 IEEE Congress on Evolutionary Computation (CEC), pp. 1311–1318. IEEE, June 2017
4. Viktorin, A., Senkerik, R., Pluhacek, M., Kadavy, T., Zamuda, A.: Distance based parameter adaptation for differential evolution. In: 2017 IEEE Symposium Series on Computational Intelligence (SSCI), pp. 1–7. IEEE, November 2017
5. Viktorin, A., Senkerik, R., Pluhacek, M., Kadavy, T., Zamuda, A.: Distance based parameter adaptation for success-history based differential evolution. Swarm and Evolutionary Computation (2018, in press). https://doi.org/10.1016/j.swevo.2018. 10.013. ISSN 2210–6502
6. Karafotias, G., Hoogendoorn, M., Eiben, Á.E.: Parameter control in evolutionary algorithms: trends and challenges. IEEE Trans. Evol. Comput. $19(2)$, 167–187 (2015)
7. Zhang, J., Sanderson, A.C.: JADE: adaptive differential evolution with optional external archive. IEEE Trans. Evol. Comput. $13(5)$, 945–958 (2009)
8. Tanabe, R., Fukunaga, A.S.: Improving the search performance of SHADE using linear population size reduction. In: 2014 IEEE Congress on Evolutionary Computation (CEC), pp. 1658–1665. IEEE, July 2014
9. Brest, J., Maučec, M.S., Bošković, B.: iL-SHADE: Improved L-SHADE algorithm for single objective real-parameter optimization. In: 2016 IEEE Congress on Evolutionary Computation (CEC), pp. 1188–1195. IEEE, July 2016

Iterative Design and Implementation of Rapid Gradient Descent Method

Wei Wei[1(✉)], Bin Zhou[2], Rytis Maskeliūnas[3],
Robertas Damaševičius[3], Dawid Połap[4], and Marcin Woźniak[4]

[1] School of Computer Science and Engineering,
Xi'an University of Technology, Xi'an 710048, China
weiwei@xaut.edu.cn
[2] College of Science, Southwest Petroleum University, Chengdu 610500, China
binzhou@swpu.edu.cn
[3] Faculty of Informatics, Kaunas University of Technology,
51368 Kaunas, Lithuania
{rytis.maskeliunas, robertas.damasevicius}@ktu.lt
[4] Institute of Mathematics, Faculty of Applied Mathematics,
Silesian University of Technology, 44100 Gliwice, Poland
{dawid.polap, marcin.wozniak}@polsl.pl

Abstract. Solvers of nonlinear systems of equations are important in software engineering. There are various methods which use gradient approach to find the solution in accordance to gradient descent. This paper presents software testing for proposed implementation of rapid gradient descent method. Results show that implementation is able to solve problems better than classic approach. The gradient path is smooth and faster converge to the final location.

Keywords: Nonlinear programming · Conjugate gradient method

1 Introduction

Optimization methods are important techniques both in applied mathematics and computer science. There are various approaches to develop an optimization and after to verify how it works. The gradient descent method, included conjugate gradient, is an approximate method which uses an information about the function shape and its steepness at the current position on the way to find minima proceeding in the direction of the steepest descent. The general form of this method, however often fails to meet requirements of certain analysis of model data, so it is necessary to do further processing of the test data samples. There are various applications of gradient methods in sensor systems [15], computer modeling [2, 3] and nuclear plant operation [12]. Also software implementation and testing [2, 6, 10, 11, 13, 17, 18] for efficient data processing [1, 7, 8, 14] is widely reported. In this article we propose rapid gradient descent method to solve optimization problem and present efficient implementation. We introduce a path-oriented testing by the use of automatic generation theory for testing results of the design and implementation. Next sections discuss automatic generation, relative knowledge and practical application of path-oriented white box testing.

© Springer Nature Switzerland AG 2019
L. Rutkowski et al. (Eds.): ICAISC 2019, LNAI 11508, pp. 530–539, 2019.
https://doi.org/10.1007/978-3-030-20912-4_48

1.1   Background and Related Works

The issue of generation of testing data is one of the basic topics in software testing field. Several approaches have proposed iterative relaxation method of linear predicate function to figure out the issue and improve the method. Other software engineering ideas employ object-oriented approach, UML design tools and C++ language to realize prototype of automatic generation of testing data. Path-oriented testing data generation (denoted as Q) is a basic and important issue in software testing field, the non-formal description can be as follow.

Given a program P and a path W and letting P input space is D, for $x \in D$, render P with input x through path W. The essence of solving Q lies in establishing and solving the restraint system.

One of the main difficulties of solving restraint system is the existing nonlinear constraint. With regard to arbitrary P and W, Weyuker [16] have proved that there is no effective algorithm to be able to generate input data which W passed by. Although theoretical results are frustrating, the need of actual application stimulates the research, furthermore, put forward the randomized method, the status method and heuristics to solve Q. Static methods include the symbolic execution method and interval arithmetic method, while dynamic methods include linear programming method. A linear predicate function to figure out the Q chooses a group of inputs arbitrarily from D to examine each branch predicate on W using program slicing ideas, and determines predicate function to the dependence of the input variables through the static and dynamic data flow analysis. Moreover, it can devise predicate pieces and dynamic slices and build linear relations of predicate function on input variables. Further linear equations system of incremental input variable can be established, in order to solve each input variable increment to obtain a new set of inputs. The biggest advantage of this method lies in the establishment of linear constraint system for each predicate function with respect to the increment of the input variables on W. When W predicate function is a linear function of the input variables, this iterative method will find the Q solution or ensure that W is not feasible. Inversely, when the predicate function contains the nonlinear function, this method may need to iterate repeatedly. The method to construct predicate slices and input dependency sets are omitted. Additionally, the method can work out the linear relations of each predicate function with respect to the input variables, then to establish a system of linear equations for input variables and obtain a new set of inputs directly after solving. However both improved method and original method are generating the same restraint system. Iterating the following processes incrementally to develop software is usually adopted UML. Software engineering and object-oriented approach to develop PTDG in accordance with the above process is widely used [2–5, 12]. In order to further study properties and ability to generate testing data of improved method, the paper bases on the original method as a core algorithm. In Linux Red Hat operating system, we have developed automatic testing data generating tool (Path wise Test Data Generator) for the C language program path with C++ and migrated PTDG to Windows operating system successfully. UML is adopted as the object-oriented standard modeling language by Object Management Group, which supports the entire software development life cycle (Fig. 1).

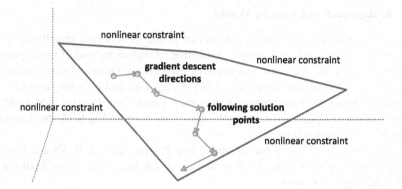

Fig. 1. Sample representation of the convergence to global solution along the direction of the gradient descent into the constraint set.

1.2 Path-Oriented Automatic Testing

PTDG system structure is mainly made up of lexical analyzer, parser, constraint constructor, constraint solver, path condition checker, data files and user interface and so on. PTDG applies lexical analysis and parse on user-specified program path to obtain the type of input variables, and transform paths to constraints construct program and path condition check program with the form of C language. Furthermore, after program is compiled the constraints constructor and paths condition checker can be generated. Constraints constructor based on the current program input, to produce the path linear constraints system of each predicate function with regard to the input variables is executed. Path condition checker is converted to linear equations system by constraint solver to obtain the new input of the program. Then inputs are checked by path condition checker. If the input meets the condition, the function ends checking, otherwise proceed according to the user path predicate functions whether they are linear function of the input variables, as well as the maximum number of iterations to decide whether to continue iterative solving. Proposed constraint solving uses the method of [16], and underlying solution tools on Linux and Windows are LAPACK++ and Matlab respectively. Not only the user input program path, initial and other input parameters, but also intermediate and final solution results in PTDG are stored into files. In addition to using the Vc++ programming environment, due to the large number of mathematical algorithms, Matlab software is needed. Taking the advantage of existing tools improves the efficiency of testing data generation.

1.3 Conjugate Gradient Method

The Conjugate Gradient Method in mathematical theory is just for a single equation solving, and requires the optimal solution, but cannot solve the problem of equations. The gradient in unconstrained optimization problems is just the gradient in a function. Clearly, the actual constraints are not necessarily only one. So here we choose multiple gradients. The forward direction is a linear combination of all negative gradients that do not meet the conditions. In other words, we can add a different coefficient before every constraint gradient to get a new direction. That is a new attempt - fast gradient method. A group of inequalities can be solved by using fast gradient descent method. The improved algorithm is based on the maximum degree that does not meet the conditions to calculate the step length. When the condition $f_i(x) < 0$ is satisfied, and get $f_1(x_0) = 10, f_2(x_0) = 2$, we choose the larger, so the step size is 10 plus step because of the unmet extent of $f_1(x) < 0$ is higher than $f_2(x) < 0$. The new method is based on the principle of gradient descent to make the resulting solution enter into the area that meets the conditions quickly and efficiently (that is the solution space). Currently, in order to explain the principle, firstly we assume that the gradient is without constraint. The case with a bit less dimension and variables will be discussed below. For example, three constraints were considered according to the following situations.

- When all the three constraints are satisfied, it means that all the gradient descent directions are positive, then the solving rate is the best, and you can follow the ideal design and fast and efficiently drop to the solution space which satisfies the condition.
- When all the three constraints cannot be satisfied, there are two approaches at this time. One approach is to change constraints which means to individually adjust all equations. The gradient direction which does not meet the requirements will be converged to the solving space which meets the conditions by gradual iteration. Another method is to add a negative sign to all equations which changes directions of all constraint vectors. When the constraints are growing fast, the first method will become very complicated and difficult to timely control. The second method is relatively easy to implement and not easily affected by the rapid growth of constraints so we choose the latter [6, 9–12].
- When there are N constraints and one constraint is met, we can let it change and get a good initial, and then find a way to try to decrease other constraints along a positive changing gradient. For example: assume that there are three constraints $\{f_1(x) < 0, f_2(x) < 0, f_3(x) < 0\}$ when only the initial value $x_0 = (t_1, t_2, t_3)$ satisfies the inequality condition $f_1(x) < 0$, try to make other possible constraints fall along the gradient of positive changes.
- When condition changes along a certain direction of no constraint gradient, task is to find the right result, but not the optimal one. We choose three constraints as an example, however it can be any number of constraints. For the condition of each inequality, we choose the smaller value as much as possible, but not the minimum. When $f_1(x) < 0$ is satisfied and $f_2(x) < 0$ is not satisfied, we try to make vector direction of $f_2(x) < 0$ change along the downward direction. We can take such as lock step interval method to let the range of variation falls in line of the required range.
- The core idea of the algorithm is that in order to meet the first positive change vector, for the other vector that does not meet the requirements, we need to do something to make the ultimate synthesis of all vector direction changes along the direction of change required by the method of variable coefficients. Assume that there are two factors a, b. The iteration gradient is determined by the gradient descent direction of last time multiplied by factor a, and then plus the result of current direction multiplied by the factor b. Because the direction plays main role,

so a, b will not affect the size of the result, which is the coefficients irrelevance. Factors that affect the outcome depends on the ratio between the coefficients. That is to say the ratio of a, b is to determine the gradient descent direction. The values of a and b can be from established formula in classic gradient algorithm. You can also determine the values of a, b through the investigation of constraint satisfaction degree.

2 Fast Gradient Descent Algorithm Based on Iterative Theory

Gradient descent method (Conjugate Gradient Method) is an effective method for solving unconstrained optimization problems. The main idea is to start from a certain initial point $x(0)$, and compute the gradient of the objective function $d(i)$, make its negative direction as the target direction, determine the appropriate steps $s(i)$, and iterate using iterative formula $x(i+1) = x(i) - s(i)d(i)$ to get the best value. We are using the improved method to get the feasible solutions of a nonlinear constrained set $g(i)[x], i = 1, \ldots, n$. If the initial point x_0 satisfies the constraint set, then it is the target point what we are looking for, otherwise we can do the following iteration using x_0 as the initial point, s_0 as a minimum step size, N as the maximum number of iterations. The method works in accordance to steps:

(1) Determine iterative direction: calculate gradient matrix of constraints set. According to the comparison of the improvement degree of each gradient vector satisfied to constraint set establish current local optimum gradient (a combination of the respective gradient vector), and combine the optimal gradient of the previous iteration to get the current optimal gradient $d(i)$.

(2) Determine the step by computing satisfaction of $x(i)$ to a set of constraints, getting the biggest dissatisfaction degree Max so step can be calculated by $s(i+1) = 0.5Max + s_0$.

(3) Do the iteration using $x(i+1) = x(i) - s(i)d(i)$.

(4) When meet the constraint set or the number of iterations is bigger than N, exit the iteration. If the latter, you might consider changing the minimum step value to do reiteration.

In short, the gradient method is to except the gradient direction becomes the direction of fastest declining rate. Its aim is to make every iteration step to be the fastest and the most effective. Ultimately, the expected solutions efficiently and quickly dropped to the solving space that meets the conditions.

Automatically generating the white-box test data is still a new field to study. The main idea of fast gradient descent algorithm based on iterative theory is to calculate each gradient of non-linear equations, reasonable gradient directions, choosing step interval and finally let all gradients along the qualifying direction go into the set of constraints efficiently. The final design of this algorithm is to adjust the step interval to achieve a set of appropriate rules in order to meet the actual needs as close as possible to the formal description of the actual system. The rules currently used are designed according to the dichotomy in mathematics. The advantages of this design is that it can simultaneously meet two requirements: meet certain growth rate and maintain the correct gradient direction. The future research will focus on developing some better rules. These rules are based on premise of analog automatic reasoning. For example, if the premise "gradient changes too fast, and step interval is not too low" is established, then it suggests that we should reduce the step interval by a certain amount. Now we adjust the step interval using dichotomy in mathematical along to change the gradient direction.

The fast decline gradient theory will be used to generate white-box testing data. The guiding ideology is converting continuous events into discrete events. When the discrete particle size is sufficiently small, the discrete object can be infinitely close to the proposed continuous objects. So we must consider using difference instead of differential, selecting step interval to trying to avoid the vector changes that tends to linear reciprocating or does similar circular closed curve direction movement. But in the actual implementation process, in order to consider the complexity of time and space, and the achieved manipulation, we do not use the idea of optimization theory mentioned above. We can just find a feasible solution when used in reality. The following algorithm design also follows this principle. The feasible solution can be reached through selecting an effective initial value and reasonable step interval. This feasible solution is processed with limited conditions and rules which can be further close to the ideal optimal solution. We need to find a reasonable input and output, and then according to the iterative approach design fast gradient descent algorithm.

Gradient descent stochastic approximation (incremental gradient descent) is mainly composed of the following:

(1) Calculate gradient: $\nabla E_D\left[\vec{\omega}\right]$

(2) Adjust weights: $\vec{\omega} \leftarrow \mu \nabla E_D\left[\vec{\omega}\right]$

(3) Error function: $E_D\left[\vec{\omega}\right] = 0.5\sum_{d\in D}(t_d - o_d)^2$, $E_d\left[\vec{\omega}\right] = 0.5(t_d - o_d)^2$

2.1 Reasoning Decision and Calculations

It's easy to find that when the two values were quantified they may comply with several rules. So how to choose the initial output value. For all in line rules, the easiest way is choosing the gradient direction which have been calculated. The other gradient changes along the right orientation. In this case, the optimal choice of step interval is essential because the appropriate step interval can not only satisfy iterative speed and time and space complexity but also enter constraints space earlier. We use dichotomy to determine the step interval, while the main data structures of the program are recording input values and the corresponding output value of step rule that can be adjusted. The main code structure is as follows:

- Solve nonlinear function and determine whether it is smaller than 0, that is to say whether the constraint condition is satisfied.
- Get the derivative, that is the gradient value to meet the right gradient direction

- The main function of the algorithm based on the input value of the initial point, by calling the gradient descent method and dynamics of rapid steps to quickly get basic feasible solution as efficient as possible is defined as follows.
- Achieve iterative function. When the number of iterations is a limited time and an initial value has been given, too small step may lead to failure, which is the small step of growth cannot complete iteration in a limited number of times. So the synthesis of gradient cannot go into the constraints set in right way.

Data type is float in algorithm temporarily. You can use double data type for a higher accuracy in the cost of running speed. So the float data type in sample program can not only meet the required speed but also satisfy accuracy requirements. In practical applications, double data is used to meet the need to reduce errors. Figure 2 illustrates successful and unsuccessful iterations. When the step size is very small, i.e. when the number of iterations is not enough, program can get the required basic feasible solution eventually increasing the number of iterations enough to reduce the negative effect of too small step size to get the correct solution. Using Matlab, a three-dimensional changes of three linear equations are illustrated in Fig. 2. Certain steps can eventually make all the gradient directions meet the requirements - decline to the required feasible solution. Since the step interval is a current difficulty in the method we use dichotomy to do iterations. Figure 2 shows an intuitive 3-D renderings from the starting point of departure, by a suitable step iterations, it eventually declines gradient in the right direction, and finally arrive at a basic feasible solution and stops. In Fig. 3 and Fig. 4 we can see comparison between classic gradient descent method and proposed improved steepest gradient descent. For both methods we solve the same set of non-linear constraints from the start point (1,1,1).

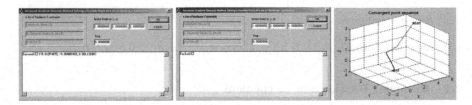

Fig. 2. Left form illustrates that appropriate step interval can be smooth along the direction of the gradient descent into the constraint set: successful calculation. Middle form illustrates improper step interval which may not be along the direction of the gradient descent into the constraint set: failed calculation. Right form illustrates using Matlab a three-dimensional changes of three linear equations.

Corresponding Matlab simulation results presented in Fig. 4 indicate that proposed method is diverging faster to meet the requirements. Improved steepest gradient decline to the convergence point smooth starting from the same demo point. The original method does not do the improvements well. We can see that corrections are done but it does not improve gradient, while in proposed method corrections are smaller however each of the improves the gradient. For the defect of fast gradient descent method, this chapter put forwards rapid gradient descent method. The proposed method has a higher

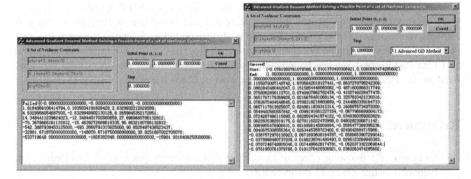

Fig. 3. Left form illustrates that classic gradient descent method cannot solve given nonlinear constrained system, while right form illustrates that proposed improved steepest gradient descent can get the correct results after demo data iteration starting from the same start point on the same step.

credibility. Through the simulation experiments was verified that the proposed method can be more effective to get correct iteration result and meet the requirements to enter the constraints set. However, it is still not perfect solution and further research will be done.

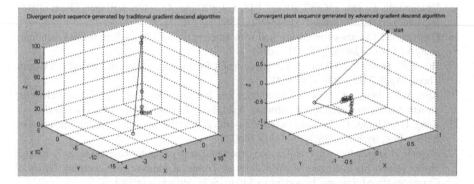

Fig. 4. Left chart demonstrates divergence for classic method, while the right chart demonstrate proposed rapid gradient descent method in Matlab simulation demo.

3   Final Remarks

This paper introduces changes of step interval for fast gradient descent algorithm. The method is oriented toward adjusting the initial start and step size in real-time processing what can improve the speed of gradient descent. Presented results show that implemented method works faster and give better results in comparison to classic approach. For further research we plan to work on dynamic adjustment of step size for input nonlinear equations.

Acknowledgements. This work is supported by the National key R&D Program of China under Grant NO. 2018YFB0203900 and the Key Research and Development Program of Shaanxi Province (No. 2018ZDXM-GY-036). This job is also supported by Scientific Research Program Funded by Shaanxi Provincial Education Department (Program No. 2013JK1139) and Supported by China Postdoctoral Science Foundation (No. 2013M542370) and the Specialized Research Fund for the Doctoral Program of Higher Education of China (Grant No. 20136118120010).

References

1. Artiemjew, P.: Boosting effect of classifier based on simple granules of knowledge. Inf. Technol. Control **47**(2), 184–196 (2018)
2. Bala, V., Duesterwald, E., Banerjia, S.: Dynamo: a transparent dynamic optimization system. ACM Sigplan Not. **46**(4), 41–52 (2011)
3. Byrd, R.H., Nocedal, J.: A tool for the analysis of Quasi-Newton methods with application to unconstrained minimization. SIAM J. Numer. Anal. **26**(3), 727–739 (1989)
4. Coleman, T.F.: Large-scale numerical optimization: introduction and overview. Cornell University (1991)
5. Eldersveld, S.K.: Large-scale sequential quadratic programming algorithms (No. SOL-92-4). STANFORD UNIVERSITY CA SYSTEMS OPTIMIZATION LAB (1992)
6. Erosa, A.M., Hendren, L.J.: Taming control flow: a structured approach to eliminating goto statements. In: Proceedings of the 1994 International Conference on Computer Languages, pp. 229–240, IEEE May 1994
7. Gabryel, M.: Data Analysis Algorithm for Click Fraud Recognition. In: Damaševičius, R., Vasiljevienė, G. (eds.) ICIST 2018. CCIS, vol. 920, pp. 437–446. Springer, Cham (2018). https://doi.org/10.1007/978-3-319-99972-2_36
8. Gabryel, M.: The bag-of-words method with different types of image features and dictionary analysis. J. UCS **24**(4), 357–371 (2018)
9. Hu, Y.F., Storey, C.: Global convergence result for conjugate gradient methods. J. Optim. Theory Appl. **71**(2), 399–405 (1991)
10. Kim, M.C., Jang, S.C., Ha, J.: Possibilities and limitations of applying software reliability growth models to safetycritical software. Nucl. Eng. Technol. **39**(2), 145–148 (2007)
11. Kang, H.G., Sung, T.: An analysis of safety-critical digital systems for risk-informed design. Reliab. Eng. Syst. Saf. **78**(3), 307–314 (2002)
12. Ragheb, H.: Operating and maintenance experience with computer-based systems in nuclear power plants. In: International Workshop on Technical Support for Licensing Issues of Computer-Based Systems Important to Safety, **5**(7). München (1996)
13. Shan, J.H., Wang, J., Qi, Z.C.: On path-wise automatic generation of test data for both white-box and black-box testing. In: Eighth Asia-Pacific Software Engineering Conference, APSEC 2001, pp. 237–240, IEEE (2001)
14. Ropiak, K., Artiemjew, P.: A Study in Granular Computing: Homogenous Granulation. In: Damaševičius, R., Vasiljevienė, G. (eds.) ICIST 2018. CCIS, vol. 920, pp. 336–346. Springer, Cham (2018). https://doi.org/10.1007/978-3-319-99972-2_27
15. Wei, W., Song, H., Li, W., Shen, P., Vasilakos, A.: Gradient-driven parking navigation using a continuous information potential field based on wireless sensor network. Inf. Sci. **408**, 100–114 (2017)
16. Weyuker, E.J.: Evaluating software complexity measures. IEEE Trans. Software Eng. **14**(9), 1357–1365 (1988)

17. Korytkowski, M.: Rough neural network ensemble for interval data classification. In: 2018 IEEE International Conference on Fuzzy Systems (FUZZ-IEEE). IEEE (2018)
18. Nowak, J., Korytkowski, M., Nowicki, R., Scherer, R., Siwocha, A.: Random Forests for Profiling Computer Network Users. In: Rutkowski, L., Scherer, R., Korytkowski, M., Pedrycz, W., Tadeusiewicz, R., Zurada, J.M. (eds.) ICAISC 2018. LNCS (LNAI), vol. 10842, pp. 734–739. Springer, Cham (2018). https://doi.org/10.1007/978-3-319-91262-2_64

The Method of Predicting Changes of a Dynamic Signature Using Possibilities of Population-Based Algorithms

Marcin Zalasiński[1][(✉)] , Krystian Łapa[1] , Krzysztof Cpałka[1] ,
and Alina Marchlewska[2,3]

[1] Institute of Computational Intelligence, Częstochowa University of Technology,
Częstochowa, Poland
{marcin.zalasinski,krystian.lapa,krzysztof.cpalka}@iisi.pcz.pl
[2] Information Technology Institute, University of Social Sciences,
90-113 Łodź, Poland
amarchlewska@san.edu.pl
[3] Clark University, Worcester, MA 01610, USA

Abstract. Verification of a signature on the basis of its dynamics is an important issue of biometrics. This kind signature is called the dynamic signature. It can be represented, among others, by the set of features determined on the basis of time characteristics: pen velocity, pen pressure on the surface of a graphics tablet, etc. Values of the features can change over time, individually for each signer. Our previous research was related to the prediction of these changes to increase the effectiveness of a signature verification process. This approach was effective. The main purpose of this work is to compare the effectiveness of the methods for a prediction of signature features changes using selected population-based algorithms. They are used for learning of the fuzzy system used for prediction. Tests of the proposed approach were performed using ATVS-SLT DB database of the dynamic signatures.

Keywords: Dynamic signature verification · Global features ·
Prediction · Fuzzy system · Population-based methods

1   Introduction

Verification of a signature on the basis of its dynamics is an important issue of biometrics. This kind signature is called the dynamic signature [16]. Dynamics of a signing process can be described by the set of features determined on the basis of time characteristics: pen velocity, pen pressure on the surface of a graphics tablet, etc. [9,15,30]. There are many effective methods for the dynamic signature verification. They select from the signature certain characteristics that have a different interpretation [33,34]. Verification of the signature performed by these methods consists in comparing the values of the signature features

© Springer Nature Switzerland AG 2019
L. Rutkowski et al. (Eds.): ICAISC 2019, LNAI 11508, pp. 540–549, 2019.
https://doi.org/10.1007/978-3-030-20912-4_49

extracted from the test signature with the averaged values of the signature features selected from the reference signatures, which are acquired and add to the database in the training phase of the biometric system.

The effectiveness of the dynamic signature verification depends on the time interval between the acquisition of the reference signatures by the user and acquisition of the test signature. If this interval is too long, the way of signing can evidently evolve, which usually reduces the effectiveness of the verification methods. This problem has been described in our previous works [35,36]. In those works, we characterized the problem of the evolution of biometric features and proposed an example method to eliminate the effects of its occurrence. That method used a fuzzy system (see e.g. [2,6–8,22,24,26–29,37]) to predict changes in the value of biometric features. It was learned using an exemplary population-based algorithm. ($\mu + \lambda$), [25]). In this work, we assumed that the effectiveness of prediction significantly depends on the adopted method of learning. Therefore, we used several selected population-based algorithms (see e.g. [10–13,31]) to optimize the fuzzy system used for prediction and compared the achieved effectiveness.

It is worth noting that in the literature there are many methods for predicting time series [18,20,32]. However, not all of them can be effectively used to verify the dynamic signature. A fuzzy system is well suited for this purpose because it can have the same structure for all users (number of rules, inputs, and outputs, etc.). Parameters of this system, different from each other for individual users, can be saved in the database along with other parameters characterizing the signatures [5]. We can also try to interpret fuzzy rules for information on the dynamic signature change trend. This can be performed independently for each user. Values of the system parameters can be selected, for example, by a population-based algorithm.

Structure of the paper is as follows: Sect. 2 describes the proposed method for prediction values of the dynamic signature global features, Sect. 3 characterizes obtained simulation results and Sect. 4 contains conclusions.

2 Method for Prediction Values of the Dynamic Signature Global Features

Remarks on the proposed method for prediction values of the dynamic signature global features can be summarized as follows:

- It uses possibilities of a fuzzy system [5,17]. The system has been used to predict changes that take place over time in the biometric features describing the dynamic signature.
- It assumes that the structure of the fuzzy system for all users is the same. Systems for individual users differ from each other by parameters which values are the result of system learning. Population-based methods can be used to perform the learning process. In simulations (see Sect. 3) we considered the following methods: genetic algorithm (GA, [25]), imperialist competitive

algorithm (ICA, [1]), golden ball algorithm (GB, [21]), differential evolution algorithm (DE, [23]), and grey wolf optimizer algorithm (GWO, [19]). The description of these algorithms can be found in the given literature.

- It allows us for prediction values of the dynamic signature global features of the individual user. It takes into account the values of the features determined during the previous training acquisition sessions of the signature (or sessions during which the signature was verified positively) and stored in the database.
- It can work for any number of the dynamic signature global features. The system used for prediction can process signals associated with any number of previous training sessions (Fig. 1).

2.1   Preparation of Learning and Testing Data

The proposed method is based on the set of global features determined for signatures created in subsequent training sessions which took place at certain time intervals. We wrote about the necessity of normalizing the values of features and their averaging in our previous work [36]. Averaged values of global features are part of the learning and testing sequence, used in the training and testing phase of the fuzzy system used for prediction. For example, the learning sequence based on the values of features from the previous session has the following form $\{\mathbf{x}_{i,s=1}, \mathbf{d}_{i,s=2}\}, \{\mathbf{x}_{i,s=2}, \mathbf{d}_{i,s=3}\}, \ldots, \{\mathbf{x}_{i,s=S-2}, \mathbf{d}_{i,s=S-1}\}$, where i is the index of the user, s is the index of the session, S is the number of sessions, $\mathbf{x}_{i,s}$ represents input vectors of the values of the features, $\mathbf{d}_{i,s} = \mathbf{x}_{i,s+1}$ represents reference vectors of the values of the features. Data from the last session can be used in testing phase, so the test set has the following form $\{\mathbf{x}_{i,s=S-1}, \mathbf{d}_{i,s=S-1}\}$. It should be noted, that the fuzzy system used for prediction can be systematically trained using the data of signatures classified as genuine.

2.2   Training and Testing

Prediction can be implemented using MIMO neuro-fuzzy system of the Mamdani-type [25]. Neuro-fuzzy systems combine the natural language description of fuzzy systems and the learning properties of neural networks (see e.g. [3,4]). Its operation can be expressed in a symbolic way as follows: $\mathbf{y}_{i,s} = \mathbf{f}_i(\mathbf{x}_{i,s})$, where $\mathbf{f}_i(\cdot)$ is a function representing system for the user i and $\mathbf{y}_{i,s} = [y_{i,n=1,s}, y_{i,n=2,s}, \ldots, y_{i,n=N,s}]$, where n is the index of the global feature, represents a vector of real answers of the system for input vector $\mathbf{x}_{i,s}$.

Improvement of the fuzzy system work for each user requires learning. It can be performed using a population-based algorithm. The purpose of the algorithm is to minimize differences between reference vectors ($\mathbf{d}_{i,s}$) and output vectors $\mathbf{y}_{i,s}$ of the considered fuzzy system. Evaluation of the system operation in the learning phase can be realized using standard RMSE error. Use of it makes sense due to the normalization of features performed earlier. The error is expressed as follows:

$$RMSE_i = \frac{1}{N} \cdot \sum_{n=1}^{N} \sqrt{\frac{\sum_{s=1}^{S-2} (d_{i,n,s} - y_{i,n,s})^2}{S - 2}}. \tag{1}$$

The error of form (1) is used in the evolutionary learning phase in order to evaluate individuals encoding parameters of the fuzzy system used for prediction. The purpose of the learning algorithm is a minimization of the error. In order to better show the accuracy of the system, we can also use a percentage measure of accuracy defined as follows:

$$ACC_i = \left(1 - \frac{\sum_{n=1}^{N} \sum_{s=1}^{S-2} |d_{i,n,s} - y_{i,n,s}|}{N \cdot (S - 2)} \right) \cdot 100\%. \tag{2}$$

Formulas (1) and (2) are related to the learning phase, but analogous formulas can be created for the testing phase. Details related to the fuzzy system and aspects of its learning can be found in our previous papers [35, 36].

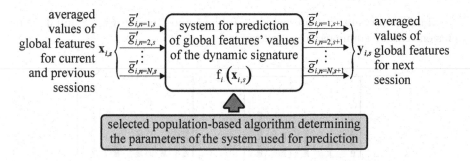

Fig. 1. The idea of prediction of the dynamic signature global features' values.

3   Simulations

Details of the simulations can be summarized as follows:

- They were performed in authorial testing environment implemented in C#.
- They were performed using ATVS-SLT DB [14] dynamic signature database which has the following structure: number of the users: $I = 27$, number of sessions: $S = 6$, and number of signatures of the user created in the sessions from 1 to 6: 4, 4, 4, 4, 15, and 15.
- Prediction was performed for 10 the best global features ($N = 10$) pointed out in [14]. Indices of these features are as follows: 3, 7, 17, 38, 45, 58, 59, 72, 93, 97.

- Prediction was performed using Mamdani-type fuzzy system characterized by the following parameters: number of rules: 3, number of inputs:
  $\{10, 20, 30, 40\}$, number of outputs: 10, fuzzy sets type: Gaussian, and triangular norms type: algebraic [25].
- For each user from the database learning of the fuzzy system is performed
  independently. The following values of the parameters of the algorithms have
  been adopted: number of steps (generations) of the algorithm: 200, number
  of repetitions of the simulation for each user: 25 (results were averaged), the
  number of individuals in the population: 100, crossing probability in GA: 0.8,
  mutation probability in GA: 0.3, the method of selecting individuals in GA,
  DE, and GB (also selection method of players that faces each other to score
  a goal): roulette wheel method, mutation range in GA: 0.2, parameter CR in
  DE: 0.5, parameter F in DE: 0.75, number of empires in ICA: 10, parameter
  ϵ in ICA: 0.1, parameter β in ICA: 2.0, parameter γ in ICA: 0.15, number of
  goal chances in GB: 20, number of teams in GB: 10, and number of matches
  in the league competition in GB: number of teams·number of teams (each
  team plays with each other).
- Moreover, in GB algorithm we assumed that each team gets a random training plan at the beginning. In this mutation range $\in [0.01, 0.30]$, crossing
  probability $\in [0.50, 1.00]$, and mutation probability $\in [0.05, 0.30]$.

Simulation results are presented in Tables 1 and 2 and in Figs. 2 and 3. Conclusions can be summarized as follows:

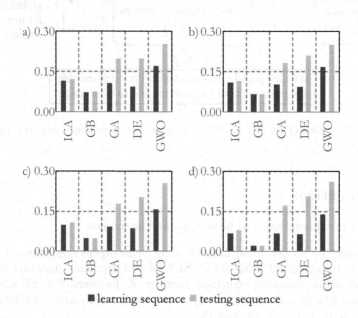

Fig. 2. RMSE error of prediction of the dynamic signature features (1) obtained for
the considered population-based algorithms and the following number of inputs: (a) 10,
(b) 20, (c) 30, (d) 40.

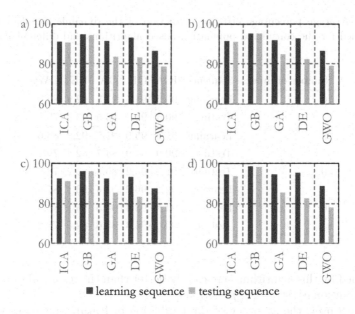

■ learning sequence ▥ testing sequence

Fig. 3. Percentage error of prediction of the dynamic signature features (2) obtained for the considered population-based algorithms and the following number of inputs: (a) 10, (b) 20, (c) 30, (d) 40.

Table 1. Average RMSE error of prediction of the dynamic signature features (1) obtained for the considered population-based algorithms and different number of inputs.

Number of inputs	Sequence	ICA	GB	GA	DE	GWO
10	Learning	0.115	0.073	0.106	0.093	0.171
	Testing	0.120	0.074	0.197	0.199	0.254
20	Learning	0.108	0.066	0.104	0.093	0.166
	Testing	0.114	0.066	0.183	0.210	0.250
30	Learning	0.097	0.048	0.093	0.087	0.156
	Testing	0.107	0.049	0.178	0.202	0.256
40	Learning	0.068	0.020	0.068	0.063	0.138
	Testing	0.080	0.021	0.173	0.205	0.261

- The highest accuracy was obtained for the golden ball algorithm (column GB, Tables 2 and 1). It was independent of the number of inputs (number of sessions) of the fuzzy system.
- The lowest accuracy was obtained for the grey wolf algorithm (column GWO, Tables 2 and 1). It was independent of the number of inputs (number of sessions) of the fuzzy system. However, it should be noted that the results

Table 2. Average percentage error of prediction of the dynamic signature features (2) obtained for the considered population-based algorithms and different number of inputs.

Number of inputs	Sequence	ICA	GB	GA	DE	GWO
10	Learning	90.9	94.5	91.5	92.9	86.3
	Testing	90.4	94.4	83.5	83.4	78.8
20	Learning	91.4	95.0	91.7	92.8	86.6
	Testing	90.9	94.9	84.7	82.4	79.2
30	Testing	91.3	96.2	85.3	83.2	78.6
	Learning	92.2	96.2	92.4	93.1	87.4
40	Learning	94.6	98.4	94.5	95.1	88.9
	Testing	93.6	98.3	85.6	82.5	78.2

obtained by this algorithm were clearly better than the results obtained using the evolutionary strategy $(\mu + \lambda)$ [36].

- For each user, the accuracy of the prediction of features increases with the increase in the number of features (number of sessions) given to the inputs of the fuzzy system (Tables 2 and 1). It was independent of the used learning algorithm.

4   Conclusions

In this article, we considered the problem of predicting changes in the value of biometric features over time. In particular, we tested various algorithms for learning a fuzzy system used to predict feature values. The simulations show that the values of dynamic signature features can be predicted with high accuracy. It results from the specificity of this problem, in which the dynamics of changes in the value of features should not be large. Nevertheless, it can cause major changes in the accuracy of the signature verification.

The choice of the learning algorithm had a great impact on the accuracy of prediction. In our simulations, the best accuracy was obtained using the golden ball algorithm. Other tested algorithms gave slightly worse results, although acceptable.

In the future, we plan to develop and test the method for the dynamic signature verification, which takes into account the conclusions of the performed simulations.

References

1. Atashpaz-Gargari, E., Lucas, C.: Imperialist competitive algorithm: an algorithm for optimization inspired by imperialistic competition. In: Proceedings of the IEEE Congress on Evolutionary Computation, vol. 7, pp. 4661–4666 (2007)
2. Beg, I., Rashid, T.: Modelling uncertainties in multi-criteria decision making using distance measure and TOPSIS for hesitant fuzzy sets. J. Artif. Intell. Soft Comput. Res. **7**, 103–109 (2017)
3. Bilski, J., Smoląg, J., Galushkin, A.I.: The parallel approach to the conjugate gradient learning algorithm for the feedforward neural networks. In: Rutkowski, L., Korytkowski, M., Scherer, R., Tadeusiewicz, R., Zadeh, L.A., Zurada, J.M. (eds.) ICAISC 2014. LNCS (LNAI), vol. 8467, pp. 12–21. Springer, Cham (2014). https://doi.org/10.1007/978-3-319-07173-2_2
4. Bilski, J., Smoląg, J.: Parallel architectures for learning the RTRN and Elman dynamic neural networks. IEEE Trans. Parallel Distrib. Syst. **26**(9), 2561–2570 (2015)
5. Cpałka, K.: Design of Interpretable Fuzzy Systems. SCI, vol. 684. Springer, Cham (2017). https://doi.org/10.1007/978-3-319-52881-6
6. Cpałka, K., Rutkowski, L.: A new method for designing and reduction of neuro-fuzzy systems. In: Proceedings of the 2006 IEEE International Conference on Fuzzy Systems (IEEE World Congress on Computational Intelligence, WCCI 2006), Vancouver, BC, Canada, pp. 8510–8516 (2006)
7. Cpałka, K., Rutkowski, L.: Evolutionary learning of flexible neuro-fuzzy systems. In: Proceedings of the 2008 IEEE International Conference on Fuzzy Systems (IEEE World Congress on Computational Intelligence, WCCI 2008), Hong Kong June 1–6, CD, pp. 969–975 (2008)
8. Cpałka, K., Rutkowski, L.: Flexible Takagi-sugeno fuzzy systems. In: Proceedings of the International Joint Conference on Neural Networks 2005, Montreal, pp. 1764–1769 (2005)
9. Doroz, R., Kudlacik, P., Porwik, P.: Online signature verification modeled by stability oriented reference signatures. Inf. Sci. **460–461**, 151–171 (2018)
10. Dziwiński, P., Avedyan, E.D.: A new method of the intelligent modeling of the non-linear dynamic objects with fuzzy detection of the operating points. In: Rutkowski, L., Korytkowski, M., Scherer, R., Tadeusiewicz, R., Zadeh, L.A., Zurada, J.M. (eds.) ICAISC 2016. LNCS (LNAI), vol. 9693, pp. 293–305. Springer, Cham (2016). https://doi.org/10.1007/978-3-319-39384-1_25
11. Dziwiński, P., Avedyan, E.D.: A new approach for using the fuzzy decision trees for the detection of the significant operating points in the nonlinear modeling. In: Rutkowski, L., Korytkowski, M., Scherer, R., Tadeusiewicz, R., Zadeh, L.A., Zurada, J.M. (eds.) ICAISC 2016. LNCS (LNAI), vol. 9693, pp. 279–292. Springer, Cham (2016). https://doi.org/10.1007/978-3-319-39384-1_24
12. Dziwiński, P., Bartczuk, Ł., Tingwen, H.: A method for non-linear modelling based on the capabilities of PSO and GA algorithms. In: Rutkowski, L., Korytkowski, M., Scherer, R., Tadeusiewicz, R., Zadeh, L.A., Zurada, J.M. (eds.) ICAISC 2017. LNCS (LNAI), vol. 10246, pp. 221–232. Springer, Cham (2017). https://doi.org/10.1007/978-3-319-59060-8_21
13. Dziwiński, P., Bartczuk, Ł., Przybyszewski, K.: A population based algorithm and fuzzy decision trees for nonlinear modeling. In: Rutkowski, L., Scherer, R., Korytkowski, M., Pedrycz, W., Tadeusiewicz, R., Zurada, J.M. (eds.) ICAISC 2018. LNCS (LNAI), vol. 10842, pp. 516–531. Springer, Cham (2018). https://doi.org/10.1007/978-3-319-91262-2_46

14. Galbally, J., Martinez-Diaz, M., Fierez, J.: Aging in biometrics: an experimental analysis on on-line signature. PLoS ONE **8**(7), e69897 (2013)
15. Galbally, J., Diaz-Cabrera, M., Ferrer, M.A., Gomez-Barrero, M., Morales, A., Fierrez, J.: On-line signature recognition through the combination of real dynamic data and synthetically generated static data. Pattern Recogn. **48**, 2921–2934 (2015)
16. Linden, J., Marquis, R., Bozza, S., Taroni, F.: Dynamic signatures: a review of dynamic feature variation and forensic methodology. Forensic Sci. Int. **291**, 216–229 (2018)
17. Łapa, K., Cpałka, K., Wang, L.: New method for design of fuzzy systems for nonlinear modelling using different criteria of interpretability. In: Rutkowski, L., Korytkowski, M., Scherer, R., Tadeusiewicz, R., Zadeh, L.A., Zurada, J.M. (eds.) ICAISC 2014. LNCS (LNAI), vol. 8467, pp. 217–232. Springer, Cham (2014). https://doi.org/10.1007/978-3-319-07173-2_20
18. McAlinn, K., West, M.: Dynamic Bayesian predictive synthesis in time series forecasting. J. Econometrics **210**, 155–169 (2018)
19. Mirjalili, S., Mirjalili, S.M., Lewis, A.: Grey wolf optimizer. Adv. Eng. Softw. **69**, 46–61 (2014)
20. Nguyen, L., Novák, V.: Forecasting seasonal time series based on fuzzy techniques. Fuzzy Sets Syst. **361**, 114–129 (2019)
21. Osaba, E., Diaz, F., Onieva, E.: Golden ball: a novel meta-heuristic to solve combinatorial optimization problems based on soccer concepts. Appl. Intell. **41**, 145–166 (2014)
22. Prasad, M., Liu, Y.T., Li, D.L., Lin, C.T., Shah, R.R., Kaiwartya, O.P.: A new mechanism for data visualization with TSK-type preprocessed collaborative fuzzy rule based system. J. Artif. Intell. Soft Comput. Res. **7**, 33–46 (2017)
23. Price, K.V., Storn, R.M., Lampinen, J.A.: Differential Evolution: A Practical Approach to Global Optimization. NCS. Springer, Heidelberg (2005). https://doi.org/10.1007/3-540-31306-0
24. Riid, A., Preden, J.S.: Design of fuzzy rule-based classifiers through granulation and consolidation. J. Artif. Intell. Soft Comput. Res. **7**, 137–147 (2017)
25. Rutkowski, L.: Computational Intelligence. Springer, Heidelberg (2008). https://doi.org/10.1007/978-3-540-76288-1
26. Rutkowski, L., Cpałka, K.: Flexible weighted neuro-fuzzy systems. In: Proceedings of the 9th International Conference on Neural Information Processing (ICONIP 2002), Orchid Country Club, Singapore, 18–22 November, CD (2002)
27. Rutkowski, L., Cpałka, K.: Neuro-fuzzy systems derived from quasi-triangular norms. In: Proceedings of the IEEE International Conference on Fuzzy Systems, Budapest, 26–29 July, vol. 2, pp. 1031–1036 (2004)
28. Rutkowski, T., Romanowski, J., Woldan, P., Staszewski, P., Nielek, R., Rutkowski, L.: A content-based recommendation system using neuro-fuzzy approach. FUZZ-IEEE **2018**, 1–8 (2018)
29. Rutkowski, T., Romanowski, J., Woldan, P., Staszewski, P., Nielek, R.: Towards interpretability of the movie recommender based on a neuro-fuzzy approach. In: Rutkowski, L., Scherer, R., Korytkowski, M., Pedrycz, W., Tadeusiewicz, R., Zurada, J.M. (eds.) ICAISC 2018. LNCS (LNAI), vol. 10842, pp. 752–762. Springer, Cham (2018). https://doi.org/10.1007/978-3-319-91262-2_66
30. Xia, X., Chen, Z., Luan, F., Song, X.: Signature alignment based on GMM for on-line signature verification. Pattern Recogn. **65**, 188–196 (2017)
31. Yang, S., Sato, Y.: Swarm intelligence algorithm based on competitive predators with dynamic virtual teams. J. Artif. Intell. Soft Comput. Res. **7**, 87–101 (2017)

32. Yin, Y., Shang, P.: Forecasting traffic time series with multivariate predicting method. Appl. Math. Comput. **291**, 266–278 (2016)
33. Zalasiński, M., Cpałka, K.: Novel algorithm for the on-line signature verification using selected discretization points groups. In: Rutkowski, L., Korytkowski, M., Scherer, R., Tadeusiewicz, R., Zadeh, L.A., Zurada, J.M. (eds.) ICAISC 2013. LNCS (LNAI), vol. 7894, pp. 493–502. Springer, Heidelberg (2013). https://doi.org/10.1007/978-3-642-38658-9_44
34. Zalasiński, M., Cpałka, K., Hayashi, Y.: New method for dynamic signature verification based on global features. In: Rutkowski, L., Korytkowski, M., Scherer, R., Tadeusiewicz, R., Zadeh, L.A., Zurada, J.M. (eds.) ICAISC 2014. LNCS (LNAI), vol. 8468, pp. 231–245. Springer, Cham (2014). https://doi.org/10.1007/978-3-319-07176-3_21
35. Zalasiński, M., Łapa, K., Cpałka, K.: Prediction of values of the dynamic signature features. Expert Syst. Appl. **104**, 86–96 (2018)
36. Zalasiński, M., Łapa, K., Cpałka, K., Saito, T.: A method for changes prediction of the dynamic signature global features over time. In: Rutkowski, L., Korytkowski, M., Scherer, R., Tadeusiewicz, R., Zadeh, L.A., Zurada, J.M. (eds.) ICAISC 2017. LNCS (LNAI), vol. 10245, pp. 761–772. Springer, Cham (2017). https://doi.org/10.1007/978-3-319-59063-9_68
37. Zhao, Y., Liu, Q.: A continuous-time distributed algorithm for solving a class of decomposable nonconvex quadratic programming. J. Artif. Intell. Soft Comput. Res. **8**, 283–291 (2018)

Pattern Classification

Application of Elastic Principal Component Analysis to Person Recognition Based on Screen Gestures

Mateusz Baran[1]([📧]) [iD], Leszek Siwik[2] [iD], and Krzysztof Rzecki[1] [iD]

[1] Faculty of Physics, Mathematics and Computer Science, Cracow University
of Technology, ul. Warszawska 24, 31-155 Kraków, Poland
{mbaran,krz}@pk.edu.pl
[2] Department of Computer Science, AGH University of Science and Technology,
Kraków, Poland
siwik@agh.edu.pl

Abstract. Person identification based on touch screen gestures is a
well-known method of authentication in mobile devices. Usually it is
only checked if the user entered the correct pattern. Taking into account
other biometric data based on the speed and shape of finger movements
can provide higher security while the convenience of this authorisation
method is not impacted. In this work the application of Sequential Joint
Functional Principal Analysis (FPCA) as a dimensionality reduction
method for gesture data is explored. Performance of the classifier is measured using 5-fold stratified cross-validation on a set of gestures collected
from 12 people. The effects of sampling rate on classification performance
is also measured. It is shown that the Support Vector Machine classifier
reaches the accuracy of 79% using features obtained using the Sequential
Joint FPCA, compared to 70% in the case of Euclidean PCA.

Keywords: Touch screen gestures · Biometrics · Classification ·
Elastic shape analysis · Pattern recognition

1 Introduction

Identification of a person based on their physiological or behavioural characteristics distinguishing them from other people is commonly referred to as biometric identification [12]. Various unique features like face images, iris, fingerprints or signature are used in such methods. Different applications have different requirements for a method used for identification. For example, most touch
screen devices lack dedicated hardware for biometric identification. Augmenting
the common gesture-based identification with biometry would improve security
without impacting user convenience [21]. Other approaches to person recognition based on hand gestures include using sequences of images from a camera
(including a depth camera) [7,24] or data from a specialized glove [4,19].

© Springer Nature Switzerland AG 2019
L. Rutkowski et al. (Eds.): ICAISC 2019, LNAI 11508, pp. 553–560, 2019.
https://doi.org/10.1007/978-3-030-20912-4_50

A very important part of data analysis is dimensionality reduction. Principal Component Analysis (PCA) is one of the most popular dimensionality reduction methods. Over the years, many variants were proposed, including Generalized PCA [29], kernel PCA and Principal Geodesic Analysis [2,9].

In recent years the elastic metric [30] has been suggested for modelling functional data. The method, partially inspired by increasingly popular data analysis using Riemannian geometry [2,11,15,28], received a significant amount of attention [1,14,16,17,23,25,28,31]. Recently, a new family of PCA variants that takes into account achievements in elastic shape analysis was proposed [6,22,26]. This family includes, among other methods, Amplitude FPCA, Phase FPCA and Sequential Joint FPCA [22,27], differing by the space in which principal components are calculated.

In this work, the elastic FPCA is applied as a dimensionality reduction method to the problem of person recognition based on a performance of a hand gesture on a touch display. The k-nearest neighbour and Support Vector Machine [8] algorithms are considered for classification in principal subspace. A set of five gestures, twelve people and five gesture executions per person is used. The evaluation is performed using stratified 5-fold cross-validation to prevent overfitting [13].

2   Materials and Methods

2.1   Gesture Data Set

The touch screen gestures were gathered using mobile devices with touchscreens (smartphones) [21]. People were performing a number of predefined types of gestures by moving a finger along a path connecting rings that were arranged in a rectangular pattern (see Fig. 1 in [20]). The task is to recognize a person given a single performance of a gesture (a survey). Each person performed each gesture a few times. This data is available for building a statistical model for this classification task. In total, $N_G = 5$ gestures performed $N_R = 5$ times by each one of $N_P = 12$ people were analysed. The data acquisition process and pattern design is detailed in a previous work [21]. Only continuous gestures (performed without raising a finger from the screen) were considered because of continuity assumption of the proposed model.

A survey can be described by a curve $f_{P,G,R}(t)\colon [0,1] \to \mathbb{R}^2$ where $P \in \{1,2,\ldots,N_P\}$ is the number of person, $G \in \{1,2,\ldots,N_G\}$ is the number of gesture used for recognition and $R \in \{1,2,\ldots,N_R\}$ is the number of repetition. The pressure data and total time of gesture execution were not taken into account in this study.

2.2   Dimensionality Reduction and Classification

Three dimensionality reduction methods are considered in this study: classical Euclidean PCA, Amplitude Functional PCA (A-FPCA) and Sequential Joint

Functional PCA (SJ-FPCA). The A-FPCA approach relies on transforming curves into the amplitude space. To do this, one has to introduce the Square Root Velocity Function (SRVF) representation. For a function $f \colon [0,1] \to \mathbb{R}^2$, its SRVF representation is expressed as a function $q \colon [0,1] \to \mathbb{R}^2$ such that $q(t) = F(\dot{f}(t))$ where $F(v) = v/\sqrt{\|v\|}$ if $\|v\| > 0$ and 0 otherwise. The first order forward finite difference formula is used to approximate the derivative of a curve.

The elastic metric has an ability to simultaneously consider bending and stretching of given curves in a principled way. In general, it is defined as a two-parameter family of Riemannian metrics on the manifold of curves. The ratio of these two parameters describes the relative weight of curve bending and stretching that should be performed to fit two given curves. However, the SRVF representation approach is compatible only with a single ratio of this two parameters.

Now, let $\mathcal{F}$ be the space of differentiable planar curves whose derivative is different from zero almost everywhere. Also, let $\tilde{\Gamma}_I$ be the space of weakly increasing absolutely continuous functions $\gamma \colon [0,1] \to [0,1]$ such that $\gamma(0) = 0$ and $\gamma(1) = 1$. This can be thought of as a special set of reparametrizations of the unit interval. With function composition operation, $\tilde{\Gamma}_I$ becomes a monoid. An action of $\tilde{\Gamma}_I$ on the space of SRVF representations of planar curves can be defined as $\gamma \cdot q = (q \circ \gamma)\sqrt{\dot{\gamma}}$. The quotient space $\mathcal{A} = \mathrm{L}^2/\tilde{\Gamma}_I$, with its quotient geometry, is called the space of amplitudes. A-FPCA is then performed in the space $\mathcal{A} \times \mathbb{R}^2$ of amplitudes and initial points of curves, $f(0)$. First, mean amplitude and mean initial values, together denoted μ, are computed for uniformly sampled input functions. Next, all SRVF representations are aligned to μ. Finally, the classical PCA is performed on resulting representations.

The SJ-FPCA works in a similar way, although the space $\mathcal{A} \times \mathbb{R}^2 \times \tilde{\Gamma}_I$ is used, where reparametrizations aligning different curves to the mean curve are also considered. Since the operation $\gamma \to \sqrt{\dot{\gamma}}$ transforms reparametrizations to the Hilbert sphere (functions from L^2 with unit norm), the geometry of $\tilde{\Gamma}_I$ is defined this way. The Principal Geodesic Analysis approach is used to handle this geometry. For more details regarding A-FPCA and SJ-FPCA see [22].

Finally, the coefficients of a gesture in the principal subspace are used for classification. Two algorithms were considered: the k-nearest neighbour and Support Vector Machine algorithms. The evaluation is performed using stratified 5-fold cross-validation.

3   Results and Discussion

The Euclidean PCA and Sequential Joint FPCA were compared in a few ways. First, Fig. 1 compares effects of different geometries of principal subspaces described by Euclidean PCA and SJ-FPCA. As can be seen, even for moderate values of coefficients in the principal subspace (most projections of surveys have coefficients with larger magnitude), the curve generated using Euclidean

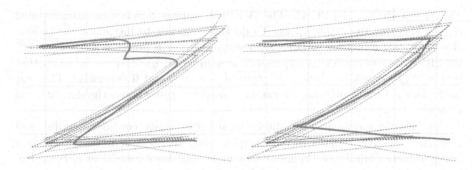

Fig. 1. Comparison of Euclidean PCA (left) and SJ-FPCA (right) for executions of
a selected gesture by a single person. Dashed lines represent input gesture curves
and thick solid line is a sample from three-dimensional principal space for coefficients
$[0.4, 0, 0]$ (Euclidean PCA) and $[5.9, -3.7, 3.0]$ (SJ-FPCA).

PCA does not resemble input curves. On the other hand, in case of the SJ-
FPCA even selecting coefficients significantly larger than these from projections
of input curves one gets a similar curve.

Table 1. Fraction of explained variance by the first 3, 5, and 7 principal components.

Δt	PCA variant	Number of principal components		
		3	5	7
0.02	Euclidean PCA	58.6%	74.6%	83.8%
	SJ-FPCA	38.8%	51.5%	60.5%
0.05	Euclidean PCA	59.4%	73.9%	83.4%
	SJ-FPCA	48.2%	61.8%	71.1%

Table 1 compares fraction of variance in the data explained by a few first
principal directions for Euclidean PCA and SJ-FPCA. Table 2 compares the
dimension of the principal subspace for both PCA algorithms. Both fraction of
explained variance and subspace dimension are averaged across all gestures and
cross-validation folds. These results indicate that the Euclidean PCA explains
more variance than SJ-FPCA for the same dimension of principal subspace.

Finally, classification results are gathered in Table 3. Three classifiers were considered: k-nearest neighbour classifier (kNN), Support Vector Machine (SVM)
with linear kernel and SVM with polynomial kernel. Values given in this Table were
obtained for kNN with $k = 1$ and a Euclidean distance function. Linear and polynomial SVM implement the C-Support Vector Classification (C-SVC) variant with
cost coefficient set to 0.5. Polynomial kernel has the form $k(x, y) = 0.5x \cdot y - 1$.
A subset of other values of classifier parameters and sampling rates was considered
but no significant improvement was achieved.

Table 2. Average dimension of the principal subspace for target explained variance 90% and 95%.

Δt	PCA variant	Target explained variance	
		90%	95%
0.02	Euclidean PCA	9.60	12.9
	SJ-FPCA	22.3	29.2
0.05	Euclidean PCA	9.68	13.0
	SJ-FPCA	15.6	20.8

Table 3. Classification accuracy in percent for considered classifiers, discretization steps, PCA methods and principal subspace size. Dimensionality of principal subspace (denoted D) is given either explicitly or as a target fraction of explained variance.

Δt		0.02				0.05			
D		3	5	90%	95%	3	5	90%	95%
kNN	Euclidean PCA	35.0	47.7	62.0	**69.7**	35.0	47.7	61.7	**66.7**
	SJ-FPCA	33.7	49.7	66.0	65.3	21.3	32.7	48.3	50.0
	No PCA	62.3				62.7			
Linear SVM	Euclidean PCA	35.0	46.7	66.7	69.7	37.7	48.0	66.7	**69.3**
	SJ-FPCA	38.0	49.7	**79.0**	78.7	29.3	36.0	56.3	57.7
	No PCA	52.3				52.7			
Polynomial SVM	Euclidean PCA	36.3	47.0	66.7	70.0	39.3	50.7	67.0	**69.7**
	SJ-FPCA	38.3	48.3	76.7	**78.0**	29.7	35.3	49.7	53.0
	No PCA	52.3				52.7			

Sampling rate $\Delta t = 0.02$ results in a significantly higher accuracy in the SJ-FPCA method than other tested sampling rate, in particular $\Delta t = 0.05$ displayed in Table 3. On the other hand, selection of sampling rate has very little effect on Euclidean PCA and classification without dimensionality reduction using considered classifiers.

The results indicate that Sequential Joint FPCA dimensionality reduction significantly improves classification accuracy and leads to a more natural geometry of the principal subspace. The accuracy is satisfactory regarding a relatively large number of people that were recognized (twelve people) and a very small set of samples per person used in building the model (four gesture executions per person).

The average time to build a SJ-FPCA model was equal to 4.6 s for 60 gestures sampled with $\Delta t = 0.02$ and the average transformation time was equal to 3.1 ms. For $\Delta t = 0.05$ these times are equal to, respectively, 550 ms and 660 μs Results were obtained on an Intel Core i7 processor using the LIBSVM library [5] and custom software written in Julia [3].

4   Conclusions

In this study the Sequential Joint FPCA dimensionality reduction method was applied to the problem of person recognition based on touch screen gestures. It was compared against the Euclidean PCA. The SJ-FPCA method enables the Support Vector Machine to achieve relatively high accuracy (79%) considering very small training set and a large number of classes. The discretization $\Delta t = 0.02$ was found to result in the highest accuracy for the SJ-FPCA method, although it does not significantly affect other considered variants.

In future work we will consider using other dimensionality reduction methods as well as feature selection algorithms [10,18]. We will also test other classifiers.

References

1. Baran, M.: Closest paths in graph drawings under an elastic metric. Int. J. Appl. Math. Comput. Sci. **28**(2), 387–397 (2018). https://doi.org/10.2478/amcs-2018-0029
2. Baran, M., Tabor, Z.: Principal geodesic analysis boundary delineation with superpixel-based constraints. Image Anal. Stereology **36**(3), 223–232 (2017). https://doi.org/10.5566/ias.1712
3. Bezanson, J., Edelman, A., Karpinski, S., Shah, V.: Julia: a fresh approach to numerical computing. SIAM Review **59**(1), 65–98 (2017). https://doi.org/10.1137/141000671
4. Blachnik, M., Głomb, P.: Do we need complex models for gestures? a comparison of data representation and preprocessing methods for hand gesture recognition. In: Rutkowski, L., Korytkowski, M., Scherer, R., Tadeusiewicz, R., Zadeh, L.A., Zurada, J.M. (eds.) ICAISC 2012. LNCS (LNAI), vol. 7267, pp. 477–485. Springer, Heidelberg (2012). https://doi.org/10.1007/978-3-642-29347-4_55
5. Chang, C.C., Lin, C.J.: LIBSVM: a library for support vector machines. ACM Trans. Intell. Syst. Technol. **2**, 1–27 (2011). http://www.csie.ntu.edu.tw/~cjlin/libsvm
6. Cheng, W., Dryden, I.L., Huang, X.: Bayesian registration of functions and curves. Bayesian Anal. **11**(2), 447–475 (2016). https://doi.org/10.1214/15-BA957
7. Cholewa, M., Głomb, P.: Estimation of the number of states for gesture recognition with hidden Markov models based on the number of critical points in time sequence. Pattern Recogn. Lett. **34**(5), 574–579 (2013). https://doi.org/10.1016/j.patrec.2012.12.002
8. Cortes, C., Vapnik, V.: Support-vector networks. Mach. Learn. **20**(3), 273–297 (1995). https://doi.org/10.1007/BF00994018
9. Fletcher, P., Lu, C., Pizer, S., Joshi, S.: Principal geodesic analysis for the study of nonlinear statistics of shape. IEEE Trans. Med. Imaging **23**(8), 995–1005 (2004). https://doi.org/10.1109/TMI.2004.831793
10. Ghosh, I.: Probabilistic feature selection in machine learning. In: Rutkowski, L., Scherer, R., Korytkowski, M., Pedrycz, W., Tadeusiewicz, R., Zurada, J.M. (eds.) ICAISC 2018. LNCS (LNAI), vol. 10841, pp. 623–632. Springer, Cham (2018). https://doi.org/10.1007/978-3-319-91253-0_58
11. Huckemann, S., Ziezold, H.: Principal component analysis for Riemannian manifolds, with an application to triangular shape spaces. Adv. Appl. Probab. **38**(2), 299–319 (2006). https://doi.org/10.1239/aap/1151337073

12. Jain, A., Hong, L., Pankanti, S.: Biometric identification. Commun. ACM **43**(2), 90–98 (2000). https://doi.org/10.1145/328236.328110

13. Japkowicz, N., Shah, M.: Evaluating Learning Algorithms: A Classification Perspective, 1st edn. Cambridge University Press, Cambridge (2011)

14. Joshi, S.H., Klassen, E., Srivastava, A., Jermyn, I.: A novel representation for Riemannian analysis of elastic curves in Rn. In: Proceedings/CVPR, IEEE Computer Society Conference on Computer Vision and Pattern Recognition, pp. 1–7. IEEE, Minneapolis, July 2007. https://doi.org/10.1109/CVPR.2007.383185

15. Mani, M., Kurtek, S., Barillot, C., Srivastava, A.: A comprehensive Riemannian framework for the analysis of white matter fiber tracts. In: 2010 IEEE International Symposium on Biomedical Imaging: From Nano to Macro, pp. 1101–1104, April 2010. https://doi.org/10.1109/ISBI.2010.5490185

16. Michor, P.W., Mumford, D.B.: Riemannian geometries on spaces of plane curves. J. Eur. Math. Soc. **8**(1), 1–48 (2006). https://doi.org/10.4171/JEMS/37

17. Mio, W., Srivastava, A., Joshi, S.: On shape of plane elastic curves. Int. J. Comput. Vis. **73**(3), 307–324 (2007). https://doi.org/10.1007/s11263-006-9968-0

18. Murphy, K.P.: Machine Learning: A Probabilistic Perspective. Adaptive Computation and Machine Learning, 1st edn. The MIT Press, Cambridge (2012)

19. Pławiak, P., Sośnicki, T., Niedźwiecki, M., Tabor, Z., Rzecki, K.: Hand body language gesture recognition based on signals from specialized glove and machine learning algorithms. IEEE Trans. Ind. Inform. **12**(3), 1104–1113 (2016). https://doi.org/10.1109/TII.2016.2550528

20. Rzecki, K., Siwik, L., Baran, M.: The elastic k-nearest neighbours classifier for touch screen gestures, in press

21. Rzecki, K., Pławiak, P., Niedźwiecki, M., Sośnicki, T., Leśkow, J., Ciesielski, M.: Person recognition based on touch screen gestures using computational intelligence methods. Inf. Sci. **415–416**, 70–84 (2017). https://doi.org/10.1016/j.ins.2017.05.041

22. Srivastava, A., Klassen, E.P.: Functional and Shape Data Analysis. SSS. Springer, New York (2016). https://doi.org/10.1007/978-1-4939-4020-2

23. Srivastava, A., Turaga, P., Kurtek, S.: On advances in differential-geometric approaches for 2D and 3D shape analyses and activity recognition. Image Vis. Comput. **30**(6–7), 398–416 (2012). https://doi.org/10.1016/j.imavis.2012.03.006

24. Suarez, J., Murphy, R.R.: Hand gesture recognition with depth images: a review. In: 2012 IEEE RO-MAN: The 21st IEEE International Symposium on Robot and Human Interactive Communication, pp. 411–417, September 2012. https://doi.org/10.1109/ROMAN.2012.6343787

25. Sundaramoorthi, G., Mennucci, A., Soatto, S., Yezzi, A.: A new geometric metric in the space of curves, and applications to tracking deforming objects by prediction and filtering. SIAM J. Imaging Sci. **4**(1), 109–145 (2011). https://doi.org/10.1137/090781139

26. Tucker, J.D., Wu, W., Srivastava, A.: Generative models for functional data using phase and amplitude separation. Comput. Stat. Data Anal. **61**, 50–66 (2013). https://doi.org/10.1016/j.csda.2012.12.001

27. Tucker, J.D., Wu, W., Srivastava, A.: Analysis of proteomics data: phase amplitude separation using an extended Fisher-Rao metric. Electron. J. Stat. **8**(2), 1724–1733 (2014). https://doi.org/10.1214/14-EJS900B

28. Turaga, P.K., Srivastava, A. (eds.): Riemannian Computing in Computer Vision. Springer, Cham (2016). https://doi.org/10.1007/978-3-319-22957-7

29. Vidal, R., Ma, Y., Sastry, S.: Generalized principal component analysis (GPCA). IEEE Trans. Pattern Anal. Mach. Intell. **27**(12), 1945–1959 (2005). https://doi.org/10.1109/TPAMI.2005.244
30. Younes, L.: Computable elastic distances between shapes. SIAM J. Appl. Math. **58**(2), 565–586 (1998). https://doi.org/10.1137/S0036139995287685
31. Younes, L.: Spaces and manifolds of shapes in computer vision: an overview. Image Vis. Comput. **30**(6–7), 389–397 (2012). https://doi.org/10.1016/j.imavis.2011.09.009

Sentiment Analysis of YouTube Video Comments Using Deep Neural Networks

Alexandre Ashade Lassance Cunha$^{(\boxtimes)}$ [ID], Melissa Carvalho Costa,
and Marco Aurélio C. Pacheco

Applied Computational Intelligence Laboratory,
Pontifical Catholic University of Rio de Janeiro, Rio de Janeiro 22430-060, Brazil
ashade@ele.puc-rio.br, melissacosta2304@gmail.com

Abstract. Over the years, social networks have become an important vehicle for communication. Many users on YouTube use comments to express opinions or critique a subject. The amount of comments, for famous videos and channels, is huge, which poses the challenge of analysing user opinions efficiently. This article proposes a sentiment analysis model of YouTube video comments, using a deep neural network. We employed an embedding layer to represent input text as a tensor, then we used a pair of convolutional layers to extract features and a fully connected layer to make the classification. The output of the neural network is the sentiment classification among negative, positive or neutral. Two videos were chosen and their comments were classified by our model, by an alternative statistical model and by humans. The human classification was considered to be 100% accurate. The results showed that our model achieves better accuracy than the statistical model, and the classification accuracy is in the range 60%–84%.

Keywords: Deep learning · Sentiment analysis ·
Deep neural networks · Opinion mining · Convolutional neural networks

1 Introduction

YouTube has become a popular form of entertainment. The term "YouTuber" is now considered a profession and many people create their videos to attract audiences and achieve monetisation through views, reputation and subscriptions on their respective channels [11].

Since YouTube is a reputation-driven platform, the income of a YouTube channel is proportional to its reputation. Hence, youtubers are continuously looking for ways to measure and increase their reputation, by adapting their content to the channel audience. However, there are few ways to measure reputation quantitatively.

Supported by Pontifical Catholic University of Rio de Janeiro
Supported by Intel® Corporation.

ⓒ Springer Nature Switzerland AG 2019
L. Rutkowski et al. (Eds.): ICAISC 2019, LNAI 11508, pp. 561–570, 2019.
https://doi.org/10.1007/978-3-030-20912-4_51

A simple way to analyse a video reputation is by the number of likes and dislikes it has. If the number of likes is much greater than the number of dislikes, then it is a good content, whereas the high number of dislikes compared to likes usually means a poor content. Although the number of likes of a video gives an overview of how successful the video is, it does not explain the underlying reasons for its success or failure.

Another way to determine a video reputation is to analyse its comments to understand how the viewers feel about the content. Before AI (artificial intelligence) and machine learning methods, it was a handmade analysis, which is barely able to review a few hundreds of comments per video. However, most big YouTube channels feature 1,000+ comments per video and posts at least 5 videos per week. Therefore, the task of hand-reviewing video comments is quickly becoming intractable and, as a consequence, machine reviewing is becoming a must-have business strategic asset for big YouTubers.

The present paper approaches an area under automatic machine reviewing of text known as sentiment analysis. In particular, we focus on the automatic classification of video comments into sentiment categories for three domains: (1) how the viewers feel about the video quality and the youtuber itself, (2) how the viewers feel about how well the topic is covered by the video, (3) how the viewers feel about how relevant the video is.

This kind of problem has been approached in the literature using machine learning. In [12], the authors combine lexical analysis and machine learning to classify sentiment polarity of Facebook messages, with 83% accuracy. In [7], the authors do opinion mining of app store comments. The goal is to automatically decide how the users feel about an app based on user reviews on the platform. The authors employed natural language processing and topic modelling techniques to extract both fine-grained and high-level features of each comment. They achieved a 59% classification accuracy analysing 7 apps from Google App Store and Apple Store user comments. In [19], the author did sentiment analysis of comments written in the Chinese language, using SVM (support vector machines) and Word2Vec. They claim high performance, achieving over 90% of accuracy in their dataset.

After the advent of deep neural networks, new studies in the field of opinion mining are emerging. The work [17] presents a deep neural network model to sentiment-analyse short texts. Moreover, [18] depicts a deep neural network for opinion mining of twitter posts. They mixed an unsupervised neural language model to determine word embeddings with a supervised deep neural network to do the actual classification. They claimed to be ranked number 2 among 11 teams on the Twitter Sentiment Analysis campaign organised by Semeval-2015 [4]. In [13], the authors do aspect mining of comments to determine what the users are complaining about. They employed a 7-layer deep convolutional neural network to tag each word in a sentence as an opinioned word or not. They combine this result with a set of linguistic patterns to develop a sentiment classifier. Their experiments applied the SemVal dataset [1] and another dataset developed by Qiu et al. [14]. The authors claimed to achieve better accuracy than state-of-the-art techniques.

Most works within the specific field of YouTube sentiment analysis do not use deep neural networks. The survey [6] reviews major contributions on sentiment analysis of YouTube comments and shows that all works are based on shallow neural networks, lexical analysis, clustering, Bayesian classifiers or other classical data mining tools.

In this context, we propose to employ deep neural networks to classify YouTube video comments written in Brazilian Portuguese language according to their writer sentiments. We used two particular videos with a high amount of comments from the channel "Joice Hasselmann", who is a journalist that posts about political facts of Brazil. This is the first work to merge sentiment analysis, YouTube comments and deep neural network classifiers.

2   Methodology

We seek to solve the problem of analysing user comments about a YouTube video, known beforehand, and classify them according to the following categories: (1) how the viewers feel about the video quality and the youtuber itself, (2) how the viewers feel about how well the topic is covered by the video, (3) how the viewers feel about how relevant the video is.

Each classification is represented by three possibilities: neutral, positive and negative.

We give a neutral classification to every comment that does not give an intuition about the feelings of its writer. For example, if we are to classify video quality and the user posts "I woke up too soon today", then this comment is assigned a neutral classification.

A positive classification is given to each comment that represents a compliment that has a relationship to the category. For instance, the post "great explanation about sports cars" is a positive comment when the category is category 2 and the video topic is sports cars.

Finally, we assign a negative classification whenever the comment represents a negative criticism about the video in the chosen classification domain.

Given a reference dataset of comments and corresponding classifications for a specific category, our AI model learns how to extract opinion features from the raw input text and then classify these features in a continuous scale within the real range $[-1; +1]$. The lower the value, the more negative is a comment; the higher the value, the more positive is a comment; 0 means a neutral comment.

Once our AI model learns from the reference dataset, we can use its inference ability to classify new posts under the specific domain used to train the AI. Therefore, for each chosen domain, there is a particular AI model instance.

Our AI model uses a combination of lexical analysis of the input text, automatic dictionary extraction of relevant words, automatic feature learning and a deep neural network. The following paragraphs explain each step of the classification process.

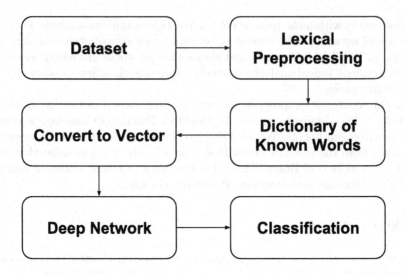

Fig. 1. Preprocessing scheme applied to original user comments.

The first step is a simple lexical preprocessing of the comment. It removes emoticons and special characters like #, , $, %, &. Then it splits hashtags into known words using a reference dictionary for the Portuguese language. Additionally, it removes words with no more than 1 letter, replaces unusual words with more common synonyms, and then removes words that appear only once.

These preprocessing tasks are employed to normalise the informal text used in YouTube posts before presenting them to the deep neural network. Since the neural network model learns from the association between sequences of words and the desired classification in the training dataset, unfrequent words or symbols tend to be useless for the learning process. Therefore, the preprocessing transform each original post into a normalised version of it, keeping the meaning and emotion.

Although this work is focused on the Portuguese language, all these preprocessing rules are applicable to the Spanish, English, French and German languages. The Fig. 2 shows our preprocessing scheme (Fig. 1).

The next step is to build a dictionary of known words. This dictionary should have words which meaning is learnable from our dataset. Therefore, unfrequent words should not be a part of this set. Hence, we build an N-sized set of the N more frequent words, where N is a positive integer parameter given beforehand. This set is our dictionary of valid words. After that, we remove unknown words (those that are not elements of the dictionary set) from the processed comments. Now the comments have only the more frequent words, which improves the learning capacity of the neural network, as discussed before.

At this point, we are able to convert our processed comments to a vector representation of dimensionality M. The integer M is chosen such that each comment is converted to an M-sized vector of integers with enough information for classification. Typically, M is the integer nearest to the average number of words in the comments of the processed dataset plus a standard deviation of that number. Thereafter, every word of each post is replaced by its numerical identification from our dictionary, and if the comment has less than M words, then the remaining positions are replaced by 0. Hence, every comment is now representable as an M-vector of integers, where 0 means no-word and any positive integer represents a particular word of our dictionary.

Now, we employ a 6-layer deep neural network to extract features and classify the input comment. The first layer is an embedding layer, useful for converting the M-sized representation to a more compact one, by removing unnecessary information. This layer is a deep learning version of the principal component analysis, that converts the input space to a new space of vectors with less dimensionality.

Next, a sequence of 2 convolution layers, of sizes 64 and 16, is used to extract different levels of features. The convolution layers are chosen because they are effective to extract features using much fewer neurons than traditional dense layers. Each layer specialises on a particular (unknown) feature, hence the more layers, the more features are extracted from the input vector. It is relevant to note that, unlike usual statistical models for classification, the neural network model does not require the input features, because it learns the features automatically using the convolutional layers. This kind of technique is the base of Artificial Intelligence: the machine model learns by example which features are useful for the classification it should perform. For a more thorough discussion on convolutional layers, please check [10].

After the convolutions, a dense layer of size 50 (50 neurons) is used to learn the association between the feature space and the output categories. This is a traditional non-linear classification layer. Finally, we add a dropout layer to avoid overfitting and a single neuron output layer with $tanh$-activation, to guarantee the output in the real range $[-1; +1]$. Then, one can use the real-valued output to measure how close to each category the input comment is, and then pick as the result the nearest of the 3 categories. The Fig. 2 depicts our deep neural network model.

Neural network training seeks to find the synapses and biases values that minimise the mean squared error of the classification of both the training set and the validation set. More details are provided in the Results section of this paper. The validation set is useful to avoid over-training the neural network, which typically provides poor inference performance.

3   Case Studies and Results

We studied two videos from the YouTube channel "Joice Hasselman":

1. #LulaNaCadeia: A ARRUAÇA DOS MORTADELAS E AS MANIFESTA-ÇÕES DO POVO DIA 24; [9] (in english: #LulaInJail: THE STREAM OF THE MORTADELLAS AND THE PEOPLE'S MANIFESTATIONS IN DAY 24)

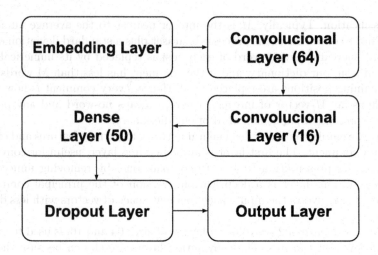

Fig. 2. Deep Neural Network Model

2. LULA ENTREGA PASSAPORTE; MPF SUGERE PRISÃO; FUGA ERA
   ÓBVIA. #JornalDaJoice [8] (in english: LULA DELIVERIES HIS PASS-
   PORT; MPF SUGGESTS PRISON; ESCAPE WAS OBVIOUS. #JoiceNews)

Each video has at least 1,000 comments. For each video, we hand-selected
a high amount of user comments (at least 700) and manually classified them
among negative/neutral/positive, using the numerical representation $-1/0/+1$,
as described in the Methodology section. Each manual classification was conducted three times, one for each category described in the Methodology section.

The manually created dataset was used for train, validation and test. From
the original dataset, we created a random partition using 70% of the data for
training, 20% for validation and 10% for testing. The training algorithm iteratively uses the training data to adapt the neural synapses to reduce the mean
squared error of predicting the classification of both the training data and the
validation data. It is a multiobjective minimisation problem that seeks to find
the synapses that minimise the mean squared error:

$$MSE = \frac{1}{N} \sum_{i=1}^{N} (f(x_i) - y_i)^2, \tag{1}$$

where x_i is the i-th input vector, y_i is its target classification value, and N is
the number of examples in the training or validation set. To avoid overfitting,
at each epoch the MSE of the validation set is computed and the optimisation
halts whenever the validation MSE increases. Therefore, we halt the optimisation
when both the validation and training errors reach a minimum.

To measure the quality of the model, we use the trained network to infer the
categories of the posts in the test set. We measure the mean squared error of
classification of the comments in the test set and the total classification error.

All the computer code of the proposed model was written in Python 3.6, using Intel® Python Distribution [2] and the Intel® Optimization for TensorFlow [3,5]. The software was run in high-end Intel® Xeon Platinum 8160 machines, awarded as a courtesy from Intel® Corporation to PUC-Rio. We also ran the proposed model on a Intel® i7 4770 CPU using the original Google TensorFlow distribution (not the Intel® Optimised version).

To compare our technique with others, this section also presents the accuracy of classification using a statistical Bayesian classifier, which employs a Gaussian mixture distribution and outputs the probability of each of the three categories. Then the category with the highest probability is selected as the result. The training uses maximum likelihood estimation and the union of the training and validation data. For more information about Bayesian classifiers, please check [15,16].

The following tables display the results of the classification for each video and each category.

Table 1. Category 1: how the viewers feel about the video quality and the youtuber itself – using the proposed model. Note: GTF means Google TensorFlow, ITF means Intel® TensorFlow.

	Training	Validation	Test
Accuracy (video 1)	97.05%	80%	84%
MSE (video 1)	0.0287	0.2159	-
Execution Time video 1 (GTF + i7 | ITF + Xeon)	132s | 69s	-	-
Accuracy (video 2)	98,18%	65%	73%
MSE (video 2)	0.0228	0.3753	-
Execution Time video 2 (GTF + i7 | ITF + Xeon)	118s | 55s	-	-

Table 2. Category 1: how the viewers feel about the video quality and the youtuber itself – using the statistical model

	Training	Test
Accuracy (video 1)	91.17%	79.22%
Execution Time video 1 (Intel i7)	71s	-
Accuracy (video 2)	83.66%	69.04%
Execution Time video 2 (Intel i7)	68s	-

Overall, Tables 1, 2, 3, 4, 5 and 6 show that the proposed model is superior to the statistical model in both accuracy and execution time (when considering the Xeon machine). The performance improvement from Google TensorFlow running on an i7 4770 CPU to Intel® Optimized TensorFlow on a Xeon Platinum 8160 CPU is due to the high parallelism and vectorisation capacity of the Xeon CPU

Table 3. Category 2: how the viewers feel about how well the topic is covered by the video – using the proposed model. Note: GTF means Google TensorFlow, ITF means Intel® TensorFlow.

	Training	Validation	Test
Accuracy (video 1)	93.29%	68%	61%
MSE (video 1)	0.0581	0.3348	-
Execution Time video 1 (GTF + i7 | ITF + Xeon)	148s | 91s	-	-
Accuracy (video 2)	93.29%	68%	62%
MSE (video 2)	0.0168	0.3481	-
Execution Time video 2 (GTF + i7 | ITF + Xeon)	141s | 85s	-	-

Table 4. Category 2: how the viewers feel about how well the topic is covered by the video – using the statistical model.

	Training	Test
Accuracy (video 1)	94.91%	60.07%
Execution Time video 1 (Intel i7)	81s	-
Accuracy (video 2)	90.63%	61.66%
Execution Time video 2 (Intel i7)	79s	-

Table 5. Category 3: how the viewers feel about how relevant the video is – using the proposed model. Note: GTF means Google TensorFlow, ITF means Intel® TensorFlow.

	Training	Validation	Test
Accuracy (video 1)	96.73%	79%	72%
MSE (video 1)	0.0397	0.1621	-
Execution Time video 1 (Google TF + i7 | Intel TF + Xeon)	112s | 63s	-	-
Accuracy (video 2)	98.05%	71%	64%
MSE (video 2)	0.0263	0.1950	-
Execution Time video 2 (GTF + i7 | ITF + Xeon)	123s | 70s	-	-

Table 6. Category 3: how the viewers feel about how relevant the video is – using the statistical model.

	Training	Test
Accuracy (video 1)	78.33%	57.92%
Execution Time video 1 (Intel i7)	75s	-
Accuracy (video 2)	93.86%	70.88%
Execution Time video 2 (Intel i7)	83s	-

and the very optimised Intel TensorFlow distribution. This is an advantage of the deep neural network model over the statistical model: the higher the CPU parallelism, the faster the neural network runs. Note that this is not true for the statistical model, which uses a sequential algorithm.

The results show that category 1 features the best accuracy. Its test set was 84% accurate, showing that the proposed model has a consistent predictive capability. On the other hand, it is also seen that the worst result belongs to category 2. We believe that this is because the content of most of the comments does not expose how well the youtuber exposes the main topic of the video. Hence, the neural network ends up having few examples to extract patterns that allow predicting sentiments related to this category.

4   Conclusions

In this work, we proposed a model for opinion mining of YouTube comments that is able to analyse user sentiments about the video. This model employs a preprocessing heuristics based on lexical analysis and then uses deep neural networks to predict user feelings from comments of any YouTube video. We considered 3 distinct categories and 2 videos, which had their comments manually selected and manually classified.

In both videos, the proposed model showed a good ability to predict user sentiments. We note that category 2 - in relation to content - is the most difficult to predict and we believe that this is due to the fact that we have few comments on our base so that the network is able to extract useful patterns. Moreover, the proposed model performed better than an alternative statistical Bayesian classifier based on Gaussian mixture distributions.

Hence, we conclude that our model has a good performance for predicting sentiment categories of YouTube videos comments. To improve the result, we suggest as future work to use a bigger dataset formed by the concatenation of comments from several videos so that the neural network can learn better with more vocabulary and better understand patterns of positivity or negativity. We also suggest investing more in preprocessing of the text. It is desirable to apply spelling and grammar correction, detection of spelling mistakes in proper names and treatment of language addictions.

References

1. Data and tools < semval 2014 task 4. http://alt.qcri.org/semeval2014/task4/index.php?id=data-and-tools. Accessed 20 Nov 2018
2. Intel distribution for python | intel software. https://software.intel.com/en-us/distribution-for-python
3. Intel optimization for tensorflow* installation guide. https://software.intel.com/en-us/articles/intel-optimization-for-tensorflow-installation-guide. Accessed May 2019
4. Semeval 2015 task 10: Sentiment analysis in twitter < semeval 2015 task 10. http://alt.qcri.org/semeval2015/task10/. Accessed 20 Nov 2018

5. Abadi, M., et al.: Tensorflow: large-scale machine learning on heterogeneous systems (2015). https://www.tensorflow.org/, software available from tensorflow.org
6. Asghar, M.Z., Ahmad, S., Marwat, A., Kundi, F.M.: Sentiment analysis on youtube: a brief survey. CoRR abs/1511.09142 (2015). http://arxiv.org/abs/1511.09142
7. Guzman, E., Maalej, W.: How do users like this feature? A fine grained sentiment analysis of app reviews. In: 2014 IEEE 22nd International Requirements Engineering Conference (RE), pp. 153–162. IEEE (2014)
8. Hasselman, J.: Lula entrega passaporte; mpf sugere prisão; fuga era óbvia. https://www.youtube.com/watch?v=JoIsGhHL9u8. Accessed 2018
9. Hasselman, J.: #lulanacadeia: A arruaça dos mortadelas e as manifestações do povo dia 24. https://www.youtube.com/watch?v=WSycy0oQITs. Accessed 2018
10. Huang, K., Hussain, A., Wang, Q.F., Zhang, R.: Deep Learning: Fundamentals, Theory and Applications., 1st edn. Springer International Publishing, Switzerland (2019)
11. Kim, J.: The institutionalization of youtube: from user-generated content to professionally generated content. Media, Cult. Soc. 34(1), 53–67 (2012). https://doi.org/10.1177/0163443711427199
12. Ortigosa, A., Martín, J.M., Carro, R.M.: Sentiment analysis in facebook and its application to e-learning. Comput. Hum. Behav. 31, 527–541 (2014)
13. Poria, S., Cambria, E., Gelbukh, A.: Aspect extraction for opinion mining with a deep convolutional neural network. Knowl.-Based Syst. 108, 42–49 (2016)
14. Qiu, G., Liu, B., Bu, J., Chen, C.: Opinion word expansion and target extraction through double propagation. Comput. Linguist. 37(1), 9–27 (2011). https://doi.org/10.1162/coli_a_00034
15. Rasmussen, C.E.: The infinite gaussian mixture model. In: Advances in Neural Information Processing Systems, pp. 554–560 (2000)
16. Reynolds, D.A., Rose, R.C.: Robust text-independent speaker identification using gaussian mixture speaker models. IEEE Trans. Speech Audio Process. 3(1), 72–83 (1995)
17. dos Santos, C., Gatti, M.: Deep convolutional neural networks for sentiment analysis of short texts. In: Proceedings of COLING 2014, the 25th International Conference on Computational Linguistics: Technical Papers, pp. 69–78 (2014)
18. Severyn, A., Moschitti, A.: Twitter sentiment analysis with deep convolutional neural networks. In: Proceedings of the 38th International ACM SIGIR Conference on Research and Development in Information Retrieval, SIGIR 2015, pp. 959–962. ACM, New York (2015). https://doi.org/10.1145/2766462.2767830
19. Zhang, D., Xu, H., Su, Z., Xu, Y.: Chinese comments sentiment classification based on word2vec and SVMperf. Expert Syst. Appl. 42(4), 1857–1863 (2015). https://doi.org/10.1016/j.eswa.2014.09.011. http://www.sciencedirect.com/science/article/pii/S0957417414005508d

Layered Geometric Learning

Hamideh Hajiabadi[1](✉), Reza Godaz[2], Morteza Ghasemi[2], and Reza Monsefi[2]

[1] Computer Engineering Department, Birjand University of Technology,
Birjand, Iran
hamideh.hajiabadi@mail.um.ac.ir
[2] Computer Engineering Department, Ferdowsi University of Mashhad (FUM),
Mashhad, Iran
{reza.godaz,morteza.ghasemi}@mail.um.ac.ir, monsefi@um.ac.ir

Abstract. Through Metric learning techniques, a metric function is learned, which shows how similar/dissimilar two samples are. From the perspective of feature selection, metric learning can be represented as a transform function mapping each sample into a new point in the new feature space. Geometric Mean Metric Learning (GMML) is one of promising methods which achieve good performance in terms of accuracy and time complexity. In this paper, we propose the use of GMML algorithm in a neural network to perform Riemannian computing on the SPD matrices which improves accuracy and reduces time complexity. We also use the eigenvalue rectification layer as a non-linear activation function to enhance the non-linearity of our model. Experimental evaluations on several benchmark data sets demonstrate that the proposed method improves accuracy in comparison with the state-of-the-art approaches.

Keywords: Metric learning · Geometric metric learning ·
Artificial Neural Network

1 Introduction

Metric Learning is a kind of data transform method, which makes similar instances closer and dissimilar ones farther. The transformed data is later used in learning algorithms (e.g., classification, regression, etc.). Metric learning can be interpreted as a feature learning [17] which maps data to a new space hoping that in the new feature space, data would be better represented (e.g., Mahalanobis distance metric). Metric learning which learns the similarity/distance metric from the annotated data is of significant practical importance, which can be considered as a pre-process of variety tasks, e.g., classification, clustering, feature extraction, feature matching, etc., [7,13,18,25]. Moreover, metric learning approaches can overcome the challenges of extreme classification [8].

Currently, best metric learning approaches make use of state-of-the-art Artificial Neural Networks (ANN), which produces the best embedding by minimizing a loss function (which is usually related to the similarity/ distance of the points) [20,21]. However, most of these techniques learn a Mahalanobis distance in the

© Springer Nature Switzerland AG 2019
L. Rutkowski et al. (Eds.): ICAISC 2019, LNAI 11508, pp. 571–582, 2019.
https://doi.org/10.1007/978-3-030-20912-4_52

Euclidean space, which can be interpreted as a linear mapping of the data. These techniques have achieved an improvement in both modeling and the algorithm.

Most deep metric learning approaches learn a Euclidean metric in a mapped space [2]. The mapped space is either a linear transform of the original space or a non-linear one. Let $x \in \mathcal{R}^d$ be an instance in the origin space and $\phi(x)$ be the corresponding instance in the mapped space, where $\phi(.)$ is either a linear function represented by $\phi(x) = A \times x$ or a non-linear function. The conventional Euclidean distance $\|\phi(x) - \phi(y)\|$ can be still used in the mapped space to estimate how dissimilar two instances are [22,26]. More precisely, letting x, y denote two samples in $\mathcal{R}^d$ space, we denote $(x-y)M(x-y)^T$ as the distance between those two samples where $M \in \mathcal{R}^{d \times d}$ is a Symmetric Positive Definite (SPD) matrix. The distance can be interpreted as a Euclidean distance, $\|\phi(x) - \phi(y)\|$, in the mapped space $\phi(.)$ where $\phi(x) = M^{\frac{1}{2}}x$. Since the distance is positive, the matrix learned through the metric learning ought to be an SPD matrix to confirm the positiveness of the distance. Some researchers make the learned matrix, symmetric-positive definite by setting the negative eigenvalues to 0, which might lead to ambiguity. This ambiguity can be prevented by making matrix space a Riemannian manifold.

In this paper, we revisit the structure of neural network and present a new ANN architecture based on geometric learning algorithms. In our proposed model, several metric learning layers are used. Each metric layer can be a new representation of a metric learning algorithm having a closed-form optimization on an SPD manifold. Through comprehensive experiments, we show the use of SPD manifold improves the performance of a ANN by experimentally evaluation on several benchmark datasets. Our main contribution is the use of geometric learning algorithms as new mertic layers in a neural network. These new layers include a Geometric Metric Mean Learning (GMML) as a transform function followed by a ReEig layer [15] which transforms data into a new space.

The rest of this paper is organized as follows. An overview of related work is briefly introduced in Sect. 2. We describe our proposed model in Sect. 3. Experimental evaluations are illustrated in Sect. 4. Finally, Sect. 5 contains conclusion with possible remarks for future works.

2   Related Works

In this section, we briefly review the promising deep distance metric learning algorithms and then concentrate on the geometric learning.

2.1   Deep Metric Learning

Since 2014 deep metric learning have been attracted by many researchers [9,10,14,19,22,24] and the idea of integrating metric learning into deep networks was first proposed in 1994 [6]. Faraki et al. combine geometrically dimension reduction and metric learning method and then integrate it into a deep framework [11]. They use Riemannian manifolds in their optimization algorithm [1] and achieve improvements.

In paper [14], a nonlinear manifold of similar face images by applying distance metric learning approaches into deep learning is learned. A joint loss function containing a logistic loss and a regularization term of network weights and biases are used. A new structure for feature embedding which learns full advantages of batches through training phase was proposed in 2016 [18]. First, some positive pairs are randomly selected and then the distances between those selected pairs and all negative pairs are calculated using $log - sum - exp$ formula.

An interesting metric learning approach which learns a map function transferring each sample to a new point in the mapped space was proposed in 2017 [22]. Some benefits of this work are as follows:- (1) A new loss is proposed which is not based on pairs or triples; therefore, data are not needed to be pre-processed to extract pairs or triples like other existing metric learning approaches. (2) During learning of embedding space, the network is encouraged to optimize a global metric for clustering; this method uses the global structure of embedding space to learn a quality metric for clustering.

An online deep metric learning framework was proposed in 2018 [16]. It consists of several metric layers in a neural network and each metric layer is actually an existing online metric learning algorithm which can be optimized in a closed form. Each metric layer is followed by a nonlinear function like $ReLu$. Let x^0, x^1 are the input and the output of the first metric layer respectively, the output is calculated as $x^1 = L^t x^0$ while $L^t L = M$ and M is the metric matrix which is calculated in a closed form optimization. The network is only updated through the forward pass. In the next subsection, We briefly overview some pioneer works that apply geometry to metric learning approaches.

2.2 Geometric Metric Learning

In 2016, a Mahalanobis-Based cost function named Geometric Mean Metric Learning (GMML) was proposed [26]. They revisited the convenient Euclidean-based optimization procedure and proposed a new geometric learning method on SPD manifolds. They then reached a geometrical closed-form solution for the Metric Learning problem, which significantly reduces the time complexity. In [23] a new local method based on GMML named L-GMML was introduced and applied to the task of ranking. Some local matrices and a corresponding anchor document were first learned and then the anchors were weighted.

A new Riemannian network architecture for deep networks using SPD matrices was proposed in [15]. They introduced some new geometric layers such as bi-linear mapping layers (BiMap), eigenvalue rectification layers (ReEig), and an eigenvalue logarithm layer (LogEig). In the following, these three layers are briefly explained.

BitMap Layer. The BiMap layer transforms an input SPD matrix to a new more compact matrix with higher ability to discriminate data. This layer uses a bi-linear mapping function f_b as follows

$$\boldsymbol{X}^k = f_b(\boldsymbol{X}^{k-1}; \boldsymbol{W}^k) = \boldsymbol{W}^k \boldsymbol{X}^{k-1} \boldsymbol{W}^{k^T} \tag{1}$$

where $\boldsymbol{X}^{k-1} \in \mathrm{Sym}^+_{d_{k-1}}$ is the input matrix of k-th layer, $\boldsymbol{W}^k \in R^{d_k \times d_{k-1}}_*, d_k <$ d_{k-1} is the connection weights and $\boldsymbol{X}^k \in R^{d_k \times d_k}$ is the output of the layer.

ReEig Layer. The ReEig layer makes input SPD matrices far away from nonpositive ones and it is formulated as follows

$$\boldsymbol{X}^k = f^{(k)}_r(\boldsymbol{X}^{k-1}) = \boldsymbol{U}^{k-1} \max(\epsilon \boldsymbol{I}, \boldsymbol{\Sigma}^{k-1}) \boldsymbol{U}^{k-1^T} \tag{2}$$

where $\boldsymbol{U}^{k-1}$ and $\boldsymbol{\Sigma}^{k-1}$ are the output of the eigenvalue decomposition and $\boldsymbol{X}^{k-1} = \boldsymbol{U}^{k-1} \boldsymbol{\Sigma}^{k-1} \boldsymbol{U}^{k-1^T}$. ϵ denotes as a rectification threshold, $\boldsymbol{I}$ is Identity matrix and $\max(\epsilon \boldsymbol{I}, \boldsymbol{\Sigma}^{k-1})$ is a diagonal matrix which is defined as follows:-

$$\boldsymbol{A}(i,i) = \begin{cases} \boldsymbol{\Sigma}^{k-1}(i,i) & , \boldsymbol{\Sigma}^{k-1}(i,i) > \epsilon \\ \epsilon & , \boldsymbol{\Sigma}^{k-1}(i,i) \leq \epsilon \end{cases} \tag{3}$$

LogEig Layer. The LogEig layer is defined as the following.

$$\boldsymbol{X}^k = f^{(k)}_l(\boldsymbol{X}^{k-1}) = \log(\boldsymbol{X}^{k-1}) = \boldsymbol{U}^{k-1} \log(\epsilon \boldsymbol{I}, \boldsymbol{\Sigma}^{k-1}) \boldsymbol{U}^{k-1^T} \tag{4}$$

where $\log(\boldsymbol{X}^{k-1})$ is the logarithm of diagonal elements. According to [3] this metric layer (Log-Euclidean Riemannian metric) provide a lie group structure to the Riemannian manifold of SPD matrices. As a result, the SPD manifold is reduced to a flat space in which conventional Euclidean computations can be simply conducted and there is no need to take the pain to do Riemannian operations such as geodesic calculations.

Riemannian Manifold Metric Learning (RMML) aims to reduce the geodesic distance of similar pairs while increasing the geometric distance of dissimilar ones on nonlinear manifolds. RMML is extended for both SPD and Grassmann manifolds, [27].

3 The Proposed Model

As discussed earlier, the aim of the metric learning approaches is to eventually obtain a metric that gives "small" distance for similar points and "large" distance for dissimilar ones. Different metric learning approaches are willing to fulfill this guideline implicitly or explicitly. Figure 1 shows the impact of learning a metric matrix M based on Mahalanobis distance.

In the Mahalanobis-based metric learning approaches, it is intended to find a matrix M through training stage where distance between ith and jth samples are defined as $d_M = (\boldsymbol{x}_i - \boldsymbol{x}_j)^T M (\boldsymbol{x}_i - \boldsymbol{x}_j)$. Matrix M must be an SPD matrix, so

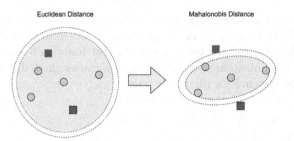

Fig. 1. Mahalanobis-based metric learning

there is a matrix W such that $W^T W = M$. We revisit the Mahalanobis distance as follows

$$
\begin{aligned}
d_M &= (\boldsymbol{x}_i - \boldsymbol{x}_j)^T W^T W (\boldsymbol{x}_i - \boldsymbol{x}_j) \\
&= (W\boldsymbol{x}_i - W\boldsymbol{x}_j)^T (W\boldsymbol{x}_i - W\boldsymbol{x}_j) \\
&= \| W\boldsymbol{x}_i - W\boldsymbol{x}_j \|_2^2.
\end{aligned}
\tag{5}
$$

We interpret $W\boldsymbol{x}_i$ as the transformed point of the original point $\boldsymbol{x}_i$ and $\| W\boldsymbol{x}_i - W\boldsymbol{x}_j \|_2^2$ as the Euclidean distance in the transformed space. So, using metric learning algorithms, data are implicitly transformed to a new space, hoping that the data would be more discriminated in the transformed space.

We propose incorporating metric learning algorithms into neural networks by introducing a geometric layer. Let $x^{(i)}$ and $x^{(i+1)} = Wx^{(i)}$ be the input and the output of the ith metric layer respectively where $M = W^t W$ is the metric matrix. Matrix M is an SPD matrix which is learned through a closed-form optimization on the SPD manifold. We use a closed-form geometric metric optimization algorithm (GMML) that has been proposed in [26]. In the following, we explain the process that has been conducted in each metric layer.

In each metric layer, we wish to find a matrix M that decrease the sum of distances over all similar points while M^{-1} increase the sum of distances over dissimilar pairs simultaneously. We propose the use of the following objective function like that was proposed by [26].

$$
\min_{M \succ 0} \sum_{(\boldsymbol{x}_i, \boldsymbol{x}_j) \in \mathcal{S}} d_M(\boldsymbol{x}_i, \boldsymbol{x}_j) + \sum_{(\boldsymbol{x}_i, \boldsymbol{x}_j) \in \mathcal{D}} d_{M^{-1}}(\boldsymbol{x}_i, \boldsymbol{x}_j)
\tag{6}
$$

where $\mathcal{S}$, $\mathcal{D}$ are sets of similar indices and dissimilar indices respectively. $d_M(\boldsymbol{x}_i, \boldsymbol{x}_j)$ is the distance between $\boldsymbol{x}_i$ and $\boldsymbol{x}_j$ and defined as $(\boldsymbol{x}_i - \boldsymbol{x}_j)M(\boldsymbol{x}_i - \boldsymbol{x}_j)^T$.

In the Euclidean space, the gradient of $d_M(\boldsymbol{x}_i, \boldsymbol{x}_j)$ with respect to M is

$$
(\boldsymbol{x}_i, \boldsymbol{x}_j)(\boldsymbol{x}_i, \boldsymbol{x}_j)^T
$$

while the gradient of $d_{M^{-1}}(\boldsymbol{x}_i, \boldsymbol{x}_j)$ is

$$
-M^{-1}(\boldsymbol{x}_i, \boldsymbol{x}_j)(\boldsymbol{x}_i, \boldsymbol{x}_j)^T M^{-1}
$$

The inner product of those two gradients is negative, so, they are in the opposite direction and an increase in the gradient of M cause a decrease in that of M^{-1}. Since the first and second terms of the cost function 6 are in the opposite direction, the minimization of the cost function causes small distance for similar pairs and large distance for dissimilar ones.

The Eq. 6 can be reformulated as follows:

$$\min_{M \succ 0} \sum_{(\boldsymbol{x}_i, \boldsymbol{x}_j) \in \mathcal{S}} tr \left(M(\boldsymbol{x}_i - \boldsymbol{x}_j)(\boldsymbol{x}_i - \boldsymbol{x}_j)^t \right)$$

$$+ \sum_{(\boldsymbol{x}_i, \boldsymbol{x}_j) \in \mathcal{D}} tr \left(M^{-1}(\boldsymbol{x}_i - \boldsymbol{x}_j)(\boldsymbol{x}_i - \boldsymbol{x}_j)^t \right) \tag{7}$$

where $tr(.)$ is the summation of diagonal elements. By considering

$$S := \sum_{(\boldsymbol{x}_i, \boldsymbol{x}_j) \in \mathcal{S}} (\boldsymbol{x}_i - \boldsymbol{x}_j)(\boldsymbol{x}_i - \boldsymbol{x}_j)^T,$$

$$D := \sum_{(\boldsymbol{x}_i, \boldsymbol{x}_j) \in \mathcal{D}} (\boldsymbol{x}_i - \boldsymbol{x}_j)(\boldsymbol{x}_i - \boldsymbol{x}_j)^T \tag{8}$$

in which $\mathcal{S}$ and $\mathcal{D}$ are:

$$\mathcal{S} := \{(\boldsymbol{x}_i, \boldsymbol{x}_j) | \boldsymbol{x}_i \text{ and } \boldsymbol{x}_j \text{ are in the same class}\},$$
$$\mathcal{D} := \{(\boldsymbol{x}_i, \boldsymbol{x}_j) | \boldsymbol{x}_i \text{ and } \boldsymbol{x}_j \text{ are in different classes}\}. \tag{9}$$

The Eq. 7 is briefed as

$$\min_{M \succ 0} \ \operatorname{tr}(MS) + \operatorname{tr}(M^{-1}D). \tag{10}$$

To achieve the optimal solution for Eq. (10), we set its derivative to zero. Derivative of Eq. (10) with respect to matrix M is as follows

$$S - M^{-1}DM^{-1} = 0 \Rightarrow MSM = D. \tag{11}$$

To obtain matrix M from the above equation, both $D \succeq 0$ and $S \succeq 0$ should hold, and it results in a positive distance as described in the following:

$$S^{1/2}MSMS^{1/2} = S^{1/2}DS^{1/2} \Rightarrow$$
$$(S^{1/2}MSMS^{1/2})^{1/2} = (S^{1/2}DS^{1/2})^{1/2} \Rightarrow$$
$$(S^{1/2}MS^{1/2}S^{1/2}MS^{1/2})^{1/2} = (S^{1/2}DS^{1/2})^{1/2} \Rightarrow$$
$$(S^{1/2}MS^{1/2}) = (S^{1/2}DS^{1/2})^{1/2} \Rightarrow \tag{12}$$
$$S^{-1/2}(S^{1/2}MS^{1/2})S^{-1/2} = S^{-1/2}(S^{1/2}DS^{1/2})^{1/2}S^{-1/2} \Rightarrow$$
$$M = S^{-1/2}(S^{1/2}DS^{1/2})^{1/2}S^{-1/2}$$

The last equation is indeed the midpoint of the geodesic joining S^{-1} to D [4]. Therefore, the obtained result automatically satisfies the constraint of $M \succeq 0$. Figure 2 shows the proposed architecture which is a conventional ANN extended with several metric layers.

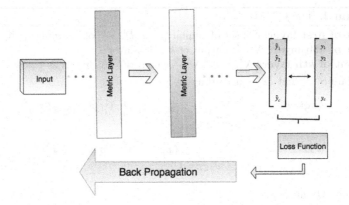

Fig. 2. Our proposed architecture

3.1 The Proposed Geometric Network

We propose a Geometric network based on SPD manifolds. We put a GMML layer as a metric layer followed by a ReEig layer. These successive layers are repeated through the network. It is noted that GMML method is fast and lead to accurate results and can be optimized in a closed-form way.

Typical neural networks apply a Stochastic Gradient Descent (SGD) algorithm for backpropagation that uses the gradient of the loss function and a learning rate to create a descent step [12], which ultimately reduces the value of loss function. In the forward path, a predicted label is produced and then is compared with the desired one to obtain the error. Afterward, the gradient of the loss function flow back through the network and update all the weights in the opposite direction of the gradient to reduce the loss value.

Alternatively, we propose to update the weights of the geometric metric layers by a closed-form optimization in two steps as follows. We first obtain the optimal matrix, M, by optimizing Eq. (7) which leads to Eq. (10). Then, as demonstrated in Eq. (5), the optimal weights of the metric layers are obtained by $W = M^{\frac{1}{2}}$. By doing so, there is no more need to update metric layers' weights through back-propagation.

As it is shown in Eq. (5), each metric layer implicitly transforms data into the new space, $X_{new} = W X_{old}$, hoping that the data in the new space would be more discriminative. W is obtained by the decomposition of the metric matrix M where $M = W^T W$. Two matrices M and W have the same dimension. The optimal value of M is obtained according to Eq. (12). We calculate the output of a metric layer by $x^{k+1} = W x^k$ where x^k is the input of the layer. The process is shown in Algorithm 1. If each metric layer is convex we will advance of using a closed-form optimization to reach a simple and global optimal value. The prove of convexity for GMML is straightforward, since it is the summation of two convex function [5]. Note that other closed form metric learning algorithm can be used instead of GMML.

Algorithm 1. The GMML Layer

Input of first layer: $\mathcal{S}^0$: set of similar pairs, $\mathcal{D}^0$: set of dissimilar pairs
Input of kth layer: X^{k-1}: output of $k - 1$th layer
Output of kth layer: $X^k = W^k X^{k-1}$ where W^k calculates as below

1: Calculate S^{k-1} and D^{k-1} according to

$$S^{k-1} := \sum_{(x_i^{k-1}, x_j^{k-1}) \in \mathcal{S}^{k-1}} (x_i^{k-1} - x_j^{k-1})(x_i^{k-1} - x_j^{k-1})^T,$$

$$D^{k-1} := \sum_{(x_i^{k-1}, x_j^{k-1}) \in \mathcal{D}^{k-1}} (x_i^{k-1} - x_j^{k-1})(x_i^{k-1} - x_j^{k-1})^T \tag{13}$$

2: Compute M^k as:

$$M^k = (S^{k-1})^{-1/2}((S^{k-1})^{1/2} D^{k-1} (S^{k-1})^{1/2})^{1/2} (S^{k-1})^{-1/2} \tag{14}$$

3: Decompose matrix $M^k = (W^k)^T (W^k)$ to obtain W^k
4: Compute the output of GMML layer as $X^k = W^k X^{k-1}$

The ReLU layer in typical neural networks includes $max(0, x)$ non-linearity. This layer is used to improve the non-linearity of the network. In the [15], the ReLU layer is replaced by a new geometric layer called ReEig. This layer recti-fies the small positive eigenvalues. We use ReEig layer instead of simple ReLu to enhance the non-linearity of the network. This layer has been defined in Eqs. (2) and (3). It prevents the input SPD matrices from having non-positive Eigenval-ues. Our proposed GMML layer and ReEig layer has been implemented in the Algorithm 1 and Algorithm 2 respectively.

Algorithm 2. The kth ReEig Layer

Input: X^{k-1}, ϵ: a rectification threshold
Output: X^k

1: Decompose $\boldsymbol{X}^{k-1}$ as $\boldsymbol{X}^{k-1} = U^{k-1} \Sigma^{k-1} (U^{k-1})^T$
2: Calculate $\boldsymbol{X}^k$ as $\boldsymbol{X}^k = f_r^{(k)}(\boldsymbol{X}^{k-1}) = U^{k-1} \max(\epsilon \boldsymbol{I}, \Sigma^{k-1})(U^{k-1})^T$ where

$$A(i,i) = \begin{cases} \Sigma^{k-1}(i,i) & , \Sigma^{k-1}(i,i) > \epsilon \\ \epsilon & , \Sigma^{k-1}(i,i) \leq \epsilon \end{cases}$$

In Fig. 2 we propose a back-propagation stage based on the SGD algorithm that can accelerate the convergence speed. As the forward propagation in the geometric layers can find new feature spaces through the close-form optimization, the back-propagation for these layers can be omitted. In the experiments, we do not use backpropagation for metric layers.

4   Experiments

In this section, we evaluate how our proposed method works in a simple classification problem. The proposed approach is evaluated on several small benchmark datasets described in Table 1 with some statistics about each.

Table 1. Description about chosen datasets

Name	# of input	# of Classes	Dimension
Breast-cancer	569	2	30
Wine	178	3	13
Iris	150	3	4
Vehicle	846	4	18
Vowel	990	11	14
German	1000	2	24

We have incorporated our proposed metric learning architecture into a Multi Layers Perceptron (MLP) to learn a metric and then classify data in the new learned space. We have first set up a network containing two metric learning layers (GMML + ReEng layer) followed by a simple MLP. The employed MLP is a network with two hidden layers including 20, 10 nodes respectively. The gradient of the Cross-entropy loss function is used for error back-propagation. In all experiments, we have used 10 fold cross validation for model selection. It means that the original dataset is partitioned into 10 disjoint subsets where 9 subsets have been used for training and the remaining one for testing.

The data have been initially normalized. Table 2 shows the experimental results on six benchmark datasets. We have compared our model with three promising metric learning algorithms including GMML, LMNN, ITML. The results show that our model performs better than others in all datasets. Results for the other methods are based on the experiments reported by [26].

Table 2. Comparison with the state-of-the-art metric learning methods

Name	GMML	ITML	LMNN	OURS
Wine	0.96	0.92	0.94	**0.96**
Iris	0.97	0.974	0.95	**0.98**
Breast cancer	0.96	0.92	0.91	**0.99**
Vehicle	0.78	0.70	0.77	**0.81**
Vowel	0.57	0.56	0.53	**0.6**
German	0.72	0.705	0.71	**0.78**

We also have explored how the number of constraints would affect the accuracy of the classification. We first picked 30% of data randomly and make similar and dissimilar sets over the selected data. We gradually increase the number of constraints and investigate the effect of increased constraints on the classification. We first pick 30% of data to generate similar and dissimilar pairs over them and explore how our proposed model work on this configuration. Figure 3 shows how an increase in the number of constraints affects the performance of the classifier.

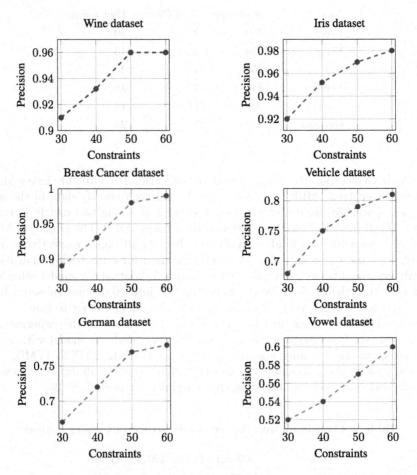

Fig. 3. Horizontal axis represents the percentage of data which are used for constraints and the vertical axis represents the precision

5   Conclusion

In this paper, we have proposed a new neural network architecture based on metric learning approaches which are updated on the SPD manifold. We focused on classification tasks and it is considered as an initial attempt to explore the use of geometric learning on neural networks. Our proposed method has been implemented and evaluated on several benchmark datasets which showed a significant improvement in comparison with the state-of-the-art metric learning algorithms. We also explored how the number of constraints affects the performance of the classifier. As a future work, we aim to integrate this architecture into more complicated deep networks. Also, we plan to incorporate more metric learning algorithms into the proposed model.

References

1. Absil, P.-A., Mahony, R., Sepulchre, R.: Optimization Algorithms on Matrix Manifolds. Princeton University Press, Princeton (2009)
2. Altiotancay, H.: Improving the k-nearest neighbour rule: using geometrical neighbourhoods and manifold-based metrics. Expert Syst. **28**(4), 391–406 (2011)
3. Arsigny, V., Fillard, P., Pennec, X., Ayache, N.: Geometric means in a novel vector space structure on symmetric positive-definite matrices. SIAM J. Matrix Anal. Appl. **29**(1), 328–347 (2007)
4. Bhatia, R.: Positive Definite Matrices, vol. 24. Princeton University Press, Princeton (2009)
5. Boyd, S., Vandenberghe, L.: Convex Optimization. Cambridge University Press, Cambridge (2004)
6. Bromley, J., Guyon, I., LeCun, Y., Säckinger, E., Shah, R.: Signature verification using a "siamese" time delay neural network. In: Advances in Neural Information Processing Systems, pp. 737–744 (1994)
7. Chopra, S., Hadsell, R., LeCun, Y.: Learning a similarity metric discriminatively, with application to face verification. In: 2005 IEEE Computer Society Conference on Computer Vision and Pattern Recognition CVPR 2005, vol. 1, pp. 539–546. IEEE (2005)
8. Choromanska, A., Agarwal, A., Langford, J.: Extreme multi class classification. In: NIPS Workshop: eXtreme Classification, vol. 1, pp. 1–2 (2013)
9. Coskun, H., Tan, D.J., Conjeti, S., Navab, N., Tombari, F.: Human motion analysis with deep metric learning. In: Ferrari, V., Hebert, M., Sminchisescu, C., Weiss, Y. (eds.) Computer Vision – ECCV 2018. LNCS, vol. 11218, pp. 693–710. Springer, Cham (2018). https://doi.org/10.1007/978-3-030-01264-9_41
10. Duan, Y., Zheng, W., Lin, X., Lu, J., Zhou, J.: Deep adversarial metric learning. In: Proceedings of the IEEE Conference on Computer Vision and Pattern Recognition, pp. 2780–2789 (2018)
11. Faraki, M., Harandi, M.T., Porikli, F.: Large-scale metric learning: a voyage from shallow to deep. IEEE Trans. Neural Netw. Learn. Syst. **29**(9), 4339–4346 (2018)
12. Hajiabadi, H., Monsefi, R., Yazdi, H.S.: Relf: robust regression extended with ensemble loss function. Appl. Intell. **49**, 1–14 (2018)
13. Hershey, J.R., Chen, Z., Roux, J.L., Watanabe, S.: Deep clustering: discriminative embeddings for segmentation and separation. In: 2016 IEEE International Conference on Acoustics, Speech and Signal Processing (ICASSP), pp. 31–35. IEEE (2016)
14. Hu, J., Lu, J., Tan, Y.-P.: Discriminative deep metric learning for face verification in the wild. In: Proceedings of the IEEE Conference on Computer Vision and Pattern Recognition, pp. 1875–1882 (2014)

15. Huang, Z., Van Gool, L.J.: A riemannian network for SPD matrix learning. In: AAAI, vol. 1, p. 3 (2017)
16. Li, W., Huo, J., Shi, Y., Gao, Y., Wang, L., Luo, J.: Online deep metric learning. arXiv preprint arXiv:1805.05510 (2018)
17. Lin, W.-C., Lu, Y.-H., Tsai, C.-F.: Feature selection in single and ensemble learning-based bankruptcy prediction models. Expert Syst. **36**(1), e12335 (2019)
18. Oh Song, H., Xiang, Y., Jegelka, S., Savarese, S.: Deep metric learning via lifted structured feature embedding. In: Proceedings of the IEEE Conference on Computer Vision and Pattern Recognition, pp. 4004–4012 (2016)
19. Schroff, F., Kalenichenko, D., Philbin, J.: Facenet: a unified embedding for face recognition and clustering. In: Proceedings of the IEEE Conference on Computer Vision and Pattern Recognition, pp. 815–823 (2015)
20. Simonyan, K., Zisserman, A.: Very deep convolutional networks for large-scale image recognition. arXiv preprint arXiv:1409.1556 (2014)
21. Sohn, K.: Improved deep metric learning with multi-class n-pair loss objective. In: Advances in Neural Information Processing Systems, pp. 1857–1865 (2016)
22. Oh Song, H., Jegelka, S., Rathod, V., Murphy, K.: Deep metric learning via facility location. In: Computer Vision and Pattern Recognition (CVPR), vol. 8 (2017)
23. Su, Y., King, I., Lyu, M.: Learning to rank using localized geometric mean metrics. arXiv preprint arXiv:1705.07563 (2017)
24. Sun, Y., Chen, Y., Wang, X., Tang, X.: Deep learning face representation by joint identification-verification. In: Advances in Neural Information Processing Systems, pp. 1988–1996 (2014)
25. Yen, I.E.-H., Huang, X., Ravikumar, P., Zhong, K., Dhillon, I.: Pd-sparse: a primal and dual sparse approach to extreme multiclass and multilabel classification. In: International Conference on Machine Learning, pp. 3069–3077 (2016)
26. Zadeh, P., Hosseini, R., Sra, S.: Geometric mean metric learning. In: International Conference on Machine Learning, pp. 2464–2471 (2016)
27. Zhu, P., Cheng, H., Hu, Q., Wang, Q., Zhang, C.: Towards generalized and efficient metric learning on riemannian manifold. In: IJCAI, pp. 3235–3241 (2018)

Fast Algorithm for Prototypes Selection—Trust-Margin Prototypes

Norbert Jankowski[✉] and Marek Orliński

Department of Informatics, Nicolaus Copernicus University, Toruń, Poland
norbert@is.umk.pl

Abstract. The k nearest neighbour method (kNN) can be used not only on an entire data set, but also after a selection of instances is performed. Selection of instances should select prototypes which well represent the knowledge about a given problem. We propose a new algorithm of prototype selection. The algorithm is based on selection of instances which represent the borders between classes and additionally they are *trustworthy* instances. Moreover, our algorithm was optimized with a forest of dedicated locality sensitive hashing (LSH) trees to speed up the prototype selection and the classification process. The algorithm's final expected complexity is $O(m \log m)$. Additionally, results show that the new algorithm lays ground for accurate classification.

1 Introduction

Let us assume that we have a learning data set $\mathcal{D} = \{\langle \mathbf{x}_i, y_i \rangle : i = 1, \ldots, m\}$ where $\mathbf{x}_i \in R^n$ are the input vectors and $y_i \in [1, \ldots, c]$ are the class labels. Selection of instances (prototypes) means that we are looking for a subset $S \subseteq \mathcal{D}$ which is enough to build a trustworthy classifier upon, for example a k nearest neighbour (kNN) classifier [1]. There are a few purposes to use instance selection. One is to remove noise or outliers to simplify the learning and classification process. Methods relevant to that use case can be seen as a filter methods. Good examples of such algorithms are the ENN [2], RNN [3] or ENRBF [4]. Another (and even more interesting) group of instance selection methods are algorithms which select a possibly small subset of $\mathcal{D}$, usually no more than around 20% of instance count. Those method we will call the prototype selection methods. Nowadays there are dozens of prototype selection algorithms, but is hard to say that all of them are really practical. We would like to recommend articles devoted to prototype selection algorithms [5–9]. In case of many of the algorithms, unfortunately, if they are accurate then their learning time is (extremely) long or the obtained reduction rate is small. Sometimes if the learning time is short then the accuracy is too poor. For example in the article [10], the authors present a method which is fast ($O(m \log m)$) and quite accurate but the reduction is average (between filter methods and prototype selection). Basing on the article by Garcia et al. [5] we made a summary in Table 1.

Column *acc* shows averaged classification accuracies on test portions from cross-validation, column *red* shows average reduction rates of a given method,

© Springer Nature Switzerland AG 2019
L. Rutkowski et al. (Eds.): ICAISC 2019, LNAI 11508, pp. 583–594, 2019.
https://doi.org/10.1007/978-3-030-20912-4_53

Table 1. The accuracies, reduction rates and times on average data sets.

Large datasets			
Method	acc	red.	time	ref
RNG	0.82	**0.2**	14635	[11]
SSMA	0.817	0.984	**45193**	[12]
RMHC	0.813	0.9	**77260**	[13]
1NN	0.8			
HMNEI	0.801	**0.6**	80	[14]
DROP3	0.795	0.884	16899	[6]
CCIS	0.795	0.92	1349	[15]
FCNN	0.777	**0.695**	100	[16]

Average datasets			
Method	acc	red.	time	ref
RMHC	0.83	0.9	**12028**	[13]
SSMA	0.829	0.98	**6306**	[12]
RNG	0.823	**0.116**	**1866**	[11]
HMNEI	0.818	**0.535**	28.98	[14]

Method	acc	red.	time	ref
ModelCS	0.816	**0.065**	15.46	[17]
CHC	0.809	0.991	**6803**	[18]
GGA	0.808	0.908	**21262**	[19]
1NN	0.806			
AllKNN	0.805	**0.21**	24.6	[20]
POP	0.803	**0.08**	0.17	[21]
RNN	0.802	0.945	**24480**	[3]
IB3	0.801	**0.767**	6.61	[20]
MSS	0.801	**0.573**	7.9	[22]
FCNN	0.796	**0.76**	3.2	[16]
CNN	0.791	**0.737**	1.1	[23]
MENN	0.784	**0.314**	37	[24]
Cpruner	0.76	0.889	35.3	[25]
Reconsistent	0.75	**0.68**	1621	[26]
DROP3	0.743	0.89	160	[6]
CCIS	0.713	0.95	12.4	[15]
MCNN	0.68	0.991	4.4	[27]
ICF	0.678	0.8	93	[28]

column *time* is the learning time in seconds. Given the above comments and an analysis of the results presented in the last Tables, we construct a new algorithm of an expected complexity of $O(m \log m)$ which is characterized by a good reduction and possibly high accuracy.

2   Trust-Margin Prototypes

For almost all known instance selection algorithms, we can say that such algorithm tries to retain *positive* instances for the classification process. However, in dozens of algorithm, it is done in several different ways. The most usual way to is define the *positivity* is the positive impact on classification, counted on the base of training data.

The main idea of our algorithm is to retain *trust-border* instances. The margins between classes look differently for different datasets. The margins differ mostly in their width and in the noise level. The margin width is the distance between the regions of two classes (if any). The noise level can be seen as percentage of enemy instances on the wrong side of a border. The width of the noisy part of the border is also crucial in classification. That's why we decided to define trust-border prototypes, as only some of the instances placed on the border can be seen as trustworthy prototypes, while others look more (or even very) noisy. The definition of a trustworthy border instance is as follows: $\mathbf{x}_i$ is a trust-border prototype if among its k nearest neighbours, there are between 1 and k' enemy instances. We choose k' to be much smaller than k (e.g. $k = 11, k' = 3$) to ensure that the prototype is not *too close* to the actual class border.

This means that primarily the prototypes are selected from border-situated instances whose neighbours are mostly from *their* class. All instances which have more than k' enemies among their k nearest neighbors are treated as not trustworthy. Such concept is aimed at *cleaning* the border.

Assume that we have an initial set of trust-border prototypes defined by:

$$S = \{\langle \mathbf{x}_i, y_i \rangle : kNN(X, \mathbf{x}_i, k, k')\} \tag{1}$$

where $kNN(X, \mathbf{x}_i, k, k')$ is *true* if between k nearest neighbours from X at least 1 and at most k' neighbours belong to the enemy, such that have a class label opposite to y_i.

Note that such strategy also rejects *clean* instances which have no enemies among their k nearest neighbours. Hence, besides trust-border instances some of the *clean* instances may be vital for the classification to be accurate. Imagine that there is an *island* of instances separated from rest of dataset. In such case not one of those island-instances becomes a prototype (because nearest neighbours do not contain any enemy) and it may happen that their closest prototype(-s) is(are) from an opposite class. Such situation leads to a case where an almost obvious classification would become inaccurate. To overcome this problem we have to add some of the clean instances which would be classified badly to represent such islands of clean instances.

To do this, we construct set of those clean instances which would be badly classified by the set of the initial prototypes S:

$$W = \{\langle \mathbf{x}_i, y_i \rangle : (\langle \mathbf{x}_i', y_i' \rangle \in kNN(X, \mathbf{x}_i, k) \Rightarrow y_i' = y_i) \wedge L_{kNN(S, \mathbf{x}_i, 1)} \neq y_i\} \tag{2}$$

where $kNN(X, \mathbf{x}_i, k)$ means the set of k nearest neighbours of $\mathbf{x}_i$ from set X. And L_A is the most frequent class label among the instances in the set A.

Now we have to select reliable instances from W as new additional prototypes to overcome the problem described above. The most reliable instances in W are those for which the distance to their closest enemy (an opposite class instance) is the smallest, but not all of them are necessary.

To include the most reliable instances from W, we first sort the elements of W according to the ascending distance to their nearest enemy. The next step is the selection of prototypes in the sorted W. We extract the first instance w from W (one with the smallest distance to the nearest enemy). This instance is added to the (primarily empty) set S'. For each instance $w' \in W$ which is *too close* to w, w' is removed from W. We assume that w' is too close to w if:

$$||\mathbf{x}_{w'} - \mathbf{x}_w|| \leq ||\mathbf{x}_w - \mathbf{x}_{w_e}||/2. \tag{3}$$

Next, we repeat the process until W becomes empty. In other words we repeatedly extract the next (in the order of ascending distance to their nearest enemy) instance w from W, add it to S' and remove the instances which are too close to w. Finally the initial set S of trust-border prototypes is extended by S'.

2.1   Random Regions Tree (LSH) and Forest of Trees

The above concept of an algorithm can be fast only if we use dedicated data structures which will support fast realization of some of the above-described actions. Plain data structures lead to complexity of $O(m^2)$. We have decided to use randomized regions with tree structures. Those structures reduce the costs to approximately $O(m \log m)$. We will use those tree structures in two modes: one just for searching for nearest neighbours, and another to search and remove nearest neighbours. Some other approaches which were also used to approximate nearest neighbours are the vantage-point trees [29], r-trees [30] or kd-trees [31].

To bring the neighbour search closer to $O(m \log m)$, especially in multidimensional spaces, we have decided to base on locality sensitive hashing (LSH). LSH was proposed in [32]. The main idea of LSH is to independently and uniformly draw random hyperplanes which divide the space $\mathcal{R}^n$ into regions (bins) of similar objects. The most important idea of the construction of random data structures was to eliminate the curse of dimensionality. We can view the set of random hyperplanes as a random binary tree. The bins contain a set of points and they serve as a source of potential neighbors of any point in the given bin. Sometimes a point may be situated near a border of its bin—in such cases not all of its actual nearest neighbors can be found in the given bin. This is the reason behind the concept of an LSH forest (LSHF) presented in [33] where the authors proposed to use a few LSH trees and search for neighbors inside the appropriate bins in each of the LSH trees.

In our algorithm we construct the LSH tree in a slightly different way. The first random division is in the root node of a tree. The random division is constructed from randomly chosen dimensions with random strength by

$$linearComb(\mathbf{y}, r^I, r^R) = \sum_{i=1}^{h} y_{r_i^I} \cdot r_i^R \qquad (4)$$

where h is the length of the random combination, r^I are random indices of selected dimensions and r^R are random coefficients of the linear combination. Next, we start independent divisions into two subtrees with appropriate subsets of vectors. This means that the division on the left branch does not divide anything in the right subtree (and vice versa). In every partition of a node, the division is shifted (if necessary) to keep a balance not worse than β (each branch has a fraction of at least β vectors in a node). This strategy keeps the number of nodes in the tree small. The tree is quite strongly balanced and there are no useless divisions. The further split of new nodes is continued if their number of vectors is still too big compared to the desired number of neighbors. The meta-code of the algorithm starts with the Algorithm RandBinsTree 1. The balanced version of partitioning is presented in Algorithm 2. The balanced version of partitioning resembles a typical partition operation (as in quicksort).

The non-leaf nodes have their sub-nodes defined, while leaf nodes an interval of a bin defined. Additionally, the pivot point is stored to define final shift of the random hyperplane. This information is necessary to define a classification process which has to traverse the tree from the root node to an appropriate bin and then select nearest neighbours among the bin items.

Algorithm 1. RandBinsTree($D, left, right, bCount$)

Data: $D = [\mathbf{y}_1, \ldots, \mathbf{y}_m]$ data vectors
$[left, right)$ interval of the current split
ids an array of vector indices
$\beta = .1$ partition threshold of minimal balance
$\alpha = 1 - (\beta + .5)/2$ threshold: whether to continue splitting
$bCount$ minimal count of elements in a bin
$h = 10$ the length of the random combination (see eq. 4)
Result: ids array of bins defined by nodes, initially: $[1, \ldots, m]$

1 **begin**
2   **for** $i \in [1, \ldots, h]$ **do**
3        $r^I[i]$=rand integer(1,n);
4        $r^R[i]$=rand real(0,1);
5   **for** $i = 1$ **to** m **do**
6        $hash[i] = linearComb(\mathbf{y}_i, r^I, r^R)$;
7     $node.div = bPartition(ids, hash, left, right, \beta)$;
8   **if** $(node.div - left) * \alpha > bCount$ **then**
9        $node.left = RandBinsTree(D, left, node.div, bCount)$
10   **else**
11       $lim = (node.div - left < bCount)$? $right : node.div$
12   node.left=new node(left,lim);
13   **if** $(right - node.div) * \alpha > bCount$ **then**
14       $node.right = RandBinsTree(D, node.div, right, bCount)$
15   **else**
16       $lim = (right - node.div < bCount)$? $left : node.div$
17   node.right=new node(lim,right);
18   **return** $node$

The trees of random bins are used to speed up the search of nearest neighbours. A forest of such trees is constructed. Divisions constructed by a single tree are quite sharp and nearest neighbours are roughly approximated by those. Using a number of trees the nearest neighbours are much better approximated. First, we collect candidate instances from each tree and then the nearest neighbours are selected from among those, see Algorithm 3. Because the number of trees and bin size is $O(1)$, the classification cost is $O(\log m)$ ($O(\log m)$ is the expected length of the longest path from the root node to a leaf).

The final complete Trust-Margin algorithm actually needs two types of LSH trees: those described above and another one which is a extension of the above random bins tree. The second type of tree must have an additional feature—it must be able to remove instances from the tree if necessary. This means that

---

Algorithm 2. bPartition($K, A, left, right, \beta$)

Data: A an array of values

K a corresponding array with keys, in case of swap in A the corresponding elements of K are also swapped

$[left, right)$ the current split's interval

β minimal proportion partition threshold

Result: *pivot* the array division point

1 **begin**
2 | $minBalance = \beta(right - left)$;
3 | $min = left + minBalance$; $max = right - minBalance$;
4 | $right - -$;
5 | $pivot = left$;
6 | **while** $left < right$ **do**
7 | | $pivot = left + (right - left)/2$; **if** $A[left] > A[pivot]$ **then**
   | | $swap(A[left], A[pivot], K[left], K[pivot])$;
8 | | **if** $A[pivot] > A[right]$ **then** $swap(A[left], A[right], K[left], K[right])$;
9 | | **if** $A[pivot] > A[right]$ **then** $swap(A[pivot], A[right], K[pivot], K[right])$;
10 | | $pivot = partition(left, right, pivot)$;
11 | | **if** $pivot < min$ **then** $left = pivot + 1$;
12 | | **else if** $pivot > max$ **then** $right = pivot - 1$;
13 | | **else return** $pivot$;
14 | **return** $pivot$;

---

we will need to alternately call to find neighbours for given instances $\mathbf{x}_i$ and to remove a given instance $\mathbf{x}_i$. What's more, we will use a forest of such trees in parallel.

Because of alternating execution of instance removal and neighbours search, the tree must adopt its structure during the removals. Otherwise, at the end, while searching for neighbours, all tree nodes would have to be analyzed as possible candidates for nearest neighbours. Such strategy would degrade computational complexity.

To overcome this problem the tree structure must be corrected from time to time—it is not necessary to modify the tree structure at every removal because leafs keep a set of instances in a bin. This means that after removing a given instance we have to check whether tree pruning is necessary. First, the procedure decrements the counter of instances in appropriate bin and triggers the prune-check procedure. The prune-check procedure starts from the leaf and travels towards the root node. At a given node it is checked whether it is necessary to concatenate a node division. The condition whether to concatenate in case of a leaf node is that if the number of elements in the bin has been reduced twice from its original value, the remaining elements are shifted to the left border of an appropriate interval in the *ids* array. Check-condition for concatenation in case of a non-leaf node tests whether both subnodes have less than *minCount* elements or whether one of the subnodes has 0 elements. If the condition is true, an appropriate concatenation is prepared.

Algorithm 3. NearestNeighbors($\mathbf{x}, T_*, k, c$)

Data: $\mathbf{x}$ define whose neighbours have to be found

$T_i, i = 1, \ldots, t$ an array of random trees, T_i consists of the root node and *ids* an array of vector indices

k desired number of neighbors

$c = 4$ an *overhead* multiplier

Result: NN set of k nearest neighbours

1 **begin**
2   **foreach** T_i **do**
3   I = items of the bin nearest to $\mathbf{x}$ in tree T_i
4          $N = N \cup I$
5   NN = find k nearest neighbours in N

2.2 Trust-Margin Prototype Selection with Tree Structures

Now we can present the fast version of the Algorithm (4). First, the tree forest for searching through all instances of X is created (first line of the code). In the next line the initial trust-border prototypes are selected as defined in Eq. 1 but here the kNN search uses the tree forest T^X instead of plainly searching in set X directly.

In line 4 collect the instances whose neighbours were from the same class but they were badly classified by selected prototypes in S. Here the kNN also works using the tree forest structures, contrary to Eq. 2. Lines 5–9 are responsible for finding the nearest enemy for each instance, so that the instances in can be sorted W according to the ascending order of nearest enemy distance. The last loop tries to add only the necessary instances as supporting prototypes from the tree T^W constructed on the instances earlier added to W. Finally the tree forest T is built to serve as the base for further classification tasks (in searching for nearest prototypes in classification).

3 Results Analysis

To present a comparison of the algorithm with known algorithms, we have take around 40 data sets from the UCI machine learning repository [34]. Data sets differ in origin, goal, the numbers of instances, features and classes, so that we can objectively present the real behavior of the proposed algorithm. We prepared a comparison of the new algorithm Trust-Margin with DROP2, DROP4 [6], Explore and Del [35] algorithms. All tests were conducted on the base of 10 times repeated 10-fold stratified cross-validation. For each test the data set was standardized. Each learning algorithm was always used with the same learning parameters (no manual parameter tuning was done).

To visualize the performance of all algorithms we present average accuracy for each benchmark data set and for each learning machine. The **ranks** are calculated for each machine for a given dataset $\mathcal{D}$. The ranks are calculated as

---

Algorithm 4. MarginProto(X, **y**)

Data: $\langle X, \mathbf{y} \rangle$ — a dataset
    k — k nearest neighbours
    k' — maximal number of enemy instances
Result: S — a set of prototypes

1   $T^X = LSHF(X)$
2   $S = \{\langle \mathbf{x}_i, y_i \rangle : kNN(\mathbf{x}_i, T^X, k, k')\}$
3   $T^S = LSHF(S)$
4   $W = \{\langle \mathbf{x}_i, y_i \rangle : (\langle \mathbf{x}_i', y_i' \rangle \in kNN(\mathbf{x}_i, T^X, k) \Rightarrow y_i' = y_i) \wedge L_{kNN(\mathbf{x}_i, T^S, 1)} \neq y_i\}$
5   **for** $i = 1$ **to** c **do**
6     $T_i = LSHF(\{\langle \mathbf{x}_j, y_j \rangle : y_j = i\})$
7   **foreach** $\langle \mathbf{x}_w, y_w \rangle \in W$ **do**
8     $w_e = \arg\min_j\{\|\mathbf{x}_j - \mathbf{x}_w\| : \langle \mathbf{x}_j, y_j \rangle \in \coprod_{i \neq y_w} kNN(\mathbf{x}_j, T_i, 1)\}$
9   sort W in order of ascending enemies;
10   $T^W = LSHFred(W)$
11   **while** $T^W \neq \emptyset$ **do**
12     $\langle \mathbf{x}_w, y_w \rangle = POP(W)$
13     $T^W = T^W - \langle \mathbf{x}_w, y_w \rangle$
14     $S' = S' + \langle \mathbf{x}_w, y_w \rangle$
15     $Q = $ extract all w' from T^W such that $\|\mathbf{x}_{w'} - \mathbf{x}_w\| \leq \|\mathbf{x}_w - \mathbf{x}_{w_e}\|/2$
16     $W = W - Q$
17   $S = S + S'$
18   $T = LSHF(S)$

---

follows: First, for a given benchmark dataset $\mathcal{D}$ the averaged accuracies of all learning machines are sorted in descending order. The machine with the highest average accuracy is ranked 1. Then, the following machines in the accuracy order whose accuracies are not statistically different from the result of the first machine are ranked 1, until a machine with a statistically different result is encountered. That machine starts the next rank group (2, 3, and so on), and an analogous process is repeated on the remaining (yet unranked) machines. Notice that each cell of the main part of Table 2 is in form: $acc + std(rank)$, where acc is average accuracy (for given data set and given learning machine), std is its standard deviation and $rank$ is the rank describe just above. If a given cell of the table is in bold it means that this result is the best for given data set or not worse then the best one (rank 1 = winners).

The new Trust-Margin algorithm has obtained the highest number of 25 wins, while the second results was 20 obtained by DROP4. Additionally, Trust-Margin had 8 unique wins (the number in brackets), which means that this algorithm was the best one and all other were statistically worse. All other algorithms had at most 2 unique wins. Two algorithms have obtained mean ranks below 2 (the best results). Those methods are DROP4 with result 1.69 and the Trust-Margin with 1.81. In case of several datasets results for Trust-Margin are much better

Table 2. Comparison of Trust-Margin prototype selection with DROP2, DROP4, Explore and Del

Dataset	Trust-Margin	Drop2	Drop4	Explore	Del
Autos	41.94 ± 9(5)	67.74 ± 11(2)	63.86 ± 12(3)	48.87 ± 9.9(4)	**70.6 ± 12(1)**
Balance-scale	**89.14 ± 2.1(1)**	74.64 ± 5.4(4)	79.82 ± 4.3(3)	81.75 ± 5.3(2)	78.83 ± 4.8(3)
Blood-transfusion	**78.76 ± 3.8(1)**	69.28 ± 6.2(4)	71.3 ± 5.8(3)	76.02 ± 1.2(2)	75.83 ± 4.2(2)
Breast-cancer-diagnostic	**95.18 ± 2.7(1)**	91.9 ± 3.3(3)	93.44 ± 3.2(2)	94.25 ± 3.9(2)	89.08 ± 5.8(4)
Breast-cancer-original	96.62 ± 1.9(1)	93.46 ± 2.8(3)	94.72 ± 2.8(2)	**96.68 ± 2(1)**	**96.3 ± 2.1(1)**
Breast-cancer-prognostic	**76.32 ± 2.2(1)**	68.87 ± 10(2)	66.96 ± 10(2)	**76.17 ± 2.7(1)**	**76.32 ± 2.2(1)**
Breast-tissue	44.56 ± 7.2(3)	**66.22 ± 12(1)**	**65.68 ± 14(1)**	61.02 ± 12(2)	**64.71 ± 13(1)**
Car-evaluation	69.64 ± 0.75(4)	**80.23 ± 2.8(1)**	**79.79 ± 2.8(1)**	70.26 ± 1.1(3)	75.57 ± 2.7(2)
Cardiotocography-1	68.4 ± 2.7(2)	**70.67 ± 3.3(1)**	**71.1 ± 3(1)**	63.13 ± 7.2(4)	67.36 ± 3.2(3)
Cardiotocography-2	**88.49 ± 1.8(1)**	86.8 ± 2.4(3)	87.34 ± 2(2)	83.4 ± 3.1(5)	84.64 ± 2.6(4)
Chess-rook-vs-pawn	85.35 ± 1.9(3)	90.46 ± 1.7(2)	**91.04 ± 1.6(1)**	76.64 ± 6.2(5)	83.24 ± 2.4(4)
CMC	**43.14 ± 3.7(1)**	42.95 ± 3.9(1)	43.01 ± 3.9(1)	43.31 ± 4(1)	41.99 ± 4(2)
Congressional-voting	**91.03 ± 5.2(1)**	81.31 ± 9.3(3)	89.35 ± 7.3(2)	**90.93 ± 6.5(1)**	87.97 ± 6(2)
Connectionist-bench-sonar	72.17 ± 8.1(3)	**81.96 ± 8.6(1)**	80.53 ± 7.9(2)	70.52 ± 10(3)	66.78 ± 10(4)
Connectionist-bench-vowel	37.73 ± 5.7(4)	**96.33 ± 2.8(1)**	**96.02 ± 3(1)**	51.92 ± 9.1(3)	95.55 ± 3.1(2)
Cylinder-bands	62.64 ± 4.8(2)	**65.43 ± 8.1(1)**	62.68 ± 8.6(2)	**64.26 ± 0.96(1)**	**64.26 ± 1.2(1)**
Dermatology	**86.7 ± 5.5(1)**	88.02 ± 5(1)	87.6 ± 4.7(1)	81.85 ± 6.1(3)	85.72 ± 6.1(2)
Ecoli	**85.14 ± 5.1(1)**	79.85 ± 6.6(3)	**84.13 ± 4.8(1)**	81.47 ± 6.5(2)	82.42 ± 6.3(2)
Glass	56.24 ± 7.7(3)	**66.53 ± 9.5(1)**	**67.22 ± 9.4(1)**	60.21 ± 9.6(2)	**65.93 ± 9.1(1)**
Habermans-survival	**74.09 ± 3.6(1)**	65.62 ± 8.9(4)	67.78 ± 6.9(3)	73.14 ± 2.2(2)	73.14 ± 3.1(2)
Hepatitis	**83.75 ± 5.8(1)**	82.25 ± 11(1)	82.38 ± 13(1)	**83.75 ± 5.8(1)**	**83.25 ± 7.4(1)**
Ionosphere	**79.89 ± 5.1(1)**	81.12 ± 6.9(1)	80.48 ± 7.4(1)	78.06 ± 7.4(2)	**81.08 ± 7.5(1)**
Iris	**93.87 ± 5.2(1)**	92.6 ± 6.7(2)	**93.87 ± 6.2(1)**	**93.47 ± 7.6(1)**	88.33 ± 8.2(3)
Libras-movement	38.53 ± 5(4)	**81.75 ± 6.7(1)**	81.5 ± 6.4(1)	56.86 ± 8.4(3)	79.75 ± 7.1(2)
Liver-disorders	**62.14 ± 8.2(1)**	61.66 ± 8.7(1)	60.29 ± 8.2(1)	58.66 ± 5.7(2)	57.69 ± 7.6(2)
Lymph	72.96 ± 12(2)	**76.7 ± 9.6(1)**	**77.19 ± 11(1)**	70.5 ± 12(2)	68.7 ± 12(3)
Monks-problems-1	80.47 ± 4.9(2)	**94.66 ± 2.9(1)**	**94.62 ± 2.9(1)**	70.42 ± 7.1(4)	74.41 ± 6.6(3)
Monks-problems-2	**65.62 ± 0.98(1)**	55.96 ± 6.5(3)	57.42 ± 6.2(2)	**65.72 ± 0.79(1)**	**65.72 ± 0.79(1)**
Monks-problems-3	**97.08 ± 2.6(1)**	93.18 ± 3.5(2)	93.39 ± 3.5(2)	84.59 ± 6.8(3)	82.52 ± 6.6(4)
Parkinsons	83.95 ± 5.9(2)	**87.73 ± 7.1(1)**	**87.82 ± 7.4(1)**	80.83 ± 7(3)	83.41 ± 7.7(2)
Pima-indians-diabetes	**74.35 ± 4(1)**	68.71 ± 5.6(4)	70.41 ± 5(3)	72.59 ± 5.7(2)	69.89 ± 5.6(3)
Sonar	72.17 ± 8.1(3)	**81.96 ± 8.6(1)**	80.53 ± 7.9(2)	70.52 ± 10(3)	66.78 ± 10(4)
Spambase	**88.59 ± 1.3(1)**	86.34 ± 1.6(3)	87.64 ± 1.6(2)	82.46 ± 4.3(5)	84.14 ± 2(4)
Spect-heart	**78.92 ± 7.1(1)**	77.5 ± 7.5(2)	77.61 ± 7.7(2)	**79.42 ± 1.7(1)**	**79.45 ± 1.8(1)**
Spectf-heart	78.74 ± 3.5(2)	67.4 ± 8.5(3)	68.22 ± 8.9(3)	**79.42 ± 1.7(1)**	**79.19 ± 2.7(1)**
Statlog-australian-credit	75.29 ± 5(3)	75.38 ± 5.7(3)	77.72 ± 5.7(2)	76.87 ± 6.5(2)	**80.64 ± 5.5(1)**
Statlog-german-credit	**71.05 ± 2.1(1)**	65.47 ± 4.9(3)	66.23 ± 4.4(3)	**70.91 ± 3(1)**	69.69 ± 3.2(2)
Statlog-heart	**79.19 ± 7.3(1)**	74.56 ± 7.6(2)	75.78 ± 7.5(2)	**78.78 ± 6.8(1)**	76.37 ± 8.8(2)
Statlog-vehicle	61.5 ± 3.5(4)	66.22 ± 4.3(2)	**67.4 ± 4.4(1)**	51.41 ± 8.5(5)	64.01 ± 4.5(3)
Thyroid-disease	**94.38 ± 0.32(1)**	87.99 ± 1.3(3)	90.65 ± 1.5(2)	**93.13 ± 7.1(1)**	88.3 ± 10(3)
Vote	**90.28 ± 6.6(1)**	85.24 ± 9.1(3)	**90.72 ± 6.6(1)**	89.26 ± 7.1(1)	87.82 ± 8.9(2)
Wine	**94.1 ± 5(1)**	93.08 ± 6.5(1)	93.54 ± 5.7(1)	93.29 ± 6.7(1)	89.93 ± 7.2(2)
Mean Accuracy	75.24 ± 4.6	77.76 ± 6.3	78.54 ± 6.1	74.44 ± 5.9	76.84 ± 5.9
Mean Rank	**1.81 ± 0.18**	2.048 ± 0.17	**1.69 ± 0.12**	2.262 ± 0.2	2.238 ± 0.16
Wins[unique]	**25[8]**	18[2]	20[2]	15[0]	12[2]

than for others. However, in case of some datasets the results are worse and we have to analyse it further detail, and probably optimize the algorithm in the future. Those results show that the new method is accurate, but its complexity $O(m \log m)$ is much better than the other algorithms' complexity of $O(m^3)$. Figure 1 presents an analysis of learning time used by the new Trust-Margin algorithm. We have tested the time for different numbers of instances of the MNIST8 dataset [36]. On the OX axis is the number of instances. On the left we show time (blue dots) and on the right (red squares) the proportion of time to the number of instances. This clearly shows that the complexity of learning is less than $O(m \log m)$.

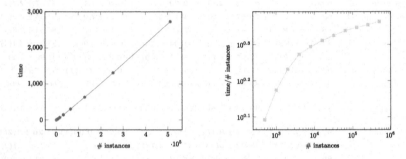

Fig. 1. Low time consumption of Trust-Margin algorithm. (Color figure online)

4 Summary

The proposed prototype selection algorithm (Trust-Margin) was constructed upon the new concept of trust-border instances, which goal is to retain only trustworthy instances on the class borders. It was presented that the algorithm can be very efficient if it is realized with supporting tree structures designed especially for this algorithm. It was shown that the algorithm has an expected complexity of $O(m \log m)$. The comparative results shows that new algorithm is accurate comparing to known algorithm but it is much faster.

References

1. Cover, T.M., Hart, P.E.: Nearest neighbor pattern classification. Inst. Electr. Electron. Eng. Trans. Inf. Theory **13**(1), 21–27 (1967)
2. Wilson, D.: Asymptotic properties of nearest neighbor rules using edited data. IEEE Trans. Syst. Man Cybern. **2**(3), 408–421 (1972)
3. Gates, G.: The reduced nearest neighbor rule. IEEE Trans. Inf. Theory **18**(3), 431–433 (1972)
4. Grochowski, M., Jankowski, N.: Comparison of instance selection algorithms II. Results and comments. In: Rutkowski, L., Siekmann, J.H., Tadeusiewicz, R., Zadeh, L.A. (eds.) ICAISC 2004. LNCS (LNAI), vol. 3070, pp. 580–585. Springer, Heidelberg (2004). https://doi.org/10.1007/978-3-540-24844-6_87

5. Garcia, S., Derrac, J., Cano, J., Herrera, F.: Prototype selection for nearest neighbor classification: taxonomy and empirical study. IEEE Trans. Pattern Anal. Mach. Intell. **34**(3), 417–435 (2012)
6. Wilson, D.R., Martinez, T.R.: Reduction techniques for instance-based learning algorithms. Mach. Learn. **38**(3), 257–286 (2000)
7. Jankowski, N., Grochowski, M.: Comparison of instances seletion algorithms I. Algorithms survey. In: Rutkowski, L., Siekmann, J.H., Tadeusiewicz, R., Zadeh, L.A. (eds.) ICAISC 2004. LNCS (LNAI), vol. 3070, pp. 598–603. Springer, Heidelberg (2004). https://doi.org/10.1007/978-3-540-24844-6_90
8. Blachnik, M.: Metody bazujące na prototypach w zastosowaniu do eksploracji danych. Silesian Technical University (2019)
9. Kordos, M.: Optimization of evolutionary instance selection. In: Rutkowski, L., Korytkowski, M., Scherer, R., Tadeusiewicz, R., Zadeh, L.A., Zurada, J.M. (eds.) ICAISC 2017. LNCS (LNAI), vol. 10245, pp. 359–369. Springer, Cham (2017). https://doi.org/10.1007/978-3-319-59063-9_32
10. Arnaiz-González, Á., Díez-Pastor, J.F., Rodríguez, J.J., García-Osorio, C.: Instance selection of linear complexity for big data. Knowl.-Based Syst. **107**, 83–95 (2016)
11. Sanchez, J., Pla, F., Ferri, F.: Prototype selection for the nearest neighbor rule through proximity graphs. Pattern Recognit. Lett. **18**(6), 507–513 (1997)
12. Garcia, S., Cano, J., Herrera, F.: A memetic algorithm for evolutionary prototype selection: a scaling up approach. Pattern Recognit. **41**(8), 2693–2709 (2008)
13. Skalak, D.B.: Prototype and feature selection by sampling and random mutation hill climbing algorithms. In: International Conference on Machine Learning, New Brunswick, NJ, USA, pp. 293–301 (1994)
14. Marchiori, E.: Hit miss networks with applications to instance selection. J. Mach. Learn. Res. **9**, 997–1017 (2008)
15. Marchiori, E.: Class conditional nearest neighbor for large margin instance selection. IEEE Trans. Pattern Anal. Mach. Intell. **32**(2), 364–370 (2010)
16. Angiulli, F.: Fast nearest neighbor condensation for large data sets classification. IEEE Trans. Knowl. Data Eng. **19**(11), 1450–1464 (2007)
17. Brodley, C.: Recursive automatic bias selection for classifier construction. Mach. Learn. **20**(1/2), 63–94 (1995)
18. Cano, J.R., Herrera, F., Lozano, M.: Using evolutionary algorithms as instance selection for data reduction in KDD: an experimental study. IEEE Trans. Evol. Comput. **7**(6), 561–575 (2003)
19. Kuncheva, L.: Editing for the k-nearest neighbors rule by a genetic algorithm. Pattern Recognit. Lett. **16**(8), 809–814 (1995)
20. Aha, D.W., Kibler, D., Albert, M.K.: Instance-based learning algorithms. Mach. Learn. **6**(1), 37–66 (1991)
21. Riquelme, J., Aguilar-Ruiz, J., Toro, M.: Finding representative patterns with ordered projections. Pattern Recognit. **36**(4), 1009–1018 (2003)
22. Barandela, R., Ferri, F., Sanchez, J.: Decision boundary preserving prototype selection for nearest neighbor classification. Int. J. Pattern Recognit. Artif. Intell. **19**(6), 787–806 (2005)
23. Hart, P.E.: The condensed nearest neighbor rule. IEEE Trans. Inf. Theory **14**(3), 515–516 (1968)
24. Hattori, K., Takahashi, M.: A new edited k-nearest neighbor rule in the pattern classification problem. Pattern Recognit. **33**(3), 521–528 (2000)

25. Zhao, K., Zhou, S., Guan, J., Zhou, A.: C-pruner: an improved instance pruning algorithm. In: Proceedings of Second International Conference on Machine Learning and Cybernetics, Xi'an, China, pp. 94–99 (2003)
26. Lozano, M.T., Sánchez, J.S., Pla, F.: Using the geometrical distribution of prototypes for training set condensing. In: Conejo, R., Urretavizcaya, M., Pérez-de-la-Cruz, J.L. (eds.) TTIA 2003. LNCS, vol. 3040, pp. 618–627. Springer, Heidelberg (2003). https://doi.org/10.1007/978-3-540-25945-9_61
27. Devi, V., Murty, M.: An incremental prototype set building technique. Pattern Recognit. **35**(2), 505–513 (2002)
28. Brighton, H., Mellish, C.: Advances in instance selection for instance-based learning algorithms. Data Min. Knowl. Disc. **6**(2), 153–172 (2002)
29. Yianilos, P.: Data structures and algorithms for nearest neighbor search in general metric spaces. In: Proceedings of the ACM-SIAM Symposium on Discrete Algorithms, pp. 311–321 (1993)
30. Manolopoulos, Y., Nanopoulos, A., Papadopoulos, A.N., Theodoridis, Y.: R-Trees: Theory and Applications. Springer, London (2006). https://doi.org/10.1007/978-1-84628-293-5
31. Brown, R.: Building a balanced k-d tree in $O(kn \log n)$ time. J. Comput. Graph. Tech. **4**(1), 50–68 (2015)
32. Har-Peled, S., Indyk, P., Motwani, R.: Approximate nearest neighbor: towards removing the curse of dimensionality. Theory Comput. **8**, 321–350 (2012)
33. Bawa, M., Condie, T., Ganesan, P.: LSH forest: self-tuning indexes for similarity search. In: Proceedings of the 14th International Conference on World Wide Web, Chiba, Japan, pp. 651–660 (2005)
34. Merz, C.J., Murphy, P.M.: UCI repository of machine learning databases (1998). http://www.ics.uci.edu/~mlearn/MLRepository.html
35. Cameron-Jones, R.M.: Instance selection by encoding length heuristic with random mutation hill climbing. In: Proceedings of the Eighth Australian Joint Conference on Artificial Intelligence, Australia, pp. 99–106 (1995)
36. Loosli, G., Canu, S., Bottou, L.: Training invariant support vector machines using selective sampling. In: Bottou, L., Chapelle, O., DeCoste, D., Weston, J. (eds.) Large-Scale Kernel Machines, pp. 301–320. MIT Press, Cambridge (2007)

Classifying Image Sequences with the Markov Chain Structure and Matrix Normal Distributions

Ewaryst Rafajłowicz[(✉)] [iD]

Faculty of Electronics, Wrocław University of Science and Technology,
Wrocław, Poland
ewaryst.rafajlowicz@pwr.edu.pl

Abstract. We consider the problem of classifying image sequences to several classes. Such problems arise in numerous applications, e.g., when a task to be completed requires that all sub-tasks are properly executed. In order to derive realistic classifiers for such complicated problems, we assume that images in the sequence form a Markov chain, while the conditional probability density function of transitions has the matrix normal distribution, i.e., it has the covariance matrix being the Kronecker product of inter-rows and inter-columns covariance matrices. Under these assumptions we derive the Bayes classifier for image sequences and its empirical version that is based on applying the plug-in rule. We also provide interpretable versions of such classifiers at the expense of additional assumptions. The proposed classifier is tested on the sequence of images from the laboratory experiments of detecting stages of an additive manufacturing process. Finally, we state conclusions and (partial) explanations on why the problem of classifying sequences of images is (much) more difficult than that of classifying individual images.

Keywords: Matrix normal distribution · Bayesian classifier ·
Classification of image sequences

1 Introduction

Our aim is discuss a way to develop a classifier for image sequences. Each sequence is considered as a whole entity that can be a member of a certain class and our aim is to build an appropriate classifier. In other words, a classifier obtains an ordered set of images as one input.

This task only seemingly reduces to known classification problems by vectorization, because then it is extremely difficult to take into account stochastic dependencies between images and their covariance structures.

A large number of examples can be pointed out when we need (or it is desirable) to classify whole image sequences. In particular, they include the following cases.

© Springer Nature Switzerland AG 2019
L. Rutkowski et al. (Eds.): ICAISC 2019, LNAI 11508, pp. 595–607, 2019.
https://doi.org/10.1007/978-3-030-20912-4_54

- Quality control of a manufacturing process when at each stage we have images of properly and improperly produced items. Then, we can classify an item as conforming only when all the sequence of images is similar to the proper sequence. This class of examples is our main focus (see Sect. 6).
- Learning and teaching of complicated tasks to be performed requiring high precision of movements. Examples include: laparoscopic surgery (see [26]), training professional sportsmen and women and autonomous parking (see, e.g., [13]).
- Collecting, e.g., cytological images of the same patient (see [2]) along time and comparing them with image sequences of other patients.
- Subsequent histological sections of the same tissue (see [5,6]), but recognized as one entity in the same spirit as in CT and in MRI images.
- When states of a dynamic systems are described as matrices or images (see, e.g. [20]), then the ability of classifying their sequences are of importance to decide at which state of the evolution the system is, e.g., whether it is still in transient states or near the equilibria states.
- Recognition of untidy hand written words by splitting them into letters, but considering them as one entity and testing to which word they are mostly similar.

The ability of classifying whole image sequences can also be useful for image understanding, but this topic is far outside the scope of this paper. We refer the reader to [24] for more detailed discussion on image understanding and the bibliography.

Clearly, it is rather impossible to construct a universal classifier for image sequences. We impose the following constraints on the class of considered classification tasks (see the next section for details):

- we confine ourselves to images represented by grey levels,
- images in a given sequence have the Markov property of the first order (a generalization to a higher order Markov chains is not difficult),
- conditional densities of the Markov chain have matrix normal distributions (MND) – see Appendix for basic properties of MND.

The last assumption is made for pragmatic reasons, otherwise we usually do not have enough observations in order to estimate the full covariance matrix of large images. An alternative approach, when we do not have enough observations, is proposed in [23].

The paper is organized as follows:

- in the following section we provide a short review of the works that have common points with this paper,
- then, in Sect. 3, we provide the problem statement and preliminary results on the Bayesian classifiers for image sequences,
- these topics are continued in the next section, in which special cases are discussed,
- in Sect. 5 we provide the empirical version of the Bayes MND classifier for image sequences, while

– a laboratory example is discussed in Sect. 5.

The paper ends by concluding remarks, including a discussion on the following question: why is the classification of an image sequence such a difficult problem?

2   Previous Work

In this section we provide a short survey of papers on classifiers that arise in cases when the assumption that class densities have the MND distribution holds. Then, we briefly discuss recent works on classifying image sequences.

The role of multivariate normal distributions with the Kronecker product structure of the covariance matrix for deriving classifiers was appreciated in [10], where earlier results are cited. In this paper the motivation for assuming the Kronecker product structure comes from repeated observations of the same object to be classified. The topic of classifying repeated measurements was further developed in [11], where repeated observations are stacked into a matrix according to their ordering along the time axis. In [11] the test for verifying the hypothesis on the Kronecker product structure of the covariance matrix was developed. The classifier based on the MND's assumption occurred to be useful for classifying images (see [17,18], where it was applied to classifying images of flames from a gas burner). In [19] it was documented – by extensive simulations – that such classifiers are relatively robust against the class imbalance.

As far as we know, classifiers that are based on MND's for recognizing image sequences, considered as entities, were not considered in the literature and this is the main topic of this paper.

The above does not mean that the topic of classifying image sequence was not considered. It was, but using other assumptions and approaches. It is worth distinguishing the following cases.

1. A rough classification of videos according to their type (comedy, drama etc.). The stream of literature on these topics is the largest. It is completely outside the scope of this paper. The closest paper in this stream is [8], in which the classification of sporting disciplines by convolutional neural networks (CNN) is discussed.
2. Detecting changes in a video stream, e.g., for safety monitoring. Here, one can distinguish two problem statements, namely,
   – the so-called novelty detection, when a proper state is known, but the type of changes is unspecified (see [21], [15])
   – a directional change detection, when the class of possible changes is a priori known. One can meet such tasks in monitoring of production processes. They are similar in spirit to pattern recognition problems (see [16] for an example).
3. The classification of (an) object(s) that are visible on several subsequent frames (see [9] and bibliography therein).
4. The classification of image sequences, where each sequence is considered as one entity. This is our main topic.

The differences between group 3 and group 4 are, in some cases, subtle. For example, consider a camera mounted over a road and two cars (say, a truck and a small car behind it). If one is interested in classifying cars into small and large ones (and possibly in classifying their types), then we are faced with case 3. However, if the small car overtakes the large one, we can ask whether the overtaking maneuver was done properly or not. This task illustrates the one from group 4, since we have to recognize all stages of this maneuver.

3   Problem Statement and Preliminary Results

By $\mathbb{X}$ we denote a sequence of ordered images $\mathbf{X}_k$, $k = 1, 2, \ldots, K$, represented by $m \times n$ matrices of grey levels that are considered to be real-valued variables. In practice, grey levels are represented by integers from the range 0 to 255, but – at this level of generality – it seems reasonable to consider them as real numbers, without imposing constraints on their range.

Sequence $\mathbb{X}$ can be classified to one of $J > 1$ classes, labeled as $j = 1, 2, \ldots, J$. The following assumptions apply to all J classes, but we avoid indexing them by class labels, unless necessary.

As (1) $\mathbb{X}$ is a random tensor, having a probability density function (p.d.f.), denoted further by $f(\mathbb{X})$ or, equivalently, by $f(\mathbf{X}_1, \mathbf{X}_2, \ldots, \mathbf{X}_K)$. Slightly abusing the notation, we shall write $f(\mathbf{X}_{L_1}, \ldots, \mathbf{X}_{L_2})$ for p.d.f.'s of subsequences of $\mathbb{X}$, where $1 \leq L_1 < L_2 \leq K$.

As (2) Elements of $\mathbb{X}$ form a Markov chain in the following sense:

$$f(\mathbf{X}_k | \mathbf{X}_{k-1}, \ldots, \mathbf{X}_1) = f_k(\mathbf{X}_k | \mathbf{X}_{k-1}), \text{ for } \quad k = 2, \ldots K, \tag{1}$$

where $f_k(\mathbf{X}_k | \mathbf{X}_{k-1})$ is the conditional p.d.f. of $\mathbf{X}_k$ when $\mathbf{X}_{k-1}$ is given. $f_k(\mathbf{X}_k | \mathbf{X}_{k-1})$ is known as the transition p.d.f. of moving from $\mathbf{X}_{k-1}$ to $\mathbf{X}_k$, for every $k > 1$.

For $k = 1$ we assume that $f_1(\mathbf{X}_1 | \mathbf{X}_0) = f_1(\mathbf{X}_1)$, i.e., f_1 is the unconditional p.d.f. of random matrix $\mathbf{X}_1$.

As (3) We assume that $\mathbf{X}_1 \sim \mathcal{N}_{n,m}(\mathbf{M}_1, U_1, V_1)$, i.e., $f_1(\mathbf{X}_1)$ is the MND with the expectation matrix $\mathbf{M}_1$ and U_1 as $n \times n$ inter-rows covariance matrix and V_1 as $m \times m$ covariance matrix between columns (see Appendix).

As (4) For $k > 1$ the transition p.d.f.'s $f_k(\mathbf{X}_k | \mathbf{X}_{k-1})$ are also assumed to have the MND's of the following form:

$$\frac{\alpha}{c} \exp\left[-\frac{1}{2} \text{tr}[U^{-1}(\mathbf{X}_k(\alpha) - \mathbf{M}_k) V^{-1} (\mathbf{X}_k(\alpha) - \mathbf{M}_k)^T\right], \tag{2}$$

where c is the normalization constant which is given by:

$$c \overset{def}{=} (2\pi)^{0.5nm} \det[U]^{0.5n} \det[V]^{0.5m}, \tag{3}$$

while $n \times m$ matrix $\mathbf{X}_k(\alpha)$ is defined as follows: for $0 \leq \alpha \leq 1$

$$\mathbf{X}_k(\alpha) = \alpha \mathbf{X}_k + (1 - \alpha) \mathbf{X}_{k-1}. \tag{4}$$

In the above, $\mathbf{M}_k$ plays the role of the mean matrix of the image sequence (video frame) at k-th step.

Several remarks are in order, concerning the above assumptions.

Remark 1 – *By selecting $0 \leq \alpha \leq 1$, one can control the influence of the previous image on the p.d.f. of the present one. The choice is case dependent. For example, when a small object is slowly moving over almost the same background, the influence of the previous frame is large, suggesting smaller values of α.*

– *For $\alpha = 1$ we obtain the independence between $\mathbf{X}_k$ and $\mathbf{X}_{k-1}$. This case can happen, e.g., when images are taken from a very fast-moving train.*

Proposition 1. *Let As (1)–As (4) hold. Tentatively, we additionally assume:*

$$U_1 = U \quad and \quad V_1 = V. \tag{5}$$

Then, each $\mathbf{X}_k$, $k = 2, \ldots, K$ has the matrix normal distribution with the expectation matrix, denoted as $\mathbf{M}_k(\alpha)$, of the following form:

$$\mathbf{M}_k(\alpha) = \alpha^{-1} \left[\mathbf{M}_k - (1 - \alpha) \mathbf{M}_{k-1}(\alpha) \right], \quad k = 2, 3, \ldots, K, \tag{6}$$

where $\mathbf{M}_1(\alpha) \stackrel{def}{=} \mathbf{M}_1$.

The covariance matrices of $\mathbf{X}_k$'s are of the form:

$$C^{k-1}(\alpha) U_1, \quad C^{k-1}(\alpha) V_1, \quad k = 2, 3, \ldots, K, \tag{7}$$

where

$$C(\alpha) \stackrel{def}{=} (1 + (1 - \alpha)^2)/\alpha^2. \tag{8}$$

Notice that $\mathbf{M}_k(\alpha) \to \mathbf{M}_k$ and $C(\alpha) \to 1$ as $\alpha \to 1$.

Proof. For $k = 2$ it suffices to integrate $f_2(\mathbf{X}_2|\mathbf{X}_1) f_1(\mathbf{X}_1)$ with respect to $\mathbf{X}_1$. The rest of the proof goes by the induction, since – after this integration – we again obtain MND with the expectation (6) and the covariances (7), when $k = 2$ is substituted.   ●

Notice the growth of the variances in (7). For this reason, it is advisable to use $\alpha < 1$, but close to 1 and to apply the Markov scheme, proposed in As (4), to rather short image sequences.

Under As (1) and As (2) it is easy to derive the following expression for the natural logarithm of f

$$\log f(\mathbb{X}) = \sum_{k=2}^{K} \log f_k(\mathbf{X}_k|\mathbf{X}_{k-1}) + \log f_1(\mathbf{X}_1). \tag{9}$$

If, additionally, As (3) and As (4) hold, then for minus $\log f(\mathbb{X})$ we obtain:

$$LLF(\mathbb{X}, \mathbb{M}, U, V) \stackrel{def}{=} -\log f(\mathbb{X}) = \log(c/\alpha) \tag{10}$$

$$+ \frac{1}{2} \sum_{k=2}^{K} \mathrm{tr}[U^{-1}(\mathbf{X}_k(\alpha) - \mathbf{M}_k) V^{-1} (\mathbf{X}_k(\alpha) - \mathbf{M}_k)^T$$

$$+ \mathrm{tr}[U_1^{-1}(\mathbf{X}_1 - \mathbf{M}_1) V_1^{-1} (\mathbf{X}_1 - \mathbf{M}_1)^T,$$

where $\mathbb{M}$ consists of $\mathbf{M}_k$, $k = 1, 2, \ldots, K$. The *LLF* also depends on K, α, m, n, but we omit displaying them as arguments, since – in a given application – they remain the same for each class.

Each class has its own p.d.f., denoted further by $f_j(\mathbb{X})$ and the corresponding minus log-likelihood function: $LLF(\mathbb{X}, \mathbb{M}^{(j)}, U^{(j)}, V^{(j)})$, where $\mathbb{M}^{(j)}$ is the sequence of means for j-th class, while $U^{(j)}$, $V^{(j)}$ are the corresponding covariance matrices, $j = 1, 2, \ldots, J$. We assume that for each class there exists a priori probability $p_j > 0$ that sequence $\mathbb{X}$ was drawn from this class. Clearly $\sum_{j=1}^{J} p_j = 1$.

It is well known (see, e.g., [4]) that for the 0-1 loss function the Bayes risk of classifying $\mathbb{X}$ is minimized by the following classification rule:

$$j^* = \arg \max_{1 \le j \le J} \ p_j \, f^{(j)}(\mathbb{X}), \tag{11}$$

where $f^{(j)}$ is the p.d.f. of sequences $\mathbb{X}$ from j-th class.

Under all the above assumptions As (1)–As (4), our aim in this paper is the following:

1. having learning sequences of mutually independent $\mathbb{X}_n^{(j)}$'s from j-th class, $n = 1, 2, \ldots, N_j$, $j = 1, 2, \ldots, J$
2. and assuming proper classifications to one of the classes
3. to construct an empirical classifier that mimics (11) decision rule in the plug-in way

and to test this rule on real data. Notice that each $\mathbb{X}_n^{(j)}$ is a sequence itself. Its elements will further be denoted as $\mathbf{X}_{k,n}^{(j)}$, $k = 1, 2, \ldots, K$.

4   Some Properties of the Bayes Classifier for Sequences

From (11) we obtain that the **Bayesian classifier for sequence** $\mathbb{X}$ is the form:

$$j^* = \arg \min_{1 \le j \le J} \ \left[-\log(p_j) + LLF(\mathbb{X}, \mathbb{M}^{(j)}, U^{(j)}, V^{(j)}) \right] \tag{12}$$

or – in the full form:

$\mathbb{X}$ is classified to class j^*, for which the following expression is minimal with respect to j:

$$\left\{ \frac{1}{2} \sum_{k=2}^{K} \mathrm{tr}[(U^{(j)})^{-1} (\mathbf{X}_k(\alpha) - \mathbf{M}_k^{(j)}) (V^{(j)})^{-1} (\mathbf{X}_k(\alpha) - \mathbf{M}_k^{(j)})^T \right. \tag{13}$$

$$\left. + \mathrm{tr}[U_1^{(j)})^{-1} (\mathbf{X}_1 - \mathbf{M}_1) (V_1^{(j)})^{-1} (\mathbf{X}_1 - \mathbf{M}_1)^T + \log(c^{(j)}) \right\} - \log(p_j).$$

Above and further on the summand $\log(1/\alpha^2)$ is omitted, since it does not depend on j.

In order to reveal the interpretation of the optimal classifier (13), it is expedient to consider the following special cases.

Corollary 1. *Let As (1)–As (4) hold and, additionally, the a priori class probabilities are equi-distributed, i.e., $p_i = 1/J$. Then, the Bayes risk is minimized by this j for which the sum of the Mahalanobis distances between $\mathbf{X}_k(\alpha)$ and $\mathbf{M}_k^{(j)}$ is minimized.*

Proof. It suffices to observe that

$$\mathrm{tr}[(U^{(j)})^{-1}\,(\mathbf{X}_k(\alpha) - \mathbf{M}_k^{(j)})\,(V^{(j)})^{-1}\,(\mathbf{X}_k(\alpha) - \mathbf{M}_k^{(j)})^T \tag{14}$$
$$= \mathrm{vec}^T(\mathbf{X}_k(\alpha) - \mathbf{M}_k^{(j)})\,\Sigma_j^{-1}\,\mathrm{vec}(\mathbf{X}_k(\alpha) - \mathbf{M}_k^{(j)}),$$

where $\Sigma_j \overset{def}{=} U_j \otimes V_j$, while $\otimes$ is the Kronecker product of matrices.   ●

Corollary 2. *If – in addition to the assumptions made in Corollary 1 – there are no correlations between rows and between columns (U_j's and V_j's are the identity matrices) and there are no correlations between images ($\alpha = 0$), then sequence $\mathbb{X}$ is classified to this class j for which*

$$\sum_{k=1}^{K} ||\mathrm{vec}(\mathbf{X}_k - \mathbf{M}_k^{(j)})||^2 \tag{15}$$

is minimal, where $||.||$ is the Euclidean norm of a vector. Thus, (15) is the nearest mean classifier in the generalized sense, i.e., the distance of all the sequence $\mathbb{X}$ is compared to the sequences of all mean matrices $\mathbb{M}^{(j)}$, $j = 1, 2, \ldots, J$ and the closest one is selected.

Corollary 2 is intuitively pleasing, but it is a very special case of (13).

Corollary 3. *For $J = 2$, if $U_1^{(1)} = U_1^{(2)}$, $V_1^{(1)} = V_1^{(2)}$ and $U_2^{(1)} = U_2^{(2)}$, $V_2^{(1)} = V_2^{(2)}$, then the classifier (13) is linear with respect to $\mathrm{vec}(\mathbf{X}_k(\alpha))$, $k = 1, 2, \ldots, K$.*

Proof. Follows directly from the right hand side of the equality in (14), since – under our assumptions – we have $\Sigma_1 = \Sigma_2$ and the quadratic terms vanish.   ●

5   An Empirical Bayes, Plug-In Classifier for Sequences of Matrices (images)

Having learning sequences of $\mathbb{X}_n^{(j)}$, $n = 1, 2, \ldots, N_j$, for each class j – $j = 1, 2, \ldots, J$ – at our disposal, we construct the empirical Bayes classifier, using the classical plug-in approach. Its derivation relays the assumptions As (1)–As (4), but – as we shall see – we can formally try to use it without imposing the MND structure of the observations. Clearly, if the observations do not follow MND, information contained in the full covariance matrix is partially lost, since we use only inter-rows and inter-columns covariances. On the other hand, however, we obtain a classifier, which is able to classify image sequences of a moderate size.

A Classifier for MND Sequences (CMNDS)

The learning phase. Firstly, p_j's are estimated as $\hat{p}_j = N_j/N$, where $N = \sum_{j=1}^{J} N_j$. The means $\mathbb{M}^{(j)}$ are estimated as the empirical means of $\mathbb{X}_n^{(j)}$, $n = 1, 2, \ldots, N_j$, but for large images and large K (long sequences) this is not a trivial computational task. These empirical means are denoted as $\hat{\mathbb{M}}^{(j)}$'s. Notice that, for practical reasons, we propose to estimate $\mathbb{M}^{(j)}$ as if $\mathbb{X}_n^{(j)}$, $n = 1, 2, \ldots, N_j$ were mutually independent, i.e., for $\alpha = 1$. We introduce $\alpha < 1$ in the testing phase only when it leads to the reduction of the classification error.

The estimation of $U^{(j)}$'s and $V^{(j)}$'s is done in a non-classic way. Details are provided in the Appendix. The resulting estimates are denoted as $\hat{U}^{(j)}$'s and $\hat{V}^{(j)}$'s.

The recognition phase. When new sequence $\mathbb{X}$ is to be classified we use the empirical version of (12) rule, i.e., it is classified to class $\hat{j}$ such that

$$\hat{j} = \arg\min_{1 \leq j \leq J} \left[-\log(\hat{p}_j) + LLF(\mathbb{X}, \hat{\mathbb{M}}^{(j)}, \hat{U}^{(j)}, \hat{V}^{(j)}) \right]. \tag{16}$$

The constant c that is present in LLF also depends on j, but our experiments indicate that in some cases it is better to consider it as a constant and to neglect it (as done in the example presented in the next section).

The assessment of the quality of learning can be done by the classic approach, namely, by the cross-validation. Notice, however, that we have to estimate two covariance matrices for each class, which may be difficult, even for small images, due to the lack of sufficiently long learning sequences. The second difficulty is the possibility that $\hat{U}^{(j)}$ and/or $\hat{V}^{(j)}$ are ill-conditioned. Even if we replace the calculations of their inversions by solving the corresponding sets of linear matrix equations, a kind of the regularization may be necessary.

6   A Laboratory Example

In order to test the CMNDS, we use the same example as in [17], but this time we consider triples of subsequent images as one sequence to be classified. These images were taken during the monitoring of a laser based additive manufacturing process of constructing a thin wall, described in more detail in [22].

The classification (and then decision) problem that arises during monitoring of this process is to determine whether the laser head is above the main body of the wall (Class 1) or near one of its ends (Class 2). This task cannot be solved just by gauging positions of the laser head, since near the ends the wall it becomes thicker and thicker as construction of the wall is progressing. Additionally, these thicker parts occupy larger and larger of the wall. Precisely this unwanted behavior is to be prevented by: firstly, recognizing that a thicker end begins and then by reducing the laser power appropriately (see [22] for details concerning the reduction of the laser power). Here, we concentrate on the recognition phase only.

Original images were down-sampled by 10 to the size 12×24. Then, they were averaged (each class separately). The resulting images are shown in Fig. 1, where the left hand side image corresponds to Class 1 and the second one is typical for Class 2.

Three element sequences, typical for Class 1, consists of:

(a) either three images as the one on the l.h.s. of Fig. 1 or
(b) two such images and the one similar to that on the r.h.s. of this figure.

Analogously, the triples typical for Class 2 contain:

(c) either three images like the one on the r.h.s. or
(d) two of this kind and one similar to the l.h.s. sub-image.

For learning and testing purposes we had 300 such triples, but classes are not well balanced, since the laser head spends much more time in the middle of the wall than near its ends.

Remark 2. *Notice that ordering of images in these two kinds of sequences is not artificial – it is natural for this process, since the laser head moves back and forth along the wall. However, the presence of the sequences like those described as (b) and such as mentioned in (d) may lead to large classification errors.*

Fig. 1. Averaged images typical for Class 1 (left panel) and for Class 2 (right panel)

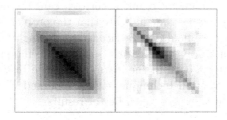

Fig. 2. Estimated V matrices for Class 1 (left panel) and Class 2 (right panel)

Matrices U and V for both classes were estimated by the method that is described in the learning phase of CMNDS and in the Appendix. The results are shown in Fig. 2 for V-type matrices and in Fig. 3 for U-type matrices. As one can observe, both U-type and V-type matrices are essentially different between

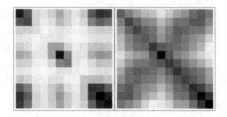

Fig. 3. Estimated U matrices for Class 1 (left panel) and Class 2 (right panel)

classes. Thus, we cannot use a linear classifier and therefore the full version of the quadratic classifier (16) was used in our example.

The following cross-validation methodology was used for testing CMNDS (see [1] for the survey of the test error estimation of classifiers). The whole sequence of triple sequences was split at random into the learning sequence of the length 125 the testing sequence of the length 175. Then, the matrices of means and covariances were estimated and plugged-in into the classifier, which was tested on the remaining 175 triples. The classification error was stored and the whole cycle of random drawing, learning and testing was repeated 1000 times. The averaged classification error (for $\alpha = 0.9$) was the following: 32% with minor fluctuations between all 1000 runs.

This result is rather disappointing, since for almost the same MND classifier, but applied to individual images, we obtained 4% of the averaged classification errors, using the same sequence of 900 images and the same methodology of testing the classifier.

One of possible reasons is that we have a relatively small number of learning and testing examples, namely, 900 images provide only 300 of triple image sequences. As a remedy in this example one may try to extend the data artificially, in a way similar to those that are used in imputation techniques, e.g., as it is proposed in [7], but this is outside the scope of this paper.

The reasons of a high recognition errors can be case-dependent (see Remark 2), but – in general – they indicate that the problem of classifying image sequences is much more difficult in practice than one might expect. Notice, however, that we do not apply any feature selection techniques, i.e., raw image triples were fed as inputs both in the learning and the testing phase. Applying a dedicated feature selection technique, e.g., a modified version of the method proposed in [3], one may expect much better results.

7   Concluding Remarks

Under several restricting, but interpretable and partly removable, assumptions the method of classifying image sequences (considered as entities) is proposed. It was extensively tested on image sequences from laboratory experiments, concerning the monitoring of the additive manufacturing, laser based, process. The results of testing indicate that the method works properly, but the percentage of correct classifications (68%) is lower than 94% obtainable under the MND assumptions, i.e., when images are considered separately. This conclusion is in agreement with the results reported in [8] that classifying individual images may sometimes lead to a better correct classification rates than classifying whole sequences. These facts indicate that problems of classifying image sequences is much more difficult than classifying individual images. It requires further research on deciding which problem statement is more appropriate in a given application.

Acknowledgements. Special thanks are addressed to Professor J. Reiner and to MSc. P. Jurewicz from the Faculty of Mechanical Engineering, Wroclaw University of Technology for common research on laser power control for additive manufacturing.

Appendix: MND and Its Estimation

The matrix normal distribution (MND) has the probability density function of the form (see, e.g., [14]):

$$f(\mathbf{X}) = \frac{1}{c} \exp\left[-\frac{1}{2} \operatorname{tr}[U^{-1}(\mathbf{X} - \mathbf{M}) V^{-1} (\mathbf{X} - \mathbf{M})^T]\right], \qquad (17)$$

where c is the normalization constant, which is given by:

$$c \stackrel{def}{=} (2\pi)^{0.5\,n\,m} \det[U]^{0.5\,n} \det[V]^{0.5\,m}, \qquad (18)$$

where $n \times m$ matrix M denotes the mean.

Concerning the covariance structure of MND densities:

1. $n \times n$ matrix U denotes the covariance matrix between rows of an image,
2. $m \times m$ matrix V stands for the covariance matrix between columns, we assume that $\det[U] > 0$, $\det[V] > 0$. We use the notation: $\mathbf{X} \sim \mathcal{N}_{n,m}(\mathbf{M}, U, V)$. The MND is a special case of a general class of Gaussian p.d.f.'s, since $\operatorname{vec}(\mathbf{X}) \sim \mathcal{N}_{nm}(\operatorname{vec}(\mathbf{M}), \Sigma)$, where $\operatorname{vec}(\mathbf{X})$ is the operation of stacking columns of matrix $\mathbf{X}$, while Σ is an $nm \times nm$ covariance matrix, which is the Kronecker product of U and V.

We assume that we have the sequence of observations: $\mathbf{X}_i$, $i = 1, 2, \ldots N$. Conditions for estimating properly the covariance matrices can be found in [12]. The maximum likelihood estimates (MLE) of the covariance matrices fulfil the following set of equations (see [12,25]):

$$\hat{U} = \frac{1}{N\,m} \sum_{i=1}^{N} (\mathbf{X}_i - \hat{\mathbf{M}}) \hat{V}^{-1} (\mathbf{X}_i - \hat{\mathbf{M}})^T, \qquad (19)$$

$$\hat{V} = \frac{1}{N\,n} \sum_{i=1}^{N} (\mathbf{X}_i - \hat{\mathbf{M}})^T \hat{U}^{-1} (\mathbf{X}_i - \hat{\mathbf{M}}). \qquad (20)$$

Equations (19) and (20) can be solved by the flip-flop method. It was proved in [25] that one iteration is sufficient to obtain the efficient estimators of U_j and V_j.

References

1. Anguita, D., Ghelardoni, L., Ghio, A., Ridella, S.: A survey of old and new results for the test error estimation of a classifier. J. Artif. Intell. Soft Comput. Res. **3**(4), 229–242 (2013)
2. Bruździński, T., Krzyżak, A., Fevens, T., Jeleń, Ł.: Web-based framework for breast cancer classification. J. Artif. Intell. Soft Comput. Res. **4**(2), 149–162 (2014)
3. Chang, O., Constante, P., Gordon, A., Singana, M.: A novel deep neural network that uses space-time features for tracking and recognizing a moving object. J. Artif. Intell. Soft Comput. Res. **7**(2), 125–136 (2017)
4. Devroye, L., Gyorfi, L., Lugosi, G.: A Probabilistic Theory of Pattern Recognition. Springer, Berlin (2013). https://doi.org/10.1007/978-1-4612-0711-5
5. Górniak, A., Skubalska-Rafajłowicz, E.: Registration and sequencing of vessels section images at macroscopic levels. In: Saeed, K., Homenda, W. (eds.) CISIM 2015. LNCS, vol. 9339, pp. 399–410. Springer, Cham (2015). https://doi.org/10.1007/978-3-319-24369-6_33
6. Górniak, A., Skubalska-Rafajłowicz, E.: Tissue recognition on microscopic images of histological sections using sequences of Zernike moments. In: Saeed, K., Homenda, W. (eds.) CISIM 2018. LNCS, vol. 11127, pp. 16–26. Springer, Cham (2018). https://doi.org/10.1007/978-3-319-99954-8_2
7. Jordanov, I., Petrov, N., Petrozziello, A.: Classifiers accuracy improvement based on missing data imputation. J. Artif. Intell. Soft Comput. Res. **8**(1), 31–48 (2018)
8. Karpathy, A., Toderici, G., Shetty, S., Leung, T., Sukthankar, R., Fei-Fei, L.: Large-scale video classification with convolutional neural networks. In: Proceedings of the IEEE Conference on Computer Vision and Pattern Recognition, pp. 1725–1732 (2014)
9. Kafai, M., Bhanu, B.: Dynamic Bayesian networks for vehicle classification in video. IEEE Trans. Industr. Inf. **8**(1), 100–109 (2012)
10. Krzyśko, M., Skorzybut, M.: Discriminant analysis of multivariate repeated measures data with a Kronecker product structured covariance matrices. Stat. Pap. **50**(4), 817–835 (2009)
11. Krzysko, M., Skorzybut, M., Wolynski, W.: Classifiers for doubly multivariate data. Discussiones Mathematicae: Probability & Statistics, p. 31 (2011)
12. Manceur, A.M., Dutilleul, P.: Maximum likelihood estimation for the tensor normal distribution: algorithm, minimum sample size, and empirical bias and dispersion. J. Comput. Appl. Math. **239**, 37–49 (2013)
13. Notomista, G., Botsch, M.: A machine learning approach for the segmentation of driving maneuvers and its application in autonomous parking. J. Artif. Intell. Soft Comput. Res. **7**(4), 243–255 (2017)
14. Ohlson, M., Ahmad, M.R., Von Rosen, D.: The multilinear normal distribution: introduction and some basic properties. J. Multivariate Anal. **113**, 37–47 (2013)
15. Prause, A., Steland, A.: Sequential detection of three-dimensional signals under dependent noise. Sequential Anal. **36**(2), 151–178 (2017)
16. Rafajłowicz, E., Steland, A.: The Hotelling-like T^2 control chart modified for detecting changes in images having the matrix normal distribution. In: Stochastic Models, Statistics and Their Applications. Springer, Cham (2019, accepted)
17. Rafajłowicz, E.: Data structures for pattern and image recognition with application to quality control Acta Polytechnica Hungarica. Informatics **15**(4), 233–262 (2018)

18. Rafajłowicz, E.: Classifiers for matrix normal images: derivation and testing. In: Rutkowski, L., Scherer, R., Korytkowski, M., Pedrycz, W., Tadeusiewicz, R., Zurada, J.M. (eds.) ICAISC 2018. LNCS (LNAI), vol. 10841, pp. 668–679. Springer, Cham (2018). https://doi.org/10.1007/978-3-319-91253-0_62

19. Rafajłowicz, E.: Robustness of raw images classifiers against the class imbalance – a case study. In: Saeed, K., Homenda, W. (eds.) CISIM 2018. LNCS, vol. 11127, pp. 154–165. Springer, Cham (2018). https://doi.org/10.1007/978-3-319-99954-8_14

20. Rafajłowicz, E., Rafajłowicz, W.: Linear matrix-state systems and their use for image-driven control. In: 10th International Workshop on Multidimensional (nD) Systems (nDS), 13–15 September 2017, Zielona Góra, Poland, Danvers, pp. 1–6. IEEE (2017)

21. Rafajłowicz, E.: Detection of essential changes in spatio-temporal processes with applications to camera based quality control. In: Steland, A., Rafajłowicz, E., Szajowski, K. (eds.) Stochastic Models, Statistics and Their Applications, pp. 433–440. Springer, Cham (2015). https://doi.org/10.1007/978-3-319-13881-7_48

22. Rafajłowicz, W., Jurewicz, P., Reiner, J., Rafajłowicz, E.: Iterative learning of optimal control for nonlinear processes with applications to laser additive manufacturing. IEEE Trans. Control Syst. Technol. (2018, accepted, available on-line)

23. Skubalska-Rafajłowicz, E.: Sparse random projections of camera images for monitoring of a combustion process in a gas burner. In: Saeed, K., Homenda, W., Chaki, R. (eds.) CISIM 2017. LNCS, vol. 10244, pp. 447–456. Springer, Cham (2017). https://doi.org/10.1007/978-3-319-59105-6_38

24. Szczepaniak, P., Tadeusiewicz, R.: The role of artificial intelligence, knowledge and wisdom in automatic image understanding. J. Appl. Comput. Sci. 18(1), 75–85 (2010)

25. Werner, K., Jansson, M., Stoica, P.: On estimation of covariance matrices with Kronecker product structure. IEEE Trans. Signal Process. 56(2), 478–491 (2008)

26. Wytyczak-Partyka, A., Nikodem, J., Klempous, R., Rozenblit, J., Klempous, R., Rudas, I.: Safety oriented laparoscopic surgery training system. In: Moreno-Díaz, R., Pichler, F., Quesada-Arencibia, A. (eds.) EUROCAST 2009. LNCS, vol. 5717, pp. 889–896. Springer, Berlin, Heidelberg (2009). https://doi.org/10.1007/978-3-642-04772-5_114

The Elastic k-Nearest Neighbours Classifier for Touch Screen Gestures

Krzysztof Rzecki[1]([✉])[iD], Leszek Siwik[2][iD], and Mateusz Baran[1][iD]

[1] Faculty of Physics, Mathematics and Computer Science,
Cracow University of Technology, ul. Warszawska 24, 31-155 Kraków, Poland
{krz,mbaran}@pk.edu.pl
[2] Department of Computer Science, AGH University of Science and Technology,
Kraków, Poland
siwik@agh.edu.pl

Abstract. Touch screen gestures are a well-known method of person authentication in mobile devices. In most applications it is, however, reduced to checking if the user entered the correct pattern. Using additional information based on the speed and shape of finger movements can provide higher security without significantly impacting the convenience of this authorization method. In this work a new distance function for the k-nearest neighbour (kNN) classifier is considered in the problem of person recognition based on touch screen gestures. The function is based on the well-known L^p distance and the elastic distance considered in elastic shape analysis. Performance of the classifier is measured using 5-fold stratified cross-validation on a set of 12 people. Only four gesture performances per gesture for each person are used to train a model. The effects of sampling rate on the classifier performance is also measured. The kNN classifier with the proposed distance function has higher accuracy than both the L^p distance and the elastic distance.

Keywords: Touch screen gestures · Biometrics · Classification ·
Elastic shape analysis · Pattern recognition

1 Introduction

Biometric identification, that is the process of identifying a person based on physiological or behavioural characteristics distinguishing them from other people [10]. Many different methods were designed based on various features like face images, iris, fingerprints or signature. Different applications have different requirements for a method used for identification. For example, most touch screen devices lack dedicated biometry hardware. Applying biometric methods to the common gesture-based identification would improve security without impacting user convenience.

In this work, the k-nearest neighbours algorithm (abbreviated kNN) is applied to the problem of person recognition based on a performance of a hand

© Springer Nature Switzerland AG 2019
L. Rutkowski et al. (Eds.): ICAISC 2019, LNAI 11508, pp. 608–615, 2019.
https://doi.org/10.1007/978-3-030-20912-4_55

gesture on a touch display. This problem has been previously studied in [21]. Other approaches to person recognition based on hand gestures include using data from a specialized glove [5,20] or sequences of images from a camera (including a depth camera) [6,23].

The kNN classifier and its variants is the most popular family of nonparametric, distance-based classification algorithms. During the years, it has received a lot of attention and many variants were proposed, for example variants based on manifold learning [15,26] or weighted kNN [7,13]. The kNN algorithm was selected for its good performance on small data sets, such as the set of available training gestures, as well as its ability to learn incrementally as the user repeatedly performs the same gesture [14].

One of the major problems of applying the kNN classifier to gesture recognition is moderately high dimensionality of the input data [19]. It has, however, been shown that appropriate selection of the distance function results in high accuracy of the constructed classifier [20].

In recent years the elastic metric [27] has been suggested for comparing functional data. The method, partially inspired by increasingly popular data analysis using Riemannian geometry [2,9,16,25], received a significant amount of attention [1,17,18,22,24,25,28], with important developments such as the Square Root Velocity Function representation [12].

In this work the classical L^p distance is extended by combining it with the elastic metric. A set of five gestures, twelve people and five gesture executions per person is used in experiments. The resulting parameter tuning is evaluated using stratified 5-fold cross-validation to prevent overfitting [11].

2   Materials and Methods

2.1   Gesture Data Set

The touch screen gesture data was gathered using mobile devices with touch screens (smartphones) [21]. People were asked to perform a predefined set of gestures, moving a finger along a certain path connecting rings arranged in a rectangular pattern (see Fig. 1). The task is to recognize a person based on a single performance of a gesture (a survey) from a predefined set of people, a special case of the classification. A few repetitions of each gesture performed by each person are available for building a statistical model for this classification task. In total, $N_G = 5$ gestures performed $N_R = 5$ times by each one of $N_P = 12$ people were analysed. Only continuous gestures (performed without raising a finger from the screen) were considered because of continuity assumption of the proposed model.

A survey can be modelled as a curve $f_{P,G,R}(t)\colon [0,1] \to \mathbb{R}^2$ where $P \in \{1,2,\ldots,N_P\}$ is the number of person, $G \in \{1,2,\ldots,N_G\}$ is the number of gesture used for recognition and $R \in \{1,2,\ldots,N_R\}$ is the number of repetition. The pressure data and total time of gesture execution, collected for previous experiments, was not used.

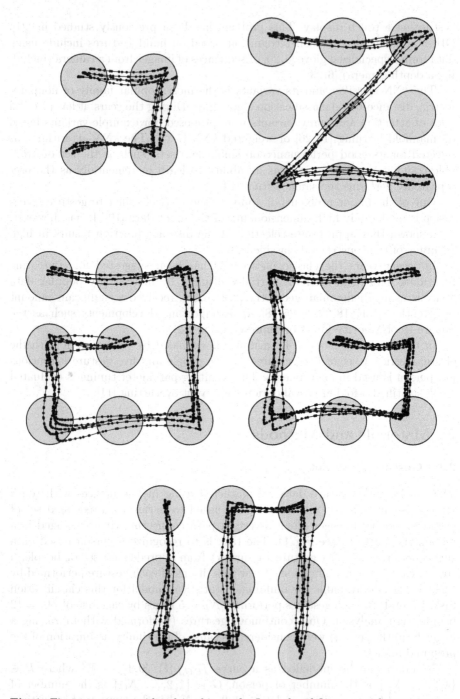

Fig. 1. Five gestures considered in this study. In each subfigure sample surveys performed by the same person are displayed. Small dots are placed in equal time intervals to show variability in speed of gesture. All gestures except the G-shaped one begin in the top left corner, whereas the G-shaped gesture begins in the top right corner.

2.2 The Classification Algorithm

The proposed distance function combines the classic L^p space distance and the elastic metric, which is most easily expressed using the Square Root Velocity Function (SRVF) representation of compared functions. For a function $f\colon [0,1] \to \mathbb{R}^2$, its SRVF representation is expressed as a function $q\colon [0,1] \to \mathbb{R}^2$ such that $q(t) = F(\dot{f}(t))$ where $F(v) = v/\sqrt{\|v\|}$ if $\|v\| > 0$ and 0 otherwise. For discretized curves, the first order forward finite difference formula is used to approximate the derivative.

The classification is performed using the k-nearest neighbour algorithm. To calculate the distance between two given surveys f_1, f_2 the following function is used:

$$d_C(f_1, f_2) = \alpha \left(\int_0^1 \|f_1(t) - f_2(t)\|^p \, dt \right)^{1/p} +$$
$$(1-\alpha) \min_{\gamma \in \Gamma} \sqrt{\int_0^1 \left\| q_1(t) - q_2(\gamma(t)) \sqrt{\dot{\gamma}(t)} \right\|^2 dt}, \tag{1}$$

where $\alpha \in [0,1]$ and $p \in (0, \infty]$ are the parameters, Γ is the set of reparametrizations, that is function $\gamma\colon [0,1] \to [0,1]$ such that $\gamma(0) = 0$, $\gamma(1) = 1$ and $\dot{\gamma}(t) > 0$ for all $t \in [0,1]$ and q_1, q_2 are SRVF representations of, respectively, f_1 and f_2. For $p \geq 1$ the function d_C, as a convex combination of two metrics, is also a metric. For details regarding calculation of the elastic metric, see [3,12]. In this paper, the dynamic programming approach is used to perform the minimization. The same discretization of the minimization over the set of reparametrizations as in [1] was used.

An important property of the elastic metric is its ability to simultaneously consider bending and stretching in a principled way (see Fig. 2). In general, it is defined as a Riemannian metric on the manifold of curves with two parameters whose ratio describes the relative weight of curve bending and stretching required to fit two given curves. However, a performant algorithm to compute this distance is known only for a single ratio of this two parameters and gives rise to the described SRVF representation framework.

2.3 Experiment Design

During the computational experiment each gesture was analysed separately. Five surveys for each person were used in evaluation based on a stratified 5-fold cross-validation. In each fold 4 surveys for each person were put in the training set and the remaining one was a part of the validation set.

The curves were discretized at regular time intervals, $t \in \{0, \Delta t, 2\Delta t, \ldots, 1\}$, for $\Delta t \in \{0.02, 0.05\}$. The parameters were optimized using full grid search over the following sets: $p \in \{0.5, 1, 2, \infty\}$, $\alpha \in \{0, 0.01, 0.1, 0.5, 0.9, 0.99, 1\}$ and $k = 1$.

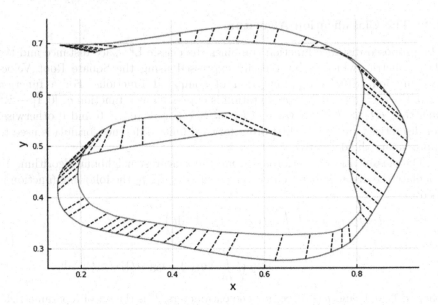

Fig. 2. Two sample gestures (shown in solid lines) and reparametrization visualised as dashed lines connecting matching point on both curves. Endpoints of dashed lines mark places on curves that correspond to sampled at a constant time interval.

Table 1. Accuracy of the elastic kNN classifier for sampling $\Delta t = 0.05$.

α	0	0.01	0.1	0.5	0.9	0.99	1
$p = 0.5$	60.0%	60.0%	60.3%	60.0%	**68.3%**	62.7%	62.7%
$p = 1$	60.0%	60.0%	60.3%	64.0%	**68.3%**	63.7%	62.7%
$p = 2$	60.0%	60.0%	60.3%	65.3%	67.0%	60.3%	62.7%
$p = \infty$	60.0%	59.7%	61.0%	63.0%	57.0%	48.7%	48.3%

Table 2. Accuracy of the elastic kNN classifier for sampling $\Delta t = 0.02$.

α	0	0.01	0.1	0.5	0.9	0.99	1
$p = 0.5$	68.0%	68.7%	70.0%	68.7%	72.3%	65.7%	64.3%
$p = 1$	68.0%	68.7%	70.0%	**73.3%**	69.0%	66.3%	65.3%
$p = 2$	68.0%	68.7%	70.3%	73.0%	66.3%	61.3%	62.3%
$p = \infty$	68.0%	69.0%	70.0%	67.7%	54.3%	49.0%	48.7%

3   Results and Discussion

Tables 1 and 2 present results of the experiments for considered values of Δt, α and p. Accuracy of the kNN classifier with $k = 1$ and distance function described by given parameters is presented and the highest accuracy for each discretization step is written in bold. The results of a kNN classifier with the L^p distance can be read from columns with $\alpha = 1$. The results for the elastic metric are in columns with $\alpha = 0$. For sampling with $\Delta t = 0.05$ the highest accuracy (68.3%) was obtained using $\alpha = 0.9$ and p equal to either 0.5 or 1. Using sampling with $\Delta t = 0.02$, even higher accuracy (73.3%) was obtained for $\alpha = 0.5$ and $p = 1$.

The results indicate that the new proposed distance function constitutes an improvement over existing functions: the L^p distance and the elastic distance. The accuracy is satisfactory regarding a very small set of samples per person used in building the model (four gesture executions per person) and a relatively large number of people that were recognized (twelve people).

Other values of Δt (0.002, 0.005, 0.01 and 0.04) and $k = 3$ were also tested in a more limited parameter space. There was no or very small improvement over presented results.

The time needed to calculate the distance d_C given by Eq. (1) is mostly spent on calculating the elastic distance. On average, it is equal to 2 ms for sampling $\Delta t = 0.02$ and 0.3 ms for $\Delta t = 0.05$. The measured time of calculation of the L^p distance was equal to about 5 μs for $\Delta t = 0.05$ and 13 μs for $\Delta t = 0.02$. The results were obtained on an Intel Core i7 processor using custom software written in Julia [4].

4   Conclusions

A new distance function for the k-nearest neighbour classifier was introduced in this study. It was compared against other known distance functions, the L^p distance and the elastic metric. The accuracy of the kNN classifier with the proposed distance function was shown to be higher than for other functions. For optimally fitted parameters, the accuracy was equal to 73.3%. Classifiers based on the L^p distance and the elastic metric reached the accuracy of only 65.3% and 68%, respectively.

The proposed variant of the kNN classifier has satisfactory accuracy even on very small datasets. Given its excellent ability to incorporate new examples into the model, it is a very good choice for person recognition based on touch screen gestures.

In future work we will consider using dimensionality reduction methods as part of preprocessing and combination with feature selection algorithms [8,19]. We will also test other variants of the kNN algorithm with the proposed distance function.

References

1. Baran, M.: Closest paths in graph drawings under an elastic metric. Int. J. Appl. Math. Comput. Sci. **28**(2), 387–397 (2018). https://doi.org/10.2478/amcs-2018-0029

2. Baran, M., Tabor, Z.: Principal geodesic analysis boundary delineation with superpixel-based constraints. Image Anal. Stereology **36**(3), 223–232 (2017). https://doi.org/10.5566/ias.1712

3. Bernal, J., Doğan, G., Hagwood, C.R.: Fast dynamic programming for elastic registration of curves. In: 2016 IEEE Conference on Computer Vision and Pattern Recognition Workshops (CVPRW), pp. 1066–1073, June 2016. https://doi.org/10.1109/CVPRW.2016.137

4. Bezanson, J., Edelman, A., Karpinski, S., Shah, V.: Julia: a fresh approach to numerical computing. SIAM Rev. **59**(1), 65–98 (2017). https://doi.org/10.1137/141000671

5. Blachnik, M., Głomb, P.: Do we need complex models for gestures? A comparison of data representation and preprocessing methods for hand gesture recognition. In: Rutkowski, L., Korytkowski, M., Scherer, R., Tadeusiewicz, R., Zadeh, L.A., Zurada, J.M. (eds.) ICAISC 2012. LNCS (LNAI), vol. 7267, pp. 477–485. Springer, Heidelberg (2012). https://doi.org/10.1007/978-3-642-29347-4_55

6. Cholewa, M., Głomb, P.: Estimation of the number of states for gesture recognition with Hidden Markov Models based on the number of critical points in time sequence. Pattern Recogn. Lett. **34**(5), 574–579 (2013). https://doi.org/10.1016/j.patrec.2012.12.002

7. Dudani, S.A.: The distance-weighted k-nearest-neighbor rule. IEEE Trans. Syst. Man Cybern. SMC **6**(4), 325–327 (1976). https://doi.org/10.1109/TSMC.1976.5408784

8. Ghosh, I.: Probabilistic feature selection in machine learning. In: Rutkowski, L., Scherer, R., Korytkowski, M., Pedrycz, W., Tadeusiewicz, R., Zurada, J.M. (eds.) ICAISC 2018. LNCS (LNAI), vol. 10841, pp. 623–632. Springer, Cham (2018). https://doi.org/10.1007/978-3-319-91253-0_58

9. Huckemann, S., Ziezold, H.: Principal component analysis for Riemannian manifolds, with an application to triangular shape spaces. Adv. Appl. Probab. **38**(2), 299–319 (2006). https://doi.org/10.1239/aap/1151337073

10. Jain, A., Hong, L., Pankanti, S.: Biometric Identification. Commun. ACM **43**(2), 90–98 (2000). https://doi.org/10.1145/328236.328110

11. Japkowicz, N., Shah, M.: Evaluating Learning Algorithms: A Classification Perspective, 1st edn. Cambridge University Press, Cambridge (2011)

12. Joshi, S.H., Klassen, E., Srivastava, A., Jermyn, I.: A novel representation for Riemannian analysis of elastic curves in Rn. In: Proceedings/CVPR, IEEE Computer Society Conference on Computer Vision and Pattern Recognition, pp. 1–7. IEEE, Minneapolis July 2007. https://doi.org/10.1109/CVPR.2007.383185

13. Kozak, K., Kozak, M., Stapor, K.: Weighted k-nearest-neighbor techniques for high throughput screening data. Int. J. Biol. Med. Sci. **1**, 155 (2006)

14. Kotsiantis, S.B.: Supervised machine learning: a review of classification techniques. In: Proceedings of the 2007 Conference on Emerging Artificial Intelligence Applications in Computer Engineering: Real Word AI Systems with Applications in eHealth, HCI, Information Retrieval and Pervasive Technologies, pp. 3–24. IOS Press, Amsterdam (2007)

15. Ma, L., Crawford, M.M., Tian, J.: Local manifold learning-based *k*-nearest-neighbor for hyperspectral image classification. IEEE Trans. Geosci. Remote Sens. **48**(11), 4099–4109 (2010). https://doi.org/10.1109/TGRS.2010.2055876

16. Mani, M., Kurtek, S., Barillot, C., Srivastava, A.: A comprehensive riemannian framework for the analysis of white matter fiber tracts. In: 2010 IEEE International Symposium on Biomedical Imaging: From Nano to Macro, pp. 1101–1104, April 2010. https://doi.org/10.1109/ISBI.2010.5490185

17. Michor, P.W., Mumford, D.B.: Riemannian geometries on spaces of plane curves. J. Eur. Math. Soc. **8**(1), 1–48 (2006). https://doi.org/10.4171/JEMS/37

18. Mio, W., Srivastava, A., Joshi, S.: On shape of plane elastic curves. Int. J. Comput. Vis. **73**(3), 307–324 (2007). https://doi.org/10.1007/s11263-006-9968-0

19. Murphy, K.P.: Machine Learning: A Probabilistic Perspective. Adaptive Computation and Machine Learning, 1st edn. The MIT Press, Cambridge (2012)

20. Pławiak, P., Sośnicki, T., Niedźwiecki, M., Tabor, Z., Rzecki, K.: Hand body language gesture recognition based on signals from specialized glove and machine learning algorithms. IEEE Trans. Ind. Inf. **12**(3), 1104–1113 (2016). https://doi.org/10.1109/TII.2016.2550528

21. Rzecki, K., Pławiak, P., Niedźwiecki, M., Sośnicki, T., Leśkow, J., Ciesielski, M.: Person recognition based on touch screen gestures using computational intelligence methods. Inf. Sci. **415–416**, 70–84 (2017). https://doi.org/10.1016/j.ins.2017.05.041

22. Srivastava, A., Turaga, P., Kurtek, S.: On advances in differential-geometric approaches for 2D and 3D shape analyses and activity recognition. Image Vis. Comput. **30**(6–7), 398–416 (2012). https://doi.org/10.1016/j.imavis.2012.03.006

23. Suarez, J., Murphy, R.R.: Hand gesture recognition with depth images: a review. In: 2012 IEEE RO-MAN: The 21st IEEE International Symposium on Robot and Human Interactive Communication, pp. 411–417 September 2012. https://doi.org/10.1109/ROMAN.2012.6343787

24. Sundaramoorthi, G., Mennucci, A., Soatto, S., Yezzi, A.: A new geometric metric in the space of curves, and applications to tracking deforming objects by prediction and filtering. SIAM J. Imaging Sci. **4**(1), 109–145 (2011). https://doi.org/10.1137/090781139

25. Turaga, P.K., Srivastava, A. (eds.): Riemannian Computing in Computer Vision. Springer, Cham (2016). https://doi.org/10.1007/978-3-319-22957-7

26. Van Der Maaten, L., Postma, E., Van den Herik, J.: Dimensionality reduction: a comparative review. Tech. Rep. TiCC TR 2009–005, Tilburg University (2009)

27. Younes, L.: Computable elastic distances between shapes. SIAM J. Appl. Math. **58**(2), 565–586 (1998). https://doi.org/10.1137/S0036139995287685

28. Younes, L.: Spaces and manifolds of shapes in computer vision: an overview. Image Vis. Comput. **30**(6–7), 389–397 (2012). https://doi.org/10.1016/j.imavis.2011.09.009

Whole Image and Modular Image Face Classification - What is Really Classified?

Ewa Skubalska-Rafajłowicz[✉] [iD]

Faculty of Electronics, Department of Computer Engineering,
Wrocław University of Science and Technology, Wrocław, Poland
ewa.rafajlowicz@pwr.edu.pl

Abstract. Our aim is to explore the importance of chosen parts of frontal face images for person recognition. We have used logistic regression as the method of face image classification based on rough image classification, and on selected parts of an image divided into rectangular image blocks. Rough image means that no image processing transformation is performed before classification. Experiments on the images of 40 persons taken from the ORL face database show that a person classification based on collections of rough face images are effective, high accuracy rates are easy to obtain, but deeper analysis based on image partitioning suggests that the most important factor for correct classification are border parts of the face image. Furthermore, the experiments confirm the thesis that randomly generated projections do not degrade, or only slightly reduce the accuracy of classification, reducing the size of the vector of features in a significant way.

Keywords: Face classification · Multinomial logistic regression ·
Spatial importance · Random projection · Privacy preserving

1 Introduction

Face recognition is a problem that has been the focus of attention from many years [1,8,9,13,18]. The face as a biometric factor [7,16] may not be the most reliable and efficient but is gaining increasing acceptance because it could work without the co-operation of the test subject. Passers-by may not even be aware of the system. In most instances, the images were not taken in a controlled environment, so illumination, facial expression, pose and other disturbances can affect the results of recognition [6,14]. Many different face classification methods use some kind of partition of a face image into rectangular image blocks, see for example, the modular PCA approach [8], the rectangular image block random projections methods [20–22], histogram of oriented gradients (HOG) based methods [4,24] or Local Binary Pattern (LBP) [17]. We do not even try to give a full overview of modular face recognition methods, i.e., methods based on a rectangular image partitioning, because of the presented results of the research concern very different conditions of performance and often require intensive processing of

© Springer Nature Switzerland AG 2019
L. Rutkowski et al. (Eds.): ICAISC 2019, LNAI 11508, pp. 616–625, 2019.
https://doi.org/10.1007/978-3-030-20912-4_56

each image prior to classification. Nevertheless, in spite of their simplicity, methods used in this work provide the hard to beat accuracy of facial recognition. Better results are possible, but are obtainable at the cost of time-consuming image processing procedures.

Our goal is to find the parts of a face image which are more important for the correct person classification than others. To do this we resign of feature selection such as, for example, eigenfaces (PCA) [23, 25, 27, 28]. In this paper, we have used pixel values as features.

Furthermore, it occurred during the simulations that the logistic regression can work efficiently with very high-dimensional feature vectors and that randomly generated projections of data do not destroy the classification results. Thus, such approaches allow us to compress efficiently the image data, additionally protecting the privacy of visualized people.

The methods examined in this paper could be used in open recognition systems. Random projection-based methods of image dimensionality reduction are independent of the data. Thus, adding or removing images from the classification system does not require any changes in transformation. The computational complexity of designing the transformation is linear with respect to the size of an image. Random projection of the whole image treated as a vector is a very simple method of obtaining low dimensional feature vectors representing large images. The block-based approach allows for even lower projection dimensions. Furthermore, the logistic regression estimates the probability of belonging to a certain class so it is possible to use the reject option when the maximum of the probability value is too low.

The main message of this paper is that border parts of the face image are the most important for correct facial classification based on a set of images taken in a changing frontal position. These border parts contain images of the subject's hair, beard, jawline, arms, forehead and ears, i.e., very soft biometric features. Experiments were performed on a set of images taken from the ORL facial database. ORL consists of 400 images of 40 persons where the images were taken at different times with different facial expressions, different facial details and head positions.

The paper is organized as follows. Section 2 provides important information about multinomial logistic regression classification method. The next Section describes classes of features used for facial recognition. Section 4 presents the ORL database details and gives the classification results based on full-size face images. These results form a base for spatial analysis of images in relation to their role in the correct person classification. Results of different sub-images classification are given in Sect. 5. Finally, some comments and conclusions are summarized.

2   Multinomial Logistic Regression

As a basic method of classification we have used multinomial logistic regression (MLR). This approach is known also as the log-linear model, softmax regression, or maximum-entropy classifier [5,10,12,15,26]. MLR is a method that attempts to separate objects belonging to different classes, and group objects belonging to the same class. The logistic regression classifier provides models of class probabilities as logistic functions of linear combinations of discriminative variables (features). The method works well even in the high-dimensional settings, so even rough images (image pixel values in a vector form) can be used as features. A symmetric formulation for multi-class logistic regression is given as:

$$Pr\{Y = c|X = x\} = \frac{\exp(w_{0c} + x^T w_c)}{\sum_{l=1}^{C} w_{0l} + x^T w_l}, \quad c = 1, \ldots, C, \tag{1}$$

where $x \in R^d$ is a feature vector, $w_c \in R^d$ is the weight vector corresponding to class c and w_{0c} is an additional, class-dependent bias parameter. The unknown weights are usually jointly estimated by maximum a posteriori (MAP) estimation using regularization of the weights (commonly as L_2 regularization term) [5]. Thus, it suffices to minimize with respect to w's the following regularized negative log-likelihood function:

$$-\sum_{c=1}^{C}\sum_{j=1}^{r_c}[(w_{0c}+w_c^T x_j(c))-\log\sum_{i=1}^{C}\exp(w_{0i}+w_i^T x_j(c))]+\rho(\sum_{c=1}^{C}(w_{0c}^2+w_c^T w_c), \tag{2}$$

where $x_1(c), \ldots x_{r_c}(c)$, $c = 1, \ldots C$ are learning feature samples and ρ is the regularization parameter. The softmax function is often used in the final layer of a neural network-based classifiers. Thus, MLR could be seen as a simple neural network with the specific method of training weights.

3   Feature used for Faces Classification

An image can be classified in a number of ways, depending on our a priori knowledge and many other factors. In this paper, we have used rough images (in vectorized form) as feature vectors and its randomly generated projections into lower dimensional space. We have used dense Gaussian projections [3,22] without any other transformations. In the first case, i.e., pixel values taken as features, partitioning of images makes no sense. The other - a random projection based approach combined with MLR classifier - consists in adding a layer of random weights preceding the softmax layer. Such a method of reducing the image's dimensions in connection with neural networks has a long history starting from the perceptron of Rosenblatt [19]. In the modular methods, i.e., in methods based on the division of the image into sub-images, we have to establish an image partitioning pattern. First, each image is divided into rectangular blocks usually of the same size. Every image block is considered as a separate image and is projected independently from other image blocks, forming only a part of a new feature vector. All these local feature vectors are concatenated, forming the feature vector of dimension kM, where M stands for a number of blocks and k is a dimension of the local random projection. It should be noted that random projection requires only $O(kd)$ operations for providing a transformation matrix whereas PCA needs $0(kd^2)$ [11].

4   Experiments

The proposed methods of classification have been conducted on the AT&T Laboratories Cambridge ORL faces database (http://www.cl.cam.ac.uk). This database contains 400 images taken from 40 persons. Each person is represented by 10 different face images. For some subjects, the images were taken at different times with different facial expressions, different facial details (with or without glasses) and head pose. The lighting conditions were also variable, though the overall quality of the photos is similar. The images of the two subjects from the ORL face database are presented in Fig. 1. All images in the database are gray-scale and normalized to a resolution of 92×112 pixels. In our experiments, the images are additionally cropped to the size of 90×108 pixels. Thus, the full dimension (d) in our experiments is equal to 9720. In the modular approach every image is split up into 30 blocks of the size 18×18 pixels. Figure 2 shows examples of partitioned images of one of the subjects. In experiments, we used 5 (or 1, or 7, or 9) images of each subject as a part of the training set. The remaining 5 (or 9, or 3 or 1) images of each subject form the testing set. The process of the learning set selection and, if applicable, the projection matrix generation, were performed many times.

Fig. 1. Sample images of the ORL database (two different subjects).

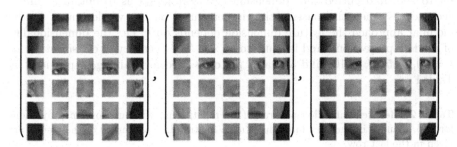

Fig. 2. Samples of partitioned images of the first subject taken from the ORL database.

So, there are 40 classes, with 200 (or 280, or 360) images used for learning and another 200 (or 120, or 40) images for testing. Notice that, if we use 5 images per person as a learning set and the remainder of the images for testing, there exist

Table 1. Mean classification accuracy (100 repetitions) with random projections of partitioned images and dimensionality of projection $k = 10$, $k = 40$, $k = 50$, and $k = 100$.

k	10	40	50	100
Accuracy %	93.11	94.41	**94.48**	94.06
Variance	3.8	3.7	2.7	3.3

about $1.14 10^{96}$ different combinations of the learning and testing sets. Thus, the accuracy of the classification was estimated by Monte-Carlo cross-validation performed on 100 repetitions.

It should be emphasized that the number of weights in the MLR classifier based on whole images, i.e., without any feature selection, is equal to 388 800. The number of the classifier parameters is comparable to the number of weight in a complicated deep-network (see for example [2]). Nevertheless, the computations performed using Mathematica 11.0 are very fast and stable. 100 repetitions of the learning process take a few minutes.

4.1   Classification of Full Dimension Images

In the first part of the experiments, we concentrate on recognition possibilities of the classification system where whole images are treated as vectors. Further, we examine the accuracy of the system based on Gaussian random projections of images (treated as vectors).

The accuracy of classification is given in Tables 2, 3. Notice, that the feature dimension equals 9720 (in the case without projections) or is equal to the dimension of the projection. In the next table (see Table 3) we present the mean accuracy of classification when rough images are projected into low-dimensional space of dimensionality from 50 to 1000. The number of training samples was set to 200. It occurred that dimension $k = 300$ allows us to obtain a similar accuracy as when the classification is performed on the whole image. In the modular approach the feature dimension depends on k, i.e., the dimensionality of random projections, and is equal to $30 \times k$. The accuracy of classification for $k = 10, 40, 50$, $k = 100$ and 5 images per class used for training, is provided by Table 1.

Table 2. Mean classification accuracy (100 repetitions) without random projections for 1, 5, 7 and 9 images per individual taken for training. Variances of the results are given in the last row.

Number of training samples	40	5 × 40	7 × 40	9 × 40
Accuracy %		66.66	**94.88**	96.15	96.48
Variance		6.26	4.6	3.5	6.8

Table 3. Mean classification accuracy (100 repetitions) with randomly generated projections of whole image and dimensionality $k = 50, 100, 200, 300, 400, 500, 600, 700,$ and $k = 1000$. The number of training samples was $5 \times 40 = 200$.

k	50	100	200	300	400	500	600	700	1000
Accuracy %	86.20	91.50	93.44	94.22	**94.86**	94.76	94.25	94.85	95.69
Variance	7.5	2.6	4.4	2.1	2.0	2.0	4.0	2.2	2.4

5   Classification Based on Selected Parts of Images

A modular approach to face images classification leads to the question which parts of the face image are important for good classification taking into account that the images are captured at different times, with different facial expressions, different facial details and head pose, and in different lighting conditions. We have examined different combinations of the modular parts of the face images, i.e., combinations of sub-images of the size 18×18 pixels. The first two rows show the mean classification accuracy for three small sub-images located in the left bottom part of each image $((1, 18) \times (1, 18)$ and $(1, 18) \times (19, 36))$ in close to the center of images $((37, 54) \times (37, 54))$, where, for example $(1, 18) \times (1, 18)$ denotes the sub-image containing the first 18 rows and columns of the full image. Figure 3 shows samples of such sub-images taken from different images of two different subjects. Results of classifications are given in Table 3. The first row of this table provides average classification accuracy for sub-images of the form $(1, 18) \times (1, 18)$ (see the first two rows in Fig. 3). We do not provide other classification results for the other image block of the size 18×18 pixels. These accuracies concentrate about 50% for blocks located close to the image borders and 20–30% when the blocks are inside.

Fig. 3. Sample sub-images $(1, 18) \times (1, 18)$ and $(37, 54) \times (37, 54)$ (two different subjects).

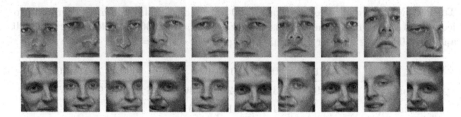

Fig. 4. Sample sub-images of the form $(19, 90) \times (19, 72)$ (two different subjects).

Relatively the most informative are the two first block-rows in combination with the last (the 6th) block-row. This part of face image allows us to predict correct person identity almost as precisely as in the case of the complete image.

Very interesting are results presented in the last row of Table 4. The classification is conducted using the central part of each image which reproduced face features of subjects (see Fig. 4 where samples of such sub-images are depicted). Results of classification based on central parts of face images are less precise than those obtained on the base of previously mentioned $(1, 36) \times (1, 90) + (91, 108) \times (1, 90)$ sub-images (Table 5).

Table 4. Mean classification accuracy for sub-images of the size 18×18 pixels (100 repetitions) 5, and 9 sub-images per individual are taken for training.

Sub-image	Mean (5) %	Variance (5)	Mean (9) %	Variance (9)
$(1, 18) \times (1, 18)$	**52.08**	6.35	57.55	42.3
$(1, 18) \times (19, 36)$	51.53	7.67	55.08	50.56
$(37, 54) \times (37, 54)$	**26.62**	6.75	31.07	36.14
$(1, 18) \times (1, 36)$	66.67	8,08	73.03	32.86
$(1, 36) \times (1, 30)$	72.63	6.54	77.30	34.3
$(1, 18) \times (1, 90)$	79.84	5.53	85.48	21.93
$(19, 36) \times (1, 90)$	76.34	8.02	83.95	29.44
$(37, 54) \times (1, 90)$	69.89	8.71	79.08	35.06
$(55, 72) \times (1, 90)$	68.79	7.49	78.97	31.11
$(73, 90) \times (1, 90)$	67.18	7.67	75.20	39.60
$(91, 108) \times (1, 90)$	78.12	6.74	86.75	26.32
$(37, 90) \times (1, 90)$	84.48	7.43	93.9	12.8
$(1, 36) \times (1, 90) +$ $(91, 108) \times (1, 90)$	**93.56**	3.26	96.3	9.27
$(19, 90) \times (19, 72)$	**79.82**	7.34	88.53	17.18

Table 5. Mean classification accuracy (100 repetitions) with random projections of chosen blocks of the image and projection dimensionality $k = 100$ and $k = 200$. The number of training samples was $5 \times 40 = 200$; variances are given in brackets.

Sub-image k	$(37, 90) \times (1, 90)$ accuracy % (variance)	$(1, 36) \times (1, 90) + (91, 108) \times (1, 90)$ accuracy % (variance)
100	82.88 (5.23)	92.85 (3.9)
200	91.43 (12.40)	92.48 (5.42)

In the modular approach the feature dimension depends on k, i.e., the dimensionality of random projections, and is equal to $30 \times k$. Table 1 provides the mean accuracy of classification for projection dimensionality $k = 10, 40, 50, k = 100$. In every case, 5 images per class are used for training.

6   Conclusions

In this paper, we have examined which parts of the face image are more important for correct person classification. Experiments strongly suggest that the most important factor in correct facial classification of parts of images taken in a changing frontal position are the border parts of the face image. These border parts contain images of the subject's hair, beard, jawline, arms, forehead and ears, i.e., very soft biometric features. Results of classification based on central parts of face images are less certain in contrast to the human experience.

The experiments presented in the paper show also that randomly generated projections do not degrade, or only slightly diminish the accuracy of classification. Moreover, the size of the vector of features is reduced in a significant way. Furthermore, during the simulation it occurred that the logistic regression can work efficiently with very high-dimensional feature vectors. Thus, such approaches allow us to compress efficiently the image data, additionally protecting the privacy of the visualized peoples.

Acknowledgments. This research was supported by scientific grant at the Faculty of Electronics, Wrocław University of Science and Technology.

References

1. Brunelli, R., Poggio, T.: Face recognition: features versus templates. IEEE Trans. PAMI **15**(10), 1042–1052 (1993)
2. Chang, O., Constante, P., Gordon, A., Singana, M.: A novel deep neural network that uses space-time features for tracking and recognizing a moving object. J. Artif. Intell. Soft Comput. Res. **7**(2), 125–136 (2017)
3. Dasgupta, S., Gupta, A.: An elementary proof of the Johnson-Lindenstrauss lemma. Random Struct. Algorithms **22**(1), 60–65 (2002)
4. Deniz, O., Bueno, G., Salido, J., De la Torre, F.: Face recognition using histograms of oriented gradients. Pattern Recognit. Lett. **32**(12), 1598–1603 (2011)

5. Friedman, J., Hastie, T., Tibshirani, R.: Regularization paths for generalized linear models via coordinate descent. J. Stat. Softw. **33**(1), 1–22 (2010)
6. Georghiades, A.S., Belhumeur, P.N., Kriegman, D.J.: From few to many: illumination cone models for face recognition under variable lighting and pose. IEEE Trans. Pattern Anal. Mach. Intell. **21**(6), 643–660 (2001)
7. Gonzalez-Sosa, E., Fierrez, J., Vera-Rodriguez, R., Alonso-Fernandez, F.: Facial soft biometrics for recognition in the wild: recent works, annotation, and COTS evaluation. IEEE Trans. Inf. Forensics Secur. **13**(8), 2001–2014 (2018)
8. Gottmukkal, R., Asari, V.K.: An improved face recognition technique based on modular PCA approach. Pattern Recognit. Lett. **24**(4), 429–436 (2004)
9. Hou, Y.-F., Pei, W.-J., Chong, Y.-W., Zheng, C.-H.: Eigenface-based sparse representation for face recognition. In: Huang, D.-S., Jo, K.-H., Zhou, Y.-Q., Han, K. (eds.) ICIC 2013. LNCS (LNAI), vol. 7996, pp. 457–465. Springer, Heidelberg (2013). https://doi.org/10.1007/978-3-642-39482-9_53
10. James, G., Witten, D., Hastie, T., Tibshirani, R.: An Introduction to Statistical Learning. Springer, New York (2013). https://doi.org/10.1007/978-1-4614-7138-7
11. Jolliffe, I.: Principal Component Analysis, 2nd edn. Springer, NewYork (2002). https://doi.org/10.1007/b98835
12. Krishnapuram, B., Carin, L., Figueiredo, M.A.T., Hartemink, A.J.: Sparse multinomial logistic regression: fast algorithms and generalization bounds. IEEE Trans. Pattern Anal. Mach. Intell. **27**(6), 957–968 (2005)
13. Learned-Miller, E., Huang, G.B., RoyChowdhury, A., Li, H., Hua, G.: Labeled faces in the wild: a survey. In: Kawulok, M., Celebi, M.E., Smolka, B. (eds.) Advances in Face Detection and Facial Image Analysis, pp. 189–248. Springer, Cham (2016). https://doi.org/10.1007/978-3-319-25958-1_8
14. Lee, K.-C., Ho, J., Driegman, D.: Acquiring linear subspaces for face recognition under variable lighting. IEEE Trans. Pattern Anal. Mach. Intell. **27**(5), 684–698 (2005)
15. Ng, A.Y., Jordan, M.I.: On discriminative vs. generative classifiers: a comparison of logistic regression and naive Bayes. In: Advances in Neural Information Processing Systems, vol. 14, pp. 841–848 (2002)
16. Ning, X., Li, W., Tang, B., He, H.: BULDP: biomimetic uncorrelated locality discriminant projection for feature extraction in face recognition. IEEE Trans. Image Process. **27**(5) (2018). https://doi.org/10.1109/TIP.2018.2806229
17. Ojala, T., Pietikainen, M., Harwood, D.: A comparative study of texture measures with classification based on feature distributions. Pattern Recognit. **29**, 51–59 (1996)
18. Proença, H., et al.: Trends and Controversies. IEEE Intell. Syst. **33**(3), 41–67 (2018). https://doi.org/10.1109/MIS.2018.033001416
19. Rosenblatt, F.: Perceptron simulation experiments. Proc. IRE **48**(3), 301–309 (1960). https://doi.org/10.1109/JRPROC.1960.287598
20. Skubalska-Rafajłowicz, E.: Spatially-organized random projections of images for dimensionality reduction and privacy-preserving classification. In: Proceedings of 10th International Workshop on Multidimensional (nD) Systems (nDS), pp. 1–5 (2017)
21. Skubalska-Rafajłowicz, E.: Open-set face classification for access monitoring using spatially-organized random projections. In: Saeed, K., Homenda, W. (eds.) CISIM 2018. LNCS, vol. 11127, pp. 166–177. Springer, Cham (2018). https://doi.org/10.1007/978-3-319-99954-8_15

22. Skubalska-Rafajłowicz, E.: Relative stability of random projection-based image classification. In: Rutkowski, L., Scherer, R., Korytkowski, M., Pedrycz, W., Tadeusiewicz, R., Zurada, J.M. (eds.) ICAISC 2018. LNCS (LNAI), vol. 10841, pp. 702–713. Springer, Cham (2018). https://doi.org/10.1007/978-3-319-91253-0_65

23. Turk, M., Pentland, A.: Eigenfaces for recognition. J. Cogn. Neurosci. **3**(1), 71–86 (1991)

24. Wang, H., Zhang, D.S., Miao, Z.H.: Fusion of LDB and HOG for face recognition. In: Proceedings of the 37th Chinese Control Conference, Wuhan, China, 25–27 July 2018, pp. 9192–9196 (2018)

25. Yang, J., Zhang, D., Frangi, A.F., Yang, J.: Two-dimensional PCA: a new approach to appearance-based face representation and recognition. IEEE Trans. Pattern Anal. Mach. Intell. **26**(1), 131–137 (2004)

26. Yu, H.-F., Huang, F.-L., Lin, C.-J.: Dual coordinate descent methods for logistic regression and maximum entropy models. Mach. Learn. **85**, 4–75 (2011)

27. Zhang, F., Yang, J., Qian, J., Yong, X.: Nuclear norm-based 2-DPCA for extracting features from images. IEEE Trans. Neural Netw. Learn. Syst. **26**(10), 2247–2260 (2015)

28. Zhou, C., Wang, L., Zhang, Q., Wei, Q.: Face recognition based on PCA and logistic regression analysis. Optik **125**, 5916–5919 (2014)

Classifier Selection for Highly Imbalanced Data Streams with *Minority Driven Ensemble*

Paweł Zyblewski[ID], Paweł Ksieniewicz[ID], and Michał Woźniak[✉][ID]

Department of Systems and Computer Networks, Faculty of Electronics,
Wrocław University of Science and Technology, Wybrzeże Wyspiańskiego 27,
50-370 Wrocław, Poland
{pawel.zyblewski,pawel.ksieniewicz,michal.wozniak}@pwr.edu.pl

Abstract. The nature of analysed data may cause the difficulty of the many practical data mining tasks. This work is focusing on two of the important research topics associated with data analysis, i.e., data stream classification as well as data analysis with imbalanced class distributions. We propose the novel classification method, employing a classifier selection approach, which can update its model when new data arrives. The proposed approach has been evaluated on the basis of the computer experiments carried out on the diverse pool of the non-stationary data streams. Their results confirmed the usefulness of the proposed concept, which can outperform the state-of-art classifier selection algorithms, especially in the case of high imbalanced data streams.

Keywords: Data streams · Concept drift · Imbalanced data ·
Classifier selection

1 Introduction

This work is focusing on the special case of data stream classification where on the one hand we may observe so-called *concept drift*, i.e., changes in incoming data distributions [11], on the other hand, we have to analyse imbalanced data [10]. This is motivated by the fact that real data streams may exhibit high and changing class imbalance ratio, which may further complicate the classification task. Nevertheless, it is also worth noting that the imbalance ratio is not the sole problem because observations from the minority class may form clusters of an unknown structure that are scattered [14]. This observation causes that the efficient classifier dedicated to solve such a task should take into consideration the local characteristics of the data. An additional complication comes from the fact that the size of minority sample set may be not sufficient enough for the learning algorithm to achieve the appropriate generalisation level and consequently, the trained model may be overfitted [3].

Many approaches have been proposed to deal with the imbalanced data distributions, which may be grouped into:

© Springer Nature Switzerland AG 2019
L. Rutkowski et al. (Eds.): ICAISC 2019, LNAI 11508, pp. 626–635, 2019.
https://doi.org/10.1007/978-3-030-20912-4_57

1. *Data preprocessing* which employs over- or undersampling approaches.
2. *Inbuilt mechanisms* adapting classification algorithms for imbalanced problems ensuring balanced accuracy for instances from both classes.
3. *Hybrid methods* combining the advantages of methods using data preprocessing with the classification methods.

Unfortunately, there are not so many works on the imbalanced data stream classification. In [7] authors employ the classifier ensembles, where each of the individual models is trained on majority class samples in the consecutive data chunks as well as on the already accumulated observations form the minority class. In [19] authors also use the ensemble approach, where prior to learning on every data chunk *undersampling* is performed based on *k-means* algorithm. Chen and He [2] present improvement of the mentioned technique and propose a family of algorithms SERA, MuSeRA and REA, which add selected incoming minority class objects to the currently processed data chunk. In [13] authors discuss a method for calculating the weights of classifiers learned on data windows and using combination rule based on weighted voting. Dizler et al. [6] extend the previously developed *Learn++* algorithm for imbalanced data (*Learn++.NIE* and *Learn++.CDS*).

Because most of the works from this domain employ the classifier ensemble [20] therefore in this work we will focus on the same approach, which is also reported as an effective tool of imbalanced data classification as well as for the nonstationary data stream classification [11]. One of the most promising approach from this domain is so-called *classifier selection* or *classifier ensemble selection* [5], where the classification model is selected for the particular region of a features space. We may distinguish two main groups of the methods. The first one proposes to partition the features space in advance (so-called *static selection*) [9,12] and a particular classifier is assigned to each partition. The second approach tries to select the classification model on fly (so-called *dynamic selection*) for each incoming observation. For each type of classifier selection the key issue is to select the most competent model from given classifiers. Most of the methods estimate their competences taking into considerations the surroundings of a classified sample [17,18].

In nutshell the main contributions of the work are as follows:

- Proposition of the *Minority Driven Ensemble* algorithm, which allows the intelligent classifier selection taking into consideration local data characteristics of each class.
- Experimental evaluation of the *Minority Driven Ensemble* algorithm on the basis of high number of diverse data streams and a detailed comparison with the state-of-art classifier selection approaches.

2   Minority Driven Ensemble

In order to deal with the problem of imbalanced data stream classification we propose the MDE (*Minority Driven Ensemble*) method, which is a combination of a chunk-based approach to ensemble learning and a classifier selection for the classification process.

2.1   Ensemble Construction

Let's assume that the data stream consists of fixed-size data chunks $\mathcal{DS}_k$, where k is the chunk index and N is the chunk size. We do not detect a concept drift, but the proposed algorithm employs a mechanism allowing it to construct self-adapting classifier ensemble E instead. As the individual classifier k-*nearest neighbors classifier* is used based on the particular data chunk devoided of *outliers* according to 5-neighbour taxonomy [15] (i.e., samples from minority class for which five nearest neighbours are majority class examples). Let Ψ_k denotes the classifier based of the kth chunk.

If the fixed ensemble size ES is exceeded, we remove from it the worst rated individual according to the *balanced accuracy* measure (BAC) [1]. Additionally, at each step we remove from the ensemble all models which BAC scores are lower than $0.5 + \alpha$, where α is the algorithm's parameter responsible for the outdated models removing rate. The pseudocode of the presented method is shown in Algorithm 1.

Algorithm 1. Ensemble construction pseudocode

Input:

    Stream of data chunks $\{\mathcal{DS}_1, \mathcal{DS}_2, ..., \mathcal{DS}_k\}$,

    Fixed ensemble size (ES),

    Outdated models removing rate (α)

1: $E \leftarrow \varnothing$

2: **for each** Data chunk $\mathcal{DS} \in Stream$ **do**

3:    $S \leftarrow scoreBaseModels(\mathcal{DS})$

4:    **if** $len(E) > 1$ **then**

5:        $E \leftarrow pruneThreshold(\alpha)$

6:    **if** $len(E) > ES - 1$ **then**

7:        $E \leftarrow pruneWorstClassifier(E, S)$

8:    $\mathcal{DS}_{filtered} \leftarrow removeOutliers(\mathcal{DS})$

9:    $\Psi \leftarrow trainNewClassifier(\mathcal{DS}_{filtered})$

10:   $E \leftarrow \Psi$

11: **end for**

2.2   Prediction

During the classification process if at least one individual classifier returns support for minority class higher than 0, then the instance is classified as the minority class example, i.e., among k nearest neighbours, at least one belongs to minority class. Based on this idea we may simplify the prediction process.

The principle of the proposed combination rule is presented in Fig. 1. The first three subplots present the decision border implementing the principle of minimum support for three subsequent processed chunks during subtle changes in the minority class distribution. The last subplot (on the right) shows the illustration of the mentioned above combination rule.

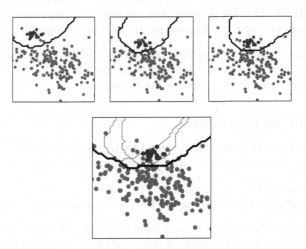

Fig. 1. Binary prediction as non-zero support for a minority class (three on the top) and a maximum from the pool (on the bottom).

3   Experimental Evaluation

This section presents the details of the experimental study that allows us to compare the classification performance of the proposed *Minority Driven Ensemble* algorithm with other state-of-art methods.

3.1   Set-Up of Experiments

Evaluation for each experiment is based on the *balanced accuracy measure* (BAC), according to scikit-learn implementation [16], employing *k-nearest neighbours classifier* as the base model for the ensemble construction. All experiments and algorithms were implemented in Python programming language and may be repeated according to source code published on *Github*[1].

3.2   Datasets

The experiments were carried out using 96 diverse data streams. Each of the streams counts one hundred thousand instances, divided into 200 chunks of 500

---

[1] https://github.com/w4k2/classifier-selection.

objects described by 8 features, and contains five *concept drifts*. The base concepts were generated according to procedure of creating the Madelon [8] synthetic classification dataset. Each of the base concepts combinations was generated three times, for the repeatability of the research, based on the determined seeds.

The variety of obtained streams was obtained by generating three streams for each combination of the following parameters of the classification task:

- *the imbalance ratio* — successively 10, 20, 30 and 40% of the minority class,
- *the level of label noise* — successively 0, 10, 20 and 30%,
- *the type of concept drift* — *gradual* or *sudden*.

3.3 Goals of the Experiments

Experiment 1 — Hyperparameters Optimization. The main goal of the first experiment was to tune the two hyperparameters of MDE:

- *ES* — ensemble size,
- α — pruning parameter responsible for the outdated models removing rate.

We have tested the mean BAC and statistical dependence for multiple values of these two parameters. Experiment was conducted on the data stream with an imbalance ratio of 1:9 and label noise of 0.1. Sudden and gradual drifts were tested separately.

Experiment 2 — Comparative Analysis of Classifier Selection Methods. During the second experiment, we compared the performance of four dynamic selection (DS) techniques implemented in DESlib [4] with MDE, depending on imbalance ratio, drift type and label noise level.

The comparative methods were:

- *Modified Classifier Ranking (Rank)* uses for classification such an individual classifier which classifies correctly the highest number of consecutive samples in the region of competence.
- *Local classifier accuracy (*LCA*)* selects for classification such an individual classifier which correctly classifies the higher number of samples within the local region, but considering only those examples where the classifier predicted the same class as the one it gave for the test instance.
- *KNORA-Eliminate (*KNORAE*)* chooses to the ensemble only the classifiers which can correctly classify all samples within the competence region. In the case if no classifier is selected the size of competence region is decreased.
- *KNORA-Union (*KNORAU*)* makes the decision on the basis of weighted voting, where the weight assigned to an individual classifier is proportional to the number of correctly classified objects in the competence region.

The detailed description of the reference methods may be found in [5]. We consider the dynamic selection dataset (DSEL) for the DS methods as the previous data chunk with the random over-sampling performed on it. Ensemble construction process is the same as described in Sect. 2.

4   Experimental Evaluation

Experiment 1 — Hyperparameters Optimization. The results of hyper-parameters' optimisation are shown in Fig. 2, which shows the relation between the α parameter (X-axis) and the ensemble size (Y-axis). Each value is equal to the mean BAC achieved by MDE for given values of ES and α. Colours correspond with the statistical dependencies between mean BAC values, according to the *Mann–Whitney U* test.

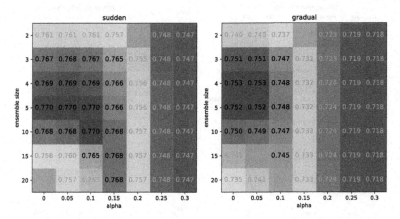

Fig. 2. Optimisation of MDE hyperparameters for sudden and gradual concept drift

Increasing the ensemble size initially stabilises the BAC, but over time degrades the ability of the ensemble to respond to the concept drift. Increasing the α removing rate parameter initially compensates for degradation in the concept drift responding time, but over time negatively affects the BAC.

The ES of three classifiers and the $\alpha = 0.05$ were chosen for further experiments.

Experiment 2 — Comparative Analysis of Classifier Selection Methods. Figure 3 shows the influence of random over-sampling on reference methods performance on data streams with high imbalance ratio (1:9). The use of oversampling equates the performance of all tested DS methods.

Figure 4 presents how performance of the methods depends on the imbalance ratio. Proposed MDE is very effective for high imbalanced data streams (10%, 20% of minority objects). Enlarging the percentage of minority class to 30% reduces the differences between MDE and reference methods. For the cases of low imbalance data (40% of minority class), MDE performs worse than reference DS methods.

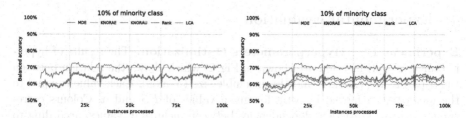

Fig. 3. Reference methods performance with (left) and without oversampling (right).

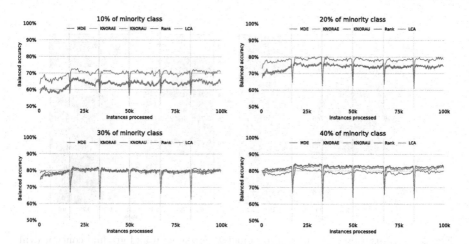

Fig. 4. Influence of imbalance scale on the quality of classification.

The aim of the following paper is to demonstrate the ability of the proposed method to classify highly imbalanced data, so all further experiments present results for streams with a percentage of a minority class not greater than 20%.

Figure 5 presents the relation between the classification quality and the type of drift. The type of drift does not affect the relation between the analysed classification methods. In either case MDE outperforms the benchmark classifiers.

Figure 6 shows the relation between the performances of the individual methods and the label noise ratio. The increase of noise has a negative effect on the overall classification quality.

The statistical analysis of the experimental evaluation is presented in Table 1. It confirms that in most cases MDE outperforms the benchmark classifier selection methods. Only for slightly imbalanced data, i.e., when imbalance ratio is small (30% of minority examples) MDE is not statistically significantly better than KNORAU and KNORAE. For almost balanced data streams (40% of minority samples), RANK, KNORAU, and KNORAE outperform MDE.

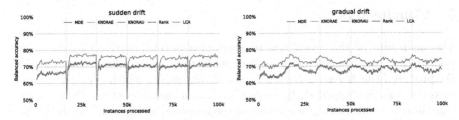

Fig. 5. Influence of concept drift type on the quality of classification.

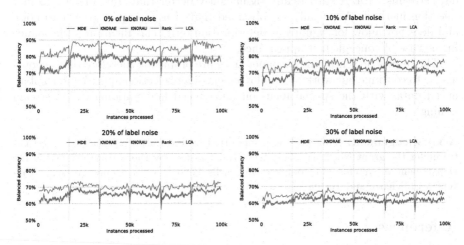

Fig. 6. Influence of label noise on the quality of classification.

Table 1. Presentation of statistical dependency of methods in all analysed contexts. Bold points the best algorithm and algorithms statistically dependent to the best.

Value	MDE	K-E	K-U	rANK	LCA
Minority class percentage					
10%	**0.697**	0.632	0.637	0.631	0.634
20%	**0.780**	0.738	0.741	0.736	0.735
30%	**0.796**	**0.794**	**0.794**	0.792	0.786
40%	0.788	**0.821**	**0.821**	**0.820**	0.811
Drift types					
incremental	**0.731**	0.675	0.680	0.675	0.674
sudden	**0.747**	0.694	0.698	0.693	0.694
Label noise					
0%	**0.851**	0.770	0.776	0.769	0.773
10%	**0.753**	0.700	0.704	0.699	0.699
20%	**0.701**	0.656	0.659	0.655	0.654
30%	**0.651**	0.614	0.617	0.613	0.611

5   Conclusions

The main aim of this work was to propose a novel, effective classifier selection method for a challenging task of imbalanced data stream classification. We proposed the *Minority Driven Ensemble* algorithm, which employs dynamic classifier selection approach to exploit local data characteristics. The computer experiments confirmed the usefulness of the proposed method and on the basis of a thorough statistical analysis we may assert that especially for high imbalanced data streams, MDE is statistically significantly better that state-of-art classifier selection methods. Especially, we observed that MDE is a quite robust to noise and does not allow for significant deterioration of its classification performance in the case of concept drift appearance.

The results presented in this paper are quite promising therefore they encourage us to continue our work on employing classifier selection approach for imbalanced data, with the special focus on imbalanced non-stationary data stream mining.

Acknowledgement. This work was supported by the Polish National Science Centre under the grant No. 2017/27/B/ST6/01325 as well by the statutory funds of the Department of Systems and Computer Networks, Faculty of Electronics, Wroclaw University of Science and Technology.

References

1. Branco, P., Torgo, L., Ribeiro, R.P.: Relevance-based evaluation metrics for multi-class imbalanced domains. In: Kim, J., Shim, K., Cao, L., Lee, J.-G., Lin, X., Moon, Y.-S. (eds.) PAKDD 2017, Part I. LNCS (LNAI), vol. 10234, pp. 698–710. Springer, Cham (2017). https://doi.org/10.1007/978-3-319-57454-7_54
2. Chen, S., He, H.: Towards incremental learning of nonstationary imbalanced data stream: a multiple selectively recursive approach. Evol. Syst. **2**(1), 35–50 (2011)
3. Chen, X.w., Wasikowski, M.: Fast: a ROC-based feature selection metric for small samples and imbalanced data classification problems. In: Proceedings of the ACM SIGKDD International Conference on Knowledge Discovery and Data Mining, pp. 124–132 (2008)
4. Cruz, R.M.O., Hafemann, L.G., Sabourin, R., Cavalcanti, G.D.C.: DESlib: a dynamic ensemble selection library in Python. arXiv preprint arXiv:1802.04967 (2018)
5. Cruz, R.M., Sabourin, R., Cavalcanti, G.D.: Dynamic classifier selection. Inf. Fusion **41**(C), 195–216 (2018)
6. Ditzler, G., Polikar, R.: Incremental learning of concept drift from streaming imbalanced data. IEEE Trans. Knowl. Data Eng. **25**(10), 2283–2301 (2013)
7. Gao, J., Yu, P.S., Fan, W., Ding, B., Han, J.: Classifying data streams with skewed class distributions and concept drifts. IEEE Internet Comput. **12**, 37–49 (2008)
8. Guyon, I.: Design of experiments of the NIPS 2003 variable selection benchmark. In: NIPS 2003 Workshop on Feature Extraction and Feature Selection, pp. 545–552 (2003)

9. Jackowski, K., Krawczyk, B., Woźniak, M.: Improved adaptive splitting and selection: the hybrid training method of a classifier based on a feature space partitioning. Int. J. Neural Syst. **24**(3) (2014)

10. Krawczyk, B.: Learning from imbalanced data: open challenges and future directions. Progress Artif. Intell. **5**(4), 221–232 (2016)

11. Krawczyk, B., Minku, L.L., Gama, J., Stefanowski, J., Wozniak, M.: Ensemble learning for data stream analysis: a survey. Inf. Fusion **37**, 132–156 (2017)

12. Kuncheva, L.I.: Clustering-and-selection model for classifier combination. In: Proceedings of the Fourth International Conference on Knowledge-Based Intelligent Information Engineering Systems & Allied Technologies, KES 2000, Brighton, UK, 30 August–1 September 2000, vol. 2, pp. 185–188 (2000)

13. Lichtenwalter, R.N., Chawla, N.V.: Adaptive methods for classification in arbitrarily imbalanced and drifting data streams. In: Theeramunkong, T., Nattee, C., Adeodato, P.J.L., Chawla, N., Christen, P., Lenca, P., Poon, J., Williams, G. (eds.) PAKDD 2009. LNCS (LNAI), vol. 5669, pp. 53–75. Springer, Heidelberg (2010). https://doi.org/10.1007/978-3-642-14640-4_5

14. Napierala, K., Stefanowski, J.: Identification of different types of minority class examples in imbalanced data. In: Corchado, E., Snášel, V., Abraham, A., Woźniak, M., Graña, M., Cho, S.-B. (eds.) HAIS 2012. LNCS (LNAI), vol. 7209, pp. 139–150. Springer, Heidelberg (2012). https://doi.org/10.1007/978-3-642-28931-6_14

15. Napierala, K., Stefanowski, J.: Types of minority class examples and their influence on learning classifiers from imbalanced data. J. Intell. Inf. Syst. **46**, 563–597 (2015)

16. Pedregosa, F., et al.: Scikit-learn: machine learning in Python. J. Mach. Learn. Res. **12**, 2825–2830 (2011)

17. Smits, P.C.: Multiple classifier systems for supervised remote sensing image classification based on dynamic classifier selection. IEEE Trans. Geosci. Remote Sens. **40**(4), 801–813 (2002)

18. Soares, R.G.F., Santana, A., Canuto, A.M.P., de Souto, M.C.P.: Using accuracy and diversity to select classifiers to build ensembles. In: Proceedings of IEEE International Joint Conference on Neural Network, pp. 1310–1316, July 2006

19. Wang, Y., Zhang, Y., Wang, Y.: Mining data streams with skewed distribution by static classifier ensemble. In: Chien, B.C., Hong, T.P. (eds.) Opportunities and Challenges for Next-Generation Applied Intelligence. SCI, vol. 214, pp. 65–71. Springer, Heidelberg (2009). https://doi.org/10.1007/978-3-540-92814-0_11

20. Woźniak, M., Graña, M., Corchado, E.: A survey of multiple classifier systems as hybrid systems. Inf. Fusion **16**, 3–17 (2014)

Artificial Intelligence in Modeling and Simulation

On Sympathy and Symphony: Network-Oriented Modeling of the Adaptive Dynamics of Sympathy States

Ilze A. Auzina, Suzanne Bardelmeijer, and Jan Treur[(✉)] [iD]

Behavioural Informatics Group, Vrije Universiteit Amsterdam,
Amsterdam, The Netherlands
ilze.amanda.auzina@gmail.com,
suzanne-bardelmeijer@live.nl, j.treur@vu.nl

Abstract. Social network analysis commonly focuses on the relationships between two actors that could represent either individuals or populations. The present paper not only introduces a new concept of sympathy states to represent a sympathy between two actors but also models how different sympathy states affect each other in an adaptive manner taking into account who expresses the sympathy and who receives it. The designed network model was designed with the Eurovision Song Contest in mind and takes into account external political events that affect the scores in this contest over the years. The properties of the model were analyzed using social network analysis. The model represents a first attempt in modeling sympathy states and their adaptive dynamics modulated by external events by Network-Oriented Modeling based on adaptive temporal-causal networks.

Keywords: Sympathy states · Social network · European countries · Hebbian learning · Adaptive network

1 Introduction

Social Network Modeling or Analysis is used to model relationships between a set of social actors. In a social network, the edges represent the connections, while the nodes are the social actors [1]. Even though Social Network Analysis (SNA) often focuses on the relationship between people, it is also used to capture connections between groups, organizations or nations [1]. Particularly, the development of worldwide social platforms, such as Facebook, has allowed modeling of social networks on a population basis between countries [2]. Nonetheless, the influence of one relationship of two social actors on another relationship of two actors has not been studied yet neither on an individual nor on a population level. Therefore, the aim of the present study is to fill in this research gap by using a Network-Oriented Modeling approach applying them to this domain.

The newly designed model is based upon temporal-causal model principles. A central role was assigned to nodes called sympathy states that represent how one actor feels connected to another actor. In the current application of the network model, the actors are based on European populations, where the sympathy states represent a sympathy from the inhabitants of one European country to those of another country,

© Springer Nature Switzerland AG 2019
L. Rutkowski et al. (Eds.): ICAISC 2019, LNAI 11508, pp. 639–651, 2019.
https://doi.org/10.1007/978-3-030-20912-4_58

as often observed for the Eurovision Song Contest. For the scope of this project, the sympathy states were created only for countries who participated in the final of Eurovision song contest of the year 2013. This selection was based upon the fact that Eurovision song contest voting system provides empirical data of sympathy between countries as a score, and that the initial sympathy state selection is based on transnational Facebook friendship data set of the year 2012 [4]. The model covers a time period of four years, from 2013 to 2016, to make the results more robust. Moreover, external political events are included in the model for each year that is modeled. These events affect the sympathy states, thus creating an adaptive dynamic model that relates to the real-life situation.

In this paper, in Sect. 2 the network model is introduced. Section 3 explains the principles used to determine the connection weights. In Sect. 4 the model is illustrated by example simulations. Analysis of the network model based on Social Network Analysis is discussed in Sect. 5. Section 6 discusses the possibility of tuning the parameters to empirical data.

2   The Designed Temporal-Causal Network Model

A dynamic modeling approach was used that enables to design complex high-level conceptual representations of adaptive dynamic models in the form of temporal–causal networks [8, 9, 16]. This approach can be considered as generic and is suitable to describe complex networks ranging from mental networks to social networks [16]. The approach can be considered as a branch in the causal modeling area which has a long tradition in AI; e.g., see [13–15]. It distinguishes itself by a dynamic perspective on causal relations, according to which causal relations exert causal effects over time, and these causal relations themselves can also change over time. The models, which can be represented conceptually or numerically by a set of parameters, are declarative and therefore not dependent on specific computational methods for simulation or analysis [8, 9, 16]. The connections represent the causal impacts according to the chosen domain which causes the state values to vary over time. When a state is affected by more than one causal relation a specific combination function is used. For example, a logistic sum is utilized to aggregate multiple impacts, where the threshold and steepness are used as parameters to define the curvature. Other parameters take the form of connection weights and speed factors. The connection weights show differences in the causal connection strengths, whereas a state's speed factor indicates the time necessary for the state to change [8]. Together the connections weights, speed factors, and combination functions define the structure of a temporal-causal network model. In the upper part of Table 1 these concepts, their notation, and explanation are shown. The corresponding numerical representation is obtained from the conceptual representation as shown in the lower part of Table 1. The following difference and differential equations are obtained:

$$
\begin{aligned}
Y(t+\Delta t) &= Y(t) + \eta_Y[\mathbf{c}_Y(\omega_{X_1,Y}X_1(t), \ldots, \omega_{X_k,Y}X_k(t)) - Y(t)]\Delta t \\
dY(t)/dt &= \eta_Y[\mathbf{c}_Y(\omega_{X_1,Y}X_1(t), \ldots, \omega_{X_k,Y}X_k(t)) - Y(t)]
\end{aligned}
\tag{1}
$$

Table 1. Conceptual and numerical representation of a temporal-causal network model

Concept	Representation	Explanation
States and connections	$X, Y, X \rightarrow Y$	Represents the structure of a network via nodes and links
Connection weight	$\omega_{X,Y}$	A connection weight $\omega_{X,Y} \in [-1, 1]$ denotes the strength of the causal impact of state X on state Y
Aggregating multiple impacts on a state	$c_Y(..)$	For each state Y a combination function $c_Y(..)$ is chosen to aggregate the causal impacts on state Y
Timing of causal effect	η_Y	For each state Y a speed factor $\eta_Y \geq 0$ is used to describe the speed of change of a state
State values over time t	$Y(t)$	At each time point t each state Y in the model has a real number value in $[0, 1]$
Single causal impact	$\mathbf{impact}_{X,Y}(t) = \omega_{X,Y}X(t)$	At t state X with a connection to state Y has an impact on Y, using connection weight $\omega_{X,Y}$
Aggregating multiple impacts	$\mathbf{aggimpact}_Y(t)$ $= c_Y(\mathbf{impact}_{X_1,Y}(t), \ldots, \mathbf{impact}_{X_k,Y}(t))$ $= c_Y(\omega_{X_1,Y}X_1(t), \ldots, \omega_{X_k,Y}X_k(t))$	The aggregated causal impact of multiple states X_i on Y at t, is determined using combination function $c_Y(..)$
Timing of the causal effect	$Y(t+\Delta t) = Y(t) + \eta_Y[\mathbf{aggimpact}_Y(t) - Y(t)]\Delta t$ $= Y(t) + \eta_Y[c_Y(\omega_{X_1,Y}X_1(t), \ldots, \omega_{X_k,Y}X_k(t)) - Y(t)]\Delta t$	The causal impact on Y is exerted over time gradually, using speed factor η_Y; here the X_i are all states with connections to state Y

A variety of standard combination functions are available that can be used to deal with multiple impacts on a state. This study uses the alogistic sum combination function in which the parameters steepness σ and threshold τ can be adjusted. For example, the model will show more abrupt behavior when high steepness values are applied. To indicate the dependence of τ and σ these are used as subscripts:

$$\mathbf{alogistic}_{\sigma,\tau}(V_1, \ldots V_k) = \left[\frac{1}{1 + e^{-\sigma(V_1 + \ldots + V_k - \tau)}} - \frac{1}{1 + e^{\sigma\tau}} \right](1 + e^{-\sigma\tau}) \qquad (2)$$

In principle parameters such as connection weights may have specific constant values. However, in adaptive cases, these parameters may change over time as well [8].

Therefore, in the adaptive network model introduced here the connection weights $\omega_{X,Y}(t)$ can be modeled as states with their own combination function. This study will use an adaptive model based on Hebbian learning. Hebbian learning was originally invented by Hebb [7] for the assumption that 'neurons that fire together, wire together' [6, 7]. In other words, when both states are often active simultaneously the connection between these states becomes stronger, which is a useful effect in the present domain of the model: if both countries exhibit high sympathy towards each other then the connection between these countries should be strengthened. Therefore, in the present model Hebbian learning is used for the connections between reciprocal sympathy states; see Fig. 1. The numerical representation used for Hebbian learning is based on the combination function

$$c(X_1, X_2, W) = X_1 X_2 (1 - W) + \mu W \tag{3}$$

where X_1 and X_2 indicate the activation level of the two connected states, W the connection weight, and μ the persistence factor; this entails the following difference and differential equation for the connection weight:

$$
\begin{aligned}
\omega_{X_1,X_2}(t+\Delta t) &= \omega_{X_1,X_2}(t) + \eta_{\omega_{X_1,X_2}}[X_1(t)X_2(t)(1 - \omega_{X_1,X_2}(t)) + \mu\omega_{X_1,X_2}(t) - \omega_{X_1,X_2}(t)]\Delta t \\
d\omega_{X_1,X_2}(t)/dt &= \eta_{\omega_{X_1,X_2}}[X_1(t)X_2(t)(1 - \omega_{X_1,X_2}(t)) + \mu\omega_{X_1,X_2}(t) - \omega_{X_1,X_2}(t)]
\end{aligned}
\tag{4}
$$

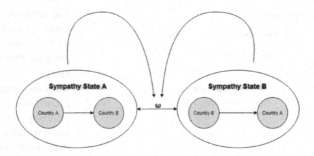

Fig. 1. The Hebbian learning principle for the connections between reciprocal sympathy states

Initially, twenty-six countries were selected to model sympathy states. This selection was based on the countries who participated in the Eurovision song contest 2013 final. Subsequently, a subset was selected from the transnational Facebook friendship data set based on the twenty-six countries chosen. The Facebook transnational data set contains information on the five countries to which people in the selected country are most connected to in terms of border-crossing Facebook Friendships [4]. Accordingly, sympathy states were created between 'sender' and 'receiver' countries where the obtained score in the Facebook matrix was at least 1. This indicates that the receiver country is the country with which sender country has the fifth-highest number of Facebook friendships [4]. This resulted in 76 sympathy states, which contained the in- formation of the sender and the receiver country. For a part of such a network model, see Fig. 2.

However, once the model was extended over multiple years, 2013, 2014, 2015 and 2016, respectively, three sympathy states had to be removed from the model due to lack of empirical data over the years. Thus, the final model contained 73 sympathy states (see Appendix A). The initial state values of these sympathy states were also based on the Facebook Friendship data set. The data set contained cell values that range from 0 to 5, where 0 indicates that country is not mentioned, and 5 that the receiver country is the country with which sender country has the highest number of Facebook friendships [4]. As mentioned earlier, only connections that had a value from 1 to 5 were included in the model. Consequently, the initial values were also based on this scoring system but converted to a range within 0 to 1. Thus, the resulting initial values ranged from 0.1 to 0.5.

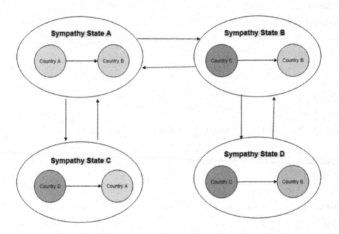

Fig. 2. Some sympathy states and their causal relations

3 Principles Determining the Nonadaptive Connection Weights

The values of the nonadaptive connection weights were based upon four basic elements: country name, sender or receiver country, geographical location, and size. The first rule stands for that country X's sympathy to country Y would affect any other sympathy state where also country X' and/or Y is a participant. This rule determines all the connections that should be established. The second rule is more elaborate as it takes into account which country is the sender and which the receiver (see Fig. 3 column 1). Furthermore, this rule was refined by implementing the location and size rule upon it (see Fig. 3 column 2–5). Figure 3 shows that the relationship of the connection is defined first. In other words, every connection is classified based on the information of why this connection is created. In total there are four categories: (1) receiving countries are the same, (2) sending countries are the same, (3) receiving country in the sender

Table 2. Connection weight principles used

	If the 3 countries are bordering	If the 3 countries are in the same neighbourhood	If from small to big country (based on European population)	Else
Receiving countries are the same				
SR* to SR* Georgia/**Germany** to Finland/**Germany**	0.8			
SR* to SR* Hungary/**Germany** to Romania/**Germany**		0.6		
SR* to SR* Hungary/**Germany** to Greece/**Germany**				0.2
Sending countries are the same				
S*R to S*R **Finland**/Norway to **Finland**/Germany	0.5			
S*R to S*R **Norway**/Iceland to **Norway**/Denmark				0.6
Receiving country and sending country in new node are the same				
SR* to S*R Estonia/**Russia** to **Russia**/Azerbaijan			0.2	
SR* to S*R Georgia/**Russia** to **Russia**/Georgia	0.8			
SR* to S*R Germany/**Netherlands** to **Netherlands**/Belgium	0.8			
SR* to S*R Hungary/**Romenia** to **Romenia**/Germany		0.6		
SR* to S*R Russia/**Belarus** to **Belarus**/Italy				0.2
SR* to S*R Netherlands/**Belgium** to **Belgium**/Spain				0.2

(continued)

Table 2. (*continued*)

	If the 3 countries are bordering	If the 3 countries are in the same neighbourhood	If from small to big country (based on European population)	Else
Sending country and receiving country in new node are the same				
S*R to SR* **Azerbaijan**/Russia to Georgia/**Azerbaijan**	0.8			
S*R to SR* **Italy**/Spain to Malta/ **Italy**		0.6		
S*R to SR* **Italy**/Spain to Belarus/ **Italy**				0.2

node and the sending country in the receiver node are the same, and (4) sending country in the sender node and the receiving country in the receiver node are the same. This creates a principle that each connection consist of three countries as one of the countries always is repeating, thus creating the connection. An exception for this rule is when the connection is reciprocal, meaning that both sympathy states consists of the same countries but in a reversed way. Then a connection weight of 0.8 was assigned and the Hebbian learning principle was implemented as discussed before.

For the remaining connections that consist of three countries it is checked whether all three of these countries are bordering; for an overview, see Table 2. If this is true, then a connection weight of 0.8 is assigned, based on the assumption that the sympathy state of bordering countries could have a strong effect on the third bordering country's sympathy as well. If the countries are not bordering, it is checked if the three countries are in the same neighborhood. If that is the case, then a connection strength value of 0.6 is assigned, meaning that the sympathy state still exhibits an influence but weaker than before. Lastly, if none of the previous constraints holds true, a value of 0.2 is assigned.

An exception of these assignment principles is possible when the connection is based on the combination of the size rule and the sender or receiver country rule category three. If the sender country is relatively small based on its population as compared to the receiver country in the sender sympathy node, for example, Estonia to Russia, then this sympathy state would have a small connection weight value to the sender node, 0.2 respectively. This is based upon the assumption that the proportion of friendships of a small population towards a large population is relatively irrelevant for the larger population's friendships to other countries. The size ranking was based upon the population of each country, where the larger countries were considered to be Russia, Germany, France, United Kingdom, and Italy (population above 60 million) [10].

The model was built upon the assumption that the results of the Eurovision song contest are influenced by political events that have happened in the preceding year, as Eurovision happens in the first half of the year. Therefore, political events in the years 2012, 2013, 2014, and 2015 that had an influence on the foreign affairs between countries were identified. Consequently, this search resulted in 12 events across the time span of 2012 to late 2015 that were thought to have an effect on the sympathy state value (see Table 3). Information about these events was obtained from news articles and European Foreign Policy Scorecards [5]. The events are independent of each other and are not affected by the sympathy states.

Table 3. Political events included in the model

Event	Year	Event	Year
Common economic space	2010	Belgium royal family visits France	2014
Russia military support	2011	Crimean crisis	2015
Eastern Partnership	2012	Poster conflict	2015
Vladimir Putin re-elected	2012	Malta security operation	2015
DCFTA	2013	Paris attacks	2015
Restored border between Russia and Belarus	2014	Railway collaboration	2015

Implementing the events allows adjusting a sympathy state value at a certain year by increasing it, positive effect, or decreasing it, negative effect. Consequently, the final model consists in total of 85 states, where 73 of these states represent sympathy states and the other 12 states represent events. A small example illustrating the final model can be found in Fig. 3.

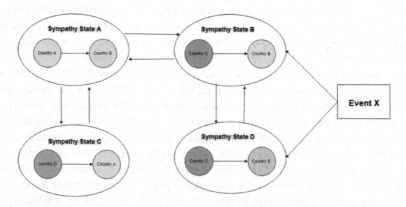

Fig. 3. Example of sympathy states in relation to relevant events

4   Example Model Simulation

As mentioned before, the main components of the model are the sympathy states that interact with each other, while the number of the events can be varied depending on the number of years included as well as whether meaningful events can be identified in the context of the sympathy states. In Fig. 4 a base scenario of the model is represented. Specifically, one event is modeled (indicated by the arrow), which has both positive, strengthening, and negative, weakening effects on specific sympathy states. In the present scenario, the speed factors for all sympathy states are set to 0.3, while the speed factor for the event is set to 0.06 to achieve that its effects only occur at a later time point. In total 60 time points were simulated, that represent 60 months or approximately 5 years. As can be seen in Fig. 4 the model does not reach an equilibrium within the considered time interval, which is a desirable effect as it is assumed that the interactions between the sympathy states change over time. This example considers only one event; by incorporating multiple events over time a realistic situation can be achieved.

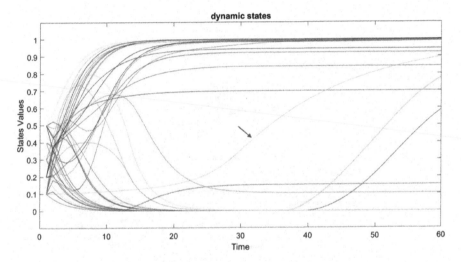

Fig. 4. Example simulation results

5   Social Network Analysis

To analyze the network the Social Network Analysis tool Gephi version 0.9.2. was used [3]. The social network consists of 85 nodes and 797 edges, where the nodes represent the sympathy states and events, and the edges represent the relationships between them. It can be observed in Fig. 5 that sympathy nodes with high betweenness centrality are located relatively more in the center of the network, meaning that these nodes are often involved between other actors in the network. Table 4 shows the top five sympathy nodes in regards to betweenness centrality, suggesting that these sympathy nodes have a high influence over the other sympathy states. Furthermore, the number of relations (edges) was analyzed. In particular, the average degree is 9.376, with a range from 1 to 36°. Table 4 indicates the sympathy nodes with the highest degree value, meaning that these nodes have the highest connections with other nodes. Lastly, the clusters were analyzed in the network. Based on modularity analysis the number of communities in this network is 5 with a modularity of 0.55.

Table 4. Top 5 sympathy states with highest degree values and top 5 sympathy states with highest betweenness centrality

Sympathy state	Degree	Sympathy state	Betweenness centrality
Finland/Russia	36	Finland/Germany	630.13
Russia/Ukraine	36	Lithuania/Russia	493.36
Lithuania/Russia	35	Finland/Russia	480.67
Ukraine/Russia	35	Finland/Norway	362.22
Georgia/Russia	33	Romania/Germany	350.19

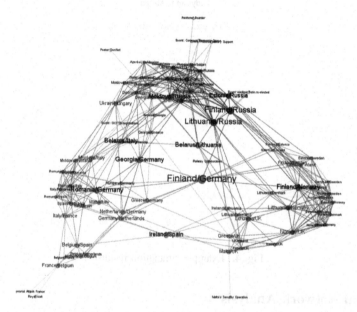

Fig. 5. Social network analysis graph with labels

6 Best Fit to the Empirical Eurovision Voting Data

Matlab v2017a was used to simulate the numerical representation of the model. An attempt has been made to exploit available empirical data based on voting in order to get a good fit of the model parameters. It was not easy to use such data in a solid way. The empirical data was obtained from Eurovision voting results from the years 2013,

2014, 2015 and 2016 [11]. The scoring system of Eurovision is based on a scale from 0 to 12, however, the model uses state values in the range between 0 and 1, thus the empirical data was converted to match this range. Initially only final voting results were taken into account, however, if the country did not participate in any of the finals after the year 2013 then a score from a semi-final was used. In a situation where empirical data could not be obtained in a certain year, because the sender and the receiver country were in a different semi-final, the approximate value was estimated using logarithmic trend-line equation using the other scoring values as reference points. Consequently, a complete empirical data set was created for four time points. Subsequently, by inter-polation this data set was extended across all months of every year using Matlab, resulting in a data set of 60 time points for all 85 states. The empirical data was compared with the model data with a step size of $\Delta t = 1$, representing a one-month interval, and the time interval from a starting point at $t = 17$ and end point at $t = 53$. Such a selection was chosen because the generated empirical data outside these boundaries was either greater than 1 or smaller than 0, which is by default outside of the range of the model. To improve the model's fit to the empirical data sympathy state speed factors were tuned using the simulated annealing algorithm in Matlab. Conse-quently, 73 parameters were optimized and the implications can be seen in Fig. 6. The optimization was based on decreasing the root mean square error (RMSE) between the model and the empirical data. After optimization, the obtained RMSE was still 0.56.

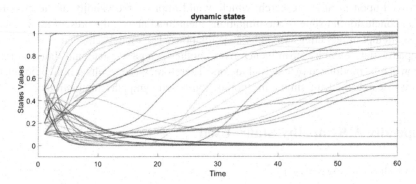

Fig. 6. Simulation results after parameter tuning

7 Discussion

The current model could be viewed as an expansion of the social influence theories. All the previous social influence theories have discussed how one person influences the release of the same behavior in others either via contagion, conformity, social facili-tation or other types of social influence [12]. This could be viewed in analogy with the sympathy states of the present model: a certain sympathy from one country to another could be viewed as an expressed social behavior on a population level. Moreover, the vicinity of the actors that often plays a role in social influence theories is also taken into account in the present model: if the participants of the sympathy states are closely located then the influence of one sympathy state to another is stronger. However, where the present model differs from the current theories is that rather than modeling whether the initial behavior is replicated by the other sympathy state, the present model attempts to show that, firstly, any behavior could have an influence on another behavior as long as at least one of the participants is part of the new behavior, and, secondly, that these behaviors can be modulated by external factors that are independent of the behaviors themselves. Nonetheless, the present model could not mimic the real world data entirely due to certain limitations.

Firstly, the empirical data was not accurate. Multiple time points had to be generated via estimation, which caused the empirical data to be unreliable and outside the range of the model state values. Consequently, a relatively high error value was generated that rather could be attributed to the imprecision of the empirical data than to the model. Secondly, due to the scope of this project only a limited amount of events, with the main focus on political events, were taken into account. However, real-world processes are more complex and cannot be summarized in twelve events, as the sum of many small events also could generate a significant impact on a sympathy state. Therefore, future research could expand the number of events included in the model, thus, resulting in a model that can better represent the complex relations between country sympathies. Thirdly, due to the time constraints, only a subset of all European countries was included in the model. Thus, perhaps important sympathy states were lost that could have improved the accuracy of the model. All of these factors could be improved upon in future research, which would improve the validity of the model.

In conclusion, in spite of the limitations mentioned above, the present model offers a first attempt in modeling sympathy state relations. The model achieved to show that a sympathy state exhibits an influence over another sympathy state and that this interaction can be modulated by external factors. Therefore, these results unfold a promising future research field for simulating population-based sympathy interactions.

Appendix A Sympathy States Used

List of all sympathy states used:

Georgia/Azerbaijan, Russia/Azerbaijan, Russia/Belarus, Ukraine/Belarus, France/ Belgium, Netherlands/Belgium, Lithuania/Denmark, Norway/Denmark, Finland/ Estonia, Estonia/Finland, Sweden/Finland, Belgium/France, Italy/France, Armenia/ Georgia, Finland/Germany, Georgia/Germany, Greece/Germany, Hungary/Germany, Netherlands/Germany, Romania/Germany, Georgia/Greece, Romania/Hungary, Ukraine/Hungary, Norway/Iceland, Belarus/Italy, Malta/Italy, Moldova/Italy, Romania/Italy, Belarus/Lithuania, Belgium/Netherlands, Germany/Netherlands, Denmark/Norway, Estonia/Norway, Finland/Norway, Iceland/Norway, Lithuania/ Norway, Sweden/Norway, Hungary/Romania, Italy/Romania, Moldova/Romania, Spain/Romania, Armenia/Russia, Azerbaijan/Russia, Belarus/Russia, Estonia/Russia, Finland/Russia, Georgia/Russia, Lithuania/Russia, Moldova/Russia, Ukraine/Russia, Belgium/Spain, Italy/Spain, Romania/Spain, Denmark/Sweden, Estonia/Sweden,

Finland/Sweden, Iceland/Sweden, Norway/Sweden, Azerbaijan/Ukraine, Belarus/
Ukraine, Georgia/Ukraine, Moldova/Ukraine, Russia/Ukraine, Greece/UK,
Iceland/UK, Lithuania/UK, Malta/UK, Norway/UK, Lithuania/Ireland, UK/Ireland,
Ireland/Spain, Ireland/UK.

References

1. Freeman, L.: The Development of Social Network Analysis. A Study in the Sociology of Science, vol. 1. Empirical Press, Vancouver (2004)
2. Barnett, G.A., Benefield, G.A.: Predicting international Facebook ties through cultural homophily and other factors. New Media Soc. **19**(2), 217–239 (2017)
3. Bastian, M., Heymann, S., Jacomy, M.: Gephi: an open source software for exploring and manipulating networks. In: International AAAI Conference on Weblogs and Social Media (2009)
4. Deutschmann, E.: The spatial structure of transnational human activity. Soc. Sci. Res. **59**, 120–136 (2016). arXiv Pre-print, http://arxiv.org/abs/1501.05921
5. European Council on Foreign Relations: The European Foreign Policy Scorecard (2012–2015). https://www.ecfr.eu/scorecard
6. Gerstner, W., Kistler, W.M.: Mathematical formulations of Hebbian learning. Biol. Cybern. **87**, 404–415 (2002)
7. Hebb, D.: The Organisation of Behavior. Wiley, New York (1949)
8. Treur, J.: Dynamic modeling based on a temporal–causal network modeling approach. Biol. Inspired Cogn. Archit. **16**, 131–168 (2016)
9. Treur, J.: Network-Oriented Modeling: Addressing Complexity of Cognitive, Affective and Social Interactions. UCS. Springer, Cham (2016). https://doi.org/10.1007/978-3-319-45213-5
10. World Population Review: Most Populous Countries (2018). http://worldpopulationreview.com/continents/europe-population/
11. Kaggle Inc.: Eurovision Song Contest scores 1975–2017 (Dataset) (2018). https://www.kaggle.com/datagraver/eurovision-song-contest-scores-19752017
12. Raven, B.H.: Social influence and power. In: Steiner, I.D., Fishbein, M. (eds.) Current Studies in Social Psychology, pp. 371–382. Holt, Rinehart & Winston, New York (1964)
13. Kuipers, B.J.: Commonsense reasoning about causality: deriving behavior from structure. Artif. Intell. **24**, 169–203 (1984)
14. Kuipers, B.J., Kassirer, J.P.: How to discover a knowledge representation for causal reasoning by studying an expert physician. In: Proceedings of the Eighth International Joint Conference on Artificial Intelligence, IJCAI 1983. William Kaufman, Los Altos (1983)
15. Pearl, J.: Causality. Cambridge University Press, Cambridge (2000)
16. Treur, J.: The ins and outs of network-oriented modeling: from biological networks and mental networks to social networks and beyond. In: Nguyen, N.T., Kowalczyk, R., Hernes, M. (eds.) Transactions on Computational Collective Intelligence XXXII. LNCS, vol. 11370, pp. 120–139. Springer, Heidelberg (2019). https://doi.org/10.1007/978-3-662-58611-2_2

Analysis of Large Scale Power Systems via LASSO Learning Algorithms

Mirosław Pawlak[1,2] and Jiaqing Lv[1,2(✉)]

[1] Electrical and Computer Engineering, University of Manitoba, Winnipeg, Canada
tvjiaqing@gmail.com
[2] Information Technology Institute, University of Social Sciences, Łódź, Poland

Abstract. In this paper, a class of modern machine learning methods is utilized for estimating the transient stability boundary characterizing the large-scale power system grids. The boundary characteristic is viewed as a highly multidimensional response of power system variables. The proposed estimation methods based on various forms of the LASSO algorithm lead to simultaneous variable selection and function recovery yielding models of the reduced complexity. The obtained models have a clear interpretation and exhibit a smaller prediction error compared with known machine learning techniques used in the existing literature on modelling of large-scale power engineering systems. The performance of our method is assessed based on the real data generated from the 470-bus power system.

Keywords: LASSO algorithms · Machine learning ·
Shrinkage methods · Sparsity · Large-scale power systems ·
Transient stability boundary

1 Introduction

Machine learning is an active field of research with numerous applications in science and engineering including modelling and prediction of power systems [1,5]. In large-scale modern data driven systems one has to cope with the high-dimensional features and limited size of training data. This large-dimensional-small data set case calls for new learning techniques that are able to perform simultaneous estimation and variable selection.

In this paper we utilize a class of such techniques (called the shrinkage learning algorithms) in the context of large-scale power systems. In fact, the proper evaluation and predictive behavior of power systems require accurate and computationally feasible machine learning methods applicable to large-dimensional data sets. Previously applied approaches to various problems of power systems include classical regression analysis, neural networks, and support vector machines, [2–4]. The particularly challenging power system problem is the functional characterization of the future behavior of the transient stability boundary. Transient stability is the ability of the power system to maintain synchronism

© Springer Nature Switzerland AG 2019
L. Rutkowski et al. (Eds.): ICAISC 2019, LNAI 11508, pp. 652–662, 2019.
https://doi.org/10.1007/978-3-030-20912-4_59

when it is subjected to severe transient disturbances such as a fault on transmission system facilities, loss of a large load, or loss of a generator. The transient stability problem is inherently high dimensional, due to the consideration of a large number of measurements existing in the given power system.

Various regression estimation approaches have been commonly used in determining future system responses for a given set of new inputs. The previous estimation methods utilize full multidimensional input signals without reducing the data dimensionality and extracting the proper features yielding the best possible prediction. There are numerous feature selection techniques like AIC, BIC, forward selection, backward selection, just to name a few, that could be applied to reduce the data dimensionality. The computational cost, however, of these methods is usually very high and therefore would be difficult to employ them in the real-time power system.

In this paper a class of modern linear regression methods called the LASSO procedure is used for prediction of the transient stability boundary of power systems. Traditionally, the various forms of the least square method have be used yielding explicit solutions. In particular, the so-called Ridge Regression, which is based on the minimization of the mean squared error penalized by the sum of square values of the regression coefficients has been utilized in the transient stability boundary problem. Different from the Ridge Regression, the LASSO approach uses the sum of absolute values of the regression coefficients as the penalty. The fundamental property of the LASSO strategy is that it automatically shrinks to zero a number of regression coefficients that seem to be redundant in the overall prediction accuracy. Thus, the LASSO approach has a potential advantage over the classical regression methods since it provides the joint automatic feature selection with model specification. This makes the method extremely suitable for the transient stability problem as well as other power engineering problems where observations are inherently high-dimensional.

This paper is organized as follows. In Sect. 3, the LASSO algorithm is briefly overviewed as well as its extensions called the adaptive LASSO and multi-step LASSO are described. A basic numerical method called "shooting algorithm" to determine the LASSO solution is also introduced. In Sect. 4, the problem of Transient Stability Boundary is described. In Sect. 5, the LASSO regression method is applied to transient stability data and its accuracy is compared with Ridge Regression and Kernel Ridge Regression techniques. The automatic feature selection property of the LASSO algorithm is revealed. We demonstrate that the LASSO method developed in this paper has superior properties over the state-of-the-art algorithms used so far in modelling of large-scale power engineering systems. The paper is the further extension of the study initiated in [10] concerning the use of modern machine learning algorithms for high-dimensional power systems.

2   LASSO Regression Methods

2.1   Regularized Least Square Regression Methods: Ridge and LASSO Algorithms

In this section we introduce the LASSO and other regression methods that minimize the constrained least square error with respect to a specific penalty.

The regression function $m(\mathbf{x}) = E[Y|\mathbf{X} = \mathbf{x}]$ represents the optimal L_2 prediction of the output scalar variable Y based on the input feature vector $\mathbf{X} \in \mathbb{R}^p$. In practice, one does not know the joint distribution of $(\mathbf{X}, Y)$ but instead observes the training data set

$$\boldsymbol{D}_n = \{(\mathbf{X}_1, Y_1), (\mathbf{X}_2, Y_2), \cdots, (\mathbf{X}_n, Y_n)\}.$$

The regression estimation problem can be viewed as a supervised machine learning case where one would like to estimate $m(\mathbf{x})$ from $\boldsymbol{D}_n$ [5]. Hence, given a new input vector $\boldsymbol{X}_{new}$, the regression analysis tries to predict the corresponding output Y_{new} using the data set $\boldsymbol{D}_n$ and often some a priori knowledge about the underlying process. For high-dimensional input vector, i.e., for a large value of p the problem of estimating the regression function $m(\mathbf{x})$ is infeasible due to the known curse of dimensionality property. Then, it is necessary to restrict the shape of $m(\mathbf{x})$ to a particular simpler form. It is common to use the following linear model

$$Y_i = \sum_{j=1}^p \beta_j X_i^{(j)} + \varepsilon_i, \quad i = 1, \ldots, n, \tag{1}$$

where $\{\varepsilon_i\}$ is a sequence of zero-mean random variables representing the noise process that is assumed to be independent of $\{\boldsymbol{X}_i\}$. Here, $\boldsymbol{X}_i = [X_i^{(1)}, \ldots, X_i^{(p)}]^T$ is the i-th input vector and $\boldsymbol{\beta} = [\beta_1, \cdots, \beta_p]^T$ is the vector of the unknown model coefficients. The linear regression model is important because many other forms of regression analysis (including generalized linear models) can be derived from the estimation theory developed for linear regression.

In practical situations, we are facing with a large number of input variables and as a result the linear model reveals the large variability and the reduced prediction accuracy. Thus, one needs to perform a search for selecting features that are important and most informative. This may result in the simplified model with the stronger prediction accuracy. The LASSO regression algorithm provides the required joint estimation-variable selection property.

To introduce the LASSO method let us begin with the classical least squares approach for the model in (1). First, note that (1) can be re-written in the matrix form

$$\mathbf{Y} = \mathbf{X}\boldsymbol{\beta} + \boldsymbol{\varepsilon}, \tag{2}$$

where $\mathbf{Y} = [Y_1, \cdots, Y_n]^T$, $\boldsymbol{\varepsilon} = [\varepsilon_1, \cdots, \varepsilon_n]^T$, and $\mathbf{X}$ is the $n \times p$ design matrix. The parameter $\boldsymbol{\beta}$ that minimizes the mean-squared error

$$\frac{1}{n}||\mathbf{Y} - \mathbf{X}\boldsymbol{\beta}||^2, \tag{3}$$

has the well-known closed-form expression

$$\hat{\beta}_{LS} = (\mathbf{X}^T\mathbf{X})^{-1}\mathbf{X}^TY. \tag{4}$$

Hence, in the least-square solution $\hat{\beta}_{LS}$, all the p coefficients are estimated including even those that have small or zero values. This property is particularly harmful if p, the number of variables, is larger than n, the size of the training set. Furthermore, the lease-square solution is not unique if the design matrix $\mathbf{X}$ is not of a full rank. These negative properties of $\hat{\beta}_{LS}$ are partially reduced by the so-called Ridge Regression [5] being the version of the least squares, where the penalized term is added. Hence, the solution of

$$\min_{\beta} \left(\frac{1}{n} ||\mathbf{Y} - \mathbf{X}\beta||^2 + \lambda ||\beta||_2 \right), \tag{5}$$

defines $\hat{\beta}_{Ridge}$ - the ridge regression estimate of β, where $||\beta||_2$ is the L_2 norm of β. In (5) the parameter $\lambda \geq 0$ controls the amount of shrinkage on β towards zero. Hence, larger λ imposes the larger shrinkage to small values. The advantage of the ridge regression is that it provides the explicit solution of the following form

$$\hat{\beta}_{Ridge} = (\mathbf{X}^T\mathbf{X} + \lambda I_p)^{-1}\mathbf{X}^T\mathbf{Y}, \tag{6}$$

where I_p is the unit matrix.

It is important to note that the ridge regression method is unable to set the coefficients exactly to zero. Hence, this approach cannot to adapt to the model sparsity. The latter is measured by the number of elements of the set $S = \{j : \beta_j \neq 0\}$, i.e., the cardinality of S denoted as p_0 is much smaller than p. Nevertheless, the ridge regression leads to the smaller mean squared error compared with the ordinary least square method and therefore it gives better prediction. The ridge regression approach to modeling the transit stability boundary in power systems has been examined in [6].

An ultimate penalization strategy applied to the mean-squared error that leads to the automatic feature selection would rely on the L_0 norm of the model coefficients. Hence, the following minimization is sought

$$\min_{\beta} \left(\frac{1}{n} ||\mathbf{Y} - \mathbf{X}\beta||^2 + \lambda ||\beta||_0 \right), \tag{7}$$

where $||\beta||_0 = \sum_{j=1}^{p} \mathbf{1}(\beta \neq 0)$. Here $\mathbf{1}(A)$ is the indicator function of the set A. The resulting optimization problem is, however, not convex and does not have the unique solution. A convex replacement for the L_0 norm is the L_1 norm penalty. This leads to the celebrated LASSO procedure [5] that seeks the solution of the following convex optimization problem

$$\min_{\beta} \left(\frac{1}{n} ||\mathbf{Y} - \mathbf{X}\beta||^2 + \lambda ||\beta||_1 \right), \tag{8}$$

where $||\beta||_1$ is the L_1 norm of β. The sought solution $\hat{\beta}_{LASSO}$ is not given in the explicit form and relies on some specialized convex optimization algorithms [9].

The geometric nature of the L_1 penalty is the origin of the sparsity property of the LASSO method that successfully shrinks the increasing number of the model coefficients toward zero as λ increases. In fact, the asymptotic analysis of the LASSO procedure reveals that the optimality model discovery property can be achieved if λ tends to infinity with n with the rate slower than $\sqrt{n}$. For the finite sample size the parameter λ must be specified via some data-driven methods, e.g., cross-validation (CV) techniques. This strategy is also adapted in this paper.

2.2   Adaptive LASSO and Multiple-step LASSO

It has been observed in [7,8] that the LASSO solution has a tendency to include more features than the true number of the relevant features, i.e., the solution $\hat{\beta}_{LASSO}$ overestimates the set $\mathcal{S} = \{j : \beta_j \neq 0\}$. This is particularly the case, when the design matrix $\boldsymbol{X}$ is strongly correlated. However, due to the screening property discussed in [7], the set $\mathcal{S}$ of the true relevant features forms a subset of the features that are selected by LASSO. A modified version of LASSO is based on putting more shrinkage to the features with smaller weights, and this idea leads to the so-called adaptive LASSO [8]. This estimate is obtained by minimizing the following criterion:

$$\frac{1}{n}||\mathbf{Y} - \mathbf{X}\beta||^2 + \lambda \sum_{j=1}^{p} \frac{|\beta_j|}{|\hat{\beta}_{init,j}|}, \tag{9}$$

where $\{\hat{\beta}_{init,j}\}$ are the initial weights selected by the aforementioned standard LASSO procedure. Hence, the features corresponding to larger weights are preserved, and the features corresponding to smaller weights experience even more shrinkage. This leads to more weights being set to zero resulting in a further simplified linear model. The recursive implementation of the adaptive LASSO algorithm yields the so-called multi-step adaptive LASSO (MSA-LASSO) regression algorithm. This method leads to the further reduction of the linear model complexity. The adaptive LASSO and MSA-LASSO can be efficiently found by convex optimization algorithms.

2.3   The Shooting Algorithm for LASSO

There are two distinct approaches for a numerical evaluation of the LASSO-type regression estimates. The first approach is based on the exact path-following method such as the LARS algorithm and its modifications [9]. The second strategy is utilizing the coordinate descent algorithm also called the shooting method [9]. The latter method is usually faster than the first one and is especially efficient in high-dimensional and sparse data settings [7]. To explain this method let us denote by $Q_\lambda(\beta)$ the criterion function in (8). Then, the gradient of $||\mathbf{Y}-\mathbf{X}\beta||^2/n$ with respect to β is given by

$$G(\beta) = 2\mathbf{X}^T(\mathbf{X}\beta - \mathbf{Y})/n.$$

The j-th coordinate of $G(\boldsymbol{\beta})$, i.e., the derivative of $G(\boldsymbol{\beta})$ with respect to β_j is equal to $G_j(\boldsymbol{\beta}) = 2\mathbf{X}_j^T(\mathbf{X}\boldsymbol{\beta} - \mathbf{Y})/n$. Then the shooting algorithm performs the following steps:

1. Let $\boldsymbol{\beta}^{(0)} \in \mathbb{R}^p$ be an initial estimator. Set $m = 0$.
2. Repeat
   - $m = m + 1$
   - For $j = 1, \cdots, p$:
   $\beta_j^{(m)} = 0$, if $|G_j(\boldsymbol{\beta}_{-j}^{(m-1)})| \leq \lambda$,
   $\beta_j^{(m)} = \arg\min_{\beta_0} Q_\lambda(\boldsymbol{\beta}_{+j}^{(m-1)})$, if $|G_j(\boldsymbol{\beta}_{-j}^{(m-1)})| > \lambda$,
   where $\boldsymbol{\beta}_{-j}^{(m-1)}$ is the vector setting the j-th component of the current solution $\boldsymbol{\beta}^{(m-1)}$ to zero and $\boldsymbol{\beta}_{+j}^{(m-1)}$ is the vector which equals to $\boldsymbol{\beta}^{(m-1)}$ except that the j-th component is equal to the scalar variable β_0 appearing in the above optimization step.
   - Until numerical convergence.

2.4 Kernel Ridge Regression

In our simulation studies, the kernel version of the Ridge Regression is used in order to be compared our proposed LASSO and MSA-LASSO procedures. The Kernel Ridge Regression is an extension of the ordinary Ridge Regression that allows nonlinear relationships between input variables. The generic formula for the kernel method is the following:

$$\hat{f}(\mathbf{x}) = \sum_{i=1}^{n} \alpha_i K(\mathbf{x}, \mathbf{X}_i), \tag{10}$$

where $K(\cdot, \cdot)$ is the proper kernel function that satisfies Mercer's conditions. The weight vector $\boldsymbol{\alpha} = [\alpha_1, \cdots, \alpha_n]^T$ can be estimated by $\hat{\boldsymbol{\alpha}} = (\mathbf{X}\mathbf{X}^T + \lambda I)^{-1}\mathbf{Y}$. In our simulation studies, the polynomial kernel $K(\mathbf{a}, \mathbf{b}) = (q + \mathbf{a}^T\mathbf{b})^d$ is used, where d is the kernel order and q is the offset parameter. To specify the Kernel Ridge Regression we use a Cross-Validation data-driven strategy to select the parameters λ, d, and q. The prediction error of the Kernel Ridge Regression is to be compared with LASSO and MSA-LASSO algorithms. It is worth noting that the Kernel Ridge Regression approach was utilized recently [6] for the problem of determination of transient stability boundary in power systems.

3 The Transient Stability Problem

Transient stability is the ability of a power system to maintain synchronism when disturbances happen due to a fault in the system such as loss of a large load, loss of a generator, or a fault on transmission facilities. It is a reflection of the capability of the power system to absorb the kinetic energy due to the imposition by the transient disturbance. The transient stability behavior of a power system, in general, is determined by the initial operating point describing the steady state before disturbance, the severity of the disturbance, and the post-fault structure of the power system. Hence, for a certain contingency and a given post-fault relay actions, transient stability is characterized only by the pre-contingency initial operating point.

The degree of the power system stability is measured by the so-called transient stability index (TSI). The TSI is a function of the initial operating point (for a given type of faults) and a post-contingency state. Hence, $TSI = f_{TSI}(\mathbf{x})$, where $\mathbf{x}$ is the p-dimensional vector describing a power flow. We use all the bus magnitudes and all bus angles to represent the pre-contingency variable $\mathbf{x}$. It is worth noting that the transient stable region is characterized by $TSI \geq TSI_0$, where TSI_0 is the threshold value. The boundary region $\{\mathbf{x} : f_{TSI}(\mathbf{x}) = TSI_0\}$ is called the transient stability boundary (TSB), and it defines the boundary between secure and insecure regions of the initial state for a given power system.

In the classical setting of power system analysis the post-contingency transient stability behavior has been determined by analyzing a large number of coupled nonlinear differential and algebraic equations in the time domain. An alternative approach is to implement machine learning techniques. Comparing with time-domain simulations, machine learning methods have an advantage with respect to speed, and easiness to implement, thus making itself feasible in real scenarios when immediate decisions are necessary.

4   Transient Stability Boundary Estimation Using the LASSO

The power system where regression estimate is performed is a medium scale real power system with 470 buses. It consists of 470 buses, 45 generating units, 214 loads and 482 transmission lines, 152 fixed shunts, and 374 adjustable transformers. All 45 generators are modeled with a 5th order generator modeled while the excitation systems of most generators are model with terminal voltage transducers, voltage regulators, exciters, and power system stabilizers. The original 470 Bus System was lightly loaded so that the system was very stable. The contingency is due to a 3-phase fault near bus 1007 on line 1007–1028 for 8 cycles and then the fault is cleared by opening line 1007–1028. This contingency is an example showing a case that the instability of the system is due to the swing of one generator against the rest of the system. Therefore for this contingency, the stability boundary is at 8 cycles. In this paper we examine the cases that a perturbation of $\pm25\%$ for active and reactive power happens, and in these cases the perturbation for generator reference voltage setting is $\pm2\%$.

Measurements are taken at the all 470 buses. Therefore, the observations include 470 bus voltages, and 469 bus angles. Therefore, the observations are 939-dimensional. For each of the observation $\mathbf{X}_i$, critical clearing time (CCT) is simulated as the response Y_i to the ith input feature vector $\mathbf{X}_i$. Here the CCT is used as a transient stability index. The mapping function from $\mathbf{X}_i$ to Y_i would define the transient stability boundary between the secure and insecure regions of operating under the certain fault and post-contingency structure already mentioned. Data set of the length 1199 is generated from the system under the above mentioned contingency. We split the data, and use the length $n = 800$ as the training set, and the rest $n' = 399$ as the testing set. The training data set $\{(\mathbf{X}_1, Y_1), ..., (\mathbf{X}_n, Y_n)\}$ is first normalized so that the input observations $\{\mathbf{X}_i\}$ as well as the responses $\{Y_i\}$ would have zero mean and unite variance. Let $\{(\tilde{\mathbf{X}}_1, \tilde{Y}_1), ..., (\tilde{\mathbf{X}}_{n'}, \tilde{Y}_{n'})\}$ denote the testing set after the normalization. In order to measure the performance of the implemented regression techniques, the following prediction error is employed

$$\text{MSE} = \frac{1}{n'} \sum_{i=1}^{n'} (\widehat{\tilde{Y}}_i - \tilde{Y}_i)^2, \tag{11}$$

where $\widehat{\tilde{Y}}_i$ is the predicted value of the testing observation $\tilde{\mathbf{X}}_i$ based on the estimated model. Hence, $\widehat{\tilde{Y}}_i = \tilde{\mathbf{X}}_i^T \hat{\beta}$, where $\hat{\beta}$ is the estimated weights derived from the original training data by using one of the regression techniques studied in this paper.

5   Prediction Based on LASSO Regression Methods

As discussed in the previous sections, regularization parameter λ plays an important role in LASSO regression as it controls the level of feature selection. For the given training set, we use the CV method to select the tuning parameter λ. We determine the CV choice of λ as the minimizer of the following criterion follows

$$\text{MSE}_{\text{CV}}(\lambda) = \frac{1}{N_{\text{CV}}} \sum_{j=1}^{N_{\text{CV}}} \frac{1}{|S_j|} \sum_{(\mathbf{X}_i, Y_i) \in S_j} (\widehat{Y}_{i,-S_j} - Y_i)^2, \tag{12}$$

where $\{S_1, \cdots, S_{N_{\text{CV}}}\}$ is the partition of data set into N_{CV} subsets. The prediction value $\widehat{Y}_{i,-S_j} = \mathbf{X}_i^T \hat{\beta}_{-S_j}(\lambda)$, where $\hat{\beta}_{-S_j}(\lambda)$ is the estimator that is based on all data but S_j. In our studies we use $N_{\text{CV}} = 3$, i.e., the 3-fold CV. We run the shooting algorithm for 2000 iterations, and then we obtain the value of $\text{MSE}_{\text{CV}}(\lambda)$. In Fig. 1(a) we plot the dependence of $\text{MSE}_{\text{CV}}(\lambda)$ on λ.

Figure 1(a) shows that $\text{MSE}_{\text{CV}}(\lambda)$ achieves minimum when $\hat{\lambda} = 0.00152$. In Fig. 1(b) we plot the number of non-zero features as a function of λ. The number of selected features by LASSO decreases as the value of λ increases. Therefore in applications when we need a smaller number of features, we can select larger λ as long as residual sum of squares is still at the acceptable low level. In our simulation studies we choose $\hat{\lambda} = 0.00152$ and perform the shooting LASSO algorithm based on 1500 iterations. This yields our final estimate $\hat{\beta}_{LASSO}(\hat{\lambda}_{\text{CV}})$ of β. We have found that among all the original 939 input features of the linear model, only 81 features are nonzero. Hence, 858 features out of the total 939 are eliminated automatically by the LASSO method. Yet the prediction error is lower than the linear model utilizing the all 939 features. As a result, a low complexity model is obtained consisting of the most informative features. Specifically, we find that the prediction error in (11) for the estimate $\hat{\beta}(\hat{\lambda}_{\text{CV}})$ is 0.07349.

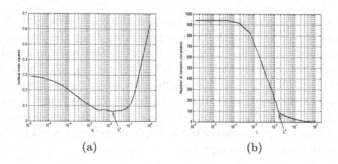

(a)   (b)

Fig. 1. (a) $MSE_{CV}(\lambda)$ vs λ, (b) Number of non-zero weights vs λ.

6   MSA-LASSO and Ridge Regression

In this section we examine the multi-step adaptive LASSO (MSA-LASSO) algorithm discussed in Sect. 2.2. The MSA-LASSO method requires the choice of the regularization parameter λ in each iteration. Table 1 shows a sequence of values of λ selected by the CV. The resulted prediction error and number of features selected in the linear model are also shown.

Table 1. Prediction results by applying the MSA-LASSO algorithm.

LASSO step k	$\hat{\lambda}_{CV}^{(k)}$	$MSE_{CV}(\hat{\lambda}_{CV}^{(k)})$	MSE for prediction	# of selected features
1	0.01519734	0.06273982	0.07349168	81
2	0.00016132	0.05442373	0.07127725	53
3	0.00014077	0.05309322	0.07101012	45
4	0.00007339	0.05266391	0.07111103	43
5	0.00011722	0.05262231	0.07091939	43
6	0.00012935	0.05260251	0.07082070	43

The Ridge Regression algorithm was also implemented with the parameter λ selected based on the 3-fold CV strategy. This estimate employs the full model dimensionality yielding the higher prediction error 0.09020790. Next, the Kernel Ridge Regression algorithm has been also implemented for different values of the order parameter d, see Sect. 2.4. The constant q and the regularization parameter λ are selected simultaneously by a 3-fold Cross-Validation. The results are summarized in Table 2. From these results, we see that Kernel Ridge Regression leads to a smaller prediction error compared with the Ridge Regression method. However, the prediction error is still larger than the one obtained using the LASSO type algorithms. It is worth mentioning that the Kernel Ridge Regression relies on the higher-order nonlinear relationships among different features, while LASSO uses merely the linear relationship in the reduced dimensionality regression model.

Table 2. Regression result by applying Kernel Ridge Regression using polynomial kernel up to order 12.

Kernel order d	$\hat{q}_{CV}^{(d)}$	$\hat{\lambda}_{CV}^{(d)}$	$\text{MSE}_{CV}(\hat{\lambda}_{CV}^{(d)}, \hat{q}_{CV}^{(d)})$	MSE for prediction
2	316228	3224.9	0.08795147	0.08513388
3	9474635	1612079.2	0.10264472	0.08146376
4	14330126	5.0646e11	0.10262463	0.08131985
5	18938420	0.01	0.10260855	0.08119592
6	23713737	0.01	0.10259889	0.08114725
⋮	⋮	⋮	⋮	⋮
12	52329912	0.01	0.10257793	0.08104084

7 Concluding Remarks

In this paper, we have examined a class of LASSO algorithms in the context of transient stability analysis. Our results show that the LASSO algorithm and its adaptive extensions outperform the commonly used techniques utilizing Ridge Regression and Kernel Ridge Regression techniques in terms of the prediction error. For the 25% perturbation data, the properly tuned LASSO regression leads to a 13.6% smaller mean square prediction error compared with Kernel Ridge Regression, or a 21.5% smaller mean square prediction error compared with Ridge Regression. Furthermore, due to the adaptive nature of LASSO algorithm, we achieve not only a smaller prediction error bust also a more parsimonious model compared with the solutions employing the L_2 penalty. Depending on the purpose of application, one can choose between the LASSO method based model that leads to more precise prediction with a larger number of features, and the one that exhibits a slightly larger error with a smaller number of feature variables.

References

1. Wehenkel, L.A.: Automatic Learning Techniques in Power Systems. Kluwer, Boston (1998)
2. Archer, B.A., Annakkage, U.D., Jayasekara, B., Wijetunge, P.: Accurate prediction of damping in large interconnected power systems with the aid of regression analysis. IEEE Trans. Power Syst. **23**, 1170–1178 (2008)
3. Gutierrez-Martinez, V.J., Cañizares, C.A., Fuerte-Esquivel, C.R., Pizano-Martinez, A., Gu, X.: Neural-network security-boundary constrained optimal power flow. IEEE Trans. Power Syst. **26**, 63–72 (2011)
4. Moulin, L.S., da Silva, A.P.A., El-Sharkawi, M.A., Marks II, R.J.: Support vector nachines for transient stability analysis of large-scale power systems. IEEE Trans. Power Syst. **19**, 818–825 (2004)
5. Hastie, T., Tibshirani, R., Friedman, J.: The Elements of Statistical Learning. Springer, New York (2009). https://doi.org/10.1007/978-0-387-84858-7

6. Jayasekara, B., Annakkage, U.: Deviation of an accurate polynomial representation of the transient stability boundary. IEEE Trans. Power Syst. **41**, 1856–1863 (2006)
7. Bühlmann, P., Van De Geer, S.: Statistics for High-Dimensional Data: Methods, Theory and Applications. Springer, Heidelberg (2011). https://doi.org/10.1007/978-3-642-20192-9
8. Zou, H.: The adaptive LASSO and its oracle properties. J. Am. Stat. Assoc. **101**, 1418–1429 (2006)
9. Friedman, J., Hastie, T., Hofling, H., Tibshirani, R.: Pathwise coordinate optimization. Ann. Appl. Stat. **1**(2), 302–332 (2007)
10. Lv, J., Pawlak, M., Annakkage, U.D.: Prediction of the transient stability boundary using the LASSO. IEEE Trans. Power Eng. **28**, 281–288 (2013)

Pattern-Based Forecasting Monthly Electricity Demand Using Multilayer Perceptron

Paweł Pełka[✉] and Grzegorz Dudek

Electrical Engineering Faculty, Czestochowa University of Technology, Częstochowa, Poland
{p.pelka,dudek}@el.pcz.czest.pl

Abstract. Medium-term electric energy demand forecasting is coming a key tool for energy management, power system operation and maintenance scheduling. This paper offers a solution to forecasting monthly electricity demand based on multilayer perceptron model which approximates a relationship between historical and future demand patterns. Energy demand time series exhibit non-stationarity, long-run trend, cycles of seasonal fluctuations and random noise. To simplify the forecasting problem the monthly demand time series is represented by patterns of yearly periods, which filter out a trend and unify data. An output variable is encoded using coding variables describing the process. The coding variables are determined on historical data or predicted using ARIMA and exponential smoothing. As an illustration, the proposed neural network model is applied to monthly energy demand forecasting for four European countries. The results confirm high accuracy of the model and its competitiveness compared to other models such as ARIMA, exponential smoothing, kernel regression and neuro-fuzzy system.

Keywords: Medium-term load forecasting · Multilayer perceptron · Pattern-based forecasting

1 Introduction

Power system load forecasting is an integral activity built into the processes of the system operation planning in a longer horizon and its current control. It is impossible to operate the system without accurate predictions. This is due to the fact that electricity cannot be stored in larger quantities and current demand has to be covered by production at any time. The accuracy of forecasts translates into production and transmission costs as well as the degree of reliability of the electricity supplies to recipients. Accurate forecasts of electricity demand are also required in competitive electricity markets. Forecasts for different time horizons and territorial areas determine the investment strategies of energy companies and allow them to optimize their market positions. This directly translates into the financial results of the competitive energy market participants.

© Springer Nature Switzerland AG 2019
L. Rutkowski et al. (Eds.): ICAISC 2019, LNAI 11508, pp. 663–672, 2019.
https://doi.org/10.1007/978-3-030-20912-4_60

Time series of the monthly electricity demand, which are the subject of this work, usually express an upward trend and yearly seasonality. The trend is correlated with the level of economic development of a given country. Seasonal fluctuations reflect the annual cycle associated with climatic factors and variability of seasons. Among the factors that disrupt both the trend and seasonal variations of the series, political decisions and factors affecting economic development are mentioned.

The methods of medium-term prediction of power systems loads can be divided into two general categories [1]: autonomous modeling approach and conditional modeling approach. In the first approach primarily historical loads and information about weather conditions are applied as input variables to predict electrical power loads. This approach is more suitable for stable economies, without sudden changes affecting the electricity demand. The conditional modeling focuses on the economic analysis and long-term planning and forecasting of energy policy. The socio-economic conditions are taken into account, which influence the energy demand in a given region. Economic growth is described by economic indicators, which constitute additional inputs of the forecasting model [1,2]. The executive parts of these both approaches employ statistical models or models based on machine learning and computational intelligence. Classical statistical models include autoregressive moving average models such as ARIMA, exponential smoothing and linear regression. Limited adaptive abilities of these methods as well as problems with modeling nonlinear relationships have resulted in increased interest in artificial intelligence techniques [3]. Artificial neural networks (NNs) are the most popular representatives of this group. They offer many advantages compared to statistical models such as identifying and modeling nonlinear functions, learning appropriate relationships directly from data, ability to generalization and parallel processing. In [3] the authors applied NNs in two variants: multilayer perceptron and radial basis function network, to forecast the trend of the monthly loads time series. The seasonal component is predicted using the Fourier series. Both forecasts, trend and seasonal fluctuations are aggregated. Due to the problem decomposition, considerable simplification of neural models has been achieved. The networks contained only two hidden neurons, which translated into faster training. Both components of the monthly load time series, a trend and seasonal fluctuations, are independently predicted in [4] using NNs. To identify the trend, the authors used moving averages and cubic splines. The combined forecast turned out to be more accurate than the forecast generated by the single NN.

NNs are often combined with other methods such as fuzzy logic and evolutionary algorithms. For example in [5] they are supported by fuzzy logic. In this work seasonal variables are defined in the form of trapezoidal indicators of the season. The authors train a collection of NNs with the same architecture but other starting weights. NNs responses are aggregated, which in effect gives more accurate forecasts. To prevent overfitting various regularization techniques are used. A weighted evolving fuzzy neural network for monthly electricity demand forecasting was proposed in [6]. Fuzzy rules implemented in neurons are introduced here additively in the training process. The novelty of this work is introducing a weighted factor to calculate the importance of each factor among the different rules. Moreover, an exponential transfer function is employed to transfer the distance of any two factors to the value of similarity among different rules. In [7] NNs trained by different heuristic algorithms, including gravitational search algorithm and cuckoo optimization algorithm, are utilized to estimate monthly electricity demands. The authors showed that the proposed approach outperforms the others and provides more accurate forecasting than traditional methods. An example of combination of NNs and genetic algorithms can be found in [8]. This work uses NNs, which architecture is developed using genetic algorithm to realize the hourly load forecasting based on the monthly total load consumption.

In this work we use multilayer perceptron for forecasting monthly electricity demand. What distinguishes the proposed model from other neural models is that it works on patterns of seasonal cycles of the time series. Patterns allows us to unify data and filter out the trend. The relationship between input and output variables in the pattern space is simpler compared to the original space. Thus, the forecasting neural model has an easier task to solve and can contain only a few neurons.

The paper is organized as follows. Section 2 presents the proposed forecasting model including time series representation using patterns. In Sect. 3 the performance of the proposed model on real-world data is evaluated. Finally, Sect. 4 is a summary of our conclusions.

2   Forecasting Model

Monthly electricity demand time series exhibit yearly cycles which we transform into input patterns. An input pattern $\mathbf{x}_i = [x_{i,1} x_{i,2} \ldots x_{i,n}]^T$ of length $n = 12$ is a vector of predictors representing n timepoints preceding the forecasted point, i.e. the time series sequence covering a seasonal cycle $X_i = \{E_{i-n+1}, E_{i-n+2}, \ldots, E_i\}$. The vector $\mathbf{x}_i$ is a normalized version of the demand vector $[E_{i-n+1} E_{i-n+2} \ldots E_i]^T$. Its components are calculated as follows [9,10]:

$$x_{i,t} = \frac{E_{i-n+t} - \overline{E}_i}{D_i} \tag{1}$$

where $t = 1, 2, \ldots, n$, $\overline{E}_i$ is the mean value of the sequence X_i, and $D_i = \sqrt{\sum_{j=1}^{n}(E_{i-n+j} - \overline{E}_i)^2}$ is a measure of its dispersion.

The normalized x-vectors for different n-length demand sequences have all the unity length, mean value equal to zero and the same variance. Thus, the input data are unified. The trend is filter out and x-patterns carry information about the shapes of the yearly cycles.

The forecasted variable is $E_{i+\tau}$, i.e. electricity demand at month $i+\tau$, where $\tau \geq 1$ is a forecast horizon. This variable is also encoded to unify data filtering the trend out. The encoded demand is:

$$y_{i,\tau} = \frac{E_{i+\tau} - \overline{E}_*}{D_*} \tag{2}$$

In this equation coding variables $\overline{E}_*$ and D_* should be determined for the seasonal cycle covering the timepoint $i + \tau$. But this future cycle is unobtainable in the moment of forecasting (timepoint i). Thus, the coding variables cannot be determined from it. We use in their place coding variables determined for the known preceding seasonal cycle X_i, i.e. $\overline{E}_* = \overline{E}_i$, $D_* = D_i$. Let us mark this approach by C1.

In the second approach, C2, $\overline{E}_*$ and D_* represents mean value and dispersion of the seasonal cycle including $i + \tau$. When the forecast horizon is $\tau \in \{1, 2, ..., 12\}$, this cycle covers the future sequence $\{E_{i+1}, E_{i+2}, ..., E_{i+12}\}$ which is unknown. We predict the coding variables for this sequence using ARIMA and exponential smoothing (ETS).

The third approach for coding variable calculation, C3, is used only for one-step ahead forecasts. In this case $\overline{E}_*$ and D_* are determined on the basis of the sequence $\{E_{i-n+2}, E_{i-n+3}, ..., E_{i+1}\}$, where the last component, E_{i+1}, is unavailable. In such case, as in C2, the coding variables are forecasted using ARIMA and ETS.

Having transformed input and output data the training set is composed. It includes pairs of x-patterns and corresponding encoded output variables y: $\Phi = \{(\mathbf{x}_i, y_{i,\tau}) | \mathbf{x}_i \in \mathbb{R}^n, y_{i,\tau} \in \mathbb{R}, l = 1, 2, ..., N\}$. The x-pattern size determines a number of NN inputs, 12. The number of hidden neurons is a variable, adjusted to the complexity of the target function which maps $\mathbf{x}$ onto y. When the forecast horizon is τ, the neural model has one output, y. This variant of the forecasting model is marked by A1 in the simulation study section. But other variant is also considered, marked by A2, where the network forecasts all seasonal cycle for the next year. In this case it has $n = 12$ outputs for $\tau = 1, 2, ..., 12$, and the training set is $\Psi = \{(\mathbf{x}_i, \mathbf{y}_i) | \mathbf{x}_i \in \mathbb{R}^n, \mathbf{y}_i \in \mathbb{R}^n, l = 1, 2, ..., N\}$, where $\mathbf{y}_i = [y_{i,1} y_{i,2} ... y_{i,n}]$. Variants A1 and A2 are used for twelve months ahead forecasts. In experimental part of the work we test the NNs also in one month ahead forecasting (variant B). In this case the training set is Φ, where $\tau = 1$ and x-pattern represents the sequence of twelve months directly preceding the forecasted month.

In all cases the NN has a single hidden layer with sigmoidal neurons. It learns using Levenberg–Marquardt algorithm with Bayesian regularization, which minimizes a combination of squared errors and the weights. This prevent overfitting. The model hyperparameters, i.e. the number of neurons, were selected in leave-one-out cross-validation. When the forecasts of the encoded demands are generated by the network, the forecasts of demands are calculated using transformed equation (2):

$$\widehat{E}_{i+\tau} = \widehat{y}_{i,\tau} D_* + \overline{E}_* \tag{3}$$

3   Simulation Study

In this section, the proposed neural model is evaluated on real-word data including monthly electricity demand for four European countries: Poland (PL), Germany (DE), Spain (ES) and France (FR). The data are taken from the publicly available ENTSO-E repository (www.entsoe.eu). They cover time period from 1998 to 2014 for PL, and from 1991 to 2014 for other countries. Our goal is to construct the forecasting models for 2014 using historical data.

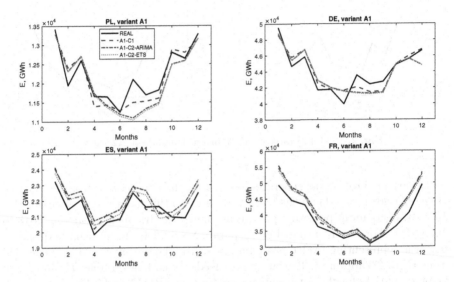

Fig. 1. Real and forecasted monthly demand for A1 variant.

We consider three variants of the forecasting procedure, A1, A2 and B. In variant A1 the model generates forecast for the k-th month of 2014 on the basis of data up to December 2013. The forecast horizon changes from $\tau = 1$ for January 2014, to $\tau = 12$ for December 2014. We train twelve NNs to generate forecasts for successive months of 2014 (each month forecasted by a separate model). Inputs of the models are the same: x-pattern representing time series fragment from January to December of the previous year. The output variable is encoded using C1 or C2 approach. In the latter case coding variables $\overline{E}_*$ and D_* for 2014 are predicted using ARIMA and ETS on the basis of their historical values.

In variant A2 instead of using twelve NNs for forecasting for individual months, we use single NN with twelve outputs. Input patterns are the same as for variant A1. Output variables are encoded using C1 or C2 approach. In C2 case we use ARIMA and ETS to forecast them.

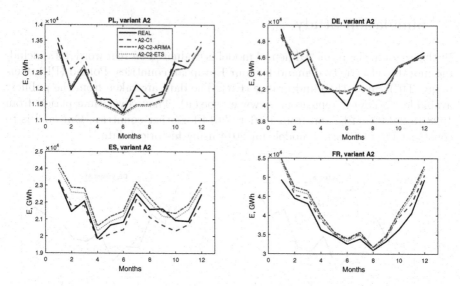

Fig. 2. Real and forecasted monthly demand for A2 variant.

In variant B the model generates forecast for the next month (from January to December 2014, $\tau = 1$) on the basis of data up to this month (e.g. the model for July 2014 gets input pattern representing time series fragment from July 2013 to June 2014). For each month we build separate NN model, which learns on the input patterns representing twelve preceding months. The output variable is encoded using C1 or C3 approach. The latter case needs the coding variables $\overline{E}_*$ and D_* to be predicted. As for the A variants we use for this ARIMA and ETS.

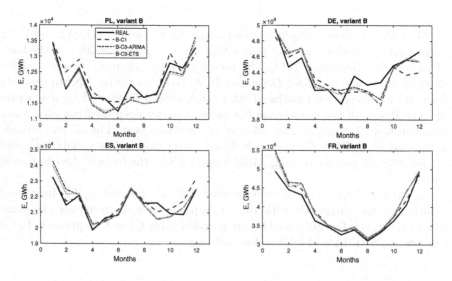

Fig. 3. Real and forecasted monthly demand for B variant.

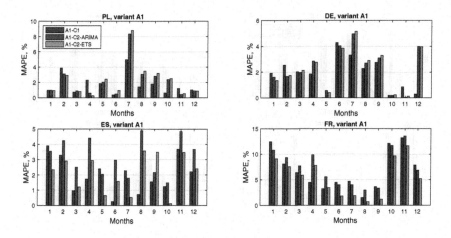

Fig. 4. Errors for A1 variant.

Figures 1, 2 and 3 show the real and forecasted monthly demand and Figs. 4, 5 and 6 show the errors (mean absolute percent errors MAPE) for each forecasted month. The forecast errors are shown in Tables 1 and 2. For comparison errors for other forecasting models are also presented: ARIMA, ETS, Nadaraya-Watson estimator NW-E [10] and neuro-fuzzy system N-FS [9]. The last two models work on patterns defined in the same way as in this work. Best results for each data are underlined. When comparing errors of all models, it should be noted that both NW-E and N-FS overcame other models in three out of eight cases each. As we can see from Tables 1 and 2, the proposed method is competitive to other ones but it is hard to indicate its best variant. However, C1 variant is usually better than C2 and C3 ones. It means that the coding variables do not have to be predicted. We can calculate them from the known preceding seasonal cycle. This simplifies the forecasting procedure.

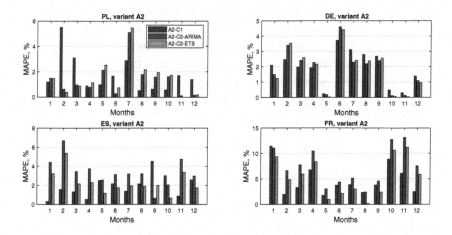

Fig. 5. Errors for A2 variant.

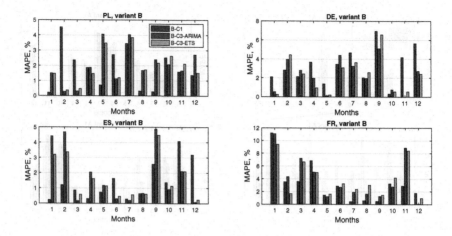

Fig. 6. Errors for B variant.

In Table 3 the number of neurons are shown selected in leave-one-out procedure. Surprisingly, NN in variant A2 having the most difficult task to forecast
twelve monthly demands at once needs the least hidden neurons: in most cases
only one. Single-output NNs need more neurons to approximate the target function: from 2.58 up to 5.92.

Table 1. MAPE for optimal number of neurons, A1 and A2 variants.

Model	PL	DE	ES	FR
A1-C1	1.76	1.86	2.02	6.84
A1-C2-ARIMA	2.17	2.31	3.21	7.47
A1-C2-ETS	2.31	2.32	2.10	5.48
A2-C1	1.75	1.93	1.90	4.71
A2-C2-ARIMA	_1.38_	1.88	3.39	7.41
A2-C2-ETS	1.55	1.86	2.28	5.42
ARIMA	3.25	4.36	1.93	10.76
ETS	6.42	2.82	2.36	6.77
N-WE	1.53	_1.80_	_1.49_	4.71
N-FS	1.57	4.94	1.67	_3.34_

Table 2. MAPE for optimal number of neurons, B variant.

Model	PL	DE	ES	FR
B-C1	1.83	3.27	1.42	3.23
B-C3-ARIMA	1.97	<u>2.29</u>	1.80	4.00
B-C3-ETS	1.87	2.30	1.62	4.00
ARIMA	1.75	2.33	1.43	4.10
ETS	2.28	2.64	2.85	3.66
N-WE	1.30	2.47	1.16	<u>2.83</u>
N-FS	<u>1.06</u>	2.87	<u>0.95</u>	5.85

Table 3. Optimal number of neurons.

Model	PL	DE	ES	FR
A1-C1	5.25	4.17	3.33	4.58
A1-C2-ARIMA/ETS	2.92	4.17	5.92	4.00
A2-C1	4	1	2	2
A2-C2-ARIMA/ETS	1	1	1	1
B-C1	4.42	4.50	3.42	4.33
B-C3-ARIMA/ETS	3.00	2.58	4.17	3.17

4   Conclusion

In this work we examine the neural network model for pattern-based forecasting monthly electricity demand. The model works on patterns representing normalized yearly seasonal cycles of the demand time series. Input patterns express shapes of the yearly cycles after filtering out a trend and unifying a variance. Also the output data are unified using coding variables which are calculated based on the historical data or they are predicted. The pattern approach simplify the forecasting problem so the forecasting model does not have to capture the complex nature of the process. This leads to model simplification and faster learning.

Multilayer perceptron provides a flexible model which can forecast both individual monthly demand and the whole yearly cycle. The proposed neural model is competitive with other state-of-the-art models such as neuro-fuzzy system and Nadaraya-Watson estimator as well as the classical statistical models including ARIMA and exponential smoothing. However, it is difficult to indicate the best variant of the model. It should be selected depending on the data, because each monthly demand time series is characterized by its own features such as the trend, variance, seasonal variations and the level of random noise.

References

1. Ghiassi, M., Zimbra, D.K., Saidane, H.: Medium term system load forecasting with a dynamic artificial neural network model. Electr. Power Syst. Res. **76**, 302–316 (2006)
2. Gavrilas, M., Ciutea, I., Tanasa, C.: Medium-term load forecasting with artificial neural network models. In: IEEE Conference on Electricity Distribution (IEE Conf. Publ No. 482) (2001)
3. González-Romera, E., Jaramillo-Morán, M.A., Carmona-Fernández, D.: Monthly electric energy demand forecasting with neural networks and Fourier series. Energy Convers. Manage. **49**, 3135–3142 (2008)
4. González-Romera, E., Jaramillo-Morán, M.A., Carmona-Fernández, D.: Monthly electric energy demand forecasting based on trend extraction. IEEE Trans. Power Syst. **21**(4), 1935–46 (2006)
5. Doveh, E., Feigin, P., Hyams, L.: Experience with FNN models for medium term power demand predictions. IEEE Trans. Power Syst. **14**(2), 538–546 (1999)
6. Pei-Chann, C., Chin-Yuan, F., Jyun-Jie, L.: Monthly electricity demand forecasting based on a weighted evolving fuzzy neural network approach. Electr. Power Energy Syst. **33**, 17–27 (2011)
7. Chen, J.F., Lo, S.K., Do, Q.H.: Forecasting monthly electricity demands: an application of neural networks trained by heuristic algorithms. Information **8**(1), 31 (2017)
8. Aquinode, R.R.B., et al.: Development of an artificial neural network by genetic algorithm to mid-term load forecasting. In: Proceedings of International Joint Conference on Neural Networks, pp. 1726–1731 (2007)
9. Pełka, P., Dudek, G.: Neuro-fuzzy system for medium-term electric energy demand forecasting. In: Borzemski, L., Świątek, J., Wilimowska, Z. (eds.) ISAT 2017. AISC, vol. 655, pp. 38–47. Springer, Cham (2018). https://doi.org/10.1007/978-3-319-67220-5_4
10. Dudek, G., Pełka, P.: Medium-term electric energy demand forecasting using Nadaraya-Watson estimator. In: IEEE 18th International Conference on Electric Power Engineering, pp. 1–6 (2017)

Squirrel-Cage Induction Motor Malfunction Detection Using Computational Intelligence Methods

Krzysztof Rzecki[1], Bartosz Wójcik[1]([✉]), Mateusz Baran[1],
and Maciej Sułowicz[2]

[1] Faculty of Physics, Mathematics and Computer Science,
Cracow University of Technology, ul. Warszawska 24, 31-155 Kraków, Poland
{krz,bartosz.wojcik,mbaran}@pk.edu.pl
[2] Faculty of Electrical and Computer Engineering,
Cracow University of Technology, ul. Warszawska 24, 31-155 Kraków, Poland
msulowicz@pk.edu.pl

Abstract. The squirrel-cage induction motors (commonly called just electric motors) are widely used in electromechanical devices. They usually act as a source of mechanical power for different types of industrial machines. There is a natural life cycle of such electric motors ending in malfunction caused by damage of particular electric or mechanical parts. Sudden and unforeseen engine failure may turn out to be a heavy cost for the company. Early detection of motor damage can minimize repair costs. In this work a machine-learning based methodology for early motor malfunction detection is presented. A test stand with a three-phase induction motor that can simulate various types of stator winding short-circuit faults under load controlled by a DC generator was build. This stand was equipped with multiple sensors for continuous monitoring. Readings from sensors were collected for different loads and types of damage. Multiple methods of preprocessing and classification were tested. Sensors types are evaluated for accuracy of malfunction recognition based on the results of computational experiments. The 5-fold stratified cross-validation was used for evaluation of preprocessing steps and classifiers. The best results were achieved for neutral voltage, axial flux, and torque sensors. Acquisition time of 0.16 s is sufficient for accurate classification.

Keywords: Induction motor · Malfunction detection · Classification · Pattern recognition · Computational intelligence methods

1 Introduction

Electric motors are used in many sectors of industry. The use of electric motors is based on their reliability, the possibility of precise control and efficiency. On the other hand, the effect of sudden and unforeseen motor failure or even unnoticed degradation of engine parts can lead to failure of the entire machine and,

© Springer Nature Switzerland AG 2019
L. Rutkowski et al. (Eds.): ICAISC 2019, LNAI 11508, pp. 673–684, 2019.
https://doi.org/10.1007/978-3-030-20912-4_61

finally, this breaks the process where the engine is used. This can increase the repair cost of the engine or a machine, or the cost related to unavailability of the machine. Mitigation of these risks requires wear monitoring and prediction of electric motor malfunction, which is fundamental for proper planning of service breaks and, consequently, cost reduction. Equipped with various electromechanical sensors, an electric motor can be monitored and sensor readings can be used by a computational intelligence system for malfunction prediction.

One of the first attempts to apply artificial intelligence techniques for detection of faults in induction motors is described in [9]. In this work the shape of the vibration spectrum was analyzed for fault symptoms. The authors assumed an ideal machine which converts all electrical energy to kinetic energy and does not produce any vibration (zero vibration energy). But in fact, a real machine produces some characteristic vibration patterns and examining whether any characteristic frequencies appear in a spectrum gives information about engine wear. Two faults were simulated in this work: a bearing fault and an imbalance in supply. A simple Artificial Neural Networks (ANN) algorithm was tested and evaluated.

In the review article [5] authors present and discuss the application of expert systems, artificial neural networks (ANNs), fuzzy logic systems and genetic algorithms to the diagnosis of electrical machine drives. The instantaneous voltages and currents are taken as input signals for the diagnostic procedure.

A Support Vector Machine (SVM) based classification for fault diagnostics of electrical machines was used in [21]. Numerical magnetic field analysis was used to generate input data for diagnosis. The four fault states (broken rotor bar, broken end-ring in rotor cage, shorted coil in stator winding and shorted turn in stator winding) and one healthy state were analyzed.

In [22] the supervised and unsupervised neural networks were applied for fault detection of electrical motors. The detection algorithm performance was verified on three fault types: air gap eccentricity, broken rotor bar, and bearing fault. The electrical supply frequency was the input signal.

In the work [15] the authors used unsupervised neural networks to detect faults of a motor stator in the three-phase induction motor. They considered alpha-beta stator currents as input signal.

The detection methods for stator turn fault and rotor bar fault were developed in [16]. Authors based their methods on calculating the cross-coupled impedance and analyzing the current frequency signature of the motor.

In work [18] a bearing fault (the outer race) detection method using the homogeneity algorithm is presented.

Authors of [11] show a methodology for vibration measurement and motor current signature analysis that enables detection of malfunctions of rotor, stator and other electric motor components.

In the study [7] the influence of a broken bar fault on the electromagnetic characteristics of the induction motor is analyzed. Authors, using an asynchronous cage motor and a finite element method-based analysis present another fault detection method.

The work [13] discusses the faults prediction of the electric motor using a Bayesian graphical model. The model was built using the knowledge about the system behavior, the degradation mechanisms, the functional decomposition and the links between the system's components. As the output, the probability of a failure is given.

Based on presented state of the art, computational intelligence methods can be useful for motor malfunction detection. It is still unknown what methods are the most appropriate for this task, which sensors give the most useful data, and what the shortest time of data acquisition for accurate malfunction recognition is. Computational intelligence methods have already been used to solve classification problems in various industrial domains [19, 20, 23, 24]. In this article, a methodology for complex diagnosis of stator coil inter-winding short circuits in three-phase squirrel-cage induction machine based on computational intelligence methods is presented.

Data was collected from specially constructed experimental setup and computational experiments were performed as described in the following sections to prove these hypotheses.

2 Materials and Methods

2.1 Experimental Setup

The subject of this study is the induction motor Sg 112M-4 produced by a Polish company Tamel. The experimental setup presented in Fig. 1 was build to collect the data. Besides motor, the setup, in general, included a DC generator with two 2 kW heaters for load simulation, two flexible couplings Rotex GS to link the motor and the generator, and an excitation regulator.

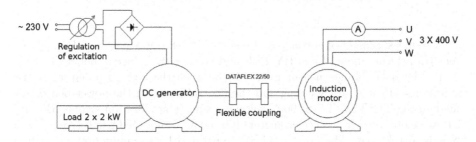

Fig. 1. Overall experimental setup diagram.

For research purposes, the taps of selected windings were led out of the casing for simple short circuits simulation. As a result, the nine classes of short circuits were simulated, between the first winding and the others as presented in Fig. 2.

The detailed schema of the experimental setup is presented in Fig. 3. It includes measuring instruments for motor monitoring.

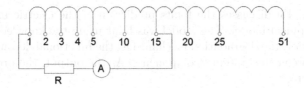

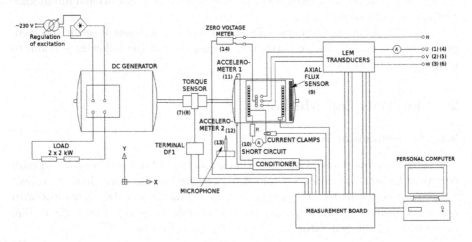

Fig. 2. Inter-winding short circuits schema.

The particular instruments (sensors marked by numbers in brackets) observations were read with the sampling frequency equal to 50 kHz by measurement board NI USB-6259.

Fig. 3. Detailed experiment schema with sensor labels.

The measurement of currents and voltages (S1–S6) was performed using current transducers model LEM HY 15-P and voltage transducers model LEM LV 25-P. The zero voltage measurement S14 between the voltage potential at the zero point of the stator winding and the neutral point on the power board was made using TESTEC TT-SI 9002 voltage probe. The vibration signals S11 and S12 were obtained from accelerometers ICP 603C01 mounted respectively in the X axis and Y axis. The noise level S13 generated by the induction motor was measured by a Roga RG-50 microphone mounted 0.5 m from the machine. The signals from both accelerometers, as well as from the microphone were directed to the PA-3000 conditioner. Electromagnetic torque S7 and rotation speed S8 were registered by the Dataflex 22/50 torque meter and DF1 connection terminal. A voltage signal proportional to derivative axial flux S9 was registered by the coil that measured the voltage that was induced on it. Finally, a current S10 in the shorted circuit was measured by Tektornix A622 current clamps. This signal was registered for control purposes only.

2.2   Materials

Five levels of load of the motor were tested by adjusting load by set stator current: idle (1 A), 2 A, 3 A, 4 A and 5 A. Then, for each load state, ten different states of malfunction (undamaged and nine short circuits) were simulated. Ten seconds of observations were recorded for each such configuration. Measurement setup was repeated twenty times for each configuration. As a result of the data acquisition $5 \times 10 \times 10 \times 50\,000 \times 20 = 0.5$ billions observations were recorded for further analysis.

The data were organized in classes of records. Each class reflects the configuration of the load of the motor and state of malfunction (or no malfunction). As a result, there were 50 classes of 20 times repeated records of 10 s each, where each record consisted of 0.5 million of observations.

The malfunction recognition task is to classify the previously unseen record of data (new signal) to one of the known classes (malfunctions).

The difference in direct signal values is easily observable as the damage severity increases for example in axial flux (unipolar) data. This is shown in Fig. 4, as well as in Fig. 5 where spectra of these signals are presented. For relatively severe damage classes recorded signals are clearly different. Note that this may not be sufficient as the focus is on achieving near perfect overall accuracy, and that requires a low classification error also for low-degree damage cases where such differentiation is not present.

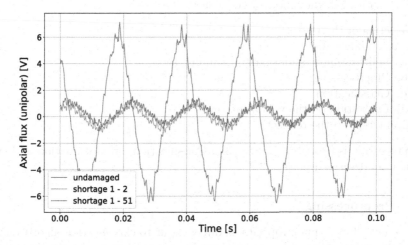

Fig. 4. Comparison of axial flux signals for three different damage classes. The blue line corresponds to signal in undamaged case, the orange one corresponds to short circuit 1–2, and the green to short circuit 1–51. (Color figure online)

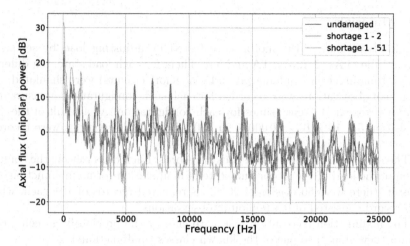

Fig. 5. Comparison of axial flux signals spectra for three different damage classes. The blue line corresponds to signal in undamaged case, the orange one corresponds to short circuit 1–2, and the green to short circuit 1–51. (Color figure online)

3 Experiments

To answer the questions set out in the Introduction computational experiments were performed in the following sequence:

1. Selection of the test set.
2. Cross-validation:
   (a) Splitting into validation and training sets.
   (b) Preprocessing.
   (c) Classification.
   (d) Evaluation on the validation set.
3. Evaluation on the test set.

Preprocessing is described in Sect. 3.1. Classification, cross-validation and evaluation are described in Sect. 3.2.

3.1 Preprocessing

Raw sensor data is inappropriate as direct input to classification algorithms, so multiple preprocessing steps are required. First, we reduce the length of the signal and apply the Fourier Transform. Using a lower resolution signal is considered to speed up the classification and classifier training, so a resampling or averaging step is needed. Applying a logarithmic transformation of the power spectrum is also considered. Standardization (or normalization) and Principal Component Analysis (PCA) [12] are the final steps of the preprocessing pipeline that were tested in classification accuracy optimization. We evaluated different combinations of these steps (including omitting some of them) and retrained our models each time. The final shape of the preprocessing pipeline is presented in Fig. 6.

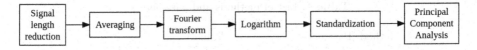

Fig. 6. Preprocessing pipeline.

Recorded signals are 10 s long, although we also consider the classification of much shorter signals. As shorter signals are easier to collect and faster to analyze, it is important to measure the trade-off between classification accuracy and speed, as outlined in the third hypothesis. As such, when investigating shorter measurement times, only a number of first samples from a record available in our dataset is taken and the rest is discarded. This has benefits similar to data reduction mentioned above, but critically this determines the time needed to classify the malfunction in the potential final detection device. We test different lengths and based on the results the selection of the shortest one that still gives good enough results can be performed.

Before transforming the data to the frequency domain, it is optionally averaged so that only a constant number of samples per signal remain, irrespective of the measurement time set in the first step.

Fast Fourier Transform is the most commonly used algorithm for obtaining frequency domain information from time series data [3]. If performed, it is applied on entire sequence obtained in the last step. We assume that classification would happen continuously, and so this results in a form of short-time Fourier Transform. The logarithm of the obtained power spectrum can be then taken.

As part of the pipeline, standardization and PCA is performed afterward. The optimal number of selected principal components of the PCA algorithm for the current pipeline is found by grid search, similarly to the parameters of the classification algorithm. It is very important to note that although standardization and PCA are usually thought of as preprocessing steps, they essentially are learning algorithms, as in both cases the results depend on training data input into them. It can result in the pipeline being inadequate for test data if training set and test set distributions vary significantly.

Data analysis was performed using the Simple Intuitive Language for Experiment Modeling (SILEM) [1], a high-level framework based on the scikit-learn Python package [17].

3.2   Classification

A test set consisting of 20% of the data was randomly selected using stratified sampling. This means data was first divided into mutually exclusive groups based on class labels, and then sampled uniformly from each group. The remaining 80% of the data was used for training and validation.

Each tested model was trained using 5-fold cross-validation. This procedure splits the training set into five disjoint subsets called folds. For each fold, a

Table 1. List of methods and parameters.

Method	Parameter	Value
PCA	number of components	10, 20, 50, 100
kNN	metric	Minkowski ($p \in \{1, 2, 3\}$)
	number of neighbours	1, 3, 5, 9, 15
SVM	kernel	polynomial, RBF, sigmoid
	C	$10^{-3}, 10^{-2}, 10^{-1}, 1, 10, 100$
MLP	activation function	logistic, relu
	sizes of hidden layers	(50), (100, 30), (100, 50, 25)
RF	number of trees	10, 20, 50, 100, 200
	criterion	gini, entropy
GB	number of trees	50, 100, 200, 500
	learning rate	$10^{-2}, 10^{-1}, 1$
NB	–	–

model score is computed using the current fold for verification while the other four folds are used for training the model. Final cross-validation score reported by the procedure is the average of the scores across all fold.

For classification purposes Multi-Layer Perceptron (MLP) [8], Support Vector Machine (SVM) [4], k-Nearest Neighbour (kNN) [2], Random Forest (RF) [10] Gradient Boosting (GB) [6] and Naive Bayes (NB) [14] algorithms were tested.

The tuning of hyperparameters, that is parameters that are set and passed to algorithms in the pipeline before the learning process, is performed using the grid search. For every hyperparameter, a list of values is specified manually. This creates a space of parameters which is then exhaustively explored. Note cross-validation as explained above is performed for each combination and the final model is refit using the whole dataset previously passed to the cross-validation procedure.

As there is no class imbalance in the collected data, choosing accuracy for this problem as the scoring metric is appropriate. Although one of the aims is to detect the malfunction as early as possible, assigning greater weight to these classes would incline the models to prioritize minor-damage detection accuracy over severe-damage detection accuracy which is not a desirable outcome.

We used the same set of grid parameters for each preprocessing pipeline and for every measurement time that was tested. The parameter values tested are given in Table 1.

4   Results and Discussion

First of all, accuracy on the test set using data from one or any two sensors was calculated. We considered different measurement time lengths in order to select one that is the shortest while still giving acceptable results. Accuracy,

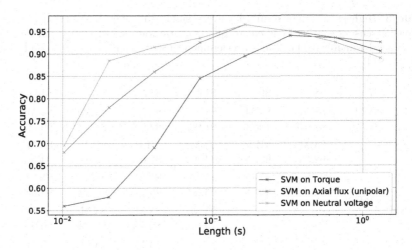

Fig. 7. Impact of measurement length on classification accuracy.

Table 2. Classifiers and parameter values that result in the highest accuracy of classification. Each row corresponds to classification using data from a single sensor.

Sensor	Classifier	Parameters	Accuracy
Torque	SVM	number of PCA components: 100, C: 100, kernel: rbf	89.5%
Rotation speed	SVM	number of PCA components: 100, C: 1, kernel: polynomial	62.5%
Axial flux	SVM	number of PCA components: 100, C: 1, kernel: polynomial	96.5%
Accelerometer – X axis	SVM	number of PCA components: 100, C: 100, kernel: RBF	79.5%
Accelerometer – Y axis	SVM	number of PCA components: 100, C: 10, kernel: RBF	81.5%
Microphone	SVM	number of PCA components: 100, C: 10, kernel: RBF	61.5%
Neutral voltage	SVM	number of PCA components: 100, C: 100, kernel: RBF	96.5%

as defined for multiclass classification, is equal to the ratio of the number of examples classified correctly to the overall number of examples.

All experiments described in this section were performed using stages listed in Sect. 3 and parameters presented in Table 1. Hyperparameters for PCA and classifiers are found by performing grid search. During averaging, $n_s = 500$ samples per signal were retained. We obtained comparable results without the standardization step and significantly worse with normalization instead of standardization.

Table 3. Highest accuracy results for every single and pair combination of sensors. Following sensors were considered: torque (S7), rotation speed (S8), axial flux (S9), X-axis accelerometer (S11), Y-axis accelerometer (S12), microphone (S13) and neutral voltage (S14).

	S7	S8	S9	S11	S12	S13	S14
S7	SVM: 89.5%	SVM: 91.5%	SVM: 100%	SVM: 91.0%	SVM: 92.5%	SVM: 86.0%	SVM: 99.5%
S8	-	SVM: 62.5%	MLP: 89.5%	SVM: 84.0%	MLP: 87.0%	MLP: 71.0%	SVM: 94.5%
S9	-	-	SVM: 96.5%	SVM: 96.5%	SVM: 99.5%	MLP: 90.5%	SVM: 99.5%
S11	-	-	-	SVM: 79.5%	SVM: 85.5%	SVM: 80.5%	SVM: 95.0%
S12	-	-	-	-	SVM: 81.5%	SVM: 81.5%	SVM: 98.0%
S13	-	-	-	-	-	SVM: 61.5%	SVM: 95.0%
S14	-	-	-	-	-	-	SVM: 96.5%

Some classifiers achieved almost perfect accuracy results with measurement time lengths longer than one second. We focused on and tested the following measurement time lengths, presented here as a number of samples: 512, 1024, 2048, 4096, 8192, 16384, 32768, 65536. Time lengths, therefore, range from 0.01 to 1.31 s. Figure 7 presents the dependency of classification accuracy on the length of analyzed signal sample for the classifiers and single sensor combinations that obtained the best result for any of the tested measurement lengths.

As can be seen in Fig. 7, there is no significant increase in accuracy for results with measurement length longer than 8192 samples. Therefore, all further discussed results assume this number of samples. Table 2 presents accuracy achieved by selecting and training a classifier based only on single sensor data. Highest achieved accuracy for data from pairs of sensors are presented in Table 3.

5   Conclusions

We infer from the results that 0.16 s is a sufficient time to accurately evaluate if this particular model of the electric motor is malfunctioning. Finest results are obtained by selecting neutral voltage, axial flux or torque as signals to build the classifier and the final malfunction detection device on. Combining two sensors does significantly improve final accuracy. SVM classifier with RBF or polynomial kernel provides the highest accuracy for this problem. Future research will include using different preprocessing methods, including wavelet transform and spectra peak detection. Performance of other classification methods like recurrent neural networks will also be investigated.

References

1. Simple intuitive language for experiment modeling. http://silem.iti.pk.edu.pl, http://silem.iti.pk.edu.pl/
2. Altman, N.S.: An introduction to kernel and nearest-neighbor nonparametric regression. Am. Stat. **46**(3), 175–185 (1992). https://doi.org/10.1080/00031305. 1992.10475879
3. Bergland, G.D.: A guided tour of the fast fourier transform. IEEE Spectr. **6**(7), 41–52 (1969). https://doi.org/10.1109/MSPEC.1969.5213896
4. Cortes, C., Vapnik, V.: Support-vector networks. Mach. Learn. **20**(3), 273–297 (1995). https://doi.org/10.1007/BF00994018
5. Fiippetti, F., Vas, P.: Recent developments of induction motor drives fault diagnosis using AI techniques. In: IECON 1998, Proceedings of the 24th Annual Conference of the IEEE Industrial Electronics Society (Cat. No.98CH36200), vol. 4, pp. 1966–1973, August 1998. https://doi.org/10.1109/IECON.1998.724019
6. Friedman, J.H.: Greedy function approximation: a gradient boosting machine. Ann. Stat. **29**(5), 1189–1232 (2001)
7. Gyftakis, K.N., Spyropoulos, D.V., Kappatou, J.C., Mitronikas, E.D.: A novel approach for broken bar fault diagnosis in induction motors through torque monitoring. IEEE Trans. Energy Convers. **28**(2), 267–277 (2013). https://doi.org/10.1109/TEC.2013.2240683
8. Hinton, G.E.: Connectionist learning procedures. Artif. Intell. **40**(1–3), 185–234 (1989). https://doi.org/10.1016/0004-3702(89)90049-0
9. Ho, S.L., Lau, K.M.: Detection of faults in induction motors using artificial neural networks. In: 1995 Seventh International Conference on Electrical Machines and Drives (Conf. Publ. No. 412), pp. 176–181, September 1995. https://doi.org/10.1049/cp:19950858
10. James, G., Witten, D., Hastie, T., Tibshirani, R.: An Introduction to Statistical Learning: With Applications in R. Springer, New York (2014). https://doi.org/10.1007/978-1-4614-7138-7
11. Jokic, S., Cincar, N., Novakovic, B.: The analysis of vibration measurement and current signature in motor drive faults detection. In: 2018 17th International Symposium INFOTEH-JAHORINA (INFOTEH), pp. 1–6, March 2018. https://doi.org/10.1109/INFOTEH.2018.8345531
12. Krzanowski, W.J. (ed.): Principles of Multivariate Analysis: A User's Perspective. Oxford University Press, Oxford (2000)
13. Lakehal, A., Ramdane, A.: Fault prediction of induction motor using Bayesian network model. In: 2017 International Conference on Electrical and Information Technologies (ICEIT), pp. 1–5, November 2017. https://doi.org/10.1109/EITech.2017.8255309
14. Manning, C.D., Raghavan, P., Schütze, H.: Introduction to Information Retrieval. Cambridge University Press, New York (2008)
15. Martins, J.F., Pires, V.F., Pires, A.J.: Unsupervised neural-network-based algorithm for an on-line diagnosis of three-phase induction motor stator fault. IEEE Trans. Ind. Electron. **54**(1), 259–264 (2007). https://doi.org/10.1109/TIE.2006.888790

16. Ostojic, P., Banerjee, A., Patel, D.C., Basu, W., Ali, S.: Advanced motor monitoring and diagnostics. IEEE Trans. Ind. Appl. **50**(5), 3120–3127 (2014). https://doi.org/10.1109/TIA.2014.2303252

17. Pedregosa, F., et al.: Scikit-learn: machine learning in Python. J. Mach. Learn. Res. **12**, 2825–2830 (2011)

18. Perez-Ramirez, C.A., Rodriguez, M.V., Dominguez-Gonzalez, A., Amezquita-Sanchez, J.P., Camarena-Martinez, D., Troncoso, R.J.R.: Homogeneity-based approach for bearing fault detection in induction motors by means of vibrations. In: 2017 IEEE International Autumn Meeting on Power, Electronics and Computing (ROPEC), pp. 1–5, November 2017. https://doi.org/10.1109/ROPEC.2017.8261624

19. Plawiak, P., Rzecki, K.: Approximation of phenol concentration using computational intelligence methods based on signals from the metal-oxide sensor array. IEEE Sens. J. **15**(3), 1770–1783 (2015). https://doi.org/10.1109/JSEN.2014.2366432

20. Plawiak, P., Sosnicki, T., Niedzwiecki, M., Tabor, Z., Rzecki, K.: Hand body language gesture recognition based on signals from specialized glove and machine learning algorithms. IEEE Trans. Ind. Inform. **PP**(99), 1 (2016). https://doi.org/10.1109/TII.2016.2550528

21. Poyhonen, S., Negrea, M., Arkkio, A., Hyotyniemi, H., Koivo, H.: Fault diagnostics of an electrical machine with multiple support vector classifiers. In: Proceedings of the IEEE International Symposium on Intelligent Control, pp. 373–378, October 2002. https://doi.org/10.1109/ISIC.2002.1157792

22. Premrudeepreechacharn, S., Utthiyoung, T., Kruepengkul, K., Puongkaew, P.: Induction motor fault detection and diagnosis using supervised and unsupervised neural networks. In: 2002 IEEE International Conference on Industrial Technology, IEEE ICIT 2002, vol. 1, pp. 93–96, December 2002. https://doi.org/10.1109/ICIT.2002.1189869

23. Rzecki, K., Pławiak, P., Niedźwiecki, M., Sośnicki, T., Leśkow, J., Ciesielski, M.: Person recognition based on touch screen gestures using computational intelligence methods. Inf. Sci. **415–416**, 70–84 (2017). https://doi.org/10.1016/j.ins.2017.05.041. http://www.sciencedirect.com/science/article/pii/S002002551730751X

24. Rzecki, K., et al.: Application of computational intelligence methods for the automated identification of paper-ink samples based on LIBS. Sensors **18**(11), 3670 (2018). https://doi.org/10.3390/s18113670

Author Index

Printed in the United States
By Bookmasters